Designing Public Policies

The second edition of this highly regarded book provides a concise and accessible introduction to the principles and elements of policy design in contemporary governance. It examines in detail the range of substantive and procedural policy instruments that together comprise the toolbox from which governments choose tools to resolve policy problems and the principles and practices that lead to their use.

Guiding readers through the study of the many different kinds of instruments used by governments in carrying out their tasks, adapting to, and altering, their environments, this book:

- Discusses current trends in instrument use linked to factors such as globalization and the increasingly networked, digital and collaborative nature of modern society;
- Considers the principles and practices behind the selection and use of specific types of instruments in contemporary government and the future research agenda of policy design studies and practices;
- Evaluates in detail the merits, demerits and rationales for the use of specific organization, regulatory, financial and information-based tools and the trends visible in their use including recent efforts to develop and deploy new tools such as nudges and choice architectures, co-production and crowd-sourcing;
- Addresses the issues surrounding not only individual tools but also concerning the evolution and development of instrument mixes, their relationship to policy styles and the challenges involved in their (re)design.

Providing a comprehensive overview of this essential component of modern governance and featuring helpful definitions of key concepts and further reading, this book is essential reading for all students of public policy, administration and management.

Michael Howlett is Burnaby Mountain Professor and Canada Research Chair (Tier 1) in the Department of Political Science at Simon Fraser University specializing in public policy analysis, political economy and resource and environmental policy.

Routledge Textbooks in Policy Studies

This series provides high-quality textbooks and teaching materials for upper-level courses on all aspects of public policy as well as policy analysis, design, practice and evaluation. Each text is authored or edited by a leading scholar in the field and aims both to survey established areas and present the latest thinking on emerging topics.

The Public Policy Primer
Managing the Policy Process
Xun Wu, M. Ramesh, Michael Howlett and Scott Fritzen

Designing Public Policies
Principles and Instruments
Michael Howlett

Making Policy Work
Peter John

Analyzing Public Policy
2nd edition
Peter John

Public Policy and Private Interest
Ideas, Self-Interest and Ethics in Public Policy
J. A. Chandler

The Public Policy Primer
Managing the Policy Process, 2nd edition
Xun Wu, M. Ramesh, Michael Howlett and Scott A. Fritzen

Designing Public Policies
Principles and Instruments, 2nd edition
Michael Howlett

Designing Public Policies

Principles and Instruments

Second edition

Michael Howlett

 Routledge
Taylor & Francis Group

LONDON AND NEW YORK

Second edition published 2019
by Routledge
2 Park Square, Milton Park, Abingdon, Oxon OX14 4RN

and by Routledge
711 Third Avenue, New York, NY 10017

Routledge is an imprint of the Taylor & Francis Group, an informa business

© 2019 Michael Howlett

First edition published by Routledge 2011

British Library Cataloguing in Publication Data
A catalogue record for this book is available from the British Library

Library of Congress Cataloging in Publication Data
Names: Howlett, Michael, 1955– author.
Title: Designing public policies : principles and instruments / Michael Howlett.
Description: Second edition. | Abingdon, Oxon ; New York, NY: Routledge is an imprint of the Taylor & Francis group, an informa business, 2019.
Series: Routledge textbooks in policy studies | Includes bibliographical references and index.
Identifiers: LCCN 2018023982| ISBN 9781138293632 (hbk) | ISBN 9781138293649 (pbk) | ISBN 9781315232003 (ebk)
Subjects: LCSH: policy sciences. | political planning.
Classification: LCC jf1525.P6 H69 2019 | DDC 320.6—dc23
LC record available at https://lccn.loc.gov/2018023982

ISBN: 978-1-138-29363-2 (hbk)
ISBN: 978-1-138-29364-9 (pbk)
ISBN: 978-1-315-23200-3 (ebk)

Typeset in Sabon
by Florence Production Ltd, Stoodleigh, Devon, UK

I profess, in the sincerity of my heart, that I have not the least personal interest in endeavouring to promote this necessary work, having no other motive than the publick good of my country, by advancing our trade, providing for infants, relieving the poor and giving some pleasure to the rich.

(A Modest Proposal – Dr Jonathan Swift, 1729)

Contents

LIST OF FIGURES ix

LIST OF TABLES xi

PREFACE xiii

ACKNOWLEDGEMENTS xv

**PART I INTRODUCTION: POLICY DESIGN AND
GOVERNANCE IN THE MODERN STATE** 1

1 Understanding the role of policy design in contemporary
policy-making 3

2 Policy design in the contemporary era: beyond globalization
and governance 23

**PART II SYSTEMATICALLY STUDYING POLICY
DESIGN**

3 What is policy design?: Key definitions and
concepts in the study of policy design 43

4 Why policy design?: Tools, mechanisms,
behaviours and the logic of policy compliance 71

PART III POLICY DESIGNING: PROCESS, PRINCIPLES AND PRACTICES   93

5 When does policy design occur?: Policy
   designing as policy formulation   95

6 Who are the policy designers and where do they work?:
   Policy advice, policy advisors and policy advisory systems   111

PART IV THE ELEMENTS OF POLICY DESIGN: POLICY INSTRUMENTS AND INSTRUMENTS MIXES   133

7 How do policy designs work?: Policy designs as
   implementation tool mixes   135

8 Organizational implementation tools   165

9 Authoritative implementation tools   191

10 Financial implementation tools   211

11 Information-based implementation tools   225

12 Traditional policy styles and contemporary
    design trends   237

PART V CONCLUSION: LESSONS FOR POLICY DESIGNS AND DESIGNERS   255

13 How to assemble and evaluate a policy design:
    character and context in policy designs   257

14 Conclusion: the capacity challenges of policy
    design over space and time   275

    BIBLIOGRAPHY   285
    INDEX   405

Figures

1.1	Policy effectiveness as the relationship between process, design and outcome	13
1.2	Five types of uncertainty designers must face	18
2.1	Modes of governance, including variation by lead actor	30
3.1	The five stages of the policy cycle and their relationship to applied problem-solving	47
3.2	An example of the range of policy instruments by governance mode and stage of the policy cycle	53
3.3	A spectrum of design processes	63
4.1	The behavioural expectations of policy design	79
4.2	Links in the policy instrument-mechanism-output chain	80
4.3	Context-related mechanism constraints	80
4.4	Links in the design chain: individual and group level	82
4.5	Links in the design chain: structural level	86
7.1	Analytical steps in social science model-building	139
7.2	Cushman's three types of policy tools	141
7.3	The Doern continuum	145
7.4	Final model of implementation tool selection process involved in policy design	151
7.5	State and societal components of 'governing resource' effectiveness	154
10.1	Spectrum of interest articulation systems	218

Tables

1.1	Cases of disproportional policy reaction and design	15
1.2	Tame and wicked problems	16
1.3	Policy-maker's knowledge and comprehension matrix	17
2.1	Modes of governance (empirical content)	31
3.1	Components of public policies involved in policy design	45
3.2	Types of policy formulation spaces: situating design and non-design processes	59
4.1	Nature of compliance of Policy Targets	76
4.2	Perceptions of policy targets after Schneider and Ingram (1993)	77
4.3	A resource-based taxonomy of procedural and substantive policy instruments	83
4.4	Behavioural needs for resource effectiveness	83
4.5	Aspects of policy processes and structures affected by procedural policy tools	87
5.1	Different kinds of uncertainty faced by policy-makers and types of policy-making responses	103
5.2	Types of policy formulation: situating design spaces	106
6.1	Ideational components of policy contents	117
6.2	The four communities of policy advisors	119
6.3	Advisory system actors by policy level	120
6.4	Capacity issues in policy design outcomes	126
7.1	Lowi's matrix of policy implementation activities	142
7.2	Hood's 1986 taxonomy of substantive policy instruments	143
7.3	A resource-based taxonomy of procedural policy instruments	149
7.4	A simplified taxonomy of substantive and procedural implementation tools	150
7.5	Ostrom's seven kinds of policy criteria/rules	152

7.6	Basic typology of portfolio designs	160
8.1	Tasks typically undertaken by government agencies	168
8.2	Examples of tasks undertaken by public enterprises (Canada – twentieth century)	171
8.3	Analytical agency network managerial tasks	183
9.1	Six types of legal instruments	194
9.2	Requisites for regulatory agency independence	195
9.3	Types of voluntary regulation	199
9.4	Actions undertaken by procedural authoritative instruments	202
9.5	Types of advisory committees	203
9.6	Purposes of advisory boards	204
9.7	US Advisory Committee Act (1972) criteria	204
9.8	Types of public consultation: design criteria	205
10.1	Average percentage of 'seed money' obtained by interest groups from each source by group type	220
10.2	Source of funding for women's groups (Canada)	222
12.1	Propensity for tool use by governance mode and resource category	239

Preface

This book introduces students to the principles and elements of policy design in contemporary governance. It does so through the detailed study of the implementation instruments used by governments in carrying out their tasks in adapting to and altering their environments and of the processes in government which lead to tool selection and enactment. These tools form the basic foundations or structures upon which all policies and programmes rest. An essential component of modern governance, the range of substantive and procedural policy instruments together comprise the toolbox from which governments select specific tools expected to resolve particular kinds of policy problems. The book begins with a discussion of several aspects of instrument use in contemporary government linked to factors such as the rise of globalization and the increasingly networked nature of modern society. It then moves on to consider the principles behind the selection and use of specific types of instruments in the process of policy formulation. The merits, demerits and rationales for the use of specific organization, regulatory, financial and information-based tools and the trends visible in their use are set out in separate sections of the book. Finally, by way of conclusion, the issue of how best to design policy programmes is addressed in a discussion of the future research agenda of policy design.

Acknowledgements

The book could not have been written without the pioneering work of the many, many scholars who individually and collectively have spent a great deal of time and effort developing the empirical cases and carefully building the many frameworks and models used throughout the text. Many colleagues have also more directly helped contribute to the ideas, models and concepts found in the book. They include M. Ramesh, Richard Simeon, Ishani Mukherjee, G. Bruce Doern, Luc Bernier, Giliberto Capano, Jeremy Rayner, Ben Cashore, Scott Fritzen, Adam Wellstead, Pearl Eliadis, Rejean Landry, Tony Zito, Margaret Hill, Azad Singh Bali, Evert Lindquist, Anthony Perl, Wu Xun, JJ Woo, Jale Tosun, Allan McConnell, Jenny Lewis, Lester Salamon, Mark Considine, Mike Mintrom, Guy Peters, Pablo del Río, Andrea Migone, Brian Head, Kent Weaver, Moshe Maor, Robert Hoppe, Martijn van der Steen, Andy Jordan, Achim Kemmerling, Namrata Chindarkar, Josh Newman, Sreeja Nair, Peter May, Daniel Béland, Eric Montpetit, Ed Araral, Don Low, Hans de Bruijn, Mark Considine, Christine Rothmayr-Allison, Frederic Varone, Ciqi Mei, Arno Simons, Jan-Peter Voss, Claire Dunlop, Darryl Jarvis, Adam Wellstead, Ching Leong and the participants in a variety of workshops and students in many classes held in North America, Europe, Asia and Australia over the years where papers on aspects of policy design and instrument choice were delivered and critiqued. A special debt is owed to Rebecca Raglon for her patience, support and encouragement. Thank you all for your ideas and inspiration.

Part I

INTRODUCTION

Policy design and governance in the modern state

Understanding the role of policy design in contemporary policy-making

Transforming policy ambitions into practice is a complex process. Historically, many efforts of policy-makers to address policy problems and maintain political order have failed due to poor designs which have not adequately incorporated this complexity in policy formulation, leading to poor decisions and difficult or ineffective implementation (Howlett 2012; Cohn 2004). These experiences have led to a greater awareness of the various obstacles that can present themselves to effective policy designs and have gradually fueled better understandings of the unique characteristics of policy formulation processes and the design spaces in which formulation efforts are embedded (Peters et al. 2018).

Policy design is itself a complex subject, however. It entails the conscious and deliberate effort to define policy aims and map them instrumentally to policy tools that aim to achieve those goals (Majone 1975; May 2003; Gilabert and Lawford-Smith 2012). In this sense, policy design signifies a particular type of policy formulation that involves activities like collecting knowledge about the outcomes of policy instrument use on policy targets and analyzing its relevance to the creation and implementation of policies meant to attain specific policy goals and aspirations (Weaver 2009b, 2010a; Bobrow and Dryzek 1987; Bobrow 2006; Montpetit 2003c).

In Davis Bobrow's (2006) apt phrase, policy design is 'ubiquitous, necessary and difficult' but surprisingly little studied and understood (Junginger 2013). Over the past three decades, it has received some treatment in the existing policy literature, but not as much, or in as much detail, as is necessary (May 1981, 1991, 2003; Weimer 1992a,b; Bobrow 2006). Within the policy sciences, it has been linked to studies of policy implementation and policy instruments (May 2003), to those of policy ideas and policy formulation (Linder and Peters 1990c,d; James and Jorgensen 2009) and has been a large, if typically implicit, part of the study of governance and even 'meta-governance'. In all these cases, however, this has typically been done without the benefit of clear and systematic analysis of how policies and governance arrangements fit together (Meuleman 2009, 2010b) and without systematic attention being paid to such basic elements as the definition of key terms and the articulation of standard concepts and principles for superior designs and design processes.

The academic enquiry of policy design – that is, self-consciously dealing with both policy processes and substance under an instrumental rubric – emerged and flourished briefly throughout the 1970s and 1980s (e.g., see Salamon 1981, 1989, 2002c) although policy design studies have been undertaken since at least the 1950s (Tinbergen 1952; Dahl and Lindblom 1953; Kirschen et al. 1964). The origins of policy design studies in the sense used in this book can be traced to the very roots of the policy sciences which espoused the overall idea of affecting better outcomes through the organized application of knowledge to policy-making, especially, but not limited to, formulation and the crafting and evaluation of policy alternatives (Wildavsky 1979; May 2003; Mintrom 2007). In the Lasswellian foundations of the policy sciences, for example, a distinction between processes of formulation and implementation was drawn in order to emphasize the significance of policy instruments and features of instrument choice to both activities (Lasswell 1954).

Most early studies focused on policy tools and had a strong focus on policy implementation issues and processes, paying much less attention to the policy development or formulation issues which are the hallmark of current studies with a design orientation (Hood 1986c; Hood and Margetts 2007).

Of course, not all work on policy design restricted itself to formulation and implementation. Larger issues about feedback processes from instrument choices to the politics of policy formation, as well as work on network governance (see Lascoumes and Legales 2007 and de Bruijn and ten Heuvelhof 1997) have examined many broader issues linked to agenda-setting and governance, among others. These are all part of design studies, given the latter's concern for understanding the inherent nuances involved in understanding and activating mechanisms to meet policy goals and considerations around political as well as technical feasibility and acceptability of policy designs.

For the first generation of policy design studies that arose from this work, the historical and institutional contexts within which policies were made were considered to significantly affect both the content and activities of design and designing (Torgerson 1985, 1990; Clemens and Cook 1999). Changes in design, then, were often understood as resulting from broader changes to the existing fabric of policy institutions within which existing policy designs were embedded. In this way of thinking, as policy conditions altered and evolved, so would the arrangements of policy means considered by policy actors engaged in formulation activity. These actors in turn were thought to be themselves impacted by evolving ideas and logics of appropriateness about particular designs flowing from dominant and evolving sets of ideas, or 'paradigms', concerning the nature and roots of policy problems and their likely means of redress (March and Olsen 2004; Goldmann 2005; Howlett 2011; Hogan and Howlett 2015).

This 'reactive' orientation toward formulation propagated a critique of early efforts toward 'design thinking' on the part of policy and organization studies scholars who emphasized the highly contingent processes of formulation followed in many instances and the resulting degree of irrationality that they argued often prevented careful analysis of knowledge and the practices of informed deliberation needed for effective policy design (Cohen et al. 1979; Dryzek 1983; Kingdon 1984). Some scholars, for example, were skeptical as to whether, given these dynamics, policy could ever actually be designed in the calm and detached ways that policy design scholars suggested should and would occur (Lindblom 1959; Dryzek and Ripley 1988; Linder and Peters 1990a; deLeon 1988).

This is a view still held by some (Eijlander 2005; Franchino and Hoyland 2009) which harkens back to post WWII criticisms of planning efforts in many countries and sectors (Lindblom 1959; Simon 1957) and the reflections on the nature of bounded rationality and incrementalism which accompanied that critique (see Baumgartner and Jones 1991, 2002; Howlett and Migone 2011). This criticism suggests a very distinct limit to the extent to which policy design is possible and promotes the view that many policy efforts occur in a 'non-design' direction, that is, one in which the formulation process is highly contingent and partisan and subject to unpredictable bargaining and other negotiative dynamics (Howlett and Mukherjee 2014, 2018).

Others, however, challenged what they felt was an overemphasis on unpredictable contextuality and irrational behaviour among policy-makers. Following the lead of Linder and Peters in a series of articles published in the late 1980s and early 1990s, they argued designs could be formulated more or less independently of contexts and then adapted to them as needed; much in the same manner that plans for buildings can be developed in the abstract but then must be adapted to fit building sites, financial constraints on owners, building codes and zoning rules and so on (Linder and Peters 1984, 1988, 1990b, 1991; Schön 1988, 1992).

This distinction allowed policy designs to be differentiated in theory and practice from both the processes of designing and activities around policy implementation and facilitated the development of a true design orientation (Schön 1988, 1992) within the policy sciences. This latter logic dominates current thinking on policy design and designs are now treated as complex entities composed of multiple elements some of which may have emerged in a largely *ad hoc* way, while others were formulated with more care given to evidence and logics of causes and effects (Howlett and Mukherjee 2017). Current studies focus both on the logic of designs themselves and upon the processes of policy advice and formulation which lead to the adoption of certain kinds of designs rather than others (van der Heijden 2011; Thelen 2003; Howlett 2004b; Craft and Howlett 2012; Howlett et al. 2015, Howlett and Lejano 2013; Howlett 2014a; Jordan et al. 2013).

The tools orientation in policy studies

In contemporary policy studies, 'design' is associated with both the analysis of the policy instruments and their implementation which comprise a design (May 2003) as well as with the study of the effect of policy advice and ideas on the process of policy formation which lead to the adoption of certain kinds of designs in specific circumstances (Linder and Peters 1990a,c). Policy designs in this sense are understood as having a *substantive* element that comprises of the technical arrangements of alternatives that can potentially resolve the policy problem at hand – and a *procedural* component that entails all the processes and activities necessary to co-ordinate the activities of policy actors in charge of formulating, making decisions and administering the alternatives (Howlett 2011). Policy design, therefore, spans both formulation and implementation in the policy process by involving the interactions between actors, ideas and interests that flow between both of these activites (Howlett et al. 2009).

These two aspects of policy designing, however, have not always received equal treatment from students of the subject. Policy design studies in the 1980s, for example, shifted from the study of 'designing' to the study of 'designs' themselves, with a specific focus on better understanding how individual implementation-related policy tools and instruments such as taxes and subsidies or regulation and public ownership operated in theory and practice (Sterner 2003; Woodside 1986; Mayntz 1983). This marked the beginning of modern studies of policy tools and this tools orientation sparked interest in a range of related subjects, such as the study of implementation failures, policy success and the linkages connecting the two, with policy scholars turning their attention to the description and classification of alternative implementation instruments and the factors which conditioned their effective use and deployment (Mayntz 1979; O'Toole 2000; Goggin et al. 1990).

At this time, for example, Bardach (1980) and Salamon (1981) went so far as to argue that the definition of policy in terms of 'issues' or 'problems' originally made by policy scholars like Lasswell at the outset of the policy studies movement (Mintrom 2007) was misguided and that policy should instead have been defined from the start in terms of the 'instruments' used in policy-making. They thus advocated shifting the focus of policy studies squarely toward the study of the design and operation of such tools (Howlett 2000c).

These students of public policy-making were joined in this effort by scholars of economics and law who studied the evaluation of policy outputs in terms of their impacts on outcomes as well as the role of law and legislation in effecting policy tool choices and designs (Stokey and Zeckhauser 1978; Bobrow and Dryzek 1987; Keyes 1996). And studies in management and administration at the time also sought to explore the linkages between politics, administration and implementation in the effort to better understand policy tool choices and patterns of use (Trebilcock and Hartle 1982). Researchers also looked at how policy instrument choices tended to shift over time (Lowi 1966, 1972, 1985), examples of which during this period included less reliance on public enterprises and regulation and the rise of privatization and deregulation (Howlett and Ramesh 1993) as well as the first wave of governance thinking advocating the enhanced use of network management or non-governmental tools in areas such as environmental regulation among others (Peters and Pierre 1998).

By the early 1980s, this tools literature had merged with the policy design orientation and emerged as a body of policy design literature in its own right. Students of policy design consequently embarked upon theory building, developing more and better typologies of policy instruments that sought to aid the conceptualization of these instruments and their similarities and differences and attempting to provide a greater understanding of the motivations and reasons underlying their use in practice as well as in theory (Salamon 1981; Tupper and Doern 1981; Hood 1986c; Bressers and Honigh 1986; Bressers and Klok 1988; Trebilcock and Hartle 1982).

This new design literature sparked interest in a range of related subjects and other scholarly work during this period served to further elucidate the nature and use of specific policy tools such as 'command-and-control' regulations and financial inducements such as tax incentives (Landry et al. 1998; Tupper and Doern 1981; Hood 1986c; Vedung et al. 1997; Howlett 1991). In general, it was believed that a greater understanding of implementation instruments and the reasons underlying instrument choice would benefit policy design both as a practice and a theoretical body of knowledge, contributing to more positive policy outcomes (Woodside 1986; Linder and Peters 1984; Mayntz 1983). Studies and practices toward pollution prevention and professional regulation, for example, benefited from advances in the systematic study of policy instruments which influenced the design and creation of new market-based tools considered to be superior alternative instruments to the state-based regulation often deployed in these and other fields (Hippes 1988; Trebilcock and Prichard 1983).

While most work focused on tool design, constructionist and behavioural perspectives were also brought to bear on the formulation processes involved in policy designing, most prominently in Schneider and Ingram's (1990, 1990a, 1994) studies of policy targets and their behaviour. These studies highlighted the manner in which opinions and views of the behaviour and worthiness of specific sections of the public affected the range and type of services they were provided and how they were treated in their provision. This provided a deeper understanding of the social and behavioural factors underpinning the use and consideration of specific kinds of policy designs in practice. Subsequent contributions by these authors as well as other scholars working in a similar vein would further advance the study of the behavioural aspects of the design process as a needed complement to studies of policy designs in themselves (Ingram and Schneider 1990; Schneider and Ingram 1997; Mondou and Montpetit 2010; Timmermans et al. 1998; Hood 2007a).

In a very important development in the late 1990s, some scholars began to progress from the study of single instrument uses to that of more complex multi-tool 'policy mixes' (Grabosky 1994; Gunningham et al. 1998; Howlett 2004b), further advancing the understanding of both the theory and practice of policy instrument choices and policy designs. And the late 1990s and early 2000s also saw a substantial shift in scholarly attention toward the more 'meta' level of policy institutions, sparked by the emergence of globalization and its preference for market-based tools as well as the start of 'governance' studies undertaken in Europe and elsewhere which emphasized the role of non-state actors – especially networks – in policy-making (Howlett and Lejano 2013). This 'globalization and governance turn' perpetuated a polarity in discussions between, for example, instruments of the 'market' and the 'state' or dichotomous governance styles such as 'hierarchies' and 'markets' which colored many design debates of the era (Howlett 2004b; Howlett 2011; Koch 2013).

By 1989, this work had progressed to the point where Salamon could argue that the design orientation and its focus on the study of implementation tools and formulation processes had become a major approach to the study of policy in and of itself. He argued this orientation would help address two main questions which had bedeviled policy scholars for decades: 'What consequences does the choice of tool of government action have for the effectiveness and operation of a government programme?' and 'What factors influence the choice of programme tools?' (265).

The contemporary design orientation

The contemporary design orientation in policy studies calls for the continued a broadening of thinking about policy design beyond individual policy tool choices, examining combinations of substantive and procedural instruments and their interactions in complex policy mixes. It also has focused on more detailed study of the actual formulation processes involved in tool and design choices as these occur and evolve over time (Linder and Peters 1990d; Schneider and Ingram 1997; Considine 2012).

These studies have obvious theoretical and practical consequences for making and understanding public policies (Braathen and Croci 2005; Braathen 2007a; Grant 2010; Skodvin, Gullberg and Aakre 2010). Environment and energy policy, for example, (Jordan et al. 2013) have both featured the development and application of 'design thinking' around areas such as emissions trading systems and sustainability transitions and these studies also have had paedagogical consequences. Rather than be confined within the technical and capacity restrictions of their policy area, for example, policy designers are now urged to 'be familiar not only with the technical aspects of the menu of instruments before them, but also with the nature of the governance and policy contexts in which they are working' (Howlett 2013). As May (2003: 226) has argued, rather than treating design as simply a technical activity of finding the best design, it should be seen to involve channeling the energies of disparate actors toward agreement in working toward similar goals.

In this regard, it is important to note that despite the vagueness and uncertainties historically associated with its principles and elements, the purpose and expectations of policy design have always been clear. That is, it is an activity conducted by a number of policy actors in the hope of improving policy-making and policy outcomes through the accurate antici-pation of the consequences of government actions (Tinbergen 1958; 1967; Schön 1992). It thus is situated firmly in the 'rational' tradition of policy studies, one aimed at improving policy outcomes through the application of policy-relevant and policy-specific knowledge to policy-making processes, specifically in the crafting of alternative possible courses of action intended to address social, political, economic and other kinds of policy problems (Cahill and Overman 1990; Bobrow 2006).

While somewhat similar in this regard to activities such as planning and strategic management, policy design is less technocratic in nature than these other efforts at 'scientific' government and administration (Forester 1989; Voss et al. 2009). However, it too is oriented toward avoiding many of the inefficiencies and inadequacies apparent in other, less knowledge-informed ways of formulating policy, such as pure political bargaining, ad hocism, or trial and error (Bobrow 2006). In general, it is less specific than planning in developing alternatives rather than detailed 'plans', fully acknowledges the uncertainty of the future and the contingent nature of policy outcomes (Voss et al. 2009) and is more open than strategic management to the idea that there are alternative sources of knowledge and design criteria than those residing in, or proposed by, experts (Fischer and Forester 1987; May 1991).

In contrast to those planning and design scholars who view policy-making as intentional and instrumentally rational, many commentators in the popular media and elsewhere have also noted many instances in which policy-making is driven by political or personal interests and where 'designs' are more or less irrational. This includes a variety of contexts in which policy formulators or decision-makers engage in interest-driven trade-offs or log-rolling between different values or resource uses, often in response to concerns about legislative expediency. These various processes and situations can be called *non-design* ones. They are situations in which policy formulation is driven neither by instrumental problem-solving nor often even socio-political concerns, but can emerge, for example, when policy-makers engage in venal or corrupt behaviour in which personal gain from a decision may trump other evaluative and decision-making criteria. Policy measures that serve symbolic, rather than practical technical or political, purposes are often produced in such non-design situations and are often the hallmark of 'non-design' outcomes and instrument choices (Mukherjee and Howlett 2014).

However, while it may not always be problem-centered, politics-centered design can also retain a design component, in the instrumental sense of the term, when its purpose is to deliberately choose instruments and design programmes which advance the interest of powerful stakeholders rather than to solve policy problems (Colebatch 2017; Turnbull 2017). This is something that occurs very often in 'clientelistic' regimes, for example, where a major criterion for tool selection and programme design is the delivery of benefits to supporters of current incumbents (Manor 2013; Gans-Morse 2014).

Policy design as a field of study

Whether it is problem or politics-centered, however, policy design differs from non-design in that it involves the deliberate and conscious attempt to define policy goals and connect them to instruments or tools expected to realize those objectives using logic, evidence and argument.

Policy design, in this sense, is a specific form of policy formulation based on the gathering and application of knowledge of the effects of policy tool use on policy targets to the development and implementation of policies aimed at the attainment of desired policy ambitions (Weaver 2009a, 2010b; Bobrow and Dryzek 1987; Bobrow 2006; Montpetit 2003b). In a time when policy-makers are often tasked with developing innovative solutions to increasingly complex policy problems, the need for intelligent design of policies and a better understanding of the policy formulation processes they involve has never been greater.

A design orientation toward formulating policies begins with the analysis of the abilities of different kinds of policy tools and resources to trigger behavioural and other mechanisms among target groups in order to affect policy outputs and outcomes (Hood 1986c). This instrumental or mechanistic knowledge is contextual in the sense that understandings of how the use of specific kinds of instruments affects outcomes such as levels of target group compliance includes consideration of many constraints on tool use originating in the limits of existing knowledge, prevailing governance structures and other arrangements which may preclude certain options and favor others. These contextual factors, including the institutional and actor arrangements and legacies which combine to create a *policy style* or favored mode of operation in many sectors and governments, are also addressed in this volume.

In general, however, a means-ends understanding of policy formulation permeates the policy design orientation (Tribe 1972; Colebatch 1998; Colebatch 2017). Although acknowledging that policy-making does not always necessarily lend itself to or result in purely instrumental thinking about policy issues, this instrumental orientation is significant in policy design studies and policy formulators operating in accordance with its strictures are expected to base their actions on analyses which are logical, knowledge and experience-based rather than, for example, from purely political calculations or bargaining or other forms of satisficing behaviour, or religious or ideological presuppositions or beliefs (Sidney 2007; Bendor et al. 2009).

Of course, this does not preclude recognition and acceptance of the fact that some policy decisions and formulation processes are in fact made in a much more highly contingent and irrational fashion in which 'design' considerations may be more or less absent (Sager and Rielle 2013). However, the extent to which considerations such as political gain or blame avoidance outweigh instrumental factors in a given instance of policy formulation is an empirical question whose answer varies in different circumstances and contexts. But, in general, this is desired to be as minimal as possible (Hood 2010).

That is, policy scholars interested in policy design have argued for several decades that in most instances, processes of policy formulation are governed less by political, religious, ideological and self-interested considerations than they are by concerns about the efficiency and effectiveness of state action in practice leading policy-makers to think more systematically and analytically about their options and alternatives (Bobrow and Dryzek 1987; Bobrow 2006). And, as noted above, even when policy processes are more contingent, the design of a policy, conceptually at least, can still be divorced from the process of its actual creation – or *designing*.

Conceptually, an instrumentally oriented policy design process begins with an assessment of the abilities of different policy tools or levers to affect policy outputs and outcomes and of availability of the kinds of resources required to allow them to operate as intended (Hood 1986c; Salamon 2002c). As Linder and Peters (1991) noted, this kind of activity is a 'spatial' or contextual one. That is, it is:

> a systematic activity composed of a series of choices . . . design solutions, then, will correspond to a set of possible locations in a design space . . . this construction emphasizes not only the potential for generating new mixtures of conventional solutions, but also the importance of giving careful attention to tradeoffs among design criteria when considering instrument choices.
>
> (130)

Instrumental knowledge is still contextual, however, in the sense that it requires a special understanding of how the use of specific kinds of instruments affects target group behaviour and compliance with government aims (Weaver 2008, 2009a,b, 2013, 2015). It thus includes knowledge and consideration of many constraints on tool use originating in the limits of existing knowledge, prevailing governance structures and other arrangements and behaviours which may preclude consideration of certain options and promote others (Howlett 2009a, 2011). Design thus requires both analytical and evidentiary capacity on the part of the government as well as the intention to exercise it, subjects which can be said to define the *design space* in which designs are formulated and emerge.

What those spaces look like and how they operate are two of the major questions addressed in this book. Past studies have helped clarify the role of historical processes, policy capacities and design intentions in affecting policy formulation processes and more recently in understanding how the bundling of multiple policy elements together to meet policy goals can be better understood and done. This literature and its implications are set out in subsequent chapters.

The general conundrum of policy design: achieving effectiveness in an uncertain world

While some aspects of studies of policy design are new, policy studies have always been interested in analyzing and improving the sets of policy tools adopted by governments to correct policy problems and in better understanding and improving processes of policy analysis and policy formulation in order to do so. While this work has progressed, however, the discussion of what general goals policy designs should serve remains disjointed. While many scholars have focused on goals like efficiency or the attainment of the greatest possible benefit at the least possible cost, a central goal, in fact, *the* central goal of policy design studies has been 'effectiveness'.

Effectiveness serves as the basic goal of any design, upon which is built other goals such as efficiency or equity (Peters et al. 2018). Effectiveness is an elusive goal, however, mainly due to the many uncertainties policy-makers face in designing policies which can attain their goals not only in the present but also into the future. Problems have different orders of complexity and as Becker and Brownson (1964) and others have pointed out. Even at a relatively simple level when a problem is well-known and knowledge is available on a subject, policy-makers may not be aware of it and thus undertake decision-making on the basis of uniformed ignorance rather than informed awareness. This becomes even more complex as collective or absolute knowledge of a subject or phenomenon is lacking or disputed, such as occurred with issues such as AIDS in the early 1980s and Climate Change in the 1990s.

Using 'effectiveness' as a criterion in judging a policy design infers that the essence of policy design resides in the articulation of policy options to meet government goals and that those designs which do this best are the most desirable (Majone 1976; Linder and Peters 1984; May 2003; Bobrow 2006). This involves the systematic effort to analyze the impacts of policy instruments on policy targets, as well as the application of this knowledge to the creation and realization of policies that can reasonably be expected to attain anticipated policy outcomes (Weaver 2009a,b; Bobrow and Dryzek 1987; Sidney 2007; Gilabert and Lawford-Smith 2012). Studies in these areas are a feature of contemporary policy design work and their content and lessons are set out in the book.

As the review of the existing policy design literature contained in this book shows, experience from a variety of sectors and jurisdictions has alluded to different aspects of what constitutes *effectiveness* and refers to this criterion in identifying and setting out *best practices* in the activity of policy design. But discussion of this latter topic is a largely scattered body of knowledge in policy studies, presenting some difficulties in drawing precise lessons about what 'effectiveness' means for the many aspects of design, ranging from abstract policy goals and instrument logics that inform the policy design environment, to the more specific mechanics of policy programmes and toolkits that help to better match particular policy objectives to individual tool settings (Howlett 2009).

In general, however, contemporary design scholars argue that feasible and realizable alternatives will be generated through better policy formulation and design processes and that such alternatives will emerge triumphant in deliberations and conflicts involved in decisions to adopt certain tools and not others. In other words, policy effectiveness is a multi-level phenomenon in which process, design and outcome are linked closely together (see Figure 1.1).

Designing public policies in the sense set out above is a difficult task in practice for any number of reasons, including lack of resources, the existence of corrupt or inefficient bureaucracies and other policy actors, the presence of powerful veto players among both state and societal actors, vague goal definition and poor implementation, evaluation and other policy practices, among others. This means there is often a high level of uncertainty in policy-making and the modern policy studies movement began with the observation that public policy-making not only commonly results from the interactions of policy-makers in the exercise of power rather than knowledge but also with the recognition that even when it is not, this does not always guarantee

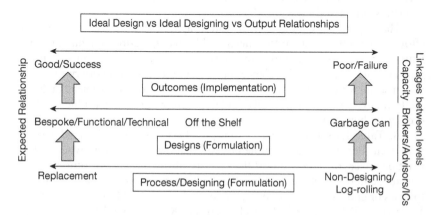

Figure 1.1 Policy effectiveness as the relationship between process, design and outcome

effective policies or the attainment of desired results (Arts and van Tatenhove 2004; Lasswell 1958; Stone 1988).

Despite these concerns, or rather precisely because these risks exist, the modern policy sciences were founded on the idea that accumulating and utilizing knowledge of the effects and impacts of a relatively well-known set of policy means developed over many years of state-building experience can effectively marshal and utilize resources and accomplish policy outcomes which enhance public value (Lasswell and Lerner 1951; Howlett and Mukherjee 2014).

As Figure 1.1 shows, the overall supposition of design studies in this field is that a good process of policy design is one in which there is an expectation that a superior process of policy formulation ('designing') will lead to a superior set of policy instruments and components ('design') which will in turn result in a superior outcome than would some other kind of process. These other kinds of processes – such as pure bargaining or log-rolling – are expected to result in an inferior mix of policy tools and elements which, by definition, would typically generate inferior results than would a set arrived at through a better, more informed process.

Dealing with uncertainty and the potential of under- and over-design

Outside of situations characterized by malfeasance and corruption where policy processes and instrument decisions are severely compromised by partisan, group and self-interest, or situations of poverty and under-development where the resources needed for effective policies and policy-making are lacking, the principal reason contemporary design scholars highlight in assessing why such linkages often do not occur automatically even in well-intentioned and well-resourced governments is *uncertainty* (Jarvis 2011b; Morgan and Henrion 1990).

That is, standard policy theory often assumes that government policy efforts can be effortlessly or 'seamlessly calibrated' to address the fundamental issue at stake with exactly the appropriate amount of effort and resources. However, much empirical evidence suggests a more complex pattern of policy response in which few efforts are well-calibrated to the problem at hand while many either systematically under- or over-react to a problem, often oscillating between these two states.

As Table 1.1 shows, in two of four possible cases, well-calibrated designs may occur but there is always the possibility of two other cases when policy reactions over- or under-'shoot' the severity of the problem or otherwise do not adequately match the nature of the underlying problem. This will lead to cases of under-reaction or over-reaction, respectively (Maor 2012b, 2014a; Jones et al. 2014; Maor 2014b; Howlett and Kemmerling 2017).

This can occur intentionally when, for example, a government wishes to display its commitment to the resolution of a problem like national security

Table 1.1 Cases of disproportional policy reaction and design

Nature of policy response	Nature of policy design problem	
	Simple	Large/complex
Simple	Proportionate design (e.g., automobile speeding)	Under-design (e.g., climate change)
Large/complex	Over-design (e.g., national security)	Proportionate design (e.g., air traffic regulation)

or crime prevention and overspends on the army or police; or in the opposite direction when it ignores opposition party demands to spend in areas its supporters consider low priority, regardless of the actual severity of the concern (Maor 2014b; Jones et al. 2014). However, it can also occur unintentionally when knowledge of the real nature of a problem is unknown or when decision-makers are over (or under) confident in the knowledge they have.

Most policy design theory operates under the assumption that governments will attempt to act as efficient policy-makers, or at least wish to do so as a normative goal, if not one always achieved in practice. This assumes government policy efforts can be 'perfectly calibrated' to seamlessly lead to the minimum appropriate amount of effort being used to maximize the solution to a policy problem. The essence of much policy analysis, modeling and advice is thus to provide templates for action appropriate to the objective characteristics and severity of policy problems.

However, this view, although pervasive in the policy sciences, is not backed up by a great deal of empirical evidence (deLeon 1999a; Hargrove 1975). As the Nobel Prize winning student of public administration, Herbert Simon (1973), pointed out many years ago, social and organizational problems come in different shapes and forms and the methods and means by which societies deal with them vary in terms of the extent of available knowledge and the ability and desire of decision-makers to incorporate that knowledge into their thinking. Some problems are 'well-structured' in the sense that their causes and effects and the means to deal with them, are well-known, while others are ill-structured in the sense that knowledge of problems and solutions is unknown or unrealized and the level of uncertainty with which they can be grappled is much higher. This was the basis for the distinction made in the 1970s by Rittel and Weber between 'wicked' and 'tame' problems (see Table 1.2).

There is much more ambiguity in scenario forecasts and projections and thus many more difficulties encountered in policy design, for example, when

Table 1.2 Tame and wicked problems

		Nature of knowledge of the problem	
		Known/well-defined and understood	Unknown/ ill-defined
Nature of knowledge of the solution	Known/well-defined and understood	Well-structured ('tame problem') e.g., automobile traffic control/ street racing	Ill-structured problem e.g., tobacco control/ addiction
	Unknown/ ill-defined	Ill-structured solution e.g., homelessness	Poorly structured ('wicked problem') e.g., climate change

critical data are lacking or non-existent. This makes it much more difficult to assign probability distributions to possible future scenarios with any confidence (McInerney et al. 2012; Lempert et al. 2002; Walker et al. 2010; Jarvis 2011a).

Historically, students of 'wicked' and 'tame' policy problems such as Churchman (1967) and Rittel and Webber (1973) thought about uncertainty in this sense (Simon 1973; Head and Alford 2015). Allowing for a greater range in estimates and efforts, as well as building in learning activities such as mid-term and first year reviews are common techniques for dealing with such issues and levels of uncertainty. However, more complex design challenges exist when both the level of 'objective' knowledge of problems as well as the relative nature of decision-makers' knowledge of that 'fact-base' are taken into account; or if there is little agreement on the choice of variables to be included in models (Walker et al. 2001; Kwakkel et al. 2010; Walker et al. 2010) (see Table 1.3).

These uncertainties can relate to 'the quality of the knowledge base' or the degree of agreement upon or the absolute size of the evidentiary support for models, or the 'value-ladenness' of policy choices, which includes different actor perspectives on the worth and value of the knowledge and information being utilized for decision-making and the presentation of arguments concerning preferred policy alternatives and pathways (Mathijssen et al. 2007). Understanding the nature of these different types and levels of uncertainty and their consequences in specific policy-making instances is thus key in policy designing (Schrader et al. 1993; Leung et al. 2015; Bond et al. 2015).

Table 1.3 Policy-maker's knowledge and comprehension matrix

		Nature of existing knowledge of a phenomenon	
		Aspects of the problem and possible solutions are known	Aspects are unknown
Nature of decision-makers' awareness of existing knowledge of a phenomenon	Aware	Known–known Key policy actors are aware of the known aspects of a phenomena (INFORMED AWARENESS)	Known–unknown Key policy actors are aware that certain aspects of the phenomenon are unknown (PRUDENT AWARENESS)
	Ignorant	Unknown–known Key policy actors are unaware of known aspects of a phenomenon (UNINFORMED IGNORANCE)	Unknown–unknown: Key policy actors are unaware that certain aspects of the phenomenon are unknown (IMPRUDENT IGNORANCE)

Thus, for example, in utilizing policy instruments, policy-makers face at least five different types of uncertainty (see Figure 1.2). This includes 'technical' uncertainty, about whether or not a specific tool or mix of tools will perform as expected, 'resource' or cost uncertainty or whether or not a government possesses adequate and plentifully available resources or capacities to implement a policy effectively, 'compliance' uncertainty or whether or not policy targets will comply with government wishes and to what extent, 'political' uncertainty over whether a design will be adopted as intended or amended or otherwise interfered with and 'effectiveness' uncertainty or whether or not the elements in a policy mix will work together toward a common aim or work at cross-purposes toward each other.

Conclusion: policy design as instrumental knowledge mobilization to promote government goals

The modern policy studies movement began with the recognition that public policy-making results from the interactions of policy-makers in the exercise of power, legitimate, or otherwise (Lasswell 1958; Arts and van Tatenhove 2004; Stone 1988). Although some of these policy-making efforts may be arbitrary or capricious, most studies urged the concerted and intentional efforts of governments to act instrumentally in a process of policy design;

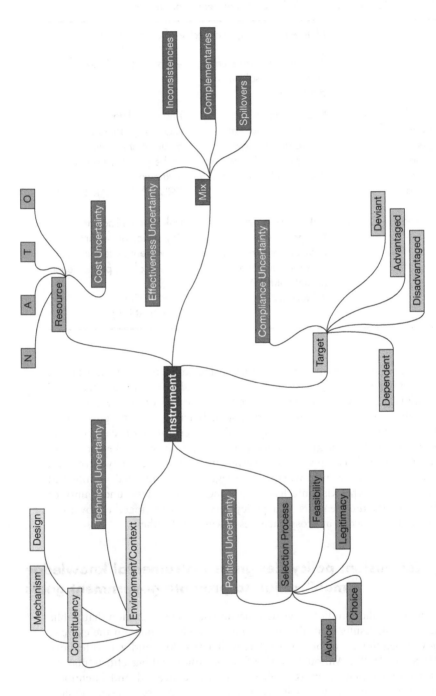

Figure 1.2 Five types of uncertainty designers must face

that is, to achieve a particular policy goal or end through the use of a set of relatively well-known set of policy means developed over many years of state-building and experience (Lasswell and Lerner 1951).

Of course, policy goals can be wide-ranging and often pose no small amount of difficulty and complexity in both their definition and diagnosis, with the implication that the formulation of solutions that are likely to succeed in addressing them necessitate the systematic consideration of the impact and feasibility of the use of specific kinds of policy means or instruments (Parsons 1995, 2001).

Thus, early work thus depicted policy design as a specific kind of policy-making in which knowledge of the policy impacts of specific policy tools was combined with the practical capacity of governments to identify and implement the most suitable technical means in the effort to achieve a specific policy aim. This activity was often expected to occur *ex ante* and independently of other considerations such as political or personal gain which might also affect formulation processes.

This 'design' activity was later recognized as requiring a situation where there was support for policy analysis and design work on the part of policy-makers and also low policy 'lock-in' on existing policy and programme arrangements. Such favorable design circumstances had to be coupled with the presence of a high level of capacity and expertise on the part of policy analysts if knowledge was to be mobilized effectively so that policy instruments were also effectively and efficiently matched to policy goals and targets (Howlett 2009a, 2010; Dunlop 2009a; Radaelli and Dunlop 2013; Howlett and Rayner 2014).

When all such conditions are present, purposive design activity is thought to be possible and preferable to other forms of policy formulation, much as is the case in the current era with recent efforts to enhance knowledge mobilization through the promotion of 'evidence-based policy-making' (Bhatta 2002; Locke 2009). When they are not, less technical and more overtly political forms of policy-making and the propensity for over- and under-design and less effective or ineffective policy outcomes are more likely to ensue (Davies 2004; Moseley and Tierney 2004; Howlett 2009b). The fervent wish of proponents of the design orientation both in the past and now is to reduce the latter instances to as few as possible by promoting the kinds of orientations and dedication of resources required for the former, in the belief that better designed policies are more likely to solve pressing problems and correct social ills (Bobrow 2006; Azuela and Barroso 2012).

Plan of the book

This book introduces students to the principles and elements of policy design in contemporary governance. It does so through the study of the implementation instruments used by governments in carrying out their tasks and adapting to and altering, their environments. These form the basic foundations or structures upon which policies and programmes rest. An essential component of modern governance, the range of substantive and procedural policy instruments together comprise the toolbox from which governments select specific tools expected to resolve policy problems.

The book begins with the discussion of several aspects of instrument use in contemporary government and then moves on to consider the logic of policy design and the principles behind the selection and use of specific types of instruments in the process of policy formulation. It then discusses in more detail when this occurs in policy-making and who makes these kinds of decisions. The merits, demerits and rationales for the use of specific organization, regulatory, financial and information-based tools and the trends visible in their use are then set out in a separate section.

This is followed by a discussion of what it is that makes and defines, a design as a good one.

Readings

Bason, C. and S. Andrea. (2014). 'Public Design in Global Perspective: Empirical Trends'. In C. Bason (ed.), *Design for Policy*. Burlington, VT: Gower, 23–40.

Bobrow, D. (2006). 'Policy Design: Ubiquitous, Necessary and Difficult'. In B. G. Peters and J. Pierre (eds), *Handbook of Public Policy*. London: Sage, 75–96.

Churchman, C. W. (1967). 'Wicked Problems'. *Management Science* 14, no. 4: B141–B142.

Clarke, A. and J. Craft. (2017). 'The Twin Faces of Public Sector Design'. *Governance* (forthcoming). Accessed 3 April 2018.

Colebatch, H. K. (2017). 'The Idea of Policy Design: Intention, Process, Outcome, Meaning and Validity'. *Public Policy and Administration* (18 May): 365–83.

Dryzek, J. S. and B. Ripley. (1988). 'The Ambitions of Policy Design'. *Policy Studies Review* 7, no. 4: 705–19.

Hansson, S. O. (1996). 'Decision Making under Great Uncertainty'. *Philosophy of the Social Sciences* 26, no. 3 (1 September): 369–86.

Hermus, M. and A. van Buuren. (2017). 'Applying Design Methodology in Public Administration. A State of the Art Based upon a Systematic Literature Review'. Presented at the ICPP, Singapore, 2017.

Howlett, M. 'Policy Design: What, Who, How and Why?' In H. Charlotte, L. Pierre and L. G. Patrick (eds), *L'instrumentation et ses effets*. Paris: Presses de Sciences Po, 281–315.

Howlett, M. and R. P. Lejano. (2013). 'Tales from the Crypt: The Rise and Fall (and Re-Birth?) of Policy Design Studies'. *Administration & Society* 45, no. 3: 356–80.

Levin, K., B. Cashore, S. Bernstein and G. Auld. (2012). 'Overcoming the Tragedy of Super Wicked Problems: Constraining Our Future Selves to Ameliorate Global Climate Change'. *Policy Sciences* 45, no. 2 (23 May): 123–52.

Linder, S. H. and B. G. Peters. (1984). 'From Social Theory to Policy Design'. *Journal of Public Policy* 4, no. 3: 237–59.

Maor, M. (2016). 'The Implications of the Emerging Disproportionate Policy Perspective for the New Policy Design Studies'. *Policy Sciences* (19 July): 1–16.

Mintrom, M. and J. Luetjens. (2016). 'Design Thinking in Policymaking Processes: Opportunities and Challenges'. *Australian Journal of Public Administration* 75, no. 3 (1 September): 391–402.

Nair, S. and M. Howlett. (2017). 'Policy Myopia as a Source of Policy Failure: Adaptation and Policy Learning under Deep Uncertainty'. *Policy & Politics* 45, no. 1 (January): 103–18.

Ralph, P. and Y. Wand. (2013). 'A Proposal for a Formal Definition of the Design Concept'. *Annual Review of Policy Design* 1, no. 1 (6 September): 1–35.

Rittel, H. W. J. and M. M. Webber. (1973). 'Dilemmas in a General Theory of Planning'. *Policy Sciences* 4: 155–69.

Schön, D. A. (1992). 'Designing as Reflective Conversation with the Materials of a Design Situation'. *Knowledge-Based Systems* 5, no. 1 (March): 3–14.

Veselý, A. (2007). 'Problem Delimitation in Public Policy Analysis'. *Central European Journal of Public Policy* 1, no. 1: 80–101.

Chapter 2

Policy design in the contemporary era

Beyond globalization and governance

Policy design studies in the sense set out in the Chapter 1 deal with the vagaries of policy formulation by separating out two dimensions of the design experience: on the one hand the exploration of the procedural aspects of design – the specific types of policy formulation activities which lead to design rather than some other form of policy generation – and the substantive – that is, the substance or content of the design itself. This is the policy-relevant articulation of the well-known distinction in design studies generally between 'design-as-verb' ('policy formulation') and 'design-as-noun' (mix of policy tools and instruments) (Hillier et al. 1972; Hillier and Leaman 1974; Gero 1990).

This orientation toward policy studies, however, declined after 1990. This was largely due to the emergence of alternative globalization and governance discourses and a research agenda in the policy sciences which shifted attention toward events occurring at the international and meta-societal levels of analysis which were often seen by proponents to dictate domestic policy tool choices, making their detailed analysis unnecessary or redundant (Howlett 2011; Howlett and Lejano 2013; Jordan et al. 2013). That is, the emergent globalization and governance literatures of the time argued that instrument choices were more or less preordained by meta-level changes in the relationships existing between states, markets and civil society organizations which favored the latter two and therefore reduced the significance and the need for sophisticated and lengthy analysis, of the former (Rhodes 1996; Kooiman 2000).

Studies in this vein promoted the use of particular types of tools – mainly market and network-based ones – regardless of context and with little regard for the appropriateness of their selection or consideration of how they might interact with pre-existing tools (Howlett and Lejano 2012). Difficulties with both the formulation and implementation of policy proposals based on such conceptions, however, led to a spate of more recent studies (see e.g., Jarvis 2011a; Ramesh and Howlett 2006; Ramesh and Fritzen 2009) which have sought to re-assert the centrality of the role of government in policy formulation and implementation (Capano 2011; Koch 2013) and the continuing importance and need for, better policy designs and understandings of design processes.

The changing context of policy design studies: the globalization and governance turns of the 1990s

Globalization involves the extensification and intensification – 'stretching and deepening' in the words of Held et al. (1999) – of cross-border interactions. While much of this process comprises trade and economic interactions, it also includes cultural, political, military and ideational relations among others.

There is a broad agreement among many popular commentators that globalization fundamentally altered many aspects of contemporary governance and policy designs. As a result of globalization, it is often alleged, for example, states' governance practices have been greatly constrained; not only in what states do but also in how they do it (Cerny 1996; Reinicke 1998). That is, as globalization has proceeded apace, states' options in terms of the policy instruments available to them in order to realize their ends have been argued to have changed in response to their growing inability to manage public policy-making processes and outcomes as they had in past eras. This process has therefore altered the nature of the kinds of policy options which are feasible in the new global circumstances, affecting the kinds of designs which emerge from policy formulation processes and can be successfully implemented.

Similarly, many commentators have also argued, either separately or in conjunction with the globalization thesis, that state practices have also been changing as societies are being transformed by improved information and communication technologies to become ever more complex networks of interorganizational actors (Mayntz 1993; Castells 1996). This increased 'networkization' of society, it is argued, has meant that many functions and activities traditionally undertaken exclusively by governments increasingly involve ever larger varieties of non-governmental actors, themselves involved in increasingly complex relationships with other societal, and state, actors (Foster and Plowden 1996). This second movement toward the development of networked societies, it is often argued, has further complicated the situation and accentuated the constraints globalization has imposed upon the capabilities of domestic states, further reducing their capacity for independent action and limiting their design choices and alternatives (Dobuzinskis 1987; Lehmbruch 1991).

Many commentators have suggested that the result of these dual processes has been that implementation practices have become more participatory and consultative over the last several decades (Alshuwaikhat and Nkwenti 2002; Arellano-Gault and Vera-Cortes 2005) as networkization has increased, while over this same time period and longer many public enterprises have also been privatized and previously government-provided services contracted-out to non-governmental organizations (NGOs) as globalization has advanced the use of market-based tools. In addition, it has also been argued that in some sectors regulatory activities have shifted from 'enforcement' to 'compliance' regimes; tax incentives have increasingly substituted for earlier systems of subsidies and grants; and many countries now place an increasing emphasis on public information and other similar types of campaigns, replacing or supplementing more coercive forms of government activity (Woodside 1983; Hawkins and Thomas 1989; Hood 1991; Howlett and Ramesh 1993; Weiss and Tschirhart 1994; Doern and Wilks 1998).

However, while the evidence of some changes in how governments function in the contemporary era is undeniable and will be discussed in depth in subsequent chapters, the scope, significance and causes of these changes remain contentious. Especially, contentious is the belief that the changes in formulation and implementation practices which have occurred have been triggered solely by the changes in the domestic and international spheres encapsulated in the dual movements of globalization and 'networkization' cited above. And even more contentious is the closely related idea that governments have no choice in their policy designs but to continue these transformations and continue to work toward the reduction of a state presence in the economy and society as these dual processes continue to unfold and intensify (Levi-Faur 2009; O'Toole and Meier 2010).

The effects of globalization and internationalization on policy design

In order to assess the actual effects and impact of environmental changes on state behaviour, it is necessary to acknowledge that serious gaps exist in our understanding of the workings and characteristics of globalization and its policy consequences (Hay 2006). Contrary to what is commonly believed and often advocated, in our global era the domestic state remains far from overwhelmed and lacking autonomous decision-making capacity (Weiss 2003; Braithwaite 2008). The source of many of the changes in the patterns of policy-making and instrument choice found in contemporary society very often lies in the domestic rather than the international arena (Scott et al. 2004; Levi-Faur 2009). Domestic states, be they national or sub-national, do not just react to changes in their international environments but also are very much still involved in the design and implementation of policies expected to achieve their ends (Lynn 1980; Vogel 2001). And to the extent that global factors have had an impact on domestic policy designs and governance practices, it is often through what can be termed more 'indirect' and 'opportunity' effects spilling over from trade and other activities, rather than from the 'direct' effects that advocates of design alterations typically cite in arguing that state behaviour must change (Howlett and Ramesh 2006).

That is, while the direct effects of globalization on instrument choice are limited, indirect effects are more substantial despite their informal nature. These consist of 'spill-over' effects and of opportunities for interaction and increased learning and lesson drawing which occur as a side effect of globalization. One of the spill-over effects of increasing integration of international markets, for example, is manifested in governments' reluctance to resort to new taxes or establish new public enterprises lest they send the 'wrong' signals to financial markets. While governments still can, and do, employ an extensive array of command and control tools, they must now anticipate adverse commercial reactions and prepare to deal with them. Deregulation and privatization measures are also widely reported in the international media and help to build the international reputation of governments undertaking them. Hence, a side effect of globalization is that governments may resort to increased use of information provision as a means to advertise a market-friendly outlook and a favorable disposition toward foreign direct investment. If these measures succeed in attracting foreign investment, the success is cited as a reason for further deregulation and privatization and for further use of state advertising.

Globalization also increases opportunities for cross-sectoral and cross-national interaction among policy practitioners and commentators. Policy-makers not only have instant access to information available on the internet but routinely get together with their foreign counterparts at countless governmental and non-governmental meetings that are held on the entire gamut of policy subjects. The meetings are forums for learning from each other's experiences and to better appreciate the technical, economic and, political potential and limitations of different policy tools. Other countries' experiences often form the starting point for governments embarking on national policy reforms. Thus, policy learning, emulation, or transfer play a critical role in efforts to reform policy instruments used to implement public policies (Huber 1991; Bennett and Howlett 1992; Hall 1993; Dolowitz and Marsh 2000; Stone 2000). Meseguer (2003) and Simmons and Elkins (2004), for instance, list learning and emulation as the key factors underlying the spread of privatization and liberalization; although the former finds no evidence that international pressures played any significant role.

Another example of policy diffusion through learning is the emulation of pollution trading rights in other areas after its perceived success in controlling the use of ozone-depleting Chloro Fluoro Carbons (CFCs) (Parson and Fisher-Vanden 1999). But again, we need to recognize that policy learning and emulation are constrained by political and institutional factors. Domestic political opposition to the adoption of measures that have successfully worked elsewhere is commonplace, forcing policy-makers to baulk or at least compromise in their use in new situations. The imperatives of path dependency – the tendency for old choices to become entrenched and institutionalized – also often make it difficult to adopt any policy instrument that is substantially different from current practice (March and Olsen 1989; Pierson 2000).

That is, there is little doubt that economic, diplomatic, military and aid-related relations among nations help shape many choices of policies and policy tools. It is well known, for example, that many countries are aggressive in pressuring other countries to weaken regulations or preferential tax or subsidy treatments that restrict international firms' business activities, and global and regional multilateral agreements are the most direct ways by which extra-territorial factors shape the choice of policy instruments. But these exist only in very few sectors and often have large areas of exclusion even when they are present. Trade and investment such as the World Trade Organization (WTO) agreements and various Free Trade Agreements, for instance, often specify in great detail the measures that governments can or cannot adopt vis-à-vis domestic and international producers. But, powerful as these treaties are, they only prohibit the use of a small number of very specific instruments such as tariffs and quotas to assist domestic producers and even then they often contain exceptions to those bans. The use of subsidies of various kinds specifically intended to assist domestic producers, for example, is restricted by countervailing duty clauses and other similar measures, but activities in the cultural and agricultural realms are often excluded from these measures as are national security issues.

Similarly, more general political agreements, whether formal or informal, can also have a constraining direct effect on the choice of policies and policy tools. The European Union is an extreme case of the formal transfer of decision-making authority to a supra-national center, for example, which often severely limits what national governments can do and the instruments they can employ to affect their decisions (Kassim and Le Galès 2010). However, even here the restrictions on national governments' abilities to employ regulatory and fiscal tools on their own are often less significant than often assumed (Halpern 2010). And, even when they are, national governments are often able to craft their own specific solutions to ongoing policy problems with little regard to EU policy through mechanisms such as 'subsidiarity' or the 'Open Method of Coordination' which allow local states to determine and design their own policy responses to EU-level initiatives (Meuleman 2010b; Heidbreder 2010; Lierse 2010; Tholoniat 2010).

Thus, while there is no doubt that the evolution of these kinds of international treaties and arrangements is an important development, in many sectors and areas of government activity they impose only very minimal or no constraints on the choice of policy tools utilized by governments; nowhere near those alleged by both proponents and opponents of globalization-led promarket reforms (see especially Palan and Abbott 1996; Clark 1998; Weiss 1999; Bernhagen 2003). There are few international agreements that specifically require governments to privatize or deregulate, for example and the sectors which have experienced the deepest deregulation and privatization in recent decades – financial, telecommunications and air transportation services – predate the General Agreement on Trade in Services (GATS) negotiated under the WTO umbrella.

Hence, to date, the actual impact of globalization on domestic state policy designs has been much less than often alleged, outside of several well-known sectors and events, and policy designs and designing activities in many sectors have not been fundamentally re-aligned as a result of these two phenomena. The direct international constraints on policy designs typically cited by proponents of the globalization thesis, for example, have largely been confined to cross-border economic exchanges and do not cover much of what governments do and how they do it. Traditional command and control instruments of governance, such as regulation by government or independent regulatory commissions, state-owned enterprises and direct taxation and subsidization, are far from antithetical to globalization as is evident in their continued and at times even increasing use in policy designs in a variety of national and sectoral settings (Jayasuriya 2001, 2004; Vogel and Kagan 2002; Jordana and Levi-Faur 2004a; Ramesh and Howlett 2006).

Changing network effects: the 'government to governance' hypothesis

Similarly, the need to shift toward the greater use of network management tools and activities put forward by adherents of the argument that states have moved 'from government to governance' as a result of changes in society and the way in which government interacts with it, is also lacking a great deal of empirical evidence (Howlett et al. 2009; Schout et al. 2010). While it is clear that the development of modern information and communications technologies have had a serious impact on the way in which individuals and organizations interact and organize themselves in contemporary societies, it is not clear that these developments have had an equally direct effect in altering traditional governance practices or policy designs (Hood 2006; Hood and Margetts 2007).

As is well known, 'governing' is what governments do: controlling the allocation of resources among social actors; providing a set of rules and operating a set of institutions setting out 'who gets what, where, when and how' in society; while at the same time managing the symbolic resources that are the basis of political legitimacy (Lasswell 1958). But this is not synonymous with 'governance'.

Governing involves the establishment of a basic set of relationships between governments and their citizens which can vary from highly structured and controlled to arrangements that are monitored only loosely and informally, if at all. In its broadest sense, 'governance' is a term used to describe the *mode* of coordination exercised by state actors in their interactions with societal actors and organizations (de Bruijn and ten Heuvelhof

1995; Kooiman 1993, 2000; Rhodes 1996; Klijn and Koppenjan 2000c). 'Governance' is thus about establishing, promoting and supporting a specific type of relationship between governmental and non-governmental actors in the governing process.

In modern capitalist societies, this means managing relationships with businesses and civil society organizations also involved in the creation of public value and the delivery of goods and services to citizens (Hall and Soskice 2001). As Steurer (2013) suggested, these three basic governance actors can be portrayed as interacting within a set of inter-related spheres of activity generating at least four ideal governance arrangements at their intersections: *market governance* between governments and business, *civil society governance* between governments and non-governmental actors, *private governance* between market and civil society actors and *network governance* between all three (see Figure 2.1).

However, this logic of governance is more extensive than Steurer suggests since different combinations of government, civil society and businesses exist and within each combination different sets of actors have different core roles and strengths. When variations on the strength of each actor in a governance relationship are included, the types of governance arrangements or 'modes' stretch to at least a dozen types, as shown in Figure 2.1.

Mark Considine and his colleagues investigated these arrangements and linkages and identified four common governance arrangements found in modern liberal-democratic states which they relate to specific policy foci, forms of state–society interactions and overall governance aims (see Table 2.1).

The mechanisms in Figure 2.1 involving the dominance of hierarchy (cells 1 and 2) can be seen to essentially involve a legal mode of governance while those featured by the dominance of market mechanisms (cells 3 and 4) form market modes of governance. Trilateral arrangements in which hierarchy dominates (cells 5 and 6), strongly or weakly, are best described as corporatist mode of governance. Trilateral mechanisms in which network or market dominates and the government plays a secondary role (cells 7, 8, 9 and 10) constitute different forms of network governance. Finally, private modes of governance involves market and network mechanisms (cells 11 and 12) with the government playing only a peripheral (albeit essential) role.

Typical management activities related to collaborative or network modes of governance are those which affect network creation, recognition, capacity-building and content creation or alteration. Robert Agranoff (Agranoff and McGuire 1999), for example, has observed that in a typical 'network management' situation 'the primary activities of ... [a] manager involve selecting appropriate actors and resources, shaping the operating context of the network and developing ways to cope with strategic and operational complexity' (21). Such definitions of network management activities, however, are very vague and their design implications unclear.

Many early proponents of the idea of increased 'networkization' simply expected governance arrangements to shift evenly away from sets of formal

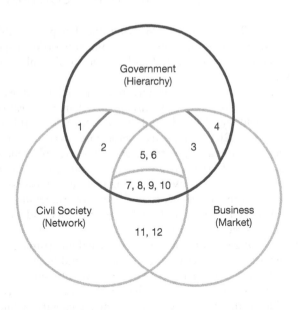

Cell #	Governance Mechanisms, by importance	Mode of Governance
1.	Hierarchy – Network	Strong Legal Governance
2.	Network – Hierarchy	Weak Legal Governance
3.	Market – Hierarchy	Strong Market Governance
4.	Hierarchy – Network	Weark market Governance
5.	Hierarchy – Market – Network	State Corporatist Governance
6.	Hierarchy – Network – Market	Societal Corporatist Governance
7.	Network – Market – Hierarchy	Network Governance
8.	Market – Network – Hierarchy	
9.	Network – Hierarchy – Market	
10.	Market – Hierarchy – Network	
11.	Market – Network	Strong Private Governance
12.	Network – Market	Weak Private Governance

Figure 2.1 Modes of governance, including variation by lead actor

Table 2.1 Modes of governance (empirical content)

Mode of governance	Central focus of governance activity	Form of state control of relationships	Overall governance aim	Prime service delivery mechanism	Key procedural tool for policy implementation
Legal governance	Legality – promotion of law and order in social relationships	Legislation, law and administration	Legitimacy – voluntary compliance	Rights – property, civil and human	Courts and litigation
Corporate governance	Management – of major organized social actors	Plans	Controlled and balanced rates of socio-economic development	Targets – operational objectives, subsidies and grants	Specialized and privileged advisory committees
Market governance	Competition – promotion of small and medium-sized enterprises	Contracts and regulations	Resource/cost efficiency and control	Regulatory boards and prices – controlling for externalities, supply and demand	Tribunals and commissions
Network governance	Relationships – promotion of inter-actor organizational activity	Collaboration	Co-optation of dissent and self-organization of social actors	Networks of governmental and non-governmental organizations	Network brokerage activities

Source: Modified from Considine, M. 2001. *Enterprising States: The Public Management of Welfare-to-Work*. Cambridge: Cambridge University Press; and English, L. M. and M. Skellern. 'Public-Private Partnerships and Public-Sector Management Reform; A Comparative Analysis'. *International Journal of Public Policy* 1, nos. 1/2 (2005): 1–21.

institutions, coercive power relations and substantive regulatory tools found in hierarchical systems toward more informal institutions, non-coercive relationships of power and a marked preference for procedural instruments and soft law in more plurilateral systems (Dunsire 1993b; Kooiman 1993). However, the possible variations in governance types and outcomes are a good deal more complicated once the possibility of sectoral variations is taken into account (van Kersbergen and van Waarden 2004; Meuleman 2009; Harrop 1992; Cerny 1993; Pontusson 1995; Daugbjerg 1998; Haas 2004; Zielonka 2007).

As observers such as Knill and Lehmkuhl have noted, governance arrangements feature different relative strengths of the public and private actors involved (Knill and Lehmkuhl 2002; Jordan et al. 2005) and vary according to whether these relationships are expressed in formal or informal terms (Treib et al. 2007; Kritzinger and Pulzl 2008). The nature of regulatory activity, for example, focuses on the formal or informal nature of the legal instruments deployed in policy implementation. 'Hard' law is thus typically conceived as synonymous with formal, state-centric, command and control types of regulation that impose generally applicable obligations onto target groups of actors, articulated with a relatively high degree of precision and directly enforceable through the courts. In contrast, 'soft' law represents a weakening (or softening) along these key metrics of obligation, precision and enforceability (Tollefson 2004; Tollefson et al. 2008).

The existence of several possible alternative types or 'modes' of governance existing simultaneously at the sectoral level suggests a more complex picture of governance arrangements, instrument choices and policy designs than the one-to-one national level, multi-sectoral shift toward the use of more participatory and less 'command and control' tools often proposed by adherents of the 'government to governance' thesis (Koppenjan and Klijn 2004; Barnett et al. 2009; Esmark 2009; Hysing 2009; Edelenbos et al. 2010; Hardiman and Scott 2010; Schout et al. 2010).

A new design research agenda beyond globalization and governance

It is only recently that policy design has re-emerged as a distinct field of inquiry as the merits of the older tools orientation was re-discovered following the failure in many jurisdictions of the overly simplistic design precepts put forward by advocates of globalization and governance thinking (Tollefson et al. 2012; Hay and Smith 2010; Jarvis 2011a).

This renewed policy design orientation is different from its predecessor, however. Like the former, it continues to advocate for the construction and analysis of ideal arrangements of policy components that can then be adapted to meet the bounds of a particular context in order to result in particular outcomes (Hood 2007a, Hood and Margetts 2007). Unlike it, however, it focusses on the articulation of design involving multiple tools, not single ones!

Dealing with policy mixes

The new design orientation focuses on bundles or portfolios of tools and the interactive effects which occur when multiple tools are used over time in policy packages operating in complex multi-policy and multi-level design contexts and often expected to address multiple goals and objectives (Howlett 2014a; Howlett and Lejano 2013; Howlett et al. 2014). The construction of policy packages operating in complex multi-policy and multi-level design contexts, rather than single instrument choices, is a key feature of contemporary design studies and practices (del Río and Howlett 2013).

Current studies seeks to better describe the nature of the bundles or portfolios of tools and to help understand the interactive effects which occur when multiple tools are used over time (Doremus 2003; Howlett 2014a; Howlett et al. 2014; Jordan et al. 2011, 2012). As such, the research agenda of the new design orientation is focused on questions which the earlier literature largely neglected, such as the trade-offs existing between different tool uses and how to deal with the synergies and conflicts which result from tool interactions.

These studies are especially interested in the different means and patterns through which policy mixes evolve over time (van der Heijden 2011, Thelen 2003, 2004; Kay 2007; Feindt 2012). They also delve more deeply than before into the behavioural characteristics of designers (Considine 2012) and into the location and activities of different kinds of advisors and experts involved in policy formulation activities (Craft and Howlett 2012) and how their activities and advice affect policy designs and designing.

Dealing with policy dynamics

A second important research area in the new policy design studies deals with better understanding the temporal processes through which designs and design spaces evolve. Where the old design orientation often assumed a constrained yet blank slate available to policy designers, newer design thinking is rooted more in an empirical experience that has generally shown policy designers having to work in spaces with already established policy mixes and significant policy legacies. They draw heavily on the work of historical and sociological neo-institutionalists such as Kathleen Thelen (2003, 2004) who noted how macro-institutional arrangements have normally been less the product of calculated planning than the result of processes of incremental modifications or reformulations such as 'layering' or 'drift' (Kay 2007; van der Heijden 2011). In the new design orientation, these processes are seen as also applying to policy mixes.

Mixes may emerge over long stretches of time as a result of earlier policy decisions. As a result, even when the initial logic of these decisions matching policy tool and target may have been clear, through multiple layering processes they can gradually transform into degenerate arrangements over time (van der Heijden 2011; Bode 2006; Howlett and Rayner 1995; Orren and Skowronek 1998; Rayner et al. 2001; Torenvlied and Akkerman 2004; Hacker 2005).

Optimizing the choice of instruments in such mixes requires an additional level of knowledge of instrument-goal interactions and considerations of both long and short-term processes of policy change. Scholars in the new design orientation, for example, are concerned with how 'unintended' policy mixes, created and limited by historical legacies, can be hampered due to internal inconsistencies, whereas other policy instrument groupings can be more successful in creating an internally supportive combination (Howlett and Rayner 2007; Grabosky 1994; Gunningham, Grabosky and Sinclair 1998; del Río 2010).

That is, in addition to questions relating to the integration of policy tools and understanding design spaces, the evolution and history of policy mixes are also of concern to the most recent generation of design thinkers. While the old orientation tended to suggest that design could only occur in spaces where policy packages could be designed 'en bloc' and 'de novo', the new orientation recognizes that most design circumstances involve building on foundations created in another era and working with sub-optimal design spaces. This contextual 'lock in' can impact the formulation process by restricting a government's ability to evaluate alternatives and plan or design in an effective manner (Howlett 2009a; Oliphant and Howlett 2010; Williams 2012).

In such situations, 'designers often attempt to patch or restructure existing policy elements rather than propose alternatives de novo although the situation may require the latter' (Howlett 2013. See also Gunningham and Sinclair 1999a; Thelen 2003, 2004; Eliadis et al. 2005). Contemporary policy design scholars are thus very interested in processes such as how policy formulators, such as software designers, can issue such 'patches' to correct flaws in existing mixes or allow them to adapt to changing circumstances (Rayner 2013; Howlett 2013; Howlett and Rayner 2014). And they are also interested in related subjects such as how policy experiments can help reveal the possibilities of re-design (Hoffman 2011) or how building temporal properties into tool mixes – 'adaptive policy-making' (Swanson et al. 2010) – can make designs more flexible or resistant to shifting conditions (Walker et al. 2010; Haasnoot et al. 2013).

Dealing with 'new' policy tools: co-production, co-design, social media and nudges

A third contemporary research area concerns the analysis and inclusion in designs of several new, or at least apparently new, policy tools (Hood and Margetts 2007). Most notable in the present era are concerns for the design and operation of collaborative tools and platforms such as crowd-sourcing, co-production and social media use, as well as behavioural tools such as the use of defaults and other tools derived from the insights of recent research in behavioural economics. The former set of tools includes the use of social media platforms (Taeihagh 2017; Liu 2017) to organize both the delivery of services – 'co-production' (Pestoff 2006; Pestoff et al. 2006) – and to influence the design process – 'co-design' (Blomkamp 2018). The latter includes a variety of tools designed to affect the automatic cognitive system in humans and 'nudge' them toward behaviours in their 'best interests' (Thaler and Sunstein 2009; Thaler et al. 2010).

The use of tools to promote collaboration and co-production, for example, is a growing area which has received very little treatment in the policy instruments literature to date and which can benefit from the insights of public management and public policy research. It concerns recent trends toward the increased promotion of collaboration and the co-production of many public services, a predominant feature of the New Public Governance (NPG) approach to public management, in the increased use of non-state actors and organizations to provide 'policy-like' outputs and activities. These range from using disability and elderly support organizations to provide services ('co-production') as well as other activities such as the use of non-governmental 'stewardship' councils to provide a basic framework of regulation ('co-management') as occurs with groups such as the Forest Stewardship Council with respect to logging activities, the Marine Stewardship Council with respect to the fisheries and many others (Ansell and Gash 2017).

Many proponents, for example, claim 'collaborative governance' combines the best of both government and market-based arrangements by bringing together key public and private actors in a policy sector in a constructive and inexpensive way (Koffijberg 2012; Rhodes 1997). Many key sectors from health to education and others now feature elements of either or both hierarchical approaches – regulation, bureaucratic oversight and service delivery – as well as market and network-based non-hierarchical approaches such as co-pays and exchanges, voluntary organizations and increasingly co-production (Brandsen and Pestoff 2006; Pestoff 2006, 2012; Pestoff et al. 2006, 2012).

As Capano (2011) and Capano et al. (2015) have noted, governance comes in many different varieties and modes. As discussed above, some of these, such as network, market and hierarchical modes are well known (Williamson 1996b). Others such as co-production (Brandsen and Pestoff 2006) and certification (Cashore 2002; Cashore et al. 2003) are much less so (Tenbensel 2005).

Although often promoted as solutions to many policies and governance challenges, any preference for collaboration has little evidence supporting it (see Adger and Jordan 2009; Howlett et al. 2009; Hysing 2009; Kjær 2004; Van Kersbergen and Van Waarden 2004; Tunzelmann 2010). In fact, a large group of 'collaborative' governance arrangements (Ansell and Gash 2008) are often prescribed without knowing exactly (a) what they are and (b) under what conditions they are likely to succeed or fail (Howlett and Ramesh 2016a,b). The use and abuse of such arrangements requires better analysis.

Unfortunately, poor definitions and poor theorization plague many accounts of collaboration in which otherwise dissimilar governance efforts are often clumped under the same rubric and their nuances and differences ignored.

Some of these tools also can be used to develop a more 'bottom-up' citizen-centered type of policy design sometimes referred to as 'co-design' (Blomkamp 2018; Bason 2014). This is an extension of older practices around public participation and collaborative governance in which an effort is made to enhance the 'wisdom of crowds' and citizen knowledge in the policy formulation and design process.

A second set of tools which has received a great deal of attention of late is those behavioural modifications premised on the notion of 'nudges' which have gained much traction within policy-making circles in recent times (see Productivity Commission 2007); Center d'analyse stratégique 2011; Dolan and Galizzi 2014). Sunstein (2014) identifies 10 important nudges types: (i) default rules; (ii) simplification; (iii) use of social norms; (iv) increases in ease and convenience; (v) disclosure; (vi) warnings, graphic, or otherwise; (vii) pre-commitment strategies; (viii) reminders; (ix) eliciting implementation intentions; and (x) informing people of the nature and consequences of their own past choices.

Most of these are variations on previous efforts to alter public and individual behaviour through information provision, although with a decidedly less conscious or rational bent (John 2013). That is, many of these efforts are geared toward what has been termed 'System 1' thinking, which is the less cognitive more automatic or reflexive mode of thinking, compared to the more conscious 'System 2' mode (Kahneman 2013a). Despite the rising popularity and promotion of the 'nudge' approach, however, it has its share of detractors. For instance, in some treatments of information tools behavioural modification is expected to follow government cues unthinkingly ('system 1' or 'instinctual' nudges) but many of the tools such as disclosure and reminders also require some aspects of 'system 2' or conscious thinking and cognition.

The role of trust and credibility of the information sent and received, for example, is also often underestimated. According to proponents of the nudge approach, for example, it is desirable and possible for public institutions to influence behaviour, while they must also respect freedom of choice (Sunstein and Thaler 2003; Thaler and Sunstein 2009). The 'libertarian paternalism' which underlies the urge to deploy nudges (Sunstein 2015), however, may well undermine these efforts at persuasion by leading to a general distrust of government (Wilkinson 2013; Mols et al. 2015; Galizzi 2014; Momsen and Stoerk 2014; Carter 2015). Critics, also argue that in seeking to exploit and improve imperfections in human judgment, nudging is a manipulative technique and thus the concept of 'liberty' on which it hinges precludes it from being empowering in any substantive sense (Goodwin 2012; Mills 2013; Wilkinson 2013). According to Wilkinson, a nudge could be manipulative yet consistent with target's autonomy, if and only if a target consents to it, something which undermines the impact and effect of many nudge techniques based on less conscious forms of reasoning.

And debate is not limited to the ethics of the approach. It has also been criticized for not being effective in changing deeply ingrained behaviour due to its overemphasis on individual preferences and reliance on an atomistic approach to social structure. Nudges may thus fail in making people think together, deliberate together and act in concert to solve large-scale problems (Goodwin 2012).

Conclusion: moving forward in policy design studies

The future research agenda for scholars in the new design orientation includes many related subjects. As set out above, three of the subjects of much current interest include outlining principles of design quality in complex multi-tiered mixes and understanding design spaces, their evolution and the evaluation of different kinds of design processes associated with them and dealing with 'new' or innovative policy tools such as co-production or behavioural nudges.

The recognition of the continued vitality of the state in a globalized environment along with the existence of multiple modern sectoral modes of governance suggests a more subtle and nuanced account of policy design trends and influences is required than is typically found in the discussions about instrument use and policy design which have flowed from many current studies of globalization and network governance. However, many existing debates about policy design often continue to fixate on the impact of these two processes and, as a result, much of the existing discussion of policy tools and policy design is characterized by misinformation, ideological predilection and unnecessarily polarized position taking.

Fortunately, other scholarship on policy design and policy instrument choice has offered pathways to a better understanding of instrument selection and policy design by grounding it more carefully in empirical studies and in more nuanced and sophisticated analyses of policy-making practices and activities (Bressers and O'Toole 1998; de Bruijn and Hufen 1998; Van Nispen and Ringeling 1998). As the discussion in this book will show, embedding the discussion of policy design in the Procrustean bed of globalization and network theory is not a useful way to advance thinking on the subject. Understanding contemporary policy design rather requires an effort to develop a more nuanced understanding of the policy formulation and implementation activities of governments than is provided by adhering to either or both of the 'globalization' and 'government to governance' hypotheses. A more detailed and systematic understanding of the kinds of policy choices open to governments and of their ability to choose specific combinations of policy tools in their efforts to create and manage public policy-making is needed to advance our understanding of policy design (Ingraham 1987). This book is intended to help facilitate this understanding.

Readings

Australian Government Productivity Commission. (2007). *Public Support for Science and Innovation*. Canberra, Australia.

Bason, C. and A. Schneider. (2014). 'Public Design in Global Perspective: Empirical Trends'. In C. Bason (ed.), *Design for Policy* (new edn). Farnham, UK; Burlington, VT: Gower, 23–40.

Blomkamp, E. (2018). 'The Promise of Co-Design for Public Policy'. *Australian Journal of Public Administration* (forthcoming). Accessed 31 October 2018.

Bovaird, T. (2007). 'Beyond Engagement and Participation: User and Community Coproduction of Public Services'. *Public Administration Review* 67, no. 5: 846–60.

Brandsen, T. and M. Honingh. (2016). 'Distinguishing Different Types of Coproduction: A Conceptual Analysis Based on the Classical Definitions'. *Public Administration Review* 76, no. 3: 427–35.

Brudney, J. L. and R. E. England. (1983). 'Toward a Definition of the Coproduction Concept'. *Public Administration Review* 43, no. 1: 59–65.

Cerny, P. G. (1996). 'International Finance and the Erosion of State Policy Capacity'. In P. Gummett (ed.), *Globalization and Public Policy*. Cheltenham, UK: Edward Elgar, 83–104.

de Bruijn, J. A. and E. F. ten Heuvelhof. (1995). 'Policy Networks and Governance'. In D. L. Weimer (ed.), *Institutional Design*. Boston, MA: Kluwer Academic Publishers, 161–79.

Hobson, J. and M. Ramesh. (2002). 'Globalisation Makes of States What States Make of It: Between Agency and Structure in the State/Globalisation Debate'. *New Political Economy* 7, no. 1: 5–22.

Howlett, M. and M. Ramesh. (2006). 'Globalization and the Choice of Governing Instruments: The Direct, Indirect and Opportunity Effects of Internationalization'. *International Public Management Journal* 9, no. 2: 175–94.

John, P. (2013). 'All Tools Are Informational Now: How Information and Persuasion Define the Tools of Government'. *Policy & Politics* 41, no. 4 (1 October): 605–20.

Johnson, E. J., S. B. Shu, B. G. C. Dellaert, C. Fox, D. G. Goldstein, G. Häubl, R. P. Larrick, *et al.* (2012). 'Beyond Nudges: Tools of a Choice Architecture'. *Marketing Letters* 23, no. 2 (June): 487–504.

Kahneman, D. (2013). *Thinking, Fast and Slow* (1st edn). New York: Farrar, Straus & Giroux.

Kooiman, J. (1993). 'Governance and Governability: Using Complexity, Dynamics and Diversity'. In J. Kooiman (ed.), *Modern Governance*. London: Sage, 35–50.

Kooiman, J. (2000). 'Societal Governance: Levels, Models, and Orders of Social-Political Interaction'. In J. Pierre (ed.), *Debating Governance*. Oxford: Oxford University Press, 138–66.

Liu, H. K. (2017). 'Crowdsourcing Government: Lessons from Multiple Disciplines'. *Public Administration Review* 77, no. 5: 656–67.

Maor, M. (2016). 'The Implications of the Emerging Disproportionate Policy Perspective for the New Policy Design Studies'. *Policy Sciences* (19 July): 1–16.

Milward, H. B. and K. G. Provan. (2000). 'Governing the Hollow State'. *Journal of Public Administration Research and Theory* 10, no. 2: 359–80.

Rhodes, R. A. W. (1996). 'The New Governance: Governing Without Government'. *Political Studies* 44: 652–67.

Schubert, C. (2017). 'Green Nudges: Do They Work? Are They Ethical?' *Ecological Economics* 132, Supplement C (1 February): 329–42.

Taeihagh, A. (2017). 'Crowdsourcing: A New Tool for Policy-Making?' *Policy Sciences* 50, no. 4 (1 December): 629–47.

Treib, O., H. Bahr and G. Falkner. (2007). 'Modes of Governance: Towards a Conceptual Clarification'. *Journal of European Public Policy* 14, no. 1: 1–20.

Van Kersbergen, K. and F. Van Waarden. (2004). '"Governance" as a Bridge Between Disciplines: Cross-Disciplinary Inspiration Regarding Shifts in Governance and Problems of Governability, Accountability and Legitimacy'. *European Journal of Political Research* 43: 143–71.

Weiss, L. (1998). *The Myth of the Powerless State: Governing the Economy in a Global Era*. Cambridge: Polity Press.

Weiss, L. (2005). 'The State-Augmenting Effects of Globalisation'. *New Political Economy* 10, no. 3: 345–53.

Part II

SYSTEMATICALLY STUDYING POLICY DESIGN

What is policy design?

Key definitions and concepts in the study of policy design

Providing a better, more nuanced understanding of policy design and the factors which influence it is the goal of this book. In attaining that goal is helpful to go back a step and provide several definitions and key concepts commonly used in the study of policy design.

What is public policy?

The first term which requires definition is 'public policy'. The most concise formal definition of a public policy was set out by Thomas Dye in his early and best-selling text on the subject where he defined policy simply as 'what government chooses to do or not to do' (Dye 1972). This is a useful definition in so far as it underscores the notions that policies are conscious choices and not accidents or accidental occurrences; that they result from government decisions and not those of other actors in society such as private companies or other non-governmental organizations; and that so-called 'negative decisions' – that is, decisions to consciously avoid changing the status quo – are just as much public policies as the more commonly understood 'positive decisions' which do in fact alter some aspect of current circumstances.

This definition, however, is not all that helpful from a design perspective because it does not reveal anything about the *processes* through which policies are made, nor the *substantive content* of government decisions and the different elements which go into making them up. In addressing these two issues, a second definition put forward almost two decades before Dye's by one of the earliest proponents of the modern policy sciences, the University of Chicago political psychologist Harold Lasswell, is quite helpful. Lasswell, like Dye, also defined public policies as government decisions but noted that they were composed of two interrelated elements: *policy goals* and *policy means* operating at different levels of abstraction (Lasswell 1958). Policy goals in this sense are the basic aims and expectations governments have in deciding to pursue (or not) some course of action, while policy means are the techniques they use to attain those goals (Walsh 1994). Both of these elements can be focused on a range of activities, from abstract principles associated with governance arrangements, to much more concrete administrative programme specifications.

In terms of *content*, this suggests that policies are composed of a number of analytically distinct elements, with some policies focused on attaining concrete outputs while others focus on less tangible normative and cognitive aspects of policy-making. However, the situation is much more complex than might first appear. A typical substantive policy, for example, involves some very abstract general 'aims' or goals, such as, in the cases of criminal justice or education policy, attaining a just society or a prosperous one; along with a set of less abstract 'objectives' actually expected to achieve those aims such as, in the examples provided above, reducing crime or providing better educational opportunities to members of the public. Further, those objectives themselves must be concretized in a set of specific targets or measures which allow policy resources to be directed toward goal attainment, such as reducing specific types of crimes to specific levels within specified periods of time or increasing post-secondary educational attendance within some set temporal period (Cashore and Howlett 2007; Kooiman 2008; Stavins 2008; Howlett and Cashore 2009).

Similarly, the means or techniques for achieving these goals also exist on several levels. These run from highly abstract preferences for specific forms of policy implementation, such as a preference for the use of market, government or non-profit forms of organization to implement policy goals in areas such as health care, or crime prevention; to the more concrete level of the use of specific governing tools or mechanisms such as regulation, information campaigns, public enterprises, or government subsidies to alter actor behaviour in order to promote or increase wellness or prevent crime; to the most specific level of deciding or determining exactly how those tools should be 'calibrated' in order to achieve policy targets. This latter activity, to continue the examples, might include providing a specific number of additional police on the streets within a specified period of time, or a specific level of subsidy to non-profit groups to provide additional hospital beds or other types of health service within the same set period of time (Howlett 2005; 2009a; Stavins 2008).

Policies are thus complex entities composed of policy goals and means arranged in several layers, ranging from the most general level of a relatively abstract governance mode, to the level of a policy regime and finally to the level of specific programme settings (Cashore and Howlett 2006; 2007; Howlett and Cashore 2009). The principle 'components' of public policies involved in any policy design, following this logic, are set out in Table 2.1.

Table 3.1 Components of public policies involved in policy design

		Policy level		
		Governance mode: high-level abstraction	Policy regime: programme-level operationalization	Programme settings specific on-the-ground measures
Policy component	Policy goals	General abstract policy aims: The most general macro-level statement of government aims and ambitions in a specific policy area	Operationalizable policy objectives: The specific meso-level areas that policies are expected to address in order to achieve policy aims	Specific policy targets: The specific, on-the-ground, aims of efforts to achieve objectives and aims
	Policy means	General policy implementation preferences The long-term preferences of government in terms of the types of organizational devices to be used in addressing policy aims	Policy tool choices The specific types of governing instruments to be used to address programme-level objectives	Specific policy tool calibrations The specific 'settings' of policy tools required to implement policy programmes

Source: Howlett et al. 2009. 'The Dependent Variable Problem in the Study of Policy Change: Understanding Policy Change as a Methodological Problem'. *Journal of Comparative Policy Analysis: Research and Practice* 11, no.1: 33–46.

In terms of policy-making *processes*, Lasswell (1956) also discussed this subject in a useful way. He did so by using one of the historically most popular models for analyzing public policy-making, which has been to think of it as a process; that is, as a set of interrelated stages through which policy issues and deliberations flow in a more or less sequential fashion from 'inputs' (problems) to 'outputs' (policies). The resulting sequence of stages is often referred to as the 'policy cycle' (Jann and Wegrich 2007; Howlett et al. 2009).

The idea of a policy cycle has received somewhat different treatment in the hands of different authors. In his own work, for example, Lasswell (1971)

divided the policy process into seven stages, which, in his view, described not only how public policies were actually made but also how they should be made: (1) intelligence, (2) promotion, (3) prescription, (4) invocation, (5) application, (6) termination and (7) appraisal. In this construct, the policy process began with intelligence-gathering, that is, the collection, processing and dissemination of information for those who participate in decision-making. It then moved to the promotion of particular options by those involved in making the decision. In the third stage, the decision-makers prescribed a course of action. In the fourth stage, the prescribed course of action was invoked alongside a set of sanctions to penalize those who fail to comply with these prescriptions. The policy was then applied by the courts and the bureaucracy and ran its course until it was terminated or cancelled. Finally, the results of the policy were appraised or evaluated against the original aims and goals.

In this view, policy-making is viewed not as primarily a random, ritualistic, or symbolic form of state activity, but as a conscious matter of attempting to match the means of policy implementation to formulated policy goals. While there is no doubt that some aspects of policy-making can be heavily symbolic and ritualized (Edelman 1964 and 1971), from a design perspective these are not the defining characteristics of policy-making, which is typically viewed as a much more pragmatic activity: that is, one intended to effectively alter practices on-the-ground in a more or less conscious or deliberate way through the efficient use of available governing resources or the creation of new ones. That is, policy-making is viewed as an *instrumental* problem-solving activity, one in which various governing resources are marshalled into a set of techniques which could at least potentially or theoretically achieve the aims, objectives and goals of policy-makers.

Lasswell's original formulation provided the basis for many other later models of the policy process (Lyden et al. 1968; Simmons et al. 1974; Brewer 1974; Anderson 1983; Brewer and deLeon 1983; Jones 1984). Each contained slightly different interpretations of the names, number and order of stages in the cycle but used the same logic to describe them; that of 'applied problem solving' (deLeon 1999b; Hill and Hupe 2006). The stages in applied problem-solving and the corresponding stages in the policy process are depicted in Figure 3.1.

In this 'standard' model, *agenda-setting* refers to the process by which problems come to the attention of governments; *policy formulation* refers to how policy options are formulated within government; *decision-making* is the process by which governments adopt a particular course of action or non-action; *policy implementation* relates to how governments put policies into effect; and *policy evaluation* refers to the processes by which the results of policies are monitored by both state and societal actors, the outcome of which may be reconceptualization of policy problems and solutions. As we have seen, policy design activity occurs at the policy formulation stage of the policy process but is not synonymous with that stage. Rather it represents the articulation of sets of ideas about policy-making and possible policy

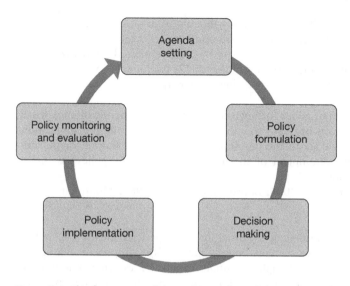

Figure 3.1 The five stages of the policy cycle and their relationship to applied problem-solving

outcomes which may or may not be actually adopted, in whole or in part, in practice (Goggin 1987).

The idea of a policy process or cycle has often been used to view policymaking in essentially pragmatic terms, as the embodiment of effort to improve the human condition through harnessing reason to guide human activities, in this case, in the process of governing (Hawkesworth 1992). In this view, policy means or instruments are often viewed mainly as *technical* mechanisms used to attain policy goals and as existing only in the stages of policy formulation – when policy means are proposed and policy implementation – when they are put into effect. However, a process model can also be used to describe policy-making as a much more overtly social or political process in which actors compete with each other in order to attain their goals or collectively 'puzzle' through toward the solution to an issue (Howlett et al. 2009; Wu et al. 2010). In this view, policy instruments are thought of as much less technical than political in nature and are typically viewed as extending to activities located in all stages of the policy process, including not just policy formulation and implementation, but also agenda-setting, decision-making and policy evaluation.

What is policy design?

As we have seen in Chapter 1 and Chapter 2, within the policy sciences, 'design' has been linked both to policy instruments and implementation (May 2003) and to the impact of policy ideas and advice on policy formulation

(Linder and Peters 1990a). It is usually thought to involve the deliberate and conscious attempt to define policy goals and connect them in an instrumental or logical fashion to the instruments or tools expected to realize those objectives (Gilabert and Lawford-Smith 2012; Majone 1975; May 2003). *Policy design*, in this sense, was defined above as

> a specific form of policy formulation based on the gathering of knowledge about the effects of policy tool use on policy targets and the application of that knowledge to the development and implementation of policies aimed at the attainment of specifically desired public policy outcomes and ambitions.
>
> (Bobrow 2006; Bobrow and Dryzek 1987; Montpetit 2003a; Weaver 2009a, 2010b)

In this sense, paralleling the situation with policies themselves, policy designs can be seen to contain both a substantive component – a set of alternative arrangements thought potentially capable of resolving or addressing some aspect of a policy problem, one or more of which is ultimately put into practice – as well as a procedural component – a set of activities related to securing some level of agreement among those charged with formulating, deciding upon and administering that alternative vis-à-vis other alternatives (Howlett 2011). Design thus overlaps and straddles both policy formulation, decision-making and policy implementation and involves actors, ideas and interests active at each of these stages of the policy process (Howlett et al. 2009). However, it also posits a very specific form of interaction among these elements, driven by knowledge and evidence of alternatives' merits and demerits in achieving policy goals rather than by other processes such as bargaining or electioneering among key policy actors.

In their many works on the subject in the late 1980s and early 1990s Stephen H. Linder and B. Guy Peters argued that, at least in theory, the actual process of public policy decision-making could, in an analytical sense, be divorced from the abstract concept of policy design, in the same way that an abstract architectural concept can be divorced from its engineering manifestation. Policy designs in this sense they argued, can be thought of as 'ideal types', that is, as ideal configurations of sets of policy elements which can reasonably be expected, within a specific contextual setting, to deliver a specific outcome. Whether or not all of the aspects of such contextual configurations are actually adopted in practice, in their view, is more or less incidental to the design, except in so far as such variations suggest the expected outcome may be less stable or reliable than the original design assumptions would augur. As Linder and Peters (1988) argued:

> Design then, is not synonymous with instrumental reasoning but certainly relies greatly on that form of reasoning. Moreover, the invention or fashioning of policy options is not designing itself and may not even call on any design. While somewhat at odds with conventional (mis)usage,

our treatment focuses attention on the conceptual underpinnings of policy rather than its content, on the antecedent intellectual scheme rather than the manifest arrangement of elements. As a result, the study of design is properly 'meta-oriented' and, therefore, one step removed from the study of policy and policy-making.

(Linder and Peters 1988: 744)

In this view, conceptually, a policy design process begins with the analysis of the abilities of different kinds of policy tools to affect policy outputs and outcomes and the kinds of resources required to allow them to operate as intended (Hood 1986c; Salamon 2002c). This instrumental knowledge is contextual in the sense that it requires a special understanding of how the use of specific kinds of instruments affects target group behaviour and compliance with government aims. It thus includes knowledge and consideration of many constraints on tool use originating in the limits of existing knowledge, prevailing governance structures and other arrangements and behaviours which may preclude consideration of certain options and promote others (Howlett 2009a, 2011). It requires both government analytical and evidentiary capacity as well as the intention to exercise it.

Such a means-ends understanding of policy-making permeates the policy design orientation but, of course, is only one possible orientation or set of practices which can be followed in policy formulation and result in policy-outputs (Colebatch 1998; Tribe 1972; Howlett and Mukherjee 2017). In the design case, policy formulators are expected as much as possible to base their analyses on logic, knowledge and experience rather than, for example, purely political calculations and other forms of satisficing behaviur which also can serve to generate policy alternatives (Bendor, Kumar and Siegel 2009; Sidney 2007).

Policy design studies deal with such alternative forms of policy formulation by separating out two dimensions of the design experience: on the one hand, the exploration of the procedural aspects of design – the specific types of policy formulation activities which lead to design rather than some other form of policy generation – and on the other the substantive components – that is, the substance or content of a design in terms of the instruments and instrument settings of which it is composed. The idea is that even when policy processes are less rational or information-driven and more political or interest-driven, the design of a policy, conceptually at least, can be divorced from the processes involved in its enactment.

Thus, regardless of the nature of the actual alternative formulation process which exists in a specific context, it is still possible to imagine a more instrumental world and hence consider or promote design alternatives 'in-themselves' as ideal-type artifacts. These can then be developed and studied in preparation for decision-making circumstances which might be propitious to their adoption either in 'pure' form or with some minor adjustments or amendments.

Again, as Linder and Peters (1990b) argued, such a:

(. . .) design orientation to analysis can illuminate the variety of means implicit in policy alternatives, questioning the choice of instruments and their aptness in particular contexts. The central role it assigns means in policy performance may also be a normative vantage point for appraising design implications of other analytical approaches. More important, such an orientation can be a counterweight to the design biases implicit in other approaches and potentially redefine the fashioning of policy proposals.

(304)

This is the bread-and-butter of policy analytical work undertaken by think tanks, policy institutes and policy schools which generally criticize existing arrangements and propose more 'rational' alternatives; that is, new or revised solutions to old or redefined problems felt more likely to achieve their goals in theory and practice or to do so more effectively.

Policy design extends to both the means or mechanisms through which goals are given effect and to the goals themselves, since goal articulation inevitably involves considerations of feasibility, or what is practical or possible to achieve in given conjunctures or circumstances considering the means at hand (Huitt 1968; Majone 1975; Ingraham 1987). Even when the goals pursued are not laudable, such as personal enrichment or military adventurism, or when the knowledge or the means utilized is less than scientific, such as religious or ideologically inspired dogma or implementation preferences and even when these efforts are much more ad hoc and much less systematic than might be desired, as long as a desire for effective resource use in goal attainment guides policy-making, it will involve some effort at design. However, this does not mean that all designs are equal or generate equal results.

Again, however, this does not preclude, but rather is built upon the recognition and acceptance of the fact that in some policy decisions and formulation processes 'design' considerations may be more or less absent and the quality of the logical or empirical relations between policy components as solutions to problems may be incorrect or ignored (Cohen et al. 1979; Dryzek 1983; Eijlander 2005; Franchino and Hoyland 2009; Kingdon 1984; Sager and Rielle 2013).

As was discussed in Chapter 1, this includes a variety of contexts in which formulators or decision-makers, for example, may engage in interest-driven trade-offs or log-rolling between different values or resource uses or, more extremely, might engage in venal or corrupt behaviour in which personal gain from a decision may trump other evaluative criteria. These 'non-design' situations are well known in political science but have not been well studied in the policy sciences and the extent to which considerations such as political gain or blame avoidance calculations outweigh instrumental factors in policy formulation is a key question in contemporary policy design studies (Hood 2010).

It is also important to note, as set out above, that policy-making and especially policy tool selection is a highly constrained process. In this regard, it is important for policy designers to incorporate into their thinking the knowledge that the exact processes by which policy decisions are taken vary greatly by jurisdiction and sector and reflect the great differences and nuances that exist between different forms of government – from military regimes to liberal democracies and within each type – as well as the particular configuration of issues, actors and problems various governments, of whatever type, face in particular areas or sectors of activity – such as health or education policy, industrial policy, transportation or energy policy, social policy and many others (Ingraham 1987; Howlett et al. 2009). In some circumstances, policy decisions will be more highly contingent and 'irrational', that is, driven by situational logics and opportunism rather than careful deliberation and assessment, than others (Cohen et al. 1979; Dryzek 1983; Kingdon 1984; Eijlander 2005; Franchino and Hoyland 2009).

Similarly, as has been discussed above, the development of programme level objectives and means choices, for example, takes place within a larger governance context in which sets of institutions, actors and practices are 'defined' which make up the 'environment' within which policy-making takes place. Some of the key elements which comprise a policy, notably, abstract policy aims and general implementation processes, are defined at this 'meta' level of policy-making. Hence, as we have seen, a legal mode of governance contains a preference for the use of laws while a market mode involves a preference for regulation and financial tools; a corporatist mode – a preference for plans and organization; and a network mode – a preference for the use of information tools. Thus, choices of programme-level tools and targets are constrained by the existing governance mode, while a policy regime logic (Skodvin, Gullberg and Aakre 2010), that is, the choices of meso-level programme objectives and policy instruments, similarly constrains micro-level targeting and programme goals. The multi-level, nested, nature of policy tool choices, therefore, must be taken into account in any effort to design or plan policy outcomes. Better designs are more effective at doing this, generating policy processes and outcomes which are more consistent with their environments.

Notwithstanding how it is conducted, however, the idea of policy design is inextricably linked with the idea of improving government actions through the conscious consideration at the stage of policy formulation of the likely outcomes of policy implementation activities. This is a concern both for non-governmental actors concerned with bearing the costs of government failures and incompetence, as well as for governmental ones who may be tasked with carrying out impossible duties and meeting unrealistic expectations. Regardless of regime and issue type and regardless of the specific weight given by governments to different substantive and procedural aims, all governments wish to have their goals effectively achieved and usually wish to do so in an efficient way, that is, with a minimum of effort and cost (Weimer 1993). Thus all governments, of whatever stripe, are interested in applying knowledge and experience about policy issues in such a way as to ensure the more or less efficient and effective realization of their aims (deLeon 1999a; Potoski 2002).

This desire to husband resources involved in goal attainment involves governments of all types and persuasions in processes of more or less conscious and rational efforts at design (Dryzek 1983). It also allows us to

> define policy designing as the effort to more or less systematically develop efficient and effective policies through the application of knowledge about policy means gained from experience and reason, to the development and adoption of courses of action that are likely to succeed in attaining their desired goals or aims within specific policy contexts.
>
> (Bobrow and Dryzek 1987; Bobrow 2006; Montpetit 2008)

What is a policy instrument?

The policy alternatives which policy designers create are composed of different sets or combinations of the policy elements described above and set out in more detail in Chapters 8–11 below. As Linder and Peters noted, policy instruments are especially significant in policy designs and designing as they are the techniques or means through which states attempt to attain their goals. Tools are the subject of deliberation and activity at all stages of the policy process and affect both the agenda-setting and policy formulation processes as well as being the subject of decision-making policy implementation and evaluation (Howlett 2005; Howlett, Ramesh and Perl 2009).

Other terms have been developed in the field of policy studies to describe the same phenomenon, such as 'governing instruments', 'policy tools' and the 'tools of government' and while these sometimes are used to refer to different mechanisms and calibrations of policy means, they are more often used synonymously.

These tools have a special place in the consideration and study of policy design because, taken together, they comprise the contents of the toolbox from which governments must choose in building or creating public policies. Policy design elevates the analysis and practice of policy instrument choice – specifically tools for policy implementation – to a central focus of study, making their understanding and analysis a key design concern (Salamon 1981; Linder and Peters 1990a). Instrument choice, from this perspective, in a sense, *is* public policy-making and understanding and analyzing potential instrument choices involved in implementation activity *is* policy design. One role of a textbook in policy design is thus assisting 'in constructing an inventory of potential public capabilities and resources that might be pertinent in any problem-solving situation' (Anderson 1975: 122).

It is important to repeat, however, that policy instruments exist at *all* stages of the policy process – with specific tools such as stakeholder consultations and government reviews intricately linked to agenda-setting activities,

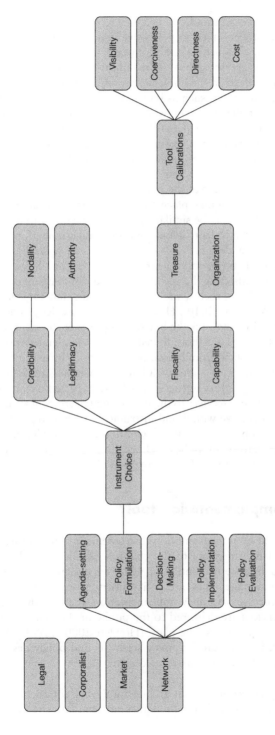

Figure 3.2 An example of the range of policy instruments by governance mode and stage of the policy cycle

ones like legislative rules and norms linked to decision-making behaviour and outcomes and others linked to policy evaluation, such as the use of ex-post, or after-the fact, cost–benefit analyses (see Figure 3.2).

Policy tools are thus in a sense 'multi-purpose', since, for example, regulation can appear in the implementation activities of several governance modes, while some tools, such as impact assessments, can also appear within several stages of the cycle. However, a regulation appearing within the implementation phase of a network mode of governance which mandates information disclosure, for example, serves a different purpose than a regulation found in a market mode which limits a firm to ownership of only a specific percentage of an industry. Similarly, consultations which take place in the agenda-setting stage of the policy process have a different purpose and effect than those which take place after a decision has been made. While the general terminology may be similar, pains must be taken to distinguish these tools and activities in order to avoid confusion and errant efforts at instrument selection and policy design.

As mentioned above, policy instruments appear in all stages of the policy process and those affecting the agenda-setting, decision-making and evaluation stages of the policy process, are very significant and important in public management (Wu et al. 2010). However most policy designs deal with plans for implementation and thus the key sets of policy instruments of concern to most policy designers are those linked to policy implementation, in the first instance and to policy formulation, in the second. In the first category, we would find examples of many well-known governing tools such as public enterprises and regulatory agencies which are expected to alter or affect the delivery of goods and services to the public and government (Salamon 2002c), while in the second we would find instruments such as regulatory impact or environmental impact appraisals which are designed to alter and affect some aspect of the nature of policy deliberations and the consideration and assessment of alternatives (Turnpenny et al. 2009).

What is an implementation tool?

The role played by implementation instruments in policy design is thus one of the central foci of many of the chapters of this book. It is they which provide the substance or content of whatever design deliberations occur at the formulation stage. They are policy instruments which affect either the content or processes of policy implementation, that is, which alter the way goods and services are delivered to the public or the manner in which such implementation processes take place (Howlett 2000c). As Linder and Peters (1984) noted, it is critical for policy scientists and policy designers alike to understand this basic vocabulary of design:

Whether the problem is an architectural, mechanical, or administrative one, the logic of design is fundamentally similar. The idea is to fashion an instrument that will work in a desired manner. In the context of policy problems, design involves both a systematic process for generating basic strategies and a framework for comparing them. Examining problems from a design perspective offers a more productive way of organizing our thinking and analytical efforts.

(253)

Understanding implementation tools is thus key to policy design. One common type of implementation instrument alters the actual *substance* of the kinds of day-to-day production, distribution and consumption activity carried out in society, while the other focuses upon altering political or policy behaviour in the *process* of the articulation of implementation goals and means. *Substantive* implementation instruments are those used to directly affect the production, distribution and consumption of goods and services in society while *procedural* implementation instruments accomplish the second purpose (Ostrom 1986; Howlett 2000c; 2005).

This distinction is apparent in common definitions of governing instruments although its significance is sometimes overlooked. Vedung, for example, has usefully defined policy instruments used in implementation activities as 'the set of techniques by which governmental authorities wield their power in attempting to ensure support and effect social change' (Vedung 1997a). This definition can be seen to include both 'substantive' tools, those Hood (1986c) defined as attempting to 'effect or detect' change in the socio-economic system, as well as those 'procedural' tools designed to 'ensure support' for government actions.

Substantive instruments are expected to alter some aspect of the production, distribution and delivery of goods and services in society. This is a large field of action since it extends not only to goods and services provided or affected by markets, but also well beyond to state or public provision and regulation, as well as to those goods and services typically provided by the family, community, non-profit and voluntary means often with neither a firm market nor state basis (Salamon 1989; 2002a). These goods and services are broadly conceived to include both mundane goods and services such as school lunches to crude vices such as gambling or illicit drug use, to more common individual virtues such as charitable giving or volunteer work with the physically challenged and include the attainment of sublime collective goals such as peace and security, sustainability, happiness and well-being.

Substantive implementation instruments can affect many aspects of production, distribution and consumption of goods and services. Production effects, for example, include determining or influencing:

1   Who produces it – for example, via licencing, bureaucracy/procurement, or subsidies for new start-ups.
2   The types of goods and services produced – for example, through bans or limits or encouragement.

3   The quantity of goods or services provided – for example, via subsidies or quotas.
4   The quality of goods or services produced – for example, via product standards, warranties.
5   Methods of production – for example, via environmental standards or subsidies for modernization.
6   Conditions of production – for example, via health and safety standards, employment standards acts, minimum wage laws and inspections.
7   The organization of production – for example, via unionization rules, antitrust or anti-combines legislation, securities legislation, or tax laws.

Consumption and distribution effects are also manifold. Some examples of these are:

1   Prices of goods and services – such as regulated taxi fares or wartime rationing.
2   Actual distribution of produced goods and services – affecting the location and types of schools or hospitals, forest tenures, or leases.
3   Level of consumer demand for specific goods – for example, through information release, nutritional and dangerous goods labeling (cigarettes), export and import taxes and bans and similar activities.
4   Level of consumer demand in general – via interest rate, monetary and fiscal policy.

Procedurally oriented implementation tools, on the other hand, affect production, consumption and distribution processes only indirectly, if at all. Rather, they instead affect the behaviour of actors involved in policy implementation. Policy actors are arrayed in various kinds of policy communities and just as tools can alter or affect the actions of citizens in the productive realm, so too can tools affect and alter aspects of policy-making behaviour (Knoke 1987; 1991; 1993). Procedural implementation tools are an important part of government activities aimed at altering policy interaction within policy subsystems but, as Klijn et al. (1995) put it, they typically 'structure . . . the game without determining its outcome' (441). That is, these behavioural modifications affect the manner in which implementation unfolds but without predetermining the results of substantive implementation activities.

Procedural implementation tools and their effects are not as well studied or understood as are substantive instruments, although several procedural techniques, such as the use of specialized investigatory commissions and government reorganizations, are quite old and well-used and have been the objects of study in fields such as public administration, public management and organizational behaviour (Woodley 2008; Schneider and Sidney 2009). Nevertheless, just like their substantive counterparts, they are a key part of policy designs and policy design activity.

Some of the kinds of implementation-related activities that can be affected by the use of procedural tools (Klijn et al. 1995; Goldsmith and Eggers 2004; Klijn and Koppenjan (2006) include:

1   changing actor policy positions
2   setting down, defining, or refining actor positions
3   adding actors to policy networks
4   changing access rules for actors to governments and networks
5   influencing network formation
6   promoting network self-regulation
7   modifying system-level policy parameters (e.g., levels of market reliance)
8   changing evaluative criteria for assessing policy outcomes, success and failure
9   influencing the pay-off structure for policy actors
10 influencing professional and other codes of conduct affecting policy actor behaviour
11 regulating inter-actor policy conflict
12 changing policy actors' interaction procedures
13 certifying or sanctioning certain types of policy-relevant behaviour
14 changing supervisory relations between actors.

As was discussed in Chapters 1 and 2 above, policy designs typically contain 'bundles' or 'mixes' of procedural and substantive implementation tools (Howlett 2000c; 2002c), a subject of some importance in policy design and to which we will return in subsequent chapters.

What isn't policy design?

As we have seen in earlier chapters, public policies are the result of efforts made by governments to alter aspects of behaviour – both that of their own agents and of society at large – in order to carry out some end or purpose. They are comprised complex arrangements of policy goals and policy means matched through some decision-making process and these policy-making efforts can be more, or less, systematic in attempting to match ends and means in a logical fashion or can result from much less systematic and rational processes.

Policy decisions can be careful and deliberate in attempting to best resolve a problem or can be highly contingent and driven by situational logics. Decisions stemming from bargaining or opportunism can also be distinguished from those which result from careful analysis and assessment. 'Policy design' implies a knowledge-based process in which the choice of means or mechanisms through which policy goals are given effect follows a logical process of inference from known or learned relationships between means and outcomes. This includes both design in which means are selected in accordance with experience and knowledge and that in which principles and relationships are incorrectly or only partially articulated or understood.

The academic enquiry of policy design – that is, self-consciously dealing with both policy processes and substance under a knowledge-driven, instrumental rubric – emerged and flourished throughout the 1970s and 1980s in studies trying to clarify what a design process involved and when it was likely to occur (see e.g., Salamon 1981, 1989, 2002c). However, these also has addressed many examples of poor designs and instances in which design considerations and intent are wholly lacking.

With respect to these latter instances of *non-design*, it bears repeating that the modern policy studies movement did begin with the clear recognition that public policy-making was not a purely technical exercise in matching means and ends but rather results from the interactions of policy-makers in the exercise of power, legitimate or otherwise (Arts and van Tatenhove 2004; Lasswell 1958; Stone 1988). Although some of these exercises were noted to be arbitrary or capricious, most were viewed as representing the concerted efforts of governments to intentionally act in an instrumental way; that is, to attempt to achieve a particular policy goal or end through the use of a relatively well-known set of policy means developed over many years of state-building experience (Lasswell and Lerner 1951). But, as discussed above, it was always acknowledged the goals pursued were wide-ranging and often posed no small amount of difficulty and complexity in both their definition and diagnosis, with the implication that the formulation of solutions that were likely to succeed in addressing them necessitated the systematic consideration of the impact and feasibility of the use of specific kinds of policy means or instruments as well as a clear understanding of the contexts of their use (Parsons 1995, 2001).

This work thus depicted instrumental policy-making as a specific kind of policy-activity which occurred in specific circumstances in which knowledge of the general impact of specific policy tools was combined with the practical capacity of governments to identify and implement the most suitable technical means in the effort to achieve a specific policy aim. This activity was expected to occur *ex ante* and independently of other considerations such as political or personal gain which might also affect decision-making and implementation processes but which should be removed from the deliberations of formulation.

Significantly for considerations of design and non-design processes, this 'design' activity was recognized as being inherently context bound, that is, requiring a situation where there was support for knowledge-based policy analysis on the part of policy-makers and where the demand for such analysis was met by a ready supply (Howlett et al. 2014). Favorable design circumstances required not only the presence of high quality information on the range and impacts of policy alternatives but also the presence of a high level of technical capacity and expertise on the part of policy analysts if knowledge was to be mobilized effectively so that policy instruments were effectively and efficiently matched to policy goals and targets (Dunlop 2009a; Howlett 2009a, 2010; Howlett and Rayner 2014; Radaelli and Dunlop 2013). Second, it was also recognized that not only 'spatial' but also 'temporal' aspects of policy formulation contexts such as policy legacies or prior commitments on the part of policy-makers limited consideration of alternatives. Where there was a relatively high policy 'lock-in' on existing tool arrangements, this could preclude adoption of potentially superior alternatives (Howlett and Rayner 2013).

When propitious conditions were present, however, purposive design activity resulting in good alternative generation and assessment was thought to be possible, much as is expected in the current era with recent efforts at improving knowledge mobilization in policy-making in the form of an emphasis upon 'evidence-based' or 'evidence-informed' policy-making (Bhatta 2002; Locke 2009; Nutley et al. 2007). When conditions are not ripe either poor designs would ensue from incomplete knowledge and information even with the best government intent, or less technical and more overtly political forms of non-design policy-making would be flow from less evidentiary and more interest-driven policy-making (Davies 2004; Howlett 2009b; Moseley and Tierney 2004).

Table 3.2 presents a schematic illustrating how these two different aspects of policy-making – a design intention and the capacity to carry it out – create different policy formulation spaces which enable very different policy design processes. This sets out a number of different formulation processes lying between the intention and ability to undertake purposive, instrumental policy design and the intention to meet more political goals coupled with the presence of significant policy resource constraints or tool lock-in affects.

Table 3.2 Types of policy formulation spaces: situating design and non-design processes

		Level of government knowledge and other constraints	
		High	Low
Government formulation intention	More instrumental	Capable policy design space Relatively unconstrained formulation via design is possible	Poor policy design space Only partially informed or restricted design is possible
	Less instrumental	Capable political non-design space Relatively unconstrained non-design processes are possible	Poor political non-design space Only poorly informed non-design is possible

What do designs and design processes look like?

As has already been noted several times, transforming policy ambitions into practice is a complex process. While formulation efforts can be done well or poorly, they reflect some wholesale or partial effort to match policy goals and means in a sophisticated way linked to improving outcomes. Non-design types also vary in the same way but more by process of decision-making than by their sphere of activity. Several common ways in which designs have emerged have been identified in the literature.

'Replacement': a relatively rare event

Fairly rapid and paradigmatic policy change has served as the orthodoxy in policy studies for the last two decades and often underlies considerations of the nature and extent of the aspirations of policy designs and designers. These latter efforts, for example, are often implicitly associated with the attainment of paradigmatic expectations and objectives, necessitating a high degree of cognitive and evaluative rationality on the part of policymakers and formulators in situations of dramatic policy reform (Hogan and Howlett 2015).

Such a view, however, (a) artificially conflates design with 'planning' and other kinds of large-scale and rapid policy reforms and (b) undermines analysis of other design processes with more limited scope and range which occur frequently and arguably with greater overall effect than wholesale paradigmatic design and re-design (Carstensen 2011). In other words, there is a tendency in the policy sciences to talk about 'design' in a manner which associates the nature and scope of design as *necessarily* wide-ranging and transformative, taking some existing policy and reforming it completely (Streeck and Thelen 2005, Thelen 2003, Mahoney and Thelen 201).

Examples of new policy 'packages' in many areas, from welfare policy to natural resource ones, however, often exist only historically, reflecting times before which there was no previous history of a policy response to a perceived policy problem. For example, the United States (US) Clean Air Act (CAA) (first enacted in 1970) was the first major federal air pollution legislation in the US that established the very first national benchmark for ambient sulfur dioxide (SO_2) (Libecap 2005; Schmalensee et al. 1998).

Such examples of new policy designs are understandably few. Most policy initiatives rather deal with already created policies that are limited by historical legacies and can be hampered due to internal inconsistencies which reforms and revisions (re-designs) attempt to address and correct. In this case, legacies from earlier rounds of decision-making affect the introduction of new elements which may conflict with pre-existing policy components.

Patching and packaging, stretching and layering as common design modalities

While early formulation and design thinking tended to suggest that the creation of instruments could only occur in spaces where new policy packages could be designed entirely *de novo,* or 'from scratch', it is now widely recognized that in most circumstances policy formulation involves building on the foundations created in another era and working with the constraints they pose.

Students of policy formulation and policy design are thus very interested, as mentioned above, in how policy formulators, such as software designers, often issue 'patches' in order to correct flaws in existing mixes or allow them to adapt to changing circumstances (Rayner 2013; Howlett 2013, Howlett and Rayner 2014).

This is not only a concern with historical accuracy in describing design processes but also due to the very practical concern that although other policy instrument groupings could theoretically be more successful in creating an internally supportive combination it may be very difficult to accomplish or even propose such changes. Designs instead often focus on reform rather than replacement of an existing arrangement (Grabosk 1994; Gunningham et al. 1998; Hou and Brewer 2010; Howlett 2004b; Howlett and Rayner 2007; del Río 2010; Barnett and Shore 2009; Blonz et al. 2008; Buckman and Diesendorf 2010; Roch et al. 2010).

This contextual 'lock in' can impact the formulation process by restricting a government's ability to evaluate alternatives and plan or design in a purely optimal instrumental manner (Howlett 2009a; Oliphant and Howlett 2010; Williams 2012). *Layering* is a typical result of processes of (re)design which alter only some aspects of a pre-existing arrangement and can thus be distinguished from processes of new policy packaging or complete replacement.

Layering, of course, is a concept developed in the neo-institutional sociological literature by some of its leading figures, namely Béland (2007), Béland and Hacker (2004), Hacker (2004b), Stead and Meijers (2004) and Thelen (2004) to explain the pattern through which social and political institutions have evolved over long-periods of time. As applied to policy-making, 'layering' connotes a process in which new elements are simply added to an existing regime often without abandoning previous ones so that polices accrete in a palimpsest-like fashion (Carter 2012). This can easily lead to internal contradictions emerging between tools and goals within policy mixes (Hacker 2004a) and mixes of policy elements can emerge over long stretches of time as a result of successive policy decisions which are not necessarily congruent.

An example of such incongruence within a policy mix can be found in the US Clean Air Act, the development of which has been heavily analyzed since the 1970s (Ackerman 1981; Greenstone 2001; among others). The 1977 amendments to the Act created a 'new source bias' as all new coal-powered plants were required to install scrubbers even if they used low-sulfur coal. This rule undermined the comparative advantage of 'cleaner' coal as the amendments raised the cost of shifting to new, less polluting plants and extended the economic lives of older, more polluting plants that did not have to shoulder the added cost of scrubbers (Libecap 2005).

This is only one small example of a general situation where the initial logic of each decision matching policy tool and target may have been clear, but through multiple layering processes they can gradually transform over time into incongruent mixes (Bode 2006; Hacker 2004c; Howlett and Rayner 1995; Orren and Skowronek 1998; Rayner et al. 2001; Torenvlied and Akkerman 2004; van der Heijden 2011). This can create policy portfolios or mixes that contain various incompatibilities, tending to frustrate the achievement of policy goals.

Distinguishing between different types of layering also allows us to further separate and identify different kinds of design and non-design processes from each other. Policy designs strongly marked by layering in this way are typically ones where new elements are added to the policy mix without the removal of older ones and existing elements are stretched to try to fit new goals and changing circumstances (van der Heijden 2011).

Hence, a key first distinction among design formulation processes concerns whether they involve '*packaging*' a new policy mix or '*patching*' an old one (Howlett 2013; Howlett and Rayner 2013; Rayner 2013). That is, in situations with significant policy legacies, designers often attempt to 'patch' or restructure existing policy elements rather than propose completely new alternative arrangements even if the situation might require the latter for the sake of enhancing coherence and consistency in the reformed policy mix (Eliadis et al. 2005; Howlett 2013; Gunningham and Sinclair 1999a,b; Thelen 2004; Thelen et al. 2003). Hence even where intentionality to systematically design may be high it may only be partial in the sense that only patching and not replacement is on the table.

Such patching or 'smart layering' has often been thought to be inherently suboptimal but patching in itself is not 'non-design', but rather constrained (re)design as a new layer is formulated in an effort to overcome anomalies or problems existing with earlier mixes (Howlett and Rayner 2013). But patching can done well if governments possess the capacity to do so but can also be done poorly if they do not. An example of poor patching is policy '*stretching*' (Feindt and Flynn 2009). This is where, operating over periods of decades or more, elements of a mix are simply extended to cover areas they were not intended to at the outset.

'Stretching' is especially problematic as small changes in the mixture of policy elements over a time period can create a situation where the elements can fail to be mutually supportive, incorporating contradictory goals or instruments whose combination create perverse incentives that frustrate initial policy goals. These problems are identified, setting the stage for further rounds of tinkering and layering that may make them worse (Feindt and Flynn 2009).

Both stretching and poor patching efforts can create a particular form of 'tense layering' (Kay 2007) which occurs when repeated bouts of layering lead to incoherence among the goals and inconsistency with respect to the instruments and settings used in a policy area. Inconsistencies arise where the means work at cross-purposes, 'providing simultaneous incentives and disincentives towards the attainment of stated goals' (Kern and Howlett 2009: 6). And incongruence occurs when an otherwise consistent mix of instruments fail to support the goals. Stretching is problematic as a design process since the addition of new goals or objectives increases the risk of incoherence, while the introduction of policy instruments through poor patching, for example, when a market orientation is introduced into an instrument set that has been based on a regulatory approach (Howlett and Rayner 2007) is also problematic.

Using the case of British food policy, Feindt and Flynn (2009), for example, describe a situation of institutional stretching where 'concerns about food supply and high productivity were overlaid with policies addressing food safety, the environment, quality foods, obesity and climate change (386)'. As a result, they argue, 'the resulting tensions ... create opportunities for more new ideas and actors to move in, fueled by a plurality of social constructions of food. Also, each new layer re-adjusts the power balance and necessitates re-interpretations of older policies' (386).

Layering and patching thus have two sides. On the one hand, negative stretching or destructive layering exacerbates tensions between regime elements and more politicized or less instrumental forms of policy-making and outcomes. However, layering can also have a positive side and help ameliorate or reduce tensions through 'smart' patching. Stretching and poor patching are thus design practices which exist at the breakpoint between design and non-design activities of government. Both these processes fall between the 'pure' design and 'pure' non-design ends of the spectrum of design processes suggested in Figure 3.3.

As Figure 3.3 shows, these forms of policy-oriented formulation processes move from highly intentional and instrumental replacement efforts to those which are more partial and less intentional such as 'smart' patching and ultimately to those which involve poor design such as 'stretching' and poor layering. In cases such as these, tense layering introduces progressively more severe inconsistencies and incongruencies and tensions between layers and policy-making and formulation may begin to take on an increasingly political complexion as the original logic and causality of a mix recedes into dim memory.

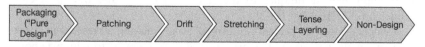

Figure 3.3 A spectrum of design processes

Non-design occurs when partisan and ideological, religious or other criteria cloud, crowd out or replace an instrumental design intentionality. Non-design mechanisms, as highlighted above, include activities such as alternative generation by bargaining or log-rolling, through corruption or co-optation efforts or through other faith-based or pure electoral calculations which are not instrumental in the same sense as are design efforts. In such contexts. the ability of policy goals to be met or the ability of means to achieve them are of secondary concern to other concerns such as ideological purity or the need to retain or augment legislative or electoral support or other similar kinds of coalition behaviour.

These too, however, can also be done well or poorly and are also affected by contextual barriers but they are not 'design' activities in the intentional instrumental public problem-solving sense set out above. That is, maximizing the return from a bargain or the returns from corruption, for example, also depends on the context, situation and expertise of actors but does not involve the same kinds of appraisal activities and competences or intentions on the part of governments as does policy design work.

These non-design processes have been studied extensively in the political science literature but less systematically in the policy sciences (Frye et al. 2012; Gans-Morse et al. 2014; Goodin 1980; Saward 1992) despite their prevalence and importance in many areas. While it is not necessary to include them in a spectrum of design work, they can be appended to a spectrum of formulation types by moving from those types of non-design work which are compatible with at least some aspects of instrumental design activities – such as bargaining among affected interests over elements of otherwise carefully designed policy alternatives – to those – such as pure electoral opportunism or corruption – where party, leader or individual self-interest replace policy instrumentalism altogether.

What makes a good policy process: evidence-based policy-making and policy design

The evidence-based policy movement mentioned above is the latest in a series of efforts undertaken by reformers in governments over the past half century to enhance the efficiency and effectiveness of public policy-making through the application to policy problems of a systematic evaluative rationality (Mintrom 2007). In all of these efforts, it is expected that through a process of theoretically informed empirical analysis, governments can better learn from experience and both avoid repeating the errors of the past as well as better apply new techniques to the resolution of old and new problems (Sanderson 2002b; May 1992).

Evidence-based or 'evidence-informed' policy-making represents an effort to reform or re-structure policy processes in such a way as to minimize non-design spaces and incidences by prioritizing evidentiary decision-making criteria in the expectation that superior policies and results will emerge from such processes than from 'non-design' ones (Nutley et al. 2007; Pawson 2006; Sanderson 2006).

Exactly what constitutes 'evidence-based policy-making' and whether analytical efforts in this regard actually result in better or improved policies, however, are subjects which remain contentious in the literature on the subject (Boaz et al. 2008; Jackson 2007; Packwood 2002; Pawson 2002). A spate of studies, for example, have questioned the value of a renewed emphasis on the collection and analysis of large amounts of data in all policy-making circumstances (Tenbensel 2004). Among the concerns raised about an increased emphasis on evidence in contemporary policy-making are:

1   That evidence is only one factor involved in policy-making and is not necessarily able to overcome other factors such as constitutional divisions of powers or jurisdictions which can arbitrarily assign locations and responsibilities for particular issue areas to specific levels or institutions of government and diminish the rationality level of policy-making by so doing (Davies 2004; Radin and Boase 2000; Young 2002);

2   That data collection and analytical techniques employed in its gathering and analysis by specially trained policy technicians may not be necessarily superior to the experiential judgments of politicians and other key policy decision-makers (Jackson 2007; Majone 1989);

3   That the kinds of 'high-quality' and universally acknowledged evidence initially proposed when 'evidence-based policy-making' first entered the lexicon of policy analysts in the healthcare field – esp. the 'systematic review' of clinical findings – often has no analog in many policy sectors where generating evidence using the 'gold standard' of random clinical trial methodologies may not be possible (Innvaer et al. 2002; Pawson et al. 2005) and;

4   That an increased emphasis on evidence-based policy making can stretch the analytical resources of participating organizations, be they governmental or non-governmental, to the breaking point (Hammersley 2005). That is, government efforts in this area may have adverse consequences both for themselves in terms of requiring greater expenditures on analytical activities at the expense of operational ones, as well as for many non-governmental policy actors, such as small-scale NGOs whose analytical resources may be non-existent and who may also be forced to divert financial, personnel and other scarce resources from implementation activities to policy-making in order to meet increased government requests for more and better data on the merits and demerits of their proposed policy solutions and programme.

(Laforest and Orsini 2005)

An increased emphasis on the use of evidence in policy-making thus requires that policy actors, and especially governmental ones, have the analytical capability required to collect appropriate data and utilize it effectively in the course of policy-making activities. As such, it highlights the fact that a significant factor affecting the ability of policy-makers to engage at all in evidence-based policy design pertains to the level of both governmental and non-governmental actors' *'policy analytical capacity'*.

Overall, Riddell (1998) summarized the requisites of policy analytical capacity as lying in:

> a recognized requirement or demand for research; a supply of qualified researchers; ready availability of quality data; policies and procedures to facilitate productive interactions with other researchers; and a culture in which openness is encouraged and risk taking is acceptable.

If evidence-based policy-making is to be achieved policy actors require the ability to collect and aggregate information in order to effectively develop medium and long-term projections, proposals for and evaluations of, future government activities. Organizations both inside and outside of governments require a level of human, financial, network and knowledge resources enabling them to perform the tasks associated with managing and implementing an evidence-based policy process. Without this they might only marshal these resources in particular areas, resulting in a 'lumpy' set of Departmental or agency competences in which some agencies are able to plan and prioritize over the long-term while others focus on shorter-term issues or if evenly distributed may only be able to react to short- or medium term political, economic, or other challenges and imperatives occurring in their policy environments (Voyer 2007).

But even in the best of circumstances and with the best of intentions, governments often grapple with complex problems involving situations in which they must deal with multiple actors, ideas and interests in complex problem environments which typically evolve and change over time. And in these and many other instances, policy decisions and 'design' considerations may be more or less absent from policy deliberations which may be overtly partisan or self-interested and not at all interested in marshalling evidence about 'what works, when' in order to attempt to deliver efficient or effective outcomes to policy clients or targets.

In such circumstances, evidence and knowledge of best practices can be ignored and the quality of the logical or empirical relations between policy components as solutions to problems may be incorrect, or also ignored (Cohen et al. 1979; Dryzek 1983; Eijlander 2005; Franchino and Hoyland 2009; Kingdon 1984; Sager and Rielle 2013). Policy formulators or decision-makers, for example, may engage in interest-driven trade-offs or legislative or bureaucratic log-rolling between different values or resource uses or, more extremely, engage in venal or corrupt behaviour in which personal or partisan gain from a decision are central preferences.

What is a superior mix of tools: coherence, consistency and congruence in policy designs

As noted in Chapter 2, a greater emphasis on tool mixes and on the processes that effectively create complex policy tool bundles has been a feature of policy design research over the last decade (Hood 2007a; Howlett 2011). These studies have increased awareness of the many dilemmas that can appear in the path of effective policy tool or 'toolkit' designs and realities (Peters and Pierre 1998; Klijn and Koppenjan 2000c; Doremus 2003; Sterner 2002).

Mixes are combinations of policy instruments that are expected to achieve particular policy objectives and which are generally seen as more efficient and effective than single instrument uses (Gunningham et al. 1998). Some instruments may work well with others by nature – as is the case with 'self-regulation' set within a regulatory compliance framework (Gibson 1999; Grabosky 1994; Trebilcock et al. 1979) – while other combinations may not, such as, notably, independently developed subsidies and regulation. Other mixes may have evolved in a certain way which has undermined, or improved, their effectiveness, while others may have never been very effective in the first place and remain so.

Explaining a superior policy design, then, is thus a matter of determining the parameters of a given policy situation and of matching the needs for action and with the supply of tools available, tasks which can be done well ('good' design) or poorly ('poor' design). Thus in 1989, for example, Linder and Peters attempted to summarize the findings of this literature and in so doing described eight 'attributes of instruments' which they felt affected specific tool choices. These were: *complexity of operation, level of public visibility, adaptability across uses, level of intrusiveness, relative costliness, reliance on markets, chances of failure and precision of targeting* (56).[1] Targeting, visibility and intrusiveness, for example, were key criteria which they felt superior designs must balance against more administratively driven preferences for 'automaticity' or cost efficient ('low maintenance') implementation.

Concerns about how to make the most of policy synergies while curtailing contradictions in the formulation of new policy packages have been a major topic of investigation within the new design orientation (Hou and Brewer 2010; Kiss et al. 2012; Lecuyer and Quirion 2013). Works on 'smart regulation' by Gunningham et al. (1998), for example, led scholars to focus on how instruments within a policy mix or 'portfolio' could effectively complement each other or conversely, resulting in fewer or greater conflicts; providing guidelines for the formulation of more sophisticated policy designs in which complementarities were maximized and conflicts avoided (Buckman and Diesendorf 2010; Roch et al. 2010; Barnett and Shore 2009; Blonz et al. 2008; del Río 2010). And a major concern of those working in contemporary policy design studies is whether reform of combinations of different policy instruments, which have evolved independently and incrementally, can accomplish complex policy goals as effectively as more deliberately customized portfolios (Howlett 2014b).

Good policy designs are thus expected to feature few contradictions and an integrated effort to match policy tools and goals (Buckman and Diesendorf 2010; Roch et al. 2010; Barnett and Shore 2009; Blonz et al. 2008; del Río 2010). Current research into how some combinations may be redundant and not achieve targets while others, albeit repetitive, may be beneficial in promoting resiliency and adaptiveness (Braathen and Croci 2005; Braathen 2007b; Swanson et al. 2010; Walker et al. 2010) have added the dimension of *robustness* to older concerns for the *coherence, consistency and congruence* of policy means and goals set out above.

Conclusion: better designs through better knowledge of policy instrument attributes and interactions

Recent policy design literature has engaged in lengthy discussions about how best to effectively integrate policy mixes so that multiple instruments are arranged together in complex but effective portfolios of policy goals and means (Gunningham et al. 1998; Doremus 2003; Briassoulis 2005a; Howlett 2011; Yi and Feiock 2012; Peters et al. 2005; Jordan et al. 2011 and 2012), often with a multi-level governance component (del Río and Howlett 2013). Effectively optimizing the choice of instruments in such mixes requires both knowledge of instrument-goal interactions and consideration of how mixes evolve over the long run, and requires an understanding of both long and short-term processes of policy change.

The components of such mixes include policy goals and policy means at various levels of generality (Howlett 2009a; Kern and Howlett 2009; Cashore and Howlett 2007) and design and instrument selection in these contexts 'are all about constrained efforts to match goals and expectations both within and across categories of policy elements' (Howlett 2009d: 74). Achieving effectiveness with respect to deploying such policy portfolios relies upon ensuring mechanisms, calibrations, objectives and settings display 'coherence', 'consistency' and 'congruence' with each other (Howlett and Rayner 2007), subjects which are taken up in detail in the chapters to follow.

Note

1 In his later work, Peters (2000b) reduced this number to seven and altered their content so that they became: directness, visibility, capital/labour intensity, automaticity or level of administration required, level of universality, reliance on persuasion vs enforcement and their 'forcing vs enabling' nature (39).

Readings

Boaz, A., L. Grayson, R. Levitt, and W. Solesbury. (2008). Does Evidence-Based Policy Work? Learning from the UK Experience. *Evidence & Policy* 4, no. 2: 233–53.

Hill, M. and P. Hupe. (2002). *Implementing Public Policy: Governance in Theory and Practice*. London: Sage.

Howlett, M. (2000). 'Managing the "Hollow State": Procedural Policy Instruments and Modern Governance'. *Canadian Public Administration* 43, no. 4: 412–31.

Howlett, M. (2005). 'What is a Policy Instrument? Policy Tools, Policy Mixes and Policy Implementation Styles'. In P. Eliadis, M. Hill and M. Howlett (eds), *Designing Government: From Instruments to Governance*. Montreal, QC: McGill-Queen's University Press, 31–50.

Howlett, M. (2009). 'Governance Modes, Policy Regimes and Operational Plans: A Multi-Level Nested Model of Policy Instrument Choice and Policy Design'. *Policy Sciences* 42, no. 1: 73–89.

Howlett, M. and I. Mukherjee. (2014). 'Policy Design and Non-Design: Towards a Spectrum of Policy Formulation Types'. *Politics and Governance* 2, no. 2 (13 November): 57–71.

Howlett, M. and J. Rayner. (2013). 'Patching vs Packaging in Policy Formulation: Assessing Policy Portfolio Design'. *Politics and Governance* 1, no. 2: 170–82.

Lasswell, H. D. (1956). *The Decision Process: Seven Categories of Functional Analysis*. College Park, MD: University of Maryland Press.

Linder, S. H. and B. G. Peters. (1990a). 'The Design of Instruments for Public Policy'. In S. S. Nagel (ed.), *Policy Theory and Policy Evaluation: Concepts, Knowledge, Causes, and Norms*. New York: Greenwood Press, 103–19.

Linder, S. H. and B. G. Peters. (1990d). 'Research Perspectives on the Design of Public Policy: Implementation, Formulation, and Design'. In D. J. Palumbo and D. J. Calista (eds), *Implementation and the Policy Process: Opening up the Black Box*. New York: Greenwood Press, 51–66.

Linder, S. H. and B. G. Peters. (1991). 'The Logic of Public Policy Design: Linking Policy Actors and Plausible Instrument'. *Knowledge in Society* 4: 125–51.

Nutley, S. M., I. Walter and H. T. O. Davies. (2007). *Using Evidence: How Research can Inform Public Services*. Bristol, UK: Policy Press.

Parsons, W. (2004). 'Not Just Steering but Weaving: Relevant Knowledge and the Craft of Building Policy Capacity and Coherence'. *Australian Journal of Public Administration* 63, no. 1: 43–57.

Peters, B. G., P. Ravinet, M. Howlett, G. Capano, I. Mukherjee, and M. H. Chou. (2018). *Designing for Policy Effectiveness: Defining and Understanding a Concept*. Elements Series. Cambridge: Cambridge University Press.

Radaelli, C. M. (1995). 'The Role of Knowledge in the Policy Process'. *Journal of European Public Policy* 2, no. 2: 159–83.

Weimer, D. L. (1992). 'The Craft of Policy Design: Can It Be More Than Art?' *Policy Studies Review* 11, nos 3/4: 370–88.

Weimer, D. L. (1993). 'The Current State of Design Craft: Borrowing, Tinkering, and Problem Solving'. *Public Administration Review* 53, no. 2 (April): 110–20.

Wu, X., M. Ramesh, M. Howlett and S. A. Fritzen. (2017). *The Public Policy Primer: Managing the Policy Process* (2nd edn). New York: Routledge.

Chapter 4

Why policy design?

Tools, mechanisms, behaviours and the logic of policy compliance

Policy sectors – such as health policy, energy policy, transport policy and many others – constitute distinct policy regimes consisting of the current collectively accepted definition of an issue, the current relevant policies (laws, regulations, fiscal instruments, government programmes and relationships) and the actors and institutions (both inside and outside government) actively engaged in implementing and modifying them (Harris and Milkis 1989; Eisner 1994a,b). These policy regimes are often viewed as examples of a general class of stable 'homeostatic' systems which, once put in place, are self-adjusting or self-equilibrating in routine circumstances and often thought of as changing only under the pressure of external shocks or 'jolts' which introduce new extraneous elements into the system, throwing them out of equilibrium (Aminzade 1992).

This notion of the exogenous nature of subsystem change focusses analytical attention on the various types of external crises which could provoke changes in policy goals and objectives and instruments or their settings, an approach which is common in comparative policy studies, for example, Wilsford (1994). However, the empirical purchase of the metaphor of contemporary policy-making as an homeostatic system has increasingly come to be challenged in the policy sciences. Contemporary policy thinking now tends to favor more adaptive constructs in which it is assumed that policy actors not only react to external changes but can also affect their own environments and, as a result, can endogenously induce significant policy change through policy design and designing (Daneke 1992; Buckley 1968; Smith 2000).

This reconceptualization has led to greater efforts to measure, chronicle and account for the precise mechanisms which are activated by policy designs and the instruments which activate them. Many of these mechanisms operate at the level of individual or group behaviour and include mechanisms such as the propensity of individuals to search for advantage or normative harmony, status and prestige, or to make utility-based calculations of costs and benefits, risks and gains, as well as group behaviour such as rent or influence-seeking which often lie behind the formation and actions of interest groups and other kinds of collective actors (Olsen 1962).

There is also third class of such mechanisms, ones in which policy network relationships alter as new nodes and links are added to policy subsystems. These structural adaptation mechanisms can be triggered by government policy interventions which introduce new actors and ideas into policy structures, often through the deployment of 'procedural' policy tools which trigger this adaptive reflex (Howlett 2000c; Lang 2016). These can precipitate and re-shape specific types of policy behaviour on the part of network members through their impact upon the nodes and links of policy subsystems, the nature of policy deliberations and discourses and ultimately policy outputs (Lang 2016).

Target behaviour, uncertain compliance and the need for persuasive designs

In 1955, Herbert Simon developed the concept of 'bounded rationality' to highlight the great distance existing between theories of human choice processes and administrative theory which often ignored cognitive and other limits in proposals for administrative and policy designs (Simon 1955, 1957). Sixty years later, public policy studies still confront the criticisms formulated by him concerning the nature of human rationality and the utilitarian assumptions commonly made about it by scholars and practitioners of public administration and public policy (Barile et al. 2015; Steg et al. 2014).

Recently, however, under the influence of findings in behavioural economics, public policy studies have gradually showed an increasing willingness to recognize the nature and extent of the limitations on rationality and have begun to apply concepts and lessons derived from this body of work to both the study of policy-maker behaviour and to that of policy targets in order to better understand and improve policy designs (Tversky and Kahneman 1974).

More work still needs to be done in both these areas but studies and practices inspired by Thaler and Sunstein in particular, captured in the notion of 'nudges' (Sunstein 2014; Thaler and Sunstein 2009) described in Chapter 1 and detailed in Chapter 11, have begun to provide insights beyond notions of utility maximization and perfect information to the basic foundations of policy implementation and design studies (Lehner et al. 2015; Rathi and Chunekar 2015; Kersh 2015; Matthies et al. 2016).

All of this work is oriented toward the articulation and successful implementation in the policy world of what has been termed 'persuasive design' (McCalley et al. 2006; Redstrom 2006) or 'design with intent' (Lockton et al. 2016). This is the effort to design an item, from a hand razor or washing machine to a public information campaign or subsidy, in such a way that the user or recipient of the good or service finds it easy to use and 'naturally' complies with its requirements and aspects. Compliance, however, is a complex subject in itself and has often been treated in a uni-dimensional way in the policy design literature, necessitating a re-thinking of the subject. This has begun to occur in recent years and has engendered some new terminology and approaches, such as the development and design of 'compliance regimes' (Weaver 2014) which policy design is now embracing.

The standard compliance-deterrence model: assumptions about human behaviour at the outset of the policy sciences and policy design literature

The aim of most public policy is to invoke behavioural change in the 'targets' of government efforts through deployment of governing resources in the form of substantive and procedural policy tools aimed at promoting relevant behaviour (Anderson 1977; Baldwin 1985). This is done in order to secure better compliance or adherence of populations to government aims and ambitions, be it in the promotion of public safety and security or in the provision of effective healthcare and social welfare. Desired changes can be large or small and the expectation of compliance can be rapid or gradual. But in all cases, some changes in behaviour in a direction congruent with government aims are expected from the utilization of state resources.

Why such compliance is not always forthcoming is a key question in the policy sciences and one which has often been examined but often in a very cursory fashion and under the burden of many, mainly economistic, assumptions about the motivations of policy targets. If perfect compliance with governments' aims existed automatically, of course, there would be little purpose in undertaking state activity beyond information provision in the first place. Recent behavioural studies have engendered their own criticisms for being overly paternalistic and top-down in their orientation toward public policies and their 'targets' (John et al. 2009; Oliver 2015; Goodwin 2012; Hausman 2010) but they have begun to shed much needed light on this hitherto under investigated aspect of policy formulation and implementation (Weaver 2014, 2015).

This is in contrast to the essentially utilitarian basis of much thinking about public policy compliance and policy implementation which has been generally pervasive in the policy sciences from the very founding of the discipline (Tribe 1972; Banfield 1977). It continues to influence even more nuanced recent thinking about tool use linked to notions of policy 'nudging' which has otherwise led the questioning of many traditional utilitarian concepts such as perfect information and reciprocal risk and benefit valuations (Stover and Brown 1975; Oliver 2015; Legett 2014; Room 2013a; John et al. 2009). Although this latter work disputes the idea of 'perfect rationality' among policy targets which often colors more traditional economistic analyses, it still accepts uncritically most of the hedonic assumptions of classic utilitarian thinking: that 'subjects' are motivated to promote pleasure and avoid pain and do so in an essentially calculating 'cost-benefit' fashion when confronted by the choice of whether or not to comply with government diktats.

Traditionally much compliance theory in economics and elsewhere has been based on the concept of 'deterrence' (Kaine et al. 2010) embodied in this way of thinking. This is based on the idea that narrow self-interest and calculable utility in enhancing pleasure and avoiding pain is the primary motivator of compliance behaviour on the part of policy actors (Kaine et al. 2010; Stover and Brown 1975), with governments enhancing pain and pleasure in efforts to deter specific kinds of activity and encourage others.

In practice this meant compliance of policy targets with government intentions was often viewed as a problem equated with the exercise of authority on the part of governments in the form of laws and regulations, a process which involved both a normative component as well as a utilitarian one with respect to the targets of taxes and rules and which was centered on deterring relatively rare non-compliant behaviour. That is, government efforts such as raising tax revenues were seen to be a kind of private–public collective action problem in which actions taken by governments on the part of the general public – such as levying taxes to pay for services – required a belief on the part of targets that the use of coercion to set and collect such taxes was legitimate and that it was in the self-interest of targets to pay them. Legitimate taxes and rules were expected to be paid and obeyed, with penalties and fines established to punish non-compliance in such a way as to 'deter' this unwanted and illegitimate behaviour (Doern and Phidd 1983). Utility calculations could then be extended to the calculation of the calibration of authority tools with penalties set at such a level as to punish those who might contest the legitimacy of such actions or deter those who might seek to free-ride on compliers.

As suggested above, however, the situation is more complex than a purely utilitarian perspective would have it, as even the most basic activities of governance such as paying taxes and obeying rules involve not just individual hedonic behaviour but also considerations on the part of targets and the public of the legality and normative 'appropriateness' of government's levying and collecting such taxes (March and Olsen 1989). Moreover, different kinds of target groups and individuals exist, and are perceived to exist, and can be, and are, treated differently by governments in terms of government expectations of the nature of compliant or non-compliant behaviour. And, of course, governments have more tools at their disposal than just authority-based ones and thus have a range of options with respect to promoting compliance, including those linked to education and persuasion as well as coercion (Hawkins and Thomas 1989; Hood 1986c).

That is, targets can be influenced through many means such as financial incentives as well as efforts at moral suasion and education to behave 'appropriately' and comply with government wishes (McLeod et al. 2015). But the compliance situation is made even more complex again by the fact that different targets have different resources and capabilities and attitudes when it comes to determining whether or not they will comply and how and to what extent, they will not (Weaver 2009b). These attitudes can be quite complex and rooted in historical and culturally specific views of government intentions and the moral and other aspects of compliant and non-compliant behaviour (Wan et al. 2014, 2015). These can include, for example, considerations of the legitimacy and illegitimacy of government actors and actions in specific fields such as constitutional, religious, or privacy-related ones but can also run into and involve the desires on the part of individuals and groups to earn praise or avoid shame or to avoid guilt and social opprobrium for their actions (Cialdini and Goldstein 2004; Beetham 1991; Weber 1978; Hofmann et al. 2014).

This variation in target motivation and compliance behaviour makes policy design a much more challenging activity than that surmised from simple hedonic utilitarian perspectives or even from more complex behaviourally inspired 'rules' of semi-rational economic calculations. The latter not being enough to capture all the considerations of cultural and psychological appropriateness cited earlier (Knetsch 2011; Koh 2011). Whether a proposed action triggers behaviour linked to 'affiliation' or 'conformity' with government wishes or results in 'boomerang' effects (encouraging the action it is aimed at discouraging or vice versa) is critical (Cialdini and Goldstein 2004; Cialdini et al. 2006) but not well-understood. Hence, for example, Kallgren et al. (2000) and de Groot and Schuitema (2012) note the manner in which norm compliance can be affected by the type of 'message' sent urging compliance and its negative or positive nature, the way it has been framed, as well as other factors linked to the character of the underlying norm itself (see also Schultz et al. 2007).

Understanding the behaviour of policy-takers: 'policy targets' and compliance issues

Policy targets come in all shapes and flavours from individuals with certain kinds of characteristics to organizations of various shapes and sizes, histories, backgrounds and memberships. The preferences of such targets are always an issue (Lichtenstein and Slovic 2006; Unsworth and Fielding 2014) and cannot simply be assumed away through the use of policy models containing implicit assumptions about the utilitarian nature of policy target behaviour and compliance (Meier and Morgan 1982).

Moreover, in all but the simplest situations governments are often faced with complex environments in which they encounter not just one but multiple actors and groups as 'targets'. Hence, for example, healthcare clients and citizens facing obesity challenges may be young or old, share some ethnic or racial characteristics, be segmented by gender and in other ways and come to a policy situation with a range of understandings of obesity science and views about food and its preparation and intake. As Weaver (2009a,b, 2014) has pointed out, this generates a spectrum of potential compliers and non-compliers ranging from unwilling ones to voluntary or willing compliers and governments need to know which specific kinds of actors fall into which group (Braithwaite 2003). What works with one group may not work with another and it is not unusual for a range of governing resources and tools to have to be deployed in order to deal with such complex, 'target-rich' environments.

In such circumstances governments must determine (a) whether or not a target is likely to comply with government actions and intentions and (b) whether any compliance is reluctant or freely given (Scholz 1991). As Table 4.1 shows estimations and diagnoses about likely compliance behaviour can usefully be linked to the general use of specific kinds of governing instruments involved in coercive versus persuasive actions on the part of governments (Hawkins and Thomas 1989).

How governments perceive these targets and classify groups within them is thus a critical aspect of policy design. But as Schneider and Ingram (1993, 1997, 2005) have repeatedly pointed out, there are some limits to the ability and desire of governments to discern the true nature of these relationships. The expected behaviour of policy targets is often framed by government agencies and policy makers using the dual aspects of 'positive' or 'negative' stereotypes and whether they are powerful or weak actors in society (Schneider and Ingram 1993, 1997, 2005). Social constructions of target populations are often stereotypes about particular groups of people that have been created

Table 4.1 Nature of compliance of policy targets

		Likelihood of compliance	
		High	Low
Willingness to comply	High	Model subjects Requires little coercion, education, or persuasion	Reluctant subjects Requires education and persuasion
	Low	Resistant subjects Requires incentives to comply	Combative subjects Requires a high level of coercion and monitoring to compel compliance

Source: Modelled after Scholz, J. T. (1991). 'Cooperative Regulatory Enforcement and the Politics of Administrative Effectiveness'. *American Political Science Review* 85, no. 1: 115–36.

Table 4.2 Perceptions of policy targets after Schneider and Ingram (1993)

		Conception of social role	
		Positive	Negative
Conception of power	Strong/ powerful	Advantaged Subsidies and incentives	Adversaries Regulation and controls
	Weak/ vulnerable	Dependents Moral suasion and exhortation	Deviants Coercion and punishments, disincentives

Source: Modelled after Schneider, A. and H. Ingram. (1993). 'Social Construction of Target Populations: Implications for Politics and Policy'. *The American Political Science Review* 87, no. 2: 334–47.

by politics, culture, socialization, history, media, literature, religion and the like. Positive constructions include images such as 'deserving', 'intelligent', 'honest', 'public spirited' and so forth. Negative constructions include images such as 'undeserving', 'stupid', 'dishonest' and 'selfish' (see Table 4.2).

In practice, therefore, the types of tools used to address problems involving these groups often vary directly according to their categorization, with positively viewed targets receiving benefits and negatively viewed ones 'burdened' by costs. More coercive measures, Schneider and Ingram argued, are often used against groups perceived as 'deviants' rather than against other groups who might actually be more resistant to government initiatives, while tools such as subsidies and other kinds of payments might be most effective if used in dealing with 'dependents' but are often given instead to advantaged groups (Schneider and Ingram 1993: 337).

This discussion highlights the significant linkages which exist between both perceptions of and actual target behaviour and government tool use. Accurately determining this requires research and clarity on the part of government and the avoidance of stereotypes and simple estimations of target group attitudes and power. Of course, while there is no denying that targets are politically and socially constructed, there is also a significant 'objective' linkage in expectations governments have about compliance. That is, advantaged groups are usually expected to comply or have similar interests or share government aspirations in general more than deviants and dependents are often able to evade controls in the same way as do adversary groups (Pierce et al. 2014).

The logic of policy design: policy change as behavioural change

The utilitarian viewpoint behind much thinking about policy design has only been seriously challenged in the policy sciences in relatively few instances where it has been undeniably apparent that target behaviour is motivated by considerations other than utility such as, for example, when logics of appropriateness clearly dominate over those of calculation in displays of patriotism or religiously inspired altruistic or resistant activity (March and Olsen 1989, 2004; Tyler 1990, 2013). Or in the negative case, as seen in the situation of behaviour that is clearly self-destructive such as drug, alcohol, or smoking addictions, which is difficult to explain or correct using a purely utilitarian framework (Vimpani 2005; McGoldrick and Boonn 2010).

Despite the relative lack of challenges to the utilitarian framework in the policy sciences, however, empirically, such a position has become increasingly difficult to hold. Consideration and plans for 'nudging' and other aspects of behavioural economics which focus on semi-conscious cues and suggestions have undermined the utilitarian paradigm alongside a new focus in contemporary policy studies on the employment of policy tools such as co-production or faith-based public service delivery (Alford 1998; Hula et al. 2007; Kissane 2007; Zehavi 2008) and, to a lesser extent, in areas affected by 'social marketing' (Pykett et al. 2014) which explicitly rely on group norms in order to be effective. These have together undermined confidence in the ability of utilitarian models to capture critical aspects of target behaviour responsible for participation in and compliance with many government schemes and intentions.

This is the case, for example, pertaining to the use of information-based tools or moral suasion to try to convince citizens to do their duty and refrain from, for instance, littering (Grasmick et al. 2001; John 2013) or to 'do the right thing', in giving up their seats on public transportation to pregnant women, the disabled, the elderly and others less fortunate than themselves (Stanbury and Fulton 1985; Bardach 1989a; Torgler 2004; Corner and Randall 2011). Such approaches have been especially significant in some jurisdictions in recent years, often displacing the deployment of regulation and financial incentives, for instance the emphasis on behavioural modification through social marketing and 'nudges' developed by the Blair government in the UK after 2008 (Chatterton and Wilson 2014). Even analyses of these tools, however, often try to link their success to issues such as 'ability' or 'capacity to comply' which reintroduces the idea of utilitarianism albeit in modified form (leavened by concerns of capability issues preventing a more straightforward compliance situation from emerging) (Winter and May 2001; Corner and Randall 2011; Chatterton and Wilson 2014; McLeod et al. 2015).

Notwithstanding this latter concern, however, this recent activity on the part of many governments raises many questions about the accuracy of the assumptions of self-interested utility maximization that underlie many existing and proposed policy designs and which have dominated the academic discourse on these subjects (DiMento 1989; Kahneman 1994; Jones et al. 2011). If target behaviour is not utilitarian, though, then what is it and how can it best be anticipated and linked in policy designs to the efficient and effective attainment of government goals, given that policy-makers themselves are behavioural agents (Viscusi and Gayer 2015) affected by the policy advice they receive and their own cognitive limitations?

Here it should be recalled that policy changes come about as governments and social actors wrestle with the basic problematic and expectations of policy interventions and adopt policies or sets of policy tools which they expect to accomplish their goals, whatever these may be. The use of policy tools is expected to activate certain propensities on the part of policy actors leading to more or less predictable changes in their behaviour and a different set of policy outputs than would have occurred with a pre-existing mix.

This is a process which is seen as involving a complex causal chain centered around existing policy behaviours and policy-making contexts and policy interventions which trigger 'targets' to change their behaviour in some new direction compatible with government aims (Falleti and Lynch 2009; Hedström and Swedberg 1996, 1998; Hedström and Ylikoski 2010). This overall logic is set out in Figure 4.1.

As Figure 4.1 illustrates, a policy design approach thus views policy-making as largely about affecting behavioural changes in target populations, with policy instruments used as the means to influence a shift from behaviour (1) to a reformed or new behaviour (1A or 2) (Balch 1980).

Despite much experience with, and study of, policy instruments, exactly which mechanisms are involved in these processes remains an active research area in the policy sciences (Howlett 2018b).

The linkages between policy instrument invocation and behavioural or policy change are very rich (see Figure 4.2). As Figure 4.2 shows, the process of behavioural change involves at least four linkages, all of which are affected

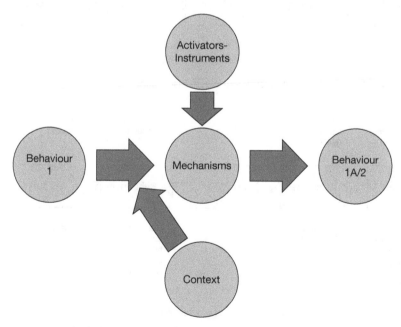

Figure 4.1 The behavioural expectations of policy design

by contextual aspects present at the exact moment at which instruments are invoked and mechanisms triggered. These are: (1) the link between tools and the governing resources present at any moment in time; (2) the link between resources and the mechanisms which tools activate and (3) the links between the mechanisms and the actual behavioural changes which occur post-activation and (4) the link between changes in behaviour and changes in policy outputs. And all four of these linkages are susceptible to various barriers and impediments to instrument choices, mechanism activation, reception and impact which make policy design and designing complex and error-prone activities. That is, each link in this chain is affected by contextual factors which can serve to block or make the linkages across the tools-output chain problematic, that is, difficult to predict and control (Falleti and Lynch 2009).

There are many such barriers and intermediating factors, which include such factors as the preferred policy style and governance mode which can affect preferences for certain tools over others (Howlett 2017; Howlett and Rayner 2013); the various capacity strengths and weaknesses which can limit

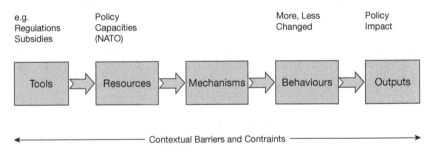

Figure 4.2 Links in the policy instrument-mechanism-output chain

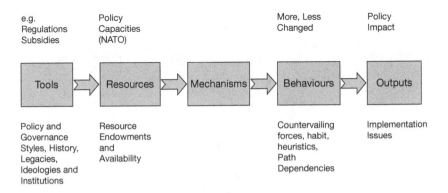

Figure 4.3 Context-related mechanism constraints

the capability of governments to use particular tools or eliminate them altogether (Wu et al. 2015b; Howlett and Ramesh 2016b); possible counter-vailing demands and constraints on behavioural change which can undermine the effect and impact of a mechanisms on subsequent behavioural change (Weaver 2014, 2015; Howlett 2018a); as well as various kinds of implemen-tation and other issues which can lessen, or enhance, policy outputs (Lindqvist 2016; Hupe and Hill 2016) (see Figure 4.3).

Policy mechanisms activated in policy designs

This discussion of the general logic policy-making and policy design, of course, begs the question of what is in the 'black box' at the center of the analysis. That is, what mechanisms drive these processes of policy change? What are the mechanisms that lead more or less regularly to one type of output even if this regularity is limited to some circumstances and not others? Who do they affect and how?

In general two kinds of mechanisms can be identified: those which more or less directly affect actor behaviour and those which involve learning and more reflective activities. These kinds of mechanisms have received treatment in the literature before which has variously termed them 'micro-meso-macro' or 'transformational', 'action-forcing', or 'situational' (Hedström and Swedberg 1998 and 1999; Hedström and Ylikoski 2010). However, these definitions are quite vague as to what exactly is micro and what macro, for example, in the case of the former and why only three types exist in the latter case. A more robust and clear way to distinguish between such mechanisms is to look at what or whose behaviour is being affected. Here a central distinction can be made between 'individual', 'group' and 'structural' mechanisms.

Individual level mechanisms

A great deal of the literature on social mechanisms in general and policy mechanisms in particular, has focussed on the individual level. Until recently these studies focussed almost exclusively on so-called 'system 2' mechanisms, that is, those which appealed to the more rational bases of human cognition, such as the ability to accurately assess the costs and benefits of specific proposed courses of action and decide upon a maximizing or optimal strategy (Elster 2009). Under the sway of behavioural economists and others, however, in recent years, as we have seen, many works dealing with 'system 2' or automatic less 'rational' motivations and cognitive strategies have increasingly been added to this lexicon (Shafir et al. 1993; Shafir 2013; Sunstein et al. 2001; Ariely 2010). Although often pitched purely at the level of individuals, many of these same mechanisms also operate at the more collective or group level (Olson 1965; Buchanon et al. 1980; Riker 1986).

In this view, at the individual level, the mechanisms activated by policy instruments in order to trigger policy change are characteristics of human behaviour such as greed, fear, risk aversion, or the use of heuristics which affect the logics of calculation and appropriateness individuals take toward issues such as whether or not to perform a crime or quit smoking or invest in a pension fund or donate to a charity (March and Olsen 2004) (see Figure 4.4).

These kinds of mechanisms are triggered or activated by 'substantive' policy instruments (Howlett 2000c) which are the typical kinds of policy tools discussed in policy design, such as in the literature around economic incentives and disincentives such as the provision of subsidies or the creation of penalty-based regulatory regimes (Tupper and Doern 1981; Hood 1986c; Howlett 1991; Hood 1995; Hood 1991; Salamon 2002c). These tools rely on a set of governing resources for their effectiveness, including 'nodality' (or information), authority, treasure, or the organizational resources of government (Hood 1986c; Anderson 1975) (see Table 4.3).

Thus information-based instruments, for example, can both facilitate the provision of information as well as suppress it and can involve the release of misleading as well as accurate information (Goodin 1980).

One of the main reasons one such tool would be chosen over another is supply-oriented: that is, that a government will utilize specific kinds of tools deploying the resources it has in ample supply or which can be easily replenished (Hood 1983). This is an important insight. But in addition to 'supply-side' capacity issues, 'demand-side' considerations are also very significant in policy design. That is, in general, each category of tool involves the use of a specific governing resource expected to trigger or lever a specific characteristic or receptor in targets, inducing a certain behavioural response. Thus, the effectiveness of the deployment of such tools is linked not just to resource availability – a precondition of their use – but also to the existence of different characteristics on the part of policy targets which make them respond in a predictable way to the use of this resource when it is deployed.

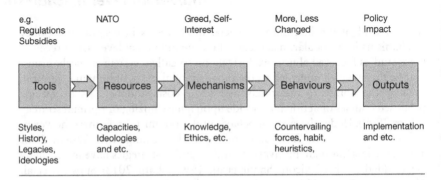

Figure 4.4 Links in the design chain: individual and group level

Table 4.3 A resource-based taxonomy of procedural and substantive policy instruments (Cells provide examples of instruments in each category)

		Governing resource and target Need			
		Information	Authority	Treasure	Organization
Purpose of tool	Substantive	Public information Campaign	Independent Regulatory agencies	Subsidies and Grants	Public enterprises
	Procedural	Official secrets acts	Administrative advisory committees	Interest group funding	Government re-organizations

Source: Adapted by Howlett, M. (2000c). 'Managing the "Hollow State": Procedural Policy Instruments and Modern Governance'. *Canadian Public Administration* 43, no. 4: 412–31 from Hood, C. (1986c). The Tools of Government. London: Chatham House.

Table 4.4 Behavioural needs for resource effectiveness

Tool type	Statecraft resource applied	Target behavioural pre-requisite
Nodality	Information	Credibility/trust – willingness to believe and act on information provided by government
Authority	Coercive power/force	Legitimacy – willingness to be manipulated by government invoked penalties and proscriptions
Treasure	Financial	Cupidity – willingness to be manipulated by gain/losses imposed by governments
Organization	Organization	Trust – willingness to receive goods and services from government and enter into partnership with it

Source: Howlett, M. (2011). *Designing Public Policies: Principles and Instruments.* New York: Routledge.

Table 4.4 presents some of the behavioural pre-requisites which governing tools rely upon for their effects.

In the case of information use, for example, tool effectiveness relies both on the availability of knowledge and the means to distribute it ('resources') and also upon the target's belief in the accuracy of the messages being purveyed, or their *credibility* ('receptor'). Similarly, the effectiveness of the use of authoritative tools, as discussed above, depends not just on the availability of coercive mechanisms and their enforcement, but also upon target perceptions of government *legitimacy*. Similarly, the effective use of treasure resources depends not just on the availability of government funding, but also on target group financial need and especially their receptivity to government funding or their *cupidity*. Likewise, the effective use of organizational tools depends both on the existence of personnel and other organizational resource but also upon target group *trust* of government fairness in the deployment and training of personnel to provide services and rules (Howlett 2017).

These are important considerations in policy design and especially in the calibration of policy tools. Thus, the use of authority-based tools such as laws and regulations, for example, involves considerations of legitimacy on the part of targets but must not over-reach or over-burden the extent of legitimacy which a government enjoys (Suchman 1995; Hanberger 2003). If a policy measure does so, it most assuredly will require much monitoring and enforcement activity in order to be even minimally effective, involving large administrative costs and burdens which may well undermine its own efficiency and effectiveness, as has occurred in the past in many countries in areas such as marijuana or alcohol prohibition (Issalys 2005).

Group level mechanisms

This same logic can be applied to groups or collections of individuals who enter into coalitions in order to pursue collective aims and goals. Such groups are sometimes viewed as mere aggregates of individual preferences with no interests or aims beyond those of their members (Olson 1965) although more careful study has shown many more complex motivations and proclivities exist at the collective or organizational level which are not reducible in such a fashion (Halpin and Binderkrantz 2011). These include propensities to search for new issues or retain existing issue orientations, decisions about whether to specialize or generalize in issue orientations and the nature of membership appeals, for example, rather than simply an interest in membership or revenue growth (Halpin et al. 2017).

Structural or sub-system level mechanisms

A third set of mechanisms is composed of those which focus on policy subsystems. According to Sabatier (1998: 99), 'A subsystem consists of actors from a variety of public and private organizations who are actively concerned with a policy problem or issue, such as agriculture and who regularly seek to influence public policy in that domain'. Such sub-systems, he argued, provide 'the most useful unit of analysis for understanding the overall policy process', superior to the use of other units such as government organizations or programmes.

A sizeable literature in the policy sciences has noted the importance to policy outputs and processes of two aspects of subsystem structure, namely the number of type of actors arrayed in a subsystem or network and especially their ability to block off or close off entry of new actors, as well as the nature of the ideas which circulate within such subsystems (Howlett 2000c; Howlett and Ramesh 1998, 2002).

That is, changes in the ends of policies, be they conceptual or practical, require new ideas to be incorporated into policy-making processes (Sabatier 1999; Campbell 1998; Blyth 1997; Hall 1993), meaning such ideas have to be able to penetrate into the policy communities and networks which control or dominate policy discourses (Howlett and Ramesh 1998). Similarly, another sizeable body of policy research links changes in the conceptual aspects of policy-making simply to the ability of actors in policy subsystems to achieve and retain 'monopoly' or hegemonic status (Baumgartner and Jones 1993; Howlett and Rayner 1995; Hoberg 1996; Jacobsen 1995; Pontusson 1995).

This set of mechanisms is quite different from the individual or group level ones in that they are less behavioural than structural in nature. This important third category of mechanisms is often ignored in the literature on policy mechanisms which overwhelmingly focusses on the micro or individual level, only occasionally venturing into a discussion of the meso or group level.

This third set of mechanisms is activated by policy tools, especially 'procedural' ones which affect the manner in which individual and groups act and interact in attempting to affect policy outcomes (Howlett 2000c). These mechanisms affect the propensity for subsystems to see the emergence of relatively consistent sets of policy actors and ideas interacting within more or less well established relational parameters or whether more chaotic relationships and interactions exist.

That is, like any kind of networks these subsystems are composed of nodes and links. And manipulating nodes and links – adding, subtracting and changing them – constitutes a set of triggers which activate a variety of mechanisms at the network level including the willingness of policy actors to enter into relationships with other, proximate, actors in the network (rather than more distant ones) or their ability to act as leaders, entrepreneurs, or brokers, between other actors and governments.

These aspects of subsystem structure have been linked to outputs in terms of affecting the propensity for specific types of policy output changes to occur. Policies goals often change, for example, when there is a simultaneous presence of new actors (as a result of systemic perturbations and/or sub-system spill-overs) as well as new ideas (emerging from policy learning and/or change in the venue where policy is made). At the opposite end, minimal changes are often seen – and often only changes in settings or tool calibrations – when stability processes such as closed networks and path dependency predominate. At any particular conjuncture, therefore, the propensity for specific types of policy change is determined by the interactive effects of policy change and stability processes on sub-system membership and deliberations, both of which can be altered by government action.

Hence there is a third major type of policy behaviour, with a specific set of mechanisms, which policy-makers can and do, activate, which are structural ones (see Figure 4.5).

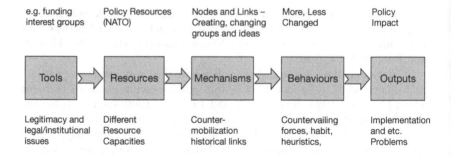

Figure 4.5 Links in the design chain: structural level

Substantive tools can also affect network structure as when, for example, subsidies to an industry lead to the creation of more firms than otherwise would exist, altering the nature of production systems and industrial ecologies. However, procedural policy tools affect aspects of sub-system structure and behaviour more directly (de Bruijn and ten Heuvelhof 1997). These tools affect many activities of actors in policy subsystems (see Table 4.5).

Examples of policy tools with this procedural orientation which triggers structural mechanisms include a government creating an advisory committee of select citizens or experts to aid it in its policy deliberations in contentious issue areas such as local housing development or chemical regulation, or its creation of a freedom-of-information or access-to-information legislation making it easier for citizens to gain access to governments records, information and documents. Re-organizing their own internal governmental structure can also have an effect on policy processes, for example, as occurs when natural resource ministries are combined with environmental ones, forcing the two to adopt some form of new operating arrangements and changing the routes and routines through which industry and environmental lobbyists and interest groups interact.

Improving policy designs through better linking tools, mechanisms and targets

The fundamental design problem for governments then, is not just determining a given governmental resource endowment or calculating the range of prison sentences or the amount of fines and subsidies to levy in some situation based on a utilitarian compliance-deterrence logic, but rather to understand on which basis compliance is likely to occur or not: that is to what extent a government enjoys legitimacy, credibility, trust and cupidity among target groups. This is a design challenge which requires detailed empirical

Table 4.5 Aspects of policy processes and structures affected by procedural policy tools

		Network structure
Process	Actors	Interactions

Formulation	Actors and preferences
	Authority
	  Restrict/invite
	  participation
	Information
	  Issuing mission statement
	Treasure
	  Funding of participants
	Organization
	  Trading influence for
	  compromise and
	  commitment
		Deliberation orientation
		Authority
		  Rules for decision making
		  (e.g., consensus vs majoritarian)
		Interaction guidelines (e.g., joint
		  declaration of intent)
		Information
		  Providing and acknowledging
		  interest positions
		Treasure
		  Establishing political opportunity
		  structures (sponsoring of
		  events/secretariat)
		Organization
		  Providing forums for
		  deliberation

Implementation	Commitment to deliver
	  results
	Authority
	  Compliance mechanism
	(binding vs non-binding)
	  Accountability
	  Effective control over
	  implementing agencies
	Information
	  Reporting
	  Monitoring
	Treasure
	  Funding of participants
	Organization
	Providing organizational
	  home/support/resources
		Joint production orientation
		Authority
		  Establishing rules for joint
		  production and collaboration
		Information
		Promotion/exhortation of
		Participation
		  Joint action plans
		Treasure
		  Incentives to collaborate (joint
		  responsibility)
		Organization
		Establishing co-ordinating and
		  service delivery agencies

Source: Adapted from Lang A. 'Collaborative Governance in Health and Technology Policy: The Use and Effects of Procedural Policy Instruments'. *Administration & Society*, (10 August 2016).

investigation and analysis in each case of tool deployment and continued monitoring over time to ensure these fundamental conditions have not changed or been undermined by any action undertaken. Governments enjoying a high level of credibility, for example, may be able to undertake actions through moral suasion while governments which do not enjoy that credibility will need to employ other tools. But whether or not this high level of credibility is being maintained is a key determinant of policy effectiveness and continual monitoring and assessment is required to ensure this remain the case and that existing tools continue to function effectively over time.

The same non-utilitarian behavioural logic extends to the use of taxes and subsidies, although the behavioural characteristics of treasure-based policy tools are not the same as for information-based ones. The former achieve their ends not through a legitimacy-coercion matrix of encouragement and deterrence but through the willingness of subjects to be manipulated, more or less voluntarily, by financial incentives and disincentives (Surrey 1970; Woodside 1979). These tools rely on the 'cupidity' of their targets and again will only be as effective as long as targets are willing to accept financial awards or penalties from governments and alter their behaviour accordingly (Braithwaite 2003). Calibrations of the settings of such tools are often claimed to be undertaken on a purely utilitarian basis but the extent of cupidity or greed on the part of policy targets varies dramatically by group and subject matter. Governments discover this whenever they attempt, for example, to discourage cigarette and tobacco or obesity by discouraging consumption through raising excise taxes on harmful products, while reducing them on others (Gulberg and Skodvin 2011; Coffman et al. 2016). Such actions may work in some cases and products or among some groups, like the elderly in the case of tobacco control, but fail in others, such as young women and younger people in general (Studlar 2002).

This behavioural pre-requisite also features in the use and effectiveness of the 'information' tools discussed above. As the poor experiences of the application of some of the insights of behavioural economics and psychology to policy-making in the form of 'nudges' or informational cues show, consideration by targets of the credibility of messages sent and received and the willingness of targets to trust their contents and promises is critical to what type and extent of behavioural response will ensue (Weiss and Tschirhart 1994). This is true of many different public information campaigns, for example, in areas of obesity and the ingestion of dangerous products, which utilize this resource (Kersh 2015; Barreiro-Hurle et al. 2010; Padberg 1992). Efforts at 'social marketing', such as these, feature the use of informational or 'nodality' tools (Hood 1986c), that appeal directly to sentiments of collective solidarity and moral duty of citizens and groups, invoking values well beyond those related to individual utility calculations (Corner and Randall 2011).

Again, while this involves a subtle effort to match resource expenditure and target behaviour as done by authority-coercion or financial incentive-based efforts, it is based upon a different compliance logic. Although some treatments of these information tools still base their analysis on behavioural assumptions in which manipulation is expected sometimes to follow government cues unthinkingly ('nudges'), this under-estimates the impact of trust and credibility of the information sent and received.

Finally, efforts at 'co-production' and co-design or co-management often aim at re-designing service delivery through various forms of partnerships in which some division of labor emerges between state and non-state actors (Pestoff et al. 2006; Voorberg 2014; Alford 1998; Braithwaite and Levi 2003). These forms of service delivery are organizational tools, which utilize state personnel and organizational resources to directly or indirectly deliver goods and services. But, again, willingness of targets to partner in these activities, as in the case of more traditional exclusively government-based ones, requires targets to assess and trust the competence of government agents to deliver or plan such services in a timely and appropriate way.

Conclusion: improving compliance regime design through policy experimentation

Several issues remain outstanding research items in this field. This includes how to ensure compliance in complex policy situations, how to move beyond heuristics in understanding and deciding on policies and how to better understand policy advice and influence.

That is, when designing for high levels of compliance, Weaver (2009a, 2014, 2015) argues the appropriate responses of governments to these challenges and barriers are to create a 'compliance regime' involving a mix of tools and elements.

A basic regime of this kind includes such traditional arrangements as:

- Providing positive incentives for compliance;
- Having negative incentives for non-compliance; and
- Providing prohibitions and requirements with punishments attached.

But it also would include less traditional elements such as:

- Providing information about what behaviour is compliant, how to comply and the advantages of compliance;
- Providing admonitions to comply on moral, self-interested, or other grounds as well as utilitarian ones;
- Providing resources to comply which may be targeted to those who would otherwise lack those resources; and
- Manipulating options and defaults (choice architecture) without substantially affecting the payoff to individuals of so doing (Weaver 2015: 6).

Weaver (2009b: 5) has also recently enumerated some of the various 'compliance problems' or 'barriers' to compliance which targets and governments face and which should be the subject of investigation and action. These include:

- **Incentive and sanction problems** where positive and or negative incentives are insufficient to ensure compliance;
- **Monitoring problems** where target compliance may be difficult or costly to monitor;
- **Resource problems** where targets lack the resources to comply even if they want to;
- **Autonomy problems** where targets do not have the power to make decisions that comply with policy even if they want to;
- **Information problems** where targets lack information that would make compliance more likely; and
- **Attitude and objectives problems** where targets are hostile/mistrustful toward providers or programmes.

What is needed for effective designs that overcome these problems is more systematic analysis and understanding of the motivations of policy targets which would allow better matching of tools and targets right at the outset of policy-making, rather than relying upon suspect utilitarian conceptions of the behaviour which lie behind policy compliance and non-compliance (Weaver 2009a,b; Braithwaite 2003; Schneider and Sidney 2009; Chatterton and Wilson 2014; Pierce et al. 2014).

A design approach to policy-making centered on an instrument-mechanism-behaviour logic has several advantages over other approaches, not least in how it clarifies the tool-to-output process of policy-making and the key factors and relationships existing in such processes. It is a key technique for developing and implementing more persuasive designs and better achieving policy goals.

Policy experiments, including pilots, play an important role in policy-relevant knowledge production which could include early evaluation of the impacts of new initiatives such as subsidies and incentive programmes for education and training of economically disadvantaged communities and utilization of data generated via these pilots (Stromsdorfer 1985). The development sector, for example, has often conducted experiments to evaluate alternative strategies and accordingly allocate resources to those that emerge as most feasible in promoting development goals (Rondinelli 1993).

Testing policy responses through active experimentation is a key tool for policy-makers interested in developing more persuasive designs. Experiments and pilot projects help them deal with different kinds of uncertainty through approaches ranging from improved knowledge of target group behaviour under different policy interventions, to improve projections of the likelihood of future states of events. Transposing the idea of 'controlled experimentation' – a concept that is well-acknowledged in the social and natural sciences, into policy research has received much attention by policy scholars and practitioners alike, attempting to deal with uncertainties in the policy environment (Anderson 1975).

Experiments have also served as a source of evidence for policy-making in many sectors including education, healthcare, environment and social welfare among others (Bennion 2011). More recently, policy pilots have also gained much attention in the transition management literature (Rotmans et al. 2001; Van den Bosch and Rotmans 2008) specifically those intended to generate long-term societal change (Bos and Brown 2012). There is little empirical analysis on the effects of policy experiments however, in particular on how their design influences their potential as 'learning incubators' (McFadgen 2013). Experimentation is nevertheless an important instrument providing a 'space' for learning to occur (Bettini et al. 2014). 'Promoting variation' (Swanson and Bhadwal 2009) by crafting multiple policy alternatives can make the emergence of a successful solution more likely (Cummings et al. 2013).

Enhanced experimentation and learning can be instrumental in 'keeping pace with the dynamic drivers and expressions of risk' in a changing policy environment (O'Brien et al. 2012), but only if the experiments themselves are designed to address the level of uncertainty involved in a specific case. The underlying motivation in designing policy experiments is that these will provide results that are largely indicative of what outputs, outcomes and challenges can be expected when programmes and policies based on results of these experiments are implemented fully, enhancing the persuasiveness of designs through proper appreciation of the compliance logics behind target behaviour (Nair and Vreugdenhil 2015).

Readings

Australian Public Service Commission. (2009). 'Smarter Policy: Choosing Policy Instruments and Working with Others to Influence Behaviour'. Canberra, ACT: Australian Public Service Commission.

Bunge, M. (1997). 'Mechanism and Explanation'. *Philosophy of the Social Sciences* 27, no. 4 (1 December): 410–65.

Bunge, M. (2004). 'How Does It Work? The Search for Explanatory Mechanisms'. *Philosophy of the Social Sciences* 34, no. 2 (1 June): 182–210.

Duesberg, S., Á. Ní Dhubháin and D. O'Connor. (2014). 'Assessing Policy Tools for Encouraging Farm Afforestation in Ireland'. *Land Use Policy* 38 (May): 194–203.

Falleti, T. G. and J. F. Lynch. (2009). 'Context and Causal Mechanisms in Political Analysis'. *Comparative Political Studies* 42, no. 9 (1 September): 1143–66.

Halpin, D. R., B. Fraussen and A. J. Nownes. (2018). 'The Balancing Act of Establishing a Policy Agenda: Conceptualizing and Measuring Drivers of Issue Prioritization within Interest Groups'. *Governance* 31, no. 2 (1 April): 215–37.

Harring, N. (2016). 'Reward or Punish? Understanding Preferences toward Economic or Regulatory Instruments in a Cross-National Perspective'. *Political Studies* 64, no. 3 (1 October): 573–92.

Hedström, P. and P. Ylikoski. (2010). 'Causal Mechanisms in the Social Sciences'. *Annual Review of Sociology* 36, no. 1: 49–67.

Heinmiller, B. T., M. A. Hennigar and S. Kopec. (2017). 'Degenerative Politics and Youth Criminal Justice Policy in Canada'. *Politics & Policy* 45, no. 3 (June): 405–31.

Howlett, M. (2018). 'Matching Policy Tools and Their Targets: Beyond Nudges and Utility Maximization in Policy Design'. *Policy & Politics* 46, no. 1 (January): 101–24.

Lockton, D., D. Harrison and N. A. Stanton. (2016). 'Design for Sustainable Behaviour: Investigating Design Methods for Influencing User Behaviour'. *Annual Review of Policy Design* 4, no. 1 (28 October): 1–10.

Porumbescu, G. A., M. I. H. Lindeman, E. Ceka and M. Cucciniello. (2017). 'Can Transparency Foster More Understanding and Compliant Citizens?' *Public Administration Review* 77, no. 6: 840–50.

Redström, J. (2006). 'Persuasive Design: Fringes and Foundations'. In W. A. IJsselsteijn, Y. A. W. de Kort, C. Midden, B. Eggen and E. van den Hoven (eds), *Persuasive Technology*, Lecture Notes in Computer Science 3962. Berlin/Heidelberg, Germany: Springer, 112–22.

Schneider, A. and H. Ingram. (1993). 'Social Construction of Target Populations: Implications for Politics and Policy'. *American Political Science Review* 87, no. 2: 334–47.

Schneider, A. and M. Sidney. (2009). 'What Is Next for Policy Design and Social Construction Theory?' *Policy Studies Journal* 37, no. 1: 103–19.

Weaver, R. K. (2009a). 'If You Build It, Will They Come? Overcoming Unforeseen Obstacles to Program Effectiveness'. The Tansley Lecture. Saskatoon, SK: University of Saskatchewan.

Weaver, R. K. (2009b). 'Target Compliance: The Final Frontier of Policy Implementation'. Research paper. Washington, DC: Brookings Institution. www.brookings.edu/research/papers/2009/09/30-compliance-weaver.

Weaver, R. K. (2014). 'Compliance Regimes and Barriers to Behavioral Change'. *Governance* 27, no. 2 (1 April): 243–65.

Weaver, R. K. (2015). 'Getting People to Behave: Research Lessons for Policy Makers'. *Public Administration Review* 75, no. 6 (1 November): 806–16.

Part III

POLICY DESIGNING

Process, principles and practices

When does policy design occur?

Policy designing as policy formulation

The foci of design activities within the policy process, as the discussion in Chapters 1–4 has shown, are around policy formulation and implementation (Hood 1986c, 2007b; Linder and Peters 1991; Varone 1998; Varone and Aebischer 2001). It is at these two stages of the policy cycle that the possible techniques to be used in realizing policy are first mooted and appraised and then, finally, executed and put into practice (Goggin 1987). The key stage of policy design, however, is policy formulation, with successful implementation and the barriers to it being one concern of formulation activity.

In general, 'policy formulation', or the pursuit of finding, devising and defining solutions, takes place once a public problem has been recognized as warranting government attention. Formulation thus follows upon an initial 'agenda setting' stage of policy-making and entails the various processes of generating options about what to do about an identified and prioritized problem. That is, during this period of policy-making, policy options that might help resolve issues and problems recognized at the agenda-setting stage are identified, refined and formalized.

Formulation activities are thus distinct from other aspects of policy-making which involve authoritative government decision-makers choosing a particular course of action, or its actual implementation on the ground (Schmidt 2008). However, the provision of solutions to problems is a complex matter and in practice, the development of options and alternatives to specific kinds of problems facing societies and governments often precedes the articulation of problems by a particular government.

Trial and error type experimental processes and learning directly or indirectly from other governments and societies' experiences with various designs, allows government to engage in emulation and other forms of design interactions during policy formulation which can serve to reduce the differences found between jurisdiction and can lead to large similarities in policy design and content among even the most diverse societies (Bennett 1991a; Bennett and Howlett 1991). However, such learning is not automatic and oftern may not occur due to time, information, ideologies or other tensions.

Policy formulation as a stage of the policy cycle

Policy formulation refers to the stage of generating options about what to do about a public problem (Sidney 2007). Once a government has acknowledged the existence of a public problem and the need to do something about it, that is, once it has entered onto the agenda of government, policy-makers are expected to decide on a course of action to follow in addressing it.

Formulating what this course of action will entail is the subject of policy formulation. It is a stage in which options that might help resolve issues and problems recognized at the agenda-setting stage are identified, refined, appraised and formalized. Although many such alternatives may have already emerged during or prior to agenda-setting (Kingdon 1984), in policy formulation some initial assessment, no matter how cursory, of the feasibility and comparative costs and benefits of different policy options is conducted (May 1981; Wildavsky 1979; Salamon 1989, 2002c; Linder and Peters 1990b,c,d; Howlett 2000c; Howlett and Ramesh 2016a,b; Howlett, Mukherjee and Woo 2015; Howlett, Ramesh and Woo 2015; Howlett, Daymer and Tolleyson 2009; Jarvis 2011b; Montpetit 2003b,c; Branthen 2007a,b; Dunlop 2009a,b). These formulation efforts and dynamics are distinct from the next stage, decision-making, where a specific course or programme of action is approved by authoritative decision-makers in government (Howlett et al. 2009) and then sent to be implemented.

As Charles Jones (1984: 7) observed, the distinguishing characteristic of policy formulation is thus simply that means are proposed in order to see if and how they could resolve a perceived societal problem or government goal. This formulation activity encompasses consideration and discussion of several elements. These include culminating in considerations of programme design and programme structure:

(a) problem conceptualization
(b) theory evaluation and selection
(c) specification of objectives
(d) programme design
(e) programme structure.

(Wolman 1981: 435)

Policy formulation, therefore, is a process of identifying and assessing possible solutions to policy problems or to put it another way, exploring the various options or alternatives available for addressing a problem through *policy analysis* (Linder and Peters 1990d). This is what Aaron Wildavsky (1979) termed finding and establishing a relationship between 'manipulable means and obtainable objectives' (15–16). It involves governments and other policy actors asking and answering questions about how societies can deal with various kinds of problems and conditions affecting citizens and organizations.

The exercise of framing problems and proposing alternatives or the matching of policy goals and means is central to the tasks and activities of policy formulation, including policy design. This is not a neutral or 'objective' or technical process. Although it may sometimes be written about or viewed in this way, as one of the earliest proponents of the policy sciences, Harold Lasswell, stated in 1936, it is a political activity thoroughly immersed and grounded in questions and conflicts about 'who gets what, when and how' in society (Lasswell 1936).

As Howlett and Ramesh noted, this is a task undertaken by governments but also affected by a wide range of state and societal actors. Public policies emanate from societies' efforts to affect changes in their own institutional or public behaviour, in order to achieve some end goal that key policy actors consider to be important. They are determined by governments but involve other actors and institutions – private, commercial, family and others – in often complex governance and governing arrangements and relationships (Howlett and Ramesh 2016a).

Design questions and concerns vary in range and scope but addressing them typically involves deliberations among a wide range of actors about what kinds of activities governments can undertake and what kinds of policy instruments or levers they can employ in crafting solutions for the public and private dilemmas they identify, or consider to be policy problems. Some problems may defy solution, such as poverty or homelessness in many countries and jurisdictions, and others may be resolvable more easily than others. But whatever solutions emerge from formulation activity are the basis of what, once adopted, becomes a public policy.

In this light, the formulation of policies and policy designs or the matching and often mismatching, of goals and means, or policy aims and instruments, occurs through the interplay of knowledge-based analytics of problems and solutions with power-based political considerations. These include actor calculations of the costs and benefits of specific problem definitions and proposed solutions, but also the partisan and electoral concerns of governments and other actors and many other matters in the realm of ideological, religious, ethical and other kinds of beliefs held by actors.

All of this activity occurs within the context of the need for policy-makers to meet and placate the diverse interests of the public, social actors and their own administrations. Not surprisingly, this process often ends with the adoption of complex assemblages or mixes of policy aims and policy tools to address policy problems and the interests of actors that are somewhat unique to each jurisdiction and which may or may not embody much in the way of 'technical' merit (Howlett and Cashore 2009).

While many policy formulation studies have been engaged in the exploration of various kinds of policy tools and how they are implemented, there has also been a dedicated focus in the literature on how policy tools and outcomes can be better matched or 'designed'. Throughout the formulation process and in subsequent activities involved in implementing initiatives and monitoring or evaluating the results of such actions, governments can and do learn from their own and others experiences and can often improve their performance and more effectively attain their aims and goals.

As discussed in earlier chapters, not all formulation activities match the criteria necessary to be called 'design'. The essence of what has come to be known as the policy design 'orientation' in the policy sciences (Howlett, Mukherjee and Woo 2015) requires a design process which is knowledge-based and intentional. While recognizing that often policy decisions and options may be made and developed in a highly contingent and irrational fashion, policy design scholars highlight the desirability of identifying ideal 'technical' models of instrument use and the need to translate them to fit context-sensitive solution conditions.

Policy formulation involves identifying both the technical and political constraints on state action (May 1981; Sidney 2007) as well as simply articulating options. It thus involves recognizing limitations on state resources such as a lack of credibility, fiscality, capacity, or legitimacy, which can limit what is considered to be *feasible* in specific circumstances (Majone 1989: 76). Politicians in most societies, for example, cannot do everything they consider would appeal to the public but also cannot ignore popular opinion and public sentiments and still maintain their legitimacy, credibility and trust. Other constraints on policy design can arise from limits on a state's administrative and financial capacity. For example, governments that have an ownership stake in economic sectors such as energy, finance and transportation may have more policy options open to them than states where the private sector exclusively delivers these goods and services, while states with well-developed and sophisticated administrative apparatuses generally also have a larger range of possible courses of action than those states lacking such resources (Ingraham 1987).

Studying policy formulation

While how policy instruments fare and how successful governments have been in their creation and deployment have always been subjects of interest among policy scholars, the literature on policy formulation has thus far remained quite rudimentary and fragmented (Sidney 2006).

The study of policy tools and their design, however, has been one major venue for building knowledge about policy options and hence policy formulation (Salamon 1989, 2002c). Policy instrument studies have over the last several decades been concerned with better understanding what Cochran and Malone (1999) deem to be the substantive 'what' questions of policy-making. That is:

> what is the plan for dealing with the problem? What are the goals and priorities? What options are available to achieve those goals? What are the costs and benefits of each of the options? What externalities, positive, or negative, are associated with each alternative?'
>
> (Cochran and Malone 1999: 46)

In parallel with this effort, the study of policy design has also dealt with the 'how', or the procedural and process-orientated questions about how best to formulate policy solutions and how such solutions have evolved over time and spread over space (Howlett 2000c; Linder and Peters 1990c; Schneider and Ingram 1997; Considine 2012).

Much useful knowledge about formulation processes and designs have emerged from these two areas of study (Howlett et al. 2015). It has been shown, for example, that governments often find themselves in the position of being leaders or laggards in terms of recognizing and addressing problems and discussing or implementing possible solutions (Gunningham et al. 1998). While there are some advantages to being leaders, the risks of failure are higher when problem definitions and solutions are innovative and laggards can benefit from both the positive and negative experiences of leaders and often can inherit an already well discussed and elaborated set of policy solutions when they do eventually turn to address a particular problem already dealt with by other jurisdictions (Béland and Howlett 2016). Monitoring events in other jurisdictions and even other branches of the same government to see how various efforts and tools aimed at providing solutions to problems have fared is often a major component of the policy formulation activity undertaken by governments and can be 'designed into' policy formulation activity through encouragement of comparative studies of policy successes and failures and by ensuring that evidence on 'best practices' in other jurisdictions enters into design deliberations and formulation practices.

What does 'policy formulation' mean?

As set out above, formulation is that stage of policy-making where a range of available options is considered and then reduced to some set that relevant policy actors, especially in government, can agree may be usefully employed to address a policy issue. This generally occurs before the issue progresses onward to official decision-makers for some definitive determination although those decision-makers may have in their public pronouncements or electoral platforms and other statements already signaled which kinds of efforts they might countenance and which they would not.

Formulation activity hence entails not only calculations of the relative benefits and risks of the various policy means that can be considered to match stated policy goals but also their potential feasibility or likelihood of acceptance and thus involves both a technical as well as a political component.

That is, once a social problem has been elevated to the formal agenda of the government, policy-makers are usually expected to act in devising alternatives or potential solutions to it. Although they may ultimately do nothing or react in a purely symbolic way, the essence of policy formulation is simply that various ways to deal with societal problems are proposed and deliberated upon by government officials and others knowledgeable about the problem. Proposals for action or inaction may come about during the initial agenda-setting discussions, during which a policy problem and a possible solution can become coupled on the government's agenda (Kingdon 1984); but they may also arise from past efforts, successful and otherwise in the originating or other jurisdictions in dealing with an issue.

This depiction paints formulation as involving several disjointed activities within a larger policy-making process that will be carried out differently in each jurisdiction and situation given the range of different actors and institutions and histories, involved in efforts to define and resolve policy issues. However, others have noted that it is possible to identify general attributes of the formulation process which are similar across jurisdictions (Howlett et al. 2009).

Several characteristics of generic policy formulation activities have been described in the policy studies literature. Jones (1984: 78), for example, depicted the following general attributes of formulation in practice:

- Formulation need not be limited to one set of actors. Thus, there may well be two or more formulation groups producing competing (or complementary) proposals.
- Formulation may proceed without a clear definition of the problem, or without formulators ever having much contact with affected groups.
- There is no necessary coincidence between formulation and particular institutions, though it is a frequent activity of bureaucratic agencies.
- Formulation and reformulation may occur over a long period of time without ever building sufficient support for any one proposal.
- There are often several appeal points for those who lose in the formulation process at any one level.
- The process itself never has neutral effects. Somebody wins and somebody loses even in the workings of science.

How does formulation occur?

Understanding the variety of inputs actors bring to the policy formulation activity and the contexts within which they function, thus can shed considerable light on topics related to why some policy options gain significant attention, while others fall by the wayside. As mentioned above, formulation can take place even without a definite depiction of the policy problem at hand (Weber and Khademian 2008) and it often proceeds over time in successive 'rounds' of formulation and reformulation of policy goals and means (Thomas 2001; Teisman 2000). Within this iterative process, while some policy-makers may look for 'win-win' solutions that maximize complementarities between the views of different actors, the costs and benefits of different policy choices are often borne disproportionately by different participants, leading to more contested processes of evaluation and deliberation (Wilson 1974).

In terms of *process*, Harold Thomas (2001) distinguished four aspects of policy formulation that are generally visible: appraisal, dialog, formulation and consolidation. During *appraisal*, information and evidence necessary to understand the issue at hand is sought and considered. This step in formulation is where data about policy problems and their solutions in the form of research reports, expertise and input from stakeholders and the general public are often considered.

Following this, a *dialog* phase between actors engaged in policy formulation typically ensues which is centered on the deliberation and exchange of different viewpoints about the policy goals and potential means to resolve them. Dialogs can be structured with the involvement of chosen experts and representatives from private sector, labor or other interest groups, or they can take place as more open and unstructured processes or in a closed and secretive fashion. This structure can make a significant difference on the impacts of that participation in the formulation process (Hajer 2005). While established expert opinion is often sought, efforts to involve participants from less established organizations and viewpoints can invigorate the discussion over policy alternatives.

Central to this process, at its core, lies the actual *formulation* phase wherein typically administrators and public officials scrutinize the costs, benefits, challenges and opportunities of various policy alternatives in the effort to consolidate a proposal or proposals about which alternatives or mix of alternatives will proceed through to consideration by authoritative decision-makers. This choice of some policy alternatives over others is likely to draw opposition from actors who have their preferred instruments sidelined and these and other forms of feedback about shortlisted policy options are commonly considered during a final *consolidation* phase in which proposed policy solutions are amended or refined before moving forward.

While some of the issues involved in formulation are technical and have a significant knowledge component, the issues that lead policy formulators to choose some policy options over others need not be based on facts (Merton 1948b). If powerful policy actors are of the belief that a policy option is unfeasible or unacceptable, this contention can be enough to exclude it from further discussion (Carlsson 2000) and vice-versa.

Policy design and the uncertainty of choices in policy formulation

While this discussion says something about 'how' a policy is formulated it is less clear 'what' is being formulated. Here it should be noted that the policy options that are considered during formulation are the embodiment of the techniques or tools of governance that, in some way, use resources of the state to define and attain government goals (Dahl and Lindblom 1953; Hood 2007b).

Policy goals result from the translation of multifaceted and interconnected societal problems into programmes of action and since this translation has implications about what items are considered to be administratively achievable, technically feasible and politically acceptable, the activities of goal selection and tool choice are often contentious (Majone 1975, 1989; Meltsner 1972; Dror 1969; Webber 1986). Indeed, even if policy-makers agree that a problem exists, they may not share an understanding of its causes or ramifications (Howlett et al. 2009: 113) or how it should be addressed.

Matching ends and means or policy goals and policy tools is thus a complex task and requires some knowledge of the problem area and potential solutions, as well as the context in which instruments will be deployed and their likely effects. This implies the use of expertise or expert advice and this is a common source of formulated content. However, many uncertainties figure or can figure even in these expert estimations and judgments. As noted in earlier chapters, different kinds of uncertainty exist and not all situations can engender the same kind of certainty in policy responses (Stirling 2010). Parameter and associated 'fuzzy' uncertainty, for example, is common in day-to-day policy-making, whereby it is often not known in real-time, to give only one instance, what is the actual unemployment rate to be used to inform interest rates or other monetary policy tools expected to overcome it (Linder and Peters 1988; deLeon 1992). Policy-makers and implementers are often somewhat surprised when particular elements of policies or their expectations fail to occur as anticipated, but they are not necessarily deeply shocked or disturbed when this happens. Even when causal relationships and future scenarios are relatively well known, there is always some uncertainty with respect to policy predictions due to statistical and uncertainties in data and estimates attached to expected relationships between policy interventions and target behaviour. Policy actors, generally, are aware of this (Jarvis 2011b; Morgan and Henrion 1990; Schrader et al. 1993) and various techniques have been developed to aid policy formulation in dealing with these kinds of uncertainty, such as conventional forecasting methods, Monte Carlo simulations and other kinds of statistical analyses which can provide likelihood estimates and probabilities which are good enough for action to be taken with the possibility of small errors and mistakes (Walker et al. 2010; Brugnach and Ingram 2012). Policies, in these instances, do not have to deal with great variation and thus do not have to be very agile, flexible, or 'robust' (see Table 5.1).

Table 5.1 Different kinds of uncertainty faced by policy-makers and types of policy-making responses

| | | Knowledge about possibilities | |
		Unproblematic	Problematic
	Unproblematic	Character of uncertainty *Risk*	Character of uncertainty *Ambiguity*
		Ameliorative techniques • Risk assessment • *Optimizing models* • *Expert consensus* • Cost–benefit analysis • Aggregated beliefs	Ameliorative techniques • Interactive modeling • Participatory deliberation • Focus & dissensus groups • Multicriteria mapping • Q-method, repertory grid
Knowledge about probabilities	Problematic	Character of uncertainty *Uncertainty*	Character of uncertainty *Ignorance*
		Ameliorative techniques • Interval analysis • Scenario methods • Sensitivity testing • Decision rules • Evaluative judgment	Ameliorative techniques • Monitoring & surveillance • Reversibility of effects • Flexibility of commitments • Adaptability, resilience • Robustness and diversity

Source: Based on Stirling, A. (2010). 'Keep It Complex'. *Nature* 468, no. 7327 (23 December): 1029–31.

While it is true that many uncertainties stem from a lack of knowledge of cause and effect relationships between policy interventions and outcomes, however, only some problems and solutions are amenable to more precise specification or assessment through better data collection and analysis. Very complex and dynamic relationships can be difficult to model or may involve a wide range of possible variation (Swanson and Bhadwal 2009). In many cases, ranging from finance and immigration to pollution and healthcare, for example, a rapid pace of change in the technological, economic and social environment may be coupled with a reduction in the ability of single jurisdictions to control internal and cross-border issue areas (Bakir 2017). And, as has often been noted, tendencies of bureaucracies to develop standard operating procedures and to 'silo' policy work in specific agencies also can ossify policy-making and reduce the scope for changes to deal with such dynamics (Yackee and Yackee 2010; Collins 2013).

Substantive constraints can also arise within the problem itself. The problem of global warming, for example, cannot be entirely eliminated because there is no known effective solution that can be employed without causing tremendous economic and social dislocations, which often leaves policy-makers to tinker with options that barely scratch the surface of the problem (Howlett et al. 2009: 112). Such constraints can be considered 'objective', since reinterpreting them or recasting them in different terms does not eliminate them.

Procedural constraints, on the other hand, are those that directly impinge upon the process of adopting policy options and are more subjective in nature and often react positively to re-formulation and re-interpretation. These constraints are embedded in the social and institutional contexts within which formulation unfolds and touch on issues related to, for example, constitutional specifications, the organization of society and the policy-making administration, electoral and legislative processes, or established patterns of ideas and beliefs that can lead decision-makers and formulators to favor some options over others (Yee 1996; Montpetit 2003b; Falkner 2000; DeLeon 1992). The specific relationships existing between social groups and the state, for example, can create 'policy horizons' or limits to the acceptability of certain kinds of policy options for certain policy actors such as treatment of disadvantaged populations for many social democratic groups and parties or various practices from abortion to same-sex marriages for various religious groups and parties (Warwick 2000; Bradford 1999). These can all affect the kind of goals considered acceptable or the means to achieve them but are not 'objective' in the sense that re-framing discussion and debate within these horizons can often lead to agreement.

Policy design and policy instrument choices as the core of policy formulation

As Charles Anderson (1971) noted, policy design is virtually synonymous with 'statecraft' or the practice of government as 'the art of the possible'. It is always a matter of making choices from the possibilities offered by a given historical situation and cultural context. From this vantage point, the institutions and procedures of the state to shape the course of economy and society become the equipment provided by a society to its leaders for the solution of public problems (121).

This applies very much to policy formulation and skilful policy designers are those who can find appropriate possibilities in the institutional equipment of ... society' to best obtain their goals. 'Designers' must avoid simply advocating 'stock' solutions unless this is called for by the limited nature of the space available for new designs (May 1981; Helms et al. 1993). Rather, they should consider the range of feasible options possible in a given circumstance and package these into sets of strategies capable of achieving policy goals (May 1981: 236, 238). Different policy spaces exist depending on how prominent are design and often concerns and these spaces condition what kinds of formulation processes are followed. As David Weimer (1992b) has noted, 'instruments, alone or in combination, must be crafted to fit particular substantive, organizational and political contexts' (373).

Formulation in space and time: the importance of context and influence

Formulation and design processes are thus wrought with both political and technical considerations. This reality, however, does not suggest that the systematic search for pairing policy means with goals is impractical and not worthwhile. Instead, it simply means that the implementation of some designs may be impossible in certain contexts and that the choice of any policy alternative involves different policy actors trying to raise and evaluate different preferred policy designs (Thomas 2001; Dryzek 1983). The evaluation of the benefits and costs of different policy options by various policy actors can still occur through more or less formal modes of policy analysis, however, and this remains a central activity during policy formulation in modern governments even in the most highly charged political circumstances (Gormley 2007; Sidney 2007; Dunn 2008).

In general, it is understood that policy formulation takes place within governance structures which have their own existing policy logic, which affects the exact process which is followed. Policy-makers need to be cognizant about the internal mechanisms of their polity and in the constituent policy sectors they are dealing with (Braathen and Croci 2005; Braathen 2007a; Grant 2010; Skodvin et al. 2010).

The amount of 'elbow room' or 'degrees of freedom' formulators have in a given formulation context heavily impacts how formulation activities proceed. Where earlier work on formulation and design often assumed a blank slate available to policy-makers, modern thinking about policy design is rooted in empirical studies and experiences that have generally shown policy designers having to work in scenarios with already established policy mixes with significant policy histories and legacies. The work of historical and sociological neo-institutionalists such as Kathleen Thelen (2003, 2004) discussed in earlier chapters has noted how macro-institutional arrangements have normally been less the product of calculated planning than the result of processes of incremental modifications or reformulations such as 'layering' or 'drift'.

That is, legacies from earlier rounds of decision-making often affect the introduction of new elements which may conflict with pre-existing policy components. As Martin Carstensen has argued, as a result policies often change through gradual processes and are often created much less through systematic reflection on (practice-derived) first principles than through processes of 'bricolage' or trial and error (Carstensen 2015).

As was discussed in Chapter 3, the contextual 'lock in' of policy alternatives often impacts formulation processes by restricting a government's ability to evaluate alternatives and plan or design in a purely optimal fashion and often leads to *layering* rather than *replacent* (Howlett 2009a; Oliphant and Howlett 2010; Williams 2012). This is a process of policy formulation and (re)design which alters only some aspects of a pre-existing arrangement and can thus be distinguished from processes proposing new policy packages or complete replacement.

While complete replacement or a brand new 'package' of policies is rare, however, there are instances whereby entirely dedicated, or 'bespoke' policy packages are created to address an unprecedented policy problem. 'Customization' of policy is somewhat more common when lessons from other similar policy contexts are tailored into new policy options.

Table 5.2 presents a schematic illustrating contemporary thinking about how the elements of capacity and government intention to alter the status quo create distinct policy design spaces which can affect whether or not policy changes are introduced within a design or non-design orientation and, within a design orientation, whether design is likely to occur by whole measures ('packaging') or in part ('patching' or 'layering') (Howlett and Mukherjee 2015).

As this table shows, in any specific design circumstance whether or not 'design' takes place at all can be seen to depend on the aim and intention of

Table 5.2 Types of policy formulation: situating design spaces

		Government's ability to alter the status quo	
		Hi	Lo
Government's intention to design	Hi	Optimal design space – Design via packaging	Incremental design space – Design via patching
	Lo	Muddling through non-design space – Formulation through incremental adaptation	Static non-design space

the government to undertake systemic thinking on a subject. But having such an intention is not enough in itself to promote replacement or design through packaging since this also depends on the government's ability or capacity to alter the status quo. In many circumstances, even when a design intent is present, the difficulties associated with altering the status quo results in design through 'patching' rather than packaging.

Determining exactly what capacities are required in order to formulate and implement complex designs is thus a subject of much interest in the field today (Considine 2012).

The pre-conditions of policy design

Favorable design circumstances within policy formulation require not only the presence of high quality information on the range and impacts of policy alternatives but also the presence of a high level of technical capacity and expertise on the part of policy analysts if that knowledge is to be mobilized effectively so that policy instruments are effectively and efficiently matched to policy goals and targets (Howlett 2009, 2010; Dunlop 2009b; Radaelli and Dunlop 2013; Howlett and Rayner 2014).

Design situations vary according to the nature of the resources available for design purposes and the constraints imposed by policy legacies. In the non-design world where the intention to design is lacking, constraints on outcomes also exist as do different processes which vary in their distance from the design ideal of public value and improving the public good (Holmberg and Rothstein 2012; Rotberg 2014).

When propitious conditions are present, purposive formulation activity resulting in good alternative generation and assessment is possible (Bhatta 2002; Locke 2009; Nutley et al. 2007). When conditions are not ripe, however, either poor designs will ensue from incomplete knowledge and information even with the best government intent, or less technical and more overtly political forms of non-design policy-making are more likely (Davies 2004; Moseley and Tierney 2004; Howlett 2009b).

Policy formulators must be aware of these differences while developing policy options and making recommendations and providing advice to governments. Policies are the result of efforts made by governments to alter aspects of their own or public behaviour in order to carry out some end or purpose they consider important but take place within specific context-bound and temporally defined spaces (Angelides and Caiden 1994) affected by current realities, emerging trends, complexities and future uncertainties.

In recent years, the policy-making environment has rapidly evolved and is no longer restricted to achieving singular purposes such as social protection, provision of health and education, or increasing civil society engagement, but rather increasingly concerned with policy integration across multiple levels of public administration and spanning multiple sectors (Angelides and Caiden 1994).

While this is clear enough conceptually, very little is actually known about the empirics of many important aspects of formulation work in public policy-making, including who is engaged in policy design and non-design efforts and why one process would emerge rather than another (deLeon 1992; Sidney 2007; Schneider and Sidney 2009).

The efforts of policy-makers often have failed due to poor designs which have inadequately incorporated the complexity of policy formulation into their considerations (Cohn 2004; Howlett 2012). These experiences have led to a greater awareness of the various obstacles that can present themselves to policy design and have gradually fueled a desire for better understanding the unique characteristics of policy formulation processes and the spaces in which design efforts are embedded as well as the merits and demerits of practical strategies and alternatives for resolving problems.

Conclusion: policy formulation and policy design beyond the technical/political divide

Transforming policy ambitions into practice is a complex process. The design orientation calls for a broadening of thinking about formulation beyond policy tool choices, examining combinations of substantive and procedural instruments and their interactions in complex policy mixes. It also has focused on the need to be more detailed study of the actual formulation processes involved in tool and design choices as these occur and have evolved over time (Linder and Peters 1990c; Schneider and Ingram 1997; Considine 2012).

Understanding which formulation process is likely to unfold or has unfolded is the key to understanding whether or not a design process is present and, if so, whether or not it is likely to generate a good or poor design effort. That is, the design of successful policies requires thinking about policy-making in such a way as to fully take into account the dual purposes – both technical/problem and political – which policies can serve and the extent to which efforts to attain those ends are adequately resourced and capable; that is, to clearly understand its 'design space' (Hillier et al. 1972; Hillier and Leaman 1974; Gero 1990). As we have seen, a very important aspect of such spaces concerns the general intention of the government in enacting policy. Much of the old design literature, as noted above, simply assumed a well-intentioned government and thus focused attention only upon 'technical' analysis; that is, upon efforts to better assess the functional potential of specific tools (Howlett 2014a). The new design literature keeps this focus but has added to it the need to also assess other factors, especially political ones affecting the design context.

The above discussion of different formulation modalities and processes does not preclude, but rather is built upon the recognition and acceptance of the fact that some policy decisions and formulation processes are highly contingent ones in which 'design' considerations may be more or less absent and where the logical or empirical relations between policy components are ignored (Kingdon 1984; Cohen et al. 1979; Dryzek 1983; Eijlander 2005; Franchino and Hoyland 2009; Sager and Rielle 2013). This includes a variety of contexts in which formulators, for example, may engage in trade-offs or log-rolling between different values or resource uses or, more extremely, engage in venal or corrupt behaviour in which personal gain from a decision may trump other criteria.

An optimal situation in public policy formulation from a design perspective is one wherein the interests and aims of both politicians and technical analysts and advisors are congruent and policy-makers seek to attain both policy and political objectives through the same tools. Key questions regarding who are the different actors involved in the process of policy formulation, in what roles, with what capacity and to what extent they are concerned with problem resolution are addressed in the following chapter.

Readings

Béland, D. and M. Howlett. (2016). 'How Solutions Chase Problems: Instrument Constituencies in the Policy Process'. *Governance* 29, no. 3: 393–409.

Caplan, N. and C. H. Weiss. (1977). *A Minimal Set of Conditions Necessary for the Utilization of Social Science Knowledge in Policy Formulation at the National Level*. Lexington, MA: Lexington Books.

DeLeon, P. (1992). 'Policy Formulation: Where Ignorant Armies Clash by Night'. *Policy Studies, Review* 11, nos 3/4: 389–405.

Dror, Y. (1969). 'The Prediction of Political Feasibility'. *Futures*, June: 282–88.

Freed, G. L, M. C. Andreae, A. E. Cowan and S. L. Katz. (2002). 'The Process of Public Policy Formulation: The Case of Thimerosal in Vaccines'. *Pediatrics* 109, no. 6: 1153–9.

Howlett, M. (2010). 'Stage Models of the Policy Process'. In B. Guy Peters (ed.) *Encyclopedia of Political Science*.

Howlett, M. (2015). 'Policy Analytical Capacity: The Supply and Demand for Policy Analysis in Government'. *Policy and Society* 34, nos 3–4: 173–82.

Howlett, M. and S. Nair. (2017). 'The Central Conundrums of Policy Formulation: Ill-Structured Problems and Uncertainty'. In I. Mukherjee (ed.), *Handbook of Policy Formulation*. New York: Routledge, 23–38.

Howlett, M., I. Mukherjee and J. Rayner. (2014). 'The Elements of Effective Program Design: A Two-Level Analysis'. *Politics and Governance* 2, no. 2 (9 June): 1–12.

Ingram, Helen, Anne L. Schneider, and Peter DeLeon. (2007). 'Social Construction and Policy Design'. In P. A. Sabatier (ed.) *Theories of the Policy Process*. Boulder, CO: Westview Press, 93–126.

James, T. E. and P. D. Jorgensen. (2009). 'Policy Knowledge, Policy Formulation, and Change: Revisiting a Foundational Question'. *Policy Studies Journal* 37, no. 1: 141–62.

Jordan, A. and J. Turnpenny (eds). (2014). *The Tools of Policy Formulation: Actors, Capacities, Venues and Effects*. Cheltenham, UK: Edward Elgar.

Klüver, H. (2013). 'Lobbying as a Collective Enterprise: Winners and Losers of Policy Formulation in the European Union'. *Journal of European Public Policy* 20, no. 1: 59–76.

Koski, C. and T. Lee. (2014). 'Policy by Doing: Formulation and Adoption of Policy through Government Leadership'. *Policy Studies Journal* 42, no. 1 (1 February): 30–54.

Lasswell, H. D. (1936). *Politics Who Gets What, When and How*. New York: McGraw Hill.

Linder, S. H. and B. G. Peters. (1987). 'A Design Perspective on Policy Implementation: The Fallacies of Misplaced Prescription'. *Review of Policy Research* 6, no. 3 (1 February): 459–75.

Linder, S. H. and B. G. Peters. (1990). 'Policy Formulation and the Challenge of Conscious Design'. *Evaluation and Program Planning* 13: 303–11.

Matheson, C. (2000). 'Policy Formulation in Australian Government: Vertical and Horizontal Axes'. *Australian Journal of Public Administration* 59, no. 2 (1 June): 44–55.

Sidney, M. S. (2007). 'Policy Formulation: Design and Tools'. In F. Fischer, G. J. Miller and M. S. Sidney (eds), *Handbook of Public Policy Analysis: Theory, Politics and Methods*. New Brunswick, NJ: CRC, Taylor & Francis, 79–87.

Sørensen, C. H., K. Isaksson, J. Macmillen, J. Åkerman and F. Kressler. (2009). 'Strategies to Manage Barriers in Policy Formation and Implementation of Road Pricing Packages'. *Transportation Research Part A: Policy and Practice* 60 (1 February): 40–52.

Thomas, H. G. (2001). 'Towards a New Higher Education Law in Lithuania: Reflections on the Process of Policy Formulation'. *Higher Education Policy* 14, no. 3: 213–23.

Turnpenny, J., C. M. Radaelli, A. Jordan and K. Jacob. (2009). 'The Policy and Politics of Policy Appraisal: Emerging Trends and New Directions'. *Journal of European Public Policy* 16, no. 4: 640–53.

Walker, W. E., S. A. Rahman and J. Cave. (2001). 'Adaptive Policies, Policy Analysis, and Policy-Making'. *European Journal of Operational Research* 128, no. 2 (16 January): 282–9.

Wood, C. H. (2008). 'Time, Cycles and Tempos in Social-Ecological Research and Environmental Policy'. *Time & Society* 17, nos 2–3: 261–82.

Chapter 6

Who are the policy designers and where do they work?

Policy advice, policy advisors and policy advisory systems

Public policies are made by decision-makers but most often on the basis of advice and information provided by other actors. The nature and influence of policy advice interacts with the bounded rationality of policy-makers, to shape their decision-making.

As Thomas' (2001) account of the different substages and activities involved in policy formulation outlined in Chapter 5 suggests, different actors are involved in different aspects of policy formulation and policy design. While powerful political and administrative leaders with decision-making authority are the ones who eventually decide on and thus 'make' public policy, in modern states they do so by following the counsel of bureaucrats, civil servants and other advisors whom they trust to evaluate and consolidate policy options into coherent designs and who provide policy leaders with expert advice about the merits and risks of the proposals being considered (MacRae and Whittington 1997; Heinrichs 2005).

It is useful to think about this wide array of policy advisors as being arranged in a *'policy advisory system'* within which proximate decision-makers occupy central positions. Studies of advisory systems in a variety of jurisdictions such as New Zealand, Israel, Canada and Australia have furthered this idea of government decision-makers operating at the center of a network of policy advisors who include both 'traditional' policy advisors, such as civil servants as well as non-state actors from NGOs and think tanks, as well as informal forms of advice supplied by colleagues, members of the public and political party affiliates, among others (Maley 2000; Peled 2002; Dobuzinskis et al. 2007).

Having a large range of actors in a policy advisory system is generally considered beneficial and indicates 'a healthy policy-research community outside the government [which] can play a vital role in enriching public understanding and debate of policy issues' serving 'as a natural complement to policy capacity within' (Anderson 1996: 486). The existence of different types of policy advisory systems, however, is linked with the nature of the demand and supply of knowledge in particular policy and governmental contexts and sectors (Halffman and Hoppe 2005). In what follows the nature of the actors involved in such systems and the impact of the advice they provide for policy design, is set out.

Policy analysis and the role of expertise in policy formulation

As Chapter 5 outlined, most policy formulation processes share certain characteristics. First and most obviously, formulation is not usually limited to one set of actors (Sabatier and Jenkins-Smith 1993a). Second, formulation may also proceed without a clear definition of the problem to be addressed (Weber and Khademian 2008) and may occur over a long period of time in 'rounds' of formulation and reformulation of policy problems and solutions (Teisman 2000). And third, the costs and benefits of different options fall disproportionately on different actors (Wilson 1974). This implies, as Linder and Peters, among others, noted, that the capability of policy designs to be realized in practice remains subject to many political as well as technical variables including who provides what kind of advice to who about how to define a problem and what can be done about it (Dryzek 1983).

The nature and sources of policy advice received by decision-makers in the policy formulation process are subjects that have received their fair share of scholarly attention. Many journals and specialized publications exist on these subjects and specialized graduate schools exist in most countries with the aim of training policy analysts to provide better advice to decision-makers (Geva-May and Maslove 2007; Jann 1991). Studies have examined hundreds of case studies of policy-making and policy formulation in multiple countries and many texts exist which chronicle various analytical techniques expected to be used in the provision of policy advice (Weimer and Vining 2004). Yet surprisingly, little systematic thinking exists about this crucial component and stage of the policy-making process (Howlett et al. 2009).

Early thinking about the content of policy advice often contrasted 'political', or partisan-ideological, value-based advice with more 'objective' or 'technical' advice and usually stressed the latter while ignoring or downplaying the former (Radin 2000). This 'positivist' or 'modern' approach to policy analysis dominated the field for decades (Radin 2000) and pre-supposed a sharp division between governmental advisors armed with technical knowledge and expertise and non-governmental actors possessing only non-technical skills and knowledge. Policy schools purporting to train professional policy advisors in government, still typically provide instruction only on a range of qualitative and quantitative techniques that analysts were expected to use in providing technical advice to decision-makers about optimal strategies and outcomes to pursue in the resolution of public problems, downplaying or ignoring political or value-laden issues and concerns (MacRae and Wilde 1979; Patton and Sawicki 1993; Vining and Weimer 1999; Irwin 2003).

The extent to which this information is used and to what extent it can be considered 'objective' and 'expert' is, of course, a continuing controversy in the policy sciences (Rein and White 1977; Lindblom and Cohen 1979; Shulock 1999; Adams 2004). And more to the point, although often implicit, a 'political' versus 'technical' advisory dichotomy often underlay models of policy advice, with advice assumed to become more technical as it moved closer to proximate decision-makers so that external actors provid political advice and internal ones technical ideas and alternatives.

It is debatable, however, to what extent such a strict separation of political and technical advice was ever true. And it is definitely the case that the supply of technical advice is no longer, if it ever was, a monopoly of governments. Various external sources of policy advice have also been found to be significant sources of substantive policy advisory content used by policy-makers to support existing policy positions and as sources of new advice (Bertelli and Wenger 2009; McGann and Sabatini 2011). Professional policy analysts, for example, are now employed not only by government departments and agencies but also by advisory system members external to government; ranging from private sector consultants to experts in think tanks, universities, political parties and elsewhere who are quite capable of providing specific suggestions about factors such as the costs and administrative modalities of specific policy alternatives (Boston 1994; Boston et al. 1996; Rhodes et al. 2010). It is also the case that many advisors both internal and external to governments, both today and in past years, provide political advice to decision-makers ranging from personal opinion and experience about public opinion and key stakeholder group attitudes and beliefs to explicit partisan electoral advice. This kind of advice has always been provided by prominent traditional inside actors such as political advisors attached to elected officials and political parties (Connaughton 2010a,b; Eichbaum and Shaw 2007, 2008; Leal and Hess 2004), as well as that stemming from the public consultation and stake-holder interventions prominent in contemporary governance (Edelenbos and Klijn 2006; Bingham et al. 2005; Pierre 1998).

While Westminster systems pride themselves on retaining at least part of this political-administrative dichotomy in the form of conventions about civil service neutrality in their specific 'civil service bargain' (Hood 2002a; Hondeghen 2011; Salomonsen and Knudsen 2011), even in this strong case, this convention has been eroded. In their study of New Zealand policy advice, for example, Eichbaum and Shaw (2008: 343) noted many instances of 'procedural politicization' that was 'intended to or has the effect of constraining the capacity of public servants to furnish ministers with (technical) advice in a free, frank and fearless manner'. It was manifested whenever a 'political' adviser 'intervenes in the relationship between a minister and his or her officials. Alternatively, it is also argued to occur due to 'conduct by ministerial advisers which is intended to or which has the effect of constraining the capacity of officials to tender frank and fearless advice by intervening in the internal workings of a department' (Eichbaum and Shaw 2008: 343). They also found many instances of 'substantive politicization', which dealt specifically with 'an action intended to, or having the effect of coloring the substance of officials' advice with partisan considerations' (Eichbaum and Shaw 2008: 343–44).

The increasingly pluralized and political nature of policy advice inputs available to decision-makers underscores that while under the older 'speaking-truth-to-power model' policy advice might often have been largely a bipartite relationship involving public servants and executive politicians, with career officials offering technical advice to cabinet ministers, this is no longer the case. Maley (2000: 453), for example, elaborated on the various policy roles for political advisers that may exist in addition to their 'in house' policy work: 'Dunn suggests an important brokering role within the executive; Ryan detects a significant role in setting policy agendas; Halligan and Power refer to advisers 'managing networks of political interaction''. Additional studies have also pointed to the role 'political' advisers can play in the brokerage, coordination and integration of various endogenous and exogenous sources of policy advice to decision-makers (Dunn 1997: 93–7; Gains and Stoker 2011; Halligan and Power 1992; Maley 2011; OECD 2011; Ryan 1995).

The content of policy advice: where policy ideas come from and how they influence policy-making and policy design thinking

It is important to note that these changes in governance practices do not just lead to a shift in the location of advice, but rather also of its content. Even in Anglo-American 'Westminster'-style political systems, the shift from the largely internal, technical, 'speaking truth' type of policy advising toward the diffuse and fragmented 'sharing of influence' approach paints a picture of contemporary policy advising that not only features the pronounced influence of external or exogenous sources of technical and political advice, but also the loss of whatever policy advisory monopoly or hegemony was once held or exercised by professional public service and advisers within government in these areas. The reduced utility of such distinctions when applied to other systems (e.g., Napoleonic, Scandinavian) with alternative administrative traditions where politico-administrative divisions may not be as pronounced, overlap, or be configured differently (Peters and Pierre 2004; Painter and Peters 2010; van den Berg 2017) is even clearer. Moving beyond simple political–technical distinctions to a more robust content-based model of policy advice is essential in order to improve the generalizability of thinking on the subject. This includes more careful thinking about the content of such 'advice'.

A key component of the content of advice relates to the type of beliefs and ideas policy advisors and policy-makers have about the feasibility, desirability and optimality of the deployment of various arrangements of policy tools to address social concerns and policy problems.

Understandably, the beliefs held by decision-makers about these policy means and other issues related to policy goals play a key part in influencing their efforts to construct policy alternatives and assess policy options (Ingraham 1987; George 1969; Mayntz 1983; Jacobsen 1995; Chadwick 2000; Gormley 2007). In the policy realm, the notion of different kinds of ideas creating claims or demands on governments was taken up by Frank Fischer and John Forester (1993) and Paul Sabatier (1987, 1988), among others writing in the 1980s and 1990s (see George 1969).

The concept of causal stories, for example, was applied to agenda-setting by Deborah Stone (1988, 1989). In Stone's view, agenda-setting usually involved constructing a 'story' of what caused the policy problem in question. As she has argued:

> Causal theories, if they are successful, do more than convincingly demonstrate the possibility of human control over bad conditions. First, they can either challenge or protect an existing social order. Second, by identifying causal agents, they can assign responsibility to particular political actors so that someone will have to stop an activity, do it differently, compensate its victims, or possibly face punishment. Third, they can legitimate and empower particular actors as 'fixers' of the problem. And fourth, they can create new political alliances among people who are shown to stand in the same victim relationship to the causal agent.
>
> (Stone 1989: 295)

But different types of ideas have different effects on different elements of policy-making and hence upon instrument choices and policy designs. Policy goals, for example, consist of a range of ideas from general philosophical and ethical principles to specific causal logics and sociological constructs. And the same is true of policy means, which can embody some knowledge of past practices and concepts of successful and unsuccessful policy implementation, but also extend beyond this to ideological and other ideational structures informing 'practical' choices for goal attainment.

Some ideas about policy instrument choices and options are likely to be more influential than others, when it comes to policy formulation, assessment and design (Lindvall 2009) and different types of ideas impact different elements of formulation. For example, abstract policy-level goals such as economic development or ecological conservation often emerge out of general ethical or political logics about the needs and benefits of goals such as alleviating poverty or protecting the environment, while more specific causal constructs about issues such as how increasing household incomes can lead to greater economic gains or how limiting agriculture near ecologically sensitive areas can result in environmental gains are more relevant at the operational or tools level. The same is true for ideas policy means that can address these kinds of goals, including ones which stem from ideas about what has worked and what has not been effective in such efforts in the past and why.

Differentiating between these different types of ideas in terms of their degree of abstraction and their normative appeal, is thus an important step in understanding the impact of policy advice in creating policy content (Campbell 1998). In their work on the influence of ideas in foreign policy-making situations, for example, Goldstein and Keohane (1993) and their colleagues noted at least three types of ideas that combined normative and cognitive elements but at different levels of generality: world views, principled beliefs and causal ideas (see also Campbell 1998; Braun 1999).

World views or ideologies, have long been recognized as helping people make sense of complex realities by identifying general policy problems and the motivations of actors involved in politics and policy. These sets of ideas, however, tend to be very diffuse and do not easily translate into specific views on particular policy problems.

Principled beliefs and causal stories, on the other hand, as Stone (1988) argued, can exercise a much more direct influence on the recognition of policy problems and on policy content. These ideas can influence policy-making by serving as 'road maps' for action, defining problems, affecting the strategic interactions between policy actors and constraining the range of policy options that are proposed (Carstensen 2010; Stone 1988, 1989). At the micro level, causal stories and beliefs about the behaviour patterns of target groups heavily influence choices of policy settings or calibrations (Stone 1989; Schneider and Ingram 1993, 1994).

As laid out in Table 6.1, ideas stemming from public sentiments or symbolic frames often appeal to the perception of appropriateness or 'legitimacy' of a certain policy choice and are largely expected to affect policy goals (Stimson 1991; Suzuki 1992; Durr 1993; Stimson et al. 1995). The policy ideas found in *public sentiments*, for example, are generally too broad and normative in nature to have much of a direct impact on programme design. However, they serve to set the context within which that design activity occurs.

Conversely, *policy paradigms* have a much greater cognitive component, allowing them to significantly influence the nature of policy means at the policy regime level. These paradigms are composed of 'a set of cognitive background assumptions that constrain action by limiting the range of alternatives that policy-making elites are likely to perceive as useful and work considering' (Campbell 2002; Surel 2000). Developed originally to describe enduring sets of cognitive ideas that are present in the natural sciences, the term 'paradigm' was later applied to long-lasting points of view on 'the way

Table 6.1 Ideational components of policy contents

| | | Level of policy debate affected | |
		Background	Foreground
Level of ideas	Normative (value)	Public sentiments	Symbolic frames
Affected	Cognitive (causal)	Policy paradigms	Programme ideas

Source: Adapted from John L. Campbell. 'Institutional Analysis and the Role of Ideas in Political Economy'. *Theory and Society* 27, no. 5 (1998): 385.

the world works' (Kuhn 1962; Kuhn and Suppe 1974; Hall 1990, 1992, 1993). The concept is closely related to traditional philosophical notions of 'ideologies' as overarching frameworks of ideas influencing action and to more recent sociological notions of 'discourses' or 'frames' (Goffman 1974; Surel 2000), but has a larger cognitive component. It helps to capture the manner in which established beliefs, values and attitudes lie behind understandings of public problems and emphasizes how paradigm-inspired notions of the feasibility of the proposed solutions are significant determinants of policy choices and alternative designs (Hall 1990: 59; Huitt 1968; Majone 1975; Schneider 1985; Webber 1986; Edelman 1988; Hilgartner and Bosk 1988).

Programme ideas, in turn, represent a selection of particular solutions from the set of options that are designated as being appropriate within a prevailing policy paradigm. Paradigms and programme ideas, thus typically have more direct influence on the selection of policy means than do public sentiments and *symbolic frames* whose influence is often indirect (Stone 1989; Hall 1993).

Distinguishing between these types of ideas and advice in terms of their level of abstraction and whether they directly affect the foreground of policy debate or its background is an important first step in discerning their impact on policy design (Campbell 1988) (see Table 6.1).

The organization of policy advice: policy advisory systems

Who holds these ideas and their relationship to advice-givers is also a significant factor in policy formulation generally and policy design activities more specifically. Generally speaking, the ideas held by central policy actors play a key role in guiding efforts to construct policy options and assess design alternatives and have a direct influence on policy content while those held by outside actors have a less direct impact (Ingraham 1987; George 1969; Mayntz 1983; Jacobsen 1995; Chadwick 2000; Gormley 2007).

Given the range of players and substages involved in it, however, policy formulation and design can be a highly diffuse and often disjointed process whose workings and results are often very difficult to discern and whose nuances in particular instances can be fully understood only through careful empirical case study. The manner in which the *policy advice system* is structured in a particular sector, however, helps us to identify the more or less influential actors involved in design decisions and policy assessments in specific sectoral subsystems or issue networks (James and Jorgensen 2009).

As mentioned above, recent studies of advice systems in countries such as New Zealand, Israel, Canada and Australia have developed this idea; that government decision-makers sit at the center of a complex web of policy advisors which include both 'traditional' political advisors in government as well as non-governmental actors in NGOs, think tanks and other similar organizations and less formal or professional forms of advice from colleagues, friends and relatives and members of the public and political parties, among others (Maley 2000; Peled 2002; Dobuzinskis et al. 2007; Eichbaum and Shaw 2007) and that this system varies by sector and by country (Hustedt and Veit 2017). Understanding the nature of policy formulation and design activities in different analytical contexts involves discerning how the policy advice system is structured and operated in the specific sector of policy activity under examination (Brint 1990; Page 2010).

The activities of policy advisory systems are central to the study of both policy formulation and policy design and to the understanding of the selection and reception given to different policy alternatives and arrangements (Brint 1990). Conceived of as knowledge utilization venues or 'marketplaces' of ideas and information, advice systems are comprised of separate components related to their role in the supply of policy advice, to its demand by government decision-makers and to the set of brokers who work as intermediaries who match knowledge supply with demand (Brint 1990; Lindquist 1998). That is, members of policy advisory systems undertake one or more of these general types of activities linked to the types of positions those participants hold in the creation and exchange of knowledge in the policy formulation process.

The first set of actors at the top of the hierarchy is composed of the 'proximate decision-makers' themselves who act as consumers of policy analysis and advice – that is, those with actual authority to make policy decisions, including cabinets and executives as well as parliaments, legislatures and congresses and senior administrators and officials delegated decision-making powers by those other bodies.

The second set, toward the bottom, is composed of those 'knowledge producers' located in academia, statistical agencies and research institutes who provide the basic scientific, economic and social scientific data upon which analyses are often based and decisions made.

The third set in between the first two is composed of those 'knowledge brokers' who serve as intermediaries between the knowledge generators and proximate decision-makers, repackaging data and information into usable form (Lindvall 2009; Page 2010). These include, among others, permanent specialized research staff inside government as well as their temporary equivalents in commissions and task forces and a large group of non-governmental specialists associated with think tanks and interest groups. Although often thought of as 'knowledge suppliers', key policy advisors almost by definition exist in the brokerage subsystem and this is where most professional policy analysts involved in policy formulation can be found (Lindvall 2009; Verschuere 2009; Howlett and Newman 2010; Page 2010).

In general, members of policy advisory systems can be identified as being in one of four 'communities' of advisors depending on the advisory role they perform as well their proximity to policy actors and their location either inside or outside of government (Table 6.2).

The *core actors* are those members of the public sector who are closest to the official policy-making units of government and include central government agencies, executive staff and professional government policy analysts. Governmental actors or *insiders* who work further away, at the periphery of policy advisory systems are those who belong to federal commissions, special committees and task forces, research councils and scientists from international organizations. From the non-governmental sector, actors who are close to the decision-makers during formulation and are considered *private sector insiders*, may include private sector consultants, political party staff, pollsters as well as donor representatives. Actors, who are considered to be farthest from the central core of policy formulators, or *outsiders*, often include those belonging to public interest groups, business associations, trade unions, independent academics, think tanks, members of the media or international non-government organizations.

Table 6.2 The four communities of policy advisors

	Proximate actors	Peripheral actors
Public/ governmental sector	Core actors Central agencies Executive staff Professional governmental Policy analysts	Public sector insiders Commissions, committees and task forces Research councils/scientists International organizations
Non-governmental sector	Private sector insiders Consultants Political party staff Pollsters Donors	Outsiders Public interest groups Business associations Trade unions Academics Think tanks Media International non- governmental organizations

Source: Howlett, M. (2014b). 'Policy Design: What, Who, How and Why?' In C. Halpern, L. Pierre and P. L. Gales (eds), *L'instrumentation et ses effets*. Paris: Presses de Sciences Po.

Table 6.3 Advisory system actors by policy level

	High level abstraction	Programme level operationalization	Specific on-the-ground measures
Policy	General abstract policy aims	Operationalizable policy objectives	Specific policy targets
Goals (normative)	Public, outsiders and insiders	Insiders and core actors	Core actors
Policy means (cognitive)	General policy implementation preferences	Operationalizable policy tools	Specific policy tool calibrations
	Public, outsiders and insiders	Insiders and core actors	Core actors

Source: Howlett, M. (2014b). 'Policy Design: What, Who, How and Why?' In C. Halpern, L. Pierre and P. L. Gales (eds), *L'instrumentation et ses effets*. Paris: Presses de Sciences Po.

In terms of the specific contribution that policy advisors and their advice can make to different policy components, these sets of actors can be thought to exist on a spectrum of influence linked to whether their advice deals with larger issues about problem definition and the articulation of policy goals, or to the technical details of policy tools and their calibrations (Table 6.3).

Members of the general public, non-governmental outsiders and insiders, for example, often impact the policy discourse at the broad level of abstract policy goals and general policy preferences, while insiders and core actors become more influential as formulation and design moves to programme level operations and then on to specifying on-the-ground measures and instruments (Page 2010).

The sources of policy advice: problem, solution and political advisors

For many years, policy-making has been envisioned as a process in which these subsets of policy actors engaged in specific types of interactions involved in the definition of policy problems, the articulation of solutions and their matching or enactment. This activity involves the definition of policy goals (both broad and specific), the creation or identification of the means and mechanisms that need to be implemented to realize these goals and the set of bureaucratic, partisan, electoral and other political struggles involved in their acceptance and transformation into action.

In much of the policy research published in recent decades, these actors are discussed in network terms as belonging to a 'subsystem' or policy 'community' (McCool 1998; Sabatier 1991). This is typically defined as a mostly undifferentiated group of actors originating in widely different areas of state and society who are united by a mutual concern for and knowledge of, a specific policy area. They are not necessarily self-interested but share some ideas and knowledge about the policy area in question, which sets them apart from other policy actors (Howlett and Cashore 2009; Howlett et al. 2009; Kingdon 2011).

These sets of actors go by a variety of different names – policy networks, policy communities, issue networks and the like – but the general 'subsystem family of concepts' emerged in the 1950s to better explain the role of discourses and interest in the policy-making process. They acknowledge the complex informal and formal exchanges that take place between both state and non-state policy actors and improve on previous work that emphasized material, self-interested activity on the part of a more limited range of actors involved in formal policy deliberations, such as think tanks, interest groups, lobbyists, bureaucrats and politicians (McCool 1998).

Early studies on subsystems were seminal in the discipline and included the articulation of a wide array of often competing concepts and terminology to describe such collectivities, such as 'iron triangles', 'sub-governments', 'cozy triangles', 'power triads', 'policy networks', 'issue communities', 'issue networks', 'advocacy coalitions', 'policy communities' and others. All these terms refer to the propensity of policy actors to create alliances surrounding substantive issues that traverse institutional boundaries and to join together both governmental and non-governmental actors in groups sharing similar perspectives on policy issues, problems and solutions (Arts et al. 2006; Freeman 1997; McCool 1998).

Sub-system theory helped distil the often informal connections between actors, ideas, interests and institutions that earlier policy studies had largely ignored when they focused on the more formal institutional linkages that exist between governmental and non-governmental agents active in policy-making (Howlett et al. 2009; McCool 1998). The concept of 'subsystem' was more nuanced than other terms in that it merged actors, ideas and institutions together, allowing policy scholars to more precisely identify the main actors in a policy process, what connects them, how they interact with each other and what effect their interactions have on policy results (Freeman and Stevens 1987; Howlett et al. 2009).

Such a unified or undifferentiated conception of a policy subsystem, however, is problematic on several scores when it comes to analyzing the sources of policy design relevant advice. In particular, the grouping of all policy actors together in a single policy subsystem has improperly and confusingly juxtaposed similar but distinct policy-related actors involved in collective activities such as problem definition, policy formulation and policy bargaining and conflict. This situation has obscured the importance and activities of such sets of actors in policy processes.

While past research on policy subsystems often assumed or implied that these tasks could be undertaken by any actor, more recent research argues that distinct sets of actors are involved in these three tasks: *epistemic communities* that are engaged in discussions about policy dilemmas and problems (Haas 1992); *instrument constituencies* that define and promote policy instruments and alternatives (Voss and Simons 2015); and *advocacy coalitions* which compete to have their choice of policy alternative and problem frames adopted (Sabatier 1988). Two of these three sets of actors are quite well known and, indeed, have their own literature about what it takes to be a member of an epistemic community or advocacy coalition, although interactions between the two are rarely discussed. The third subset, the instrument constituency, is much less well studied but is concerned exclusively with the articulation and promotion of policy solutions (Béland and Howlett 2016; Voss and Simons 2014; Mann and Simons 2014).

Distinguishing clearly between these three sets of actors and activities allows researchers and practitioners to better capture how policy problems are designated and defined and how they move forward through the political processes. It allows each different subgroup to be analyzed as a discrete entity rather than being obscured within the multiple tasks undertaken by the subsystem as a whole.

Actors in the problem stream: epistemic communities

While it would be possible, in answering the question about who is active in policy formulation and what they do, to develop new terminology to describe each subgroup, adequate terms already exist in the policy literature that can be used for this purpose. In this light, the concept of epistemic communities, which emerged out of the international relations literature to identify groups of scientists involved in defining and delimiting problem spaces in areas such as oceans policy and climate change (Gough and Shackley 2001; Haas 1992; Zito 2001), can be used as the basis for understanding the first set of actors involved mainly in defining policy problems and providing and packaging policy advice related to those definitions.

Academic explorations of epistemic communities have thus far mainly used examples from environmental policy, a field that is constantly engaged in connecting scientific findings to policy-making. Haas (1992) first described the epistemic communities involved in deliberations in the environmental sector as a diverse group of policy actors including scientists, academics experts, public sector officials and other government agents who are united by a common interest in or a shared interpretation of the science behind an environmental dilemma (Gough and Shackley 2001; Haas 1992). These epistemic communities, he found, influenced 'policy innovation not only through their ability to frame issues and define state interests but also through their influence on the setting of standards and the development of regulations' (Adler and Haas 1992: 378).

Information regarding a policy problem is the glue that bonds actors within an epistemic community together, differentiating them from those actors involved in political negotiations and practices around policy goals and solutions, as well as from those, discussed below, who specialize in the development, design and articulation of policy tools or solutions (Biddle and Koontz 2014). Several studies exist supporting this view of the perceptions of epistemic community members and the problem-framing role they play in policy-making (Lackey 2007; Meyer et al. 2010; Nelson and Vucetich 2009).

In his studies of global oceans research and policy, Rudd (2014, 2015), for example, provides important empirical findings related to scientists' framing of environmental dilemmas at the science-policy interface. In his large-N, quantitative study spanning 94 countries and meant to comprehensively cover the role of scientists in oceans policy-making, Rudd points out conclusively the uniformity regarding research priorities across the globe. He writes that:

> once evidence is assembled and knowledge created, it must also be effectively communicated, sometimes in politicized environments, ensuring that it is effectively brought to bear on sustainability challenges. Demands on scientists to increase the level of integration and synthesis in their work and to communicate increasingly sophisticated information to policymakers and society, will only grow.
>
> (Rudd 2015: 44)

Actors in the policy stream: instrument constituencies

Epistemic communities are conceptually distinct from a second group of actors, instrument constituencies, whose focus is much less upon problems than upon providing advice to government about potential policy solutions. 'Instrument constituencies' is a term recently developed in the comparative public policy field to describe the set of actors involved in solution articulation, independent of the nature of the problem to be addressed (Voss and Simons 2014).

The policy instruments that are devised or revised, considered and assessed in the process of matching problems and solutions can be viewed as the cognitive constructs of these actors as they grapple with policy-making. Such constituencies advocate for particular tools or combinations of tools to address a range of problem areas. They are united by their adherence to the design and promotion of specific policy instruments as the solutions to general sets of policy problems, usually in the abstract, which are then applied to real-world conditions. They are hence active in the 'policy' stream Kingdon (1984) identified, one that increases its activity as policy alternatives and instruments are formulated and combined to address policy aims.

That is, unlike epistemic communities that pursue the translation of broad issues into distinct problems that policy-makers can act upon, instrument constituencies are more concerned with policy tools and supplying policy-makers with information and advice about the design and mechanics of these tools. Think tanks, for example, often fall into this category, as they provide policy-makers with 'basic information about the world and societies they govern, how current policies are working, possible alternatives and their likely costs and consequences' (McGann et al. 2014: 31).

In a series of studies on how various emission trading schemes emerged in Europe (Mann and Simons 2014; Voss and Simons 2014), Voss and Simons have noted that, just as epistemic communities perpetuate ideas of policy problems and advocacy coalition members are occupied with political beliefs, members of instrument constituencies are distinct and stay cohesive due to their unified identification not with a problem definition or political agenda, but rather with their support of a particular policy tool or a specific combination of policy tools. These constituencies are thus 'networks of heterogeneous actors from academia, policy consulting, public policy and administration, business and civil society, who become entangled as they engage with the articulation, development, implementation and dissemination of a particular technical model of governance' (Voss and Simon 2014: 738). They promote and further develop a particular instrument and are part of conscious groupings that attempt to realize their particular version of that instrument.

The practices of such actors thus 'constitute and are constituted by the instrument' and develop 'a discourse of how the instrument may best be retained, developed, promoted and expanded' (Voss and Simons 2014). What brings them together is the role they play in articulating 'the set of stories, knowledge, practice and tools needed to keep an instrument alive both as model and implemented practice' (Voss and Simons 2014).

Actors in the politics stream: advocacy coalitions

The 'politics' stream (Kingdon 1984) is the milieu where a third distinct set factors – 'advocacy coalitions' are most active. Although the term 'advocacy coalition' is used by students of American policy-making in the context of earlier, less well differentiated, sub-system theory to describe the activities of those involved in the political struggle surrounding the matching of problem definitions and policy tools (Sabatier and Weible 2007; Schlager and Blomquist 1996) it is also useful in the context of the analysis of this specific set of activities within policy advice provision. As is well known, Paul Sabatier and Hank Jenkins-Smith (1993a) first advanced the idea of advocacy coalitions during the 1980s as a response to perceived limitations of existing policy process research programmes: the shortcomings of the stages heuristic in establishing a causal theory of the policy process, the poor discussion about the role of scientific knowledge in policy-making, the polarity of the top-down and bottom-up perspectives of policy implementation, and the need to consider time horizons of a decade or more when investigating the policy process and the need to acknowledge the bounded rationality of policy actors. Since then advocacy coalitions have inspired a strong research programme, with many works developing different sets of propositions about advocacy coalition behaviour and activity (see Sabatier 1987, 1988, 1998; Sabatier and Jenkins-Smith 1993b; Sabatier and Weible 2007; Weible et al. 2009; Weible et al. 2011).

These actors and advisors are often situated in key decision-making institutions of government and compete to get their choice of problem definitions as well as solutions adopted during the policy process, working within and against epistemic communities and instrument constituencies in order to do so.

Such politically active policy actors are usually more publicly visible than the members of those groups of substantive experts who collaborate in the formulation of policy alternatives or problem definition who often constitute a 'hidden cluster' of actors including for example, policy consultants and experts in aid agencies and international NGOs. More visible actors in the politics stream can include, as in the case of the US Congress Kingdon examined, 'the president and his high-level appointees, prominent members of the congress, the media and such elections-related actors as political parties and campaigns' (Kingdon 1984: 64), while less visible members include lobbyists, political party brokers and fixers and other behind-the-scenes advisors and participants.

As Sabatier and his colleagues (1988) argued, the relative success of a coalition in furthering its preferred match of policy goals and tools depends on a number of factors, including external factors such as their financial resource endowments, level of expertise and number of supporters. Other external factors that have also been found to be important in advocacy behaviour include public opinion as coalition members employ knowledge about what the competing views on important policy problems or solutions are for a 'variety of uses from argumentation with opponents to mobilization of supporters' (Weible and Nohrstedt 2011).

What are designers capable of doing? Capacity issues in policy advice and policy design

Transforming intentions and ideas into practice is a complex process and many noble efforts of policy-makers fail due to lack of capacity for designing effective policies. A critical enabling condition is required for effective policy designs to emerge from policy formulation activity: enough *policy analytical capacity* to allow a government to acquire and process the information and knowledge required to conduct a sophisticated policy analysis of problems and alternatives (Wu et al. 2015a; Howlett and Ramesh 2015).

This capacity relates to the sets of skills, competences, resources and institutional arrangements and capabilities with which key tasks and functions in policy process are structured, staffed and supported, including the provision of policy advice. The extent to which the principle actors involved in the policy process are able to gather advice, evaluate its merits and carry out their functions depends on their organization's data collection and analysis

Table 6.4 Capacity issues in policy design outcomes

		Level of governance (political and operational) capacity	
		High	Low
Level of analytical capacity	High	**Capable design** Effective policies are possible	**Poor political design** Good technical designs may be weakly supported
	Low	**Capable political design** Good political designs are possible which may be technically poor	**Poor design** Only ineffective and poorly supported policies are possible

capabilities. This includes their ability or capability to store and disseminate operationally relevant information. And each organization's analytical competences allow its members to identify and understand policy problems, canvass for solutions, assess alternatives based on comparative assessment and evaluate the impacts of chosen policies (Howlett 2009d, 2015) to a greater or lesser extent (see Table 6.4).

Effective policies can emerge only if governments possess high levels of governance capacity as well as a high level of analytical capability. Conversely, the absence of both types of capabilities allow only for only weak design efforts and increase the probability of ineffective policies emerging from this process.

Capacity constraints may be so strong that the ultimate design of policies is only distantly related to solving the originally highlighted problem. When policy tools are used in combination, as is often the case in social policy, for example, or when they are layered on top of earlier tools, there are additional complexities that promote synergies and complementarities, but also allow for contradictions and conflicts in expected and unexpected ways. Only a high level of policy capacity can help advisors and analysts predict and avoid these situations (Howlett and Rayner 2007).

Other problems in policy advising: decision-maker heuristics, disproportionality and the social construction of policy targets

As previous chapters have set out, decision-makers are cognitively constrained in terms of their information processing capacities. They lack complete knowledge of consequences, of all possible alternatives and face difficulties associated with anticipation. In order to deal with these gaps, decision-makers seek out advice but also frequently employ heuristic principles in order to reduce complex tasks that involve assessing probabilities and predicting values, to simpler judgmental operations (Tversky and Kahneman 1974: 1124). These heuristics are mental shortcuts that reduce the cognitive burden associated with decision-making (Shah and Oppenheimer 2008).

Decision-maker heuristics and the social construction of policy targets

An important heuristic particularly relevant in policy analysis which affects policy designs is the use of mental models (Hendrick 1994; World Bank 2015). These models are the internal representations created to interpret the environment by individual cognitive systems, with some types of mental models shared inter-subjectively (Denzau and North 1994).

The social constructions of target population discussed above are an example of such heuristics that may exert a powerful influence on policy design (Schneider and Ingram 1993). Socially reinforced choices and shared mental models can affect policy design by blocking choices, preventing even conceiving of certain courses of action while promoting certain others. To the extent that policy-makers themselves are behavioural agents, their judgements all suffers from such psychological biases (Viscusi and Gayer 2015).

These biases may present themselves in the selection of policy advice and its utilization. For instance, a bias frequently identified with policy-makers is the 'confirmation bias', that is, the selective gathering of, or giving undue weight to, certain information in order to support a previously held belief (Nickerson 1998). Another bias that policy-makers often exhibit is their tendency to continue on a project once an initial investment of resources has been made: the 'sunk cost bias' (Arkes and Blumer 1985).

(Dis)Proportionality in policy designing: the role of policy advisors in over and under-reactions

As has also been discussed in earlier chapters, in an ideal world, designing policies involves governments acting as efficient policy-makers. As a consequence, any errors in decision-making – over or under-reacting to the nature of a problem – can be attributed to idiosyncratic errors such as poor information control and management, personality conflicts, or miscalculation of costs and benefits of public action. In this sense, the task of policy advisors and of a policy advisory system as a whole is to provide templates for action appropriate to the objective characteristics and severity of a policy problem: in other words, to provide an adequate policy design given the nature of the problem at hand.

However, it is well known that this simple 'proportionality' is less common than might be assumed (deLeon 1999a; Hargrove 1975). In fact, studies of policy success and failure suggest more complex patterns in which relatively few efforts are well calibrated as most either under- or over-react to problems, or oscillate between these two states (Maor 2012a, 2014a; de Vries 2010). While some poorly calibrated efforts may only be temporary in nature, reflecting a sort of poor marksmanship in the early stages of a trial and learning approach to resolve a problem which will be corrected in future, many instances involve sustained periods of over- (and under) reaction in which either government resources are wasted or problems continue to be unresolved (de Vries 2010). These systematic over and under-reactions and specifically sustained under-reactions, are the subject of much interest (Maor 2014a, Jones et al. 2014).

At least some of the blame for over and under-reactions and over and under designs often falls on policy advisors. Though the social and political construction of underlying policy problems (e.g., Zuckerman 2012) always gives room for political controversy and disagreement in assessing exactly what is the nature of the problem at hand and therefore what is a reasonable or proportionate response to it, as many have argued, feedback loops between policy-makers, expert advisors and the public play a major role in creating both inflationary and deflationary pressures upon problem definitions and policy solutions (Jacobs and Weaver 2014; also Patashnik 2003).

Jones et al. (2014), for example, argue the origins of a many over-reactions are biases in information processing which occur at least in part due to the lack insulation of policy-making elites from public sentiments. Similarly, Maor (2014a) explains policy over-reaction by looking at valence politics or differences between the emotional and unemotional content of specific policy issues, especially considering the role of extreme forms of public sentiment such as moral outrage or panics in promoting policy over-reaction.

In the case of policy over-reactions, it is argued that this reaction is sustained by cognitive, ideational and institutional processes such as interest group support or the persuasiveness of causal narratives favoring action over inaction (Stone 2011). Institutional fragmentation into several policy subsystems more susceptible to groupthink and less autonomous from interest groups and the public than larger more unified ones has also been noted to lead to this type of disproportionate response (May et al. 2009). However, even in larger subsystems, over-reactions can follow a 'naïve' contagion process, in which policy (mis)learning contributes to over-reaction. Herd behaviour of advisors in support of particular actions can lead governments – similar to the financial investors acting in concert in the case of asset bubbles – to copy policy practices from other jurisdictions without considering their limitations or contextual constraints (Jarvis 2014).

Compared to that on over-reactions, the literature on under-reaction is much less well developed (but see Maor 2014b). Empirically, of course, one can find many illustrations of this phenomenon. Harmful international tax competition (e.g., Kemmerling 2011; Holzinger 2005) in which countries are slow to respond to changes in other jurisdictions or the slow reaction of agencies to epidemics such as the 'mad cow disease' (BSE) and other health issues (Leiss and Powell 2004; Smith 2004; Oosterveer 2002) are prime examples of policy underinvestment which, again, are closely linked to the nature of the advice policy-makers receive from epistemic communities, instrument constituencies and advocacy coalitions.

Conclusion: policy design as constrained expert discourse

Policy design – in the social policy sphere and all others – is most productive when the government enjoys legitimacy and broad political support. Design will be strong or weak depending on the organizational and analytical competences governments possess to formulate and implement their policy preferences and this, in turn, is linked to the nature of policy advisors and their interactions with decision-makers.

It is common to find statements such as Halligan's (1995) assertion that a good advice system should consist of:

> at least three basic elements within government: a stable and reliable in-house advisory service provided by professional public servants; political advice for the minister from a specialized political unit (generally the minister's office); and the availability of at least one third-opinion option from a specialized or central policy unit, which might be one of the main central agencies.
>
> (162)

Balancing political and technical objectives is only part of the policy design challenge and is only one kind of policy advice, however. The receptiveness of decision-makers to advice and their need for it will vary from case to case. In many design situations, for example, general abstract policy definitions, aims and implementation preferences can often be taken as given, establishing the context in which design decisions relating to programme-level and on-the-ground specifications are made by policy insiders and core actors and reducing the role played by epistemic communities in the provision of policy advice, while enhancing that of instrument constituencies. In other less well-defined circumstances, advocacy coalitions may play a stronger role.

How the temporal and spatial elements of a policy process fit together, then, is a critical determinant of how key actors view and articulate the range of policy alternatives available to them and their need and desire for specific kinds of advice.

In all cases, however, a critical component of policy formulation and policy design is related to the ideas and knowledge policy-makers and advisors hold about the nature of policy instruments and their configurations. This subject is set out in the six chapters which comprise the next Part of the book.

Readings

Campbell, J. L. (1998). 'Institutional Analysis and the Role of Ideas in Political Economy'. *Theory and Society* 27, no. 5: 377–409.

Caplan, N. and C. H. Weiss. (1977). *A Minimal Set of Conditions Necessary for the Utilization of Social Science Knowledge in Policy Formulation at the National Level*. Lexington, MA: Lexington Books.

Craft, J. and M. Howlett. (2012). 'Policy Formulation, Governance Shifts and Policy Influence: Location and Content in Policy Advisory Systems'. *Journal of Public Policy* 32, no. 2: 79–98.

Craft, J. and M. Howlett. (2013). 'The Dual Dynamics of Policy Advisory Systems: The Impact of Externalization and Politicization on Policy Advice'. *Policy and Society* 32, no. 3: 187–97.

Eichbaum, C. and R. Shaw. (2008). 'Revisiting Politicization: Political Advisers and Public Servants in Westminster Systems'. *Governance* 21, no. 3: 337–63.

Fleischer, J. (2009). 'Power Resources of Parliamentary Executives: Policy Advice in the UK and Germany'. *West European Politics* 32, no. 1: 196–214.

Fraussen, B. and D. Halpin. (2017). 'Think Tanks and Strategic Policy-Making: The Contribution of Think Tanks to Policy Advisory Systems'. *Policy Sciences* 50, no. 1 (1 March): 105–24.

Goldstein, J. and R. O. Keohane. (1993). 'Ideas and Foreign Policy: An Analytical Framework'. In J. Goldstein and R. O. Keohane (eds), *Ideas and Foreign Policy: Beliefs, Institutions and Political Change*. Ithaca, NY: Cornell University Press, 3–30.

Hall, P. A. (1993). 'Policy Paradigms, Social Learning and the State: The Case of Economic Policy Making in Britain'. *Comparative Politics* 25, no. 3: 275–96.

Heinrichs, H. (2005). 'Advisory Systems in Pluralistic Knowledge Societies: A Criteria-Based Typology to Assess and Optimize Environmental Policy Advice'. In S. Maasen and P. Weingart (eds), *Democratization of Expertise?* Vol. 24. Berlin/Heidelberg: Springer-Verlag, 41–61.

Hustedt, T. and S. Veit. (2017). 'Policy Advisory Systems: Change Dynamics and Sources of Variation'. *Policy Sciences* 50, no. 1 (1 March): 41–6.

Jacobs, A. M. (2008). 'How Do Ideas Matter? Mental Models and Attention in German Pension Politics'. *Comparative Political Studies* 42, no. 2: 252–79.

James, T. E. and P. D. Jorgensen. (2009). 'Policy Knowledge, Policy Formulation, and Change: Revisiting a Foundational Question'. *Policy Studies Journal* 37, no. 1: 141–62.

Lindvall, J. (2009). 'The Real but Limited Influence of Expert Ideas'. *World Politics* 61, no. 4: 703–30.

Maley, M. (2000). 'Conceptualising Advisers' Policy Work: The Distinctive Policy Roles of Ministerial Advisers in the Keating Government, 1991–96'. *Australian Journal of Political Science* 35, no. 3: 449–70.

Manwaring, R. (2017). 'Understanding Impact in Policy Advisory Systems: The Australian Case of the "Thinker in Residence"'. *International Journal of Public Administration* 41, no. 11 (24 March): 1–12.

Maor, M. (2012). 'Policy Overreaction'. *Journal of Public Policy* 32, no. 3: 231–59.

Maor, M. (2014). 'Policy Persistence, Risk Estimation and Policy Underreaction'. *Policy Sciences* 47, no. 4 (9 July): 425–43.

Nilsson, M., A. Jordan, J. Turnpenny, J. Hertin, B. Nykvist and D. Russel. (2008). 'The Use and Non-Use of Policy Appraisal Tools in Public Policy Making: An

Analysis of Three European Countries and the European Union'. *Policy Sciences* 41: 335–55.

O'Faircheallaigh, C. (2010). 'Public Participation and Environmental Impact Assessment: Purposes, Implications and Lessons for Public Policy Making'. *Environmental Impact Assessment Review* 30: 19–27.

Radaelli, C. M. (2005). 'Diffusion without Convergence: How Political Context Shapes the Adoption of Regulatory Impact Assessment'. *Journal of European Public Policy* 12, no. 5: 924–43.

Schmidt, V. A. (2010). 'Taking Ideas and Discourse Seriously: Explaining Change Through Discursive Institutionalism as the Fourth New Institutionalism?' *European Political Science Review* 2, no. 1: 1–25.

Schneider, A. and H. Ingram. (1994). 'Social Constructions and Policy Design: Implications for Public Administration'. *Research in Public Administration* 3: 137–73.

Sidney, M. S. (2007). 'Policy Formulation: Design and Tools'. In F. Fischer, G. J. Miller and M. S. Sidney (eds), *Handbook of Public Policy Analysis: Theory, Politics and Methods*. New Brunswick, NJ: CRC, Taylor & Francis, 79–87.

Simons, A. and J.-P. Voss. (2017a). 'The Concept of Instrument Constituencies: Accounting for Dynamics and Practices of Knowing Governance'. *Policy and Society* 37, no. 1 (2 January): 14–35.

Simons, A. and J.-P. Voss. (2017b). 'Policy Instrument Constituencies'. In M. Howlett and I. Mukherjee (eds), *Handbook of Policy Formulation*. Cheltenham, UK: Edward Elgar, 355–72.

Weible, C. M. (2008). 'Expert-Based Information and Policy Subsystems: A Review and Synthesis'. *Policy Studies Journal* 36, no. 4: 615–35.

Wu, X., M. Ramesh and M. Howlett. (2015). 'Policy Capacity: A Conceptual Framework for Understanding Policy Competences and Capabilities'. *Policy and Society* (Special issue on The Dynamics of Policy Capacity) 34, nos 3–4 (September): 165–71.

Zito, A. R. (2001). 'Epistemic Communities, European Union Governance and the Public Voice'. *Science and Public Policy* 28, no. 6: 465–76.

Part IV

THE ELEMENTS OF POLICY DESIGN

Policy instruments and instruments mixes

How do policy designs work?

Policy designs as implementation tool mixes

A significant part of policy design activity, as we have seen in previous chapters, involves matching policy goals with the ideas formulators hold about feasible and desirable mixes of policy means or tools. Understanding policy instrument choices and the range of possibilities present in any design situation is a key factor for both policy advisors and decision-makers and requires both an understanding of what kinds of instrument options exist, which subset of those is generally considered feasible or possible in a given context and which among that smaller subset of all possible tools is deemed by policy experts and the public to be the most appropriate to use at a given time.

In the effort to help deal with these questions, students of policy formation and policy instruments in a variety of academic disciplines have over the years developed several models or conceptual schemes which help to explain how policy instruments differ and how those different ones can be used in specific circumstances to achieve specific kinds of ends. This study of the 'tools of government' has a long history and a rich tradition of research in the policy sciences, much of it borrowed from public administration, law and regulatory studies, public management and many sectoral fields, from telecommunications and environmental regulation to social policy and educational studies. The main findings and currents of thinking in this area are set out below, providing a template for the study of the elements of policy designs which informs the details and analysis of specific kinds of tools in Chapters 8–11.

The origins of policy instrument study as field of academic inquiry

Fields interested in studying public policy, such as political science and political sociology, have traditionally been concerned with studying policy 'inputs' or the dynamics of public policy formation. For example, in political science, a key focus has been upon the role played by public opinion, political party activities, elections and similar phenomena in affecting policy-making processes and defining policy content, while, in the case of political sociology, a key focus has been on understanding the roles played by social structure in defining actor 'interests' and positions in policy-making processes (Mayntz 1983).

Studies in these disciplines revealed a great deal about policy formation processes but tended to neglect the implementation component of policy-making. Studies in other fields such as public administration and management and organization studies, on the other hand, following the admonitions of early students of the field such as the US president and political scientist Woodrow Wilson (1887) traditionally focused their efforts on the study of the inner workings of government, especially upon the study of behavioural and management issues involved in such tasks as financial administration and budgeting, ministerial responsibility and accountability, the operation of the merit principle and human resources/personnel administration. While these studies often purposely avoided considering the more political aspects of policy processes, they provided a great deal of information on implementation issues and processes which have helped inform policy instrument and policy design studies.

In his pathbreaking early works on public policy-making, Harold Lasswell drew on both these literatures not only to define public policy, clarify important aspects of policy-making such as the number and type of stages involved in policy deliberations and emphasize the importance of context to its workings (Torgerson 1985, 1990), but also to think about the main instruments of policy-making. Lasswell (1954) noted the extent to which governments could affect policy-making through manipulations involving, among other things, 'symbols, signs and icons' and argued that a principal task of the policy sciences must be to understand the nuances of these actions and their effects (Lasswell 1954, 1971).

Like others of Lasswell's insights, this orientation was retained by many later students of policy-making who developed very flexible notions of the multiple means by which governments could affect, or give effect to, policy. In these early works, 'policy instruments' were defined very broadly so as to include a wide range of tools or techniques of governance used at different stages of the policy process. However, in the 1970s as the effort to improve policy-making through improved policy designs took shape, work turned to focus on the evaluation of the impact on policy outcomes of specific kinds of implementation-related tools, primarily economic ones like subsidies and taxes (Mayntz 1983; Woodside 1986; Sterner 2002) but later extended to many more types and variations.

Many authors and scholars, following this lead, argued for a fundamental recasting of policy studies along the lines of implementation research. Bardach (1980) and Salamon (1981), for example, both argued in the early 1980s that policy studies had 'gone wrong' right at the start by defining policy in terms of 'issues', 'areas', or 'fields' rather than in terms of 'instruments'. As Salamon put it:

> The major shortcoming of current implementation research is that it focuses on the wrong unit of analysis and the most important theoretical breakthrough would be to identify a more fruitful unit on which to focus analysis and research. In particular, rather than focusing on individual programmes, as is now done, or even collections of programmes grouped according to major 'purpose', as is frequently proposed, the suggestion here is that we should concentrate instead on the generic tools of government action, on the 'techniques' of social intervention.
>
> Salamon (1981: 256)

Following these kinds of injunctions, other scholars began to investigate the links between implementation failures and policy success in more detail and turned their gaze directly on the subject of how implementation alternatives were crafted and formulated (Mayntz 1979; Goggin et al. 1990; O'Toole 2000). Studies in economics and law which focused on the 'ex-post' evaluation of the impact of policy outputs (Bobrow 1977; Stokey and Zeckhauser 1978), for example, began the more systematic appraisal of implementation alternatives. Many lessons about policy instruments and policy design were also drawn from legal studies, for example, which revealed a great deal about how tools such as laws, regulations and other mechanisms involved in the delivery of various kinds of goods and services operate and upon procedural aspects of formulation and implementation activities such as the passage of legislation and forms of administrative rule-making, while organization, management and administrative studies provided insights into the links between administrative systems and governance modes, among others (Peters and Pierre 1998; Pierre and Peters 2005). Ultimately, insights gleaned from a wide body of interdisciplinary literature concerning policy inputs and governmental processes were combined in the 1980s and 1990s in the explicit study of policy instruments and their role in policy design.

Studies from the early 1980s focused on the need to more precisely categorize types of policy instruments in order to better analyze the reasons for their use (Salamon 1981; Tupper and Doern 1981; Trebilcock and Hartle 1982; Bressers and Honigh 1986; Bressers and Klok 1988). Careful examination and systematic classification of implementation instruments and instrument choices, it was argued, would not only lead to insights into the factors driving the policy process and the characterization of long-term patterns of public policy-making, as Lasswell had hoped, but would also allow practitioners to more readily draw lessons from the experiences of others with the use of particular techniques in specific circumstances and hence improve policy designs and outcomes (Mayntz 1983; Linder and Peters 1984; Woodside 1986).

During this period, studies in Europe and North America shed a great deal of light on the construction and establishment of regulatory and other political and administrative agencies and enterprises; traditional financial inducements and the 'command-and-control' measures adopted by administrative agencies, during this period (Tupper and Doern 1981; Hood 1986a; Howlett 1991; Vedung 1997b; Landry et al. 1998). And this new emphasis upon the systematic study of policy instruments quickly generated a sizable academic literature and resulted in immediate application in the design of many new policy initiatives in emerging areas such as pollution prevention and professional regulation (Trebilcock 1983; Hippes 1988). Significant subjects such as the reasons behind shifts in patterns of instrument choices associated with the waves of privatization and deregulation which characterized the period also received attention (Howlett and Ramesh 1993).

Most of these studies, however, focused exclusively upon what were referred to in previous chapters as 'substantive instruments'; that is, those which directly affect the production and delivery of goods and services in society. These early studies failed to adequately address procedural tools and consequently until around the year 2000 developed only a partial description of policy tools and an understanding of how instrument choices related to policy design.

Nevertheless, by the late 1980s the field of instrument studies had advanced enough that Salamon (1989) could argue that the 'tools approach' had become a major approach to policy studies in its own right, bringing a unique perspective to the policy sciences with its focus on policy outputs. Salamon argued that this perspective had revealed that not only did, as traditional studies had maintained, 'politics determine policy', but also the reverse (Landry et al. 1998). That is, via the feedback mechanism in the policy cycle (Pierson 1992, 1993), tool choices led to the establishment of a 'political economy' of a policy regime: a tool choice such as, for example, a decision to use tax incentives to accomplish some end, created a constituency for continuation of that incentive (and sometimes one opposed to it), affecting future policy deliberations and decisions including those related to instrument choices (Linder and Peters 1984; Bobrow and Dryzek 1987; Dryzek and Ripley 1988).

At this point, Salamon framed two important research questions to be addressed in future analyses of the tools of government action: 'What consequences does the choice of tool of government action have for the effectiveness and operation of a government programme?' and 'What factors influence the choice of programme tools?' (265). These questions were taken up by the 'tools approach' and the policy design literature in the 1990s.

The development of models in the study of policy tools

Assessing and answering Salomon's questions required scholars interested in policy design to engage in a lengthy process of social scientific analysis and model-building related to the study of implementation tools. These efforts expanded the number of preliminary questions which needed to be answered before Salamon's queries could be addressed (Salamon 1981; Timmermans et al. 1998; Hood 2007b) to include:

(1) What potential tools does any government have?
(2) How can these be classified?
(3) How have these been chosen in the past?
(4) Is there a pattern for this use?
(5) If so, how can we explain this (or these) pattern(s)?
(6) Can we improve on past patterns of use?

In order to answer these questions, policy scientists pursuing the tools approach followed, not necessarily as systematically as might be hoped, a

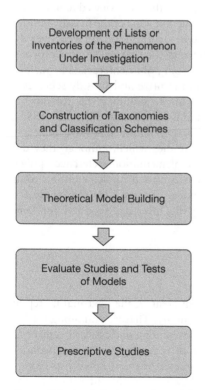

Figure 7.1 Analytical steps in social science model-building

five-stage research and analytical model-building strategy; one quite typical of the social sciences (see Figure 7.1) (McKelvey 1978, 1982; Stevens 1994). Each of the stages in this process is set out and described below.

The construction of empirical inventories

As Figure 7.1 shows, the first step in the systematic study of policy instruments, as in any other similar endeavor in the social sciences, is the establishment of an inventory of the dependent variable. While there were many scholars who had looked at specific tools in the past (such as Cushman's 1941 study of regulatory agencies which was often cited by early students of the field), the first effort to systematically define the range of possible instruments which could be used in a policy design originated in the post-World War II planning exercises undertaken by the United Nations and the Organization for Economic Co-operation and Development (OECD) in Europe.

Key figures in this research included Nobel Prize winning development economists such as E. S. (Etienne) Kirschen and Jan Tinbergen, who published groundbreaking studies including *Economic Policy in Our Times* (1964) dealing with the instruments for economic policy they had viewed in operation in the process of post-war European reconstruction. One of the first inventories of instruments was Kirschen et al.'s (1964) identification of well over 40 different types of implementation instruments then prevalent in European economic policy-making activities, ranging from public enterprises to various forms of government procurement and tax incentive and subsidy schemes.

Such studies were followed by many others examining the instruments prevalent in other areas, such as banking and foreign policy (Hermann 1982), adding to the list tools such as interest rate determination and other monetary and fiscal tools. These were pathbreaking studies which, although they did not make any distinctions between general implementation preferences, policy mechanisms or calibrations and very often confused implementation tools and instruments used at other stages of the policy process, laid the groundwork for such future refinements by providing the raw data required for later classification efforts.

The development of taxonomies

Once a fairly exhaustive inventory has been created, the next major step in theory construction is to move toward taxonomy. That is, examining the list of the phenomena under consideration and attempting to classify or categorize the subject matter into a smaller number of mutually exclusive categories which, together, retain the exhaustive character of the original lists. Many such schemes were developed in the policy instruments literature of the 1960s–1980s.

Kirschen et al. (1964), for example, utilized a resource-based taxonomy of governing instruments to group instruments into five general 'families' according to the 'governing resource' they used: public finance, money and credit, exchange rates, direct control and changes in the institutional framework (16–17). However, this scheme was very sectorally specific and focused on the specific problem of achieving economic development goals. More generic schemes were developed such as that put forward by Theodore Lowi (1966, 1972), which heavily influenced later thinking on the subject.

Lowi developed the insight first put forward by students of public administration in the USA like Cushman (see Figure 7.2), that governments had only a small number of alternative choices in any given regulatory situation, depending on the amount of coercion they wished to employ in that situation – in Cushman's case, choosing either to regulate or not and, if so, to regulate either by the use of public enterprises or regulatory commissions. This analysis, among other things, introduced the idea that instrument choices were multi-level and nested, an insight which would be further developed in the years to come.

In his own work, however, Lowi argued that a four-cell matrix based on the specificity of the target of coercion and the likelihood of its actual application would suffice to distinguish all the major types of government implementation activity. The original three policy types he developed included the weakly sanctioned and individually targeted 'distributive' policies; the individually targeted and strongly sanctioned 'regulatory' policy; and the strongly sanctioned and generally targeted 'redistributive' policy. To these three Lowi later added the weakly sanctioned and generally targeted category of 'constituent' policy (see Table 7.1).

This was a significant advance, since it attempted to reduce the complexity of instrument choice to a single two-dimensional framework. However, Lowi's categories of tools – distributive, redistributive, constituent and regulatory – did not fit well with existing tool inventories and hence were difficult to operationalize and test (Roberts and Dean 1994). As a result, many other classification schemes emerged in the literature in the mid-to-late 1980s.

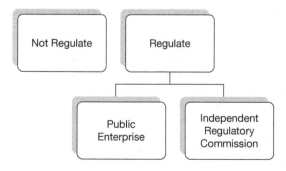

Figure 7.2 Cushman's three types of policy tools

Table 7.1 Lowi's matrix of policy implementation activities

		Specificity of target	
		Specific	General
Likelihood of sanctions	High	Regulatory	Re-distributive
	Low	Distributive	Constituent

Many of these efforts, but not all, followed Lowi and Cushman's lead in focusing on some aspect of coercion as the key element differentiating policy instrument types. In a key development, however, some also introduced a greater number of differentiating criteria. Balch (1980), for example, talked about both 'carrots' (inducements or incentives) and 'sticks' (coercion or disincentives), while Bardach (1980) argued that government had three 'technologies' which they could utilize in any given choice situation: enforcement, inducement and benefaction; and that these strategies required different combinations of four critical governmental resources: money, political support, administrative competency and creative leadership. Elmore (1987) identified four major classes of instruments: mandates, inducements, capacity-building and system-changing.

Further studies moving in the design direction refined this idea of only a limited number of 'governing resources' lying behind each tool. As we have already seen in earlier chapters, Christopher Hood (1983, 1986a) generated a major work on the subject in 1986 which was heavily influenced by detailed studies of the British and German policy implementation processes undertaken previously by Dunsire (1978) and Mayntz (1975). It involved the elaboration of a fourfold resource-based categorization scheme for policy instruments which served as an admirable synthesis of the other, earlier, models.

Hood argued that governments have essentially four resources at their disposal which they can use to either effect changes in their environment or detect them: *nodality*, meaning the resource that existed simply by nature of the fact that governments existed at the 'centre' of social and political networks but which can also be thought of as 'information' or 'knowledge'; *authority*; *treasure*; and *organization* (or 'NATO' in Hood's terminology). In Hood's scheme, implementation instruments are grouped together according to which of the NATO resources they *most* or *primarily* relied upon for their effectiveness, fully recognizing that most used some combination of these resources in practice (Anderson 1977; Hood 1986a).

A government regulation requiring a license in order to use a particular pesticide, for example, is a policy tool expected to give effect to a set of policy objectives (in this case a problem with externalities from pollution and information asymmetries between producers and consumers of sophisticated chemical products) within a set of aims (such as environmental protection and species preservation) and preferred implementation preferences (such as

Table 7.2 Hood's 1986 taxonomy of substantive policy instruments

		Governing resource			
		Nodality	Authority	Treasure	Organization
Principle use	Detectors Effectors	Surveys Public information campaign	Licencing Regulation	Policing Subsidies	Record-keeping Government agencies

Source: Adapted from Christopher Hood (1986c). *The Tools of Government*. Chatham: Chatham House.

market-based service delivery within a market mode of governance). Such a mechanism requires an organization to implement it, some funding to pay the personnel involved in that activity, information notices to regulatees that a license is required and that the requirement will be enforced and some legal authority to create a license scheme and enforce it. Such an instrument thus involves the use of many types of governing resources, but the *primary* resource it relies upon is the legal authority to enforce compliance, without which all of the other resources would be ineffective and unnecessary.

This taxonomy proved useful in providing a limited number of eight clearly differentiated categories of instruments (see Table 7.2).

Contemporary conceptions of instrument choice

As Linder and Peters (1990b: 307) noted, once the tools of government have been inventoried and classified, 'the need to do something more becomes irresistible'. The next logical step was 'to explore functional connections' involving 'matching instruments to goals, policy problems, social impact and organizations'. Taking this next step toward the idea of policy design, as we have seen, requires clarifying the nature of the criteria by which experts assess policy tools and the nature of the contexts in which they can reasonably be anticipated to perform as expected.

Kirschen et al., in their early 1964 work, had already gone some distance toward that goal by arguing that the key determinants of policy choice in the case of the economic instruments they had identified were the economic objective or goal pursued and the structural and conjunctural context of the choice. The economic objectives, they argued, were determined by the interaction of political parties and their representatives in government, administrators and interest groups (1964: 224–36), while the structural and conjunctural context, in turn, was affected by the influence of long-term economic processes and structures and current economic conditions (236–38). They argued that the actual choice of instrument from within the set that fit these epistemic and contextual constraints should be made on essentially technical grounds, according to efficiency and cost criteria; although the political preferences of interest groups and governments – including sociological and ideological constraints – and the institutional limitations of the political system itself had to be taken into account as factors influencing key decision-makers (238–44).

This was a prescient analysis of the overall set of factors affecting instrument choices (Majone 1976, 1989), combining as it did both technical and political factors. However, it was also one which was not adequately grounded in a classification of instruments so as to be able to produce specific recommendations or hypotheses concerning appropriate instrument selections and policy designs in different circumstances or times.

The first models of instrument choices which were so grounded attempted to identify a limited number of criteria upon which policy tools varied; creating single or multiple 'spectrums' or 'continuums' of instrument characteristics which it was hoped could then be associated with specific government preferences among these criteria. Dahl and Lindblom, for example, as early as 1953 had argued that the number of alternative politico-economic instruments is virtually infinite and proposed five long continua as a method of assessing tool preferability in specific contextual situations (Dahl and Lindblom 1953). Their first continuum ranged instruments according to whether they involved public or private enterprises or agencies; the second according to whether they were persuasive or compulsory; the third according to whether they involved direct or indirect controls over expenditures; the fourth according to whether they involved organizations with voluntary or compulsory membership; and the fifth according to whether government agencies were autonomous or directly responsible to legislators or executive members. Although Dahl and Lindblom did not pursue any further the question of whether and to what extent governments actually used these criteria in order to choose a particular instrument, their idea of arranging instruments on a continuum in order to better clarify the reasons behind their choice was adopted by many authors. Salamon and Lund (1989), for example, suggested that different instruments involve varying degrees of effectiveness, efficiency, equity, legitimacy and partisan support that affect their appropriateness for a particular situation.

A simplified version of this model was put forward by a group of Canadian scholars including Bruce Doern, Richard Phidd, Seymour Wilson and others,[1] who published a series of articles and monographs in the late 1970s and early 1980s that turned Lowi's two-dimensional matrix of policy choices into a single continuum of policy instruments based on the 'degree of government coercion' each instrument choice entailed. They first placed only self-regulation, exhortation, subsidies and regulation on this scale (Doern 1981) but later added in categories for 'taxation' and public enterprise (Tupper and Doern 1981) and finally, an entire series of finer 'gradiations' within each general category (Phidd and Doern 1983) (see Figure 4.3).

For Doern and his colleagues, the development of their coercion spectrum model led to the hypothesis of a twofold rationale of instrument choice: one that fitted very well with the notion of a 'continuum' of choices and which offered a great deal of explanatory power in the context of liberal-democratic states. This rationale was based on an appreciation of the ideological preferences of liberal-democratic governments for limited state activity and on the difficulties posed to this principle by the relative political 'strength' of the societal actors in resisting government efforts to shape their behaviour. Assuming that all instruments were more or less technically 'substitutable' – or could perform any task although not necessarily as easily or at the same cost – they argued that in a liberal-democratic society, governments, for ideological reasons, would prefer to use the least coercive instruments available and would only 'move up the scale' of coercion as far as was necessary in order to overcome societal resistance to attaining their goal. As Doern and Wilson put it:

> politicians have a strong tendency to respond to policy issues, (any issue) by moving successively from the least coercive governing instrument to the most coercive. Thus they tend to respond first in the least coercive fashion by creating a study, or by creating a new or reorganized unit of government, or merely by uttering a broad statement of intent. The next least coercive governing instrument would be to use a distributive spending approach in which the resources could be handed out to constituencies in such a way that the least attention is given as to which taxpayers' pockets the resources are being drawn from. At the more coercive end of the continuum of governing instruments would be a larger redistributive programmeme, in which resources would be more visibly extracted from the more advantaged classes and redistributed to the less advantaged classes. Also at the more coercive end of the governing continuum would be direct regulation in which the sanctions or threat of sanctions would have to be directly applied.
>
> (Doern and Wilson 1974: 339)

This model was lauded for its simplicity and elegance but, as critics pointed out, was still problematical in its application to policy design decisions

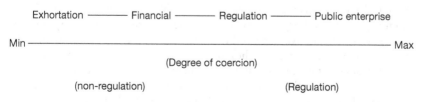

Figure 7.3 The Doern continuum

since 'coercion' appears to be indivisible, or at best, still very difficult to operationalize with the degree of precision required by the model (Trebilcock et al. 1982).

This formulation has many advantages, however. It is not unidimensional, although it might appear so on first reading, because it, like Kirschen, does take into account several political and contextual variables and it, like Cushman, assumes instrument choices are multi-level, with finer calibrations of instruments emerging after initial broad selections have been made. That is, it assumes that both states and societal interests in liberal-democratic regimes prefer a minimal state and choose instruments accordingly after that initial decision has been made. Preferring 'self-regulation', governments would first attempt to influence overall target group performance through exhortation and then add instruments only as required in order to compel recalcitrant societal actors to abide by its wishes, eventually culminating, if necessary, in the take-over of individual firms.

This is not an unreasonable conclusion, based as it is on much observation of the practices of such governments and hints at the 'nested' nature of instrument choices, a subject not previously as well developed in instrument studies. However, as Woodside (1986) argued:

> Experience suggest that governments do not always seek to avoid coercive solutions, but indeed, may at times seem to revel in taking a hard line from the start. While there are undoubtedly many reasons for these heavy-handed responses, surely some of the most important ones include the constituency or group at which the policy is aimed, the circumstances in which the problem has appeared and the nature of the problem involved.
>
> Woodside (1986: 786)

Trebilcock et al. questioned the likelihood of state actors adhering to a minimalist notion of their own proper role in society, preferring public choice inspired notions about bureaucratic expansionism and political credit-mongering motivating administrative and political policy-makers; especially notions of a political cost–benefit calculus aimed at vote maximization (Trebilcock et al. 1982).

These authors also questioned the notion of instrument substitutability found in Doern's work, arguing that constitutional restraints, financial limitations and other technical criteria prevented certain instruments from being utilized in specific circumstances (Trebilcock and Prichard 1983). Thompson and Stanbury did much the same, focusing on visibility and its linkages to political advantage and disadvantage as a criterion of instrument choice. Democratic politicians, they argued, are not ideologically predisposed toward a small state or minimal instruments but would adopt whatever instrument generates the most political benefits for them while minimizing the political costs (Howard and Stanbury 1984; Stanbury 1986). Baxter-Moore, from a neo-Marxist perspective, similarly challenged Doern's notion that the state is committed to a minimal role in society. He argued that 'the state will generally use less intrusive instruments when seeking the compliance of the dominant capitalist class and deploy more intrusive measures to direct or control the behaviour of subordinate classes' (Baxter-Moore 1987: 346). However, despite these criticisms, the Doern model remains one of the dominant ones in studies of public policy tools; its virtues of simplicity and parsimony outweighing its empirical and conceptual difficulties.

Improving on Hood's taxonomy of policy instruments: adding in procedural tools

Fortunately, however, earlier generations of implementation scholars had not completely neglected procedural instruments and other works, like those of Gunningham and his colleagues (Gunningham et al. 1998) had begun to deal with the problem of the design of policy mixes.[2] And others, like those of Schneider and Ingram, developed more sophisticated notions of the inter-relationships existing between governance modes and target group behaviour (Schneider and Ingram 1997). Meanwhile other scholars such as Salamon had also turned their attention to the issue of micro-calculations and calibrations and developed ideas about the sets of factors policy formulators take into account in fine-tuning their instrument choices (Salamon 1989, 2002a).

In the case of procedural instruments, several works dealing with aspects of the subject provided a broad sense of which direction to pursue in attempting to elevate this area of instrument studies to the level that substantive implementation instrument research had attained through taxonomy construction and model-building (Walker 1983, 1991; Qualter 1985).

In their 1988 work, for example, Bressers and Klok (1988) had noted the ways in which 'subjective rational actors' can be influenced by manipulation of the alternatives placed before them and that different instruments can affect the number of policy options developed in the policy process, or the calculations of costs and benefits of alternative courses of action made by policy actors. While some of the instruments they examined were 'substantive' (e.g., the use of licenses to affect the cost of certain activities), most of the instruments captured by their scheme were procedural; especially those dealing with the selective creation, provision and diffusion of information to policy actors.

On the basis of this analysis Schneider and Ingram, following Elmore and his colleagues, identified five general types of instruments corresponding to these 'behavioural assumptions'. These they called 'authority', 'incentives', 'capacity-building', 'symbolic and hortatory' and 'learning' instruments. As was the case with Bressers and Klok, this scheme included both 'procedural' and 'substantive' tools. While their discussion, like many in the USA at the time, virtually ignored pure public provision of goods and services by government agencies and corporations (Leman 1989), the 'authority' and 'incentive' examples cited are typical substantive instruments involving mixed provision of goods and services by a combination of private and public actors. 'Capacity', 'symbolic' and 'learning' tools, however, are much more procedurally oriented, affecting the policy institutions and processes within which policy decisions take place.

Taken together, the works of Bressers and Klok, along with that of Schneider and Ingram and others in the USA and Europe, identified a large number of procedural instruments; their inventory, like that in the case of substantive tools, being accompanied by several ideas about how to classify them (Chapman 1973; Weiss and Tschirhart 1994). These authors identified, among others, tools involved in education, training, institution creation, the selective provision of information, formal evaluations, hearings and institutional reform (Wraith and Lamb 1971; Chapman 1973; Kernaghan 1985; Peters 1992b; Weiss and Tschirhart 1994; Bellehumeur 1997).

Research into the tools and mechanisms used in intergovernmental regulatory design also identified several other such instruments, including intergovernmental 'treaties' and a variety of 'political agreements' that can affect target-group recognition of government intentions and vice versa (Bulmer 1993; Doern and Wilks 1998; Harrison 1999). Other research into interest-group behaviour and activities highlighted the existence of tools related to group creation and manipulation, including the role played by private or public-sector patrons in aiding the formation and activities of such groups (Burt 1990; Phillips 1991; Pal 1993; Finkle et al. 1994; Nownes and Neeley 1996; Lowry 1999). Still other specialized research into aspects of contemporary policy-making highlighted the use of procedural techniques such as the provision of research funding for and access to, investigative hearings and tribunals (Salter and Slaco 1981; Gormley 1989; Cairns 1990; Jenson 1994).

While most researchers focused on the manner in which these instruments were used to enhance 'desirable' traits in public policy-making such as enhanced participation and the wider dissemination of policy-relevant knowledge, some scholars like Saward (1992) also emphasized that procedural tools were also used to 'negatively' affect interest groups' and other actors' behaviour: that is, to restrict their freedom to associate and engage in policy influencing activities.

This latter research highlighted the role such tools have played on the 'dark side' of politics and policy-making; for example, suppressing government enemies and rewarding friends via punishment, exclusions and denial of information (Goodin 1980; Saward 1990, 1992). Examples of 'negative' procedural policy tools identified at this time included co-opting opponents through provision of funds and other privileges, denying information, keeping opponents' views from the public, penalizing opponents by denying funding or recognition and fragmenting opposition – divide and conquer – by selective rewarding, rewarding 'neutrals', adding administrative hurdles and costs to opponents and many more. These latter studies, however, all existed outside the mainstream of policy instrument research, which continued to focus almost exclusively on substantive implementation tools but were ready to be used when policy design and implementation studies moved in a procedural direction in the late 1990s.

Hood's taxonomy of substantive instruments can be modified to help make sense out of this disparate list of procedural tools and this task was undertaken in the late 1990s in several quarters. Classifying procedural instruments just as Hood had done for their substantive counterparts, that is, in accordance with the type of 'governing resource' on which they primarily rely for their effectiveness, generates a useful preliminary taxonomy of procedural tools.

Drawing a distinction between 'positive' and 'negative' uses of governing resources in terms of whether they encourage or discourage actor participation in policy processes further parallels the 'effector–detector' distinction made in Hood's original discussion of substantive tools (Howlett 2000c) (see Table 7.3).

As was the case with Hood's discussion of substantive instruments, this taxonomy is useful in so far as it highlights a small number of different basic resources used by different types of procedural tools and therefore allows a virtually unlimited number of such instruments to be placed in a limited number of general categories, preparing the ground for the development of improved understandings of the basic contours and possibilities of tool selection and of policy designs.

This insight allows a simplified NATO model to be set out in Table 7.4, which includes both procedural and substantive tools as well as a clearer idea of what constitutes a basic governing resource. It is this model which is used in Chapters 8–11 to set out and describe the basic subtypes and most common individual kinds of implementation instruments used in contemporary policy designs.

Table 7.3 A resource-based taxonomy of procedural policy instruments

		Governing resource			
		Nodality	Authority	Treasure	Organization
Principle use	'Positive'	Freedom of information	Mandated participatory processes	Interest-group funding	Conferences and commissions
	'Negative'	Propaganda	Preferential access to policy-makers	Targeted campaign funding	Red tape

Source: Adapted from Howlett, M. 'Managing the 'Hollow State': Procedural Policy Instruments and Modern Governance'. *Canadian Public Administration* 43, no. 4 (2000): 412–31.

Table 7.4 A simplified taxonomy of substantive and procedural implementation tools

		Governing resource			
		Information	Authority	Treasure	Organization
Purpose	Substantive of tool	Public information campaigns	Independent regulatory agencies	Subsidies and grants	Public enterprises
	Procedural	Official secrets acts	Administrative advisory committees	Interest-group funding	Government reorganizations

Improving on micro-level models of tool calibrations: Linder and Peters' clarification of the attributes of instruments choice and Ostrom's institutional rules

While helpful, however, these insights remain firmly at the 'meso' level of tool preferences and need to be applied to the 'micro' level of the choice of specific tool calibrations.

In 1989, Linder and Peters first described eight 'attributes of instruments' which they argued affected specific micro-level tool choices. These were: complexity of operation, level of public visibility, adaptability across uses, level of intrusiveness, relative costliness, reliance on markets, chances of failure and precision of targeting (1989: 56).[1] In his later work, however, Peters (2000a) reduced this number to seven and altered their content so that they became: directness, visibility, capital/labor intensity, automaticity or level of administration required, level of universality, reliance on persuasion versus enforcement and their 'forcing vs enabling' nature (39). This was no doubt due to the conclusion he drew from further study that drawing a sharp distinction between 'market-based' and 'state-based' tools is less useful than thinking about these as 'modes of governance; while 'chances of failure' is also a highly contextual item which does not 'adhere' to an instrument as a fundamental characteristic.

The other difference between the two lists is the addition of several sub-elements to 'level of intrusiveness' which, if removed, leaves five main instrument characteristics or appraisal criteria: *automaticity, visibility, intrusiveness, cost* and *precision of targeting*. The first four criteria all deal with the level of resource intensiveness of an instrument choice: that is, to the degree to which it utilizes, respectively, organizational, nodality, treasure, or authority resources. Precision of targeting, on the other hand, is a key criterion related to tool calibrations or 'settings'.

Putting these considerations together with those found at the governance mode and policy regime lever generates a set of nested implementation tool criteria involved in a typical design situation, as set out in Figure 7.4.

These micro-level tool considerations extend beyond these criteria, however. In her work on environmental policy design, for example, the Nobel Prize winning political scientist Eleanor Ostrom argued that most policies articulate at least seven different kinds of rules governing everything from who is included in a policy, to who can contest it and what kinds of payoffs and penalties are levied on targets (see Table 7.5).

Taken together, these provide a clear set of guidelines to policy designers about what a policy should entail and provide some insights into the kinds of 'settings' required to put such considerations or rules in place and make them stick.

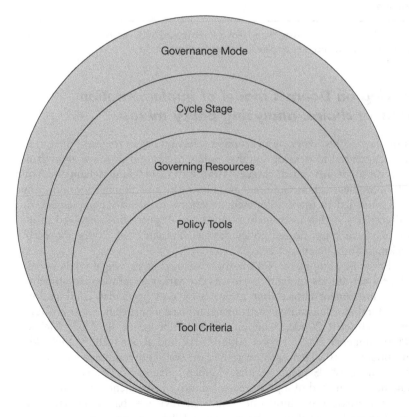

Figure 7.4 Final model of implementation tool selection process involved in policy design

Table 7.5 Ostrom's seven kinds of policy criteria/rules

Boundary rules that specify how actors were to be chosen to enter or leave these positions

Position rules that specify a set of positions and how many actors hold each one

Choice rules that specify which actions are assigned to an actor in a position

Information rules that specify channels of communication among actors and what information must, may, or must not be shared

Scope rules that specify the outcomes that could be affected

Aggregation rules (such as majority or unanimity rules) that specify how the decisions of actors at a node were to be mapped to intermediate or final outcomes

Payoff rules that specify how benefits and costs were to be distributed to actors in positions

---

Source: Adapted from Ostrom, Elinor, Nobel Prize Lecture 2009 'Beyond Markets and states: Polycentric Governance of Complex Economic Systems'.

Improving on Doern's model of implementation instrument choice: analyzing policy mixes

In the late 1990s, work on instrument selection began to assess the question of the potential to develop optimal policy mixes and to move away from a focus on single instrument choices (Grabosky 1994; Gunningham and Young 1997). Studies such as Gunningham, Grabosky and Young's work on 'smart regulation' led to the development of efforts to identify complementarities and conflicts within instrument mixes or tool 'portfolios' involved in more complex and sophisticated policy designs (Barnett et al. 2008; Shore 2009; Buckman and Diesendorf 2010).

For these authors, the key question was no longer 'why do policy-makers utilize a certain instrument?' as it was for earlier generations of students of policy instrument choice, but rather 'why is a particular combination of procedural and substantive instruments utilized in a specific sector?' (Dunsire 1993b; Howlett 2000c; Salamon 2002c; Cubbage et al. 2007; Gleirscher 2008; Gipperth 2008; Taylor 2008; Clark and Russell 2009; McGoldrick and Boonn 2010). Hence, for example, the well-known implementation style found in many US policy sectors, dubbed 'adversarial legalism' by Robert Kagan, is composed of a preferred substantive instrument – regulation – and a characteristic procedural one – judicial review – based on widespread, easily accessible, legal procedures (Kagan 1991).

This new generation of design scholars began to develop what may be described as a 'scalpel' – as opposed to the more blunt 'hammer' – approach to instrument use; one that emphasizes the importance of designing policies that employ a mix of policy instruments carefully chosen to create positive interactions with each other (Sinclair 1997).[3] Proponents of 'smarter' regulation, for example, proposed the development of sophisticated policy instrument mixes in which government's combined a range of market solutions and public and private orderings in order to overcome societal resistance and effectively attain their policy goals in an expeditious and efficient manner (Gunningham et al. 1998; Santos et al. 2010; Gossum et al. 2010).

As we have seen policy tools, or the instruments or techniques used by government in order to implement policy goals (Howlett 2005), have a special place in considerations and studies of policy design. This is because this approach is based on the preparation of plans for tool use with a reasonable chance of achieving a specific goal or target (Howlett 2004b). Choosing policy tools becomes more complex when multiple goals and multiple policies are involved within the same sector and government, as is very common in many policy-making situations (Doremus 2003; Jordan et al. 2012; Howlett et al. 2009).

These latter kinds of multi-policy, multi-goal and multi-instrument mixes – what Milkman (2012) calls 'policy bundles', Chapman (2003) and Hennicke (2004) a 'policy mix' and Givoni et al. (2012) 'policy packages' – are examples of complex portfolios of tools. These mixes typically involve much more than functional logics linking tools to a goal but also deal with ideological or even 'aesthetic' preferences in tool choices and goal articulation which involve trade-offs and bargaining between actors in choosing one set of tools, goals and policies over another (Béland and Wadden 2012; Williams and Balaz 1999). This makes their formulation or design especially problematic (Peters 2005b; Givoni 2013; Givoni et al. 2012). Most often the focus should move from the design of specific instruments to the appropriate design of instrument mixes. This is more difficult to do when instruments belong to different territorial/administrative levels.

Key design questions about such portfolios with which contemporary scholars and practitioners grapple include the issues of avoiding both 'over' and 'under' design (Haynes and Li 1993; Maor 2012b): how to achieve 'complementarity' and avoid 'redundancy' or counter-productive mixes (Grabosky 1995; Hou and Brewer 2010; Justen et al. 2013), how to enhance or alter mixes over time so that they are able to continue to meet old goals and take on new ones (van der Heijden 2011; Kay 2007) and how to sequence or phase in instruments over time (Taeihagh et al. 2013).

In their 1990 study of policy targets and their behaviour, Schneider and Ingram also began to systematically pursue Doern's insight that the extent of a government's willingness to alter the underlying behaviour of key policy actors was a major factor affecting its choice of policy implementation tool. They argued that policy-making 'almost always attempts to get people to do things that they might not otherwise do' and noted that:

If people are not taking actions needed to ameliorate social, economic or political problems, there are five reasons that can be addressed by policy: they may believe that law does not direct them or authorize them to take action; they may lack incentives or capacity to take the actions needed; they may disagree with the values implicit in the means or ends; or the situation may involve such high levels of uncertainty that the nature of the problem is not known and it is unclear what people should do or how they might be motivated.

Schneider and Ingram (1990a: 513–14)

That is, they recognized that each of Hood's 'statecraft' resources required not only state capacity in that area – that is, a plentiful supply of the 'resource' – but also a corresponding belief or endowment on the part of target groups which would allow that capacity to be utilized effectively (Schneider and Ingram 1990a, 1990b, 1993, 1994, 1997).

Thus, as pointed out in Chapter 4, the effective use of 'nodality', for example, requires the transmission of information to targets, 'authority' requires the enforcement capability to coerce or force targets to do something they might not otherwise wish to do, 'treasure' requires having the fiscal capacity to provide targets with incentives or disincentives to act in certain ways and 'organization' requires the administrative capacity to provide them with some good or service directly. But in order to be effective not only must governments have an adequate 'supply' of these resources, but targets must also be susceptible to their deployment: effective information transmission requires *credibility* or the belief among targets that a government is telling the truth; the effective use of authority requires *legitimacy* or the belief among the target population that the use of authority is legally and morally appropriate; the effective use of treasure resources requires *cupidity* or the willingness on the part of actors to accept payments or make them; and the effective use of organization requires *trust* on the part of the target group that an administration is competent and capable of actually delivering the promised goods or services.

The relationship between government organizational capacity, resource availability and target beliefs is set out in (creating Figure 7.5). That is, as Schneider and Ingram noted, each 'resource' is not an absolute entity but a

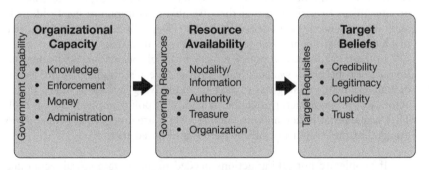

Figure 7.5 State and societal components of 'governing resource' effectiveness

relationship, composed of both a state capacity and a target group belief creating a 'governance' relationship between the two parties to a policy arrangement.

In what follows below several distinctions are drawn between mix types based on the complexity of design variables including the number of instruments, the number of policy goals, the number of sectors and the levels of government and sectors involved in the construction and maintenance of a portfolio. It is argued that if policy design theory is to improve and better inform policy practice, then it requires better understanding the dimensions of these design spaces and the kinds of formulation processes which they encounter (Howlett 2011).

Problems with existing portfolio analyses

Although thinking about the design of policy portfolios has been at the forefront of much current research work on policy design (Howlett 2005; Howlett 2011; Howlett and Lejano 2012), existing studies of such bundles of tools do not use consistent terminology and fail to define the dependent variable carefully enough (Howlett et al. 2006). As a result, the cumulative impact of empirical studies has not been great, theorization has lagged and understanding of the mix phenomena, despite many observations of its significance, has not improved very much over past decades (Chapman 2003; Ring and Schroter-Schlaack 2010).

As we have seen above, most older literature on policy tools focused on single instrument choices and designs (Tupper and Doern 1981; Salamon 1989; Trebilcock and Prichard 1983) and these studies provide only limited insights into the complex arrangements of multiple policy instruments which are commonly found in all policy fields (Jordan et al. 2011, 2012; Givoni 2013). Many significant issues related to the manner in which tool choices in bundles are made and how tool bundles evolve over time affect the propensity for designs to avoid the twin shoals of over and under-reacting to problems (Maor 2012a; Howlett and Rayner 2007) while incorporating better knowledge of both synergistic and counter-productive tool relationships and interactions (del Río 2010; LePlay and Thoyer 2011; Grabosky 1995; Justen et al. 2013).

First, there are a series of questions about how exactly tools fit together, or should fit together, into a mix. In such mixes, the instruments are not isolated from each other and tools in such mixes interact leading to the potential for negative conflicts ('one plus one is less than two') and synergies ('one plus one is more than two') (Lecuyer and Bibas 2011; Philibert 2011). In such cases, different design principles are required to help inform portfolio structure. Here, the question of tool complementarity looms large. As Tinbergen (1952) noted, additional tools – 'supplementary' or 'complementary' ones – are often required to control side-effects or otherwise bolster the use of a 'primary' tool. Bundling or mixing policy tools together in complex arrangements, however, raises many difficult questions for students and practitioners when there are significant interactive effects among policy tools (Boonekamp 2006; Yi and Feiock 2012), some of which may be very difficult to anticipate or quantify using standard analytical tools (Justen et al. 2013).

A second and related set of issues involves determining how many tools are required for the efficient attainment of a goal or goals. This concern has animated policy design studies from their outset and an example of an oft-cited rule in this area originating in very early years of policy design studies is that the optimal ratio of the number of tools to targets or goals in any portfolio is 1:1 (Knudson 2009).

This is a rule-of-thumb design principle toward which Tinbergen (1952) provided some logical justification in his discussion of the information and administrative costs associated with the use of redundant tools in the area of economic policy. Most observers, however, dispute that such a simple situation was ever 'normal' and instead argue that combinations of tools are typically found in efforts to address multiple policy goals (Jordan et al. 2012). The issue of potentially under or over-designing a mix arises in all such circumstances and is made more complex because in some instances, for example, arrangements may be unnecessarily duplicative while in others some redundancy may be advantageous in ensuring that goals will be met (Braathen and Croci 2005; Braathen 2007a). Tinbergen analyzed what he termed the 'normal' case in which it was possible to match one goal with one target so that one instrument could fully address its task and accomplish the goal set out for it. As Tinbergen (1952: 37) himself argued, however, '*a priori* there is no guarantee that the number of targets always equals the number of instruments' and (71) 'it goes without saying that complicated systems of economic policy (for example) will almost invariably be a mixture of instruments'.

A third set of concerns relates to how any optimum figure can be attained in practice. This concern is less a spatial than a temporal one as the existing evidence shows that sub-optimal situations are very common in many existing mixes which have developed haphazardly through processes of policy layering (Thelen 2004; van der Heijden 2011). This is a process in which new tools and objectives have been piled on top of older ones, creating a mixture of quite possibly inconsistent and somewhat incoherent policy elements (Howlett and Rayner 2007; Carter 2012). These processes and change dynamics focus attention on the sequencing of instrument choices (Taeihagh et al. 2009, 2013b) and especially upon the fact that many existing mixes have developed without any sense of an overall conscious design. These kinds of 'unintentional' mixes can be contrasted with 'smarter' designs which involve creating new sets of tools specifically intended to overcome or avoid the problems associated with layering but which may be harder to put into practice (Gunningham et al. 1998; Kiss et al. 2012).

In other words, intelligent design of policy mixes begins with ensuring a good fit not only between packages of tools and government goals and their institutional and behavioural contexts at a specific moment in time (Considine 2012; Lejano and Shankar 2013), but also across time periods as new instruments appear and old ones evolve or are eliminated. That is, design analyses must extend beyond questions of tool synergies and optimal design to consideration of how and why mixes change over time and how the processes of policy formulation followed in adopting such complex designs take place (Larsen et al. 2006; Kay 2007; Feindt and Flynn 2009).

Better defining the design space: vertical and horizontal levels of complexity in policy portfolios

Most work on the subject of policy portfolio design fails to define the design space carefully enough to be able to distinguish the impact on different design choices of the spatial and temporal factors influencing the portfolio design process. Most studies, for example, fail to differentiate between simple and complex contexts and simple and complex designs and mixes (Howlett 2004b; Howlett et al. 2006). But, as the discussion of the Tinbergen Rule above illustrated, incorporating the level of complexity of a mix is an important characteristic of the problem context which principles of portfolio design must take into account. Providing a better model of policy design spaces helps reveal some important variations in terms of who makes or is capable of making design decisions, as well as upon the likely content of that decision in specific contexts (Howlett 2011).

In addressing the issue of design spaces and their impact on policy designs and designing a first-order distinction must be drawn between single 'level' mixes and those with a more complex structure. That is, in addition to the 'horizontal' issue addressed by many students of policy mixes – pertaining to the kind of relationships existing between tools, goals and policies within a single level of government or sector of policy-making – a second, 'vertical' dimension is present and often ignored in these studies. This vertical dimension involves not just the number of instruments, goals and policies found in a mix, but also the number of policy sectors they involve and the number of governments active in policy formulation in this area (del Río 2009).

Such a framework allows room for many more complex interactions between bundle elements than typically envisioned or analyzed in existing studies. That is, conflicts and synergies between tools, goals and policies can be identified both at the horizontal level, for example, between different types of instruments and goals within each level of analysis and/or at the vertical, that is, across and between different policy sectors and/or administrative levels. These variations have significant implications for both the number and type of actors involved in policy design and the processes through which formulation unfolds, as well as for the complexity of design itself. While some aspects of horizontal interactions can be addressed in largely technical ways – so that, for example, some conflicts can be mitigated just by selecting certain instruments over others – in more complex cases, such analyses must be supplemented by other political, administrative and organizational logics and policy formulation processes become more difficult. These challenges are multiplied as mixes evolve over time.

That is, vertical designs cutting across sectors and governments require efforts aimed at achieving administrative coordination and policy integration suitable to the complexity of context which horizontal mixes generally do not. In the former situation relevant coordination, for example, needs to be in place between different administrative levels and across policy subsystems which are not needed in simpler horizontal contexts. The configuration of elements in a vertical mix must relate to preferences for different instruments favored in multiple sectors and governments rather than just among a single set of actors (Freeman 1985; Howlett 2009a). And shifts in these preferences over time require changes to existing mixes which may be more or less easy to achieve and require special handling or developmental techniques and analysis.

Developing a basic taxonomy of policy mixes

Developing a typology of policy mixes based on the level of complexity of design spaces is a useful first step in advancing design studies beyond their current weak status. Mixes can be assessed at a general level by identifying spaces of conflicts, complementarities and synergies between policy fields, but those interactions also depend on the type of tools being adopted and the specific design elements of the instruments adopted within those policy fields. The choice of specific instruments and design elements within interacting policy fields may contribute to mitigate conflicts and promote complementarities and synergies or not. Coordination is easier under certain instruments and design elements than under others.

The first key dimension in constructing such a taxonomy relates to distinguishing between mixes according to the number of instruments, goals and policies found within the horizontal level. Additional scenarios then exist for vertical mixes in situations in which multiple instruments and goals exist across sectors and governments. Like at the horizontal level, at these levels tools and goals may complement each other while in others or in some aspects, they might not (Hull 2008; Flanagan et al. 2011).

While relatively simple mix design processes may be dominated by expert actors (Dunlop 2009a) and decided upon according to technical or functional criteria (Braathen 2007a) moving toward multiple goals brings in additional actors such as those arrayed in 'epistemic communities' (Marier 2008) and involves more sophisticated evidence and ideas than is found in more simple contexts (Sanderson 2002a). In such multi-level government and governance contexts (Hooghe and Marks 2003), different levels of government are likely to have some common, but also different goals and instrument preferences (Enderlein et al. 2011) and reconciling them typically involves the use of the overt political calculus of intra- or intergovernmental bargaining and decision-making (Bolleyer and Borzel 2010; Kaiser 2012).

Increasing complexity from horizontality to verticality brings in cross-sectoral or cross-national epistemic actors (Haas 1992), including political ones and often involves the assessment and use of politically contested evidence and criteria (Gilabert and Lawford-Smith 2012). The most sophisticated design spaces involve the most complex design processes and the full range of subsystem actors operating across multiple governance levels (McCool 1998; Hooghe and Marks 2003). Here, in a context of vested interests, lobbying pressures and intergovernmental jurisdictional disputes, fully blown political criteria such as blame-avoidance, credit claiming, bargaining and log-rolling relevant information (Hood 2010) are features of policy formulation and designs take on new forms and patterns.

Taking these 5 aspects of horizontality and verticality into account and assuming simple binary measures of complexity at each level, yields 32 possible configurations of portfolios. This complexity can be greatly reduced, however, by restricting analysis to only complex tool mixes; that is, eliminating from further analysis half the circumstances whereby only a single instrument is utilized. Combining both cross-sectoral and multi-governmental vertical elements into a single multi-level variable then reduces this to eight basic types (see Table 7.6).

In this model, mixes can be seen to range from the simplest type when multiple tools are an issue (Type I) to the most complex multi-level, multi-policy and multi-goal type (Type VIII). Four of these eight types, are *'instrument mixes'* which involve single policy contexts (Types I, II, V and VI) and therefore are less complex than their multi-policy counterparts (Types III, VII and VIII) which can be termed *'policy mixes'*.

Are all these eight types equally likely to occur? Although much of the literature seems to suggest that Type I situations are the norm, empirical studies suggest this is not the case (Howlett et al. 2006; Hosseus and Pal 1997) and that more complex design spaces and hence policy portfolios are commonplace and growing. Factors such as the administrative and legislative arrangements present in federal and non-federal systems affect the likelihood of appearance of multi-governmental mixes (Howlett 1999; Bolleyer and Borzel 2010), while increasing efforts to promote collaborative or horizontal governance arrangements, for example, will affect the number of multi-sectoral and multi-policy situations which exist (Peters 1998; Koppenjan et al. 2009).

Conclusion: the multi-dimensional nature of contemporary policy designs and design thinking

This chapter has chronicled the development of the main elements of theoretical work on policy tools which can help to clarify the different types of policy portfolios which are currently often ignored or improperly juxtaposed in the

Table 7.6 Basic typology of portfolio designs

Dimension	Types							
	I	II	III	IV	V	VI	VII	VIII
Multi-Level	No	No	No	No	Yes	Yes	Yes	Yes
Multi-Policy	No	No	Yes	Yes	No	No	Yes	Yes
Multi-Goal	No	Yes	No	Yes	No	Yes	No	Yes
	Simple Single-level Instrument Mix	Complex Single-level Instrument Mix	Simple Single-Level Policy mix	Complex Single-level Policy mix	Simple Multi-level Instrument Mix	Complex Multi-level Instrument Mix	Simple Multi-level Policy mix	Complex Multi-level Policy mix

literature on policy design. This was done in an effort to provide the basis not only for better designs but also for improved considerations of the formulation processes and actors involved in such complex policy-making efforts. The discussion thus contributes to efforts currently being made to assess the success or optimality of complex policy mixes (Mandell 2008; Howlett and Rayner 2013; del Río 2014) and advances the project of revitalizing policy design studies as urged by Howlett and Lejano (2013).

Current policy design theory is based on the insights developed during this period that while policy goals are manifold and alter over time and while the choice of policy means is context driven and resource contingent, the toolbox with which designers must work is essentially generic (Majone 1989). That is, as Hood, Lowi and others noted, the reasons behind the actual choice a government may make to implement its policy goals may be complex, but the set of possible choices is limited in nature, bound as they are to the limited number of types of different governing resources they have at their disposal. Understanding the basic types of instruments available to policy-makers and establishing the criteria that policy experts use for assessing the advantages and disadvantages of their use is essential knowledge required to understand how designs emerge and thus to aid in the creation of new ones as well as the assessment and improvement of existing ones (Gibson 1999). That is, as Renate Mayntz (1983) argued, 'to approach the problems of effective programmeme design', it was 'necessary first to identify the relevant programmeme elements and characteristics which are the object of decision in a process of programmeme design' (126).

As this discussion has shown, over the course of the past 30 years, the study of policy implementation instruments has advanced through the various stages of social scientific theory construction and now contributes a great deal of knowledge to policy formulation and policy design (Hood 2007; Lascoumes and Le Galès 2007).

The multi-dimensional nature of policy mixes, however, is a phenomena which has been ignored in most of the policy instrument choice and policy design literature until recently, resulting in a lack of clarity and difficulties associating different kinds of actors and evaluation criteria with mixes (Leutz 1999; Justen et al. 2013) and the continual use of outdated or inappropriate design maxims in their construction which significantly enhance the potential for over and under-designing. Even with only three main portfolio dimensions – goals, policies and levels – the design situation is more complex and nuanced than is normally depicted in the existing policy instrument literature.

Mitigating the conflicts and encouraging synergies within these mixes through effective policy design first requires recognizing these different design spaces and their implications for what is being designed and by whom (Howlett 2013). Only then can efforts take place to enhance relevant horizontal and vertical coordination between and within different administrative levels and sectors relating to different instruments, goals and policies contained within a mix.

Notes

1 Their work on instrument choice influenced others working on the subject at the University of Toronto, such as Michael Trebilcock, Donald Dewees, Robert Pritchard and others, who took part in a detailed discussion of instrument choice issues commissioned as part of a government 'regulation reference' in the late 1970s (Trebilcock and Hartle 1982; Trebilcock et al. 1982).

2 This also was investigated by Tinbergen and later Mundel in the economics literature. On the Tinbergen–Mundell theorem that 'there must be as many independent policy instruments as there are policy targets and secondly that a policy instrument should be assigned to the policy target on which it has the maximal effect', see Ergas (2010).

3 Assessing these interaction effects in practice can be quite difficult. For examples of sophisticated, if somewhat subjective, efforts to do so, primarily in the energy and climate change areas (see Bonnekamp 2006; Oikonomou and Grajakos 2010; and del Río 2010).

Readings

Bemelmans-Videc, M.-L. and E. Vedung. (1997). 'Conclusion: Policy Instrument Types, Packages, Choices and Evaluation'. In M.-L. Bemelmans-Videc, R. C. Rist and E. Vedung (eds), *Carrots, Sticks and Sermons: Policy Instruments and Their Evaluation*. New Brunswick, NJ: Transaction, 249–73.

de Bruijn, J. A. and E. F. ten Heuvelhof. (1997). 'Instruments for Network Management'. In W. J. M. Kickert, E.-H. Klijn and J. F. M. Koppenjan (eds), *Managing Complex Networks: Strategies for the Public Sector*. London: Sage, 119–36.

Doern, G. B. and V. S. Wilson. (1974). 'Conclusions and Observations'. In G. B. Doern and V. S. Wilson (eds), *Issues in Canadian Public Policy*. Toronto, ON: Macmillan, 337–45.

Goodin, R. E. (1980). *Manipulatory Politics*. New Haven, CT: Yale University Press, 1–36.

Hood, C. (1983). 'Using Bureaucracy Sparingly'. *Public Administration* 61, no. 2: 197–208.

Hood, C. (2007). 'Intellectual Obsolescence and Intellectual Makeovers: Reflections on the Tools of Government after Two Decades'. *Governance* 20, no. 1: 127–44.

Howlett, M. (1991). 'Policy Instruments, Policy Styles, and Policy Implementation: National Approaches to Theories of Instrument Choice'. *Policy Studies Journal* 19, no. 2: 1–21.

Howlett, M. (2000). 'Managing the "Hollow State": Procedural Policy Instruments and Modern Governance'. *Canadian Public Administration* 43, no. 4: 412–31.

Howlett, M. (2004). 'Beyond Good and Evil in Policy Implementation: Instrument Mixes, Implementation Styles and Second-Generation Theories of Policy Instrument Choice'. *Policy and Society* 23, no. 2: 1–17.

Howlett, M. and J. Rayner. (2007). 'Design Principles for Policy Mixes: Cohesion and Coherence in "New Governance" Arrangements'. *Policy and Society* 26, no. 4: 1–18.

Howlett, M. and P. del Río. (2015). 'The Parameters of Policy Portfolios: Verticality and Horizontality in Design Spaces and Their Consequences for Policy Mix Formulation'. *Environment and Planning* C 33, no. 5: 1233–45.

Kickert, W. J. M. and J. F. M. Koppenjan. (1997). 'Public Management and Network Management: An Overview'. In W. J. M. Kickert, E.-H. Klijn and J. F. M. Koppenjan (eds), *Managing Complex Networks: Strategies for the Public Sector*. London, Sage, 35–61.

Kirschen, E. S., J. Benard, H. Besters, F. Blackaby, O. Eckstein, J. Faaland, F. Hartog, L. Morissens and E. Tosco. (1964). *Economic Policy in Our Time*. Chicago, IL: Rand McNally.

Linder, S. H. and B. G. Peters. (1989). 'Instruments of Government: Perceptions and Contexts'. *Journal of Public Policy* 9, no. 1: 35–58.

Lowi, T. J. (1972). 'Four Systems of Policy, Politics and Choice'. *Public Administration Review* 32, no. 4: 298–310.

Salamon, L. M. (1981). 'Rethinking Public Management: Third-Party Government and the Changing Forms of Government Action'. *Public Policy* 29, no. 3: 255–75.

Saward, M. (1990). 'Cooption and Power: Who Gets What from Formal Incorporation'. *Political Studies* 38: 588–602.

Schneider, A. L. and H. Ingram. (1994). 'Social Constructions and Policy Design: Implications for Public Administration'. *Research in Public Administration* 3: 137–73.

Woodside, K. (1986). 'Policy Instruments and the Study of Public Policy'. *Canadian Journal of Political Science* 19, no. 4: 775–93.

Chapter 8

Organizational implementation tools

Organizational implementation instruments include a broad range of governing tools which rely upon the use of government and non-governmental institutions and personnel to affect policy output delivery and policy process change. There is a wide variety of *substantive organizational tools* available to affect both the production and consumption/distribution of goods and services in society. However, these generally fall into two main types depending on the proximity of their relationship to government and hence the ability of government to control the effects of their utilization: direct government and quasi-governmental or societally-based organizational tools. *Procedural organizational tools* generally involve the organization and reorganization of government agencies and policy processes in order to affect key parameters of governmental activity and that of the policy communities' governments face in making public policies.

Each type of tool is closely associated with a different mode of governance. Direct government tools, for example, are a principle component of legal modes of governance, while quasi-governmental tools are a feature of corporatist modes and procedural organizational tools are commonly used to construct market and network governance arrangements and architectures which, in turn, often utilize non-state tools.

Substantive organizational instruments

There are many types of substantive instruments which rely for their effectiveness upon the organizational resources of governments and non-governmental agencies and actors. Most involve (and rely primarily) on the use of government personnel to achieve government goals, usually operating in structures created and controlled by governments. These are 'direct' government organizations, but can also include 'indirect' or quasi- or parastatal ones; the best-known example of which is the state-owned or 'public enterprise' – which itself comes in many shapes, sizes, colors and flavors (Bernier 2011) – as well as non-state ones such as co-production or certification (Cashore 2002; Voorberg et al. 2015).

Direct government

The direct use of government agencies for substantive policy purposes involves the 'delivery of a good or service by government employees, funded by appropriations from government treasury' (Leman 1989 and 2002). This is what has sometimes been referred to as 'the forgotten fundamental' (Leman 1989) within policy instrument studies, as its ubiquitous nature is often ignored in studies focusing on more esoteric kinds of tools.

Within this general type of direct government organizational tool, there are several common forms or subtypes found in many jurisdictions. These include the following.

Line departments

In most countries, government agencies undertake a wide variety of tasks on a direct basis. These include, but are certainly not limited to, those listed in (Table 8.1).

These services are provided at all levels of government (central or federal, provincial, state or regional, as well as urban or local) in slightly different configurations in different countries. Unemployment, welfare, or social security payments, for example, can be the task of central governments in some countries and eras and of provincial or local governments in others.

Typically, modern government agencies follow what is known in the public administration literature as a Weberian 'monocratic bureaucracy' form of organization (Brubaker 1984; Beetham 1987). This is a type of organizational structure first systematically described and analyzed by the German political sociologist Max Weber in his early twentieth-century work, *Economy and Society*. Weber argued that although bureaucratic forms of organization had a long history, a significant change had occurred in the modern era as such organizations had come to be viewed as providing services to the public rather than being the property of a monarch or emperor to do with as he or she pleased. The main characteristics of a modern government agency, in Weber's view, were:

- Personnel are appointed on the basis of a merit system of appointment, retention and recruitment.
- Office holders do not own the office in which they work, but hold it subject to the provisions of the merit system.

- Those offices tend to be organized in a hierarchical fashion with a relatively small span of control and multiple levels.
- Activities in the agency operate according to the rule of law – office holders are not above the law and must operate within its limits (including provisions for their accountability – via some form of a 'chain of account-ability' to representative assemblies in modern liberal democracies who actually establish and promulgate laws.

(Albrow 1970; Weber 1978)

What are commonly referred to as 'line' departments (in order to distinguish them from central, headquarters, or 'staff' units) have this 'classic' hierarchical Weberian monocratic bureaucratic form and are thoroughly embedded in legal forms of governance. Such units are typically organized in a pyramidal shape linking offices of civil servants in various branches and sections to a single department head, such as a department of health or a department of highways. A subvariation of this is the 'ministry'; a form in which, typically multiple pyramids of departments culminate in a single head (e.g., a ministry of lands, parks and housing) or an 'agency', which operates separately from the policy-making level of managerial control (Verhoest et al. 2010).

These forms of government organization are the 'workhorses' of publicly provided goods and service delivery in most modern states (see Table 8.1 for an example of their use in government service delivery in a modern state, Canada).

Although many modern states originally practiced legal modes of governance in most sectors, establishing legal rules and forms of legitimation through the rule of law, they have grown dramatically through the creation and expansion of ministries, departments and agencies in areas such as defence, transportation and, later, social welfare, education and health provision. This has resulted in the conversion of many sectors from legal modes of governance to more corporatist ones featuring larger and active state organizations, often with a monopoly over the goods and services they provide. These kinds of organizations can be very large (the US Department of Defense, for example, has over 2 million employees, including approximately 750,000 civilians) and can be subdivided into hundreds of separate branches, bureaus, sections and agencies. They employ the most personnel and deliver by far the largest percentage of state-provided goods and services in liberal-democratic and virtually all other, forms of modern government.

The 'government employees' employed in line departments are typically civil or public servants. In most liberal-democratic countries, these are unionized and well-paid positions and although this is not the case in many other countries where officials may supplement their wages illegally through various forms of corruption ('kickbacks', bribes, 'service' payments, expediting 'fees' and so on), in either case the use of public servants to directly deliver public services is an expensive proposition, which in itself discourages its use.

Table 8.1 Tasks typically undertaken by government agencies

Task	Examples
Facilitating commerce	Mint, standards of weights and measures bureaus
Managing public lands	Commissioners of public lands, ministries of lands and parks, or environment or natural resources
Constructing public works	Departments of public works – airports, highways
Research, testing and statistics	National statistical agencies
Law and justice	Courts, solicitor-general or attorney general offices, corrections and prisons and policing
Technical assistance, record-keeping	Farm extension, ministries of agriculture, and libraries national archives, national libraries
Health care	Ministries of health – hospitals. clinics, dentists, nursing, home care.
Social services	Ministries of welfare and social, family, or community services
Education and training	Ministries of education, post-secondary education colleges and universities, technical and training institutes
Labor relations	Ministries of labour and labour relations
Marketing	Tourism, ministries of small business and ministries of trade and commerce
Defence	Ministries of defence, army, navy, air force and coast guard
Supplying internal government needs	Ministries of supply and services, Queen's printers
Finance	Ministries of finance and treasury boards
International affairs	Ministries of external or foreign affairs

Source: Adapted from Hodgetts, J. E. 1973. *The Canadian Public Service: A Physiology of Government 1867–1970*. Toronto: University of Toronto Press.

How well these officials are educated and trained and what kinds of facilities and information they have to work with also affects their capacity and perceived competence and, along with cost, can play a significant role in their placement within a policy design (Brunsson 2006). Countries or sectors with well-resourced administrative systems regarded as highly efficient and competent by their citizenry are more likely to feature direct government service provision in their policy designs than countries with corrupt or inefficient civil services, given the advantages the former often hold for governments in terms of cost and ease of programme administration.

Central support agencies

These are agencies which are similar in appearance to line departments, but often act more like private companies; delivering services within governments rather than to external constituencies. Some of these are very old (like government stationers and printers) while others (like government systems and information technology units) are much more recent. Many of these agencies are quite large and since they often serve functions similar to private companies they are and have often been, primary targets for government efforts to develop market modes of governance in some sectors through contracting out or privatizing government services – that is, they are simply turned into 'firms' supplying government services by severing their funding through general appropriations revenue and establishing autonomous boards of directors. Cost issues are typically a major factor influencing their inclusion in policy designs.

Social and health insurance and pension plans

Social and health insurance and pension schemes like those used in many countries for unemployment insurance, elderly income support and health care are other government organization-based schemes, ones in which all individuals in certain categories are mandated to make payments to a government agency which acts, usually, as a monopoly insurance provider for that group (Katzman 1988; Moss 2002). Some of these schemes, of course, are among the largest areas of government expenditure and are virtually identical in organizational form to direct government organizational tools given their universal and mandated nature – with the main difference being that programme funds come from dedicated insurance payments rather than general tax revenue. These schemes are generally very high profile and targeted to specific kinds of outputs. They are often intended to be revenue-neutral, although any short-term shortfalls in these schemes typically have to be made up by governments. They also can provide large pools of capital which governments can use to finance infrastructure and other kinds of investments. As such, they are very popular and found throughout the world, although their configuration and extent of private sector involvement varies greatly from country to country. Countries which do not have such schemes typically cite reasons related to costs or intrusiveness upon already existing private sector programmes.

Quasi-governmental organizational forms

All of this type of government agencies have an essentially bureaucratic organizational structure and also exist largely as Weberian forms of administration – although most are structured in a more 'business-like' fashion with fewer rules and regulations guiding their behaviour than government departments and agencies. These include the following main types.

Public enterprises and other corporate forms

Public enterprises or 'state-owned enterprises' (SOEs) are the most common and well-known type of quasi-governmental substantive organizational tool. SOEs undertake or have undertaken a wide variety of tasks in many jurisdictions (see Table 8.2).

There are many different definitions of public enterprises with different levels of public ownership ascribed to these organizations. Hence, for example, in Canada the Ontario Auditor's Act defines 'public enterprise' as:

> a corporation which is not an agency of the Crown and having 50 percent or more of its issued and outstanding shares vested in the government or having the appointment of a majority of its Board of directors made or approved by the Lt. Gov in Council

thus including a specified level of ownership and a means of control within the definition itself (Prichard 1983).

Perry and Rainey (1988) developed an exhaustive typology of these kinds of government organizations by examining the different types of ownership, sources of funding and mode of social control exercised over them. The key feature of these organizations, however, is that they have a corporate form and are not administrative agencies. That is, they operate under separate legislation or under general corporate legal principles and government control is exercised indirectly as a function of government share ownership; typically through voting control over appointments to the company board of directors – who usually can be removed 'at pleasure' by the government. The board of directors then hires and fires senior management so that government control is indirect and 'arm's-length', unlike the management and control of direct government administrative agencies.

Some public enterprises can raise and borrow money on their own authority, while others are limited in their sphere of independence and must

Table 8.2 Examples of tasks undertaken by public enterprises (Canada – twentieth century)

Task	Example (Canada, twentieth century)
Housing	Canadian mortgage and housing Corporation
Finance	Bank of Canada, small business Development Bank, Caisse de Depot et Placement de Quebec
Wartime production	Canadian Arsenals
Transportation	Canadian National Railways, Via Rail, Air Canada/ Trans-Canada Airlines, St Lawrence Seaway Co., BC Ferries, Northern Transportation Company Ltd
Strategic industries	Atomic Energy of Canada Ltd, Petro-Canada
Communications	Canadian Broadcasting Corporation, Radio-Canada
Cultural industries	Canadian Film Development Corporation, National Film Board, National Museum Corps
Utilities	SaskTel, Hydro Quebec, Ontario Hydro and BC Hydro
Infant industries	Petrosar, Athabaska Tar Sands, Canadian Development Corporation
Sick industries	Skeena Cellulose, BC Resources Investment Corporation
Property management	British Columbia Building Corporation
Regional development	Prince Rupert Coal Corporation, DEVCO, Cape Breton Development Corp
Lotteries and vice	BC Liquor Stores, Société des Alcools de Quebec, Casino Nova Scotia, Lotto-Canada
Local utilities	Translink, Edmonton Telephones
Marketing boards	Canada Wheat Board, British Columbia Egg and Milk Marketing Board and Freshwater Fish Marketing Board

Source: Adapted from Vining, A. R. and R. Botterell. 1983. 'An Overview of the Origins, Growth, Size and Functions of Provincial Crown Corporations'. In J. R. S. Pritchard (ed.), Crown Corporations: The Calculus of Instrument Choice. Toronto: Butterworths, 303–68.

seek funding or permission to borrow from governments. Similarly, some are free to set whatever prices they would like for their products while others must seek government permission to alter prices and may be subsidized to provide a good or service at below market value. While government share ownership can drop below 50 percent and still exercise control if the remainder of the shares is widely held, it is more common for a government to own 50 percent or more of voting shares (in fact it is very common for them to own 100 percent). However, there is a growing number of 'mixed' enterprises with joint public–private or multiple government ownership.

These companies can be exceedingly large, although they can also be much smaller, in some cases limited to one or two factories or offices. Sovereign wealth funds, holding the proceeds of oil and gas or pension revenues in countries such as Singapore and Dubai, for example, are among the largest firms in terms of assets and can control hundreds of billions of dollars in investments (Elson 2008), while large public hydroelectrical or petrochemical utilities in countries such as Canada, Norway, Mexico, Iran and Venezuela also rank first among companies in those countries based on size of assets controlled (Laux and Molot 1988).

The use of state-owned enterprises is common in corporatist forms of governance which prize their high levels of automaticity, intrusiveness and visibility as well as their generally low cost and ability to be precisely targeted to different sectors and policy areas. However, there have been many efforts to privatize these companies, or move their ownership from the government to the private sector as some governments have attempted to shift from corporatist to more market modes of governance or cut costs or reduce their balance sheets or level of debt (Savas 1989).

These efforts have been successful in sectors where competition exists, such as marketing boards, product producing companies and property management (Savas 1987; Laux 1993) but have generally foundered in other areas where the privatized corporation has simply become a monopoly service provider. This has often been the case with large-scale utilities such as water, electricity, or public transportation providers where natural monopoly conditions often exist (Chapman 1990; Gayle and Goodrich 1990; Bos 1991). In these cases, they have often been re-nationalized or re-regulated through the creation of regulatory oversight agencies and mechanisms (see Chapter 9) (Mees 2005; Leland and Smirnova 2009). Policy designers now very much take these contextual circumstances into account in proposing or recommending either the creation or privatization of SOEs.

Table 8.2 provides examples of the many public enterprises used in Canada in the twentieth century, a country which has not been at the forefront of the deployment of such tools.

Organizational hybrids (alternative service delivery)

In recent years, numerous hybrid forms of indirect government organizations have also been developed and implemented in many jurisdictions. These have often been proposed in situations where governments would like to privatize or contract out government services but where there is not a competitive market; thereby limiting the utility of outright sale or divestment by a government (Mathur and Skelcher 2007).

Examples of these types of tools include so-called 'special operating agencies' (SOAs) (Koppell 2003; Birrell 2008) which were established in many countries in the 1980s and 1990s in the effort to grant more autonomy to central service agencies and remove them from day-to-day government control. This was typically done by 'outsourcing' whatever services could be secured from a competitive external marketplace, while allowing agencies providing those goods and services which could not be so relocated to charge real prices to purchasers and to retain their earnings and make their own reinvestment decisions (Aucoin 2006; Flumian et al. 2007).

A second type of hybrid is the 'quasi-autonomous non-governmental organization' or *quango*, an organizational form in which a non-governmental agency is established and given a grant of authority by a government to provide a particular good or service (Hood 1986b). These can be precisely targeted and many airports, ports and harbors are run by such 'independent authorities' which rely on governments for their monopoly position but which are answerable to their own boards for their activities rather than to the government itself (Kickert 2001). These agencies are usually then able to charge their own prices for the good or service they provide, retain their earnings and raise funds on capital markets for investments, removing these items from government books and balance sheets (Flinders and McConnel 1999; Lovink 1999; Advani and Borins 2001).

There can be serious principle-agent problems with these kinds of agencies, however, which can affect their use in fields with legal or corporatist modes of governance (Koppell 2003). Maintaining the arm's-length nature of the relationship of public enterprises and quangos to government is difficult and such agencies may not have enough autonomy for governments to avoid the consequences of scandals or other problems associated with them. That is, these relationships can be either too close (day-to-day interference) or too distant (agencies become distant and aloof powers unto themselves). Utilizing this form of substantive organizational tool can be also very expensive and linked to unpopular actions with political and economic consequences for governments – such as price increases, political scandals and high-profile financing and operational issues. Many public agencies also do not have to face the discipline of the market in terms of meeting shareholder or investor expectations for profitability and hence lack at least this incentive to operate in a cost-efficient manner, raising difficulties for many governments practicing market forms of governance in specific sectors (Kernaghan 1993; Ford and Zussman 1997; Flumian et al. 2007). These kinds of visibility and cost issues generally discourage the inclusion of these agencies in policy designs.

Partnerships, commissioning and contracting out

More recent efforts on the part of some governments to shift some sectors from legal or corporatist to market modes of governance – that is, to offload legal and financial responsibility for goods and service delivery and have existing goods and services delivered through the private or quasi-governmental sector – have evolved into several distinct forms of organization which are more private than public, with the public sector acting mainly as a purchaser of goods and services provided by private companies (Grimshaw et al. 2001; Grimsey and Lewis 2004; Greener 2006).

One typical form of such activity is 'contracting out' or outsourcing, in which internal provision of some good or service is simply replaced with a source external to government (Zarco-Jasso 2005). This can be more complicated if a non-governmental provider does not exist for a particular product or service, so that a government must first, or simultaneously, create a non-governmental provider (Brown et al. 2008). Outsourcing of highway and railway maintenance in many countries in the 1980s and 1990s, for example, involved government managers creating their own firms, which then bid on and received government contracts to provide maintenance services; those companies then immediately hired former government workers and in some cases used former government equipment, to provide the same service (McDavid and Clemens 1995).

More recently this form of activity has moved to the capital goods sector with the development of so-called 'P3s' or 'public-private partnerships' in which governments encourage private sector firms to build and operate public infrastructure such as schools, office buildings, hospitals and sports facilities and even prisons and transportation infrastructure such as bridges and roads, in return for a government guarantee of a long-term lease or use agreement with the provider (English and Skellern 2005). The net effect of this activity is to remove capital costs from government budgets while retaining the service (Rosenau 1999; Boase 2000).

Different kinds of these partnerships exist, such as collaborative partnerships with NGOs to control hospital admissions for the disabled, operational partnerships with companies and other governments, to share costs for many of the items discussed above; and contributory partnerships where governments may provide funding without necessarily controlling the use of such funds, as occurs when matching funds are provided for local or community-based environmental improvement projects (Kernaghan 1993; Daniels and Trebilcock 1996; Hodge and Greve 2007).

Although popular in some countries and sectors in recent years as examples of 'collaborative' or 'joined-up' government, such schemes often stretch the resources of non-profit or volunteer organizations and can result in inefficient or incompetent goods and services delivery (Evans et al. 2005; Riccucci and Meyers 2008; Smismans 2008; Tsasis 2008). These kinds of cost and reliability issues increasingly have affected considerations of such tools and their inclusion in policy designs.

Commissioning

Commissioning is the most recently recognized collaborative technique in which, as Taylor and Migone (2017) put it:

Generally refers to a more strategic and dynamic approach to public service design and delivery with a clear focus on aligning resources to desired outcomes by injecting greater diversity and competition into the public service economy. By creating public service markets, the expertise and resources of the private and not-for-profit sectors can be harnessed and leveraged through new business and delivery models.

Commissioning goes well beyond traditional procurement and outsourcing agendas (Tanner 2007; Macmillan 2010; Martikke and Moxham 2010) with the aim of increasing service levels from both private and community partners by involving 'third sector' actors, such as NGOs in both service target formulation and design ('co-design') as well as service delivery ('co-management'). The provision of stable funding and ongoing interactions with government funding agencies, it is argued, allows the capacity of third sector actors to be enhanced at the same time that co-design and co-management ensures that outcomes match the expectations of clients rather than agencies (Bovaird et al. 2014).

Commissioning suffers from many capacity issues, however. Again, as Taylor and Migone (2017) also note:

This means that the various organizations involved redefine their relations with the public administration on one level, with the clients/users of the services on another and finally with each other. A critical element in this relationship is the creation of high level trust relations among the stakeholders. This trust will affect the flow of information and help in the creation of a contestable environment where multiple parties can move away from hindrances to outcome-based approaches such as overly legalistic contracts, enable the devolution of meaningful autonomy to those who are ultimately accountable and responsible for the delivery of services.

As they note in some cases the new relationship will modify established sets of interactions, such as when increased competitiveness of non-profit organizations results in decreased cooperation among the providers (Buckingham 2009; Mills, Meek and Gojkovic 2011).

Contracting

Contracting is probably the most well-known such activity and involves governments in reducing the level of direct state involvement in the provision of public services, including internal state services, through the replacement of civil servants and internal procurement processes with contractual arrangements with, usually, non-governmental organizations, primarily businesses (Ascher 1987; Vincent-Jones 2006). Various forms of contracting out exist, such as the PPPs or Public–Private Partnerships discussed above,

175

which have grown in popularity in areas involving large-scale infrastructure investments, whereby private firms absorb many investment costs and construct or rehabilitate infrastructure projects in water, highways, dams and other such areas, in exchange for long-term contracts to operate and profit from them (English and Skellern 2005; Vining et al. 2005). Other less rigorous forms of contracting out exist in areas such as healthcare, education and prisons, in which contracts may not involve large investments and profit sharing but rather simply remove major expenditure areas, such as penitentiaries, from government books and budgets (Thadani 2014; Roehrich et al. 2014).

In the case of contracting, many supporters of the concept have noted significant limitations which can prevent contracting from functioning effectively. The 2016 Nobel Prize in Economics, for example, was awarded to two economists who specialize in detailing the significant flaws and limits of contracting in areas such as prisons and healthcare (Hart 2017; Holmström and Milgrom 1991). Their concern is with the difficulty encountered by governments in enforcing quality control in such contracts when the nature of the service provided (i.e., its quality) is dependent on difficult to monitor interactions between, for example, patients and doctors or prisoners and prison guards. However, many other criticisms of such partnerships exist (Newman 2014) which highlight the need to carefully negotiate realistic contracts and the information asymmetries and knowledge gaps linked to them, as well as other issues such as difficulties encountered cancelling contracts or preventing contractees from simply reneging on their contracted obligations (Jensen 2017).

Non-state and society-based tools: co-production and certification

Efforts at policy reform have been omnipresent in many developed and developing countries over the past several decades and have often featured efforts to reduce the number of state-based tools and shift their activities toward either hybrid instruments or in some cases away from state-based organizations altogether. Many of these efforts have featured waves of management reforms and administrative re-structuring, including privatizations, de-regulation and re-regulation and the like (Ramesh and Howlett 2006). 'Anything but the government', for example, was a popular sentiment in public policy reform for at least two decades (Christensen and Lægreid 2008). These efforts led to the articulation and promotion of several alternative modes of governing to more traditional 'hierarchical' or state-led ones.

Many of these techniques are 'market-based' and constitute efforts to replace government activity with private sector actions (Savas 1987). However, others are focused less on zero-sum notions of state-market relations but rather involve more complex ideas about involving 'civil society' actors more directly in 'collaborative' policy-making, administration and implementation

(Brudney 1987; Salamon 1989). These kinds of activities come in many forms but two which have received a great deal of attention in recent years are 'co-production' and 'certification'.

Certification

Certification is a term used to capture the activities of many non-state actors involved in areas such as forestry, fisheries, organic foods and other similar areas in which quality control and enforcement of standards is accomplished less directly than is the case with traditional command and control regulation (Cashore et al. 2004; Cutler et al. 1999; Gulbrandson 2010). In these cases, for a variety of reasons from cost to ideology, 'certification' of standards is undertaken by civil society organizations such as the Forestry Stewardship Council or the Marine Stewardship Council which lack the formal authority to compel business and industries to abide by regulatory standards but which utilize (often negative) publicity, boycotts and other actions to encourage compliance (Cashore 2002; Pérez-Ramírez 2012).

These tools are often referred to as non-state market-based (NSMD) tools (Cashore 2002) since they do not rely upon state authority for their power and legitimacy to regulate private sector activity, but rather do so through market activities such as product labeling and producer certifications; affecting consumer behaviour and preferences for, for example, organic produce or sustainably harvested timber, fish or coffee, among others.

While it is debatable if they could work without the 'iron-fist' of a threat of potential government regulation lurking in the background, it is clear that their impact and operation is through market mechanisms, affecting the supply and demand for products and services by affecting consumer views of their costs and benefits.

Almost all products can be certified in this sense, although many do not need to be if consumers can themselves judge their quality and desirability. When information is lacking on, for example, the provenance or production techniques used in wine or food products such as olive oil, however, certification can enhance prices and encourage consumption, as occurs, for example, with the certification of 'pre-owned' (i.e., used) cars, electronic equipment, or art works.

Such schemes rely heavily on the reputation of the certifier for honesty, accuracy and precision. In the case of certification, legitimacy and trust are key aspects of the certifying organizations and predictors of the success of voluntary certification arrangements (Bernstein and Cashore 2007). Certification only functions effectively if trust exists between the public and certifiers and between the certifiers and certified companies and governments. Concerns about second-class regulation or corrupt standards can easily undermine years of work building up a certified brand. Similarly competing or dueling certifiers can also undermine existing schemes and lead to their ineffectiveness (Zelli et al. 2017). If their reputation is damaged, as has happened from time to time with products such as wine or olives in which additives were added or cheaper products substituted for expected ones, such schemes can collapse and require either substantial reform or government takeover, revealing their dependence on government, ultimately, to serve as the guarantor of quality.

Co-production

Co-production is a short-hand term for a variety of governance arrangements which involve citizens in the production and delivery of public services. First set out by Elinor Ostrom (Parks et al. 1981) in her work on community policing in the 1960s, the term has been expanded and popularized by Victor Pestoff and Taco Brandsen in their many books and writings in the years since then (Brandsen and Pestoff 2006; Pestoff et al. 2012).

The idea of co-production can be traced back to Ostrom's (1973) study of the Chicago police force and is part of her theory of polycentric governance (Ostrom 1996). In the US, these ideas generated interest among public administration scholars in the 1970s and the 1980s (Parks et al. 1999; Brandsen and Pestoff 2006) and experienced a revival in the decades after the turn-of-the-century (Pestoff et al. 2012). The idea has since been picked up and studied by scholars around the world (e.g., Whitaker 1980; Parks et al. 1981; Ostrom 1996; Alford 2002; Brandsen and Pestoff 2006; Prentice 2006; Bovaird 2007; Pestoff and Brandsen 2009; Pestoff et al. 2012).

Originally, co-production was narrowly defined as the 'involvement of citizens, clients, consumers, volunteers and/or community organizations in producing public services as well as consuming or otherwise benefiting from them' (Alford 1998: 128). Drawing on the experience of countries in Scandinavia in areas such as parent-teaching associations, Brandsen and Pestoff highlighted the extent to which many governance arrangements, even those thought to be purely hierarchical, such as public schooling, in fact combine aspects of hierarchical or state-based governance with elements of civil society mobilization (Pestoff 2006).

In early studies of activities such as parent–teacher interactions, this involvement in co-production activity was typically voluntary, meaning it existed as a positive externality reducing production and delivery costs of public services. This made it very attractive to governments seeking cost reductions in public service delivery, especially ones favorable to notions of 'social enterprise' and enhanced community participation seen as an end- or good-in-itself (Parks et al. 1981; Salamon 1981 and 1987).

Although co-production emerged as a concept that emphasized citizens' engagement in policy design and delivery, its meaning has evolved in recent years to include both individuals (i.e., citizens and quasi-professionals) and organizations (citizen groups, associations and non-profit organizations) collaborating with government agencies (Alford 1998; Poocharoen and Ting 2015). In this sense, as public management studies have showed, non-governmental organisations can act as effective facilitators of the participation by individual citizens while managerial reliance on trust and shared responsibility can discourage competitiveness and foster knowledge sharing among participating organisations (Pestoff and Brandsen 2010; Poocharoen and Ting 2015).

Two aspects of the use of co-production as a policy tool are critical. First, at the macro-level, governance arrangements, actors and their interaction matter to co-production success, just as is the case with any policy tool, highlighting the need to combine policy and public management thinking in order to achieve service delivery success. Second, at the meso and micro level, some balancing of state and societal roles are required if co-production is to be sustained (Howlett 2000c, 2004a).

Like all others, co-production also has a downside as a policy tool. In the case of co-production, it has long been recognized that expectations of free labor from co-producers may not materialize (Sorrentino 2015; Brudney and England 1983) and schemes to incentivize co-producers through payments are susceptible to all of the usual harms of public expenditures, including corruption, clientelism and goals displacement, among others (Howlett et al. 2017).

Procedural organizational instruments

Substantive tools, of course, are only one half of the uses toward which government and non-governmental organizational resources can be put. The second use is procedural. This involves the use of the organizational resources such as personnel, staffing, institutionalization and internal procedures to alter or affect policy processes in order to better achieve general government aims or specific programme activities.

It bears repeating that these tools do not involve direct or indirect goods and service delivery mechanisms, as do their substantive counterparts, but rather affect procedural activities, generally efforts aimed at creating or restructuring policy community structure and/or behaviour through government leadership or 'network management' efforts.

According to Agranoff and McGuire (1999: 21), this latter activity involves 'network managers' in 'selecting appropriate actors and resources, shaping the operating context of the network and developing ways to cope with strategic and operational complexity'. The key dimensions or tasks involved in these kinds of network management activities include the identification of potentially compatible network actors, given the issue at hand; limiting potential conflicts that would hinder flexibility; recognizing legal requirements; balancing political objectives/conflicts with policy objectives; and assigning costs in implementation.

That is, any policy process, policy managers need to work with the structure and operation of any network which already exists in the area; recognize potential new actors, limit the role of ineffective actors; balance their time and resource commitments (money, technology, expertise, etc.); maintain the focus of the network in achieving goals; and build trust between actors/reduce possible conflicts (Mandell 1994; 2000; Agranoff 1998; Agranoff and McGuire 1999; Koppenjan and Klijn 2004; Wu et al. 2010). In order to achieve these ends, various kinds of organizational network management tools can be used. Several of the most common of these are set out below.

Network management tools

There are many different types of procedural tools linked with the use of specific government organizational resources which can affect various aspects of policy subsystem behaviour in policy processes. Interest in these tools has grown as many governments, as discussed in Chapter 1, have moved in the direction of more overt network management in some sectors in recent years.

Staff or central (executive) agencies

This is an old form of government organization, one in which a small, co-ordinating government agency, rather than one which directly delivers services to the public, is created to centralize agency initiatives in some area. Such 'staff or 'central' agencies are generally created as a means to control other administrative agencies and are often linked very closely to the political executive (Bernieret al. 2005). In Westminster-style parliamentary systems, for example, older examples include Privy Council offices and treasury board secretariats, while newer ones include presidential, premier and prime minister's offices, ministries of state, communication units, intergovernmental secretariats and various kinds of implementation units (Chenier 1985; Savoie 1999; Lindquist 2006).

Although small (even most prime minister's offices until recently had less than 100 personnel, most of whom handled correspondence) these are central co-ordinating units which exercise a great deal of control over other bureaucratic agencies through their links to the executive and to the budgetary and policy processes in government. They have seen much growth in recent years as political executives have sought to re-establish control over far flung administrative apparatuses (Campbell and Szablowski 1979; Rhodes and Weller 2001; Bevir et al. 2003; Bernier et al. 2005).

Unlike line departments, these staff or central agencies are less, or non-hierarchical, flatter organizations typically staffed by political appointees, although others also employ permanent officials as well. Key officials are chiefs of staff, principle secretaries and specialized positions such as a clerk of the Privy Council or cabinet secretary. These agencies play a major and increasing role in designing and coordinating policies and policy-making, ensuring accountability to legislatures and controlling the budgets, activities and plans of line departments and ministries. Their small cost is a major design consideration although this is often offset by their high visibility and high level of intrusiveness in the affairs of the government agencies they control or co-ordinate.

Tribunals and other quasi-judicial bodies

These are created by statute and perform many administrative functions, such as hearing appeals concerning licencing (e.g., of pesticides), certification (of personnel or programmemes) and permits (e.g., for disposal of effluents). Appointed by government, they usually represent, or purport to represent, some diversity of interests and expertise.

Administrative hearings are conducted by tribunals in a quasi-judicial fashion, often in order to aid tribunals in their activities. These hearings are bound by rules of natural justice and procedures may also be dictated by statutory provisions. The decisions of tribunals are designed to be binding on the ministry in question but may be subject to various political, administrative and judicial appeals. Public hearings may be statutorily defined as a component of the administrative process.

In the framework of administration, tribunals are directed toward securing compliance with administrative edicts and the achievement of identified standards of behaviour by both governmental and non-governmental actors. They may act as a mechanism with which to appeal administrative decisions, but in most cases, proceedings are held at the discretion of a decision-making authority and public hearings are often 'after the fact' public information sessions rather than being true consultative devices (Grima 1985; Stewart and Sinclair 2007). They can be precisely targeted and are an important component of legal modes of governance which are generally low cost and nearly invisible. However, in other forms of governance, like market or corporatist modes, their relatively high levels of intrusiveness can diminish their appeal in the eyes of policy designers.

Creating or reorganizing government agencies

Another fairly commonly used procedural organizational tool is to establish new government agencies or reform existing institutions in order to focus or re-focus state and societal activities on specific problems or issue areas (Goetz 2007; Durant 2008). Setting up a new government ministry for technology or a new research council to promote advanced technologies such as biotechnology, e-technologies, or other high technology sectors, for example, is a common action on the part of governments wanting to target a new area of activity for further development (Hood 2004; Lindquist 2006; van Thiel 2008). However, such actions are highly visible and, if repeated too often, quite costly. They are also quite intrusive and, as a result, are proposed and used, only infrequently.

Establishing analytical units

Some governments have also set up internal think tanks or research institutes in order to provide policy advice to governments (Dobuzinskis et al. 2007; Marchildon 2007). Many government departments and agencies also have established specialized policy units designed to generate studies and reports which can influence or help to persuade both government officials and non-governmental actors of the merits of government plans. These agencies also often employ outside consultants to bring additional expertise and knowledge to policy formation, implementation and evaluation (Schwartz 1997; Perl 2002; Speers 2007). The knowledge they generate is used to inform internal policy-making processes and also to garner support for government positions from outside groups (Whiteman 1985 and 1995).

New analytical units such as those policy shops created in many jurisdictions in the 1970s and 1980s in order to promote formal policy analysis and what is now referred to as 'knowledge-based' or 'evidence-based' policy-making are good examples of procedural organizational tools (Prince 1979; Prince and Chenier 1980; Chenier 1985; Hollander and Prince 1993; Lindquist 2006). These agencies can be precisely targeted and are generally low cost and have low visibility. However, their impact on policy-making can raise the ire of stakeholders and others in market, corporatist and network forms of governance, while other agencies in more legal modes also find them to be rivals. Such considerations have dampened enthusiasm for such units in many jurisdictions and sectors and reduced their appeal in policy designs in recent years.

Establishing clientele units

New administrative units in areas like urban affairs, science, technology and other areas flourished in the 1970s, as did new environmental units in many countries in the 1970s and 1980s; they were joined by units dealing with areas such as youth and small business in the 1990s; while in the post-1990 period other new units were developed in countries such as Canada and Australia to deal with aboriginal affairs and in many countries to promote multiculturalism, women's and human rights. Human rights units dealing with minorities and the disabled are good examples of network mobilization and activation occasioned by government organizational (re)engineering (Malloy 1999, 2003; Teghtsoonian and Grace 2001; Teghtsoonian and Chappell 2008; Osborne et al. 2008).

In general, these agencies can be precisely targeted in order to undertake the management functions set out in Table 8.3. They are very popular in network governance modes given their generally low cost, high visibility and high levels of automaticity. They are also popular in policy designs in legal governance given their relatively high levels of intrusiveness.

Table 8.3 Analytical agency network managerial tasks

---

1   Vertical and horizontal co-ordination
2   Overcome institutional blockages such as federalism and divisions of power
3   'Mainstreaming'
4   Building commitments
5   Building legitimacy/developing visions and agreement on alternatives
6   Building coalitions
7   Structuring NGO activity, for example, lobbying activities

---

Source: Adapted from Mandell, M. P. 'A Revised Look at Management in Network Structures'. *International Journal of Organizational Theory and Behaviour* 3, nos.1/2 (2000): 185–210.

Establishing government reviews, ad hoc task forces, commissions, inquiries and public hearings

A sixth common procedural organizational tool used by governments is the establishment of a government review. These range from formal, mandated, periodic reviews of legislation and government activity by congressional or parliamentary committees and internal administrative bodies to 'ad hoc' processes such as task forces or inquiries designed to activate or mobilize network actors to support government initiatives (Gilmore and Krantz 1991; Bellehumeur 1997; Marchildon 2007; Sulitzeanu-Kenan 2007, 2010; Rowe and McAllister 2010).

Ad hoc task forces and inquiries are typically temporary bodies, much shorter term and often more issue related than institutionalized advisory committees. Ad hoc commissions are also created as instruments to consult a variety of interests with regard to economic and other areas of planning activity. These range from the presidential or royal commissions to those created at the departmental level. Presidential and royal commissions are the most formal and arm's length and therefore, are the most difficult for governments to control and predict and therefore are used less often (Maxwell 1965; Doern 1967; Clokie and Robinson 1969; Wilson 1971; Chapman 1973; Flitner 1986; Salter 1990; Jenson 1994).

Task forces have been created in many jurisdictions for planning, consultation, or conflict resolution concerning many specific issues. The task force may be invoked by a government when there is an area of conflict in which different groups have different interests and perspectives or where they require information in order to arrive at a decision or judgment (Marier 2009; Rowe and McAllister 2006).

The subject matter of an ad hoc commission is typically urgent, of concern to more than one ministry and level of government and is the subject of some controversy (Resodihardjo 2006; Sulitzeanu-Kenan 2010). It is invoked at the discretion of government and is subject to political, economic and social pressures. Indeed, the very initiation of the commission is likely to be the product of pressure by public groups. But, as Chapman (1973: 184) noted 'Commissions may also play a significant political role and are often used as a method for postponing to an indefinite future decision on questions which appear to be embarrassing but not urgent'. Employment of these instruments for this purpose can result in serious legitimation problems for governments utilizing these policy tools, however, given their high level of visibility (Heinrichs 2005; Hendriks and Carson 2008; Stutz 2008; Marier 2009).

Public participation through hearings is the most common type of public or network consultation in many sectors (Rowe and Frewer 2005). Hearings vary by degree of formalization and when they occur in a policy process. The most effective and influential are often flexible processes that are geared toward policy formulation such as project reviews or environmental assessments, but the most common are rigid processes that take place in or after the implementation stage of a process, such as a formal policy evaluation exercise (Dion 1973; Baetz and Tanguay 1998; Edelenbos and Klijn 2005). Public hearings are often mandated by legislation and most often occur after a decision has been taken – that is, purely as information and/or legitimation devices. Actual instances of open, truly empowered public hearing processes are very rare (Riedel 1972; Grima 1985; Torgerson 1986).

Although sometimes used for other purposes such as information collection or blame attribution, these tools are often also used to overcome institutional 'blockages' and veto points such as those which are commonly found in federal–state or intergovernmental relations or in interdepartmental jurisdictional struggles (Ben-Gera 2007). They can also help bolster the capacity of groups to become more involved in the policy process if funding is extended to their participants, thereby promoting network governance (Robins 2008). They can be precisely targeted and are generally low cost. However, their high level of visibility can cause problems for governments and results in their less frequent appearance in policy designs than would otherwise be the case (Rowe and Frewer 2005).

Legislative and executive oversight agencies

This category of organizational tools also includes specialized agencies with very different policy-making functions, such as arm's-length independent auditor-generals or access to information commissioners, which are units typically attached to legislatures, providing some oversight or control over executive branch activities (Campbell-Smith 2008). Many principle-agent problems can also be overcome through administrative procedures mandating oversight agency reviews of government actions (McCubbins and Lupia 1994; McCubbins et al. 1987), especially if these are linked to funding and budgetary issues (Hall 2008). These latter units are usually fairly small, inexpensive and highly visible and there has been a proliferation of such units in recent years dealing with areas such as corruption, human rights and the promotion of ethnic and gender equality (Malloy 2003). They often represent an effort to promote legal governance in sectors typically configured in other modes.

Conclusion: organizational tools – the forgotten fundamental in policy design studies

Practical experience and ideological predilections have shaped the substance of much of the debate on governance, ranging from preferences for democracy, popular participation and collaboration to concerns about budget deficits and public sector inefficiencies in hierarchy-based systems. These have often driven preferences for the use of specific forms of governance from hierarchical ones to market or network-based ones.

In recent years, however, for a variety of reasons a strong preference for shifts toward non-hierarchical forms of governance coupled with discontent with the results of market-based reforms in the 1970s–1990s has led to increasing attention being paid to different kinds of more civil-society or networked forms of governance, often referred to by the shorthand term 'collaborative governance' (Meuleman 2009).

Lost in the identification of alternative forms of collaboration followed by governments around the world in a variety of sectors, however, has been the understanding of exactly what kind of governance arrangement is 'collaborative' and especially, under what conditions a preferred governance mode could actually address a particular sector's problems.

Given that all collaborative modes are vulnerable to specific kinds of failures due to these inherent vulnerabilities when governments reform or try to shift from one mode to another mode, policy-makers and advisors need to understand not only the nature of the problem they are trying to address and the skills and resources they have at their disposal to address it, but especially the innate features of each potential governance tool and the capabilities and competences each requires in order to operate at a high level of performance. How specific government capabilities and competences can be bolstered or augmented by collaborative arrangements when governance reforms are contemplated or implemented will vary from case to case depending on the distribution of available capacities.

Organization-based implementation tools are generally costly and have high visibility. This is because they rely on government personnel funded by appropriations from general revenue raised through taxes or royalties, although some are also funded from market revenue stemming from the sale of goods or services. The use of tax-based funding makes the use of public servants expensive in the sense that governments tend to have a limited capacity to tax citizens to pay for services and incur opportunity costs no matter which activity they choose to adopt. It can also lead to governance failures, as the link between system outputs and inputs (expenditures and revenues) is usually not clear, providing the opportunity for funds to be misallocated and effort misspent, all in the fishbowl environment of public government (Le Grand 1991).

However, in some countries additional sources of revenue – such as those accruing from natural resources rents or 'royalties' – especially from oil and natural gas activities in many states in the contemporary era – can make the expenses involved in direct delivery appear less onerous for the public at large and in such circumstances such tools are much easier for governments to establish and maintain. It is also the case that some publicly delivered goods and services can be charged for – for example, through highway or bridge tolls, or publicly run electricity, fuel or food services, among many others – and can be priced like any other private good or service, helping to explain why many resource-rich countries have large public sectors and why many countries of all types have large public sectors and state-owned enterprises.

Despite their real or perceived cost and in spite of many efforts to create or replace them with other forms of service and goods delivery, direct delivery of goods and services by public agencies remain 'the forgotten fundamental' of implementation instruments and policy designs. That is, much attention has been focused in the past three decades on the privatization of public goods and service production and distribution facilities and organizations and many efforts have been made to replace chargeable publicly provided goods ('toll' or 'club' goods such as toll bridges or publicly run recreational facilities) (Potoski and Prakash 2009) with privately supplied ones, largely in the effort to improve productivity or reduce the burden on taxpayers and governments of the wages of public servants involved in direct government provision (Dunleavy 1986; Ascher 1987; Cook and Kirpatrick 1988; Donahue 1989; Finley 1989; Cowan 1990; Hanke and Walters 1990; Heald 1990; Connolly and Stark 1992). However, these efforts have generally been less successful than often thought or alleged.

Many new hybrid and non-state practices from contracting to partnerships were also a key component of 'New Public Management' (NPM) thinking in the 1980s and 1990s in many countries and are a key component of many contemporary efforts to promote 'public-private partnerships' and 'collaborative government' (Linder 1999). However, it is sometimes overlooked that 'old-fashioned' government agencies are still the most common and pervasive policy instrument in most sectors (Leman 1989; Aucoin 1997; Olsen 2005). Even in the ostensibly most private sector-oriented market governance systems (like the USA or, more recently, New Zealand), direct government goods and service production usually reaches close to 50 percent of gross national product (GNP) – that is, half of the dollar value of all goods and services produced in a country in one year – while direct civil service employment typically hovers in the area of 15–20 percent of the labor force but can also be much higher (Christensen and Pallesen 2008; Derlien 2008; Busemeyer 2009). The difference between the two figures having to do with the fact that many expenditures are composed of transfers to individuals which can involve large sums but only a small administrative overhead – for example, unemployment insurance or old age security payments.

This organizational activity is somewhat sectorally focused, due to large publicly provided expenditures on direct government activities such as defence and the military which cannot be delivered by the private sector and/or items such as health care, social security, education and pensions associated with the development of modern welfare states and the extension of legal rights to these services to members of the public. It also includes what statistical agencies refer to as the 'MUSH' sector – municipalities, universities, schools and hospitals – which in many countries are established as autonomous or semi-autonomous operating agencies of more senior levels of government. In many countries, MUSH sector agencies are among the largest employers since the activities they undertake – such as education and health care, as well as sewer, road and parks maintenance – are very labor intensive.

Many of the recent innovations in organizational forms, from special operating agencies, to quangos, private–public partnerships and various kinds of hybrid organizations, have emerged largely in the effort to reduce the size of existing organizations and transform some sectoral activities from legal and corporatist to market modes of governance (Hardiman and Scott 2010). This is done in the name of improving the efficiency of service delivery, or in order to try to reduce the resource burden large public service delivery agencies place on budgets and taxpayer loads (Verhoest et al. 2007; O'Toole and Meier 2010).

Either way, it has promoted the frequent appearance of experiments in alternate instruments and policy designs, although much less often their realization in practice. Significant areas of public expenditure and effort such as health care and education, for example, have generally proved immune to privatization efforts given their overall cost structures, mandatory service delivery nature and high levels of citizen support (Le Grand 2009). Most successes have come in either small-scale direct service privatizations or in single-industry company privatizations which have generally not altered earlier governance modes (Verhoest et al. 2010).

Procedural organizational instruments have also been growing in frequency of appearance, but for different reasons: under efforts to shift sectoral activity undertaken through older legal forms of governance to more corporatist or network forms. Government reorganizations are increasingly common and these reorganizations and the new agencies often created alongside them often are intended to use government organizational resources to refocus government efforts and interactions with policy community/network members rather than directly improve the delivery of particular types of goods and services (Herranz 2007; Bache 2010).

As Peters (1992a) noted, re-organization of existing departments and agencies serves to refocus government efforts and reposition government administration within policy networks, bringing together policy community members to reconsider the effectiveness of network management activities

(Banting 1995; de la Mothe 1996), improving management of complex areas by restructuring relationships (May 1993; Metcalfe 2000) and can insert government actors between competing private actors in networks by, for example, creating consumer departments to sit between producers and (un)organized consumers (Bache 2010). These moves are often accompanied by the increasing use of government reviews and inquiries, as well as consultative conferences and other similar organizational forms for stakeholder and public consultation (Crowley 2009; Lejano and Ingram 2009).

Readings

Alford, J. (1998). 'A Public Management Road Less Travelled: Clients as Co-Producers of Public Services'. *Australian Journal of Public Administration* 57, no. 4 (1 December): 128–37.

Bellehumeur, R. (1997). 'Review: An Instrument of Change'. *Optimum* 27, no. 1: 37–42.

Bovaird, T., I. Briggs and M. Willis. (2014). 'Strategic Commissioning in the UK: Service Improvement Cycle or Just Going Round in Circles?' *Local Government Studies* 40, no. 4 (4 July): 533–59.

Brandsen, T. and V. Pestoff. (2006). 'Co-Production, the Third Sector and the Delivery of Public Services'. *Public Management Review* 8 (December): 493–501.

Cairns, B., M. Harris and P. Young. (2005). 'Building the Capacity of the Voluntary Nonprofit Sector: Challenges of Theory and Practice'. *International Journal of Public Administration* 28: 869–85.

Cantor, R., S. Henry and S. Rayner. (1992). *Making Markets: An Interdisciplinary Perspective on Economic Exchange*. Westport, CT: Greenwood Press.

Cashore, B., G. Auld and D. Newsom. (2003). 'Forest Certification (Eco-Labeling) Programs and Their Policy-Making Authority: Explaining Divergence Among North American and European Case Studies'. *Forest Policy and Economics* 5: 225–47.

Fledderus, J., T. Brandsen and M. E. Honingh. (2015). 'User Co-Production of Public Service Delivery: An Uncertainty Approach'. *Public Policy and Administration* 30, no. 2 (1 April): 145–64.

Goldsmith, S. and W. D. Eggers. (2004). 'Designing the Network'. In *Governing by Network: The New Shape of the Public Sector*. Washington, DC: Brookings Institution, 55–92.

Hatanaka, M., C. Bain and L. Busch. (2005). 'Third-Party Certification in the Global Agrifood System'. *Food Policy* 30: 354–69.

Hood, C. (2004). 'Controlling Public Services and Government: Towards a Cross-National Perspective'. In C. Hood, O. James, B. G. Peters and C. Scott (eds), *Controlling Modern Government; Variety, Commonality and Change*. Cheltenham, UK: Edward Elgar, 3–21.

Howlett, M., A. Kekez, and O.-O. Poocharoen. (2017). 'Understanding Co-Production as a Policy Tool: Integrating New Public Governance and Comparative Policy Theory'. *Journal of Comparative Policy Analysis: Research and Practice* 19, no. 5 (20 October): 487–501.

Kelman, S. J. (2002). 'Contracting'. In L. M. Salamon (ed.), *The Tools of Government: A Guide to the New Governance*. New York: Oxford University Press, 282–318.

Kernaghan, K. (1993). 'Partnership and Public Administration: Conceptual and Practical Considerations'. *Canadian Public Administration* 36, no. 1: 57–76.

Leman, C. K. (2002). 'Direct Government'. In L. M. Salamon (ed.), *The Tools of Government: A Guide to the New Governance*. New York: Oxford University Press, 48–79.

Migone, A. and M. Howlett. (2012). 'From Paper Trails to DNA Barcodes: Enhancing Traceability in Forest and Fishery Certification'. *Natural Resources Journal* 25, Fall: 421–41.

Olsen, J. P. (2005). 'Maybe It Is Time to Rediscover Bureaucracy'. *Journal of Public Administration Research and Theory* 16, no. 1: 1–24.

Peters, B. G. (1992). 'Government Reorganization: A Theoretical Analysis'. *International Political Science Review* 13, no. 2: 199–218.

Poocharoen, O. and B. Ting. (2013). 'Collaboration, Co-Production, Networks: Convergence of Theories'. *Public Management Review*, 18 (December): 1–28.

Posner, P. L. (2002). 'Accountability Challenges of Third-Party Government'. In L. M. Salamon (ed.), *The Tools of Government: A Guide to the New Governance*. New York: Oxford University Press, 523–51.

Riccucci, N. M. and M. K. Meyers. (2008). 'Comparing Welfare Service Delivery among Public, Nonprofit and For-Profit Work Agencies'. *International Journal of Public Administration* 31: 1441–54.

Savas, E. S. (1989/90). 'A Taxonomy of Privatization Strategies'. *Policy Studies Journal* 18, no. 2: 343–55.

Stanton, T. H. and R. C. Moe. (2002). 'Government Corporations and Government-Sponsored Enterprises'. In L. M. Salamon (ed.), *The Tools of Government: A Guide to the New Governance*. New York: Oxford University Press, 80–116.

Vining, A. R., A. E. Boardman and F. Poschmann. (2005). 'Public–Private Partnerships in the US and Canada: "There are No Free Lunches"'. *Journal of Comparative Policy Analysis* 7, no. 3: 199–220.

Chapter 9

Authoritative implementation tools

There are many types of 'authoritative' implementation instruments that are part of, and often central features of, many policy designs. All involve and rely primarily upon, the ability of governments to direct or steer targets in the directions they would prefer them to go through the use of the real or perceived threat of state-enforced sanctions. While treasure resources, discussed in Chapter 10, are often used to encourage 'positive' behaviour – that is, behaviour which is aligned with government goals – authoritative actions can be used for this purpose, but are often also used in a 'negative' sense, that is, to prevent or discourage types of behaviour which are incongruent with government expectations (Ajzen 1991).

The use of the coercive power of the state to achieve government goals through the control or alteration of societal (and governmental) behaviour is the essence of *regulation*, the most common type of governing instrument found in this category and the one most compatible with legal forms of governance.

With regulation, the government does not provide goods and service delivery 'directly' through the use of its organizational resources but rather allows this to occur in a controlled fashion through an intermediary – usually a private company or market enterprise, but also sometimes state-owned enterprises or more commonly, NGOs such as churches, voluntary organizations and association, trade unions and professional bodies. Depending on how this is done, this can be compatible with either market or corporatist types of governance (Mitnick 1978; Scott 2001). Other procedural authoritative tools are also compatible with network governance.

Substantive authoritative instruments

In general, all types of regulation involve the promulgation of more or less binding rules which circumscribe or alter the behaviour of particular target groups (Hood 1986a; Kiviniemi 1986). As it has been succinctly described by Barry Mitnick, this involves the 'public administrative policing of a private activity with respect to a rule prescribed in the public interest' (Mitnick 1978).

Rules take various forms and include standards, permits, prohibition and executive orders. Some regulations, like ones dealing with criminal behaviour, are *laws* and involve the police and judicial system in their enforcement. Most regulations, however, are *administrative edicts* created under the terms of enabling legislation and administered on a continuing basis by a government department or a specialized, quasi-judicial government agency (Rosenbloom 2007). In relatively rare cases, the authority to enact, enforce, or adjudicate regulations can also be delegated to NGOs in various forms of 'voluntary' or 'self-regulation'. All of these types are set out and their strengths and weaknesses in policy designs described below.

Direct government regulation

Regulation is a fundamental technique or tool of legal governance. Although citizens may not always be aware of their presence, among other things regulations govern the price and standards of a wide variety of goods and services they consume, as well as the quality of water they drink and the air they breathe.

There are numerous definitions of regulation, but a good general one is offered by Michael Reagan (1987), who defines it as:

> a process or activity in which government requires or proscribes certain activities or behaviour on the part of individuals and institutions, mostly private but sometimes public and does so through a continuing administrative process, generally through specially designated regulatory agencies.

Thus, in this view, regulation is a prescription by the government which must be complied with by the intended targets; failure to do so usually involves a penalty, sometimes financial but also often involving incarceration and imprisonment.

This type of instrument is often referred to as 'command and control' regulation since it typically involves the government issuing a 'command' to some target group in order to 'control' their behaviour. 'Control' also sometimes refers to the need for governments to monitor and enforce target group activity in order for a 'command' to be effective.

This type of regulation is very common in both social and economic spheres in order to encourage 'virtues' and discourage 'vices', however those are defined at the time. Thus the criminal law, for example, is a kind of regulatory activity, as are common laws and civil codes, which all countries have and which states develop and implement, usually relatively non-controversially (May 2002; Cismaru and Lavack 2007). Although much less significant in terms of the day-to-day lives of many citizens, much more attention is paid in the policy tools literature to economic regulation which affects aspects of established markets for goods and service production and is often resisted by target companies and industries if they feel it undermines their competitive position either domestically or internationally (Baldwin and Cave 1999; Crew and Parker 2006).

It is sometimes difficult for governments to 'command and control' their targets if these targets resist regulatory efforts (Scholz 1991) or if governments do not have the capacity or legitimacy required to enforce their orders. As a result of these difficulties other types of regulation exist in which rules are vaguer and the threat of penalties may be, at best, remote. These different types of regulation are discussed below.

Laws

Law is an important tool of modern government and the very basis of legal modes of governance (Ziller 2005). Several different types of laws exist, however. These include distinctions often drawn by legal scholars between private and public law; private civil or tort law and common law; public criminal and administrative law; and hybrids such as class action suits which combine features of public and private law. These different types of law vary substantially in terms of what kinds of situations they can be applied to, by whom and to what effect (Keyes 1996; Scheb and Scheb 2005).

All of these laws can be thought of as 'regulations' since all involve the creation of rules governing individual behaviour (Williamson 1975; 1996a; Ostrom 1986). However, in the form it is usually discussed by policy scholars, 'regulation' is typically thought of as a form of public law; although even then it can also involve criminal and individual or civil actions (Kerwin 1994, 1999; West 2005).

Keyes (1996) has usefully described the six types of legal instruments which can be used by governments when they wish to invoke their authority to try to direct societal behaviour (see also Brandsen et al. 2006). These are shown in Table 9.1.

While laws can prohibit or proscribe many kinds of behaviour (and encourage others either by implication or overtly), in order to move beyond the symbolic level, they all require a strong enforcement mechanism, which includes various forms of policing and the courts (Edelman 1964, 1988). And even here a considerable amount of variation and discretion is possible since inspections and policing can be more or less onerous and more or less frequent, can be oriented toward responding to complaints or actively looking for transgressions ('police patrols' vs 'fire alarms') and can be focused on punishment of transgressions or prevention, in the latter case often with a strong educational component designed to persuade citizens and others to adopt modes of behaviour more congruent with government aims and objectives (McCubbins and Schwartz 1984; Hawkins and Thomas 1989;

Table 9.1 Six types of legal instruments

1 Statutes
2 Delegated legislation between levels of government
3 Decisions of regulatory bodies and courts
4 Contracts or treaties
5 Quasi-legislation such as tax notices and interpretative bulletins
6 Reference documents such as background papers, other legislation, standing orders, etc.

Source: Adapted from Keyes, J. M. 1996. 'Power Tools: The Form and Function of Legal Instruments for Government Action'. *Canadian Journal of Administrative Law and Practice* 10: 133–74.

McCubbins and Lupia 1994; May and Winter 1999). A desire for 100 percent compliance on the part of governments requires a high level of scrutiny and thus some kind of ongoing, institutionalized and regulatory presence within a government organization or agency: typically a line department such as a police department or some other similar administrative bureau with investigatory and policing powers.

All laws are intrusive and many are highly visible. A significant problem with the use of laws in policy designs, however, pertains to cost, automaticity and precision of targeting. With respect to the first two, while passage of a law is usually not all that costly, the need for enforcement is. Laws have a low degree of automaticity as they rely upon citizen's goodwill and perceptions of legitimacy for them to be obeyed. Inevitably this will not ensure 100 percent compliance and will thus require the establishment of an enforcement agency, such as the police, customs agencies, immigration patrols, coastguards and the courts. Precision of targeting is also an issue since most laws have general applicability and often cannot single out specific groups or targets for differential treatment. These problems have led to the use of alternate forms of regulation expected to reduce these costs and allow for improved targeting of specific actors such as firms involved in specific kinds of economic activities.

Independent regulatory commissions

Direct administrative implementation of legislative rules is very common in legal modes of governance. However, in the economic realm, especially, it often raises concerns about corruption and patronage, that is, in the abuse of administrative discretion to either ease enforcement in certain cases or administer it capriciously in others. Checks on administrative discretion usually exist through the court system, whereby those who feel they have been unfairly treated can often appeal administrative decisions and seek their overturn (Jaffe 1965; Edley 1990). This can be a very time-consuming and expensive process, however and several distinct forms of regulatory agencies with semi-independent, quasi-judicial status have been developed in order to avoid governance problems associated with direct departmental regulation.

The most well-known of these is the *independent regulatory commission* or IRC used in corporatist modes of governance. Although some early exemplars of this instrument can be found in canal authorities in Great Britain and other European railway, highway and transportation regulatory authorities of the eighteenth and nineteenth centuries, the IRC as it is currently known stems mainly from concerns raised in the post-Civil War USA about unfair practices in railway transportation pricing and access. These led to the creation of an innovative organizational regulatory form in the 1887 US Pendleton Act which established the US Interstate Commerce Commission, a quasi-judicial body operating at arms length from government which was intended to act autonomously in the creation and enforcement of regulations and which remained in operation for over 100 years (until 1995) (Cushman 1941).

Independent regulatory commissions evolved from the transportation sector to become common in many other sectors, not limited to those dealing with economic issues. They are 'semi-independent' administrative agencies in the sense that, as was the case with public enterprises, government control is indirect and exercised via the appointment of commissioners who are more or less difficult to remove from office (Stern 1997; Gilardi 2005b,c; Jacobzone 2005; Majone 2005; Christensen and Laegreid 2007).

Irene Wu has listed 11 aspects of their organization, staffing and function which make such agencies 'independent' (Wu 2008; Wonka and Rittberger 2010) (see Table 9.2).

IRCs are quasi-judicial in the sense that one of their main activities is adjudicating disputes over the interpretation and enforcement of rules – a task

Table 9.2 Requisites for regulatory agency independence

---

1 An independent leader
2 Exclusive licensing authority
3 Independent funding
4 Private sector regulatees
5 Little movement of staff between industry and regulator
6 Consumer offices
7 Universal service offices
8 Notice and comment decision-making
9 Rules against gifts
10 Rules against conflicts of interest
11 Post-employment rules

Source: Adapted from Wu, Irene. 'Who Regulates Phones, Television and the Internet? What Makes a Communications Regulator Independent and Why It Matters'? *Perspectives on Politics* 6, no. 4 (2008): 769–83.

taken away from the courts in order to ensure that expertise in the specific activities regulated is brought to bear on a case in order to have more expert, timely and predictable results. Decisions of independent regulatory commissions are still subject to judicial review, although often this is only in terms of issues relating to procedural fairness, rather than the evidentiary basis of a decision (Edley 1990; Berg 2000; Laegreid et al. 2008; Lehmkuhl 2008).

IRCs are relatively inexpensive, specialized bodies that can remove a great deal of the routine regulatory burden in many areas of social and economic life from government departments and are quite popular with governments wishing to simplify their agendas and reduce their need to supervise specific forms of social behaviour on a day-to-day basis.

In the contemporary period, independent regulatory commissions are involved with all aspects of market behaviour, production, distribution and consumption, as well as many areas of social life. Many specialized forms of IRCs exist, such as the use of 'marketing boards', or arm's length regulatory bodies often staffed by elected representatives of producers and granted specific rights to control prices and/or supply, thereby creating and enforcing pricing and supply regimes on producers. This has occurred primarily in areas affected by periodic bouts of over or under-supply and can be found in areas such as bulk agricultural commodities such as wheat or milk which are very sensitive to price fluctuations, but also in areas such as liver and heart transplants subject to chronic supply shortages (Weimer 2007; Royer 2008). These boards typically act as rationing boards charged with allocating supply quotas and setting prices in order to smooth out supply fluctuations in the activity involved.

Although it began with regulation of trade, commerce and distribution, primarily railways and transport, the IRC instrument quickly moved to production and in the post-World War I era in many countries IRCs were implemented in areas such as labor and industrial dispute regulation, as well as the commodity-based marketing boards mentioned above. In the post-World War II era, they were used to cover a range of emerging consumer and consumption issues such as consumer rights, landlord–tenant interactions, human rights disputes and others (Hodgetts 1973).

As Berg (2000) and Stern and Holder (1999) noted, in addition to questions related to their level of independence or autonomy, additional design criteria include the clarity of their roles and objectives; their degree of accountability of governments or the public; their level and type of participation and transparency; and ultimately their predictability in terms of being bound by precedents either of their own making or through judicial review (see also Berg et al. 2000).

IRCs, like more direct government regulation, have been the subject of efforts at *deregulation* as some governments attempted to move some sectors away from legal and corporatist governance forms toward more market modes of operation. Some high-profile privatization and deregulation in transportation, telecommunication and financial industries in many countries occurred as a result of these effort (Levi-Faur 2003).

The reality, however, is that there has been no across the-board reduction in the use of more directive tools (Drezner 2001a; Vogel 2001; Wheeler 2001). Like privatization, deregulation is nowhere as widespread as claimed by both enthusiasts and critics (Iacobucci et al. 2006). Even in banking, the most globalized sector, there is little or no evidence of an overall decline of regulation and the market and credit crises of 2008 have led to *increased* moves in a re-regulatory direction in many countries, from Iceland to the USA (Busch 2002; Harris 2004). Indeed, regulations have been expanded in many sectors to compensate for the loss of state control following privatization of public enterprises (Jordana and Levi-Faur 2004b; Braithwaite 2008) and IRCs are among the most favored means of re-regulating deregulated or privatized industries and activities (Ramesh and Howlett 2006).

With respect to targeting, including precision and selectivity among groups and policy actors, the information needed to establish regulation is less than with many other tools because a government need not know in advance the subject's preferences, as is necessary in the case of some other instruments. It can just establish a standard, for example, a permitted pollution level and expect compliance. This is also unlike the situation with financial incentives, for example, which will not elicit a favorable response from regulatees unless their intended subjects have a preference for them (Mitnick 1980).

There are still some concerns about the use of this instrument in policy designs, however, linked to considerations of cost and visibility. The cost of enforcement by regulatory commissions can be quite high depending on the availability of information and the costs of investigation and prosecution in highly legalistic and adversarial circumstances can also be very large. Regulations also are often inflexible and do not permit the consideration of individual circumstances and can result in decisions and outcomes not intended by the regulators (Bardach 1989b; Dyerson and Mueller 1993). They quite often distort voluntary or private sector activities and can promote economic inefficiencies, for example. Price regulations and direct allocation, for example, restrict the operation of the forces of demand and supply and affect the price mechanism, thus causing sometimes unpredictable economic distortions in the market. Similarly, restrictions on entry to and exit from industrial sectors, for example, can reduce competition and thus have a negative impact on prices. Regulations can also inhibit innovation and technological progress because of the market security they afford existing firms and the limited opportunities for experimentation they might permit. For these and other reasons, they are often labeled as overly intrusive by many firms and actors.

Indirect government regulation

A third form of regulation is 'indirect regulation' which is very compatible with corporatist modes of governance. There are several different types of such regulation, however, which vary in terms of their design attributes.

Delegated professional regulation

This is a relatively rare form of regulatory activity which occurs when a government transfers its authority to license certain practices and discipline transgressors to non-governmental or quasi-governmental bodies whose boards of directors, unlike the situation with independent regulatory commissions, they typically do not appoint (Elgie 2006; Kuhlmann and Allsop 2008).

Delegated regulation typically involves legislatures passing special legislation empowering specific groups to define their own membership and regulate their own behaviour. Brockman (1998) defines it as:

> the delegation of government regulatory functions to a quasi-public body that is officially expected to prevent or reduce both incompetence (lack of skill, knowledge or ability) and misconduct (criminal, quasi-criminal or unethical behaviour) by controlling the quality of service to the public through regulating or governing activities such as licencing or registration – often involving a disciplinary system (fines, licences, suspension or revocation) and codes of conduct/ethics, etc.

This occurs most commonly in the area of professional regulation where many governments allow professions such as doctors, lawyers, accountants, engineers, teachers, urban planners and others to control entrance to their profession and to enforce professional standards of conduct through the grant of a licencing monopoly to an organization such as a bar association, a college of physicians and surgeons, or a teachers' college (Tuohy and Wolfson 1978; Trebilcock et al. 1979; Tuohy 1992, 1999; Sinclair 1997). Typically, appeals of the decisions of delegated bodies may also be heard by the courts or specialized administrative tribunals (Trebilock 2008).

The idea behind delegated regulation, as with independent regulatory commissions, is that direct regulation through government departments and the courts is too expensive and time-consuming to justify the effort involved and the results achieved. Rather than tie up administrators and judges with many thousands of cases resulting from, for example, professional licensing or judicial or medical malpractice, these activities can be delegated to bodies composed of representatives of the professional field involved who are the ones most knowledgeable about best practices and requirements in the field. Governments have neither the time nor expertise required to regulate multiple interactions between lawyers and their clients, teachers and students, or doctors and patients, for example and a form of 'self-regulation' is more practical and cost-efficient.

Scandal in areas such as business accounting in many countries in recent years, however, can undermine confidence in a profession's ability or even willingness to police itself and can lead to a crisis in confidence in many aspects of delegated self-regulation (Vogel 2005; Bernstein and Cashore 2007; Tallontire 2007). Of course, any delegation of government regulatory authority can be revoked if misbehaviour ensues.

Voluntary or incentive regulation

Another form of indirect or 'self-regulation' has a more recent history than delegated regulation and has been extended to many more areas of social and economic life. This is typically a form found in market governance systems in which, rather than establish an agency with the authority to unilaterally direct targets to follow some course of action with the ability to sanction those actors who fail to comply, instead a government tries to persuade targets to voluntarily adopt or conform to government aims and objectives.

Although these efforts often exist 'under the shadow of hierarchy' (Heritier and Lehmkuhl 2008) – that is, where a real threat of enhanced oversight exists should voluntary means prove insufficient to motivate actors to alter their behaviour in the desired fashion – they also exist in realms where hierarchies don't exist, such as the international realm when a strong treaty regime, for example, cannot be agreed upon (Dimitrov 2002, 2005, 2007). A major advantage often cited for the use of voluntary standard-setting is cost savings, since governments do not have to pay for the creation, administration, enforcement and renewal of such standards, as would be the case with traditional command and control regulation whether implemented by departments or independent regulatory commissions. Such programmes can also be effective in international settings, where establishment of effective legally-based governmental regimes can be especially difficult (Schlager 1999; Elliott and Schlaepfer 2001; Cashore et al. 2003; Borraz 2007).

Moffet and Bregha set out the main types of voluntary regulation (see Table 9.3) found in areas such as environmental protection.

These tools attempt such activities as inducing companies to exceed pollution targets by excluding them from other regulations or enforcement actions; establishing covenants in which companies agreed to voluntarily abide by certain standards; establishing labeling provisions or fair trade programmes; providing favorable publicity and treatment for actors exceeding

Table 9.3 Types of voluntary regulation

1	Legislated compliance plans
2	Regulatory exemption programmes
3	Government–industry negotiated agreements
4	Certification
5	Challenge programmes
6	Design partnerships
7	Standards auditing and accounting

Source: Adapted from Moffet, J. and F. Bregha. 1999. 'Non-Regulatory Environmental Measures'. In R. B. Gibson (ed.), *Voluntary Initiatives: The New Politics of Corporate Greening*. Peterborough: Broadview Press.

existing standards; promoting co-operation over new innovations; and attempting to improve standards attainment by targeted actors through better auditing and evaluation. These are all forms of what Sappington (1994) has termed 'incentive regulation'.

The role played by governments in voluntary regulation is much less explicit than in traditional regulation, but is nevertheless present. Unlike the situation with command and control or delegated regulation, in these instances governments allow non-governmental actors to regulate themselves without creating specific oversight or monitoring bodies or agencies or empowering legislation. As Gibson (1999: 3) defined it:

> By definition voluntary initiatives are not driven by regulatory require-
> ments. They are voluntary in the sense that governments do not have to
> order them to be undertaken . . . [but] governments play important roles
> as initiators, signatories, or behind-the-scenes promoters.

While many standards are invoked by government command and control regulation, others can be developed in the private sphere, such as occurs in situations where manufacturing companies develop standards for products or where independent certification firms or associations guarantee that certain standards have been met in various kinds of private practices (Gunningham and Rees 1997; Andrews 1998; Iannuzzi 2001; Cashore 2002; Eden 2009; Eden and Bear 2010).

These kinds of self-regulation, however, are often portrayed as being more 'voluntary' than is actually the case. That is, while non-governmental entities may, in effect, regulate themselves, they typically do so, as Gibson notes, with the implicit or explicit permission of governments, which consciously refrain from regulating activities in a more directly coercive fashion (Gibson 1999; Ronit 2001). As long as these private standards are not replaced by government enforced ones, they represent the acquiescence of a government to the private rules, a form of delegated regulation (Haufler 2000, 2001; Knill 2001b; Heritier and Eckert 2008; Heritier and Lehmkuhl 2008).

That is, as a 'public' policy instrument, 'self-regulation' still requires some level of state action – either in supporting or encouraging development of private self-regulation or retaining the 'iron fist' or the threat of 'real' regulation if private behaviour does not change (Cutler et al. 1999; Gibson 1999; Cashore 2002; Porter and Ronit 2006). This is done both in order to ensure that self-regulation meets public objectives and expectations (see e.g., Hoek and King's (2008) analysis of the ineffective self-regulation practiced by TV advertisers in New Zealand) and to control the kinds of 'club' status which self-regulation can give to firms and organizations which agree to adhere to 'voluntary' standards (Potoski and Prakash 2009).

The certification schemes discussed in Chapter 8, for example, can closely approximate cartel-like arrangements which allow premiums to accrue to club members rather than to the public. As Delmas and Terlaak (2001) noted, joining or participating in voluntary schemes entails both costs and benefits to companies, which undertake detailed cost-benefit calculations about whether or not to join voluntary associations. This is one of the 'limits of virtue' which David Vogel (2005) noted in his studies of various corporate social responsibility (CSR) schemes in the late 1990s and first decade of the twenty-first century (see also Tallontire 2007; Steurer 2010; and Natural Resources Canada 2003).

It is also the case that any possible savings in administrative costs over more direct forms of legal regulation must be balanced against additional costs to society which might result from ineffective or inefficient administration of voluntary standards, especially those related to non-compliance (Gibson 1999; Karamanos 2001; Henriques and Sadorsky 2008).

Market creation and maintenance

Paradoxically as it might seem from its title, another form of an indirect regulatory instrument used by the government is the use of co-called 'market-based' instruments (Hula 1988; Fligstein 1996). These refer to a particular type of regulatory tool in which governments establish property rights frameworks or regimes which establish various kinds of limits or prices for certain goods and services and then allow market actors to work within these 'markets' to allocate goods and services according to price signals (Averch 1990; Cantor et al. 1992).

Such schemes have often been proposed mostly in the area of environmental and resource policy, from land and water use (Murphy et al. 2009) and bio-conservation (ecosystem services) (Wissel and Watzold 2009) to climate change-related emissions control systems (Sovacool 2011), but have also been used in areas such as fisheries and taxi services, in the form of individual transferable quotas (ITQs) or tokens (Pearse 1980; Townsend et al. 2006) and with respect to the control of greenhouse gas regulation, such as the 'cap and trade' systems created in the European Union and other countries associated with the Kyoto Protocol and climate change mitigation efforts (Heinmiller 2007; Voss 2007; Hahn 2008; Toke 2008; Pope and Owen 2009).

However, despite much publicity, few of these schemes have been implemented given the difficulties of setting prices and limits on items such as pollutants, problems with leakage and poor enforcement in the system and dangers associated with market failures, as well as the inability of governments to bear the blame for problems with these systems, despite their ostensibly arm's length character (Stavins 1998, 2001; Mendes and Santos 2008; Keohane et al. 2009). Unlike traditional regulation, these designs can be higher cost and less automatic than expected and also are very difficult, if not impossible, to target toward specific actors and groups (Krysiak and Schweitzer 2010; Mickwitz et al. 2008).

Procedural authoritative instruments

Procedural authority-based instruments typically involve the exercise of government authority to recognize or provide preferential access or treatment to certain actors – and hence to fail to recognize others – in the policy process, or to mandate certain procedural requirements in the policy-making process in order to ensure it takes certain views or perspectives into account. These instruments perform a wide variety of network management functions (Agranoff and McGuire 1999), very often in order to gain support or marginalize policy opponents but also to ensure certain standards and standard practices are followed in policy choices (Goodin 1980; Saward 1992).

Policy network activation and mobilization tools

In terms of network management activities, many procedural authoritative tools are involved largely in the 'selective activation' of policy actors and/or their 'mobilization' through the extension of special recognition in a policy process. The key use of authority is in the extension of preferential access to decision-makers or regulators for certain views and actors and not others, or at least to a lesser extent (Doerr 1981).

Procedural authoritative tools attempt to ensure efficiency and effectiveness of government actions through activation of policy actor support. Networks may be structured, for example, through the creation of various advisory processes which all rely on the exercise of government authority to recognize and organize specific sets of policy actors and give them preferential access to government officials and decision-makers (Pierre 1998; Hall and O'Toole 2004). These include advisory councils, ad hoc task forces and inquiries, consultations and public hearings oriented toward extending special authoritative status to certain societal interests or 'stakeholders', that is, those actors with a financial or some other form of 'stake' in a particular state activity (Hall and O'Toole 2004).

Table 9.4 Actions undertaken by procedural authoritative instruments

---

Problem identification
Mobilizing interest
Spanning and bridging activities
Claims-making
Knowledge acquisition
Convening and deliberating
Community capacity-building
Transparency, evaluation and feedback

Source: Adapted from Phillips, S. D. and M. Orsini. 2002. 'Mapping the Links: Citizen Involvement in Policy Processes'. Ottawa: Canadian Policy Research Networks.

Phillips and Orsini (2002) list the types of policy process activities which advisory committees undertake (see Table 9.4).

Several distinct types of authoritative network management tools can be identified in this group. Prominent ones include the following list.

Advisory councils

Advisory councils are the best example of procedural authoritative instruments and are very common in market and corporatist governance arrangements. These are more or less permanent bodies established to provide advice to governments – either political-executive or administrative – on an ongoing basis. They are often established on a sectoral (e.g., industry specific such as an automobile trade advisory committee) basis, but also can be topical (e.g., biomedical ethics) (Gill 1940; Brown 1955; Smith 1977). These committees play a major role in many areas but are especially prominent in areas of new technologies where they play a significant role in linking governments to various kinds of expert or 'epistemic' communities (Haas 1992; Jasanoff 1998; Heinrichs 2005; Dunlop 2009a).

The archetypal advisory council is a more or less permanent body used to institutionalize interest group members in government deliberations (Heinrichs 2005). They are at least partially if not fully co-optive in nature

Table 9.5 Types of advisory committees

1	General advisory committees – to discuss policy alternatives generated by government, comment on current policies, examine trends and needs and suggest alternatives to status quo
2	Science and technology advisory committees – to provide expert advice in narrow specialist areas
3	Special clientele advisory committees – to assist governments to make and implement policies in special sectors of the economy or society
4	Research advisory committees – lengthy, research-oriented to tackle large questions
5	Public conferences – e.g., citizens' assemblies, national forest congresses, etc.
6	Geographic-based advisory committees – to deal with geographic particularities, e.g., in agriculture
7	Intergovernmental advisory committees – to co-ordinate between government levels
8	Interdepartmental committees – to achieve vertical and horizontal coordination in government

Sources: Adapted from Smith, T. B. 'Advisory Committees in the Public Policy Process'. *International Review of Administrative Sciences* 43, no. 2 (1977):153–66; Brown-John, C. L. 'Advisory Agencies in Canada: An Introduction'. *Canadian Public Administration* 22, no. 1 (1979): 72–91.

and intended to align the ideas and actions of the regulated group and the government ministry to which they are attached. However, they can also be more standalone and independent sources of expert advice to governments such as science and technology councils, councils of economic advisors and others (Phidd 1975; Doern 1971).

Smith (1977) and Brown-John (1979) identify eight main types of advisory committees commonly found in modern liberal-democratic governments. These are set out in Table 9.5.

Brown (1955) lists several purposes of such bodies which stress their network nature (see Table 9.6).

These boards are generally very inexpensive and almost invisible. They can be precisely targeted and enhance the automaticity of government. They are also viewed, generally, as non-intrusive. As a result, they have proliferated in all governments in recent years. This proliferation has led in some countries to the passage of legislation to control and standardize the number of advisory

Table 9.6 Purposes of advisory boards

1	Source of advice
2	A source of support for regulators
3	A means of popularizing a regulatory regime
4	A 'listening post' for industry and government to listen to each other
5	A means of reaching an agreement and resolving conflicts between government and interests
6	An agency for special inquiries
7	A device for patronage
8	A set of ambassadors for an administrative agency

Source: Adapted from Brown, D. S. 'The Public Advisory Board as an Instrument of Government'. *Public Administration Review* 15 (1955): 196–201.

Table 9.7 US Advisory Committee Act (1972) criteria.

1	Written charter explaining role of committee
2	Timely notice of committee meetings in Federal register
3	Fair and balanced representation on committees
4	Sponsoring agencies prepare minutes of meetings
5	Open committee meetings to the public wherever possible
6	Provide public access to information used by the committee
7	Government given sole authority to convene and adjourn meetings
8	Committees terminated in two years unless renewed or otherwise provided by statute

Source: Adapted from Smith, T. B. 'Advisory Committees in the Public Policy Process'. *International Review of Administrative Sciences* 43, no. 2 (1977): 153–66.

committees and their behaviour. The US Advisory Committee Act (1972), for example, specifies membership and guidelines and standard operating procedures for these types of committees (Brown 1955; Cronin and Thomas 1970; Brown 1972; Smith 1977; Heinrichs 2005) (see Table 9.7).

Public consultation, stakeholder and consensus conferences

In addition to more permanent bodies, governments can also organize short-term and long-range mechanisms to provide input and legitimate government policy-making (Leroux et al. 1998). Increasingly, the role of the public in these processes has been expanded to include participation in the design of the consultation process as well as in making policy recommendations to the government (Abelson et al. 2003; Dryzek and Tucker 2008). Sometimes mandated by legislation, appropriate levels of government will often elicit public involvement in administrative activities such as regulatory monitoring and environmental impact assessment.

Abelson et al. (2003) have noted that these participation efforts can be classified by looking at the procedures, representation and information involved and by looking at their outcomes. Key issues in the design of consultative processes are first who is involved and who is not (e.g., whether elites or the public are involved; or whether only stakeholders rather than the public, per se, are consulted) and who makes this determination, for example, government or representative groups (Howlett 1990).

Many of these efforts are structured as 'stakeholder' representative groups, but 'stakeholder' is a very poorly defined term. Glicken (2000: 306), for example, defines it very broadly as: 'A stakeholder is an individual or group influenced by – and with an ability to significantly impact (either directly or indirectly) – the topical areas of interest'. It is also critical what resources they have, such as access to funding; access to staff; access to politicians; access to information; or access to witnesses (Salter and Slaco 1981); and

Table 9.8 Types of public consultation – design criteria

---

1 From the point of view of publicity: how private and secret these consultations are, versus public, open and transparent
2 From the point of view of official status: whether consultations are unofficial, semi-official, or official
3 From the point of view of origin: whether the consultations are 'organic' (traditional) or 'inorganic' (imposed)
4 From the point of view of imperiousness: whether participation is optional or compulsory

---

Source: Adapted from Dion, L. 'The Politics of Consultation'. Government and Opposition 8, no. 3 (1973): 332–53.

whether or not their recommendations are binding (Webler and Tuler 2000; Margerum 2008). Dion lists several of these design criteria on several conjoint continua in Table 9.8.

These consultations can cover an extraordinarily wide range of topics – from constitutional issues related to voting systems and the like (Kogan 2010) to much more mundane ones such as city zoning changes. They are typically organized by private government agencies, although in some jurisdictions, such as Australia, consultants specializing in the organization and delivery of consultation exercises have become much more prominent in recent years (Hendriks and Carson 2008).

Conclusion: regulation – a very flexible instrument

The evolution of regulation as a key policy instrument in the toolbox of modern government is a well-known story. From the development of the principle of delegated legislation in the early years of the evolution of the modern state (Page 2001; Gilardi 2002; Thatcher and Stone-Sweet 2003) to the first creation of specialized quasi-judicial independent regulatory commissions in the USA after the Civil War (Huntington 1952; Eisner 1994a,b), the gradual development of bureaucratic expertise and capacity in the social and economic realms is a defining characteristic of the legal and corporatist modes of governance found in many policy sectors and a central feature in many policy designs (Berg 2000; Howlett 2002b; Howlett 2004b; Scherer 2008).

Debates about the merits of this development continue in many areas, however, especially those sectors which could be organized along market lines. For example, a large literature exists on whether or not regulations serve the public or the private interest (Posner 1974; Stigler 1975a) and whether or not they contribute to economic efficiency by correcting market failures (Croley 2007) or instead create new government ones (Wolf 1979, 1987; Le Grand 1991; Zerbe and McCurdy 1999). The discussion has generated a plethora of studies about the merits of particular types of regulation over others (Hawkins and Thomas 1989; Williams 2000; Ringquist et al. 2003), the problems of regulatory capture (Laffont and Tirole 1991) and the difficulties of legislative and judicial oversight of regulatory activities (de Smith 1973; Angus 1974; McCubbins and Schwartz 1984; McCubbins and Lupia 1994; Gilardi 2005a).

This discussion has often led to the linking of specific instrument choices to larger issues such as levels of trust in government (Levy and Spiller 1994) and other aspects of administrative traditions and governance modes (see McAllister 2009; Kagan 2001; Klijn et al. 2010). A general tendency to shift regulatory activity from enforcement to persuasion has been noted but also with significant variations by nation and sector (Pautz 2009; McAllister et al. 2010) as governments attempt to deal with the nature of targets and their behaviour in complex coercion–avoidance–persuasion games (Scholz 1984, 1991).

The early 1980s was a turning point in the debate on regulation in many countries, as the idea that regulations were conceived and executed solely in the public interest came under heavy attack from a wide range of critics. Much of this criticism relied heavily on works by authors and economists of the Chicago (Stigler 1971; Peltzman 1976; Becker 1983) and Virginia (Posner 1974; Landes and Posner 1975; Buchanan and Tollison 1984; Tollison 1991) schools of political economy who argued that many regulations were inefficient as well as inequitable. Governments led by right-wing politicians in many countries, such as Ronald Reagan in the USA and Margaret Thatcher in the UK, but also Labor governments in New Zealand and elsewhere, further fanned popular sentiment against regulations by putting deregulation and the search for alternatives to traditional 'command and control' regulation at the center of policy reform agendas designed to address declines in productivity and persistent inflation and high unemployment present at the time (Howlett and Ramesh 2006). Many governments began at this time to experiment with forms of 'voluntary regulation'.

Many 'deregulation' measures, however, are common sense reforms intended to iron out shortcomings, anomalies and obsolescence in existing regulations rather than a response to any particular systemic pressure (Wilson 2003). The nature and extent of problems change, as do solutions available to deal with them (Frischtak 1995). The campaign for removal or at least weakening of such regulations is often led by businesses which find complying with them in new technological environments to be onerous. Their efforts find ready support among voters who have their own reasons for disaffection with outdated, inappropriate and seemingly meaningless regulations which can impose costs on them for various services – such as telephones and television – which seem unwarranted. The regulators' frustration with the costs of their implementation further reinforces calls for reform.

Understanding why deregulation occurs has proved to be a challenge to regulatory theorists, since many of the imperatives regarded as the source of regulation – such as industry collusion and the desire to retain market share through the erection of barriers to entry to new firms – continue to be vital in the deregulatory context (Crew and Rowley 1986). Some analysts have therefore searched for exogenous causes – such as foreign or technical pressures for regulatory harmonization (Derthick and Quirk 1985; Libecap 1986; Quirk 1988; Lazer and Mayer-Schonberger 2002; Garcia-Murillo 2005).

However, it must also be noted that at the same time that some deregulation has occurred, re-regulation of many sectors has also taken place. And, as the discussion in this chapter has shown, an explosion of the use of procedural authoritative implementation tools has also occurred. While some of this activity can be traced to attempts to shift governance modes in various sectors, it is also the case that changes have occurred as policy design ideas have changed, given different configurations of costs and other instrument attributes in some sectors, sometimes undermining long established policy styles and policy-making routines.

Readings

Bryson, J. M. and B. C. Crosby. (1993). 'Policy Planning and the Design and Use of Forums, Arenas, and Courts'. In B. Bozeman (ed.), *Public Management: The State of the Art*. San Francisco, CA: Jossey-Bass, 323–44.

Cantor, R., S. Henry and S. Rayner. (1992). *Making Markets: An Interdisciplinary Perspective on Economic Exchange*. Westport, CT: Greenwood Press.

Cook, D. (2002). 'Consultation, for a Change? Engaging Users and Communities in the Policy Process'. *Social Policy and Administration* 36, no. 5: 516–31.

Cordes, J. J. (2002). 'Corrective Taxes, Charges and Tradable Permits'. In L. M. Salamon (ed.), *The Tools of Government: A Guide to the New Governance*. New York: Oxford University Press, 255–81.

Crew, M. A. and C. K. Rowley. (1986). 'Deregulation as an Instrument in Industrial Policy'. *Journal of Institutional and Theoretical Economics* 142: 52–70.

Doern, G. B. (2004). 'Institutional and Public Administrative Aspects of Voluntary Codes'. In K. Webb (ed.), *Voluntary Codes: Private Governance, the Public Interest and Innovation*. Ottawa, ON: Carleton Research Unit on Innovation, Science and Environment, 57–76.

Eisner, M. A. (1994). 'Economic Regulatory Policies: Regulation and Deregulation in Historical Context'. In D. H. Rosenbloom and R. D. Schwartz (eds), *Handbook of Regulation and Administrative Law*. New York: Marcel Dekker, 91–116.

Hall, T. E. and L. J. O'Toole. (2004). 'Shaping Formal Networks through the Regulatory Process'. *Administration and Society* 36, no. 2: 186–207.

Heinrichs, H. (2005). 'Advisory Systems in Pluralistic Knowledge Societies: A Criteria-Based Typology to Assess and Optimize Environmental Policy Advice'. In S. Maasen and P. Weingart (eds), *Democratization of Expertise? Exploring Novel Forms of Scientific Advice in Political Decision-Making*. Dordrecht, Netherlands: Springer, 41–61.

Keyes, J. M. (1996). 'Power Tools: The Form and Function of Legal Instruments for Government Action'. *Canadian Journal of Administrative Law and Practice* 10: 133–74.

Lowndes, V. and C. Skelcher. (1998). 'The Dynamics of Multi-Organizational Partnerships: An Analysis of Changing Modes of Governance'. *Public Administration* 76, Summer: 313–33.

McCubbins, M. D., R. G. Noll and B. R. Weingast. (1987). 'Administrative Procedures as Instruments of Political Control'. *Journal of Law, Economics, and Organization* 3, no. 2: 243–77.

Mitchell, R. K., B. R. Agle and D. J. Wood. (1997). 'Toward a Theory of Stakeholder Identification and Salience: Defining the Principle of Who and What Really Counts'. *Academy of Management Review* 22, no. 4: 853–86.

Pal, L. A. (1993). *Interests of State: The Politics of Language, Multiculturalism, and Feminism in Canada*. Kingston, ON: McGill-Queen's University Press.

Phillips, S. D. (1991). 'How Ottawa Blends: Shifting Government Relationships with Interest Groups'. In F. Abele (ed.), *How Ottawa Spends 1991–92: The Politics of Fragmentation*. Ottawa, ON: Carleton University Press, 183–228.

Pierre, J. (1998). 'Public Consultation and Citizen Participation: Dilemmas of Policy Advice'. In B. G. Peters, and D. J. Savoie (eds), *Taking Stock: Assessing Public Sector Reforms*. Montreal, QC: McGill-Queen's Press, 137–63.

Salamon, L. A. (2002). 'Economic Regulation'. In L. M. Salamon (ed.), *The Tools of Government: A Guide to the New Governance*. New York: Oxford University Press, 117–55.

Sovacool, B. K. (2011). 'The Policy Challenges of Tradable Credits: A Critical Review of Eight Markets'. *Energy Policy* 39, no. 2 (February): 575–85.

Townsend, R. E., J. McColl and M. D. Young. (2006). 'Design Principles for Individual Transferable Quotas'. *Marine Policy* 30: 131–41.

West, W. (2005). 'Administrative Rulemaking: An Old and Emerging Literature'. *Public Administration Review* 65, no. 6: 655–68.

Wu, I. (2008). 'Who Regulates Phones, Television, and the Internet? What Makes a Communications Regulator Independent and Why It Matters?' *Perspectives on Politics* 6, no. 4: 769–83.

Chapter 10

Financial implementation tools

Financial substantive tools are not synonymous with all government spending since much of this goes to fund direct service delivery and also support regulatory agencies (as well as to provide information, which will be discussed in Chapter 11). Rather, such tools are specific techniques of governance involved in transferring treasure resources to or from other actors in order to encourage them to undertake some activity desired by governments through the provision of financial incentives or to discourage them through the imposition of financial costs.

Like organizational and authoritative tools, there are many different permutations of these instruments and mechanisms. In fact, they can be calibrated down to the decimal point, since they involve the transfer of money or goods and services with a calculable dollar value, between governments and between governments and non-governmental actors and organizations. And, as such, their exact configuration is virtually infinite in variety. Nevertheless, like organizational and authority-based tools, their basic types are few and categorizable according to what kind of treasure resource they rely upon to extract expected behaviour from targeted organizations, groups and individuals. Transfers can be either in cash or tax-based but also can be made through a wide range of 'cash equivalents', for example, procurement, loan guarantees, insurance, or vouchers among others. Both principal types and some of the many alternate means and variations are discussed below.

Substantive financial instruments

The use of treasure resources in policy designs in order to allow states to obtain their substantive goals is very common and is compatible with several modes of governance, but especially market-based ones. Modern liberal democratic states spend billions annually on many different programmes involving the use of these tools. However, in some areas, such as industrial activity, some efforts have been made in recent years – through provisions of free trade treaties and the like – to restrict their use. These efforts have been only partially successful, though, often resulting in the transformation of cash-based incentives and disincentives to other forms of financial tools rather than their complete abandonment.

Cash-based financial tools

Grants, subsidies and user fees

Haider defines grants as 'payments in cash or in kind (or charges) to lower units of government, non-profits or profit-seeking companies, NGOs (and individuals) to support public purposes' (Haider 1989: 94). All substantive grants are subsidies or 'unearned savings to offset production costs' and are one of the oldest forms of the financial tools through which governments pay companies, organizations, or individuals to do (or not to do – such as agricultural subsidies for not growing corn or wheat, etc.) some (un)desired form of activity (Lybecker and Freeman 2007). This is the 'carrot' in instrument and implementation models based on the idea of the use of 'carrots and sticks' (regulations or penalties by governments in their efforts to influence non-governmental actors). Many, many such schemes exist, from the use of Feed-in-Tariffs to promote the use of renewable energy supplies such as solar panels and wind power (DeShazo et al. 2017) to the payment of cash to parents to send their children to school in various kinds of 'Conditional Cash Transfers' or CCTs found in countries from the Philippines to Brazil and Ghana (Brooks 2015).

User fees are the most straightforward financial disincentive (one of the 'sticks' available to governments) as they, too, simply affect target behaviour by increasing the cost of doing some action. While straightforward in principle, however, in practice their design can be quite complex depending on exactly what it is that governments wish to accomplish through their imposition, for example, revenue generation, goods or service rationing or some combination of the two, and how non-governmental actors are likely to react to such charges (Deber et al. 2008).

These kinds of cash-based tools use the direct transfer of treasure resources from governments to some other actor in the form of monetary payments. They vary along several dimensions. They can, to cite only a few examples, be large or small; a single instance or multi-year in nature; tax deductible (which increases their size) or not; used alone or in combination with other instruments (for instance, in conjunction with the use of public enterprises in regional development programmes); matched or not by recipients; or linked to some other item (e.g., a per capita grant) (Woodside 1979; Leeuw 1998; Haider 1989). They typically can be very precisely targeted down to the level of the individual and individual firm or plant and can be very precisely calibrated. They are also quite visible as they appear in public accounts and are considered to be more intrusive than information-based tools, but less so than authority or organization-based ones. They can also be designed in such a way as to enhance their automaticity, although this is more the case with tax- and royalty-based payments, as discussed below.

Tax- or royalty-based financial instruments

The second main type of substantive treasure-based instrument involves those which are based not on direct cash transfers, but rather on indirect transfers mediated through the tax system, or in some countries, through the use of royalty systems designed to capture natural resource rents. In these systems, a government can forego tax or royalty income they would otherwise have collected from an individual, organization, or firm, which serves as an incentive to targets to undertake the activity receiving favorable tax treatment; or, in the case of tools which increase taxes on certain kinds of activity, to not undertake that activity or to undertake less of it.

Tax- and royalty-based expenditures

Tax expenditures or 'tax incentives' come in many kinds. Maslove defines them as 'special provisions in the tax law providing for preferred treatment and consequently resulting in revenue losses (or gains)' (Maslove 1978; Surrey 1979). These can be 'paid in advance' and can be carried forward for numbers of years and, like cash-based schemes, can be 'matched' by other sources of funds, range in size and significance and can be used in conjunction with other instruments.

Different subtypes exist depending on 'where' government tax reve is forgone. *Tax incentives* generally involve deductions from corporate o personal income, meaning their actual effect on a target group is determined by the marginal rate of taxation individual persons or firms must pay. Their effect, therefore, varies from group to group. *Tax credits,* on the other hand, are direct deductions from taxes owed and therefore their size is the same regardless of the tax rates individual taxpayer's face. Tax credits are typically the only ones which can be 'negative', in the sense that they can be used to push a taxpayer's tax load beyond zero so that a refund (or real cash transfer) may ensue. However, most tax expenditures will only push a taxpayer's tax to zero, meaning their effect also remains conditional on the amount of tax targets pay.

These same schemes can also be developed with transfers from non-tax based revenue in mind, such as resource royalty payments or other forms of economic rents. Governments often, for example, promote oil and gas exploration by allowing energy companies to write off some portion of their exploration costs against royalties they would otherwise have to pay.

Excise taxes

Excise taxes are another treasure-based tool, one that acts as a disincentive for individuals, organizations and groups to undertake specific actions and activities. Cnossen (2005: 2) defines these as 'all selective taxes and related levies and charges on goods and services'. They have several general purposes: (1) to raise revenue for general purposes, (2) to offset 'external costs', (3) to discourage consumption and (4) to pay for public goods (Nowlan 1994).

Raising revenue through taxes is, of course, the oldest technique of government practiced, from taxes placed on-road use by the Romans to the tea tax US colonists rebelled against at the Boston Tea Party.

In this form, excise taxes typically support legal modes of governance. Using taxes to offset costs of production – to pay for pollution cleanup or health consequences of tobacco use in order to correct production or consumption 'externalities' such as pollution or carbon emissions or ill-health which otherwise would be passed onto the general public – is a much newer form and is more compatible with market governance modes (Mandell 2008; Toke 2008; Pope and Owen 2009). A similar effort involves so-called 'vice taxes' for activities such as gambling, alcohol consumption, lotteries, or more frequently in recent years, various forms of 'virtuous' 'green' taxes such as those designed to cover the cost of recycling car batteries or used oil or paint, or even returnable bottle deposits, all designed to offset the social costs of the activities concerned (Cnossen 2005; Eloi 2009). The use of motor fuel taxes to cover the cost of road construction or mass transit is an example of the fourth of Nowlan's purposes.

Such taxes generally discourage the taxed activity by raising its price. This, of course, can be a mixed blessing for activities such as public transit and can often result in unintended consequences for items taxed in order to raise revenues, both in terms of taxpayer resistance and upset and in the unintended encouragement of the increased use of non-taxed items or substitute goods and services such as an increase in motorcycle use if cars are taxed. They are generally inexpensive to establish, although they require an extensive revenue collection and enforcement presence to avoid evasion and can be either highly visible, if added on to prices, or almost invisible if included with posted prices. They can be targeted to specific kinds of goods and services and set up to be highly automated. They are generally considered to be quite intrusive by those paying them, however, which is the main reason they are often excluded from policy designs.

Cash or tax-equivalent financial tools

Both cash and tax or royalty-based transfers provide financial incentives and disincentives to policy actors to undertake or refrain from undertaking specific activities encouraged or discouraged by governments. However, such encouragement and discouragement do not always require a direct or indirect cash transfer. Governments are also able to provide financial incentives through the much less direct use of their spending powers to offset costs or provide additional benefits to policy targets. Several of the more prominent of these tools are discussed below.

Preferential procurement

Preferential procurement involves the use of government purchases to subsidize companies or investors which agree to abide by specific provisions of government contracts. These can extend to preferential treatment for firms which, for example, employ the disabled or women, or ethnic or linguistic minorities, but also often extend to special favorable treatment for small business; national defense contractors; and regional development schemes in which investors receive government contracts if they agree to locate factories or distribution or other services in specially designated regions (Bajari and Tadelis 2001; Rolfstam 2009).

Such procurement schemes play a major part in efforts by governments to promote 'third sector' or volunteer and community group-based delivery of public services and are often a part of corporatist governance arrangements. In many cases, it may be illegal or unconstitutional for a government to directly deliver funding to such groups, especially since many have a religious or 'faith base' which can violate constitutional limits separating church and state activities (Dollery and Wallis 2003; Black et al. 2004; Kissane 2007; Hula et al. 2007; Zehavi 2008). However, these groups may still be able to receive favorable treatment such as in bidding for government contracts, making procurement an important part of their funding base and of efforts to enhance their policy delivery capacity (Carmel and Harlock 2008; Chapman et al. 2008; Diamond 2008; Hasan and Onyx 2008; Walsh et al. 2008).

Like direct cash subsidies, many trade agreements attempt to ban procurement plans which favor national over international suppliers but these provisions do not extend to favorable treatment for marginalized groups or individuals. Such procurement schemes, of course, by extending favorable treatment to some contractors also act as a disincentive to non-favored groups and firms which are discouraged from bidding for contracts and other services to the extent of the subsidy provided (McCrudden 2004). The main advantage of such forms of subsidy over other forms of payments is their low visibility profile, which encourages their use.

Favorable insurance and loan guarantees

Insurance or loan guarantees also act as a subsidy to the extent that government backing helps to secure loans thereby raising the reliability of borrowers, altering the types of borrowers who might otherwise not qualify for loans, or reducing interest payments and charges that individuals and companies would otherwise have to pay (Maslove 1983). The difference in cost constitutes a subsidy.

Such guarantees are very common in areas such as student loans, for example, in which governments agree to serve as the guarantor of loans to banks which otherwise would reject most students as too risky. They are also common in areas such as export development, whereby a government may provide insurance to a domestic firm to help it offset the risk of undertaking some action in a foreign country, or provide a foreign company or government with assurance that a contract will be fulfilled by the supplying firm.

Some loans can also be made directly to individuals and firms on a 'conditionally repayable' basis; that is, whereby a loan turns into a grant if the conditions are successfully met, for example, in making housing payments. These tools are almost invisible, can be precisely targeted and are often considered to be less intrusive than grants and direct cash or tax transfers, making them a popular choice for policy designs in sectors in which governments are pursuing market modes of governance.

Vouchers for public services

Vouchers are 'money replacements' provided by governments to certain groups in order to allow them to purchase specified goods and services in specific amounts. These are typically used when a government does not trust someone to use a cash transfer for its intended purpose, for example, with vouchers for food (food stamps), child care, or welfare hotel/housing payments.

Some governments such as Denmark and Sweden, however, also use these to provide some freedom of choice for consumers to select particular kinds of public services (usually education) in order to promote competition within monopoly provision systems or to allow equitable funding arrangements between providers based on specific attributes – such as schools provided by different religious denominations (Le Grand 2007; Andersen 2008; Klitgaard 2008). These can lead to grey markets (when food stamps, for example, are sold at a discount to 'undeserving' recipients) and may not improve service delivery if there is little choice provided in the supply of goods and services for which vouchers are issued (Valkama and Bailey 2001). As a result, although often mooted, vouchers appear only rarely in policy designs.

Sales of state assets at below market prices

Governments can also sell off or 'rent out' certain items – from the TV and radio spectrum to old or surplus equipment, buildings and land. If prices are set below market rates then this is a subsidy to investors and businesses, etc. (Sunnevag 2000). Many privatizations of formerly state-owned firms in collapsed socialist countries in the 1990s, for example, involved this kind of sale, including for lucrative mineral and oil and gas rights, which made billions of dollars for the many former officials who were often favored in these deals (Newbery 2003). Given the costs involved and their generally high profile, however, this tool also does not feature very often in policy designs in countries which are stable and solvent.

Procedural financial instruments

Treasure resources, of course, just as organizational and authoritative ones, can also be used to alter the nature of policy processes. Procedural financial tools are generally used to attempt to alter or control aspects of the interest articulation and aggregation systems in contemporary states by creating or encouraging the formation of associations and groups where this activity might not otherwise occur, or, more prosaically, by rewarding government friends and punishing enemies through various kinds of payment schemes or penalties.

Phillip Schmitter, in his comparative studies of European systems, argued that the interest articulation systems in different countries form a spectrum from 'free market', 'competitive' pluralism to 'state-sponsored oligarchic corporatism' (see Figure 10.1). In Schmitter's (1977, 1985) view pluralism is a system of interest articulation in which interest groups are 'free-forming', have voluntary membership and are multiple and non-monopolistic/ competitive. That is, more than one group can represent individual members. This closely approximates the situation with network and market governance regimes at the sectoral level.

Corporatist regimes are the opposite – they require state licensing, have compulsory membership and are monopolistic. Corporatism was the official fascist mode of social organization. In order to avoid this association and connotation, modern studies tend to use the term 'neocorporatism' to distinguish modern forms of (liberal-democratic) corporatism found in states such as Austria or Sweden from older ones – though examples also exist of this form in liberal-democratic states in crises, for example, during wartime or, during the Great Depression-era Rooseveltian New Deal. Other variants also exist, such as, for example, consociationalism – where corporatist systems exist but divisions are on ethnic or religious grounds (e.g., The Netherlands); or 'concertations' (France) where there is more pluralism in some areas than others (e.g., social vs economic planning); or 'parentela pluralism' (Atkinson and Coleman 1989a) where divisions are partisan (e.g., Italy) (Lijphart 1969; Lehmbruch 1979).

Until recently, interest group theorists in North America claimed it was largely pluralist (Bentley 1908; Truman 1964) whereby it was argued that interest group formation was a quasi-automatic, 'naturalistic process' in which state activity was minimal. The empirical basis for this assessment, however, was lacking (see Mancur Olson 1965; Salisbury 1969; Bachrach and Baratz 1970; and especially Jack Walker 1991 and later Anthony Nownes

2000). Neo-pluralism is a modern version of pluralism which takes into account some state activity in this area and can be considered the analog of legal governance at the sectoral level.

Olson's (1965) view of the 'collective action problems' interest groups face in these different governance contexts is an important insight helpful to understanding the rationales for the government use of procedural financial instrument in these situations. Olson argued that in any political system, some individuals have fewer incentives and more disincentives to form and join interest groups than others – for example, someone benefiting from some proposed government action might have a stronger motivation to lobby for it, than would someone who stood neither to gain nor suffer from it. As a result, in a 'free association' system, there would be a tendency for specific affected interests – for example, businesses negatively affected by regulation– to form groups and pressure governments, while other more general interests – for example, to retain tough environmental standards on industry – would be poorly represented. Due to this unequal distribution of the costs and benefits of political action, in many issue areas, Olson argued, in pluralist systems 'general interest' groups were unlikely to form, or if they did would be quickly captured by 'special interests' who had more to gain from their existence and activities (Strolovitch 2006).

Olson had the idea that this could be overcome by providing 'selective incentives' for membership in mass groups – a practice followed, for example, by many environmental groups who offer a variety of services and free goods, such as calendars and book discounts, to attract and retain members. More recent works, however, point to the significance of a variety of factors in the process of group creation, such as the nature of a country's associational rights, the existence of 'focusing events' raising the public profile of an issue and especially the presence of outside funds for seed money, as key factors in the creation and growth of interest groups.

Governments, can play a major, though little studied, role in affecting this general pattern of interest group behaviour by either encouraging or discouraging interest group formation and activity. These activities are little known but quite common in many countries. Governments can do this, for example, by creating (or not) systems of associational rights which allow groups to form, using their actions and resources to publicize events and issues and providing funds for the creation and maintenance of groups. Procedural financial tools are key ones used to affect these kinds of interest group system behaviour.

These tools generally fall into two types, those which are used to create or help support the formation of interest groups and those which help to

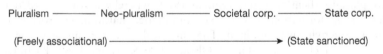

Figure 10.1 Spectrum of interest articulation systems

activate or mobilize them. The latter can be thought as 'network creation tools' while the latter can be considered as 'network mobilization tools'.

Financial policy network creation tools

Although their activities in this domain are often hidden from view, governments practicing network and corporatist governance modes are very often actively involved in the creation and organization of policy networks and many key policy actors. An important activity in this regard is the use of government financial resources to create either the organizations themselves which go into the establishment of a policy network – research institutes, think tanks, government departments and the like – or to facilitate the interaction of already existing but separate units into a more coherent network structure (Hudson et al. 2007).

Funding is very often provided to think tanks and other policy research units and brokers by governments, either in the form of direct funding or as contracts (Rich 2004; Abelson 2007). More controversial, however, and at the same time not very well understood, is the role governments play in funding interest groups (Anheier et al. 1997).

Interest group creation

Provision of seed money is a key factor in interest group creation (Nownes 2004). King and Walker (1991), for example, found that the percentage of groups that received aid from outside groups in startups in the USA was 34 percent for profit sector groups, non-profit 60 percent and citizens' groups 89 percent. Nownes and Neeley (1996) surveyed 121 national public interest groups in the USA in the mid-1990s and uncovered a pattern of extensive foundation support in terms of how their origin was financed (Table 10.1). While this survey revealed no direct government involvement, it did show that foundations provided a large percentage of the funding for pressure group creation and since these operate under special tax treatment in the USA, this gives the US federal government a substantial indirect role in interest group creation in that country (Lowry 1999; Carmichael 2008).

In other countries, however, a much more direct role is played by governments, sometimes also with a substantial indirect role through foundations, but sometimes not. In Canada, for example, Pal (1993) noted that many of the prominent national interest groups in specific sectors, such as the Canadian Day Care Advocacy Association, the Canadian Congress for Learning Opportunities among Women, the Canadian Ethnocultural Council and others had emerged from conferences and workshops organized by federal government departments in the 1980s and 1990s (see also Finkle et al. 1994). Similar results can be found in many other jurisdictions. This activity is generally low profile and inexpensive, but can be considered intrusive and

Table 10.1 Average percentage of 'seed money' obtained by groups from each source by group type

Source	Type of group (%)				
	Patronage	Societal disturbance	Personal disturbance	Splinter	Generic entrepreneurial
Foundations	38	38	0	23	19
The government	0	0	0	0	0
Corporations	0	1	17	3	2
Other					
Associations	32	11	3	0	2
Individuals	19	18	3	28	29
Personal funds	0	31	60	43	43
Other*	11	1	17	3	5
Total	100	100	100	100	100
n	10	12	6	16	16

Note: * Includes loans, merchandise sales, fees for service and special events.

Source: Adapted from Nownes, A. and G. Neeley. 'Toward an Explanation for Public Interest Group Formation and Proliferation: 'Seed Money', Disturbances, Entrepreneurship and Patronage'. *Policy Studies Journal* 24, no. 1 (1996): 74–92.

is not all that easily targeted, making it a less popular instrument in policy designs than network mobilization (see below). However, where interest groups do not exist, governments may have little choice but to facilitate their creation if they wish to practice a network or corporatist form of governance.

Financial network mobilization tools

A second key type of activity undertaken by governments through the use of procedural financial policy tools relates less to the creation of new groups and networks than to the reorientation of older, already existing ones. Again, in the case of think tanks and other such actors, this can be accomplished through various forms of government contracting and procurement, notably consulting (Speers 2007). A significant target for this kind of funding, however, is interest groups.

Interest group alteration/manipulation/co-optation

Cash funds or the tax system are used in many countries to alter interest group behaviour. The aim may be simply to neutralize or co-opt a vocal opponent of government (Kash 2008), but can also be a more broad-based effort to 'even out the playing field' for groups which lack the kinds of resources available to other groups (such as business) to mobilize and pressure governments to adopt policies of which they approve (Furlong and Kerwin 2004; Boehmke 2005).

Most business groups, as well as many others, prefer 'insider action' and only revert to 'outside agitation' in order to attract new members in a competitive situation with other groups (Binderkrantz 2005).

Designing these programmes can, therefore, be quite complex (Phillips et al. 2010). Governments often use this tool to counterbalance, for example, lobbying on the part of business interests.

Lowry (1999) found that two main types of foundations exist in the USA–company sponsored and independent – and both take active roles not only in interest group creation (discussed above) but also in funding interest group activities. In the USA in 1992, for example, he uncovered 463 grants made by 37 company foundations and 125 independent foundations just to environmental groups, $32.6 million from independent foundations versus only $1.5 million from company-sponsored foundations. Again, given the favorable tax treatment foundations enjoy in the USA, this gives the US government a substantial indirect role in interest group activity as well as their creation.

In other countries, as with interest group creation, foundations are less important and governments also provide 'sustaining' funding after groups are created. Stanbury, for example, examined the Canadian federal public accounts for 1986–87 and found 17 federal departments gave $185 million to over 500 groups (excluding non-policy groups like those providing shelters for battered women). Over 50 organizations in Stanbury's sample were funded by a single federal agency – the Federal Secretary of State–mainly in the area of multiculturalism.

Similarly, Pal found a total of $80 million going from the Federal Secretary of State to minority language groups over the period 1970–82, $50 million in 1978–82 alone while multicultural groups received over $125 million from 1976–88 and $94 million in 1983–88. Women's programmes received $63 from 1973–88 and $46 million over 1984–88 (Stasiulis 1988; Pal 1993; Stanbury 1993). Phillips (1991) found the Federal Secretary of State to have spent $130 million over much the same period on over 3,000 groups with 5 major areas accounting for about one-third of all recipients: 337 groups for official languages; 457 women's groups; 195 disabled groups; 160 aboriginal groups; and 175 multicultural groups.

A total of 160 of these groups were defined only as 'public interest groups' (or classical pressure groups) and received $24 million from federal departments alone that year. Burt (1990) similarly surveyed the sources of funding received by 144 women's groups (24 percent of the estimated 686 such groups in Canada at the time) in the early 1980s and found the government was the single largest donor by far for most types of groups, far outstripping membership dues (see Table 10.2).

Table 10.2 Source of funding for women's groups (Canada)

Most important source of funds	Type of group (%)			
	Traditional	Status of women	Service	Shelter
Government	33	40	38	52
Dues	8	20	9	0
Fund-raising	17	7	2	11
Other n/a	42	33	51	37
	100	100	100	100

Source: Adapted from Burt, Sandra. 'Canadian Women's Groups in the 1980s: Organizational Development and Policy Influence'. *Canadian Public Policy* 16, no. 1 (1990): 17–28.

In Europe, Mahoney and Beckstrand (2009) similarly identified 1,164 civil society groups that received funding from the European Commission in 2003–07. They shared in 120 million euros of funding at the EU level and another 75 million in international, national and sub-national-level funding. These were primarily groups operating at the EU level in areas such as youth, sports, education and cultural activities in support of the EC mandate to develop a supra-national EU civil society.

This funding is almost invisible, can be precisely targeted and although often considered intrusive in legal and market governance modes, is quite compatible with network and corporatist activities. As a result, it is a growing area and a prominent feature of many contemporary policy designs.

Conclusion: treasure – an effective but depletable resource

The use of financial resources is one of the oldest forms of government activity and instrument use. The use of substantive treasure-based instruments is quite common in designs and in terms of size and impact, it is as significant as direct government service delivery or regulation.

The use of this resource, as Hood (1983, 1986c) noted, is sometimes restricted by a lack of treasure resources, either because a country is poor and simply cannot generate revenue or, as has happened in jurisdictions such as California, for example, because of various measures which prevent or limit government access to substantial taxpayer wealth. However, notwithstanding these limitations, in general, all governments spend considerable sums encouraging certain activities and discouraging others through the use of various kinds of fiscal and monetary tools and techniques. An important trend in this area, as noted by Howard (1993, 1995, 1997), is toward the increased use of tax-based incentives rather than subsidies. This is due to a number of reasons but often reflects concerns with visibility and automaticity.

As for procedural financial tool uses, as mentioned above, the use of these techniques in sectors employing corporatist and network modes of governance is also increasing at a substantial rate, although the exact mechanisms used vary from country to country, such as the use of indirect foundations in the USA, compared to more direct government allocations in many other jurisdictions.

Readings

Bangalore, M., G. Hochman and D. Zilberman. (2016). 'Policy Incentives and Adoption of Agricultural Anaerobic Digestion: A Survey of Europe and the United States'. *Renewable Energy* 97 (November): 559–71.

Beam, D. A. and T. J. Conlan. (2002). 'Grants'. In L. M. Salamon (ed.), *The Tools of Government: A Guide to the New Governance*. New York: Oxford University Press, 340–80.

Brooks, S. M. (2015). 'Social Protection for the Poorest: The Adoption of Antipoverty Cash Transfer Programs in the Global South'. *Politics & Society* 43, no. 4 (1 December): 551–82.

Cnossen, S. (2005). 'Economics and Politics of Excise Taxation'. In S. Cnossen (ed.), *Theory and Practice of Excise Taxation: Smoking, Drinking, Gambling, Polluting and Driving*. Oxford: Oxford University Press, 1–19.

Cordes, J. J. (2002). 'Corrective Taxes, Charges and Tradable Permits'. In L. M. Salamon (ed.), *The Tools of Government: A Guide to the New Governance*. New York: Oxford University Press, 255–81.

Deber, R., M. J. Hollander and P. Jacobs. (2008). 'Models of Funding and Reimbursement in Health Care: A Conceptual Framework'. *Canadian Public Administration* 51, no. 3: 381–405.

DeShazo, J. R., T. L. Sheldon and R. T. Carson. (2017). 'Designing Policy Incentives for Cleaner Technologies: Lessons from California's Plug-In Electric Vehicle Rebate Program'. *Journal of Environmental Economics and Management* 84 (July): 18–43.

Howard, C. (2002). 'Tax Expenditures'. In L. M. Salamon (ed.), *The Tools of Government: A Guide to the New Governance*. New York: Oxford University Press, 410–44.

Juillet, L., C. Andrew, T. Aubry and J. Mrenica. (2001). 'The Impact of Changes in the Funding Environment on Nonprofit Organizations'. In K. L. Brock and K. G. Banting (eds), *The Nonprofit Sector and Government in a New Century*. Montreal, QC: McGill-Queen's University Press, 21–62.

Klitgaard, M. B. (2008). 'School Vouchers and the New Politics of the Welfare State'. *Governance* 21, no. 4: 479–98.

Leeuw, F. L. (1998). 'The Carrot: Subsidies as a Tool of Government'. In M.-L. Bemelmans-Videc, R. C. Rist and E. Vedung (eds), *Carrots, Sticks and Sermons: Policy Instruments and Their Evaluation*. New Brunswick, NJ: Transaction, 77–102.

Louhaichi, M., Y. A. Yigezu, J. Werner, L. Dashtseren, T. El-Shater and M. Ahmed. (2016). 'Financial Incentives: Possible Options for Sustainable Rangeland

Management?' *Journal of Environmental Management* 180 (15 September): 493–503.

Maddison, S. (2005). 'Democratic Constraint and Embrace: Implications for Progressive Non-Government Advocacy Organisations in Australia'. *Australian Journal of Political Science* 40, no. 3: 373–89.

Nownes, A. and G. Neeley. (1996). 'Toward an Explanation for Public Interest Group Formation and Proliferation: "Seed Money", Disturbances, Entrepreneurship, and Patronage'. *Policy Studies Journal* 24, no. 1: 74–92.

Pal, L. A. (1993). *Interests of State: The Politics of Language, Multiculturalism, and Feminism in Canada*. Kingston, ON: McGill-Queen's University Press.

Phillips, S. D. (1991). 'How Ottawa Blends: Shifting Government Relationships with Interest Groups'. In F. Abele (ed.), *How Ottawa Spends 1991–92: The Politics of Fragmentation*. Ottawa, ON: Carleton University Press, 183–228.

Sharpe, D. (2001). 'The Canadian Charitable Sector: An Overview'. In J. Phillips, B. Chapman and D. Stevens (eds), *Between State and Market: Essays on Charities Law and Policy in Canada*. Toronto, ON: University of Toronto Press.

Stanton, T. H. (2002). 'Loans and Loan Guarantees'. In L. M. Salamon (ed.), *The Tools of Government: A Guide to the New Governance*. New York: Oxford University Press, 381–409.

Surrey, S. S. (1970). 'Tax Incentives as a Device for Implementing Government Policy: A Comparison with Direct Government Expenditures'. *Harvard Law Review* 83, no. 4 (1 February): 705–38.

Woodside, K. (1979). 'Tax Incentives vs. Subsidies: Political Considerations in Governmental Choice'. *Canadian Public Policy* 5, no. 2: 248–56.

Wu, J. and A. Tal. (2017). 'From Pollution Charge to Environmental Protection Tax: A Comparative Analysis of the Potential and Limitations of China's New Environmental Policy Initiative'. *Journal of Comparative Policy Analysis: Research and Practice* (25 September): 1–14.

Chapter 11

Information-based implementation tools

Information-based tools are those based on the last of the four categories of resources set out by Hood (1986c): 'nodality' or 'centrality' or, as we have defined it, involved in communicating 'knowledge' or 'information' to target groups in the expectation this will alter their behaviour. These are the 'sermon' in the 'carrots, sticks and sermons' formulation of policy instruments.

Exactly what is meant by the term 'information' or 'communication', varies from author to author, ranging from its association with all forms of political activity (Deutsch 1963; Bang 2003) to a very specific focus on one type of action, like public service or political advertising (Firestone 1970; Young 2007). These different foci make classifying and analyzing the wide range of activities and tasks more difficult than it should be (Ledingham 2003).

As Evert Vedung defines them, information-based policy tools are 'efforts to use the knowledge and data available to governments to influence consumer and producer behaviour in a direction consistent with government aims and wishes and/or gather information in order to further their aims and ambitions' (Vedung and van der Doelen 1998).

This definition, however, while useful, is limited in that it conceals or elides the two different general purposes to which these tools can be put to use (Howlett et al. 2010). These are the familiar procedural versus substantive distinction used throughout this book – whether these activities are intended to serve as devices primarily oriented toward the manipulation of the behaviour of policy actors in policy processes (Edelman 1988; Saward 1992; Mikenberg 2001; Sulitzeanu-Kenan 2007) or as social and economic ones involved in and affecting the production, distribution and consumption of different types of goods and services (Hornik 1989; Salmon 1989a; 1989b; Jahn et al. 2005; Howlett 2009b). Disentangling the two is necessary in order to provide a clear analysis of the role each plays in policy designs.

It is also important to note that many new communication practices have emerged in recent years, at least in part due to the development of new information technologies, notably computerization and the internet (Feldman and Khademian 2007) which have broadened the range and menu of government nodality tools. These include the development and use of instruments which promote citizen empowerment such as freedom of information (FOI) legislation, the use of public performance measures, various forms of e- or 'digital' government and the increased use of government surveys and advertising among others (Hood and Margetts 2007).

Substantive informational instruments

Following Vedung's lead we can define substantive government communication policy instruments as those policy techniques or mechanisms which rely on the use of information to directly or indirectly affect the behaviour of those involved in the production, consumption and distribution of different kinds of goods and services in society.

The most high profile and thus most commonly observed and chronicled type of substantive tool is the instrument focused on the effort to alter consumer behaviour: the *government information campaign*. This includes various campaigns waged by governments to encourage citizens to, for example, eat well, engage in fewer vices and otherwise behave responsibly, which are common especially in market modes of governance.

However, communication activities aimed at altering producer behaviour through provision of product and process information to customers (*labeling and product information*) are also very prominent. As Hood (1986c) noted, these kinds of tools can be targeted at different levels of society – individuals, groups and populations as a whole and according to whether they are intended to collect or disseminate information.

Information dissemination tools

Information dissemination tools like public service advertizing are classic 'persuasion instruments' and are the most studied substantive information implementation tools. Adler and Pittle define these instruments as those 'persuasion schemes [which] convey messages which may or may not contain factual information which overtly seek to motivate target audiences to modify their behaviour' (Adler and Pittle 1984: 160). These tools are used often, as they are fairly inexpensive. However, they remain controversial as the line between communications and intrusive propaganda is one which is easily blurred and their effectiveness is difficult to gauge (Gelders and Ihlen 2009, 2010).

Exhortation and moral suasion

The most prominent type of substantive information tool designed to persuade is the appeal from political leaders to various social actors, urging them to follow a government's lead in some area of social or economic life. Stanbury and Fulton (1984) provide a list of 'exhortation' and 'moral suasion' activities which include 'pure political leadership such as appeals for calm, better behaviour, high principles and whereby voluntary action is urged under threat of coercion if refused' (304).

Such forms of 'moral suasion' are often specifically aimed or targeted at individual producers or sectors and are typically used within the context of an already existing regulatory regime. These can help governments regulate a variety of activities without necessarily creating new legal instruments in order to do so. Many countries, for example, administer important aspects of their financial systems in this fashion, asking banks, taxpayers and other financial institutions to act in a certain way (e.g., keep interest rates low, or allow certain groups to borrow funds) with the implicit or explicit threat of direct government regulation if such requests are ignored or go unfulfilled (Bardach 1989a). Government requests are often very focused and can be quite secretive (e.g., in the immediate aftermath of the 9/11 airline hijackings when the US government urged credit card companies to provide records of suspicious activities by suspected hijackers).

Information campaigns

Mass media and targeted information campaigns, on the other hand, are much more visible, by definition and tend to be aimed less at producers than at consumers. Adler and Pittle (1984) describe these tools as 'notification instruments' which:

> Convey factual information to the intelligent target. Implicit in the notification approach is the belief that the target, once apprised of the facts, will make the appropriate decision.

Some notification tools do attempt to be purely factual, ongoing and passive in nature, such as nutritional labeling on foodstuffs or health warnings on cigarettes (Padberg 1992; Baksi and Bose 2007). They are usually enacted in regulations (i.e., disclosure is mandatory) and are aimed at providing information to consumers allowing them to make better decisions, or overcome information asymmetries between producers and consumers, with the expectation that consumers will change their behaviour in some way consistent with government goals – for example, reducing smoking, exercising more, or eating nutritional foods rather than snacks (Jahn et al. 2005). Although the evidence of the effectiveness of such campaigns is mixed (Mann and Wustemann 2009; Barreiro-Hurlé et al. 2010), this has not dampened their growth.

Other information campaigns are more active and less factual, but have the same intent; that is, providing social actors with more information about aspects of their behaviour and its advantageous or deleterious quality, urging enhancement of the former and a diminishment of the latter. The information often transmitted through such information instruments is not always so factual, however, but can be used to 'sell' a government's policies in the same way that other products are marketed. Such campaigns are often conducted at the mass level and use a variety of mass-media delivery mechanisms (commercials, broadcasts, newspaper advertisements and the like). High profile campaigns in many countries to prevent drinking and driving or encourage the purchase of war bonds during wartime are good examples of the use of this kind of instrument.

This kind of mass campaign began with the emergence of mass media and is now common in most countries. Many national governments are now the largest purchasers of advertising in their countries and far outstrip national brands well known for their advertising overkill, such as alcoholic beverage and soft drink companies, as well as fast food chains. The federal government of Canada, for example, has been the largest advertiser in the country since 1976 (Stanbury et al. 1983) with the larger provincial governments in the top 10 as well. Ryan (1995) noted that federal advertising expanded from $3.4 million in 1968 to $106.5 million in 1992, a 3000 percent increase. Even inflation adjusted this amounted to a 665 percent increase in 25 years.

Specific national issue campaigns, however, can be very costly. Alasdair Roberts and Jonathan Rose (1995), for example, conducted an in-depth study of a mass media campaign conducted by the Federal Government of Canada to introduce a new goods and services tax (GST) in 1989–90. They found the federal Department of Finance to have spent $11.6 million on public education in a combined print/radio/TV campaign, $5 million on direct mail materials, $5 million on a call center; Revenue Canada (Customs) to have spent $10.6 million on advertising, $9.2 million on instructional material; Revenue Canada (Taxation) to have spent a further $28 million advertising a GST credit, while a specially created GST Consumer Information Office spent $7.4 million on advertising and $6.9 million on production. The total for this one campaign was $85 million. This was more than the largest private sector advertisers spent in all of 1989. For example, Proctor and Gamble, with its hundreds of consumer products, had a total advertising budget of $56.7 million. This has led to some calls in some countries for greater regulation or control on government advertising, but these proposals have shown few results (Young 2007).

Although they can be costly, such campaigns are generally less expensive than many other alternatives, although the costs of non-compliance must also be taken into account (Pellikaan and van der Veen 2002). Generally, governments will tend to include information tools and government communications in policy designs only when:

(1) 100 percent compliance is not required for a policy to be effective;
(2) government and public interests coincide (e.g., on health awareness) so that government appeals are likely to be favorably received; and
(3) only in relatively short-term crisis situations when other tools may require too much lead time to be effective; where
(4) it is otherwise difficult to impose sanctions and where
(5) the issue in question is not very complex (technological or legal) in nature but can be reduced to the level of advertising slogans.
  (See Rose 1993; Romans 1966; Vedung and van der Doelen 1998)

Nudges and information-based choice architectures

In recent years, as we have seen, much attention has been paid to information provision as a governing tool as a result of work based in behavioural economics which promotes the use of 'nudges' or cues to encourage or discourage certain kinds of behaviour at a less 'conscious' level (Thaler and Sunstein 2010). These cues are more subtle than traditional information and media-based campaigns and are often targeted at the unconscious or semi-conscious level of individual behaviour. They can include such micro-level interventions as changing the default opt-in on organ donation forms to a default opt-out, for example, or painting walking path lines in subway stations that lead to stairs rather than escalators in order to encourage exercise.

Sunstein (2014) identified 10 important types of nudges, many of which have been discussed in earlier chapters. They are all efforts to alter citizen behaviour by altering the informational environment in which they operate, especially through activation of so called 'system 1' or quasi-automatic cognitive responses (Kahneman 2013b; Strassheim 2018). These include:

(1) Changing default rules such as making people opt out rather than in to some scheme,
(2) Simplification of the options presented to individuals, such as a shortened contract,
(3) Use of social norms to encourage people to conform with certain practices, such as not littering or jaywalking,
(4) Increases in ease and convenience such as making bike paths and exercise areas common and easily accessible,
(5) Disclosure, that is, mandating the provision of certain kinds of information, like the real interest rate charged to credit card debt,
(6) Warnings, graphic, or otherwise to discourage behaviour, such as mandatory pictures of cancer victims on cigarette packages,
(7) Pre-commitment strategies such as the provision of peer-supported anti-obesity or alcoholism support groups such as Weight Watchers or Alcoholics Anonymous,
(8) Reminders of important activities such as children's dental appointment or vaccination schedules,

(9) Eliciting implementation intentions through various campaigns such as voter registration drives or pension planning,

(10) Informing people of the nature and consequences of their own past choices such as informing them of the amount they have spent on electricity in past months or years on their current bill.

Many of these items are included with bills or forms or mailings of various kinds and are intended to provide information about their behaviour to consumers which might otherwise be difficult or impossible for them to collect, such as the fluctuations in their monthly electricity or water consumption.

Although the idea of 'nudging' received a surge of attention after 2010, the effectiveness of such measures is unclear. Evidence suggests, for example, that they may have a role to play in solving large scale policy issues but only when they are exercised in tandem with other policy tools such as financial incentives or penalties (Mills 2012), such as a sliding scale of water or electricity prices in the example above, designed to discourage higher levels of consumption.

Moreover, there may be an unintended 'behavioural spillover' of nudges (Dolan and Galizzi 2015). That is, there is a risk of infantilizing and diminishing of people's autonomous decision-making capacities by constantly manipulating them (Hausman and Welch 2010; Bovens 2009) and also a concern regarding the potential for abuse in the use of nudging to shape people's choices in pro-government ways (Hausman and Welch 2010). Governments may also be unable to counter 'nudge' style tactics employed by private market institutions which, for example, encourage people to spend rather than save, or smoke or gamble rather than abstain, to name only a few (Bovens 2009; Loewenstein et al. 2015).

Hagman et al. (2015) also find significant differences in the receptiveness of different populations to nudging activity. They find a high degree of acceptance toward 'nudge' policies among a sample population drawn from Sweden and the USA but also a majority of the respondents perceiving such policies to be intrusive to their freedom of choice. Policies that the researchers classified as pro-social (i.e., focusing on social welfare) also had a significantly lower acceptance rate compared to pro-self nudge policies (i.e., focusing on private welfare). In addition, 'overt' nudges, that is, those that target conscious, higher-order cognitive processes of decision-making were preferred by people over 'covert' nudges (i.e., those that target subconscious, lower-order processes of decision-making). However, while this was true in most contexts, such as eating, purchasing, exercising and making investment decisions, it wasn't true in another context-that of workplace productivity decisions (Felsen, Castelo and Reiner 2013).

Regardless of the behavioural tool being employed, whether a nudge, shove, or budge, in cases where incentives for non-compliance are high, such information-based tools may be unlikely to secure compliance by themselves. In such cases, policy-makers need to think about both the barriers that may be preventing compliance and how to match a variety of policy tools to the most important barriers, taking into account the heterogeneity within the given population in terms of their receptiveness to different tool use (Weaver 2015).

Information and knowledge collection tools

Information collection is the key to many and better policies (Nutley et al. 2007) and, as Hood (1986c) pointed out, many implementation instruments exist to collect information for governments and can contribute to enhanced 'evidence-based' policy-making. This extends to the use of licensing provisions in which information may be collected before or after a license is granted, but can also involve the use of research and generation of new policy-relevant knowledge through special forums such as inquiries and commissions.

Inquiries and commissions

One fairly common and high-profile means by which governments collect information is the use of official inquiries such as a judicial inquiry or executive commission. These exist on a spectrum depending on their relationship to government agencies and according to their functions. Some inquiries and task forces are largely internal to government and intended to mobilize network actors. These have been discussed in Chapter 8 in the context of procedural organizational tools. Other kinds of commissions, however, are designed primarily to collect information (Sulitzeanu-Kenan 2010; Rowe and McAllister 2006). Many judicial inquiries fall into this category and have a great deal of autonomy from governments. They are a common feature of legal modes of governance and enjoy a variety of different relationships with their commissioners. Presidential and royal commissions, for example, are independent and autonomous although they still depend on government for budgets and resources. Others are less 'arms-length' and expected to report back to specific agencies on specific subjects with no guarantee that their reports will ever be released to the public. All of these devices can be used to summarize existing knowledge or generate new data on a subject (Chapman 1973; Bulmer 1981; Sheriff 1983; Clark and Majone 1985; d'Ombrain 1997; Elliott and McGuinness 2001; Montpetit 2003c; 2008; Salter 2003; Prasser 2006).

Statistical agencies and units

Another such information collecting and disseminating tool is the use of statistical agencies which are specifically tasked with collecting data on a wide variety of social activities of individuals, groups and firms. These typically operate using internationally recognized standards for classifying these activities and may rely more or less heavily on voluntary disclosure of information. These agencies may conduct surveys on specialized topics and/or periodic censuses of national or sub-national populations (Anderson and Whitford 2018).

This information is often used to determine such factors as the level of per capita grants transferred between governments, or the number and types of hospitals and medical facilities which should be built and where these and other public institutions like schools and offices, should be located. National and other level statistical agencies are expensive to establish and maintain but once in operation can be used to collect information on many subjects at relatively low cost and often provide otherwise very hard to collect information to the public as well as governments through, for example, time series databases on a wide range of issues from housing starts to consumer savings rates.

Surveys and polling

In many countries, governments are now the largest purchasers of surveys (Hastak et al. 2001) and many government agencies now undertake surveys on a regular basis, both as environmental scans in order to try to anticipate issues, but also in order to determine public opinion on agency performance (Rothmayr and Hardmeier 2002; Page 2006).

Procedural informational instruments

In order to pursue their preferred policy initiatives, governments can also use procedural tools based on government information resources in order to attempt to alter the behaviour of policy network members involved in policy-making processes (Burris et al. 2005), just as they attempt to alter consumer and producer behaviour through the employment of substantive information-based tools.

Information-based procedural policy tools are those designed to affect policy processes in a way consistent with government aims and ambitions through the control and selective provision of information. As Hood suggested, these are 'nodality' instruments because the information exchanged is valuable largely as a function of the government's position as a key nodal link in a policy network. Some of these efforts are aimed at promoting information release while others are aimed at preventing it.

Both European and American studies have found that governments have increasingly employed a variety of procedural information-based instruments to indirectly affect the outcomes of the policy process in ways that are consistent with their aims and objectives (Kohler-Koch 1996; Johansson and Borell 1999; Hall and O'Toole 2000). The most commonly observed and chronicled category of procedural tool is the type which focuses on the use of *general information prevention or disclosure laws and other tools* – such as access to information laws – in order to provide policy network actors with the knowledge required to effectively filter and focus their demands on government for new policy measures or reforms to older ones. However, governments are also very much involved in the use of communications on government websites and through other means (Gandy 1982; Hood and Margetts 2007) to provide additional information to policy network members in specific sectoral or issue areas in order to both enhance their credibility and effectiveness but also to promote evidence-based rather than pure advocacy activity. These tools fall into two types depending on whether they facilitate or withhold information.

Information release tools

Stanbury and Fulton (1984) describe two common types of procedural information release or disclosure tools: *information disclosure* (e.g., through formal FOI and privacy laws) and *consultation/co-optation tools*, such as public hearings, the discreet use of confidential information such as planned leaks to the press, or planned public disclosure of government intentions.

Freedom of information and E- or digital government legislation and other initiatives

FOI provisions allow access to an individual's own records and those of others – with numerous mainly benign exemptions – (to protect other individuals from unnecessary disclosure) and allowing access to documents and records of others – with numerous exemptions – again mainly benign and intended to protect individuals from unnecessary disclosure. These legislative arrangements were a feature of the centuries-old Scandinavian ombudsman system of administrative control and were introduced in many other countries in the 1970s and 1980s (Relyea 1977; Bennett 1988, 1990, 1991a, 1992; Bennett and Raab 2003; Bennett and Bayley 1999; Howe and Johnson 2000).

These are sometimes accompanied by other tools such as 'whistleblower' acts; that is, bills intended to protect people who speak out about problems in the government's bureaucracy. Through such legislation, bureaucrats are often offered legal protection against reprisals for reporting government wrongdoing. Both represent popular forms of procedural information tool design.

Various kinds of open data and e-government projects, often referred to collectively as 'digital government', which move previously in-person service delivery online also often have an information release component to them, collecting data on users, or providing additional venues for users to obtain information on government programmes and other options (Clarke and Craft 2017; Clarke et al. 2017).

Information release prevention tools

There is also a wide range of such tools designed to protect certain kinds of information on government activities or in government files and prevent its distribution to the public. These include protecting not only information collected by governments but that which comes into their possession (e.g., from a foreign government or via documents filed in court cases and the like). These range from wartime (and peacetime, for example, a film review board) censorship and bans on political parties and speech such as hate crimes legislation, to official secrets acts with various levels of confidentiality and penalties imposed for publicizing or releasing government secrets, especially but not exclusively around areas such as national security.

Censorship

This has occurred in many countries during wartime but also in peacetime, for example, as media, film, or theater censorship. This latter use has been slowly whittled away in most advanced countries as individual rights in democratic states have been ruled to trump government or collective ones but wartime prohibitions remain very common (Qualter 1985).

Official secrets acts

Official secrets acts are a replacement for censorship in many areas. They are often the most important statute relating to national security in many countries and are designed to prohibit and control access to and the disclosure of sensitive government information (Pasquier and Villeneuve 2007). Offences tend to cover espionage and leakage of government information. The term 'official secret' varies dramatically in meaning from country to country but, broadly, allows governments to classify documents and prohibit release of different categories for sometimes very long periods of time (e.g., 50–75 years). All countries have some form of official secrecy although the legislative and executive basis for such laws varies quite dramatically between countries.

Privacy and data protection acts

These acts exist in many jurisdictions as a counterpoint to access to information laws in which various types of personally specific information is excluded from such acts. Some jurisdictions have specific legislation devoted to this subject, usually with a focus on protecting personal information in areas such as health, financial, or tax matters and with respect to criminal proceedings.

These instruments are also quite varied but in general it is fair to say that restricting information is low cost to initiate but high cost to monitor and maintain, while the reverse is true of information disclosure. In terms of targeting, it is true of both sets of instruments that it is very difficult to target either secrecy or disclosure on specific groups. As a result, these actions are typically more difficult to set up and take more time and effort than is often thought to be the case, making them an infrequent component of many policy designs, although increasingly demanded in an era of computer hacking and data breaches.

Conclusion: information-cost efficient but often ineffective

As has been set out above, there are many different kinds of government communication and information activities and in the past the lack of an effective taxonomy or framework for their analysis has made generalizing about their impact and patterns of use quite difficult. Describing information-based policy tools in the terms set out above helps to highlight the similarities and differences between different instruments and helps develop a relatively parsimonious taxonomy of their major types which can facilitate national and cross-national studies of their use and impact.

Information dissemination activities remain relatively low cost in terms of financial and personnel outlays, but compliance is a major issue and, as in all advertising activities, evaluating the impact of these campaigns is very uncertain (Salmon 1989a, 1989b). Adler and Pittle (1984: 161), for example, found 'many of these programmes require more careful planning, larger expenditures and longer implementation periods than they usually receive'.

The assumption that greater knowledge always equals greater compliance with government aims, for example, is not always the case. Alcoholism and drug abuse, to give only two prominent examples, are complex problems that are not 'rational' in the sense that individuals continue to consume or engage in them while knowing their destructive attributes (so-called 'demerit goods') (see Walsh 1988; Weiss and Tschirhart 1994). Greater knowledge may not affect or alter their behaviour in such cases.

Thus while it may be the dream of many governments that simply monitoring and communicating with people will accomplish all of their ends, this is not usually the case. The benefits to government in using such tools may thus be much lower than anticipated if such a high visibility instrument is perceived to have failed and the blame for a continuing policy problem is focused squarely on governments (Hood 2007b). Such considerations are a prominent feature in the design of policy alternatives envisioning the use of such tools, often resulting in their use in combination with other tools rather than as the sole tool deployed in a policy area of interest.

Readings

Anderson, D. M. and A. Whitford. (2018). 'Designing Systems for the Co-Production of Public Knowledge: Considerations for National Statistical Systems'. *Policy Design and Practice* 1, no. 1 (2 January): 79–89.

Bardach, E. and R. A. Kagan. (1982). 'Mandatory Disclosure'. In E. Bardach and R. A. Kagan (eds), *Going by the Book: The Problem of Regulatory Unreasonableness.* Philadelphia, PA: Temple University Press, 242–70.

Bennett, C. and R. Bayley. (1999). 'The New Public Administration: Canadian Approaches to Access and Privacy'. In M. W. Westmacott and H. P. Mellon (eds), *Public Administration and Policy: Governing in Challenging Times.* Scarborough, ON: Prentice Hall/Allyn & Bacon, 189–201.

Bougherara, D., G. Grolleau and N. Mzoughi. (2007). 'Is More Information Always Better? An Analysis Applied to Information-Based Policies for Environmental Protection'. *International Journal of Sustainable Development* 10, no. 3: 197–213.

Bulmer, M. (1981). 'Applied Social Research? The Use and Non-Use of Empirical Social Inquiry by British and American Governmental Commissions'. *Journal of Public Policy* 1: 353–80.

Cairns, A. C. (1990). 'Reflections on Commission Research'. In A. P. Pross, I. Christie and J. A. Yogis (eds), *Commissions of Inquiry.* Toronto, ON: Carswell, 87–110.

Chapman, R. A. (1973). 'Commissions in Policy-Making'. In R. A. Chapman (ed.), *The Role of Commissions in Policy-Making.* London: George Allen & Unwin, 174–88.

Clarke, A. and J. Craft. (2017). 'The Vestiges and Vanguards of Policy Design in a Digital Context'. *Canadian Public Administration* 60, no. 4 (1 December): 476–97.

Howells, G. (2005). 'The Potential and Limits of Consumer Empowerment by Information'. *Journal of Law and Society* 32, no. 3: 349–70.

Jahn, G., M. Schramm and A. Spiller. (2005). 'The Reliability of Certification: Quality Labels as a Consumer Policy Tool'. *Journal of Consumer Policy* 28: 53–73.

Salmon, C. (1989). 'Campaigns for Social Improvement: An Overview of Values, Rationales, and Impacts'. In C. Salmon (ed.), *Information Campaigns: Managing the Process of Social Change.* Newbury Park, CA: Sage, 1–32.

Sheriff, P. E. (1983). 'State Theory, Social Science, and Governmental Commissions'. *American Behavioural Scientist* 26, no. 5: 669–80.

Vedung, E. and F. C. J. van der Doelen. (1998). 'The Sermon: Information Programs in the Public Policy Process – Choice, Effects and Evaluation'. In M.-L. Bemelmans-Videc, R. C. Rist and E. Vedung (eds), *Carrots, Sticks and Sermons: Policy Instruments and Their Evaluation.* New Brunswick, NJ: Transaction, 103–28.

Weiss, J. A. (2002). 'Public Information'. In L. M. Salamon (ed.), *The Tools of Government: A Guide to the New Governance.* New York: Oxford University Press, 217–54.

Chapter 12

Traditional policy styles and contemporary design trends

As the discussion in Chapters 8–11 has shown, there are many different kinds of instruments which can be used in a policy design and many ways in which instruments of different types can be combined into a policy mix.

Given this variation, the extent of the permutations and combinations possible within it and the complex nature of the policy advice systems in which design decisions are taken, one might expect each policy design to be idiosyncratic and for there to be an incredibly wide range of designs, much as there is in the area of ship design, for example, whereby boats can take on almost any shape and structure imaginable.

However this is not the case in the policy sphere. Rather designs are fairly limited and the same general design, for example, utilizing a combination of regulation and stakeholder advisory councils, is very common and operates in a very similar manner across a wide range of domains and problem areas. It is also the case that with an extremely wide range of permutations, it would be very difficult if not impossible to identify and talk about any specific trends in design activity. However with a much smaller number of designs, it is possible to identify several general trends and directions in policy design, much as is the case with, for example, men's fashion.

As we saw in Chapter 2, for example, many scholars have argued that in coming to terms with the challenges of globalization and the increasing networkization of society, governments have developed a renewed interest in a particular set of policy tools appropriate to market or network modes of governance. Because of this purported shift in governance contexts – the presence of more flexible economic and political circumstances than have existed in the past (Lenihan and Alcock 2000) – contemporary policy designs in many advanced countries, it has been argued, have changed. Specifically, unlike in past epochs, they are argued to have become more indirect and subtle, more often much less visible than was previously the case, and more similar (Rhodes 1997).

As also discussed in Chapter 2, it has been argued in many circles that in response to the increased complexity of society and the international environment, governments in many countries in Western Europe, in particular, have turned away from the use of a relatively limited number of traditional, more or less command-and-control oriented, 'substantive' policy tools such as public enterprises, regulatory agencies, subsidies and exhortation and begun to increasingly use their organizational resources to support a different set of 'procedural' tools (Klijn and Teisman 1991; Peters 1998) such as government reorganizations, reviews and inquiries, government–NGO partnerships and stakeholder consultations. These all act to guide or steer policy processes in the direction government wishes through the manipulation of policy actors and their interrelationships and constitute a 'new governance' system (Bingham et al. 2005).

Even contemplating statements of this kind would be impossible if designs were plentiful and hundreds or even thousands of discrete types existed. Why this is not the case and what it is that holds variation in policy designs down to a minimum is discussed in this chapter, as well as identifying what are the main trends in designs utilizing each of the major NATO categories set out in Chapters 8–11. As this discussion shows, the basic context of institutions and structures in which design activities occur, serves to create a jurisdiction's 'policy style' (Richardson et al. 1982; Howlett and Tosun 2019) or long-term preference for a certain mode of policy-making and a certain choice of instruments, creating a governance mode which is difficult to change and which structures instrument choices and design decisions in predictable ways.

Understanding contemporary policy designs

Table 12.1 shows how the mode of governance found in a jurisdiction includes a specific set of tool preferences; the use of those tools and their interactions being more or less coherent and compatible with that mode. Legal governance modes, for example, are correlated closely with preferences for the use of direct government, laws and direct regulation, the use of excise taxes and insurance and, often, censorship and privacy laws; while alternate modes such as corporatist governance are correlated with a preference for the use of state-owned enterprises, independent and other forms of delegated regulation, the use of subsidies and grants, interest group mobilization and information campaigns. The same is true of market governance modes which are correlated with a preference for contracting out, voluntary regulation and deregulation, tax incentives and data collection; and network governance modes with the use of clientele agencies, co-production, consultation mechanisms, interest group creation and access to information.

Experts in government are familiar with these modes and see the links between policy components in terms of their compatibility with each mode

Table 12.1 Propensity for tool use by governance mode and resource category

		Governance Mode			
		Legal	Corporatist	Market	Network
	Organization	Direct government Administrative tribunals	State-owned enterprises	Privatization Contracting out Special operating agencies Private–public partnerships	Clientele agencies Task forces Public hearings
NATO resource category	Authority	Laws Direct regulation Administrative procedures	Independent regulatory commissions Delegated regulation Advisory councils	Deregulation Voluntary and self-regulation	Stakeholder conferences
	Treasure	Excise taxes Insurance	Subsidies, grants and interest group mobilization	Tax incentives Procurement and vouchers Exhortation and suasion	Interest group creation
	Informational	Product information campaigns Censorship Official secrets	Government information campaigns Surveys	Statistics and data collection	Freedom of information

as well as their inner coherence within a policy mix. From their positions in policy advisory networks they are able to develop policy alternatives which combine these elements in more or less consistent ways, since choosing particular tools based on factors such as political, social and economic feasibility, government capacity and target group structure and calibrating specific tool components means taking into account factors around the nature of the predominant mode of governance found in that jurisdiction.

These factors and calculations do change over time as the context of policy-making changes and shifts in governance modes and policy regime logics occur, as globalization and network theorists rightly noted, leading to changes in overall policy design preferences.

However policy styles do not change quickly and changes are also infrequent (Howlett and Tosun 2019), meaning there is a great deal of continuity in policy designs across most sectors and issue areas. It is also the case that these changes occur at different times and with different impacts in each policy sector and it is a mistake to think that a general macro-level societal movement such as networkization will manifest itself equally in all areas of state activity. This can be seen from even a rudimentary examination of the globalization and network literature which, in fact, argue equally vehemently that such shifts are occurring, but in two different directions: toward either the general adoption of market governance, or network governance, respectively.

In fact, as the discussion in the previous chapters has indicated, within the context of these general trends several distinct meso-level trends can be observed in the use of particular types of governing tools in contemporary public policy designs. Some of the more evident of these latter trends are set out in more detail below.

Patterns of organizational tool use: direct and indirect instrument designs

Despite some moves toward the increased use of procedural tools more compatible with network modes of governance – such as public hearings, task forces and the establishment of clientele agencies – most policy sectors in most governments remain firmly based in legal or corporatist modes of governance established decades ago and featuring a prominent role for direct government goods and service delivery: what Chapter 8 described as the 'forgotten fundamental' of policy instruments and policy designs (Leman 1989; Majone 1997).

In recent years, direct forms of government goods and service delivery have continued to grow in most sectors, although the attention paid to this continued growth has often been overshadowed in the academic literature by that paid to continued, but much smaller scale experimentation with alternate forms of indirect government organization (Aucoin 1997). However, the pattern of change in the use of this dominant policy tool has been very uneven as governments have expanded in spurts and starts punctuated by major crises, especially in times of war or financial crises and their aftermath when more corporatist modes of governance have often flourished (Bird 1970; Hodgetts 1973).

Public enterprises, for example, grew dramatically in many countries, both in the developed world in association with war efforts and in developing countries as a function of decolonization and drives toward economic development. The spread of privatization in almost every country over the last three decades reflected a rapid and fundamental change in expert attitudes toward the use of this instrument, as governments tried to move many sectors away from corporatist modes of governance under the pressure of cost and other constraints (Le Grand 1984; Walker 1984; Savas 1987; Veljanovski 1988; Kamerman and Kahn 1989; MacAvoy et al. 1989; Salamon 1989; Starr 1989, 1990a; Ikenberry 1990; Richardson 1990, 1990b; Suleiman and Waterbury 1990; Kemp 1991; Marsh 1991).

The term 'privatization', however, carries at least two different, albeit related, meanings (Starr 1989, 1990a, 1990b). In one common usage, the term is sometimes inaccurately used as a shorthand reference for general efforts made to reduce the scale or scope of government. In this sense, the term is used to denote a basic shift in the overall relationship or governance mode existing between a government and its constituent society toward a more market mode of co-ordination. In the second sense, however, privatization refers only to those specific efforts made by the state to replace organizational instruments based on government ownership with those based on more indirect controls – such as independent regulatory commissions – which does not necessarily entail a corresponding shift toward a market governance mode.

In this more restricted sense, for example, a government's commitment to an existing mode remains unchanged; what changes instead is the general manner in which it meets its commitments: shifting from the use of organizational resources to more authoritative ones. Similarly, instead of regulating a company's, to provide another example, polluting activities, the government may offer it a financial incentive to modernize its equipment and curb pollution. Again this does not represent a shift in the fundamental governance mode but rather a change of regime logic within an existing one.

Patterns of authoritative tool use: indirect regulation and increased public participation

Looking at the use and promotion of authority-based substantive policy tools, the discussion in Chapter 9 showed that regulations are compatible with most modes of governance, depending on how state directed they are. Many policy designs have indeed changed over the past two decades in this tool area. Within an existing governance mode, for example, many regulatory activities have shifted from 'enforcement' to 'compliance' regimes (Hawkins and Thomas 1989; Doern and Wilks 1998). But these activities remain compatible with pre-existing modes of governance and do not necessarily infer a shift toward market or network forms of governance as proponents of phenomena such as deregulation – often linked to patterns of globalization and networkization – have alleged.

Nevertheless, it is true that many governments in recent years have made varying levels of effort, albeit often more in formulation than implementation, to deregulate important sectors of their economies; that is, to shift from earlier legal or corporatist governance modes to a more market or network mode. Many such efforts failed to produce qualitatively superior results to the regimes they replaced, leading to a movement back toward 're-regulation' in the policy designs adopted or proposed in many jurisdictions (Jordana and Levi-Faur 2004a; Ramesh and Howlett 2006).

While these different phases of regulatory activities are little studied, Bernstein (1955) postulated the existence of a regulatory 'life cycle' moving from birth to senescence and regulatory decline and termination or *deregulation*. In Bernstein's work, the idea was that a regulatory agency or regime would gradually suffer a decline in autonomy due to the accumulation of decisions which would generate a cadre of skilled regulators who moved back and forth between regulators and regulatees, undermining the independence of the regulating body and its legitimacy as an impartial protector of the public interest. Eventually the regulator would be 'captured' by the regulatee and the regime would decline into oblivion (Bernstein 1955). However the linkages between the different phases are not well understood and recent studies suggest that rather than just decline into abolition, regulatory agencies and regimes move in cycles of regulation – deregulation – re-regulation (Jordana and Levi-Faur 2004b; Ramesh and Howlett 2006).

While deregulation certainly occurred in many areas in the 1980s and 1990s, studies are very limited with respect to clarifying the general historical processes through which this step took place and whether or not this was due only, or always, to regulatory capture. Some early studies of deregulation initiatives in North America and Europe do exist (Swann 1988; Rubsamen 1989; Gayle and Goodrich 1990; Richardson 1990; Beesley 1992; Collier 1998), as do some theoretical works attempting to explain the origins of that deregulatory initiative (Crew and Rowley 1986; Derthick and Quirk 1985; Hammond and Knott 1988; Daugbjerg 1997; Lazer and Mayer-Schonberger 2002) but they are far from conclusive.

These studies generally show that regulatory regimes everywhere evolved gradually, emerging in response to the turbulence caused by industrialization and the growth of unfettered market capitalism (Eisner 1993, 1994a,b). Their development, in fact, is co-terminate with that of the enhancement of the bureaucratic capacity of the modern state (Hodgetts 1964; Skowronek 1982). As an inexpensive and plentiful source of government control, regulation was often invoked by governments eager to reduce their direct government agency-level involvement in the provision of goods and services in society but unwilling to fully trust politically important functions entirely to market actors. Although regulation was often initially opposed by industry and many professional economists as promoting inefficiency, it was generally accepted in mainstream policy circles as essential for addressing market imperfections and dealing with the uncertainties of modern economic and social life. It is only recently that a broad body of opinion emerged which regards regulations as often inefficient and burdensome for the state itself (Cheung 2005).

The expansion of reservations and even antipathy toward regulations led to two quite distinct movements: toward, on the one hand, 'regulatory reform' and, on the other, 'deregulation'. These two movements are quite different and represent two separate approaches to resolving 'the regulatory dilemma' highlighted in Bernstein's work (Birch 1984). However, as Eisner has pointed out, deregulatory activities and regulatory reforms, or streamlining, are often incorrectly juxtaposed (Eisner 1994a). While regulatory reform has involved activities such as the mandating of cost–benefit analyses before the enactment of any new rules, deregulation involves the wholesale roll back and even abolition of existing rules (McGarity 1991).

In addition to these developments in the substantive arena, with respect to procedural authoritative instruments, Chapter 9 also underscored the development of, compatible with the networkization thesis, demands for enhanced participation and consultation in government policy-making driven by domestic groups (Kernaghan et al. 2000).

But this is not a new phenomenon and there has been substantial growth in the use of consultative forums and mechanisms in many sectors and countries over the past half century. This extends from the increased use of public hearings to the increased creation (and regulation) of advisory committees. As David Brown noted as early as 1955 in the USA, for example, while in 1938 there were perhaps 100 advisory boards in the US federal government, by 1955, there were 50 in the US Department of Agriculture alone (vs four in 1938). Smith (1977) also noted that this phenomenon varied by jurisdiction and that while by 1962–63 the US federal government had over 900 advisory committees and the UK in 1960 about 500, Australia only about 200 by 1975.[1]

Institutionalized forms of citizen involvement in policy-making attempt to replace agenda-setting and policy influence by only those actors intimately involved in project or policy proposals with a process in which 'outsiders' as well as 'insiders' can promote new and alternative perspectives on these issues and can be viewed as generally attempting to move legal, corporatist and market modes of governance toward more 'network' types (Marchildon 2007). But advisory committees, commissions, task forces and round tables already exist in many sectors and are compatible with other governance modes, not just network ones.

As Dion argued as early as 1973, at least part of the growth noted by Brown, Smith and others was due to the decline of political parties as a vehicle to aggregate public interests and of legislative and representative institutions to articulate them and is very compatible with corporatist and other forms of governance (Dion 1973). Over the past several decades new avenues for public participation – various kinds of boards, commissions and tribunals – have provided more institutionalized means for citizen involvement. In many countries and sectors, the 1990s in particular ushered in an era in which a number of new procedural authoritative instruments were established through which the public's participation was actively sought by the state. Environmental task forces, round tables, land-use planning commissions and other advisory tools have been used by governments in various countries and sectors, while new legislation – embodying processes such as mandatory environmental assessment reviews – created additional instruments mandating public participation. However problems with limited community group resources and too many consultative exercises can lead to diminishing returns and ineffectiveness if they are utilized too often (Cook 2002; Ross et al. 2002) and regulations preventing participatory abuses, such as legislation controlling lobbyists through mandatory registration, have also been deployed (Chari et al. 2007).

Patterns of financial tool use: from visible to invisible instruments

There have been some interesting developments in the patterns of use found in this very old set of instruments and some interesting tool dynamics well worth additional study. While most economic theories push for visible taxes and incentives in order to promote virtues and discourage vice, the reality in most countries is a trend toward more and more hidden financial tools – especially tax-based ones which are difficult to trace and quantify.

Howard (1993, 1995, 1997, 2002), for example, estimated that the US welfare system in the mid-1990s included $896 million in direct expenditures but also $437.9 million in tax expenditures (1995: 26). This 'hidden welfare system' he argued, since it is based primarily on non-refundable tax incentives, mainly favored the middle class, that is, those with taxable incomes who can benefit from these programmemes – such as pensions plans (US$76 billion in 1995); home mortgage deductions (US$50 billion in 1995); deferral of capital gains on home sales (US$17 billion); and employer health insurance (US$77 billion). He estimated tax expenditures in the USA grew by an average 4.8 percent over the period 1967–95 versus 5.9 percent for direct expenditure on income security, health and housing, but over the period 1980–90 grew at a faster rate than direct expenditures (3.9 vs 3.1 percent annual growth) with a similar pattern over the period 1975–95 (the 'Republican era' in US politics) in what was ostensibly a deficit cutting/free trade era of market-based governance.

This expansion has been fueled by shifts in implementation preferences owing a great deal to the assessment criteria of visibility, intrusiveness, automaticity and cost. The tax system is already in place, along with a collections and enforcement apparatus, so changes to create new incentives or disincentives are largely matters of administration. There is some risk involved in their use, though, as it is often difficult to control whether or not a recipient will actually do what a government wants them to with the transferred funds. Besides problems with black and grey markets, market distortions and international prohibitions associated with this tool, agents can also often simply take the money offered with few results in terms of achievement of a principle's intentions. Avoiding such principle – agent problems can involve costly and visible enforcement agencies, which negates some of the advantages of the use of these instruments in contemporary policy designs.

With respect to procedural financial tools, a pattern in many countries and sectors has been for their increased use over the past 30 years in the effort to enhance and control the operation of interest articulation and aggregation systems in many sectors. This is compatible in many jurisdictions with pre-existing corporatist modes of governance but many groups in other governance modes now receive direct funding from governments while others are funded indirectly through tax systems which allow for transfers of funds to non-profit and charitable groups either directly or through foundations (Pross and Stewart 1993; Phillips 2001; Sharpe 2001; Carmichael 2010; Wood and Hagerman 2010). This pattern of government funding typically has some negative consequences for recipient groups (De Vita and Twombly 2005; Pittel and Rubbelke 2006; Guo 2007; Knott and McCarthy 2007).

As Laforest and Orsini argued:

> Rather than seeing a multiplicity of innovative practices, voluntary organizations are actually using fewer tools and fewer strategies to influence the policy process, investing most of their energy in research and evidence-based advocacy ... becoming depoliticized and professionalized as they engage more in research and develop finely honed analytical skills. ... While voluntary organizations are increasingly being consulted and engaged in policy-making, the basis of these interventions too often lies in their capacity to generate empirical evidence and data, not in their ability to articulate the interests of their constituents.
>
> (Laforest and Orsini 2005: 482; *see also* Cairns et al. 2005)

The use of such procedural financial tools is generally very inexpensive and can be precisely targeted, making them a preferred tool for government managers eager to control their policy environments. There are some risks involved in such activities though, since outside funding promotes oligarchy/formalization in voluntary associations and can lead to discontent both among 'co-opted' group memberships as well as from groups which do not receive funding (Saward 1990, 1992; Lowndes and Skelcher 1998; Smith 2005a,b). Ideological predispositions toward 'free association' in deliberative democratic practices, too, are jeopardized by government manipulation of interest articulation systems, which can lead to further difficulties for governments who engage in this practice in a substantial way, although the lack of visibility and accountability of such practices reduces this concern (Beetham 1991; Phillips 1991; Stanbury 1993; Webb 2000; Maddison 2005; Carmichael 2010).

Patterns of informational tool use: the growth of exhortation, nudges and public information campaigns

It is now very much a matter of course for information campaigns to accompany many government initiatives and Chapter 11 showed how expenditures, laws and programmes in this area have grown as they have been included in more and more policy designs. This is explicable given the non-coercive nature of this tool, which accords well with the ideology and imperatives of liberal-democratic governments and their preferred legal and corporatist-based governance modes.

Information dissemination remains relatively low cost in terms of financial and personnel outlays as well, but compliance with government urgings is a major issue – and as in all advertising (Pepsi, Coke, etc.) evaluating the impact of these campaigns is very uncertain (Salmon 1989a,b). Consumers may not pay attention to information provided by, for example, nutritional or eco-labels, or may become inured to messages repeated too often (Howells 2005). Effective campaigns can also take some time to get started and evoke any behavioural response and behaviour can revert back to old habits and patterns once a campaign stops. Or, where too much information is provided ('information overload') intended targets may stop listening, also leading to diminishing returns over time (Bougherara et al. 2007).

The political risks to government in using this tool also may be high if such high visibility instruments are perceived to have failed to alter behaviour in the desired direction, leading to demands for greater government efforts.

Moreover, as the discussion of privacy and official secrets legislation in Chapter 11 showed any moves in a more network governance direction are often offset by similar moves toward a legal governance mode involving knowledge suppression, either for state or individual privacy purposes. Any general diminishment of state power in this area can be easily reversed in times of war or crisis, as has been the case in many countries in the post 9/11 environment of the US-led 'war on terror'. Freedom of information versus privacy balancing, for example, is very important ideologically in many liberal-democratic countries as it pits individual rights to know what a government is doing against individual rights to privacy (De Saulles 2007). And concerns with state and collective security in times of war or terrorism can lead to a renewed emphasis on restricting information disclosure, as we have seen recently in many countries.

While in recent years more attention has been paid to information-based tools as a result of the 'nudge' movement described above and in earlier chapters, to date the actual implementation of such measures has been very minor, extending largely to re-writing forms and contracts to alter defaults, as in the case of organ donation provisions on driver's licences and some minor adjustment to traffic laws, and efforts to have citizens engage in more healthy life choices, such as walking up stairs rather than always riding escalators (Lorenco et al. 2016; Moseley and Stoker 2015).

Overall patterns and trends in contemporary policy designs

As this discussion has shown, the patterns of tool use in contemporary policy designs are much more varied than simply involving a cross-sectoral, government-wide shift toward policy mixes associated with enhanced market and network governance but also not wildly disparate in terms of their content and evolution.

In the case of organizational tools, there has been a noticeable movement in many sectors away from the use of direct government instruments and public enterprises and toward the use of more indirect means of goods and service delivery such as partnerships, special operating agencies and quangos. However, this movement should not lead us to underestimate the resilience and continued presence of traditional direct government tools, especially line departments, which remain the backbone of most policy sectors.

In the case of organization-based procedural tools, there has been a simultaneous movement toward the use of government organizational resources to involve larger components of the public or affected 'stakeholders' in policy deliberations. These moves, again while certainly not new, do reflect a shift in some policy sectors from state-led toward more societally driven modes of organization as efforts have been made in many countries to implement some aspects of network governance.

With respect to authoritative substantive instruments, this same pattern appears once again as traditional direct and indirect regulatory mechanisms which are a feature of implementation in legal and corporatist modes of governance and remain predominant there, have been augmented by efforts to promote more voluntary regulatory regimes in a wide variety of issue areas – from environmental protection to food safety.

This deregulatory movement has been offset in many jurisdictions and sectors, however, by the return to direct or indirect regulation through re-regulation of areas such as telecommunications and energy in many countries (Majone 1997). The relative stasis in this category of tool choice is also visible in its procedural components, as traditional mechanisms such as advisory committee creation continue to be used extensively, whether the context is regulation, deregulation, or re-regulation.

In the area of financial tools, however, changes in policy designs have been more unidirectional, with most countries seeing a cross-sectoral government-wide shift in recent years from an emphasis on the use of more visible subsidies to a preference in many sectors for less visible forms of tax- and royalty-based expenditures.

On the procedural front, there is not a great deal of information available from which to judge, but it appears that, in many countries, more or less covert efforts to correct collective action problems through the use of tools such as interest group creation have been attempted in many sectors, but this is a policy design which is compatible with already existing corporatist modes of governance as well as the development of new network ones.

Finally, in the area of information-based tools, the propensity for governments to undertake large-scale public information campaigns has accelerated, as has their use of devices such as surveys and other techniques for monitoring their populations. On the procedural side, however, an earlier generation's efforts at enhancing information access for the public has been somewhat curtailed in the post-9/11 environment of enhanced security and state secrecy.

The general picture this provides, in terms of measures of government involvement in specific tool choices and policy designs, is of a number of shifts, but much less *between* governance modes, as suggested by the globalization and 'government to governance' thesis, than *within* them.

This is not to say that major shifts never happen, but that they are rare. In some cases, for example, some efforts have been made to shift designs toward more market- or network-based ones, with some success. As Hood et al. and Majone have argued in the European case, for example, 'modern states are placing more emphasis on the use of authority, rules and standard-setting, partially displacing an earlier emphasis on public ownership, public subsidies and directly provided services' (Hood et al. 1999; see also Majone 1997). However, even here, most sectors in Europe remain firmly entrenched in traditional and long-lasting corporatist governance modes.

These trends, therefore, are much less dramatic than those suggested by the network-globalization hypothesis and suggest a much greater resilience and continued high capacity of the state in the face of these two macro-level trends than is often alleged (Aucoin 1997; Lynn 2001; Hill and Lynn 2004; Hamelin 2010).

It suggests, among other things, that governance modes are more difficult to change in many sectors than is often argued and provides additional evidence for the contention that policy designs must be compatible with previously existing governance modes if they are to survive the formulation process and be implemented successfully. Empirical evidence of the existence of these kinds of long-term overall governance arrangements also exists in the work of Theodore Lowi, for example, who noted that while the historical record in general throughout the world has been one featuring the constant expansion of the range and scope of instruments used in governance, that in the case of the USA, at least, these arrangements proceeded through four principle periods.

As he argued in 'Four Systems of Policy, Politics and Choice' (Lowi 1972: 300): 'It is not hard to document historically that the overwhelming proportion of policies produced by the U.S. federal government during the 19th century were distributive', while regulatory policies were introduced in the late nineteenth century and redistributive ones in the twentieth (see also

Orren and Skowronek 1998 and Skowronek 1982). These arrangements roughly correspond to rotating periods of Considine's legal, market and corporate modes of governance but over a very long two century period.

Explaining these patterns: governance modes and policy styles

As this discussion has shown, the insights gained from studies of policy instruments and policy design is that, because macro-level arrangements such as governance modes typically change only very slowly over time, patterns of government instrument choices tend to exhibit a surprising amount of similarity within policy sectors and over time (de Vries 1999, 2002, 2005). A focus on relatively long-standing structural or institutional factors in the policy formulation process which affect state capacity and network complexity helps to explain why long-lasting patterns of instrument choice such as those discussed above exist at both the sectoral and national levels.

And these studies have also identified the key agents responsible for this lack of movement, underlining the key role played by policy experts at the policy formulation stage of the policy-making process and how they ensure policy alternatives are developed which accord with their conceptions of feasibility, meaning focusing a great deal of attention on their congruence with existing governance norms and contextual dynamics.

These policy experts, as guardians of knowledge and ideas about the appropriate relationships existing between policy tools and governance modes, occupy key positions in policy advice systems and play a key role in influencing policy formulation in such a way as, normally, outside of periods of turbulence in governance ideas and policy regimes, ensures continuity in favored policy designs or the adoption and maintenance of a distinct 'policy style'.

The concept of a policy style

In describing long-term continuity in policy-making, policy studies typically draw on the notion of 'policy regimes' or long-term arrangements which include the following elements: a common set of policy ideas (policy paradigm), a long-lasting governance arrangement (policy mix), a common or typical policy process (policy style) and a more or less fixed set of policy actors (policy subsystem or policy monopoly). Together, these elements combine to ensure policy outputs remain very much within a range of options compatible with the pillars of the regime.

In his work on social policy, for example, Gosta Esping-Andersen found 'specific institutional arrangements adopted by societies in the pursuit of work and welfare. A given organization of state–economy relations is associated with a particular social policy logic' (Rein et al. 1987). Similarly, in their work on US policy-making, Harris and Milkis (1989: 25) found

249

regimes developed as a 'constellation' of (1) ideas justifying governmental activity, (2) institutions that structure policy-making and (3) a set of policies. Eisner, similarly, defined a regime as a 'historically specific configuration of policies and institutions which establishes certain broad goals that transcend the problems' specific to particular sectors (Eisner 1993: xv; see also Eisner 1994a). From this perspective, a policy style can be thought of as existing as part of a larger 'policy regime' that emerges over time as policy succession takes place and stabilizes many aspects of policy-making.

The concept of a *policy style* is useful not only for helping to describe typical policy processes and deliberations, but also for capturing an important aspect of policy dynamics, that is, the relatively enduring nature of these arrangements (Larsen et al. 2006). Numerous case studies over the last three decades have highlighted the manner in which ideological and institutional factors insulate policies from pressures for change. Pierson's (2000) work on path dependence and Grossback et al.'s (2006) study on the role of ideology for policy diffusion are just examples of this strand of research. By the mid-1970s, it was apparent to many observers that actors in the policy processes, as Simmons et al. (1974: 461) put it, tended to 'take on, over a period of time, a distinctive style which affects#. . .#policy decisions, that is, they develop tradition and history which constrains and refines their actions and concerns'.

The general idea of polities developing a characteristic way of doing things, or a style of governing or ruling, of course, is not new. It has clear links to the foundational studies of bureaucracy and bureaucratization developed by Weber and others in the late nineteenth and early twentieth centuries (Weber 1978; Eisenstadt 1963). It also was a major part of the first wave of comparative administrative studies carried out after the World War II which focused on the identification and elaboration of national administrative cultures (Waldo 1948; Barker 1944).

The concept of such styles re-emerged in the late 1990s, however, in the works of, among others, Héritier et al. (1996), Knill (1998, 1999) and Bekke et al. (1993, 1996a,b, 2000, 1999), scholars interested in, among other things, the difficulties encountered in the countries of the European Union (EU) in adopting and implementing EU-wide administrative initiatives. This scholarship suggested the critical importance of the concept of policy styles in assessing the role played by existing administrative systems in affecting public policy processes and outcomes, including impeding efforts to reshape the administration itself.

The first modern studies of policy styles argued that public policy outcomes varied directly according to the nature of the political system found in each country (Peters et al. 1978). Although some empirical evidence of substantial differences in *outcomes* was uncovered in empirical tests of this hypothesis (Castles 1998; Obinger and Wagschal 2001), it was soon suggested that the concept could be more fruitfully applied not to outcomes but to the policy *process* in a particular country. Each country or groups of countries were said to have its or their own pattern of policy-making, which characterized its policy processes and the resulting policy decisions.

The volume *Policy Styles in Western Europe*, edited by Jeremy Richardson and his colleagues (Richardson et al. 1982), first addressed this concept systematically. It sought to address whether distinct cultural and institutional features of modern states in the 1980s had implications for the making and implementation of public policy decisions within them.

That book looked at the similarities and differences that existed among the countries of Western Europe in terms of their propensity to take *anticipatory or reactive* decisions and, in either case, whether they tended to do so in a *top-down state driven or bottom-up societally driven* fashion. More precisely, chapters looked at (then West) France, Germany, the Netherlands, Sweden, Norway and the United Kingdom.

Although not inclusive of all aspects of a regime, the manner in which policy deliberations take place and the kinds of instruments chosen to implement policies constitute a policy style. This style is exercised within the constraints imposed by institutional arrangements, which shape its contours, such as political and electoral conventions and institutions, as well as within a policy paradigm that shapes its content. However, a style is important in such a regime as it helps determining the range and type of alternatives and final policy outputs, which occur as policy issues are processed within the regime.

As such, it is a useful term for describing long-term patterns found in the process and eventually also in the substance of policy-making in a particular sector. The general idea is that sectoral policy-making tends to develop in such a way that the same actors, institutions, instruments and governing ideas tend to dominate sectoral policy-making for extended periods of time, infusing a policy sector with both a consistent content and a set of typical policy processes or procedures and actors (Tosun and Lang 2017). Understanding how policy styles – along with – paradigms and regimes – form, how they are maintained and how they change, therefore, is an important aspect of the study of public policy and is helpful in explaining divergences and convergences in patterns of policy designs (Kuks 2004; de Vries 2005).

The fundamental idea of policy styles is to establish similarities between different types of policy-making and the ways in which they are made. With regard to public policies, the concept of policy styles refers to the 'standard operating procedures' of governments in the making and implementing of public policies (Richardson et al. 1982: 2). Put differently, policy styles relate to durable and systematic approaches to policy problems (Freeman 1985: 474). Such persistent forms of interaction and behavioural patterns should be observed during the formulation and implementation of a policy.

Ultimately in assessing regulatory behaviour at the sectoral level in Europe, Knill (1998) focused on similar criteria to those put forward by Richardson et al. in their work on national styles. As he argued:

The dimension of regulatory styles is defined by two related aspects: the mode of state intervention and administrative interest intermediation; i.e. patterns of interaction between administrative and societal actors. (These include) dimensions (such as) hierarchical versus self-regulation, as well as uniform and detailed requirements versus open regulation allowing for administrative flexibility and discretion. In the same way different patterns of interest intermediation can be identified, such as formal versus informal, legalistic versus pragmatic and open versus closed relationships.

In other words, policy styles are sturdy because they are intimately linked with governance contexts and institutional arrangements (Howlett 2002c). National policy systems, for example, can be seen as the offshoots of larger national governance and administrative traditions or cultures (Dwivedi and Gow 1999; Bevir and Rhodes 2001) such as parliamentary or republican forms of government and federal or unitary states. This leads to different concentrations of power in the central institutions of government, degrees of openness and access to information and patterns of reliance on certain kinds of governing instruments rather than others. Civil service organizations have rules and structures affecting policy and administrative behaviour such as the constitutional order establishing and empowering administrators and affecting patterns and methods of recruiting civil servants and how they interact with each other and the public which make their deployment by governments more or less difficult and (in)flexible (Bekke et al.1993).

The relationship between legislative and executive is also of crucial importance. In parliamentary models, the executive is a group of ministers elected from the very parliament, while in pure presidential systems the two branches of government are separate. In this context, Lijphart (1999) claims that, despite strong variations among countries, democratic systems tend to fall into two categories: majoritarian and consensus democracies. The majoritarian system – which is generally associated with the UK and hence is also known as the 'Westminster model' – concentrates power and fuses executive and legislative powers in the classic parliamentary manner (e.g., Colombia, Costa Rica, France, Greece and New Zealand (before 1996), blocking or diminishing opportunities for 'bottom-up' innovation while simultaneously increasing the likelihood of inter-state learning and policy transfer and diffusion.

Conclusion: continuity in policy styles and policy designs

Students of public policy-making in many countries have begun to move beyond simple macro-level models and theories of policy design and have developed a renewed interest in the meso- and micro-aspects of policy formulation and the investigation of the ways in which governments actually propose and utilize the multiple different types of policy instruments available to them (Goggin et al. 1990; Dunsire 1993a). And this is just as true for practitioners as it is for theorists and academics. As Evert Lindquist (1992) argued close to two decades ago, in the modern era officials need:

> new analytical tools that will help them to diagnose and map the external environments of public agencies, to recognize the inherent tensions and dynamics in these environments as they pertain to policy development and consensus-building and to develop new strategies for 'working' these environments in the interests both of their political masters and those of the broader communities they serve. . . . If public servants are to learn from the experience of colleagues working in other sectors and levels of government, they will need a vocabulary to facilitate the dialogue.
>
> (128–9)

This pre-supposes that official and others are aware both the range of tools at their disposal, as set out in Chapters 8–11 and the factors which limit their possible combinations and deployments. Concepts such as governance modes and policy styles are critical in this regard and form the necessary backdrop to any efforts to outline or detail 'best practices' in policy design and designing.

It is to the articulation of these best principles and practices that we now turn in Part V.

Note

1   Lloyd Brown-John (1979) counted 1500 in the USA at the state and federal levels.

Readings

Adam, C., S. Hurka and C. Knill. (2015). 'Four Styles of Regulation and Their Implications for Comparative Policy Analysis'. *Journal of Comparative Policy Analysis: Research and Practice* (21 September): 1–18.

Agranoff, R. and M. McGuire. (2001). 'Big Questions in Public Network Management Research'. *Journal of Public Administration Research and Theory* 11, no. 3: 295–326.

Bingham, L. B., T. Nabatchi and R. O'Leary. (2005). 'The New Governance: Practices and Processes for Stakeholder and Citizen Participation in the Work of Government'. *Public Administration Review* 65, no. 5: 547–58.

Derthick, M. and P. J. Quirk. (1985). *The Politics of Deregulation*. Washington, DC: Brookings Institution.

Dion, L. (1973). 'The Politics of Consultation'. *Government and Opposition* 8, no. 3: 332–53.

Eisner, M. A. (1994). 'Discovering Patterns in Regulatory History: Continuity, Change and Regulatory Regimes'. *Journal of Policy History* 6, no. 2: 157–87.

Enkler, J., S. Schmidt, S. Eckhard, C. Knill and S. Grohs. (2016). 'Administrative Styles in the OECD: Bureaucratic Policy-Making beyond Formal Rules'. *International Journal of Public Administration* 40, no. 8 (13 July): 1–12.

Freeman, G. P. (1985). 'National Styles and Policy Sectors: Explaining Structured Variation'. *Journal of Public Policy* 5, no. 4: 467–96.

Hammond, T. H. and J. H. Knott. (1988). 'The Deregulatory Snowball: Explaining Deregulation in the Financial Industry'. *Journal of Politics* 50, no. 1: 3–30.

Howard, C. (1993). 'The Hidden Side of the American Welfare States'. *Political Science Quarterly* 108, no. 3: 403–36.

Howlett, M. (1991). 'Policy Instruments, Policy Styles and Policy Implementation'. *Policy Studies Journal* 19, no. 2: 1–21.

Howlett, M. (2004). 'Administrative Styles and the Limits of Administrative Reform: A Neo-Institutional Analysis of Administrative Culture'. *Canadian Public Administration* 46, no. 4: 471–94.

Howlett, M. and M. Ramesh. (1993). 'Patterns of Policy Instrument Choice: Policy Styles, Policy Learning and the Privatization Experience'. *Policy Studies Review* 12, no. 1: 3–24.

Jordana, J. and D. Levi-Faur. (2004). 'The Politics of Regulation in the Age of Governance'. In J. Jordana and D. Levi-Faur (eds), *The Politics of Regulation: Institutions and Regulatory Reforms for the Age of Governance.*, Cheltenham, UK: Edward Elgar, 1–28.

Kammerman, S. B. and A. J. Kahn. (1989). *Privatization and the Welfare State.* Princeton, NJ: Princeton University Press.

Libecap, G. D. (1986). 'Deregulation as an Instrument in Industrial Policy: Comment'. *Journal of Institutional and Theoretical Economics* 142: 70–4.

Majone, G. (1997). 'From the Positive to the Regulatory State: Causes and Consequences of Changes in the Mode of Governance'. *Journal of Public Policy* 17, no. 2: 139–67.

Moran, M. (2002). 'Review Article: Understanding the Regulatory State'. *British Journal of Political Science* 32, no. 2: 391–413.

Rhodes, R. A. W. (1994). 'The Hollowing Out of the State: The Changing Nature of the Public Service in Britain'. *The Political Quarterly* 65, no. 2: 138–51.

Richardson, J., G. Gustafsson and G. Jordan. (1982)'.The Concept of Policy Style'. In J. J. Richardson (ed.), *Policy Styles in Western Europe*. London: George Allen & Unwin, 1–16.

Vogel, D. (2005). *The Market for Virtue: The Potential and Limits of Corporate Social Responsibility*. Washington, DC: Brookings Institution.

Part V

CONCLUSION

Lessons for policy designs and designers

How to assemble and evaluate a policy design

Character and context in policy designs

As Stephen Linder, B. Guy Peters, Davis Bobrow, Peter May, Patricia Ingraham, Christopher Hood, Renate Mayntz and the other pioneers of policy design research in the 1980s and 1990s argued, like other kinds of design activities in manufacturing and construction, policy design involves three fundamental aspects: (1) knowledge of the basic building blocks or materials with which actors must work in constructing a (policy) object; (2) the elaboration of a set of principles regarding how these materials should be combined in that construction; and (3) understanding the process by which a design becomes translated into reality.

In a policy context, this means understanding the kinds of implementation tools governments have at their disposal in attempting to alter some aspect of society and societal behaviour; elaborating a set of principles concerning which instruments should be used in which circumstances; and understanding the nuances of policy formulation and implementation processes in government.

The first and third of these three topics have been addressed in Parts II, III and IV of this book. Here in Part V the second needed component of a full exploration of policy design work is set out.

CONCLUSION

Articulating basic principles of policy design

As we have seen in earlier chapters, design tasks are undertaken by experts in policy advice systems, utilizing different sets of ideas they and other policy actors, have about the normative and cognitive contents of policies. It is in this sense that one can talk about policies being designed or consciously crafted and constructed by state actors.

As we have noted, this does not mean that design is always done well – no more than this is the case in architecture or industrial design – and it does not mean that design is not the only activity important to studying or making public policy. Other equally important activities include 'understanding' policy-making or researching its nature and processes (Howlett et al. 2009); 'managing' public policy, or ensuring that planned objectives are actually met in practice (Wu et al. 2010); and 'analyzing' public policy, for example, that is, evaluating the experiences of past or existing policies in order to better inform future policies and developing methodologies for policy alternative appraisal and evaluation (Weimer and Vining 2004; Dunn 2008).

Like all these other tasks, design can be done well or poorly, depending on the skills and knowledge of the designer and the amount of time, information and other resources at his or her disposal in the design task. Designers must not always be simply reacting to circumstances or engaging in a process of incremental policy-making, but require some autonomy and capability to systematically evaluate their circumstances and the range of instrument choices they might make if design is to occur in any meaningful sense.

Design is nevertheless a crucial activity in policy-making and considerations of policy success or failure (Marsh and McConnell 2010; McConnell 2010) since it embodies the lessons learned from other policy activities at the moment in time when a new policy is being developed or an old one reformed. Like architecture or engineering, it is critical to policy-making that the lessons of past efforts – both successes and failures – are encapsulated into principles of sound design which can offer the best chance of the attainment of government goals and objectives in prevalent circumstances (May 1981; Schneider and Ingram 1988; Weimer 1992a; Rose 1993; 2005; Grabosky 1995; Gunningham and Sinclair 1999a).

Principles of effective policy designs based on the character of tools

The literature on policy design reviewed in earlier section of the book has highlighted several key principles for effective policy designs based on the 'character' or innate characteristics of the tools set out in Chapters 8–11. These principles can inform policy design considerations in this area. Three of these principles are listed below.

Parsimonious tool use and the Tinbergen Rule

The older literature on policy design suggested several maxims or heuristics which can be used to head off common errors in policy-making. The first and oldest of these is to observe parsimony in tool selection.

An oft-cited rule in this area, discussed above, for example, is that the optimal ratio of the number of tools to goals is 1:1 (Knudson 2009) an axiom first put forward by Tinbergen (1952) who argued that the number of policy tools in any mix should roughly match the number of goals or objectives set for the policy. This is a reasonable rule-of-thumb, for which Tinbergen provides some logical justification in his discussion of information and administrative costs associated with redundant tools in the area of economic policy. Assuming that utilizing more instruments costs less than fewer and that redundancy is not a virtue, this maxim translates easily enough into a basic efficiency calculus for the attainment of policy ends.

Sequencing: moving up the scale of coercion in instrument choices

A second principle of policy design found in the older literature on the subject was not only to be parsimonious in the number of instruments chosen at a specific point in time to attain a goal, but also dynamically or sequentially, as noted above. In the mid-1970s and early 1980s, for example, Bruce Doern, Richard Phidd and Seymour Wilson argued that different policy instruments varied primarily in terms of the 'degree of government coercion' each instrument choice entailed (Doern 1981; Doern and Phidd 1983; Doern and Wilson 1974; Tupper and Doern 1981). They argued that tool choices should only 'move up the spectrum' of coercion from minimum toward maximum if and when necessary.

This rationale is again based on a cost-effort calculation but linked to an appreciation of the ideological preferences of liberal-democratic governments for limited state activity and on the difficulties posed to the exercise of state power and policy compliance by the relative political 'strength' of the societal actors able to resist government efforts to shape their behaviour. Assuming that all instruments were more or less technically 'substitutable' or could perform any task – although not necessarily as easily or at the same cost – Doern and his colleagues argued that in a liberal democratic society, governments, for both cost and ideological reasons, would prefer to use the least coercive instruments available and would only 'move up the scale' of coercion as far as was necessary in order to overcome societal resistance to attaining their policy goals (Howlett 1991). Preferring 'self-regulation' as a basic default, for example, they argued governments should first attempt to influence overall target group performance through exhortation and then only add instruments as required in order to compel recalcitrant societal actors to abide by their wishes, eventually culminating, if necessary, in the fully public provision of goods and services.

Principles of policy design based on the character of tool mixes

The studies cited in earlier chapters also provide admonitions to policy designers and articulate principles of policy formulation and design linked to the characteristics of policy *portfolios* as well as individual tools. Five of these are set out below.

Utilize coherence, consistency and congruence as measures of the design integrity and superiority of a mix

Much work on policy design and policy mixes has focused on the need for the various parts of a mix or portfolio to be *integrated* for maximum effectiveness (Briassoulis 2005a,b). Policies are composed of several elements and some correspondence across these elements is required if policy goals are to be integrated successfully with policy means (Cashore and Howlett 2007).

These include criteria such as '*consistency*' (the ability of multiple policy tools to reinforce rather than undermine each other in the pursuit of policy goals), '*coherence*' (or the ability of multiple policy goals to co-exist with each other and with instrument norms in a logical fashion, the relationships within the shaded area in figure) and '*congruence*' (or the ability of goals and instruments to work together in a uni-directional or mutually supportive fashion) as important measures of optimality in policy mixes following this integrative logic (Lanzalaco 2011; Howlett and Rayner 2007; Kern and Howlett 2009).

However, while clear enough in theory, empirical work on the evolution of policy mixes has highlighted how these three criteria are often weakly represented in existing mixes, especially those which have evolved over a long period of time (Howlett and Rayner 2006b; Rayner and Howlett 2009). That is, discussions of policy designs do not take place in an historical vacuum and an issue which is especially vexing for design studies is the extent of the constraints imposed on design by the *temporal* evolution of tool portfolios (Miller and Winterberger 1990).

Many existing studies assume, whether explicitly to implicitly, that *any* combination of tools is possible in any circumstance. That is, that decision-makers have unlimited degrees of freedom in their design choices. Empirical studies, however, have noted this kind of freedom in combining design elements is only to be found in very specific circumstances – what Thelen (2003) terms 'replacement' or 'exhaustion' – when older tool elements have been swept aside or abandoned and a new mix can be designed or adopted *de novo*. These circumstances are quite rare and most existing mixes or portfolios have been found to have emerged from a gradual historical process in which a policy mix has slowly built up over time through processes of incremental change or successive reformulation – processes that historical institutionalists, such as Thelen (2003), Hacker (2004b, 2005) and others, term 'layering', 'drift', or 'conversion' (Bode 2006). This aspect of designing and design work is discussed further in the next section.

Maximizing complementary effects and minimizing counter-productive ones

Recent design thinking and earlier work on 'smart regulation' both underlined the importance of considering the full range of policy instruments when designing a mix rather than assuming that a choice must be made between only a few alternatives such as regulation versus market tools (Gunningham et al. 1998).

However, a major issue for such studies is the fact that not all of the tools involved and invoked in a mix are inherently complementary (Tinbergen 1952; Grabosky 1995; Gunningham et al. 1998; Gunningham and Sinclair 1999a; del Río et al. 2011; Boonekamp 2006) in the sense that they evoke contradictory responses from policy targets (Schneider and Ingram 1990a,b, 1993, 1994, 1997, 2005). Some combinations, of course, may be more virtuous in providing a reinforcing or supplementing arrangement (Hou and Brewer 2010). And some other arrangements may also be unnecessarily duplicative while in others some redundancy may be advantageous (Braathen and Croci 2005; Braathen 2007a).

That is, as Grabosky (1995) and others suggested, some tools counteract each other – for example, using command and control regulation while also attempting voluntary compliance – while, as Hou and Brewer (2010) argued, other tools complement or supplement each other – for example, using command and control regulation to prevent certain behaviour deemed undesirable and financial incentives to promote more desired activities.

A key principle of current policy design thinking, therefore, is to try to maximize supplementary effects while minimizing counterproductive ones. 'Smart' design implies creating packages which take these precepts into account in their formulation or packaging (Gunningham et al. 1998; Gunningham and Sinclair 1999b; Eliadis et al. 2005).

However, when multiple tools are involved in a mix, the tools involved and invoked in a mix may be inherently contradictory (Tinbergen 1952; Grabosky 1995; Gunningham et al. 1998) in the sense that they evoke contradictory responses from policy targets (Schneider and Ingram 1990a,b, 1993, 1994, 1997, 2005), while other combinations may be more virtuous in providing a reinforcing or supplementing arrangement (Hou and Brewer 2010).

Although a consensus does not exist on the terms and definitions of conflicts, complementarities and synergies (Oikonomou and Jepma 2008; Oikonomou et al. 2010, 2011a), nevertheless it can be argued that the types of interaction found between tools will vary such that in some cases there will be:

(1) a strong conflict: where the addition of an instrument (X) leads to a reduction of the effect of a second instrument (Y) in the combination: $0 < X + Y < 1$;
(2) a weak conflict (partial complementarity) where the addition of an instrument to another leads to a positive effect on the combination, but lower than the one that would take place if both were used separately: $1 < X + Y < 2$;
(3) a situation of full complementarity where X adds fully to the effect of Y in the combination: $X + Y = 2$; and
(4) a situation of synergy where adding X to Y magnifies the impact of the combination: $X + Y > 2$ (del Río 2013).

Such interactions can range from 'no effect' to 'direct interaction' with effects ranging from 'duplication' (positive or negative redundancy) to 'extended coverage' (positive redundancy) (del Río 2007: 1368–9). Effective design would involve avoiding strong conflicts, minimizing weak ones and promoting complementarity and synergies.

Here the idea would be to attempt to avoid conflicts of both types while promoting tool combinations which are complementary or synergistic. While this becomes more difficult to do as the level of complexity of the design space increases, it remains a central goal of a portfolio design. It may be impossible to satisfy all assessment criteria with different instruments when more than one goal, policy or government is involved, however. The best way to address trade-offs and conflicts between criteria is to adopt a multi-criteria framework which makes those conflicts explicit. This allows policy makers to give weights to those criteria and decide on the trade-off according to their preferences.

Linking tools and goals is a second area in which synergies and complementarities can be sought. Criteria such as 'congruence' and level of 'integration' have been suggested as useful in this area of portfolio design (Howlett and Rayner 2007; Lanzalaco 2011; Mandell 2008; Howlett and Rayner 2007; Kern and Howlett 2009). Work on mixes in sectors such as climate change mitigation and renewable energy support (del Río et al. 2007 and 2011; del Río 2009, 2010; Boonekamp 2006) leads the way in this regard.

As del Río (2009) has argued, design principles to promote integration in complex mixes require a broader view of the elements found in policy mixes than is typically found in the literature on the subject (da Costa 2013). That is, appropriate policy evaluation, appraisal and design cannot be conducted in a narrow context. The focus should not be on the functioning of specific instruments with respect to one specific criterion, but rather upon the functioning of the whole policy mix and the conflicts and synergies with respect to several goals and criteria in this portfolio. This is a particular challenge with overlapping policies and governments. What might be regarded as conflictive in the interactions within an instrument mix might not be so problematic when a broader picture of a policy or governmental mix is considered.

But both horizontal and vertical coordination are very difficult to achieve. There is certainly a role for coordination between goals and instruments to mitigate conflicts and to promote complementarities and synergies in policy mixes. But the existence of different goals at different administrative levels complicates vertical coordination. Different benefits and costs for different constituencies stemming from supranational policies may lead to low levels of social acceptability and considerations of political feasibility. Different goals may create winners and losers at lower administrative levels and, thus, lead to unacceptable distributional effects. All of these factors must enter into design considerations.

Avoiding over and under-designing

Prima facie, simple Tinbergen-type single instrument, single-goal, single policy, single government instrument mixes represent only one of many possible types of instrument mixes. And this means that the standard Tinbergen design maxim of 'one goal – one tool' proposed as a suitable design maxim to address the issue of instrument optimality is unlikely to be put into practice very often and other principles need to be developed to take its place within more complex designs if over and under-designing is to be avoided.

This means utilizing only the number of tools required to reasonably attain policy goals and achieve compliance with government wishes and no more than that. While it may not be clear at the start what is that number, beginning with a smaller number and adding tools as needed to ensure compliance and monitoring the impact and effect of each additional tool can help identify it.

Promoting patching as well as packaging in portfolio design

There is another issue related to the temporal development of mixes and how to handle it which earlier chapters have shed light on. This has to do with consideration of how best to overcome temporal legacies in existing portfolios.

That is, as we have seen in earlier chapters, at least two distinct design techniques emerge from formulation efforts which may take the form of policy 'packaging', that is the creation of new mixes or 'patching' in which only selected aspects of existing mixes are altered.

Recognizing the drawbacks of layering, conversion and drift as often promoting unintentional mixes, many critics have increasingly argued for the promotion of complex policy mixes through replacement. However multiple policy tool portfolios which have evolved over a long period time through processes of incremental layering often cannot easily be replaced. Policy 'patching' is a more realistic design modality in such contexts and, if done properly, with a clear eye on promoting coherence and integration in complex environments can achieve complex and ambitious policy goals in as efficient and effective a way as those designs which are consciously created as interlocking packages of measures (Feindt and Flynn 2009; Kay 2007; Howlett and Rayner 2014).

Better matching tools and target behaviours in compliance regimes

There also is a significant behavioural component to the design of policy mixes which is critical to policy success and failure (Weaver 2009b; Lynn 1986; Schneider and Ingram 1990a; Shafir 2013). That is, as discussed in Chapter 4 in some detail, it is critically important for policy-making that the behaviour resulting from policy activity and the expenditure of governing resources matches that anticipated prior to deployment (May 2004; Kaine et al. 2010; Duesberg et al. 2014).

Policy tool use and behavioural expectations are linked in the sense that the use of policy tools involves implicit or explicit assumptions and expectations about the effect tool deployment will have upon those impacted by it. In most cases, with the exception of those symbolic instances where 'over-design' is welcomed, such as in areas such as national security or crime prevention (Maor 2013, 2014a, 2016), efficient policy designs are those that affect only those targets whose behaviour it is necessary to change and with only the minimum necessary levels of coercion and display.

Policy designs themselves, however, have often been developed with only the most rudimentary and cursory knowledge of how those expected to be affected by an instrument are in fact likely to react to it (Lewis 2007; Corner and Randall 2011; Taylor et al. 2013; Duesberg et al. 2014). Regardless of whether those targets are purely social constructions with few empirical referents (Schneider and Ingram 1993, 2005) or if they reflect more objective assessment of the actual behaviour of relevant groups of policy actors, however, it is critical for effective policy-making that actual target behaviour matches expectations and this is thus a key aspect of effective policy design (Grabosky 1995; Weaver 2009a,b, 2013, 2015; Winter and May 2001; Neilson and Parker 2012).

Much work in this area is often focused around the idea of 'getting incentives right' or calibrating incentives and disincentives, within financial tools in order to achieve expected levels of compliance and outcomes rather than upon examining other, more normative or culturally determined aspects of target reactions. Policy designs in areas such as environmental policy-making developed in the 1980s reflected this economistic orientation with policy initiatives in areas such as pollution prevention and professional regulation assuming a distinctly utilitarian bent in so doing (Hippes 1988; Trebilcock 1983; González-Eguino 2011). This tendency has changed somewhat in recent years as scholars and practitioners alike, many under the influence of behavioural economics, have come to better appreciate that members of the public and other policy actors often behave in less than perfectly rational ways (Ariely 2010; Thaler et al. 2010; Thaler and Sunstein 2009; Mulgan 2008; Bason 2014).

Weaver (2009b: 5), for example, has enumerated some of the various 'compliance problems' or 'barriers' to compliance which governments face when putting their policies into practice which policy instruments must overcome. These include incentive and sanction problems where positive and or negative incentives are insufficient to ensure compliance, but also monitoring problems where target compliance may be difficult or costly to monitor; resource problems where targets lack the resources to comply even if they want to; autonomy problems where targets do not have the power to make decisions that comply with policy even if they want to; information problems where targets lack information that would make compliance more likely and attitude and objectives problems where targets are hostile/mistrustful toward providers or programmes.

Addressing such considerations requires more than one tool and how these tools interact in a 'compliance regime' is an important but understudied aspect of policy designs.

It is also a situation which has a temporal as well as a spatial dimension since many regimes have developed haphazardly over time. That is, across time periods new instruments appear and old ones may have evolved or been eliminated. How the processes of policy formulation followed in adopting such complex designs take place is a subject of much interest in the design world (Larsen et al. 2006; Kay 2007; Feindt and Flynn 2009).

The existing evidence, for example, shows that suboptimal situations are very common in many existing mixes which have developed through processes of policy layering (Thelen 2004; van der Heijden 2011). These kinds of 'unintentional' mixes can be contrasted with 'smarter' designs which involve creating new sets of tools specifically intended to overcome or avoid the problems associated with layering but which may be harder to put into practice (Gunningham et al. 1998; Kiss et al. 2012). Both these processes and change dynamics again focus attention on the *need to properly sequence* instrument choices within mixes (Taeihagh et al. 2009, 2013b; Daugbjerg 2009).

Principles of policy design based on the design context

While knowledge of the character of individual tools and mixes is important in developing principles for policy design, the policy design *context* is equally so (deLeon 1988). Kirschen et al., for example, noted very early on that the key determinants of the policy choices they examined were the economic objectives pursued and the structural and conjunctural context of the choice. While the choice of a specific instrument could be made on essentially technical grounds, according to criteria such as efficiency, cost, or effectiveness, it was also affected by the political preferences of interest groups and governments and a variety of sociological and ideological constraints which would also inform tool choices and preferences (238–44). Lasswell (1954) too noted the extent to which governments could affect every aspect of policy-making though such manipulations varied depending upon the circumstances and actors involved in any given context, and argued that a principal task of the policy sciences must be to understand the nuances of these situations and calibrate their actions and their effects accordingly (Lasswell 1954, 1971; Doern and Phidd 1988; Doern and Wilson 1974).

These authors and others identified a host of contextual factors that come into play in instrument choices and design decisions and different governments do choose different instruments given their particular mix of partisan, electoral, legislative and other preferences including their habits and historical *modus operandi* or policy style. As the discussion in Chapter 12 noted, this latter subject influences assessments of the nature and impact of governance modes on design decisions and helps explain common patterns and motifs in the construction of common policy designs in different jurisdictions reflecting these concerns (Richardson et al. 1982; Howlett 2004a; Howlett 2009d).

Such decisions about tools and designs are not random and context, like character, can be systematically modeled and analyzed in its effects on the process of policy designing.

In other words, the design of policy mixes encompasses the need to ensure a good fit not only between packages of tools and government goals but also their institutional and behavioural contexts at specific moments in time (Considine 2012; Lejano and Shankar 2013). As noted in earlier chapters, existing work on the subject of policy portfolio design has helped to address this issue by differentiating between design spaces which are simple and more complex (Howlett 2004b, 2011; Howlett et al. 2006;).

Thus, for example, it is possible to categorize policy mixes in terms of whether they are single level 'horizontal' mixes and those with a more complex 'vertical' structure (del Río 2009; Howlett and del Río 2015). Such a framework allows room for many more complex interactions between bundle elements than typically envisioned or analyzed in existing studies. That is, conflicts and synergies between tools, goals and policies can be identified both at the horizontal level, for example, between different types of instruments and goals within each level of analysis and/or at the vertical, that is, across and between different policy sectors and/or administrative levels.

These variations have significant implications for both the number and type of actors involved in policy design and the processes through which formulation unfolds, as well as for the complexity of design itself.

Other work has examined a second aspect of 'context', that is, the question of the ability or capacity and intent of governments to undertake this kind of design activity. Having the necessary skills or *competences* to make policy are crucial to policy and governance success. However, they also rely on their availability and the availability of adequate resources to allow them to be mobilized. These resources or *capabilities* must exist at the individual, organizational and system levels in order to allow individual policy workers and managers to participate in and contribute to designing, deploying and evaluating policies. It includes not only their ability to analyze but also to learn and adapt to changes as necessary (Wu et al. 2015a).

Analytical competences allow policy alternatives to be effectively generated and investigated; managerial capacities allow state resources to be effectively brought to bear on policy issues; and political capacities allow policy-makers and managers the support required to develop and implement their ideas, programmes and plans. The skills and competences of key policy professionals, such as policy-makers, public managers and policy analysts, play a key role in determining how well various tasks and functions in policy process but require various kinds of resources if they are to be exercised fully or to the extent they are needed. But resources must also be available at the level of the organization if their members' ability to perform policy functions as needed is to exist.

System level capabilities include the level of support and trust a public agency enjoys from its political masters and from the society at large as well as the nature of the economic and security systems within which policy-makers operate. Such factors are critical determinant of organizational capabilities and thus of public managers' and analysts capability to perform their policy work. Political support for both from both above and below is also vital because agencies and managers must be considered legitimate in order to access resources from their authorizing institutions and constituencies on a continuing basis and such resources must also be available for award in the first place (Woo et al. 2015).

Just as was the case with single instrument and mix characteristics, it is also possible to highlight several design principles which flow from the analysis of the design contexts set out above. These include the question of *goodness of fit* of proposed designs with pre-existing governance preferences and the need for an accurate analysis of the *degrees of freedom* designers have to innovate at any specific moment in time.

Goodness of fit: the need for designs to match governance mode and policy regime capacities

Design choices emerge from and must generally be congruent with the governance modes or styles practiced in particular jurisdictions and sectors (Howlett 2009c). 'Goodness of fit' between tool and context is thus a key concern in contemporary policy design considerations and can be seen to occur at several different levels (Brandl 1988). That is, different orientations toward state activity require different capabilities on the part of state and societal actors and since different governance modes or styles rely on these to greater or lesser degrees, policy designs must take into account both the desired governance context and the actual resources available to a governmental or non-governmental actor in carrying out its appointed role.

Thus, for example, planning and 'steering' involve direct co-ordination of key actors by governments, requiring a high level of government policy capacity to identify and utilize a wide range of policy tools in a successful policy 'mix' or 'arrangement' (Arts et al. 2006; Arts and van Tatenhove 2000). Again, work on 'policy styles' and administrative traditions (Kagan 2001, Richardson et al. 1982, Freeman 1985; Knill 1998) have identified common patterns and motifs in the construction of typical policy designs in different jurisdictions reflecting such concerns (Kiss et al. 2012; Howlett 2009a, 2011) and leading to preferences for particular kinds of tools which make their design and adoption simpler than non-traditional ones.

Degrees of freedom in policy designs: matching policy designing and policy designs over time

Second, as noted above, empirical studies in many policy areas have shown that many existing policy mixes were not 'designed' in the classical sense of conscious, intentional and deliberate planning according to well established or oft-used governance principles but rather evolved through processes of layering and others. As Christensen et al. (2002) have argued the issue here is the leeway or degrees of freedom policy designers have in developing new designs given existing historical arrangements, path dependencies, policy legacies and lock-in effects.

That is, in addition to the requirements of 'goodness of fit' with prevailing governance modes with respect to the logic of policy design there are also constraints imposed on designs by existing sectoral trajectories of policy development. As Christensen et al. note, 'these factors place constraints on and create opportunities for purposeful choice, deliberate instrumental actions and intentional efforts taken by political and administrative leaders to launch administrative reforms through administrative design' (2002: 158). Determining how much room to maneuver or the degrees of freedom designers have to be creative (Considine 2012) or, to put it another way, to what degree they are 'context bound' in time and space (Howlett 2011) is a key one for contemporary design studies.

Designing and assessing policy prototypes through experiments and pilot projects

Although policies may be difficult to change and governance modes and policy styles long-term and persistent, erstwhile policy designers do not always have to work within these contexts and may propose radical or innovative designs which would greatly alter the status quo. Although, for the reasons pointed out above, these might not prove immediately feasible or popular, designers can advocate the development of pilot projects or policy experiments in which new designs and ideas are tried out and proven prior to their being 'scaled up' or 'scaled down' and put into widespread practice.

Such policy experimentation can be used to pre-test different programmes and policies for their likely impacts, process of implementation and stakeholder acceptability prior to launching these fully or on a large-scale. Policy experimentation provides meaning by helping in framing or projecting the future, deriving alternate response strategies and monitoring any changes in the policy environment.

Pilots can aid in policy appraisal (Turnpenny et al. 2009) and provide useful insights for dealing with complex policy issues and high uncertainty (Vreugdenhil et al. 2010). The small-scale and experimental nature of pilots can encourage policy innovations (Cabinet Office 2003) and policy-makers are thus often urged or consider pilot projects and other forms of policy experiments in order to test new policy and programme approaches (Martin and Sanderson 1999; Vreugdenhil et al. 2010).

Policy pilots form a common and important form of policy experimentation and involve the introduction of major government policies or programmes at a 'controlled small-scale' (Weiss 1975) or in a phased manner, 'allowing them to be tested, evaluated and adjusted before being rolled out' (Cabinet Office 2003). Planning 'well-designed pilots' alongside a fully functioning policy can also help test a policy's performance along with the identification of emerging issues and make necessary policy adjustments (Swanson and Bhadwal 2009). A pilot in this sense can form an important step of regular policy monitoring and evaluation over the long-term (Cabinet Office 2003).

However, there are several challenges posed to realizing the benefits of policy experimentation in practice which need to be overcome if success is to be achieved in this area. The study of the impact of pilots on policy development is often limited to 'learning from failure'. Furthermore, the factors leading to success of a pilot and links between pilot diffusion and transition to policies are not well-established, theoretically or empirically (Vreugdenhil et al. 2009).

Designing for robustness and resilience: dealing with surprise, agility and improvisation in policy design

How to best deal with uncertainty and surprise is another issue which has troubled policy studies for some time. Studies of policy uncertainty and policy failure have emphasized the need to have policies able to improvise in the face of an uncertain future, meaning there is a need to design and adopt policies featuring agility, improvisation and flexibility.

By definition, these kinds of designs require redundant resources and capabilities and this need is in strong opposition to ideas about design which equate better designs with efficiency and the allocation of the minimum amount of resources, and to those which emphasize routinization and the replication of standard operating procedures and programme elements.

While these latter designs may be appropriate in some circumstances where competition might provide a degree of system-level resilience and or in well-known or stable environments where surprise is unlikely, this is not true in many public sector activities where government is the sole provider of particular goods and services and future scenarios are unknown, contested, or un-predictable. As studies of crisis management and other similar situations have emphasized, in these instances, robustness is needed and can be planned for.

Governments grapple with complex problems involving situations in which they must deal with multiple actors, ideas and interests in complex problem environments which typically evolve and change over time. This means there is often a high level of uncertainty in policy-making and the modern policy studies movement began with the observation that public policy-making not only commonly results from the interactions of policy-makers in the exercise of power rather than knowledge and also with the recognition that this does not always guarantee effective policies or the attainment of desired results (Arts and van Tatenhove 2004; Lasswell 1958; Stone 1988).

The modern policy sciences are founded on the idea that accumulating and utilizing knowledge of the effects and impacts of a relatively well-known set of policy means developed over many years of state-building experience can more effectively marshal and utilize them than is likely to occur with such purely power-driven process (Lasswell and Lerner 1951; Howlett and Mukherjee 2014). However, more recently, there has been a recognition that even in cases of well-thought out and intentioned or otherwise well-designed policies, failures commonly occur over time (Nair and Howlett 2017; Howlett et al. 2015). That is, even when policies are designed with a clear evidentiary basis in a model process they may still fail if they do not adapt to changings circumstances and concerns as policy implementation proceeds and the policy is put into action (Nair and Howlett 2017).

While some policies are intended only to be short-term fixes, studies of policy uncertainty and policy failure have emphasized the need in many cases to design agility, improvisation and flexibility, or *robustness*, and resilience into policies in order for them to be able to adapt to deal with surprise and uncertain futures over the medium-to-long-term (Walker et al. 2010, 2013; Kwakkel et al. 2010; Capano and Woo 2017). Studies of policy uncertainty, crisis management, policy learning and policy capacity (Moynihan 2009a), for example, have all emphasized this need. This means to design policies capable of maintaining the same performance in the face of any type of internal/external perturbation (Capano and Woo 2017) in order to deal with surprise and avoid policy failure caused by unexpected or unknown occurrences which upset initial design specifications and assumptions (Howlett et al. 2015), Swanson and Bhadwal (2009), for example, emphasize the importance of formal policy review and continuous learning (regular review process even when the policy is functioning well) as one of several process tools that can help policies deal effectively with anticipated and unanticipated conditions.

Designing policies which are robust and resilient over such a wide range of unknowns and uncertainties is a major challenge. On a substantive level, 'robust' policies are those which incorporate some slack, allowing room for adjustments as conditions change. Robust policies, as in the case of a bridge or building, need to be 'overdesigned' or 'over-engineered' in order to allow for a greater range of effective, responses across contexts and time. This can be effective and even efficient over the long-term, for example, in the case of 'automatic stabilizers' such as welfare payments or unemployment insurance payments in the event of an economic downturn, maintaining some level of spending and saving despite a general economic contraction and removing some funds from investment availability during boom times (Salamon 2002b; Sterner 2003). Organizations can become too lean (Radnor and Boaden 2004) and may eliminate elements that could be useful when circumstances change, thus restricting the ability of an organization to respond to surprises (Lai 2012). The ability to alter and adapt policies on the fly – to improvise effectively – requires some level of redundancy in programme resources and parameters but may involve significant administrative and other redundancies and expenses in the short-term which may make them difficult to enact or implement.

And such minimum levels of robustness may not be enough in dealing with deeper levels of uncertainty. These circumstances require not just robust policies but also policy processes that promote robustness. That is, policy robustness in such circumstances requires a style of decision-making which allows response to surprises to be improvised and implemented in an effective way *as they occur* (Room 2013a,b), such as built-in policy reviews and mechanisms for outside evaluation and control including provisions for future public hearings and information access, disclosure and dissemination which can allow more significant adjustments to changing circumstances to occur (Lang 2016).

The European Environment Agency (2001) report on long-term policies, for example, has repeatedly emphasized the importance of building into policies various processes to recognize early warnings of changes in policy environments, especially as new knowledge emerges. The report noted the rising degrees of uncertainty about the the suitability of existing policy solutions to address specific policy problems in the future, but that many of the serious problems posed by deep uncertainties at present could be reduced if *policy-making* remained flexible and adaptive, or robust and resilient. This can include actions promoting informal relationships, personal connections and past experiences which are the prerequisites for collaboration in extreme events or, what Lai (2012) call 'auto-adaptation to initial conditions', the frequent re-examination and adaptation to changes of initial conditions and assumptions.

Conclusion: better design and better design processes

Transforming policy ambitions into practice is a complex process and intentionally creating the best possible arrangement of policy elements is not always the first item on a government's mind, nor necessarily within its reach. Many noble efforts of policy-makers have failed due to poor design capacity or the inability or lack of desire to alter elements of existing policies in a more logical, instrumental, fashion (Howlett 2012; Cohn 2004). These experiences have led to a greater awareness of the various obstacles that can present themselves to policy design efforts and have gradually fueled a desire for better understanding the unique characteristics of policy instruments and the different contexts within which policy design work proceeds, as well as to articulate principles of policy decision, which are themselves robust across jurisdictions, sectors and time periods, and provide instructions to those attempts to improve policy making and policy outcomes through better policy designing.

Readings

Berg, S. V., A. N. Memon and R. Skelton. (2000). 'Designing an Independent Regulatory Commission'. IRC Research Paper.

Bryson, J. M., K. S. Quick, C. S. Slotterback and B. C. Crosby (2013). 'Designing Public Participation Processes'. *Public Administration Review* 73, no. 1 (1 January): 23–34.

Capano, G. and J. J. Woo. (2017). 'Resilience and Robustness in Policy Design: A Critical Appraisal'. *Policy Sciences* 37, no. 4 (5 January): 1–28.

Capano, G., M. Howlett and M. Ramesh. (2018). 'Designing for Robustness: Surprise, Agility and Improvisation in Policy Design'. *Policy & Society* 37, no. 4: 1–22.

Fung, A. (2003). 'Survey Article: Recipes for Public Spheres: Eight Institutional Design Choices and Their Consequences'. *Journal of Political Philosophy* 11, no. 3 (1 September): 338–67.

Gilardi, F. (2005). 'The Formal Independence of Regulators: A Comparison of 17 Countries and 7 Sectors'. *Swiss Political Science Review* 11, no. 4: 139–67.

Grabosky, P. (1995). 'Counterproductive Regulation'. *International Journal of the Sociology of Law* 23: 347–69.

Holland, S. P. and M. R. Moore. (2013). 'Market Design in Cap and Trade Programs: Permit Validity and Compliance Timing'. *Journal of Environmental Economics and Management* 66, no. 3 (November): 671–87.

Hood, C. (1983). 'Using Bureaucracy Sparingly'. *Public Administration* 61, no. 2: 197–208.

Hou, Y. and G. Brewer. (2010). 'Substitution and Supplementation between Co-Functional Policy Instruments: Evidence from State Budget Stabilization Practices'. *Public Administration Review* 70, no. 6: 914–24.

Howlett, M. and S. Nair. (2017). 'From Robustness to Resilience: Avoiding Policy Traps in the Long-Term'. *Sustainability Science* 11, no. 6: 909–17.

Howlett, M. and M. Ramesh. (2016). 'Achilles' Heels of Governance: Critical Capacity Deficits and Their Role in Governance Failures'. *Regulation & Governance* 10, no. 4 (1 December): 301–13.

Howlett, M., I. Mukherjee and J. Rayner. (2014). 'The Elements of Effective Program Design: A Two-Level Analysis'. *Politics and Governance* 2, no. 2 (9 June): 1–12.

Howlett, M., J. Vince and P. del Río. (2017). 'Policy Integration and Multi-Level Governance: Dealing with the Vertical Dimension of Policy Mix Designs'. *Politics and Governance* 5, no. 2 (5 May): 69–78.

Justen, A., N. Fearnley, M. Givoni and J. Macmillen. (2014). 'A Process for Designing Policy Packaging: Ideals and Realities'. *Transportation Research Part A: Policy and Practice, Policy Packaging* 60 (February): 9–18.

Justen, A., J. Schippl, B. Lenz and T. Fleischer. (2013). 'Assessment of Policies and Detection of Unintended Effects: Guiding Principles for the Consideration of Methods and Tools in Policy-Packaging'. *Transportation Research Part A: Policy and Practice* 60 (February): 19–30.

Kempf, R. J. (2015). 'Crafting Accountability Policy: Designing Offices of Inspector General'. *Policy & Society* 34, no. 2: 137–49.

May, P. J. (1981). 'Hints for Crafting Alternative Policies'. *Policy Analysis* 7, no. 2: 227–44.

Mayntz, R. (1983). 'The Conditions of Effective Public Policy: A New Challenge for Policy Analysis'. *Policy & Politics* 11 (April): 123–43.

Mees, H. L. P., J. Dijk, D. van Soest, P. P. J. Driessen, M. H. F. M. W. van Rijswick and H. Runhaar. (2014). 'A Method for the Deliberate and Deliberative Selection of Policy Instrument Mixes for Climate Change Adaptation'. *Ecology and Society* 19, no. 2: 58.

Nair, S. and M. Howlett. (2016a). 'Meaning and Power in the Design and Development of Policy Experiments'. *Futures*, 76 (February): 67–74.

Nair, S. and M. Howlett. (2016b). 'From Robustness to Resilience: Avoiding Policy Traps in the Long-Term'. *Sustainability Science* 11, no. 6: 909–917.

Optic, Optimal Policies for Transportation in Combination. (2014). 'Best Practices and Recommendations on Policy Packaging'. *Annual Review of Policy Design* 2, no. 1 (8 November): 1–10.

de la Rue du Can, S., G. Leventis, A. Phadke and A. Gopal. (2014). 'Design of Incentive Programs for Accelerating Penetration of Energy-Efficient Appliances'. *Energy Policy* 72 (September): 56–66.

Skeete, J.-P. (2017). 'Examining the Role of Policy Design and Policy Interaction in EU Automotive Emissions Performance Gaps'. *Energy Policy* 104 (May): 373–81.

Taeihagh, A., M. Givoni and R. Bañares-Alcántara. (2013). 'Which Policy First? A Network-Centric Approach for the Analysis and Ranking of Policy Measures'. *Environment and Planning B: Planning and Design* 40, no. 4: 595–616.

Vining, A. R. and A. E. Boardman. (2008). 'Public–Private Partnerships: Eight Rules for Governments'. *Public Works Management & Policy* 13, no. 2 (1 October): 149–61.

Whitten, S. M. (2017). 'Designing and Implementing Conservation Tender Metrics: Twelve Core Considerations'. *Land Use Policy* 63 (April): 561–71.

Chapter 14

Conclusion: the capacity challenges of policy design over space and time

In what follows below, two central points in the book concerning the nature of policy design and the preconditions for its success are set out. These are: (1) the need for designers to thoroughly analyze and understand the 'policy space' in which they are working; and (2) the need for them to be aware of and deal with the temporal and contextual dimensions of this space.

Understanding the design space

The chapters in this book have highlighted many significant aspects of the policy formulation and design processes, describing both how these processes work, who is involved with them, their impact on policy outcomes and lessons from the existing design literature on best practices for practitioners and erstwhile designers as they go about their work.

This is ongoing work and the ongoing research agenda of the new design orientation is focused on many questions which an earlier literature on the subject largely neglected, such as the trade-offs existing between different tools in complex policy mixes and how to deal with the synergies and conflicts which result from tool interactions; as well as the different means and patterns – such as layering – through which policy mixes evolve over time (Thelen 2004).

Understanding the design space available in any design situation is critical. Many formulation situations, for example, involve information and knowledge limits or involve multiple actors whose relationships may be more adversarial or competitive than is typically associated with a design process and outcome

(Schon 1988; Gero 1990). That is, not all policy-making is logic or knowledge-driven and how closely policy-makers approximate the instrumental logic and reasoning which is generally thought to characterizes an intellectually-driven design situation in this field or any other is a function of the 'space' in which formulation considerations take place (Howlett et al. 2009). As we have seen, some of these spaces are conducive to policy design, while others – 'non-design' spaces – are not.

But even within a design space, some situations are more propitious for large-scale or fundamental reforms or policy 'packaging' than others which tends toward policy 'patching' or 'stretching'. As we have seen, policy formulation typically occurs within the confines of an existing governance mode and policy logic which both simplifies and constrains the task of policy design. It does this by restricting the number of alternatives which are considered feasible in any given situation. This can reduce to manageable proportions the otherwise almost infinite range of possible specific micro-level instrument choices (Meuleman 2010b) and promote 'smart' layering; but only if these contextual constraints are diagnosed accurately.

Establishing the nature of the policy design 'space' is, therefore, a crucial activity for policy designers. That is, the process of design and instrument selection is made simpler once the fact that some of the elements of public policies remain more amenable to careful thought and deliberate government manipulation than others is recognized.

Designing successful policies also requires thinking about policy-making in such a way as to fully take into account the dual purposes–substantive and procedural – which policies can serve and the nature of the multiple levels of policy elements or components which make up a typical policy. But understanding exactly how instrument choices are constrained by higher-order sets of variables is crucial to making good policy design decisions in specific policy-making contexts.

As set out in this book, adopting a multi-level, nested model of policy context helps clarify what 'room' exists at what level of policy for new or alternative policy design elements (Hamdouch and Depret 2010). As the discussion here has shown, high-level abstract 'macro' level policy goals typically vary in accordance with the nature of the governance mode found in a particular sector at a specific time which itself encompasses the set of political actors, ideas and institutional rules which are prevalent in that jurisdiction at the moment at which policy deliberations and decision making takes place (Moore 1988; Braun 1999; Howlett and Ramesh 2003). The existence of these fairly long-term and stable governance arrangements helps maintain relatively constant general formulation and implementation preferences or 'styles', since these derive from and are constrained by the same set of factors which influence and inform the development and articulation of abstract policy goals and means (Howlett 1991; May 1991; Dunsire 1993a; Kooiman 2000, 2008).

As the discussion in Chapters 8–11 has shown, the existence of a dominant governance mode in a particular sector or issue area generates certain propensities for the use of specific kinds of tools within and across Hood's resource categories. That is, these different governance modes involve different overall preferences for general kinds of substantive and procedural policy instruments expected to attain the general aims of government. Different countries and sectors share these styles and they are the first important overall determinant of the policy design space found in specific policy and issue areas (Meuleman 2010a; Hardiman and Scott 2010; Howlett and Tosun 2019).

As we have seen in many countries, the preferred instruments for policy implementation in many sectors have been configured as largely legal and corporatist rather than market or network based. Although the context, style and substance of both the marketplace and the network has infiltrated the policy formulation process in recent years (Majone 1989), as the discussion in the book has shown, the policy design space in most sectors remains firmly fixed within earlier modes, especially, in many countries in Europe, Asia and Latin America, for example, within corporatist modes (Heritier et al. 1996; Knill 2001b; Pollitt 2001a). Hence, although compliance with government intentions has been approached in some sectors in these countries in terms of market-based factors – profit margins and the economic viability of industry, employment patterns and international competitiveness – any new emphasis on the deployment of market-based policy tools has had little effect on already long-standing and implemented policy designs in many sectors (Rhodes 1996; Salamon 2001; O'Toole and Meier 2010).

This underlines the linkages which exist between patterns of policy instrument choices and general governance preferences and the need for policy designers to be thoroughly aware of this aspect of the nature of the design space within which they are working.

But there is more to the impact of design spaces on policy designs and designing than this. Promoting 'integrated' policy mix designs congruent with existing design spaces, for example, multiplies the problems designers face in making choices and selecting instruments (Meijers and Stead 2004; Stead et al. 2004; Briassoulis 2005b,c). Doing so, however, assumes the existence of a great deal of administrative and analytical capacity on the part of state actors that may or may not exist in different sectors and countries (Howlett 2009d; Howlett and Newman 2010).

That is, in order for 'design' to meaningfully occur at all, policy designers need a great deal of knowledge and insight into the workings of their polity and specific policy sectors, raising to the forefront questions about the capacity of policy experts and advisors involved in the policy formulation process (Bye and Bruvoll 2008; Schön 1992). In order to be able to make an appropriate decision about when to introduce new instruments and when to renew old ones, they must be familiar not only with the technical aspects of the menu of instruments before them, but also with the nature of the governance and policy contexts in which they are working and thus require training and experience in both these aspects of the policy design process if design is to occur at all (Braathen 2005, 2007b; Grant 2010; Skodvin et al. 2010).

Whether or not such expertise exists within a design space is a further criteria of design success of which both students and practitioners of policy design must be fully aware.

Understanding the temporality of design choices

As the discussion in the book has also repeatedly noted, specific instrument choices are embedded decisions, existing within a nested, multi-level environment of governance modes, policy regime logics and tool calibrations and are heavily context-laden. The basic nature of possible governance regimes, however, is well known and the general implementation preferences they entail are also quite clear. That leaves the essential design challenge in many sectors as one of the identification and articulation of specific policy measures, more or less carefully calibrated, from within each resource category, within an already existing governance mode.

However, the common existence of fairly 'routine' design situations should not be taken to suggest complete stability in all areas and it is certainly the case that preferred governance modes do change as some governments have moved away, for example, from legalistic and corporatist modes toward more flexible modes associated with market and network governance and governance styles. Such movements, as adherents of the globalization and government-to-government hypotheses have articulated, can have a large impact on the types of policy design choices taken by government, such as a shift away from 'direct' government activities toward an increased reliance on the indirect manipulation of market and policy network actors found in some sectors such as energy and education policy in recent years.

There is thus a temporal aspect to policy designs contexts, which policy designers must also take into account. As Christensen et al. (2002) have argued, the leeway or degree of maneuverability policy designers have in developing new designs is influenced not only by existing contextual factors and polity features but also by historical-institutionalist ones.

That is, except in the case of completely new policy areas, which are relatively rare, designers are typically faced with a situation in which an existing set of policy goals and a mix of policy instruments is already in place (Thelen 2003, 2004). These arrangements commonly have emerged or evolved over relatively long periods of time through previous design decisions and as the discussion in this book has shown, even if they had a clear logic and plan at the outset they may no longer do so (Bode 2006). This is because they may have evolved through such temporal processes as layering in which instruments and goals are simply added to existing ones without abandoning the previous ones, a process which has been linked to both incoherence among the policy ends and inconsistency with respect to policy means (Howlett and Rayner 1995; Orren and Skowronek 1999; Rayner et al. 2001).

In these contexts, designers are faced with the challenge of redesign or the replacement of only some of the existing regime elements in which the design space has been altered by the continued existence of the remnants of earlier policy efforts. In such situations, designers often attempt to patch or restructure existing policy elements rather than propose alternatives *de novo* (Gunningham and Sinclair 1999a; Thelen 2003, 2004; Eliadis et al. 2005). In such redesigns, Howlett and Rayner (2007) and Kern and Howlett (2009) have focused attention on the importance of designers aiming to achieve 'coherence, consistency and congruence' in any new design. That is, designers should ensure that any new design elements are coherent in the sense that they are logically related to overall policy aims and objectives; that they be consistent in that they work together to support a policy goal; and that both policy goals and means should be congruent, rather than working at cross purposes.

Again, this requires a great deal of analytical and implementation capacity on the part of policy-makers and policy designers which may or may not exist. Capacity, therefore, emerges as a key criteria for designing effective policies over both space and time.

Overcoming capacity and competence challenges to effective design

As the above discussion suggests, governments face a variety of empirical, capacity and knowledge-related circumstances which pose significant challenges to their designing effective of policies.

The desire to create effective policies in areas such as climate change, for example, where problems are expected to mount in number and persist over the long-term, needs to not only be based on evidence and logic but also to embody flexibility in order to still be able to deliver on expectations about programmeme and policy goals and objectives (Jordan 2014; Leone 2010).

Attaining robust, resilient and effective policies requires a conscious effort to diagnose existing arrangements and levels of uncertainty and design policies and policy-making processes capable of adapting to a wide range of potential future circumstances (Day and Klein 1989; Capano and Woo 2017). Formulating and implementing policy processes and programmemes which promote agility is not automatic, however, but requires care and forethought. Failing to correctly identify the bounds and range of these uncertainties, for example, is a major cause of policy over and under-reaction (Maor 2012a,b) and unwanted over and under-policy design.

The need for leadership, brokerage and entrepreneurship in policy design implementation

Even where suitable capacity exists to design an effective policy, however, this does not guarantee that the design will effectively be implemented. In dealing with higher levels of uncertainty, policy-makers must operate as

279

'continuous policy-fixers' (Ingraham 1987) and their role oscillates between that of a policy 'architect', 'facilitator' and 'learner' in the policy process to appropriately 'adjust' a design in response to changing conditions over time (Howlett and Mukherjee 2014; Junginger 2013; Bason 2013; Mulgan 2008; Chiarini 2012).

Brokerage, for example, is an important task that needs to be undertaken in ensuring not only that knowledge and power are brought together in the right combination to result in problem-centered policy-making (Christopoulos and Ingold 2011) but that implementation proceeds effectively. Its prevailing function in a policy design perspective is bridging and connecting different groups in a network or different actors on a common project of design, or in channeling improvisation according to the planned design in order to maintain of facilitate agility.

Entrepreneurship (Schneider and Teske 1995; Kingdon 1984; Mintrom 1997; Mintrom and Norman 2009; Wijen and Ansari 2007; Levy and Scully 2007) is also important as entrepreneurs can be the bearers of innovation or act to enlighten policy-makers with respect to the real meaning of new evidence-based knowledge (Argote et al. 1990; Darr et al. 1995).

And leadership is also significant (Weber 1978; Blondel 1987) as transformational and transactional leadership (cf. Burns 2012; Selznick 1984; Gronn 2009; Pfeffer 1977; Svara 1994; Stiller 2009), each activate different mechanisms of followership critical in steering the policy design process by 'constraining' or encouraging policy-makers to maintain their commitment toward design-orientated formulation and implementation (OECD 2011).

Conclusion: dealing better with uncertainty – the task of policy design in contemporary government

Policy design, in this sense, is a specific form of policy formulation based on the gathering of knowledge about the effects of policy tool use on policy targets and the application of that knowledge to the development and implementation of policies aimed at the attainment of specifically desired public policy outcomes and ambitions (Bobrow 2006; Bobrow and Dryzek 1987; Montpetit 2003b; Weaver 2009b, 2010b). It involves the deliberate and conscious attempt to define policy goals and connect them in an instrumental fashion to tools expected to realize those objectives (Gilabert and Lawford-Smith 2012; Majone 1975; May 2003).

Within the policy sciences, the 'design' orientation addresses key questions about policy instrument characteristics and choice and about the factors behind successful design formulation and implementation (May 2003; Linder and Peters 1990a). These include such important questions as the trade-offs existing between different tools in complex policy mixes and how to deal with the synergies and conflicts which result from tool interactions; as well as the different means and patterns – such as layering – through which policies evolve over time (van der Heijden 2011; Howlett 2014b; Howlett and Lejano 2013; Howlett et al. 2014; Doremus 2003; Jordan et al. 2011, 2012; del Río and Howlett 2013).

Studies in fields such as political science, economics, law and public administration have all underlined that translating policy aims and objectives into practice is not as simple a task as might at first appear. Policies are made by a variety of different actors interacting with each other over a relatively long period of time within the confines of a set of political and economic institutions and governing norms, each with different interests and resources and all operating within a climate of uncertainty caused both by context and time-specific knowledge and information limitations (Bressers and O'Toole 1998, 2005). Understanding who these actors are and why and how they act the way they do is a critical aspect of all public policymaking activity, including policy instrument selection and in policy design (Skodvin et al. 2010).

The analysis presented in this book suggests that many traditional ways of thinking about these activities and their impact on policy instrument choices and policy designs are out of date. Dichotomous sets of policy alternatives – such as 'market versus state' – and metaphors – such as 'carrots versus sticks', for example, – lend themselves to blunt thinking about instruments and their modalities. Administrators and politicians involved in policy design need to expand the menu of government choice to include both substantive and procedural instruments and a wider range of options of each and to understand the important context-based nature of instrument choices.

Beyond such obvious points, however, theorists and practitioners also both need to move beyond simple notions of the pervasive impact of large-scale macro developments such as globalization and networkization. Understanding the precise nature of a policy space and its history of development over time are prerequisites of successful design (Schön 1992). Innovative policy design, especially, requires that the parameters of instrument choice be well understood, both in order to reduce the risk of policy failure and to enhance the probability of policy success (Linder and Peters 1990a; Schneider and Ingram 1997).

Given the complexity of policy making it is not surprising that many noble efforts by governments and citizens to create a better and safer world have foundered on poor policy design. However, while not an optimal outcome, this has led to a greater appreciation of the difficulties encountered in designing public policies and the attempt to correct gaps in our understanding, a process which albeit slowly, has improved our knowledge of the principles and elements of the nature of policy instruments and their governance contexts of policy design.

The challenge for a new generation of design studies is to develop not only the conceptual clarity and the methodological sophistication needed to identify changes in policy contexts, but also the techniques for understanding the influences of interaction between these contexts and the other elements of policy (Eliadis et al. 2005; Yeung and Dixon-Woods 2010; del Río 2010;

Hamelin 2010). Blunt choices lend themselves to blunt thinking about instruments and their modalities which is not helpful in conducting or thinking about policy design.

As the basis for the design and implementation of carefully calibrated policy measures, the templates developed by Doern, Hood, Linder and Peters; Schneider and Ingram; and Salamon in the mid-1980s are still very useful in helping to organize the literature and focus design discussions. But, in spite of this work and the centrality and importance of design to public policy-making, the subject still remains in many respects a 'missing link' in policy studies (Hargrove 1975). Scholars need more empirical analysis in order to test their models and provide better advice to governments about the process of tool selection and how to better match tools for the job at hand. But while the design process is complex, often internally orchestrated between bureaucrats and target groups and usually much less accessible to public scrutiny than many other kinds of policy deliberations, this should not be allowed to stand in the way of its further elaboration and refinement (Kiviniemi 1986; Donovan 2001).

Readings

Balch, G. I. (1980). 'The Stick, the Carrot, and Other Strategies: A Theoretical Analysis of Governmental Intervention'. *Law and Policy Quarterly* 2, no. 1: 35–60.

Bason, C. (2014). *Design for Policy*. Farnham, UK; Burlington, VT: Gower.

Baxter-Moore, N. (1987). 'Policy Implementation and the Role of the State: A Revised Approach to the Study of Policy Instruments'. In R. J. Jackson, D. Jackson and N. Baxter-Moore (eds), *Contemporary Canadian Politics: Readings and Notes*. Scarborough, ON: Prentice Hall, 336–55.

Coletti, P. (2015). 'Public Policy Design: How to Learn From Failures'. *World Political Science* 11, no. 2: 325–45.

Gunningham, N., P. Grabosky and D. Sinclair. (1998). *Smart Regulation: Designing Environmental Policy*. Oxford: Clarendon Press, 422–53.

Howlett, M. (2014). 'From the "Old" to the "New" Policy Design: Design Thinking beyond Markets and Collaborative Governance'. *Policy Sciences* 47, no. 3 (28 May): 187–207.

Howlett, M. (2018a). 'The Criteria for Effective Policy Design: Character and Context in Policy Instrument Choice'. *Journal of Asian Public Policy* 11, no. 3 (6 December): 245–66.

Howlett, M. and I. Mukherjee. (2018). 'The Contribution of Comparative Policy Analysis to Policy Design: Articulating Principles of Effectiveness and Clarifying Design Spaces'. *Journal of Comparative Policy Analysis: Research and Practice* 20, no. 1 (1 January): 72–87.

Howlett, M., I. Mukherjee and J. J. Woo. (2015). 'From Tools to Toolkits in Policy Design Studies: The New Design Orientation towards Policy Formulation Research'. *Policy & Politics* 43, no. 2: 292–311.

Johnson, J. and M. Cook. (2014). 'Policy Design: A New Area of Design Research and Practice'. In M. Aiguier, F. Boulanger, D. Krob and C. Marchal (eds). *Complex Systems Design & Management*. Cham, Germany: Springer, 51–62.

Justen, A., N. Fearnley, M. Givoni and J. Macmillen. (2014). 'A Process for Designing Policy Packaging: Ideals and Realities'. *Transportation Research Part A: Policy and Practice, Policy Packaging*, 60 (February): 9–18.

Lindquist, E. A. (1992). 'Public Managers and Policy Communities: Learning to Meet New Challenges'. *Canadian Public Administration* 35, no. 2: 127–59.

Lockton, D., D. Harrison and N. A. Stanton. (2016). 'Design for Sustainable Behaviour: Investigating Design Methods for Influencing User Behaviour'. *Annual Review of Policy Design* 4, no. 1 (28 October): 1–10.

Madrian, B. C. (2014). 'Applying Insights from Behavioral Economics to Policy Design'. *Annual Review of Economics* 6, no. 1: 663–88.

Mintrom, M. and J. Luetjens. (2016). 'Design Thinking in Policymaking Processes: Opportunities and Challenges'. *Australian Journal of Public Administration* 75, no. 3: 391–402.

Mukherjee, I. and S. Giest. (2017). 'Designing Policies in Uncertain Contexts: Entrepreneurial Capacity and the Case of the European Emission Trading Scheme'. *Public Policy and Administration* (20 September).

Öberg, P. O., M. Lundin and J. Thelander. (2015). 'Political Power and Policy Design: Why Are Policy Alternatives Constrained?' *Policy Studies Journal* 43, no. 1 (1 February): 93–114.

Peters, B. G., P. Ravinet, M. Howlett, G. Capano, I. Mukherjee and M. H. Chou. (2018). *Designing for Policy Effectiveness: Defining and Understanding a Concept*. Elements Series. Cambridge: Cambridge University Press.

Salamon, L. M. and B. G. Peters. (2002). 'The Politics of Tool Choice'. In L. M. Salamon (ed.), *The Tools of Government: A Guide to the New Governance*. New York: Oxford University Press, 552–64.

Turnbull, N. (2017). 'Policy Design: Its Enduring Appeal in a Complex World and How to Think It Differently'. *Public Policy and Administration* 33, no. 4: 357–64.

Vancoppenolle, D., H. Sætren and P. Hupe. (2015). 'The Politics of Policy Design and Implementation: A Comparative Study of Two Belgian Service Voucher Programs'. *Journal of Comparative Policy Analysis: Research and Practice* (21 April): 1–17.

Van Kersbergen, K. and F. van Waarden. (2004). ' "Governance" as a Bridge Between Disciplines: Cross-Disciplinary Inspiration Regarding Shifts in Governance and Problems of Governability, Accountability and Legitimacy'. *European Journal of Political Research* 43, no. 2: 143–72.

Webb, K. (2005). 'Sustainable Governance in the Twenty-First Century: Moving Beyond Instrument Choice'. In P. Eliadis, M. Hill and M. Howlett (eds), *Designing Government: From Instruments to Governance*. Montreal, QC: McGill-Queen's University Press, 242–80.

Woodside, K. (1986). 'Policy Instruments and the Study of Public Policy'. *Canadian Journal of Political Science* 19, no. 4: 775–93.

Bibliography

Abelson, D. E. (2002). *Do Think Tanks Matter? Assessing the Impact of Public Policy Institutes.* Kingston, ON: McGill-Queen's University Press.

Abelson, D. E. (2007). 'Any Ideas? Think Tanks and Policy Analysis in Canada'. In L. Dobuzinskis, M. Howlett and D. Laycock (eds), *Policy Analysis in Canada: The State of the Art.* Toronto, ON: University of Toronto Press, 298–310.

Abelson, J., P. G. Forest, J. Eyles, P. Smith, E. Martin and F. P. Gauvin. (2003). 'Deliberations about Deliberative Methods: Issues in the Design and Evaluation of Public Participation Processes'. *Social Science and Medicine* 57: 239–51.

Aberbach, J. D. and B. A. Rockman. (1989). 'On the Rise, Transformation and Decline of Analysis in the US Government'. *Governance* 2, no. 3: 293–314.

Ackerman, B. (1981). *Clean Coal/Dirty Air: or How the Clean Air Act Became a Multibillion-Dollar Bail-Out for High-Sulfur Coal Producers,* Vol. 23. New Haven, CT: Yale University Press.

Adam, C., S. Hurka and C. Knill. (2015). 'Four Styles of Regulation and Their Implications for Comparative Policy Analysis'. *Journal of Comparative Policy Analysis: Research and Practice* (21 September): 1–18.

Adamowicz, W. (2007). 'Reflections on Environmental Policy in Canada'. *Canadian Journal of Agricultural Economics* 55: 1–13.

Adams, D. (2004). 'Usable Knowledge in Public Policy'. *Australian Journal of Public Administration* 63, no. 1: 29–42.

Adcroft, A. and R. Willis. (2005). 'The (Un)Intended Outcome of Public Sector Performance Measurement'. *International Journal of Public Sector Management* 18, no. 5: 386–400.

Adelle, C. and D. Russell. (2013). 'Climate Policy Integration: A Case of Déjà Vu?' *Environmental Policy and Governance* 23, no. 1: 1–12.

Adger, W. N. and Jordan, A. J. (eds). (2009). *Governing Sustainability.* Cambridge: Cambridge University Press.

Adger, W. N., I. Lorenzoni and K. L. O'Brien (eds). (2010). *Adapting to Climate Change: Thresholds, Values, Governance* (reissue). Cambridge: Cambridge University Press.

Adler, E. and P. M. Haas. (1992). 'Conclusion: Epistemic Communities, World Order, and the Creation of a Reflective Research Program'. *International Organization*, 46: 367–90.

Adler, R. S. and R. D. Pittle. (1984). 'Cajolry or Command: Are Education Campaigns an Adequate Substitute for Regulation?' *Yale Journal on Regulation* 1, no. 2: 159–93.

Advani, A. and S. Borins. (2001). 'Managing Airports: A Test of the New Public Management'. *International Public Management Journal* 4: 91–107.

Agranoff, R. (1998). 'Multinetwork Management: Collaboration and the Hollow State in Local Economic Policy'. *Journal of Public Administration Research and Theory* 8, no. 1: 67–92.

Agranoff, R. and M. McGuire. (1999). 'Managing in Network Settings'. *Policy Studies Review* 16, no. 1: 18–41.

Agranoff, R. and M. McGuire. (2001). 'Big Questions in Public Network Management Research'. *Journal of Public Administration Research and Theory* 11, no. 3: 295–326.

Ajzen, I. (1991). 'The Theory of Planned Behavior'. *Organizational Behavior and Human Decision Processes* 50, no. 2: 179–211.

Albrow, M. (1970). *Bureaucracy*. London: Pall Mall Press.

Alexander, E. (1982). 'Design in the Decision-Making Process'. *Policy Sciences* 14: 279–92.

Alford. J. (1998). 'A Public Management Road Less Traveled: Clients as Co-Producers of Public Services'. *Australian Journal of Public Administration* 57, no. 4: 128–37.

Alford, J. (2002). 'Why Do Public-Sector Clients Coproduce? Toward a Contingency Theory'. *Administration & Society* 34, no. 1: 32–56.

Alford, R. (1972). 'The Political Economy of Health Care: Dynamics Without Change'. *Politics and Society* 2: 127–64.

Allcott, H. (2011). Social Norms and Energy Conservation. *Journal of Public Economics* 95, nos 9–10: 1082–95.

Allcott, H. and T. Rogers. (2014). 'The Short-Run and Long-Run Effects of Behavioral Interventions: Experimental Evidence from Energy Conservation'. *American Economic Review*, 104, no. 10: 3003–37.

Allison, G. T. and M. H. Halperin. (1972). 'Bureaucratic Politics: A Paradigm and Some Policy Implications'. *World Politics* 24, Supplement: 40–79.

Alonso, S., J. Keane and W. Merkel. (eds) (2011). *The Future of Representative Democracy*. Cambridge: Cambridge University Press.

Alshuwaikhat, H. M. and D. I. Nkwenti. (2002). 'Visualizing Decisionmaking: Perspectives on Collaborative and Participative Approach to Sustainable Urban Planning and Management'. *Environment and Planning B: Planning and Design* 29: 513–31.

Altman, D. (2010). *Direct Democracy Worldwide*. Cambridge: Cambridge University Press.

Ambali, A. R. (2010). 'E-Government in Public Sector: Policy Implications and Recommendations for Policy-Makers'. *Research Journal of International Studies* 17: 133–45. www.eurojournals.com/RJIS_17_10.pdf.

Amenta, E. and B. G. Carruthers. (1988). 'The Formative Years of US Social Spending Policies: Theories of the Welfare State and the American States during the Great Depression'. *American Sociological Review* 53: 661–78.

Aminzade, R. (1992). 'Historical Sociology and Time'. *Sociological Methods and Research*, 20, no. 4: 456–80.

Andersen, S. C. (2008). 'Private Schools and the Parents that Choose Them: Empirical Evidence from the Danish School Voucher System'. *Scandinavian Political Studies* 31, no. 1: 44–68.

Anderson, C. W. (1971). 'Comparative Policy Analysis: The Design of Measures'. *Comparative Politics* 4, no. 1: 117–31.

Anderson, C. W. (1977). *Statecraft: An Introduction to Political Choice and Judgement.* New York: John Wiley & Sons.

Anderson, G. (1996). 'The New Focus on the Policy Capacity of the Federal Government'. *Canadian Public Administration* 39, no. 4: 469–88.

Anderson, J. E. (1975). *Public Policymaking.* New York: Praeger.

Anderson, P. A. (1983). 'Decision Making by Objection and the Cuban Missile Crisis'. *Administrative Science Quarterly* 28: 201–22.

Andrews, R. (1998). 'Environmental Regulation and Business "Self-Regulation"'. *Policy Sciences* 31: 177–97.

Angelides, C. and G. Caiden. (1994). 'Adjusting Policy-thinking to Global Pragmatics and Future Problematics'. *Public Administration and Development* 14: 223–39.

Angus, W. H. (1974). 'Judicial Review: Do We Need It?' In D. J. Baum (ed.), *The Individual and the Bureaucracy.* Toronto, ON: Carswell, 101–35.

Anheier, H. K., S. Toepler and S. W. Sokolowski. (1997). 'The Implications of Government Funding for Non-Profit Organizations: Three Propositions'. *International Journal of Public Sector Management* 10, no. 3: 190–213.

Anker, H., V. Nellemann and S. Sverdrup-Jensen. (2004). 'Coastal Zone Management in Denmark: Ways and Means for Further Integration'. *Ocean and Coastal Management* 47: 495–513.

Ansell, C. and A. Gash. (2008). 'Collaborative Governance in Theory and Practice'. *Journal of Public Administration Research and Theory* 18, no. 4: 543–71.

Ansell, C. and A. Gash. (2017). 'Collaborative Platforms as a Governance Strategy'. *Journal of Public Administration Research and Theory* 28, no. 1 (13 December): 16–32.

Antonson, H. and A. Åkerskog. (2015). '"This Is What We Did Last Time". Uncertainty Over Landscape Analysis and Its Procurement in the Swedish Road Planning Process'. *Land Use Policy* 42 (January): 48–57.

Araña, J. E. and C. J. León. (2013). 'Can Defaults Save the Climate? Evidence from a Field Experiment on Carbon Offsetting Programs'. *Environmental and Resource Economics* 54, no. 4: 613–26.

Arellano-Gault, D. and G. Vera-Cortes. (2005). 'Institutional Design and Organisation of the Civil Protection National System in Mexico: The Case for a Decentralised and Participative Policy Network'. *Public Administration and Development* 25: 185–92.

Argote, L., S. L. Beckman and D. Epple. (1990). 'The Persistence and Transfer of Learning in Industrial Settings'. *Management Science* 36, no. 2: 140–54.

Ariely, D. (2010). *Predictably Irrational, Revised and Expanded Edition: The Hidden Forces That Shape Our Decisions* (expanded revised edition). New York: Harper Perennial.

Arkes, H. R. and C. Blumer. (1985). 'The Psychology of Sunk Cost'. *Organizational Behavior and Human Decision Processes* 35, no. 1: 124–40.

Armstrong, D. (1998). 'Globalization and the Social State'. *Review of International Studies* 24: 461–78.

Arrow, K. J. (1958). 'Tinbergen on Economic Policy'. *Journal of the American Statistical Association* 53, no. 281 (March): 89–97.

Arts, B. and J. van Tatenhove. (2004). 'Policy and Power: A Conceptual Framework Between the "Old" and "New" Policy Idioms'. *Policy Sciences* 37: 339–56.

Arts, B., P. Leroy and J. van Tatenhove. (2006). 'Political Modernisation and Policy Arrangements: A Framework for Understanding Environmental Policy Change'. *Public Organization Review* 6, no. 2: 93–106.

Ascher, K. (1987). *The Politics of Privatisation: Contracting Out Public Services.* London: Macmillan.

Atkinson, M. M. and W. Coleman. (1989a). *The State, Business and Industrial Change in Canada.* Toronto, ON: University of Toronto Press.

Atkinson, M. M. and W. Coleman. (1989b). 'Strong States and Weak States: Sectoral Policy Networks in Advanced Capitalist Economies'. *British Journal of Political Science* 19: 47–67.

Atkinson, M. M. and W. D. Coleman. (1992). 'Policy Networks, Policy Communities and the Problems of Governance'. *Governance* 5, no. 2: 154–80.

Atkinson, M. M. and R. A. Nigol. (1989). 'Selecting Policy Instruments: Neo-Institutional and Rational Choice Interpretations of Automobile Insurance in Ontario'. *Canadian Journal of Political Science* 22, no. 1: 107–35.

Aucoin, P. (1990). 'Contribution of Commissions of Inquiry to Policy Analysis: An Evaluation'. In A. P. Pross, I. Christie and J. A. Yogis (eds), *Commissions of Inquiry.* Toronto, ON: Carswell, pp. 197–207.

Aucoin, P. (1995). *The New Public Management: Canada in Comparative Perspective.* Montreal, QC: Institute for Research on Public Policy.

Aucoin, P. (1997). 'The Design of Public Organizations for the 21st Century: Why Bureaucracy Will Survive in Public Management'. *Canadian Public Administration* 40, no. 2: 290–306.

Aucoin, P. (2006). 'Accountability and Coordination with Independent Foundations: A Canadian Case of Autonomization'. In T. Christensen, and P. Laegreid (eds), *Autonomy and Regulation: Coping with Agencies in the Modern State.* Cheltenham, UK: Edward Elgar, 110–33.

Aucoin, P. and H. Bakvis. (2005). 'Public Service Reform and Policy Capacity: Recruiting and Retaining the Best and the Brightest'. In M. Painter, and J. Pierre (eds), *Challenges to State Policy Capacity: Global Trends and Comparative Perspectives.* London: Palgrave Macmillan, pp. 185–204.

Auer, M. (1998). 'On Agency Reform as Decision Process'. *Policy Sciences* 31: 81–105.

Australian Public Service Commission. (2009). *Smarter Policy: Choosing Policy Instruments and Working with Others to Influence Behaviour.* Canberra, ACT: Australian Public Service Commission. http://trove.nla.gov.au/version/45613174.

Averch, H. (1990). *Private Markets and Public Interventions: A Primer for Policy Designers.* Pittsburgh, PA: University of Pittsburgh Press.

Ayres, I., S. Raseman and A. Shih. (2013). 'Evidence from Two Large Field Experiments that Peer Comparison Feedback Can Reduce Residential Energy Usage'. *The Journal of Law, Economics, and Organization* 29, no. 5, 992–1022.

Azuela, G. E. and L. A. Barroso. (2012). *Design and Performance of Policy Instruments to Promote the Development of Renewable Energy: Emerging Experience in Selected Developing Countries.* Washington, DC: World Bank Publications.

Bache, I. (2010). 'Partnership as an EU Policy Instrument: A Political History'. *West European Politics* 33, no. 1: 58–74.

Bachrach, P. and M. S. Baratz. (1970). *Power and Poverty: Theory and Practice.* New York: Oxford University Press.

Baetz, M. C. and A. B. Tanguay. (1998). ' "Damned if You Do, Damned if You Don't": Government and the Conundrum of Consultation in the Environmental Sector'. *Canadian Public Administration* 41, no. 3: 395–418.

Bajari, P. and S. Tadelis. (2001). 'Incentives Versus Transaction Costs: A Theory of Procurement Contracts'. *RAND Journal of Economics* 32, no. 3: 387–407.

Bakir, C. (2017). 'How Can Interactions Among Interdependent Structures, Institutions, and Agents Inform Financial Stability? What we have Still to Learn from Global Financial Crisis'. *Policy Sciences* 50, no. 2 (1 June): 217–39.

Baksi, S. and P. Bose. (2007). 'Credence Goods, Efficient Labeling Policies and Regulatory Enforcement'. *Environmental and Resource Economics* 37: 411–30.

Bakvis, H. (1997). 'Advising the Executive: Think Tanks, Consultants, Political Staff and Kitchen Cabinets'. In P. Weller, H. Bakvis and R. A. W. Rhodes (eds), *The Hollow Crown: Countervailing Trends in Core Executives*. New York: St Martin's Press.

Bakvis, H. (2000). 'Rebuilding Policy Capacity in the Era of the Fiscal Dividend: A Report from Canada'. *Governance* 13, no. 1: 71–103.

Balch, G. I. (1980). 'The Stick, the Carrot, and Other Strategies: A Theoretical Analysis of Governmental Intervention'. *Law & Policy* 2, no. 1: 35–60.

Baldwin, D. A. (1985). *Economic Statecraft*. Princeton, NJ: Princeton University Press.

Baldwin, R. and M. Cave. (1999). *Understanding Regulation: Theory, Strategy and Practice*. Oxford: Oxford University Press.

Bali, A. S. and M. Ramesh. (2015). 'Health Care Reforms in India: Getting It Wrong'. *Public Policy and Administration* 30, nos 3–4: 300–19.

Banerjee, A. and E. Duflo. (2011). *Poor Economics: A Radical Rethinking of the Way to Fight Global Poverty* (Reprinted). New York: Public Affairs.

Bang, H. P. (2003). *Governance as Social and Political Communication*. Manchester, UK: Manchester University Press.

Banting, K. (1995). 'The Social Policy Review: Policy Making in a Semi-Sovereign Society'. *Canadian Public Administration* 38, no. 2: 283–90.

Bardach, E. (1977). *The Implementation Game: What Happens after a Bill Becomes a Law*. Cambridge, MA: MIT Press.

Bardach, E. (1980). 'Implementation Studies and the Study of Implements'. Paper presented to the American Political Science Association. Berkeley, CA: University of California, Graduate School of Public Policy.

Bardach, E. (1989a). 'Moral Suasion and Taxpayer Compliance'. *Law and Policy* 11, no. 1: 49–69.

Bardach, E. (1989b). 'Social Regulation as a Generic Policy Instrument'. In L. M. Salamon (ed.), *Beyond Privatization: The Tools of Government Action*. Washington, DC: Urban Institute, pp. 197–229.

Barker, E. (1944). *The Development of Public Services in Western Europe 1660–1930*. Oxford: Oxford University Press.

Barnett, C. K. and B. Shore. (2009). 'Reinventing Program Design: Challenges in Leading Sustainable Institutional Change'. *Leadership & Organization*, 30, no. 1: 16–35.

Barnett, P., T. Tenbensel, J. Cuming, C. Alyden, T. Ashton, M. Pledger and M. Burnette. (2009). 'Implementing New Modes of Governance in the New Zealand Health System: An Empirical Study'. *Health Policy* 93: 118–27.

Barr, M. S., S. Mullainathan and E. Shafir. (2009). 'The Case for Behaviorally Informed Regulation'. In *New Perspectives on Regulation*. Cambridge, MA: The Tobin Project, pp. 25–62.

Barreiro-Hurlé, J., A. Gracia and T. de-Magistris. (2010). 'Does Nutrition Information on Food Products Lead to Healthier Food Choices?' *Food Policy* 35, no. 3 (June): 221–9.

Bartle, I. and P. Vass. (2007). 'Self-Regulation within the Regulatory State: Towards a New Regulatory Paradigm?' *Public Administration* 85, no. 4: 885–905.

Barzelay, M. and N. Fuchtner. (2003). 'Explaining Public Management Policy Change: Germany in Comparative Perspective'. *Journal of Comparative Policy Analysis* 5, no. 1: 7–28.

Bason, C. (2014). *Design for Policy*. Farnham, UK; Burlington, VT: Gower.

Batlle, C. and I. J. Perez-Arriaga. (2008). 'Design Criteria for Implementing a Capacity Mechanism in Deregulated Electricity Markets'. *Utilities Policy* 16: 184–93.

Bator, F. M. (1958). 'The Anatomy of Market Failure'. *Quarterly Journal of Economics* 72, no. 3: 351–79.

Bauer, J. (2006). *International Forest Sector Institutions and Policy Instruments for Europe: A Source Book*. Geneva, Switzerland: FAO/UNECE.

Baumgartner, F. R. and B. D. Jones. (1991). 'Agenda Dynamics and Policy Subsystems'. *The Journal of Politics* 53, no. 4: 1044–74.

Baumgartner, F. R. and B. D. Jones. (1993). *Agendas and Instability in American Politics*. Chicago, IL: University of Chicago Press, 26, 239–41.

Baumgartner, F. R. and B. D. Jones. (2002). *Policy Dynamics*. Chicago, IL: University of Chicago Press.

van Bavel, R., B. Herrmann, G. Esposito and A. Proestakis. (2013). *Applying Behavioural Sciences to EU Policy-Making*. Institute for Prospective Technological Studies. Luxembourg: Publications Office of the European Union.

Baxter-Moore, N. (1987). 'Policy Implementation and the Role of the State: A Revised Approach to the Study of Policy Instruments'. In R. J. Jackson, D. Jackson and N. Baxter-Moore (eds), *Contemporary Canadian Politics*. Scarborough, ON: Prentice Hall.

Bearce, D. H. (2008). 'Not Complements but Substitutes: Fixed Exchange Rate Commitments, Central Bank Independence and External Currency Stability'. *International Studies Quarterly* 52: 807–24.

Becker, G. S. (1983). 'A Theory of Competition Among Pressure Groups for Political Influence'. *Quarterly Journal of Economics* 98 (August): 371–400.

Becker, S. W. and F. O. Brownson. (1964). 'What Price Ambiguity? Or the Role of Ambiguity in Decision-Making'. *Journal of Political Economy* 72, no. 1 (1 February): 62–73.

Beesley, M. E. (1992). *Privatization, Regulation and Deregulation*. New York: Routledge.

Beetham, D. (1987). *Bureaucracy*. Milton Keynes, UK: Open University Press.

Beetham, D. (1991). *The Legitimation of Power*. London: Macmillan.

Behn, R. D. (1981). 'Policy Analysis and Policy Politics'. *Policy Analysis* 7, no. 2: 199–226.

Bekke, H. A. G. M. (1999). 'Studying the Development and Transformation of Civil Service Systems: Processes of De-Institutionalization'. *Research in Public Administration* 5: 1–18.

Bekke, H. A. G. M. and F. M. van der Meer (eds). (2000). *Civil Service Systems in Western Europe*. Cheltenham, UK: Edward Elgar.

Bekke, H. A. G. M., J. L. Perry and T. A. J. Toonen. (1993). 'Comparing Civil Service Systems'. *Research in Public Administration* 2: 191–212.

Bekke, H. A. G. M., J. L. Perry and T. A. J. Toonen. (eds). (1996a). *Civil Service Systems in Comparative Perspective*. Bloomington, IN: Indiana University Press.

Bekke, H. A. G. M., J. L. Perry and T. A. J. Toonen. (1996b). 'Introduction: Conceptualizing Civil Service Systems'. In H. A. G. M. Bekke, J. L. Perry and T. A. J. Toonen (eds), *Civil Service Systems in Comparative Perspective*, Bloomington, IN: Indiana University Press, 1–12.

Béland, D. (2007). 'Ideas and Institutional Change in Social Security: Conversion, Layering and Policy Drift'. *Social Science Quarterly* 88, no. 1: 20–38.

Béland, D. and J. Hacker. (2004). 'Ideas, Private Institutions, and American Welfare State "Exceptionalism"'. *International Journal of Social Welfare* 13, no. 1: 42–54.

Béland, D. and M. Howlett. (2016). 'How Solutions Chase Problems: Instrument Constituencies in the Policy Process'. *Governance* 29, no. 3: 393–409.

Béland, D. and A. Waddan. (2012). 'The Obama Presidency and Health Insurance Reform: Assessing Continuity and Change'. *Social Policy and Society* 11, no. 3: 319–30.

Bellehumeur, R. (1997). 'Review: An Instrument of Change'. *Optimum* 27, no. 1: 37–42.

Bemelmans-Videc, M.-L. (1998). 'Introduction: Policy Instrument Choice and Evaluation'. In M. L. Bemelmans-Videc, R. C. Rist and E. Vedung (eds), *Carrots, Sticks and Sermons: Policy Instruments and Their Evaluation*, New Brunswick, NJ: Transaction, 21–58.

Bemelmans-Videc, M.-L., R. C. Rist and E. Vedung (eds). (1998). *Carrots, Sticks and Sermons: Policy Instruments and Their Evaluation*. New Brunswick, NJ: Transaction.

Bendor, J., S. Kumar and D. A. Siegel. (2009). 'Satisficing: A "Pretty Good" Heuristic'. *The B.E. Journal of Theoretical Economics* 9, no. 1.

Ben-Gera, M. (2007). *The Role of Ministries in the Policy System: Policy Development, Monitoring and Evaluation*. Paris: OECD.

Benjamin, L. M. (2008). 'Bearing More Risk for Results: Performance Accountability and Nonprofit Relational Work'. *Administration and Society* 39, no. 8: 959–83.

Bennett, C. (1988). 'Different Processes, One Result: The Convergence of Data Protection Policy in Europe and the United States'. *Governance* 4, no. 1: 415–41.

Bennett, C. J. (1990). 'The Formation of a Canadian Privacy Policy: The Art and Craft of Lesson-Drawing'. *Canadian Public Administration* 33, no. 4: 551–70.

Bennett, C. J. (1991a). 'How States Utilize Foreign Evidence'. *Journal of Public Policy* 11, no. 1: 31–54.

Bennett, C. J. (1991b). 'Review Article: What is Policy Convergence and What Causes It?' *British Journal of Political Science* 21, no. 2: 215–33.

Bennett, C. J. (1992). *Regulating Privacy: Data Protection and Public Policy in Europe and the United States*. Ithaca, NY: Cornell University Press.

Bennett, C. J. (1997). 'Understanding Ripple Effects: The Cross-National Adoption of Policy Instruments for Bureaucratic Accountability'. *Governance* 10, no. 3: 213–33.

Bennett, C. J. and R. Bayley. (1999). 'The New Public Administration: Canadian Approaches to Access and Privacy'. In M. W. Westmacott and H. P. Mellon (eds), *Public Administration and Policy: Governing in Challenging Times*. Scarborough, ON: Prentice Hall/Allyn & Bacon, 189–201.

Bennett, C. J. and M. Howlett. (1992). 'The Lessons of Learning: Reconciling Theories of Policy Learning and Policy Change'. *Policy Sciences* 25, no. 3: 275–94.

Bennett, S. and M. McPhail. (1992). 'Policy Process Perceptions of Senior Canadian Federal Civil Servants: A View of the State and Its Environment'. *Canadian Public Administration* 35, no. 3: 299–316.

Bennett, C. J. and C. D. Raab. (2003). *The Governance of Privacy: Policy Instruments in Global Perspective*. Aldershot, UK: Ashgate.

Bentley, A. F. (1908). *The Process of Government*. Chicago, IL: University of Chicago Press.

Berg, S. V. (2000). 'Sustainable Regulatory Systems: Laws, Resources and Values'. *Utilities Policy* 9: 159–70.

Berg, S. V., A. N. Memon and R. Skelton. (2000). *Designing an Independent Regulatory Commission*. IRC Research Paper.

Berger, S. (1981). *Organizing Interests in Western Europe: Pluralism, Corporatism and the Transformation of Politics*. Cambridge: Cambridge University Press.

Bernhagen, P. (2003). 'Is Globalization What States Make of It? Micro-Foundations of the State–Market Condominium in the Global Political Economy'. *Contemporary Politics* 9, no. 3: 257–76.

Bernier, L. (2011). 'The Future of Public Enterprises: Perspectives from the Canadian Experience'. *Annals of Public and Cooperative Economics* 82, no. 4 (1 December): 399–419.

Bernier, L., K. Brownsey and M. Howlett (eds). (2005). *Executive Styles in Canada: Cabinet Structures and Leadership Practices in Canadian Government*. Toronto, ON: University of Toronto Press.

Bernstein, M. H. (1955). *Regulating Business by Independent Commission*. Princeton, NJ: Princeton University Press.

Bernstein, S. and B. Cashore. (2007). 'Can Non-State Global Governance Be Legitimate? An Analytical Framework'. *Regulation and Governance* 1: 347–71.

Berry, W. D., R. C. Fording and R. L. Hanson. (2003). 'Reassessing the "Race to the Bottom" in State Welfare Policy'. *The Journal of Politics* 65, no. 2: 327–49.

Bertelli, A. (2006). 'The Role of Political Ideology in the Structural Design of New Governance Agencies'. *Public Administration Review* 66, no. 4: 583–95.

BETA. (2016). 'Behavioural Economics Team of the Australian Government | Department of the Prime Minister and Cabinet [Text]' (22 April). www.dpmc. gov.au/domestic-policy/behavioural-economics. Retrieved 4 April 2017.

Bevir, M. (ed.). (2007). *Public Governance*, Vol. 4. London: Sage.

Bevir, M. and R. A. W. Rhodes (2001). 'Decentering Tradition: Interpreting British Government'. *Administration and Society* 33, no. 2: 107–32.

Bevir, M., R. A. W. Rhodes and P. Weller. (2003). 'Traditions of Governance: Interpreting the Changing Role of the Public Sector'. *Public Administration* 81, no. 1: 1–17.

Bhatta, G. (2002). 'Evidence-Based Analysis and the Work of Policy Shops'. *Australian Journal of Public Administration* 61, no. 3: 98–105.

Biddle, J. C. and T. M. Koontz. (2014). 'Goal Specificity: A Proxy Measure for Improvements in Environmental Outcomes in Collaborative Governance'. *Journal of Environmental Management* 145: 268–76.

Binderkrantz, A. (2005). 'Interest Group Strategies: Navigating Between Privileged Access and Strategies of Pressure'. *Political Studies* 53: 694–715.

Bingham, L. B., T. Nabatchi and R. O'Leary. (2005). 'The New Governance: Practices and Processes for Stakeholder and Citizen Participation in the Work of Government'. *Public Administration Review* 65, no. 5: 547–58.

Birch, A. H. (1984). 'Overload, Ungovernability and Delegitimization: The Theories and the British Case'. *British Journal of Political Science* 14: 136–60.

Bird, R. M. (1970). *The Growth of Government Spending in Canada*. Toronto, ON: Canadian Tax Foundation.

Birkland, T. A. (1997). *After Disaster: Agenda Setting, Public Policy and Focusing Events*. Washington, DC: Georgetown University Press.

Birkland, T. A. (1998). 'Focusing Events, Mobilization, and Agenda Setting'. *Journal of Public Policy* 18, no. 1: 53–74.

Birkland, T. A. (2009). 'Disasters, Lessons Learned, and Fantasy Documents'. *Journal of Contingencies and Crisis Management* 17, no. 3: 146–56.

Birrell, D. (2008). 'Devolution and Quangos in the United Kingdom: The Implementation of Principles and Policies for Rationalisation and Democratisation'. *Policy Studies* 29, no. 1: 35–49.

Bishop, P. and G. Davis. (2002). 'Mapping Public Participation in Policy Choices'. *Australian Journal of Public Administration* 61, no. 1: 14–29.

Black, A. E., D. L. Koopman and D. K. Ryden. (2004). *Of Little Faith: The Politics of George W. Bush's Faith-Based Initiative*. Washington, DC: Georgetown University Press.

Blaikie, P. and H. Brookfield. (1987). *Land Degradation and Society*. London: Methuen.

Blair, R. (2002). 'Policy Tools Theory and Implementation Networks: Understanding State Enterprise Zone Partnerships'. *Journal of Public Administration Research and Theory* 12, no. 2: 161–90.

Blankart, C. (1985). 'Market and Non-Market Alternatives in the Supply of Public Goods: General Issues'. In F. Forte and A. Peacock (eds), *Public Expenditure and Government Growth*. London: Basil Blackwell, 192–201.

Blind, P. K. (2006). *Building Trust in Government in the Twenty-First Century: Review of Literature and Emerging Issues*. New York: UNDESA.

Blomkamp, E. (2018). 'The Promise of Co-Design for Public Policy'. *Australian Journal of Public Administration*. Forthcoming.

Blondel, J. (1987). *Political Leadership: Towards a General Analysis*. London; Beverly Hills, CA: Sage.

Blonz, J. A., S. P. Vajjhala and E. Safirova. (2008). *Growing Complexities: A Cross-Sector Review of US Biofuels Policies and Their Interactions*. Washington, DC: Resources for the Future.

Blyth, M. M. (1997). '"Any More Bright Ideas?" The Ideational Turn of Comparative Political Economy'. *Comparative Politics* 29: 229–50.

Boardman, A. E., D. H. Greenberg, A. R. Vining and D. L. Weimer. (2001). *Cost-Benefit Analysis: Concepts and Practice*. Upper Saddle River, NJ: Prentice Hall.

Boase, J. P. (2000). 'Beyond Government: The Appeal of Public Private Partnerships'. *Canadian Public Administration* 43, no. 1: 75–91.

Boaz, A., L. Grayson, R. Levitt and W. Solesbury. (2008). 'Does Evidence-Based Policy Work? Learning from the UK Experience'. *Evidence & Policy* 4, no. 2: 233–53.

Bobrow, D. B. (1977). 'Beyond Markets and Lawyers'. *American Journal of Political Science* 21, no. 2: 415–33.

Bobrow, D. B. (2006). 'Policy Design: Ubiquitous, Necessary and Difficult'. In B. G. Peters and J. Pierre (eds), *Handbook of Public Policy*. London: Sage, pp. 75–96.

Bobrow, D. B. and J. S. Dryzek. (1987). *Policy Analysis by Design*. Pittsburgh, PA: University of Pittsburgh Press.

Bode, I. (2006). 'Disorganized Welfare Mixes: Voluntary Agencies and New Governance Regimes in Western Europe'. *Journal of European Social Policy* 16, no. 4: 346–59.

Boehmke, F. J. (2005). *The Indirect Effect of Direct Legislation*. Columbus, OH: Ohio State University Press.

Bogart, W. A. (2002). *Consequences: The Impact of Law and Its Complexity*. Toronto, ON: University of Toronto Press.

Bolleyer, N. and T. A. Borzel. (2010). 'Non-Hierarchical Policy Coordination in Multilevel Systems'. *European Political Science Review* 2, no. 2: 157–85.

Bond, A., A. Morrison-Saunders, J. A. E. Gunn, J. Pope and F. Retief. (2015). 'Managing Uncertainty, Ambiguity and Ignorance in Impact Assessment by Embedding Evolutionary Resilience, Participatory Modeling and Adaptive Management'. *Journal of Environmental Management* 151 (15 March): 97–104.

Boonekamp, P. G. M. (2006). 'Actual Interaction Effects Between Policy Measures for Energy efficiency – A Qualitative Matrix Method and Quantitative Simulation Results for Households'. *Energy* 31, no. 14 (November): 2848–73.

Borenstein, S. (2013). *A Microeconomic Framework for Evaluating Energy Efficiency Rebound and Some Implications* (Working Paper No. 19044). Washington, DC: National Bureau of Economic Research.

Borins, S. F. (1982). 'World War Two Crown Corporations: Their Wartime Role and Peacetime Privatization'. *Canadian Public Administration* 25, no. 3: 380–404.

Borins, S. F. (2001). 'Public Management Innovation in Economically Advanced and Developing Countries'. *International Review of Administrative Sciences* 67: 715–31.

Borraz, O. (2007). 'Governing Standards: The Rise of Standardization Processes in France and in the EU'. *Governance* 20, no. 1: 57–84.

Bos, D. (1991). *Privatization: A Theoretical Treatment*. Oxford: Clarendon Press.

Boston, J. (1994). 'Purchasing Policy Advice: The Limits of Contracting Out'. *Governance* 7, no. 1: 1–30.

Boston, J., J. Martin, J. Pallot, and P. Walsh. (1996). *Public Management: The New Zealand Model*. Auckland, New Zealand: Oxford University Press.

Bostrom, A., R. E. O'Connor, G. Böhm, D. Hanss, O. Bodi, F. Ekström, ... I. Sælensminde. (2012). 'Causal Thinking and Support for Climate Change Policies: International Survey Findings'. *Global Environmental Change* 22 no. 1: 210–22.

Bougherara, D., G. Grolleau and N. Mzoughi. (2007). 'Is More Information Always Better? An Analysis Applied to Information-Based Policies for Environmental Protection'. *International Journal of Sustainable Development* 10, no. 3: 197–213.

Bourgon, J. (1996). 'Strengthening Our Policy Capacity'. In Canadian Centre for Management Development (ed.), *Rethinking Policy: Strengthening Policy Capacity – Conference Proceedings*. Ottawa, ON: Ministry of Supply and Services, 22–30.

Bovaird, T. (2007). 'Beyond Engagement and Participation: User and Community Co-Production of Public Services'. *Public Administration Review* 67, no. 5: 846–60.

Bovaird, T., I. Briggs and M. Willis. (2014). 'Strategic Commissioning in the UK: Service Improvement Cycle or Just Going Round in Circles?' *Local Government Studies* 40, no. 4 (4 July): 533–59.

Bovens, L. (2009). 'The Ethics of Nudge'. In T. Grüne-Yanoff and S. O. Hansson (eds), *Preference Change*. Dordrecht, Netherlands: Springer 207–19.

Bovens, M. and P. 't Hart. (1995). 'Frame Multiplicity and Policy Fiascos: Limits to Explanation'. *Knowledge and Policy* 8, no. 4: 61–83.

Bovens, M. and P. 't Hart. (1996). *Understanding Policy Fiascoes*. New Brunswick, NJ: Transaction.

Bovens, M., P. Hart and B. G. Peters. (2001). 'Analysing Governance Success and Failure in Six European States'. In M. Bovens, P. 't Hart and B. G. Peters (eds), *Success and Failure in Public Governance: A Comparative Analysis*. Cheltenham, UK: Edward Elgar, 12–32.

Braathen, N. A. (2007a). *Instrument Mixes Addressing Non-Point Sources of Water Pollution*. Paris: OECD.

Braathen, N. A. (2007b). 'Instrument Mixes for Environmental Policy: How Many Stones Should Be Used to Kill a Bird?' *International Review of Environmental and Resource Economics* 1, no. 2 (16 May): 185–235.

Braathen, N. A. and E. Croci. (2005). 'Environmental Agreements Used in Combination with Other Policy Instruments'. In *The Handbook of Environmental Voluntary Agreements*, Vol. 43. Dordrecht, Netherlands: Springer, 335–64.

Brabham, D. C. (2008). 'Crowdsourcing as a Model for Problem Solving: An Introduction and Cases'. *Convergence* 14, no. 1 (1 February): 75–90.

Brabham, D. C., K. M. Ribisl, T. R. Kirchner and J. M. Bernhardt. (2014). 'Crowdsourcing Applications for Public Health'. *American Journal of Preventive Medicine* 46, no. 2 (February): 179–87).

Bradford, N. (1999). 'The Policy Influence of Economic Ideas: Interests, Institutions and Innovation in Canada'. *Studies in Political Economy*, 59: 17–60.

Brady, M. (2011). 'Improvisation versus Rigid Command and Control at Stalingrad'. *Journal of Management History* 17, no. 1 (11 January): 27–49.

Braithwaite, J. (2008). *Regulatory Capitalism: How It Works, Ideas for Making It Work Better*. Cheltenham, UK: Edward Elgar.

Braithwaite, J., J. Walker and P. Grabosky. (1987). 'An Enforcement Taxonomy of Regulatory Agencies'. *Law and Policy* 9, no. 3: 323–51.

Brandl, J. (1988). 'On Politics and Policy Analysis as the Design and Assessment of Institutions'. *Journal of Policy Analysis and Management* 7, no. 3: 419–24.

Brandsen, T. and M. Honingh. (2016). 'Distinguishing Different Types of Coproduction: A Conceptual Analysis Based on the Classical Definitions'. *Public Administration Review* 76, no. 3: 427–35.

Brandsen, T. and V. Pestoff. (2006). 'Co-Production, the Third Sector and the Delivery of Public Services'. *Public Management Review* 8: 493–501.

Brandsen, T., M. Boogers and P. Tops. (2006). 'Soft Governance, Hard Consequences: The Ambiguous Status of Unofficial Guidelines'. *Public Administration Review* 66, no. 4: 546–53.

Brändström, A. and S. Kuipers. (2003). 'From "Normal Incidents" to Political Crisis: Understanding Selective Politicization of Policy Failures'. *Government and Opposition* 38, no. 3: 279–305.

Braun, B. (2013). 'Preparedness, Crisis Management and Policy Change: The Euro Area at the Critical Juncture of 2008–2013'. *The British Journal of Politics & International Relations* 17, no. 3: 419–41.

Braun, D. (1999). 'Interests or Ideas? An Overview of Ideational Concepts in Public Policy Research'. In D. Braun, and A. Busch (eds), *Public Policy and Political Ideas*. Cheltenham, UK: Edward Elgar, 11–29.

Bregha, F., J. Benidickson, D. Gamble, T. Shillington and E. Weick. (1990). *The Integration of Environmental Considerations into Government Policy*. Ottawa, ON: Canadian Environmental Assessment Research Council.

Bressers, H. T. A. (1998). 'The Choice of Policy Instruments in Policy Networks'. In B. G. Peters and F. K. M. Van Nispen (eds), *Public Policy Instruments: Evaluating the Tools of Public Administration*, New York: Edward Elgar, 85–105.

Bressers, H. T. A. and M. Honigh. (1986). 'A Comparative Approach to the Explanation of Policy Effects'. *International Social Science Journal* 108: 267–88.

Bressers, H. T. A. and P.-J. Klok. (1988). 'Fundamentals for a Theory of Policy Instruments'. *International Journal of Social Economics* 15, nos 3/4: 22–41.

Bressers, H. T. A. and L. J. O'Toole. (1998). 'The Selection of Policy Instruments: A Network-Based Perspective'. *Journal of Public Policy* 18, no. 3: 213–39.

Bressers, H. T. A. and L. J. O'Toole. (2005). 'Instrument Selection and Implementation in a Networked Context'. In P. Eliadis, M. Hill and M. Howlett (eds), *Designing Government: From Instruments to Governance*, Montreal, QC: McGill-Queen's University Press, 132–53.

Bressers, H. T. A., D. Fuchs and S. Kuks. (2004). 'Institutional Resource Regimes and Sustainability: Theoretical Backgrounds and Hypotheses'. *Environment and Policy* 41: 23–58.

Brewer, G. D. (1974). 'The Policy Sciences Emerge: To Nurture and Structure a Discipline'. *Policy Science* 5, no. 3: 239–44.

Brewer, G. and P. de Leon. (1983). *The Foundations of Policy Analysis*. Homewood, IL: Dorsey.

Breyer, S. (1979). 'Analyzing Regulatory Failure: Mismatches, Less Restrictive Alternatives and Reform'. *Harvard Law Review* 92, no. 3: 549–609.

Breyer, S. (1982). *Regulation and Its Reform*. Cambridge, MA: Harvard University Press.

Briassoulis, H. (2005a). 'Analysis of Policy Integration: Conceptual and Methodological Considerations'. In *Policy Integration for Complex Environmental Problems: The Example of Mediterranean Desertification*. Aldershot, UK: Ashgate, 50–80.

Briassoulis, H. (2005b). 'Complex Environment Problems and the Quest of Policy Integration'. In *Policy Integration for Complex Environmental Problems: The Example of Mediterranean Desertification*. Aldershot, UK: Ashgate, 1–49.

Briassoulis, H. (ed.). (2005c). *Policy Integration for Complex Environmental Problems: The Example of Mediterranean Desertification*. Aldershot, UK: Ashgate.

Bridge, L. and A. Salman. (2000). *Policy Instruments for ICZM in Nine Selected European Countries*. Leiden, Netherlands: EUCC.

Brinkerhoff, D. W. (2009). 'Developing Capacity in Fragile States'. *Public Administration and Development* 30, no. 1: 66–78.

Brinkerhoff, D. W. and B. L. Crosby. (2002). *Managing Policy Reform: Concepts and Tools for Decision-Makers in Developing and Transitional Countries*. Bloomfield, CT: Kumarian Press.

Brinkerhoff, D. W. and P. J. Morgan. (2010). 'Capacity and Capacity Development: Coping with Complexity'. *Public Administration and Development* 30, no. 1: 2–10.

Brint, S. (1990). 'Rethinking the Policy Influence of Experts: From General Characterizations to Analysis of Variation'. *Sociological Forum* 5, no. 3 (September): 361–85.

Brockman, J. (1998). '"Fortunate Enough to Obtain and Keep the Title of Profession": Self-Regulating Organizations and the Enforcement of Professional Monopolies'. *Canadian Public Administration* 41, no. 4: 587–621.

Brooks, S. (1989). *Public Policy in Canada: An Introduction*. Toronto, ON: McClelland & Stewart.

Brooks, S. M. (2015). 'Social Protection for the Poorest: The Adoption of Antipoverty Cash Transfer Programs in the Global South'. *Politics & Society* 43, no. 4 (1 December): 551–82.

Brown, C. (1994). 'Politics and the Environment: Nonlinear Instabilities Dominate'. *American Political Science Review* 88, no. 2: 292–303.

Brown, C. L. and Krishna, A. (2004). 'The Skeptical Shopper: A Metacognitive Account for the Effects of Default Options on Choice'. *Journal of Consumer Research* 31, no. 3: 529–39.

Brown, D. S. (1955). 'The Public Advisory Board as an Instrument of Government'. *Public Administration Review* 15: 196–201.

Brown, D. S. (1972). 'The Management of Advisory Committees; An Assignment for the '70's'. *Public Administration Review* 32: 334–42.

Brown, D. and J. Eastman. (1981). *The Limits of Consultation*. Ottawa, ON: Science Council of Canada.

Brown, M. P. (1992). 'Organizational Design as a Policy Instrument'. In R. Boardman (ed.), *Canadian Environmental Policy: Ecosystems, Politics and Processes*. Toronto, ON: Oxford University Press, 24–42.

Brown, T. and J. Wyatt. (2010). 'Design Thinking for Social Innovation (SSIR)'. *Stanford Social Innovation Review* Winter.

Brown, T. L. and M. Potoski. (2003). 'Transaction Costs and Institutional Explanations for Government Service Production Decisions'. *Journal of Public Administration Research and Theory* 13, no. 4: 441–68.

Brown, T. L., M. Potoski and D. M. Ven Syke. (2008). 'Changing Modes of Service Delivery: How Past Choices Structure future Choices'. *Environment and Planning C: Government and Policy* 26: 127–43.

Brown-John, C. L. (1979). 'Advisory Agencies in Canada: An Introduction'. *Canadian Public Administration* 22, no. 1: 72–91.

Brubaker, R. (1984). *The Limits of Rationality: An Essay on the Social and Moral Thought of Max Weber*. London: Allen & Unwin.

Brudney, J. L. (1987). 'Coproduction and Privatization: Exploring the Relationship and Its Implications'. *Nonprofit and Voluntary Sector Quarterly* 16, no. 3 (1 July): 11–21.

Brudney, J. L. and R. E. England. (1983). 'Toward a Definition of the Coproduction Concept'. *Public Administration Review* 43, no. 1: 59–65.

Brugnach, M. and H. Ingram. (2012). 'Ambiguity: The Challenge of Knowing and Deciding Together'. *Environmental Science & Policy* 15, no. 1 (January): 60–71.

de Bruijn, H. and A. L. Porter. (2004). 'The Education of a Technology Policy Analyst – To Process Management'. *Technology Analysis and Strategic Management* 16, no. 2: 261–74.

de Bruijn, J. A. and E. F. ten Heuvelhof. (1991). 'Policy Instruments for Steering Autopoietic Actors'. In T. Veld, L. Schaap, C. J. A. M. Termeer and M. J. W. van Twist (eds), *Autopoiesis and Configuration Theory: New Approaches to Societal Steering*. Dordrecht. Netherlands: Kluwer, 161–70.

de Bruijn, J. A. and E. F. ten Heuvelhof. (1995). 'Policy Networks and Governance'. In D. L. Weimer (ed.), *Institutional Design*. Boston, MA: Kluwer Academic, 161–79.

de Bruijn, J. A. and E. F. ten Heuvelhof. (1997). 'Instruments for Network Management'. In W. J. M. Kickert, E.-H. Klijn and J. F. M. Koppenjan (eds), *Managing Complex Networks: Strategies for the Public Sector*. London: Sage, 119–36.

de Bruijn, J. A. and H. A. M. Hufen. (1998). 'The Traditional Approach to Policy Instruments'. In B. G. Peters and F. K. M. V. Nispen (eds), *Public Policy Instruments: Evaluating the Tools of Public Administration*, New York: Edward Elgar, 11–32.

Brunsson, N. (2006). *Mechanisms of Hope: Maintaining the Dream of the Rational Organizaton*. Copenhagen, Denmark: Copenhagen Business School Press.

Bryner, G. (2008). 'Failure and Opportunity. Environmental Groups in US Climate Change Policy'. *Environmental Politics* 17, no. 2: 319–36.

Bryson, J. M., B. C. Crosby and L. Bloomberg. (2014). 'Public Value Governance: Moving Beyond Traditional Public Administration and the New Public Management'. *Public Administration Review* 74, no. 4: 445–56.

Bryson, J. M., K. S. Quick, C. S. Slotterback and B. C. Crosby. (2013). 'Designing Public Participation Processes'. *Public Administration Review* 73, no. 1 (1 January): 23–34.

Brzezinski, Z. (2005). 'The Dilemma of the Last Sovereign'. *The American Interest* 1.

Buchanan, J. M. (1980). 'Rent Seeking and Profit Seeking'. In J. M. Buchanan, R. D. Tollison and. G. Tullock (eds), *Toward a Theory of the Rent-Seeking Society*. College Station, TX: Texas A&M University Press.

Buchanan, J. M. and R. D. Tollison (eds). (1984). *The Theory of Public Choice – II*. Ann Arbor, MI: University of Michigan Press.

Buchanan, J. M., R. D. Tollison and G. Tullock. (1980). *Toward a Theory of the Rent-Seeking Society*. College Station, TX: Texas A&M University Press.

Buckingham, H. (2009). 'Competition and Contracts in the Voluntary Sector: Exploring the Implications for Homelessness Service Providers in Southampton'. *Policy & Politics* 37, no. 2: 235–54.

Buckley, W. (1968). 'Society as a Complex Adaptive System'. In W. Buckley (ed.), *Modern System Research for the Behavioural Scientist*, Chicago, IL: Aldine.

Buckman, G. and M. Diesendorf. (2010). 'Design Limitations in Australian Renewable Electricity Policies'. *Energy Policy* 38, no. 7: 3365–76.

Bulkley, H. (2000). 'Discourse Coalition and the Australian Climate Change Policy Network'. *Environment and Planning C: Government and Policy* 18: 727–48.

Bullock H., J. Mountford and R. Stanley. (2001). *Better Policy-Making*. London: Centre for Management and Policy Studies.

Bulmer, M. (1981). 'Applied Social Research? The Use and Non-Use of Empirical Social Inquiry by British and American Governmental Commissions'. *Journal of Public Policy* 1: 353–80.

Bulmer, S. J. (1993). 'The Governance of the European Union: A New Institutionalist Approach'. *Journal of Public Policy* 13, no. 4: 351–80.

Bunge, M. (1997). 'Mechanism and Explanation'. *Philosophy of the Social Sciences* 27, no. 4 (1 December): 410–65.

Bunge, M. (2004). 'How Does It Work? The Search for Explanatory Mechanisms'. *Philosophy of the Social Sciences* 34, no. 2 (1 June): 182–210.

Burke, F. G. (1969). 'Public Administration in Africa: The Legacy of Inherited Colonial Institutions'. *Journal of Comparative Administration* 1, no. 3: 345–78.

Burns, J. M. G. (2012). *Leadership*. New York: Open Road Media.

Burns, J. P. and B. Bowornwathana. (1993). *Civil Service Systems in Asia*. Cheltenham, UK: Edward Elgar.

Burris, S., P. Drahos and C. Shearing. (2005). 'Nodal Governance'. *Australian Journal of Legal Philosophy* 30: 30–58.

Burstein, P. (1991). 'Policy Domains: Organization, Culture and Policy Outcomes'. *Annual Review of Sociology* 17: 327–50.

Burt, S. (1990). 'Canadian Women's Groups in the 1980s: Organizational Development and Policy Influence'. *Canadian Public Policy* 16, no. 1: 17–28.

Busch, A. (2002). *Divergence or Convergence? State Regulation of the Banking System in Western Europe and the United States.* Contribution to the Workshop on Theories of Regulation, Nuffield College, Oxford, 25–6 May.

Busemeyer, M. R. (2009). 'From Myth of Reality: Globalisation and Public Spending in OECD Countries Revisited'. *European Journal of Political Research* 48: 455–82.

van Buuren, A. and E.-H Klijn. (2006). 'Trajectories of Institutional Design in Policy Networks: European Interventions in the Dutch Fishery Network as an Example'. *International Review of Administrative Sciences* 72, no. 3: 395–415.

van Buuren, A. and D. Loorbach. (2009). 'Policy Innovation in Isolation? Conditions for Policy Renewal by Transition Arenas and Pilot Projects'. *Public Management Review* 11, no. 3: 375–92.

Bye, T. and A. Bruvoll. (2008). 'Multiple Instruments to Change Energy Behaviour: The Emperor's New Clothes?' *Energy Efficiency* 1, no. 4 (1 November): 373–86.

Cabinet Office Behavioural Insights Team. (2010). *Applying Behavioural Insight to Health.* London: Cabinet Office Behavioural Insights Team. www.gov.uk/government/publications/applying-behavioural-insight-to-health-behavioural-insights-team-paper.

Cabinet Office Behavioural Insights Team. (2011). *Behaviour Change and Energy Use* (Research and analysis). Cabinet Office Behavioural Insights Team. Retrieved from www.gov.uk/government/publications/behaviour-change-and-energy-use.

Cabinet Office Behavioural Insights Team. (2014). *EAST: Four Simple Ways to Apply Behavioural Insights.* London: Cabinet Office Behavioural Insights Team. www.behaviouralinsights.co.uk/publications/east-four-simple-ways-to-apply-behavioural-insights/.

Cahill, A. G. and E. S. Overman. (1990). 'The Evolution of Rationality in Policy Analysis'. In S. S. Nagel (ed.), *Policy Theory and Policy Evaluation: Concepts, Knowledge, Causes and Norms.* New York: Greenwood Press, 11–27.

Cairney, P. and M. D. Jones. (2016). 'Kingdon's Multiple Streams Approach: What is the Empirical Impact of this Universal Theory?' *Policy Studies Journal* 44, no. 1: 37–58.

Cairns, A. C. (1990). 'Reflections on Commission Research'. In C. Innis, J. A. Yogis and A. P. Pross (eds), *Commissions of Inquiry.* Toronto, ON: Carswell, 87–110.

Cairns, B., M. Harris and P. Young. (2005). 'Building the Capacity of the Voluntary Nonprofit Sector: Challenges of Theory and Practice'. *International Journal of Public Administration* 28: 869–85.

Cameron, D. R. (1978). 'The Expansion of the Public Economy: A Comparative Analysis'. *American Political Science Review* 72, no. 4: 1243–61.

Camilleri, A. R. and R. P. Larrick. (2013). 'Metric and Scale Design as Choice Architecture Tools'. *Journal of Public Policy & Marketing* 33, no. 1: 108–25.

Campanella, M. L. (1993). 'The Effects of Globalization and Turbulence on Policy-Making Processes'. *Government and Opposition* 28, no. 2: 190–205.

Campbell, C. and G. J. Szablowski. (1979). *The Superbureaucrats: Structure and Behaviour in Central Agencies.* Toronto, ON: Macmillan.

Campbell, H. E., R. M. Johnson and E. H. Larson. (2004). 'Prices, Devices, People or Rules: The Relative Effectiveness of Policy Instruments in Water Conservation'. *Review of Policy Research* 21, no. 5: 637–62.

Campbell, J. L. (1998). 'Institutional Analysis and the Role of Ideas in Political Economy'. *Theory and Society* 27, no. 5: 377–409.

Campbell, J. L. (2002). 'Ideas, Politics and Public Policy'. *Annual Review of Sociology* 28, no. 1: 21–38.

Campbell-Smith, D. (2008). *Follow the Money: The Audit Commission, Public Money and the Management of Public Services, 1983–2008.* London: Allen Lane.

Canadian Government. (1996). 'Strengthening Our Policy Capacity'. Report of the Task Force on Strengthening the Policy Capacity of the Federal Government. Ottawa, Canada: Ministry of Supply and Services.

Cantor, R., S. Henry and S. Rayner. (1992). *Making Markets: An Interdisciplinary Perspective on Economic Exchange.* Westport, CT: Greenwood Press.

Capano, G. (2011). 'Government Continues to Do Its Job. A Comparative Study of Governance Shifts in the Higher Education Sector'. *Public Administration* 89, no. 4: 1622–42.

Capano, G. (2012). 'Policy Dynamics and Change: The Never-Ending Puzzle'. In E. Araral, S. Fritzen, M. Howlett, M. Ramesh and X. Wu (eds), *Routledge Handbook of Public Policy.* New York: Routledge, 451–72.

Capano, G. and J. J. Woo. (2017). 'Resilience and Robustness in Policy Design: A Critical Appraisal'. *Policy Sciences* (5 January): 1–28.

Capano, G., M. Howlett and M. Ramesh (eds). (2015). *Varieties of Governance. Studies in the Political Economy of Public Policy.* Basingstoke, UK; New York: Palgrave Macmillan.

Capano, G., M. Howlett and M. Ramesh. (2018). 'Designing for Robustness: Surprise, Agility and Improvisation in Policy Design'. *Policy & Society.* Forthcoming.

Cardozo, A. (1996). 'Lion Taming: Downsizing the Opponents of Downsizing'. In G. Swimmer (ed.), *How Ottawa Spends 1996–97: Life under the Knife.* Ottawa, ON: Carleton University Press, 303–36.

Carlsson, L. (2000). 'Policy Networks as Collective Action'. *Policy Studies Journal* 28, no. 3: 502–20.

Carmel, E. and J. Harlock. (2008). 'Instituting the "Third Sector" as a Governable Terrain: Partnership, Procurement and Performance in the UK'. *Policy and Politics* 36, no. 2: 155–71.

Carmichael, C. M. 'Doing Good Better? The Differential Subsidization of Charitable Contributions'. *Policy and Society* 29, no. 3: 201–17.

Carstensen, M. B. (2010). 'The Nature of Ideas and Why Political Scientists Should Care: Analysing the Danish Jobcentre Reform from an Ideational Perspective'. *Political Studies* 58, no. 5: 847–65.

Carstensen, M. B. (2011). 'Paradigm Man vs. the Bricoleur: Bricolage as an Alternative Vision of Agency in Ideational Change'. *European Political Science Review* 3, no. 1: 147–67.

Carstensen, M. B. (2015). 'Bringing Ideational Power into the Paradigm Approach: Critical Perspectives on Policy Paradigms in Theory and Practice'. In J. Hogan, and M. Howlett (eds), *Policy Paradigms in Theory and Practice.* Basingstoke, UK: Palgrave Macmillan.

Carter, P. (2012). 'Policy as Palimpsest'. *Policy & Politics* 40, no. 3: 423–43.

Cashore, B. (2002). 'Legitimacy and the Privatization of Environmental Governance: How Non-State Market-Driven (NSMD) Governance Systems Gain Rule-Making Authority'. *Governance* 15, no. 4: 503–29.

Cashore, B. and M. Howlett. (2006). 'Behavioural Thresholds and Institutional Rigidities as Explanations of Punctuated Equilibrium Processes in Pacific Northwest Forest Policy Dynamics'. In R. Repetto (ed.), *Policy Dynamics*. New Haven, CT: Yale University Press, 137–61.

Cashore, B. and M. Howlett. (2007). 'Punctuating Which Equilibrium? Understanding Thermostatic Policy Dynamics in Pacific Northwest Forestry'. *American Journal of Political Science* 51, no. 3: 532–51.

Cashore, B., G. Auld and D. Newsom. (2003). 'Forest Certification (Eco-Labeling) Programs and their Policy-Making Authority: Explaining Divergence Among North American and European Case Studies'. *Forest Policy and Economics* 5: 225–47.

Cashore, B., G. Auld and D. Newsom. (2004). *Governing Through Markets: Forest Certification and the Emergence of Non-State Authority* (1st edn). New Haven, CT: Yale University Press.

Castells, M. (1996). *The Information Age: Economy, Society and Culture*, Vol. I, *The Rise of Network Society*. Malden, MA: Blackwell.

Castles, F. G. (1998). *Comparative Public Policy: Patterns of Post-War Transformation*. Cheltenham, UK: Edward Elgar.

Castles, F. G. (2001). 'On the Political Economy of Recent Public Sector Development'. *Journal of European Social Policy* 11, no. 3: 195–211.

Castree, N. (2008). 'Neoliberalising Nature: The Logics of Deregulation and Reregulation'. *Environment and Planning A* 40: 131–52.

Centre d'analyse stratégique. (2011). *Green Nudges: New Incentives for Ecological Behaviour*. Paris: Premier Ministre Republique Francaise. http://archives.strategie. gouv.fr/cas/system/files/2011-03-09-na-216-nudgesvertsgb_0.pdf.

Centre for Sustainable Energy/Environmental Change Institute, University of Oxford. (2012). *Factors Influencing Energy Behaviours and Decision-Making in the Non-Domestic Sector: A Rapid Evidence Assessment* (Policy Paper). Department of Energy & Climate Change, UK. www.gov.uk/government/publications/factors-influencing-energy-behaviours-and-decision-making-in-the-non-domestic-sector-a-rapid-evidence-assessment.

Cerny, P. G. (1990). *The Changing Architecture of Politics*. Beverly Hills, CA: Sage.

Cerny, P. G. (1993). 'Plurilateralism: Structural Differentiation and Functional Conflict in the Post-Cold War World Order'. *Millenium* 22, no. 1: 27–51.

Cerny, P. G. (1996). 'International Finance and the Erosion of State Policy Capacity'. In P. Gummett (ed.), *Globalization and Public Policy*, Cheltenham, UK: Edward Elgar, 83–104.

Cerny, P. G. (2010). 'The Competition State Today: From Raison d'État to Raison du Monde'. *Policy Studies* 31, no. 1: 5–21.

Chadwick, A. (2000). 'Studying Political Ideas: A Public Political Discourse Approach'. *Political Studies* 48: 283–301.

Chapman, B. (1971). *The Profession of Government*. London: Unwin.

Chapman, C. (1990). *Selling the Family Silver: Has Privatization Worked?* London: Hutchinson Business Books.

Chapman, R. (2003). 'A Policy Mix for Environmentally Sustainable Development – Learning from the Dutch Experience'. *New Zealand Journal of Environmental Law* 7, no. 1: 29–51.

Chapman, R. A. (1973). 'Commissions in Policy-Making'. In R. A. Chapman (ed.), *The Role of Commissions in Policy-Making*. London: George Allen & Unwin, 174–88.

Chapman, R. A. (ed.). (1973). *The Role of Commissions in Policy-Making*. Sydney, NSW: Allen & Unwin.

Chapman, T., J. Brown and R. Crow. (2008). 'Entering a Brave New World? An Assessment of Third Sector Readiness to Tender for the Delivery of Public Services in the United Kingdom'. *Policy Studies* 29, no. 1: 1–17.

Chari, R., G. Murphy and J. Hogan. (2007). 'Regulating Lobbyists: A Comparative Analysis of the United States, Canada, Germany and the European Union'. *The Political Quarterly* 78, no. 3: 422–38.

Charih, M. and A. Daniels (eds). (1997). *New Public Management and Public Administration in Canada*. Toronto, ON: IPAC, 143–63.

Chávez, C. A., M. G. Villena and K. Stranlund. (2009). 'The Choice of Policy Instruments to Control Pollution Under Costly Enforcement and Incomplete Information'. *Journal of Applied Economics* 12 (November): 207–27.

Chelariu, C., W. J. Johnston and L. Young. (2002). 'Learning to Improvise, Improvising to Learn: A Process of Responding to Complex Environments'. *Journal of Business Research, Marketing Theory in the Next Millennium* 55, no. 2 (February): 141–7.

Chenier, J. A. (1985). 'Ministers of State to Assist: Weighing the Costs and the Benefits'. *Canadian Public Administration* 28, no. 3: 397–412.

Cheung, A. B. L. (2005). 'The Politics of Administrative Reforms in Asia: Paradigms and Legacies, Paths and Diversities'. *Governance* 18, no. 2: 257–82.

Chiarini, A. (2012). *Lean Organization: From the Tools of the Toyota Production System to Lean Office* (2013 edn). Milan, Italy; New York: Springer.

Christensen, J. G. and T. Pallesen. (2008). 'Public Employment Trends and the Organization of Public Sector Tasks'. In H.-U. Derlien and B. G. Peters (eds), *The State at Work*, Vol. 2: *Comparative Public Service Systems*. Cheltenham, UK: Edward Elgar.

Christensen, T. and P. Lægreid (eds). (2001). *New Public Management: The Transformation of Ideas and Practice*. Aldershot, UK: Ashgate.

Christensen, T. and P. Lægreid. (2007). 'Regulatory Agencies – The Challenges of Balancing Agency Autonomy and Political Control'. *Governance* 20, no. 3: 499–520.

Christensen, T. and P. Lægreid. (2008). 'NPM and Beyond – Structure, Culture and Demography'. *International Review of Administrative Sciences* 74, no. 1 (1 March): 7–23.

Christensen, T. and P. Lægreid. (2012). 'Governance and Administrative Reforms'. In D. Levi-Faur (ed.), *The Oxford Handbook of Governance*. Oxford: Oxford University Press, 255–68.

Christensen, T., P. Lægreid and L. R. Wise. (2002). 'Transforming Administrative Policy'. *Public Administration* 80, no. 1: 153–79.

Christopoulos, D. and K. Ingold. (2011). 'Distinguishing between Political Brokerage and Political Entrepreneurship'. *Procedia – Social and Behavioral Sciences* 10: 36–42.

Churchman, C. W. (1967). 'Wicked Problems'. *Management Science* 14, no. 4: B141–B142.

Cialdini, R. B. (2003). 'Crafting Normative Messages to Protect the Environment'. *Current Directions in Psychological Science* 12, no. 4: 105–9.

Cialdini, R. B. (2008). *Influence: Science and Practice* (5th edn). Boston, MA: Allyn & Bacon.

Cicin-Sain, B. and R. Knecht. (1998). *Integrated Coastal and Ocean Management: Concepts and Practices*. Washington, DC: Island Press.

Cismaru, M. and A. M. Lavack. (2007). 'Tobacco Warning Labels and the Protection Motivation Model: Implications for Canadian Tobacco Control Policy'. *Canadian Public Policy* 33, no. 4: 477–86.

Citi, M. and A. M. Rhodes. (2007). 'New Modes of Governance in the EU: Common Objectives Versus National Preferences'. European Governance Papers, No. N-07-01. www.connex-network.org/eurogov/pdf/egp-newgov-N-07-01.pdf. Accessed 29 February 2008.

Clark, C. D. and C. S. Russell. (2009). 'Ecological Conservation: The Problems of Targeting Policies and Designing Instruments'. *Journal of Natural Resources Policy Research* 1, no. 1: 21–34.

Clark, I. (1998). 'Beyond the Great Divide: Globalization and the Theory of International Relations'. *Review of International Studies* 24: 479–98.

Clark, W. C. and G. Majone. (1985). 'The Critical Appraisal of Scientific Inquiries with Policy Implications'. *Science, Technology and Human Values* 10, no. 3: 6–19.

Clarke, A. and J. Craft. (2017). 'The Vestiges and Vanguards of Policy Design in a Digital Context'. *Canadian Public Administration* 60, no. 4 (1 December): 476–97.

Clarke, A., E. A. Lindquist and J. Roy. (2017). 'Understanding Governance in the Digital Era: An Agenda for Public Administration Research in Canada'. *Canadian Public Administration* 60, no. 4 (1 December): 457–75.

Clarke, H. (2010). 'Formulating Policy Responses to Global Warming in the Face of Uncertainty'. *Agenda: A Journal of Policy Analysis and Reform* 17, 33–54.

Clayton, S. (2012) 'Will People Act to Mitigate Climate Change?' *Analyses of Social Issues and Public Policy* 12, no. 1, 221–4.

Clemens, E. S. and J. M. Cook. (1999). 'Politics and Institutionalism: Explaining Durability and Change'. *Annual Review of Sociology* 25: 441–66.

Clokie, H. M. and J. W. Robinson. (1969). *Royal Commissions of Inquiry: The Significance of Investigations in British Politics*. New York: Octagon Books.

Cnossen, S. (2005). 'Economics and Politics of Excise Taxation'. In *Theory and Practice of Excise Taxation: Smoking, Drinking, Gambling, Polluting and Driving*, S. Cnossen (ed.). Oxford: Oxford University Press, 1–19.

Cobb, R. W. and C. D. Elder. (1972). *Participation in American Politics: The Dynamics of Agenda-Building*. Boston, MA: Allyn & Bacon.

Cochran, C. L. and E. F. Malone (1999). *Public Policy: Perspectives and Choices*. Boulder, CO: Lynne Rienner.

Codagnone, C., Bogliacino, F. and Veltri, G. (2013). *Testing CO2/Car Labelling Options and Consumer Information* (Final Report). Brussels, Belgium: European Commission. http://ec.europa.eu/clima/policies/transport/vehicles/labelling/docs/report_car_labelling_en. pdf.

Coglianese, C. (1997). 'Assessing Consensus: The Promise and Performance of Negotiated Rulemaking'. *Duke Law Journal* 46, no. 6: 1255–1349.

Cohen, M. D., J. G. March and J. P. Olsen. (1972). 'A Garbage Can Model of Organizational Choice'. *Administrative Science Quarterly* 17, no. 1: 1–25.

Cohen, M. D., J. G. March and J. P. Olsen. (1979). 'People, Problems, Solutions and the Ambiguity of Relevance'. In *Ambiguity and Choice in Organizations*. Bergen, Norway: Universitetsforlaget, 24–37.

Cohen, M. A. and V. Santhakumar. (2007). 'Information Disclosure as Environmental Regulation: A Theoretical Analysis'. *Environmental and Resource Economics* 37: 599–620.

Cohen, M. G. and S. McBride (eds). (2003). *Global Turbulence: Social Activists' and State Responses to Globalization*. Aldershot, UK: Ashgate.

Cohen, W. M. and D. A. Levinthal. (1990). 'Absorptive Capacity: A New Perspective on Learning and Innovation'. *Administrative Sciences Quarterly* 35: 128–52.

Cohn, D. (2004). 'The Best of Intentions, Potentially Harmful Policies: A Comparative Study of Scholarly Complexity and Failure'. *Journal of Comparative Policy Analysis* 6, no. 1: 39–56.

Cole, D. H. and P. Z. Grossman. (1999). 'When Is Command-and-Control Efficient – Institutions, Technology, and the Comparative Efficiency of Alternative Regulatory Regimes for Environmental Protection'. *Wisconsin Law Review* 887–937.

Colebatch, H. K. (1998). *Policy*. Minneapolis, MN: University of Minnesota Press.

Colebatch, H. K. (2005). 'Policy Analysis, Policy Practice and Political Science'. *Australian Journal of Public Administration* 64, no. 3: 14–23.

Colebatch, H. K. (2006a). 'What Work Makes Policy?' *Policy Sciences* 39, no. 4 (November): 309–21.

Colebatch, H. K. (ed.). (2006b). *The Work of Policy: An International Survey*. New York: Rowman & Littlefield.

Colebatch, H. K. (2018). 'The Idea of Policy Design: Intention, Process, Outcome, Meaning and Validity'. *Public Policy and Administration* 33, no. 4 (18 May): 365–83.

Colebatch, H. K. and B. A. Radin. (2006). 'Mapping the Work of Policy'. In H. K. Colebatch (ed.), *The Work of Policy: An International Survey*. New York: Rowman & Littlefield, 217–26.

Colebatch, H. K., R. Hoppe and M. Noordegraaf (eds). (2011). *Working for Policy*. Amsterdam, Netherlands: Amsterdam University Press.

Coleman, W. D. (1991). 'Monetary Policy, Accountability and Legitimacy: A Review of the Issues in Canada'. *Canadian Journal of Political Science* 24, no. 4: 711–34.

Coleman, W. D. (1996). *Financial Services, Globalization and Domestic Policy Change: A Comparison of North America and the European Union*. Basingstoke, UK: Macmillan.

Coletti, P. (2015). 'Public Policy Design: How to Learn From Failures'. *World Political Science* 11, no. 2: 325–45.

Collier, U. (1998). *Deregulation in the European Union: Environmental Perspectives*. London: Routledge.

Collins, A. and G. Judge. (2008). 'Client Participation in Paid Sex Markets under Alternative Regulatory Regimes'. *International Journal of Law and Economics* 28: 294–301.

Collins, A. E. (2013). 'Applications of the Disaster Risk Reduction Approach to Migration Influenced by Environmental Change'. *Environmental Science & Policy* 27, Supplement 1 (March): S112–S125.

Comfort, L. K. (2010). *Designing Resilience: Preparing for Extreme Events* (1st edn). Pittsburgh, PA: University of Pittsburgh Press.

Comfort, L. K. (2012). 'Designing Disaster Resilience and Public Policy: Comparative Perspectives'. *Journal of Comparative Policy Analysis: Research and Practice* 14, no. 2 (1 April): 109–13.

CommGAP. (2009). 'Communication for Good Governance'. Washington, DC: Communication for Governance and Accountability Program, World Bank. www.gsdrc.org/go/display&type=Document&id=3718.

Compston, H. and I. Bailey. (2012). *Feeling the Heat. The Politics of Climate Change Policy in Rapidly Industrializing Countries*. Basingstoke, UK; New York: Palgrave Macmillan.

Conn, W. D. (2009). 'Applying Environmental Policy Instruments to Used Oil'. *Journal of Environmental Planning and Management* 52, no. 4: 457–75.

Connolly, M. E. H. and A. W. Stark. (1992). 'Policy Making and the Demonstration Effect: Privatization in a Deprived Region'. *Public Administration* 70, no. 3: 369–85.

Connor, L. H. and N. Higginbotham. (2013). '"Natural Cycles" in Lay Understanding of Climate Change'. *Global Environmental Change* 23, no. 6: 1852–61.

Considine, M. (2001). *Enterprising States: The Public Management of Welfare-to-Work*. Cambridge: Cambridge University Press.

Considine, M. (2012). 'Thinking Outside the Box? Applying Design Theory to Public Policy'. *Politics & Policy* 40, no. 4: 704–24.

Considine, M. and J. M. Lewis. (2003). 'Bureaucracy, Network, or Enterprise? Comparing Models of Governance in Australia, Britain, the Netherlands and New Zealand'. *Public Administration Review* 63, no. 2: 131–40.

Considine, M., D. Alexander and J. M. Lewis. (2009). *Networks, Innovation and Public Policy: Politicians, Bureaucrats and Pathways to Change Inside Government*. Basingstoke, UK: Macmillan.

Considine, M., D. Alexander and J. M. Lewis. (2014). 'Policy Design as Craft: Design Expertise Using a Semi-experimental Approach'. *Policy Sciences* 47, 209–25.

Cook, D. (2002). 'Consultation, for a Change? Engaging Users and Communities in the Policy Process'. *Social Policy and Administration* 36, no. 5: 516–31.

Cook, P. and C. Kirpatrick. (1988). *Privatization in Less Developed Countries*. New York: St Martin's Press.

Cooke, P. (2007). 'Building a Partnership Model to Manage Irish Heritage: A Policy Tools Analysis'. *Irish Journal of Management* 27, no. 2: 75–97.

Corner, A. and A. Randall. (2011). 'Selling Climate Change? The Limitations of Social Marketing as a Strategy for Climate Change Public Engagement'. *Global Environmental Change* 21, no. 3 (August): 1005–14.

da Costa Canoquena, J. M. (2013). 'Reconceptualising Policy Integration in Road Safety Management'. *Transport Policy* 25 (January): 61–80.

Cowan, L. G. (1990). *Privatization in the Developing World*. New York: Greenwood Press.

Cowles, M. G., J. Caporaso and T. Risse (eds). (2001). *Transforming Europe: Europeanization and Domestic Change*. Ithaca, NY: Cornell University Press.

Cox, R. W. (1996). *Approaches to World Order*. Cambridge: Cambridge University Press, 296–313.

Craft, J. and M. Howlett. (2012). 'Policy Formulation, Governance Shifts and Policy Influence: Location and Content in Policy Advisory Systems'. *Journal of Public Policy* 32, no. 2: 79–98.

Craft, J. and M. Howlett. (2013). 'The Dual Dynamics of Policy Advisory Systems: The Impact of Externalization and Politicization on Policy Advice'. *Policy and Society* 32, no. 3: 187–97.

Craft, J., M. Howlett, M. Crawford and K. McNutt. (2013). 'Assessing Policy Capacity for Climate Change Adaptation: Governance Arrangements, Resource Deployments, and Analytical Skills in Canadian Infrastructure Policy Making'. *Review of Policy Research* 30, no. 1: 42–65.

Crew, M. and D. Parker (eds). (2006). *International Handbook on Economic Regulation*. Cheltenham, UK: Edward Elgar.

Crew, M. A. and C. K. Rowley. (1986). 'Deregulation as an Instrument in Industrial Policy'. *Journal of Institutional and Theoretical Economics* 142: 52–70.

Croley, S. P. (2007). *Regulation and Public Interests: The Possibility of Good Regulatory Government*. Princeton, NJ: Princeton University Press.

Cronin, T. E. and N. C. Thomas. (1970). 'Educational Policy Advisors and the Great Society'. *Public Policy* 18, no. 5: 659–86.

Cross, M. K. D. (2015). 'The Limits of Epistemic Communities: EU Security Agencies'. *Politics and Governance* 3, no. 1: 90–100.

Cross, W. (2007). 'Policy Study and Development in Canada's Political Parties'. In L. Dobuzinskis, M. Howlett and D. Laycock (eds), *Policy Analysis in Canada: The State of the Art*. Toronto, ON: University of Toronto Press, 233–42.

Crowley, K. (2009). 'Can Deliberative Democracy be Practiced? A Subnational Policy Pathway'. *Politics and Policy* 37, no. 5: 995–1021.

Cubbage, F., P. Harou and E. Sills. (2007). 'Policy Instruments to Enhance Multifunctional Forest Management'. *Forest Policy and Economics* 9: 833–51.

Cunha, M. P. E., K. Kamoche and J. V. D. Cunha. (2002). *Organizational Improvisation*. London; New York: Routledge.

Cushman, R. E. (1941). *The Independent Regulatory Commissions*. London: Oxford University Press.

Cutler, A. C., V. Haufler and T. Porter. (1999). 'The Contours and Significance of Private Authority in International Affairs'. In A. C. Cutler, V. Haufler, and T. Porter (eds), *Private Authority and International Affairs*. Albany, NY: State University of New York, 333–76.

Cyert, R. M. and J. G. March. (1992). *Behavioral Theory of the Firm* (2nd edn). Cambridge, MA: Wiley-Blackwell.

Dacey, R. and L. J. Carlson. (2004). 'Traditional Decision Analysis and the Poliheuristic Theory of Foreign Policy Decision Making'. *The Journal of Conflict Resolution* 48, no. 1: 38–55.

Dahl, R. A. and C. E. Lindblom. (1953). *Politics, Economics and Welfare: Planning and Politico-Economic Systems Resolved into Basic Social Processes*. New York: Harper & Row.

Dahlberg, L. (2005). 'Interaction Between Voluntary and Statutory Social Service Provision in Sweden: A Matter of Welfare Pluralism, Substitution or Complementarity?' *Social Policy and Administration* 39, no. 7: 740–63.

Dahlström, C., J. Lindvall and B. Rothstein. (2013). 'Corruption, Bureaucratic Failure and Social Policy Priorities'. *Political Studies* 61, no. 3 (1 October): 523–42.

Dalal-Clayton, B. and B. Sadler. (2005). *Strategic Environmental Assessment: A Sourcebook and Reference Guide to International Experience*. London: Earthscan.

Daneke, G. A. (1992). 'Back to the Future: Misplaced Elements of Political Inquiry and the Advanced Systems Agenda'. In W. N. Dunn and R. M. Kelly (eds), *Advances in Policy Studies Since 1950*. New Brunswick, NJ: Transaction, 267–90.

Daniels, R. J. and M. J. Trebilcock. (1996). 'Private Provision of Public Infrastructure: An Organizational Analysis of the Next Privatization Frontier'. *University of Toronto Law Journal* 46: 375–426.

Darr, E. D., L. Argote and D. Epple. (1995). 'The Acquisition, Transfer, and Depreciation of Knowledge in Service Organizations: Productivity in Franchises'. *Management Science* 41, no. 11 (1 November): 1750–62.

Datta, S. and S. Mullainathan. (2014). 'Behavioral Design: A New Approach to Development Policy'. *Review of Income and Wealth* 60, no. 1: 7–35.

Datta, S., J. J. Miranda, L. Zorattoa, O. Calvo-González, M. Darling and K. Lorenzana. (2015). *A Behavioral Approach to Water Conservation: Evidence from Costa Rica*. Washington, DC: The World Bank.

Daugbjerg, C. (1997). 'Policy Networks and Agricultural Policy Reforms: Explaining Deregulation in Sweden and Re-Regulation in the European Community'. *Governance* 10, no. 2: 123–42.

Daugbjerg, C. (1998). *Policy Networks Under Pressure: Pollution Control, Policy Reform and the Power of Farmers*. Aldershot, UK: Ashgate.

Daugbjerg, C. (2009). 'Sequencing in Public Policy: The Evolution of the CAP over a Decade'. *Journal of European Public Policy* 16, no. 2: 395–411.

Daugbjerg, C. and D. Marsh. (1998). 'Explaining Policy Outcomes: Integrating the Policy Network Approach with Macro-Level and Micro-Level Analysis'. In David Marsh (ed.), *Comparing Policy Networks*. Buckingham, UK: Open University Press, 52–71.

Daugbjerg, C. and G. T. Svendsen. (2003). 'Designing Green Taxes in a Political Context: From Optimal to Feasible Environmental Regulation'. *Environmental Politics* 12, no. 4: 76–95.

Davies, H. T. O., S. M. Nutley and P. C. Smith (eds). (2000). *What Works? Evidence-based Policy and Practice in Public Services*. Bristol, UK: Policy Press.

Davies, P. (2004). *Is Evidence-Based Government Possible?* London: Polity Press.

Day, P. and R. Klein. (1989). 'Interpreting the Unexpected: The Case of AIDS Policy Making in Britain'. *Journal of Public Policy* 9, no. 3: 337–53.

Deber, R., M. J. Hollander and P. Jacobs. (2008). 'Models of Funding and Reimbursement in Health Care: A Conceptual Framework'. *Canadian Public Administration* 51, no. 3: 381–405.

Debus, M. and J. Müller. (2013). 'The Programmatic Development of CDU and CSU Since Reunification: Incentives and Constraints for Changing Policy Positions in the German Multi-Level System'. *German Politics* 22, nos 1–2: 151–71.

DECC/Behavioural Insights Team. (2014). *Evaluation of the DECC and John Lewis Energy Labelling Trial* (Research and Analysis No. 14D/320). Department of Energy & Climate Change, UK. www.gov.uk/government/publications/evaluation-of-the-decc-and-john-lewis-energy-labelling-trial.

del Río, P. (2007). 'The Interaction between Emissions Trading and Renewable Electricity Support Schemes. An Overview of the Literature'. *Mitigation and Adaptation Strategies for Global Change* 12, no. 8: 1363–90.

del Río, P. (2009). 'Interactions between Climate and Energy Policies: The Case of Spain'. *Climate Policy* 9, no. 2: 119–38.

del Río, P. (2010). 'Analysing the Interactions Between Renewable Energy Promotion and Energy Efficiency Support Schemes: The Impact of Different Instruments and Design Elements'. *Energy Policy* 38, no. 9 (September): 4978–89.

del Río, P. (2014). 'On Evaluating Success in Complex Policy Mixes: The Case of Renewable Energy Support Schemes'. *Policy Sciences* 47, no. 3: 267–87.

del Río, P. and M. P. Howlett. (2013). *Beyond the 'Tinbergen Rule' in Policy Design: Matching Tools and Goals in Policy Portfolios* (8 April). SSRN Scholarly Paper. Rochester, NY: Social Science Research Network. http://papers.ssrn.com/abstract=2247238.

del Río, P., J. Carrillo-Hermosilla and T. Könnölä. (2010). 'Policy Strategies to Promote Eco-Innovation'. *Journal of Industrial Ecology* 14, no. 4: 541–57.

del Río, P., A. C. Silvosa and G. I. Gómez. (2011). 'Policies and Design Elements for the Repowering of Wind Farms: A Qualitative Analysis of Different Options'. *Energy Policy* 39, no. 4 (April): 1897–1908.

Delacourt, S. and D. G. Lenihan (eds). (2000). *Collaborative Government: Is there a Canadian Way?* Toronto, ON: Institute of Public Administration of Canada.

DeLeon, P. (1979). *Development and Diffusion of the Nuclear Power Reactor: A Comparative Analysis*. Cambridge, MA: Ballinger.

DeLeon, P. (1988). 'The Contextual Burdens of Policy Design'. *Policy Studies Journal* 17, no. 2: 297–309.

DeLeon, P. (1992). 'Policy Formulation: Where Ignorant Armies Clash by Night'. *Review of Policy Research* 11, nos 3–4: 389–405.

DeLeon, P. (1999a). 'The Missing Link Revisited: Contemporary Implementation Research'. *Policy Studies Review* 16, no. 3: 311–38.

DeLeon, P. (1999b). 'The Stages Approach to the Policy Process: What Has It Done? Where Is It Going?' In P. A. Sabatier (ed.), *Theories of the Policy Process*. Boulder, CO: Westview, 19–34.

Delmas, M. A. and A. K. Terlaak. (2001). 'A Framework for Analyzing Environmental Voluntary Agreements'. *California Management Review* 43, no. 3: 44–63.

Delmas, M. A., M. Fischlein and O. I. Asensio. (2013). 'Information Strategies and Energy Conservation Behavior: A Meta-Analysis of Experimental Studies from 1975 to 2012'. *Energy Policy* 61: 729–39.

Derlien, H.-U. (2008). 'Conclusion'. In H.-U. Derlien and B. G. Peters (eds), *The State at Work*, Vol. 1, *Public Sector Employment in 10 Countries*. Cheltenham, UK: Edward Elgar, 283–91.

Derthick, M. and P. J. Quirk. (1985). *The Politics of Deregulation*. Washington, DC: Brookings Institution.

Dery, D. (1984). *Problem Definition in Policy Analysis*. Lawrence, KS: University of Kansas.

Dery, D. (1999). 'Policy by the Way: When Policy is Incidental to Making Other Policies'. *Journal of Public Policy* 18, no. 2: 163–76.

Desch, M. C. (2007/8). 'America's Liberal Illiberalism. The Ideological Origins of Overreaction in US Foreign Policy'. *International Security* 32(3): 7–43.

DeShazo, J. R., T. L. Sheldon and R. T. Carson. (2017). 'Designing Policy Incentives for Cleaner Technologies: Lessons from California's Plug-in Electric Vehicle Rebate Program'. *Journal of Environmental Economics and Management* 84 (July): 18–43.

Deutsch, K. W. (1963). *The Nerves of Government: Models of Political Communication and Control*. New York: Free Press.

Deverell, E. (2009). 'Crises as Learning Triggers: Exploring a Conceptual Framework of Crisis-Induced Learning'. *Journal of Contingencies and Crisis Management* 17, no. 3: 179–88.

Dewees, D. N. (1983). 'Instrument Choice in Environmental Policy'. *Economic Inquiry*. 31: 53–71.

Diamond, J. (2008). 'Capacity Building in the Voluntary and Community Sectors: Towards Relative Independence – Limits and Possibilities'. *Public Policy and Administration* 23, no. 2: 153–66.

Diamond, L. J. (2002). 'Thinking About Hybrid Regimes'. *Journal of Democracy* 13, no. 2: 21–35.

Diani, M. (1992). 'Analysing Social Movement Networks'. In M. Diani and R. Eyerman (eds), *Studying Collective Action*. London: Sage, 107–37.

Dietzenbacher, E. (2000). 'Spillovers of Innovation Effects'. *Journal of Policy Modeling* 22, no. 1: 27–42.

Dimitrov, R. (2002). 'Confronting Nonregimes: Science and International Coral Reef Policy'. *The Journal of Environment Development* 11, no. 1 (March): 53–78.

Dimitrov, R. (2005). 'Hostage to Norms: States, Institutions and Global Forest Politics'. *Global Environmental Politics* 5, no. 4: 1–24.

Dimitrov, R. S., F. S. Detlef, G. M. DiGiusto and A. Kelle. (2007). 'International Nonregimes: A Research Agenda'. *The International Studies Review* 9: 230–58.

Dinner, I., E. J. Johnson, D. G. Goldstein and K. Liu. (2011). 'Partitioning Default Effects: Why People Choose not to Choose'. *Journal of Experimental Psychology. Applied* 17, no. 4: 332–41.

Dion, L. (1973). 'The Politics of Consultation'. *Government and Opposition* 8, no. 3: 332–53 (p. 339).

Dobbin, F., B. Simmons and G. Garrett. (2007). 'The Global Diffusion of Public Policies: Social Construction, Coercion, Competition, or Learning?' *Annual Review of Sociology* 33: 449–72.

Dobuzinskis, L. (1987). *The Self-Organizing Polity: An Epistemological Analysis of Political Life*. Boulder, CO: Westview.

Dobuzinskis, L., M. Howlett and D. Laycock (eds). (2007). *Policy Analysis in Canada: The State of the Art*. Toronto, ON: University of Toronto Press.

Doern, G. B. (1967). 'The Role of Royal Commissions in the General Policy Process and in Federal–Provincial Relations'. *Canadian Public Administration* 10, no. 4: 417–33.

Doern, G. B. (1971). 'The Role of Central Advisory Councils: The Science Council of Canada'. In G. B. Doern and P. Aucoin (eds), *The Structures of Policy-Making in Canada*. Toronto, ON: Macmillan, 246–66.

Doern, G. B. (1974). 'The Concept of Regulation and Regulatory Reform'. In G. B. Doern and V. S. Wilson (eds), *Issues in Canadian Public Policy*. Toronto, ON: Macmillan, 8–35.

Doern, G. B. (1981). *The Nature of Scientific and Technological Controversy in Federal Policy Formation*. Ottawa, ON: Science Council of Canada.

Doern, G. B. (1983). 'The Mega-Project Episode and the Formulation of Canadian Economic Development Policy'. *Canadian Public Administration* 26, no. 2: 219–38.

Doern, G. B. and R. W. Phidd. (1983). *Canadian Public Policy: Ideas, Structure, Process* (1st edn). Toronto, ON: Methuen.

Doern, G. B. and R. W. Phidd. (1988). *Canadian Public Policy: Ideas, Structure, Process* (2nd edn). Toronto, ON: Nelson.

Doern, G. B. and S. Wilks. (1998). *Changing Regulatory Institutions in Britain and North America*. Toronto, ON: University of Toronto Press.

Doern, G. B. and V. S. Wilson. (1974). 'Conclusions and Observations'. *Issues in Canadian Public Policy* 339, Toronto, Canada: Methuen, 337–45.

Doerr, A. D. (1981). *The Machinery of Government in Canada*. Toronto, ON: Methuen.

Doerr, A. D. (1982). 'The Role of Coloured Papers'. *Canadian Public Administration* 25, no. 3: 366–79.

Dolan, P. and M. M. Galizzi. (2014). 'Getting Policy-Makers to Listen to Field Experiments'. *Oxford Review of Economic Policy* 30, no. 4: 725–52.

Dolan, P. and M. M. Galizzi. (2015). 'Like Ripples on a Pond: Behavioral Spillovers and Their Implications for Research and Policy'. *Journal of Economic Psychology* 47: 1–16.

Dolan, P. and R. Metcalfe. (2013). *Neighbors, Knowledge, and Nuggets: Two Natural Field Experiments on the Role of Incentives on Energy Conservation* (CEP Discussion Paper, No. CEPDP1222). London: Centre for Economic Performance,

London School of Economics and Political Science. http://cep.lse.ac.uk/_new/publications/series.asp?prog=CEP.

Dolan, P., M. Hallsworth, D. Halpern, D. King and I. Vlaev. (2010). *Mindspace: Influencing Behaviour Through Public Policy*. London: Institute for Government. www.instituteforgovernment.org.uk/sites/default/files/publications/MINDSPACE.pdf.

Dollery, B. and J. Wallis. (1999). *Market Failure, Government Failure, Leadership and Public Policy*. London: Macmillan.

Dollery, B. and J. Wallis. (2003). *The Political Economy of the Voluntary Sector: A Reappraisal of the Comparative Institutional Advantage of Voluntary Organizations*. Cheltenham, UK: Edward Elgar.

Dolowitz, D. P. and D. Marsh. (2000). 'Learning from Abroad: The Role of Policy Transfer in Contemporary Policy-Making'. *Governance* 13, no. 1: 5–23.

Donahue, J. D. (1989). *The Privatization Decision: Public Ends, Private Means*. New York: Basic Books.

Donovan, M. C. (2001). *Taking Aim: Target Populations and the Wars on Aids and Drugs*. Washington, DC: Georgetown University Press.

van Dooren, W. (2004). 'Supply and Demand of Policy Indicators: A Cross-Sectoral Comparison'. *Public Management Review* 6, no. 4: 511–30.

Doremus, H. (2003). 'A Policy Portfolio Approach to Biodiversity Protection on Private Lands'. *Environmental Science & Policy* 6: 217–32.

Dowd, K. (1999). 'Too Big to Fail? Long-Term Capital Management and the Federal Reserve'. *Cato Institute Briefing Papers* no. 52. www.cato.org/pubs/briefs/bp52.pdf.

Downs, A. (1972). 'Up and Down with Ecology: The Issue-Attention Cycle'. *Public Interest* 28: 38–50.

Doz, Y. and M. Kosonen. (2014). *Governments for the Future: Building the Strategic and Agile State*. Helsinki, Finland: SITRA.

Drezner, D. W. (2001a). 'Globalization and Policy Convergence'. *International Studies Review* 3, no. 1 (Spring): 53–78.

Drezner, D. W. (2001b). 'Reflection and Reappraisal: Globalization and Policy Convergence'. *International Studies Review* 3, no. 1: 53–78.

Drezner, D. W. (2005). 'Globalization, Harmonization and Competition: The Different Pathways to Policy Convergence'. *Journal of European Public Policy* 12, no. 5: 841–59.

Dror, Y. (1964). 'Muddling Through – "Science" or Inertia'. *Public Administration Review* 24, no. 3: 154–7.

Dryzek, J. (1983). 'Don't Toss Coins in Garbage Cans: A Prologue to Policy Design'. *Journal of Public Policy* 3, no. 4: 345–67.

Dryzek, J. S. and B. Ripley. (1988). 'The Ambitions of Policy Design'. *Policy Studies Review* 7, no. 4: 705–19.

Dryzek, J. S. and A. Tucker. (2008). 'Deliberative Innovation to Different Effect: Consensus Conferences in Denmark, France and the United States'. *Public Administration Review* 68, no. 5: 864–76.

Duesberg, S., Á. N. Dhubháin and D. O'Connor. (2014). 'Assessing Policy Tools for Encouraging Farm Afforestation in Ireland'. *Land Use Policy* 38 (May): 194–203.

Dunleavy, P. (1986). 'Explaining the Privatization Boom: Public Choice Versus Radical Approaches'. *Public Administration* 64, no. 1: 13–34.

Dunleavy, P. and C. Hood. (1994). 'From Old Public Administration to New Public Management'. *Public Money and Management* 14, no. 3: 9–16.

Dunlop, C. A. (2009a). 'The Temporal Dimension of Knowledge and the Limits of Policy Appraisal: Biofuels Policy in the UK'. *Policy Sciences* 43, no. 4 (October): 343–63.

Dunlop, C. A. (2009b). 'Policy Transfer as Learning: Capturing Variation in What Decision-Makers Learn from Epistemic Communities'. *Policy Studies* 30, no. 3: 289–311.

Dunn, W. N. (1986). *Policy Analysis: Perspectives, Concepts and Methods.* New Brunswick, NJ: JAI Press.

Dunn, W. N. (2008). *Public Policy Analysis: An Introduction.* Upper Saddle River, NJ: Pearson/Prentice Hall.

Dunsire, A. (1986). 'A Cybernetic View of Guidance, Control and Evaluation in the Public Sector'. In F.-X. Kaufman, G. Majone and V. Ostrom (eds), *Guidance, Control and Evaluation in the Public Sector.* Berlin, Germany: Walter de Gruyter, 327–46.

Dunsire, A. (1993a). *Manipulating Social Tensions: Collibration as an Alternative Mode of Government Intervention* (Discussion Paper 93/7). Cologne, Germany: Max Planck Institute for the Study of Societies.

Dunsire, A. (1993b). 'Modes of Governance'. In J. Kooiman (ed.), *Modern Governance.* London: Sage, 21–34.

Durant, R. F. (2008). 'Sharpening a Knife Cleverly: Organizational Change, Policy Paradox and the "Weaponizing" of Administrative Reform'. *Public Administration Review* 68, no. 2: 282–94.

Durning, D. and W. Osama. (1994). 'Policy Analysts' Roles and Value Orientations: An Empirical Investigation Using Q Methodology'. *Journal of Policy Analysis and Management* 13, no. 4: 629–57.

Durr, R. H. (1993). 'What Moves Policy Sentiment?' *American Political Science Review* 87: 158–72.

Dwivedi, O. P. (ed.). (1982). *The Administrative State in Canada: Essays in Honour of J.E. Hodgetts.* Toronto, ON: University of Toronto Press.

Dwivedi, O.P. and J. I. Gow. (1999). *From Bureaucracy to Public Management: The Administrative Culture of the Government of Canada.* Toronto, ON: IPAC.

Dye, T. R. (1972). *Understanding Public Policy.* Englewood Cliffs, NJ: Prentice-Hall.

Dyerson, R. and F. Mueller. (1993). 'Intervention by Outsiders: A Strategic Perspective on Government Industrial Policy'. *Journal of Public Policy* 13, no. 1: 69–88.

Easton, D. (1965). *A Systems Analysis of Political Life.* New York: Wiley.

Ebeling, F. and S. Lotz. (2015). 'Domestic Uptake of Green Energy Promoted by Opt-Out Tariffs'. *Nature Climate Change* 5, no. 9: 868–71.

Economic Council of Canada. (1979). *Responsible Regulation.* Ottawa, ON: Ministry of Supply and Services.

Edelenbos, J. and E.-H. Klijn. (2005). 'Managing Stakeholder Involvement in Decision-Making: A Comparative Analysis of Six Interactive Processes in the Netherlands'. *Journal of Public Administration Research and Theory* 16, no. 3: 2.

Edelenbos, J., A. van Buuren and N. van Schie. (2011). 'Co-Producing Knowledge: Joint Knowledge Production between Experts, Bureaucrats and Stakeholders in Dutch Water Management Projects'. *Environmental Science & Policy* 14, no. 6 (October): 675–84.

Edelenbos, J., N. van Schie and L. Gerrits. (2010). 'Organizing Interfaces between Government Institutions and Interactive Governance'. *Policy Sciences* 43, no. 1: 73–94.

Edelman, M. (1964). *The Symbolic Uses of Politics*. Chicago, IL: University of Illinois Press.

Edelman, M. (1971). *Politics as Symbolic Action: Mass Arousal and Quiescence*. Chicago, IL: Markham Publishing.

Edelman, M. (1988). *Constructing the Political Spectacle*. Chicago, IL: University of Chicago Press.

Eden, S. (2009). 'The Work of Environmental Governance Networks: Traceabilty, Credibility and Certification by the Forest Stewardship Council'. *Geoforum* 40: 383–94.

Eden, S. and C. Bear. (2010). 'Third-Sector Global Environmental Governance, Space and Science: Comparing Fishery and Forestry Certification'. *Journal of Environmental Policy and Planning* 12, no. 1: 83–106.

Edley, C. F. J. (1990). *Administrative Law: Rethinking Judicial Control of Bureaucracy*. New Haven, CT: Yale University Press.

Edwards, L. (2009). 'Testing the Discourse of Declining Policy Capacity: Rail Policy and the Department of Transport'. *Australian Journal of Public Administration* 68, no. 3: 288–302.

EEA (European Environment Agency). (2001). *Environmental Signals 2001*. Brussels, Belgium: EEA. www.eea.europa.eu/publications/signals-2001.

Egeberg, M. (1999). 'The Impact of Bureaucratic Structure on Policy Making'. *Public Administration*. 77, no. 1: 155–70.

Eichbaum, C. and R. Shaw. (2008). 'Ministerial Advisers and the Politics of Policy-Making: Bureaucratic Permanence and Popular Control'. *The Australian Journal of Public Administration* 66, no. 4: 453–67.

Eijlander, P. (2005). 'Possibilities and Constraints in the Use of Self-Regulation and Co-Regulation in Legislative Policy: Experiences in the Netherlands – Lessons To Be Learned for the EU'. *Electronic Journal of Comparative Law* 9, no. 1: 1–8.

Eikenberry, A. M. (2007). 'Symposium-Theorizing Governance Beyond the State'. *Administrative Theory and Praxis* 29: 193–7.

Eisenstadt, S. E. (1963). *The Political Systems of Empires*. London: Collier.

Eisner, M. A. (1993). *Regulatory Politics in Transition*. Baltimore, MD: Johns Hopkins University Press.

Eisner, M. A. (1994a). 'Discovering Patterns in Regulatory History: Continuity, Change and Regulatory Regimes'. *Journal of Policy History*. 6, no. 2: 157–87.

Eisner, M. A. (1994b). 'Economic Regulatory Policies: Regulation and Deregulation in Historical Context'. In D. H. Rosenbloom and R. D. Schwartz (eds), *Handbook of Regulation and Administrative Law*. New York: Marcel Dekker, 91–116.

Elgie, R. (2006). 'Why Do Governments Delegate Authority to Quasi-Autonomous Agencies? The Case of Independent Administrative Authorities in France'. *Governance* 19, no. 2: 207–27.

Eliadis, P., M. Hill and M. Howlett (eds). (2005). *Designing Government: From Instruments to Governance*. Montreal, QC: McGill-Queen's University Press.

Eliste, P. and P. G. Fredriksson. (1998). *Does Open Trade Result in a Race to the Bottom? Cross Country Evidence*. Washington, DC: World Bank.

Elkin, S. L. (1986). 'Regulation and Regime: A Comparative Analysis'. *Journal of Public Policy* 6, no. 1: 49–72.

Elkins, Z. and B. Simmons. (2005). 'On Clusters, Waves and Diffusion: A Conceptual Framework'. *Annals of the American Association of Political and Social Science* 598: 33–51.

Ellig, J. and D. Lavoie. (1995). 'The Principle–Agent Relationship in Organizations'. In P. Foss (ed.), *Economic Approaches to Organizations and Institutions: An Introduction*. Aldershot, UK: Dartmouth.

Elliott, C. and R. Schlaepfer. (2001). 'The Advocacy Coalition Framework: Application to the Policy Process for the Development of Forest Certification in Sweden'. *Journal of European Public Policy* 8, no. 4: 642–61.

Elliott, D. and M. McGuinness. (2001). 'Public Inquiry: Panacea or Placebo?' *Journal of Contingencies and Crisis Management* 10, no. 1: 14–25.

Elmore, R. F. (1978). 'Organizational Models of Social Program Implementation'. *Public Policy* 26, no. 2: 185–228.

Elmore, R. F. (1987). 'Instruments and Strategy in Public Policy'. *Policy Studies Review* 7, no. 1: 174–86.

Eloi, L. (2009). 'Carbon Tax: The French Connection'. *The Economists' Voice* (December): 1–4.

Elsen, M., R. Giesen and J. Leenheer. (2015). *Milan BExpo 2015 Behavioural Study on Food Choices and Eating Habits: Final Report*. Luxembourg: European Commission. http://bookshop.europa.eu/uri?target=EUB:NOTICE:DS0415694:EN:HTML.

Elson, A. (2008). 'The Sovereign Wealth Funds of Singapore'. *World Economics* 9, no. 3: 73–96.

Elster, J. (1989). *The Cement of Society: A Study of Social Order*. Cambridge, UK; New York: Cambridge University Press.

Elster, J. (2009). *Reason and Rationality*. Princeton, NJ: Princeton University Press.

Enderlein, H., S. Wälti and M. Zürn. (2011). *Handbook on Multi-Level Governance*. Cheltenham, UK: Edward Elgar.

Engels, A., O. Hüther, M. Schäfer and H. Held. (2013). 'Public Climate-Change Skepticism, Energy Preferences and Political Participation'. *Global Environmental Change* 23, no. 5: 1018–27.

English, L. M. and M. Skellern. (2005). 'Public–Private Partnerships and Public Sector Management Reform: A Comparative Analysis'. *International Journal of Public Policy* 1, nos 1/2: 1–21.

Enkler, J., S. Schmidt, S. Eckhard, C. Knill and S. Grohs. (2016). 'Administrative Styles in the OECD: Bureaucratic Policy-Making Beyond Formal Rules'. *International Journal of Public Administration* (13 July): 1–12.

EPA (Environmental Protection Agency). (2001). *The United States Experience with Economic Incentives for Protecting the Environment* (No. EPA-240-R-01-001). National Center for Environmental Economics: Office of Policy, Economics, and Innovation Office of the Administrator US Environmental Protection Agency.

Ergas, H. (2010). 'New Policies Create a New Politics: Issues of Institutional Design in Climate Change Policy'. *Australian Journal of Agricultural and Resource Economics* 54, no. 2: 143–64.

Erwin C. (1975). *The Missing Link: The Study of the Implementation of Social Policy*. Washington, DC: Urban Institute.

Escribano, G. (2013). 'Ecuador's Energy Policy Mix: Development Versus Conservation and Nationalism with Chinese Loans'. *Energy Policy* 57(c): 152–9.

Esmark, A. (2009). 'The Functional Differentiation of Governance: Public Governance beyond Hierarchy, Market and Networks'. *Public Administration* 87, no. 2: 351–70.

Esping-Andersen, G. (1990). *The Three Worlds of Welfare Capitalism*. Cambridge: Polity Press.

Europæiske, M. (2013). *Adaptation in Europe: Addressing Risks and Opportunities from Climate Change in the Context of Socio-Economic Developments.* Copenhagen, Denmark: European Environment Agency.

Evangelista, M. (1995). 'The Paradox of State Strength: Transnational Relations, Domestic Structures, and Security Policy in Russia and the Soviet Union'. *International Organization.* 49, no. 1: 1–38.

Evans, B., T. Richmond and J. Shields. (2005). 'Structuring Neoliberal Governance: The Nonprofit Sector, Emerging New Modes of Control and the Marketisation of Service Delivery'. *Policy and Society* 24, no. 1: 73–97.

Evans, P. (1997). 'The Eclipse of the State? Reflections on Stateness in an Era of Globalization'. *World Politics* 50, no. 1: 62–87.

Everitt, J. and B. O'Neill (eds). (2002). *Citizen Politics: Research and Theory in Canadian Political Behaviour.* Toronto, ON: Oxford University Press.

Evers, A. (2005). 'Mixed Welfare Systems and Hybrid Organizations: Changes in the Governance and Provision of Social Services'. *International Journal of Public Administration* 28: 737–48.

Evers, A. and H. Wintersberger (eds). (1990). *Shifts in the Welfare Mix: Their Impact on Work, Social Services and Welfare Policies.* Frankfurt, Germany; Boulder, CO: Campus/Westview.

Executive Research Group. (1999). *Investing in Policy: Report on Other Jurisdictions and Organizations.* Toronto, ON: Ministry of the Environment.

Falk, R. A. (1997). 'State of Siege: Will Globalization Win Out?' *International Affairs* 73, no. 1: 123–36.

Falkenmark, M. (2004). 'Towards Integrated Catchment Management: Opening the Paradigm Locks between Hydrology, Ecology and Policy-Making'. *Water Resources Development* 20, no. 3: 275–82.

Falkner, G. (2000). Policy Networks in a Multi-Level System: Convergence Towards Moderate Diversity? *West European Politics* 2, no. 4: 94–120.

Falleti, T. G. and J. F. Lynch. (2009). 'Context and Causal Mechanisms in Political Analysis'. *Comparative Political Studies* 42, no. 9: 1143–66.

Farazmand, A. (1999). 'Globalization and Public Administration'. *Public Administration Review.* 59, no. 6: 509–22.

Fehr, E. and K. M. Schmidt. (2003). 'Theories of Fairness and Reciprocity: Evidence and Economic Applications'. In M. Dewatripont, L. P. Hansen and S. J. Turnovsky (eds), *Advances in Economics and Econometrics.* Cambridge, UK: Cambridge University Press, 208–57.

Feindt, P. H. (2012). 'The Politics of Biopatents in Food and Agriculture, 1950–2010: Value Conflict, Competing Paradigms and Contested Institutionalisation in Multi-level Governance'. *Policy and Society* 31, no. 4 (November): 281–93.

Feindt. P. and A. Flynn. (2009). 'Policy Stretching and Institutional Layering: British Food Policy Between Security, Safety, Quality, Health and Climate Change'. *British Politics* 4, no. 3: 386–414.

Feiock, R. C., A. F. Tavares and M. Lubell. (2008). 'Policy Instrument Choices for Growth Management and Land Use Regulation'. *Policy Studies Journal* 36, no. 3: 461–80.

Feldman, M. S. and A. M. Khademian. (2007). 'The Role of the Public Manager in Inclusion: Creating Communities of Participation'. *Governance* 20, no. 2: 305–24.

Fellegi, I. (1996). *Strengthening Our Policy Capacity.* Ottawa, ON: Deputy Ministers Task Force.

Ferlie, E., A. Pettigrew, L. Ashburner and L. Fitzgerald. (1996). *The New Public Management in Action*. New York: Oxford University Press.

Ferraro, P. J. and Price, M. K. (2013). 'Using Nonpecuniary Strategies to Influence Behavior: Evidence from a Large-Scale Field Experiment'. *The Review of Economics and Statistics* 95, no. 1: 64–73.

Ferraro, P. J., J. J. Miranda and M. K. Price. (2011). 'The Persistence of Treatment Effects with Norm-Based Policy Instruments: Evidence from a Randomized Environmental Policy Experiment'. *American Economic Review* 101, no. 3: 318–22.

Ferreira, A. and D. Otley. (2009). 'The Design and Use of Performance Management Systems: An Extended Framework for Analysis'. *Management Accounting Research*, online.

Festinger, L. (1962). *A Theory of Cognitive Dissonance*. Stanford, CA: Stanford University Press.

Finer, D., P. Tillgren, K. Berensson, K. Guldbrandsson and B. Hagland. (2005). 'Implementation of a Health Impact Assessment (HIA) Tool in a Regional Health Organization in Sweden – A Feasibility Study'. *Health Promotion International* 20, no. 3: 277–84.

Finer, S. E. (1997). *The History of Government From the Earliest Times*, Vol. III: *Empires, Monarchies and the Modern State*. Oxford: Oxford University Press; especially Chapter 7 'The Transplantation of European State-Models, 1500–1715'.

Finkle, P., K. Webb, W. Stanbury and P. Pross. (1994). *Federal Government Relations with Interest Groups: A Reconsideration*. Ottawa, ON: Privy Council Office.

Finley, L. K. (ed.). (1989). *Public Sector Privatization: Alternative Approaches to Service Delivery*. New York: Quorum Books.

Firestone, O. J. (1970). *The Public Persuader: Government Advertising*. Toronto, ON: Methuen.

Fischer, C. (2010). 'Combining Policies for Renewable Energy: Is the Whole Less Than the Sum of Its Parts?' *International Review of Environmental and Resource Economics* 4, no. 1 (30 June): 51–92.

Fischer, F. and J. Forester. (1987). *Confronting Values in Policy Analysis: The Politics of Criteria*. Beverly Hills, CA: Sage.

Fischer, F. and J. Forester. (1993). *The Argumentative Turn in Policy Analysis and Planning*. Durham, NC: Duke University Press.

Fischhoff, B. (2010). 'Judgment and Decision Making'. *Wiley Interdisciplinary Reviews: Cognitive Science* 1, no. 3: 724–38.

Flanagan, K., E. Uyarra and M. Laranja. (2011). 'Reconceptualising the "Policy Mix" for Innovation'. *Research Policy* 40, no. 5 (June): 702–13.

Fleischer, J. (2009). 'Power Resources of Parliamentary Executives: Policy Advice in the UK and Germany'. *West European Politics* 32, no. 1: 196–214.

Fligstein, N. (1996). 'Markets as Politics: A Political-Cultural Approach to Market Institutions'. *American Sociological Review* 61 (August): 656–73.

Flinders, M. V. and H. McConnel. (1999). 'Diversity and Complexity: The Quango-Continuum'. In M. V. Flinders, and M. J. Smith (eds), *Quangos, Accountability and Reform: The Politics of Quasi-Government*. Sheffield, UK: Political Economy Research Centre, 17–39.

Flitner, D. (1986). *The Politics of Presidential Commissions*. New York: Transnational.

Flora, P. and A. J. Heidenheimer (eds). (1981). *The Development of Welfare States in Europe and America*, New Brunswick, NJ: Transaction.

Flumian, M., A. Coe and K. Kernaghan. (2007). 'Transforming Service to Canadians: The Service Canada Model'. *International Review of Administrative Sciences* 73, no. 4: 557–68.

Ford, R. and D. Zussman. (1997). *Alternative Service Delivery: Sharing Governance in Canada*. Toronto, ON: KPMG/IPAC.

Forester, J. (1983). 'What Analysts Do'. In W. N. Dunn (ed.), *Values, Ethics and the Practice of Policy Analysis*. Lexington, KY: Lexington Books, 47–62.

Forester, J. (1989). *Planning in the Face of Power*. Berkeley, CA: University of California Press.

Forsyth, A., C. S. Slotterback and K. J. Krizek. (2010). 'Health Impact Assessment Review'. *Environmental Impact Assessment Review* 30: 42–51.

Foster, C. D. and F. J. Plowden. (1996). *The State under Stress: Can the Hollow State Be Good Government?* Buckingham, UK; Philadelphia, PA: Open University Press.

Foster, E., M. Haward and S. Coffen-Smout. (2005). 'Implementing Integrated Oceans Management: Australia's South East Regional Marine Plan (SERMP) and Canada's Eastern Scotian Shelf Integrated Management (ESSIM) Initiative'. *Marine Policy* 29: 391–405.

Franchino, F. and B. Hoyland. (2009). 'Legislative Involvement in Parliamentary Systems: Opportunities, Conflict and Institutional Constraints'. *American Political Science Review* 103, no. 4: 607–21.

Franz, J. S. and C. Kirkpatrick. (2008). 'Improving the Quality of Integrated Policy Analysis: Impact Assessment for Sustainable Development in the European Commission'. *Evidence & Policy* 4, no. 2: 171–85.

Fraussen, B. and D. Halpin. (2017). 'Think Tanks and Strategic Policy-Making: The Contribution of Think Tanks to Policy Advisory Systems'. *Policy Sciences* 50, no. 1 (1 March): 105–24.

Frederick, S., G. Loewenstein and T. O'Donoghue. (2002). Time Discounting and Time Preference: A Critical Review. *Journal of Economic Literature* 40, no. 2: 351–401.

Frederiks, E. R., Stenner, K. and Hobman, E. V. (2015). Household Energy Use: Applying Behavioural Economics to Understand Consumer Decision-Making and Behaviour. *Renewable and Sustainable Energy Reviews* 41, 1385–94.

Freeman, G. P. (1985). 'National Styles and Policy Sectors: Explaining Structured Variation'. *Journal of Public Policy* 5, no. 4: 467–96.

Freeman, J. (1997). 'Collaborative Governance in the Administrative State'. *UCLA Law Review* 45, no. 1: 77–177.

Freeman, J. R. (1989). *Democracy and Markets: The Politics of Mixed Economies*. Ithaca, NY: Cornell University Press.

French, R. (1980). *How Ottawa Decides: Planning and Industrial Policy-Making 1968–1980*. Toronto, ON: Lorimer.

Friedman, T. L. (1999). *The Lexus and the Olive Tree*. New York: HarperCollins.

Frischtak, C. R. (1995). 'The Changed Role of the State: Regulatory Policies and Reform in a Comparative Perspective'. In C. R. Frischtak (ed.), *Regulatory Policies and Reform: A Comparative Perspective*. New York: World Bank, 1–15.

Frye, T., O. J. Reuter and D. Szakonyi. (2012). *Political Machines at Work: Voter Mobilization and Electoral Subversion in the Workplace*. SSRN Scholarly Paper. Rochester, NY: Social Science Research Network. http://papers.ssrn.com/abstract=2110201.

Fukuyama, F. (2013). 'What Is Governance?' *Governance* 26, no. 3: 347–68.

Fung, A. (2003). 'Survey Article: Recipes for Public Spheres: Eight Institutional Design Choices and Their Consequences'. *Journal of Political Philosophy* 11, no. 3 (1 September): 338–67.

Furlong, S. R. and C. M. Kerwin. (2004). 'Interest Group Participation in Rule Making: A Decade of Change'. *Journal of Public Administration Research and Theory* 15, no. 3: 353–70.

Gabrielian, V. and F. Fischer. (1996). 'Reforming Eastern European Bureaucracy: Does the American Experience Apply?' In H. K. Asmerom and E. P. Reis (eds), *Democratization and Bureaucratic Neutrality*, London: Macmillan, 109–26.

Gadamer, H. (1989). *Truth and Method*. New York: Cross Road.

Gage, R. W. and M. P. Mandell (eds). (1990). *Strategies for Managing Intergovernmental Policies and Networks*. New York: Praeger.

Gailmard, S. and J. W. Patty. (2007). 'Slackers and Zealots: Civil Service, Policy Discretion, and Bureaucratic Expertise.l' *American Journal of Political Science* 51, no. 4: 873–89.

Galanter, M. (1980). 'Legality and Its Discontents: A Preliminary Assessment of Current Theories of Legalization and Delegalization'. In E. Blankenburg, E. Klausa and H. Rottleuthner (eds), *Alternative Rechtsforen und Alternativen Zum Recht*, Bonn, Germany: Westdeutscher Verlag, 11–26 .

Gall, G. L. (1983). *The Canadian Legal System*. Toronto, ON: Carswell.

Gandrud, C. and C. Grafström. (2015). 'Inflated Expectations: How Government Partisanship Shapes Monetary Policy Bureaucrats' Inflation Forecasts'. *Political Science Research and Methods* 3, no. 2: 353–80.

Gandy, O. H. (1982). *Beyond Agenda Setting: Information Subsidies and Public Policy*. Norwood, NJ: Ablex.

Ganghof, S. (2006). 'Tax Mixes and the Size of the Welfare State: Causal Mechanisms and Policy Implications'. *Journal of European Social Policy* 16, no. 4: 360–73.

Gans-Morse, J., S. Mazzuca and S. Nichter. (2014). 'Varieties of Clientelism: Machine Politics during Elections'. *American Journal of Political Science* 58, no. 2 (1 April): 415–32.

Garcia Martinez, M. (2015). 'Solver Engagement in Knowledge Sharing in Crowdsourcing Communities: Exploring the Link to Creativity'. *Research Policy* 44, no. 8 (October): 1419–30.

Garcia-Murillo, M. (2005). 'Regulatory Responses to Convergence; Experience from Four Countries'. *Info – The Journal of Policy, Regulation and Strategy for Telecommunications* 7, no. 1: 20–40.

Garson, G. David. (1986). 'From Policy Science to Policy Analysis: A Quarter Century of Progress'. In W. N. Dunn (ed.), *Policy Analysis: Perspectives, Concepts and Methods*. Greenwich, CT: JAI Press, 3–22.

Gayle, D. J. and J. N. Goodrich (eds). (1990). *Privatization and Deregulation in Global Perspective*. Westport, CT: Quorum Books.

Gehring, T. and S. Oberthur. (2009). 'The Causal Mechanisms of Interaction Between International Institutions'. *European Journal of International Relations* 15, no. 1: 125–56.

Gelders, D. and O. Ihlen. (2009). 'Minding the Gap: Applying a Service Marketing Model into Government Policy Communications'. *Government Information Quarterly* 27, no. 1: 34–40.

Gelders, D. and O. Ihlen. (2010). 'Government Communication about Potential Policies: Public Relations, Propaganda or Both?' *Public Relations Review* 36, no. 1: 59–62.

George, A. L. (1969). 'The "Operational Code": A Neglected Approach to the Study of Political Leaders and Decision-Making'. *International Studies Quarterly* 13: 190–222.

Gerard, D. and Lave, L. (2007). 'Experiments in Technology Forcing: Comparing the Regulatory Processes of US Automobile Safety and Emissions Regulations'. *International Journal of Technology, Policy and Management* 7, no. 1: 1.

Gero, J. S. (1990). 'Design Prototypes: A Knowledge Representation Schema for Design'. *Text Serial Journal* 11, no. 4 (15 December): 26–36.

Geva-May, I. and A. M. Maslove. (2006). 'Canadian Public Policy Analysis and Public Policy Programs: A Comparative Perspective'. *Journal of Public Affairs Education* 12, no. 4: 413–38.

Geva-May, I. and A. M. Maslove. (2007). 'In Between Trends: Developments of Public Policy Analysis and Policy Analysis Instruction in Canada, the United States and the European Union'. In L. Dobuzinskis, M. Howlett and D. Laycock (eds), *Policy Analysis in Canada: The State of the Art*. Toronto, ON: University of Toronto Press, 186–216.

Gibson, R. B. (1999). *Voluntary Initiatives and the New Politics of Corporate Greening*. Toronto, ON: University of Toronto Press.

Giebels, D., A. van Buuren and J. Edelenbos. (2015). 'Using Knowledge in a Complex Decision-Making Process – Evidence and Principles from the Danish Houting Project's Ecosystem-Based Management Approach'. *Environmental Science & Policy* 47 (March): 53–67.

Gifford, R. and L. A. Comeau. (2011). 'Message Framing Influences Perceived Climate Change Competence, Engagement, and Behavioral Intentions'. *Global Environmental Change*, 21, no. 4: 1301–7.

Gilabert, P. and H. Lawford-Smith. (2012). 'Political Feasibility: A Conceptual Exploration'. *Political Studies* 60, no. 4: 809–25.

Gilardi, F. (2002). 'Policy Credibility and Delegation to Independent Regulatory Agencies: A Comparative Empirical Analysis'. *Journal of European Public Policy* 9, no. 6: 873–93.

Gilardi, F. (2005a). 'Evaluating Independent Regulators'. In OECD Working Party on Regulatory Management and Reform (ed.), *Designing Independent and Accountable Regulatory Authorities for High Quality Regulation – Proceedings of an Expert Meeting in London, United Kingdom 10–11 January 2005*. Paris: OECD, 101–25.

Gilardi, F. (2005b). 'The Formal Independence of Regulators: A Comparison of 17 Countries and 7 Sectors'. *Swiss Political Science Review* 11, no. 4: 139–67.

Gilardi, F. (2005c). 'The Institutional Foundations of Regulatory Capitalism: The Diffusion of Regulatory Agencies in Western Europe'. *Annals of the American Academy of Political and Social Science* 595, no. 1: 84–101.

Gill, N. N. (1940). 'Permanent Advisory Committees in the Federal Government'. *Journal of Politics* 2: 411–25.

Gilmore, T. N. and J. Krantz. (1991). 'Innovation in the Public Sector: Dilemmas in the Use of Ad Hoc Processes'. *Journal of Policy Analysis and Management* 10, no. 3: 455–68.

Gipperth, L. (2008). 'The Legal Design of the International and European Union Ban on Tributyltin Antifouling Paint: Direct and Indirect Effects'. *Journal of Environmental Management* 90, Supplement: S86–S95.

Givoni, M. (2014). 'Addressing Transport Policy Challenges through Policy-Packaging'. *Transportation Research Part A: Policy and Practice* 60 (February): 1–8.

Givoni, M., J. Macmillen, D. Banister and E. Feitelson. (2013). 'From Policy Measures to Policy Packages'. *Transport Reviews* 33, no. 1: 1–20.

Gleeson, D. H., D. Legge, D. O'Neill and M. Pfeffer. (2011). 'Negotiating Tensions in Developing Organizational Policy Capacity: Comparative Lessons To Be Drawn'. *Journal of Comparative Policy Analysis: Research and Practice* 13, no. 3 (June): 237–63.

Gleeson, D. H., D. G. Legge and D. O'Neill. (2009). 'Evaluating Health Policy Capacity: Learning from International and Australian Experience'. *Australia and New Zealand Health Policy* 6, no. 1 (26 February).

Gleirscher, N. (2008). 'Policy Instruments in Support of Organic Farming in Austria'. *International Journal of Agricultural Resources, Governance and Ecology* 7, nos 1/2: 51–62.

Glennan, S. (2002). 'Rethinking Mechanistic Explanation'. *Proceedings of the Philosophy of Science Association*, no. 3: 342–53.

Glennerster, R. and K. Takavarasha. (2013). *Running Randomized Evaluations: A Practical Guide*. http://public.eblib.com/choice/publicfullrecord.aspx?p=1458376.

Glicken, J. (2000). 'Getting Stakeholder Participation "Right": A Discussion of Participatory Processes and Possible Pitfalls'. *Environmental Science and Policy* 3: 305–10.

Goetz, A. M. (2007). 'Manouevring Past Clientelism: Institutions and Incentives to Generate Constituencies in Support of Governance Reforms'. *Commonwealth and Comparative Politics* 45, no. 4: 403–24.

Goffman, E. (1974). *Frame Analysis: An Essay on the Organization of Experience*. Cambridge, MA: Harvard University Press.

Goggin, M. L. (1987). *Policy Design and the Politics of Implementation: The Case of Child Health Care in the American States*. Knoxville, TN: University of Tennessee Press.

Goggin, M. L., A. O. M. Bowman, J. P. Lester and L. J. O'Toole. (1990). *Implementation Theory and Practice: Toward a Third Generation*. Glenview, IL: Scott, Foresman/Little, Brown.

Goldmann, K. (2005). 'Appropriateness and Consequences: The Logic of Neo-Institutionalism'. *Governance* 18, no. 1: 35–52.

Goldsmith, S. and W. D. Eggers. (2004). *Governing by Network: The New Shape of the Public Sector*. Washington, DC: Brookings Institution.

Goldstein, J. and R. O. Keohane (eds). (????). *Ideas and Foreign Policy: Beliefs, Institutions and Political Change*. Ithaca, NY: Cornell University Press.

Goldstein, N. J., R. B. Cialdini, V. Griskevicius and J. D. Article. (2008). 'A Room with a Viewpoint: Using Social Norms to Motivate Environmental Conservation in Hotels'. *Journal of Consumer Research* 35, no. 3: 472–82.

González-Eguino, M. (2011). 'The Importance of the Design of Market-Based Instruments for CO_2 Mitigation: An AGE Analysis for Spain'. *Ecological Economics* 70, no. 12 (October): 2292–2302.

Goodin, R. E. (1980). *Manipulatory Politics*. New Haven, CT: Yale University Press.

Goodin, R. E. and M. Rein. (2001). 'Regimes on Pillars: Alternative Welfare State Logics and Dynamics'. *Public Administration* 79, no. 4: 769–801.

Goodwin, T. (2012). 'Why We Should Reject "Nudge"'. *Politics* 32, no. 2 : 85–92.

Gormley, W. T. (1989). *Taming the Bureaucracy: Muscles, Prayers and Other Strategies*. Princeton, NJ: Princeton University Press.

Gormley, W. T. (1998). 'Regulatory Enforcement'. *Political Research Quarterly* 51, no. 2: 363–83.

319

Gormley, W. T. (2007). 'Public Policy Analysis: Ideas and Impact'. *Annual Review of Political Science* 10: 297–313.

Gossum, P., B. Arts and K. Verheyen. (2010). 'From "Smart Regulation" to "Regulatory Arrangements"'. *Policy Sciences* 43, no. 3: 245–61.

Gough, C. and S. Shackley. (2001). 'The Respectable Politics of Climate Change: The Epistemic Communities and NGOs'. *International Affairs* 77: 329–46.

Goulder, L. H. and A. R. Schein. (2013). 'Carbon Taxes Versus Cap and Trade: A Critical Review'. *Climate Change Economics* 4, no. 3: 1–28.

Gourevitch, P. (2004). 'Corporate Governance: Global Markets, National Politics'. In M. Kahler and D. Lake (eds), *Governance in a Global Economy*. Princeton, NJ: Princeton University Press, 305–31.

Gow, J. I. and S. L. Sutherland. (2004). 'Comparison of Canadian Masters Programs in Public Administration, Public Management and Public Policy'. *Canadian Public Administration*. 47, no. 3: 379–405.

Grabosky, P. N. (1994). 'Green Markets: Environmental Regulation by the Private Sector'. *Law and Policy* 16, no. 4, 419–48.

Grabosky, P. N. (1995). 'Counterproductive Regulation'. *International Journal of the Sociology of Law* 23: 347–69.

Graham, K. A. and S. D. Phillips. (1997). 'Citizen Engagement: Beyond the Customer Revolution'. *Canadian Public Administration* 40, no. 2: 225–73.

Grant, W. (2010). 'Policy Instruments in the Common Agricultural Policy'. *West European Politics* 33, no. 1: 22–38.

Grant, W. and A. MacNamara. (1995). 'When Policy Communities Intersect: The Cases of Agriculture and Banking'. *Political Studies* 43: 509–15.

Grantham A. (2001). 'How Networks Explain Unintended Policy Implementation Outcomes: The Case of UK Rail Privatization'. *Public Administration* 79, no. 4: 851–70.

Greener, I. (2002). 'Understanding NHS Reform: The Policy-Transfer, Social Learning and Path Dependency Perspectives'. *Governance* 15, no. 2: 161–83.

Greener, I. (2006). 'Markets in the Public Sector: When Do They Work and What Do We Do When They Don't'. *Policy and Politics* 36, no. 1: 93–108.

Greenstone, M. (2001). *The Impacts of Environmental Regulations on Industrial Activity: Evidence from the 1970 & 1977 Clean Air Act Amendments and the Census of Manufactures*. No. w8484. Washington, DC: National Bureau of Economic Research.

Greenwood, D. J. J. (2005). 'Democracy and Delaware: The Mysterious Race to the Bottom/Top'. *Yale Law and Policy Review* 23, no. 2: 402–25.

Griffin, R. (2013). 'Auction Designs for Allocating Wind Energy Leases on the US Outer Continental shelf'. *Energy Policy* 56 (May): 603–11.

Grima, A. (1985). 'Participatory Rites: Integrating Public Involvement in Environmental Impact Assessment'. In J. B. R. Whitney and V. W. Maclaren (eds), *Environmental Impact Assessment: The Canadian Experience*. Toronto, ON: University of Toronto Institute for Environmental Studies, 33–51.

Grimsey, D. and M. K. Lewis. (2004). *Public Private Partnerships: The Worldwide Revolution in Infrastructure Provision and Project Finance*. Cheltenham, UK: Edward Elgar.

Grimshaw, D., S. Vincent and H. Willmott. (2001). 'New Control Modes and Emergent Organizational Forms: Private–Public Contracting in Public Administration'. *Administrative Theory and Practice* 23, no. 3: 407–30.

Grimshaw, J. M., M. P. Eccles, J. N. Lavis, S. J. Hill and J. E. Squires. (2012). 'Knowledge Translation of Research Findings'. *Implementation Science* 7, no. 1 (31 May): 50.

Grin, J. and H. V. De Graaf. (1996). 'Implementation as Communicative Action: An Interpretative Understanding of Interactions between Policy Actors and Target Groups'. *Policy Sciences* 29: 291–319.

Gromet, D. M., H. Kunreuther and R. P. Larrick. (2013). 'Political Ideology Affects Energy-Efficiency Attitudes and Choices'. *Proceedings of the National Academy of Sciences* 110, no. 23: 9314–19.

Gronn, P. (2009). 'Leadership Configurations'. *Leadership* 5, no. 3 (1 August): 381–94.

Gross, M. (2010). *Ignorance and Surprise: Science, Society, and Ecological Design.* Cambridge, MA: MIT Press.

Grossback, L. J., S. Nicholson-Crotty and D. A. Peterson. (2004). 'Ideology and Learning in Policy Diffusion'. *American Politics Research* 32, no. 5: 521–45.

Grüne-Yanoff, T. and R. Hertwig. (2016). 'Nudge Versus Boost: How Coherent are Policy and Theory?' *Minds and Machines* 26, nos 1–2: 149–83.

Gulbrandsen, L. H. (2010). *Transnational Environmental Governance: The Emergence and Effects of the Certification of Forests and Fisheries.* Cheltenham, UK: Edward Elgar.

Gunningham, N. and J. Rees. (1997). 'Industry Self-Regulation: An Institutional Perspective'. *Law and Policy* 19, no. 4: 363–414.

Gunningham, N. and D. Sinclair. (1999a). 'New Generation Environmental Policy: Environmental Management Systems and Regulatory Reform'. *Melbourne University Law Review* 22, no. 3: 592–616.

Gunningham, N. and D. Sinclair. (1999b). 'Regulatory Pluralism: Designing Policy Mixes for Environmental Protection'. *Law and Policy* 21, no. 1: 49–76.

Gunningham, N. and D. Sinclair. (2002). *Leaders and Laggards: Next Generation Environmental Regulation.* Sheffield, UK: Greenleaf.

Gunningham, N. and M. D. Young. (1997). 'Toward Optimal Environmental Policy: The Case of Biodiversity Conservation'. *Ecology Law Quarterly* 24: 243–98.

Gunningham, N., P. Grabosky and D. Sinclair. (1998). *Smart Regulation: Designing Environmental Policy.* Oxford: Clarendon Press.

Guo, C. (2007). 'When Government Becomes the Principal Philanthropist: The Effects of Public Funding on Patterns of Nonprofit Governance'. *Public Administration Review* 67, no. 3: 458–73.

Gupta, J., C. Termeer, J. Klostermann, S. Meijerink, M. van den Brink, P. Jong, S. Nooteboom and E. Bergsma. (2010). 'The Adaptive Capacity Wheel: A Method to Assess the Inherent Characteristics of Institutions to Enable the Adaptive Capacity of Society'. *Environmental Science & Policy* 13, no. 6 (October): 459–71.

Haas, E. B. (1958). *The Uniting of Europe: Political, Social and Economical Forces 1950–1957.* London: Stevens & Sons.

Haas, P. M. (1992). 'Introduction: Epistemic Communities and International Policy Coordination'. *International Organisation* 46: 1–36.

Haas, P. M. (2001). 'Policy Knowledge: Epistemic Communities'. In *International Encyclopedia of the Social and Behavioral Sciences.* Oxford: Pergamon, 11578–86.

Haas, P. M. (2004). 'When Does Power Listen to Truth? A Constructivist Approach to the Policy Process'. *Journal of European Public Policy* 11, no. 4: 569–92.

Haasnoot, M., J. H. Kwakkel, W. E. Walker and J. ter Maat. (2013). 'Dynamic Adaptive Policy Pathways: A Method for Crafting Robust Decisions for a Deeply Uncertain World'. *Global Environmental Change* 23, no. 2: 485–98.

Habermas, J. (1973). 'What Does a Legitimation Crisis Mean Today? Legitimation Problems in Late Capitalism'. *Social Research* 40, no. 4: 643–67.

Habermas, J. (1975). *Legitimation Crisis*. Boston, MA: Beacon Press.

Hacker, J. S. (2004a). 'Privatizing Risk without Privatizing the Welfare State: The Hidden Politics of Social Policy Retrenchment in the United States'. *American Political Science Review* 98: 243–60.

Hacker, J. S. (2004b). 'Reform without Change, Change without Reform: The Politics of US Health Policy Reform in Comparative Perspective'. In M. A. Levin, and M. Shapiro (eds), *Transatlantic Policymaking in an Age of Austerity: Diversity and Drift*. Washington, DC: Georgetown University Press, 13–63.

Hacker, J. S. (2004c). 'Review Article: Dismantling the Health Care State? Political Institutions, Public Policies and the Comparative Politics of Health Reform'. *British Journal of Political Science*. 34: 693–724.

Hacker, J. S. (2005). 'Policy Drift: The Hidden Politics of US Welfare State Retrenchment'. In W. Streek, and K. Thelen (eds), *Beyond Continuity: Institutional Change in Advanced Political Economies*. Oxford: Oxford University Press, 40–82.

Hagman, W., D. Andersson, D. Västfjäll and G. Tinghög. (2015). 'Public Views on Policies Involving Nudges'. *Review of Philosophy and Psychology* 6, no. 3: 439–53.

Hahn, R. W. (2008). *Greenhouse Gas Auctions and Taxes: Some Practical Considerations*. Washington, DC: AEI Centre for Regulatory and Market Studies, Working Paper 8–12.

Haider, D. (1989). 'Grants as a Tool of Public Policy'. In L. M. Salamon (ed.), *Beyond Privatization: The Tools of Government Action*. Washington, DC: Urban Institute, 93–124.

Haider, H., C. Mcloughlin and Z. Scott. (2011). *Communication and Governance*. The World Bank.

Hajer, M. A. (1997). *The Politics of Environmental Discourse: Ecological Modernization and the Policy Process*. Oxford: Oxford University Press.

Hajer, M. A. (2005). 'Setting the Stage: A Dramaturgy of Policy Deliberation'. *Administration and Society* 36, no. 6: 624–47.

Halffman, W. and R. Hoppe. (2005). 'Science/Policy Boundaries: A Changing Division of Labour in Dutch Expert Policy Advice'. In S. Maasen, and P. Weingart (eds), *Democratization of Expertise?* Dordrecht, Netherlands: Springer, 135–51.

Hall, M. and K. Banting. (2000). 'The Nonprofit Sector in Canada: An Introduction'. In Keith Banting (ed.), *The NonProfit Sector in Canada: Roles and Relationships*. Montreal, QC: McGill-Queen's University Press, 1–28.

Hall, P. A. (1986). *Governing the Economy: The Politics of State Intervention in Britain and France*. Cambridge: Polity Press.

Hall, P. A. (1989a). 'Conclusion: The Political Power of Economic Ideas'. In Peter A. Hall (ed.), *The Political Power of Economic Ideas: Keynesianism Across Nations*. Princeton, NJ: Princeton University Press, 361–92.

Hall, P. A. (1989b). *The Political Power of Economic Ideas: Keynesianism Across Nations*. Princeton, NJ: Princeton University Press.

Hall, P. A. (1990). 'Policy Paradigms, Experts, and the State: The Case of Macroeconomic Policy-Making in Britain'. In S. Brooks and A. G. Gagnon (eds), *Social Scientists, Policy and the State*. New York: Praeger, 53–78.

Hall, P. A. (1992). 'The Change from Keynesianism to Monetarism: Institutional Analysis and British Economic Policy in the 1970s'. In S. Steinmo, K. Thelen and

F. Longstreth (eds), *Structuring Politics: Historical Institutionalism in Comparative Analysis*, Cambridge: Cambridge University Press, 90–114.

Hall, P. A. (1993). 'Policy Paradigms, Social Learning and the State: The Case of Economic Policy-Making in Britain'. *Comparative Politics* 25, no. 3: 275–96.

Hall, P. A. and D. Soskice. (2001). 'Varieties of Capitalism: The Institutional Foundations of Comparative Advantage'. In Peter A. Hall and David Soskice (eds), *An Introduction to Varieties of Capitalism*. New York: Oxford University Press, 1–70.

Hall, P. A. and R. C. R. Taylor. (1996). 'Political Science and the Three New Institutionalisms'. *Political Studies* 44: 936–57.

Hall, T. (2008). 'Steering Agencies with Short-Term Authorizations'. *Public Administration Review* 68, no. 2: 366–79.

Hall, T. E. and L. J. O'Toole. (2000). 'Structures for Policy Implementation: An Analysis of National Legislation, 1965–66 and 1993–94'. *Administration and Society* 31, no. 6: 667–86.

Hall, T. E. and L. J. O'Toole. (2004). 'Shaping Formal Networks through the Regulatory Process'. *Administration and Society* 36, no. 2: 186–207.

Halligan, J. (1995). 'Policy Advice and the Public Sector'. In B. G. Peters and D. T. Savoie (eds), *Governance in a Changing Environment*, Montreal, QC: McGill-Queen's University Press, 138–72.

Hallsworth, M. (2016). 'Behavioural Insights: The Road to "Better" Policies?' www.hertie-school.org/the-governance-post/2016/08/behavioural-insights-road-better-policies. Accessed 1 August.

Halpern, C. (2010). 'Governing Despite Its Instruments? Instrumentation in EU Environmental Policy'. *West European Politics* 33, no. 1: 39–57.

Halpern, D. (2015). *Inside the Nudge Unit: How Small Changes Can Make a Big Difference*. London: W. H. Allen.

Halpin, D. R., B. Fraussen and A. J. Nownes. (2018). 'The Balancing Act of Establishing a Policy Agenda: Conceptualizing and Measuring Drivers of Issue Prioritization within Interest Groups'. *Governance* 31, no. 2 (1 April): 215–37.

Hamalainen, T., M. Kosonen and Y. L. Doz. (2012). *Strategic Agility in Public Management*. SSRN Scholarly Paper. Rochester, NY: Social Science Research Network. http://papers.ssrn.com/abstract=2020436. Accessed 12 March.

Hamdouch, A. and M.-H. Depret. (2010). 'Policy Integration Strategy and the Development of the "Green Economy": Foundations and Implementation Patterns'. *Journal of Environmental Planning and Management* 53, no. 4: 473.

Hamelin, F. (2010). 'Renewal of Public Policy via Instrumental Innovation: Implementing Automated Speed Enforcement in France'. *Governance* 23, no. 3: 509–30.

Hammersley, M. (2005). 'Is the Evidence-Based Practice Movement Doing More Good Than Harm? Reflections on Iain Chalmers' Case for Research-Based Policy Making and Practice'. *Evidence & Policy* 1, no. 1: 85–100.

Hammond, T. H. (1986). 'Agenda Control, Organizational Structure, and Bureaucratic Politics'. *American Journal of Political Science* 30, no. 2: 379–420.

Hammond, T. H. and J. H. Knott. (1988). 'The Deregulatory Snowball: Explaining Deregulation in the Financial Industry'. *Journal of Politics* 50, no. 1: 3–30.

Hammond, T. H. and J. H. Knott. (1999). 'Political Institutions, Public Management, and Policy Choice'. *Journal of Public Administration Research and Theory* 9, no. 1: 33–85.

Hanke, S. H. and S. J. K. Walters. (1990). 'Privatization and Public Choice: Lessons for the LDCs'. In D. J. Gayle and J. N. Goodrich (eds), *Privatization and Deregulation in Global Perspective*. New York: Quorum Books, 97–108.

Hansen, R., N. Fruntzeskaki, T. McPhearson, E. Roll, N. Kabisch, A. Kaczorowska, J.-H. Kain, M. Artmann and S. Pauleil. (2015). 'The Uptake of the Ecosystem Services Concept in Planning Discourses of European and American Cities'. *Ecosystem Services* 12 (April): 228–46.

Hanson, M. (1974). 'Organizational Bureaucracy in Latin America and the Legacy of Spanish Colonialism'. *Journal of Inter-American Studies and World Affairs* 16, no. 2: 199–219.

Hardiman, N. and C. Scott. (2010). 'Governance as Polity: An Institutional Approach to the Evolution of State Functions in Ireland'. *Public Administration* 88, no. 1: 170–89.

Hardin, G. (1968). 'The Tragedy of the Commons'. *Science* 162: 1243–8.

Hardin, R. (1982). *Collective Action*, Baltimore, MD: Johns Hopkins University Press.

Hardisty, D. J., E. J. Johnson and E. U. Weber. (2010). 'A Dirty Word or a Dirty World? Attribute Framing, Political Affiliation, and Query Theory'. *Psychological Science* 21, no. 1: 86–92.

Hargadon, A. B. and Y. Douglas. (2001). 'When Innovations Meet Institutions: Edison and the Design of the Electric Light'. *Administrative Science Quarterly* 46, no. 3: 476.

Hargrove, E. L. (1975). *The Missing Link: The Study of the Implementation of Social Policy*. Washington, DC: Urban Institute.

Harring, N. (2016). 'Reward or Punish? Understanding Preferences toward Economic or Regulatory Instruments in a Cross-National Perspective'. *Political Studies* 64, no. 3 (1 October): 573–92.

Harrington, W., R. D. Morgenstern and T. Sterner. (2004). 'Comparing Instrument Choices'. In W. Harrington, R. D. Morgenstern and T. Sterner (eds). *Choosing Environmental Policy: Comparing Instruments and Outcomes in the United States and Europe*. Washington, DC: RFF Press, 1–22.

Harris, P. (2007). 'Collective Action on Climate Change: The Logic of Regime Failure'. *Natural Resources* 47, no. 1: 195–224.

Harris, R. and S. Milkis. (1989). *The Politics of Regulatory Change*. New York: Oxford University Press.

Harris, S. L. (2004). 'Financial Sector Reform in Canada: Interests and the Policy Process'. *Canadian Journal of Political Science* 37, no. 1: 161–84.

Harrison, D., A. Foss, P. Klevnas and D. Radov. (2011). 'Economic Policy Instruments for Reducing Greenhouse Gas Emissions'. www.oxfordhandbooks.com/view/10.1093/oxfordhb/9780199566600.001.0001/oxfordhb-9780199566600-e-35.

Harrison, K. (1999). 'Retreat from Regulation: The Evolution of the Canadian Environmental Regulatory Regime'. In G. B. Doern, R. J. Schultz and M. M. Hill (eds), *Changing the Rules: Canadian Regulatory Regimes and Institutions*. Toronto, ON: University of Toronto Press, 122–42.

Harrison, K. and L. M. Sundstrom (eds). (2010). *Global Commons, Domestic Decisions: The Comparative Politics of Climate Change*. Cambridge, MA; London: The MIT Press.

Harrop, M. (1992). *Power and Policy in Liberal Democracies*. Cambridge: Cambridge University Press.

Hart, O. (2017). 'Incomplete Contracts and Control'. *American Economic Review* 107, no. 7: 1731–52.

Harter, P. J. and G. C. Eads. (1985). 'Policy Instruments, Institutions and Objectives: An Analytical Framework for Assessing "Alternatives" to Regulation'. *Administrative Law Review* 37: 221–58.

Hartle, D. G. (1978). *The Expenditure Budget Process in the Government of Canada*. Toronto, ON: Canadian Tax Foundation.

Hasan, S. and J. Onyx (eds). (2008). *Comparative Third Sector Governance in Asia*. Dordrecht, Netherlands: Springer.

Hastak, M., M. B. Mazes and L. A. Morris. (2001). 'The Role of Consumer Surveys in Public Policy Decision Making'. *Journal of Public Policy and Marketing* 20, no. 2: 170–85.

Haufler, V. (2000). 'Private Sector International Regimes'. In R. A. Higgott, G. R. D. Underhill and A. Bieler (eds), *Non-State Actors and Authority in the Global System*. London: Routledge, 121–37.

Haufler, V. (2001). *A Public Role for the Private Sector: Industry Self-Regulation in a Global Economy*. Washington, DC: Carnegie Endowment for International Peace.

Hausman, D. M. and B. Welch. (2010). 'Debate: To Nudge or Not to Nudge'. *Journal of Political Philosophy* 18, no. 1: 123–36.

Hawke, G. R. (1993). *Improving Policy Advice*. Wellington, New Zealand: Victoria University Institute of Policy Studies.

Hawkesworth, M. (1992). 'Epistemology and Policy Analysis'. In W. Dunn, and R. M. Kelly (eds), *Advances in Policy Studies*. New Brunswick, NJ: Transaction, 291–329.

Hawkins, K. and J. M. Thomas. (1989). 'Making Policy in Regulatory Bureaucracies'. In K. Hawkins and J. M. Thomas (eds), *Making Regulatory Policy*. Pittsburgh, PA: University of Pittsburgh Press, 3–30.

Hay, C. (2006). 'Globalization and Public Policy'. In M. Moran, M. Rein and R. E. Goodin (eds), *The Oxford Handbook of Public Policy*. Oxford: Oxford University Press, 587–604.

Hay, C. and N. J.-A. Smith. (2010). 'How Policy-Makers (Really) Understand Globalization: The Internal Architecture of Anglophone Globalization Discourse in Europe'. *Public Administration* 88, no. 4: 903–27.

Hayes, M. (2007). 'Policy Making Through Disjointed Incrementalism'. In G. Morcol (ed.), *Handbook of Decision Making*. New York: CRC/Taylor & Francis, 39–59.

Haynes, K. E. and Q. Li. (1993). 'Policy Analysis and Uncertainty: Lessons from the IVHS Transportation Development Process'. *Computers, Environment and Urban Systems* 17, no. 1 (January): 1–14.

Head, B. W. (2008). 'Three Lenses of Evidence-Based Policy'. *Australian Journal of Public Administration* 67, no. 1: 1–11.

Head, B. W. and J. Alford. (2015). 'Wicked Problems: Implications for Public Policy and Management'. *Administration & Society* 47, no. 6: 711–39.

Heady, F. (1996). 'Configurations of Civil Service Systems'. In H. A. G. M. Bekke, J. L. Perry and T. A. J. Toonen (eds), *Civil Service Systems in Comparative Perspective*. Bloomington, IN: Indiana University Press, 207–26.

Heald, D. (1990). 'The Relevance of Privatization to Developing Economies'. *Public Administration and Development* 10, no. 1.

Heclo, H. (1974). *Modern Social Politics in Britain and Sweden: From Relief to Income Maintenance*. New Haven, CT: Yale University Press.

325

Hedström, P. and R. Swedberg. (1996). 'Social Mechanisms'. *Acta Sociologica* 39, no. 3 (1 July): 281–308.

Hedström, P. and R. Swedberg (eds). (1998). *Social Mechanisms: An Analytical Approach to Social Theory*. Cambridge; New York: Cambridge University Press.

Hedström, P. and P. Ylikoski. (2010). 'Causal Mechanisms in the Social Sciences'. *Annual Review of Sociology* 36, no. 1: 49–67.

Heggers, D., M. Lamers, A. van Zeijl-Rozema and C. Dieperink. (2012). 'Conceptualising Joint Knowledge Production in Regional Climate Change Adaptation Projects: Success Conditions and Levers for Action'. *Environmental Science & Policy* 18 (April): 52–65.

Heidbreder, E. (2011). 'Structuring the European Administrative Space: Policy Instruments of Multi-Level Administration'. *Journal of European Public Policy* (June).

Heilman, J. G. and R. W. Walsh. (1992). 'Introduction: Energy Program Evaluation and Policy Design'. *Policy Studies Journal* 20, no. 1: 42–7.

Heinmiller, B. T. (2007). 'The Politics of "Cap and Trade" Policies'. *Natural Resources Journal* 47, no. 2: 445–67.

Heinmiller, B. T., M. A. Hennigar and S. Kopec. (2017). 'Degenerative Politics and Youth Criminal Justice Policy in Canada'. *Politics & Policy* 45, no. 3 (June): 405–31.

Heinrichs, H. (2005). 'Advisory Systems in Pluralistic Knowledge Societies: A Criteria-Based Typology to Assess and Optimize Environmental Policy Advice'. In S. Maasen and P. Weingart (eds), *Democratization of Expertise? Exploring Novel Forms of Scientific Advice in Political Decision-Making*. Dordrecht, Netherlands: Springer, 41–61.

Heinz, J. P., E. O. Laumann, R. H. Salisbury and R. L. Nelson. (1990). 'Inner Circles or Hollow Cores'. *Journal of Politics* 52, no. 2: 356–90.

Held, D., A. McGrew, D. Goldblatt and J. Perraton. (1999). *Global Transformations: Politics, Economics and Culture*. Cambridge: Polity Press.

Helleiner, E. (1994). *States and the Reemergence of Global Finance*. Ithaca, NY: Cornell University Press.

Helms, L. B., S. B. Kurtt and A. B. Henkin. (1993). 'Assuring Failure: Implementation Design and Policy Environment of a Federal Program Provision'. *The American Review of Public Administration* 23, no. 3 (1 September): 263–77.

Hendrick, R. (1994). 'A Heuristic Approach to Policy Analysis and the Use of Sensitivity Analysis'. *Public Productivity & Management Review* 18, no. 1: 37–55.

Hendriks, C. (2009). 'Deliberative Governance in the Context of Power'. *Policy and Society* 28, no. 3: 173–84.

Hendriks, C. and L. Carson. (2008). 'Can the Market Help the Forum? Negotiating the Commercialization of Deliberative Democracy'. *Policy Sciences* 41, no. 4: 293–313.

Hennicke, P. (2004). 'Scenarios for a Robust Policy Mix: The Final Report of the German Study Commission on Sustainable Energy Supply'. *Energy Policy* 32, no. 15 (October): 1673–8.

Henriques, I. and P. Sadorsky. (2008). 'Voluntary Environmental Programs: A Canadian Perspective'. *Policy Studies Journal* 36, no. 1: 143–66.

Heritier, A. (2001). 'Market Integration and Social Cohesion: The Politics of Public Services in European Regulation'. *Journal of European Public Policy* 8, no. 5: 825–52.

Heritier, A. and S. Eckert. (2008). 'New Modes of Governance in the Shadow of Hierarchy: Self-Regulation by Industry in Europe'. *Journal of Public Policy* 28, no. 1: 113–38.

Heritier, A. and D. Lehmkuhl. (2008). 'Introduction: The Shadow of Hierarchy and New Modes of Governance'. *Journal of Public Policy* 28, no. 1: 1–17.

Heritier, A., C. Knill and S. Mingers. (1996). *Ringing the Changes in Europe: Regulatory Competition and the Transformation of the State. Britain, France, Germany.* Berlin, Germany: Walter de Gruyter.

Hermann, C. F. (1982). 'Instruments of Foreign Policy'. In P. Callahan, L. P. Brady and M. G. Hermann (eds), *Describing Foreign Policy Behaviour*. Beverly Hills, CA: Sage, 153–74.

Hernes, G. (1976). 'Structural Change in Social Processes'. *American Journal of Sociology* 82, no. 3: 513–47.

Herranz, J. (2007). 'The Multisectoral Trilemma of Network Management'. *Journal of Public Administration Research and Theory* 18, no. 1: 1–31.

Herrick, C. (2004). 'Objectivity versus Narrative Coherence: Science, Environmental Policy and the US Data Quality Act'. *Environmental Science and Policy* 7, no. 5: 419–33.

Hesse, J. J. (1997). 'Rebuilding the State: Public Sector Reform in Central and Eastern Europe'. In J.-E. Lane (ed.), *Public Sector Reform: Rationale, Trends and Problems*. London: Sage, 114–45.

Hessing, M., M. Howlett and T. Summerville. (2005). *Canadian Natural Resource and Environmental Policy: Political Economy and Public Policy*. Vancouver, BC: University of British Columbia Press.

Hickle, G. T. (2014). 'Moving Beyond the "Patchwork": A Review of Strategies to Promote Consistency for Extended Producer Responsibility Policy in the US'. *Journal of Cleaner Production* 64, no. 1: 266–276.

Hicklin, A. and E. Godwin. (2009). 'Agents of Change: The Role of Policy Managers in Public Policy'. *Policy Studies Journal* 37, no. 1: 13–20.

Hicks, R. and P. Watson. (2007). *Policy Capacity: Strengthening the Public Service's Support to Elected Officials*. Edmonton, AB: Government of Alberta.

Hilgartner, S. and C. L. Bosk. (1988). 'The Rise and Fall of Social Problems: A Public Arenas Model'. *American Journal of Sociology* 94, no. 1: 53–78.

Hill, C. J. and L. E. Lynn. (2004). 'Is Hierarchical Governance in Decline? Evidence from Empirical Research'. *Journal of Public Administration Research and Theory* 15, no. 2: 173–95.

Hill, M. and P. L. Hupe. (2006). 'Analysing Policy Processes as Multiple Governance: Accountability in Social Policy'. *Policy and Politics* 34, no. 3: 557–73.

Hill, M. and P. L. Hupe. (2014). *Implementing Public Policy: An Introduction to the Study of Operational Governance* (3rd edn). London: Sage.

Hillier, B. and A. Leaman. (1974). 'How is Design Possible: A Sketch for a Theory'. *DMG-DRS Journal: Design Research and Methods* 8, no. 1: 40–50.

Hillier, B., J. Musgrave and P. O'Sullivan. (1972). 'Knowledge and Design'. In W. J. Mitchell (ed.), *Environmental Design: Research and Practice*. Los Angeles, CA: University of California – Los Angeles, 29.3.1–29.3.14.

Hills, J. and M. Michalis. (2000). 'Restructuring Regulation: Technological Convergence and European Telecommunications and Broadcasting Markets'. *Review of International Political Economy* 7, no. 3: 434–64.

Hippes, G. (1988). 'New Instruments for Environmental Policy: A Perspective'. *International Journal of Social Economics* 15, nos 3/4: 42–51.

Hira, A., D. Huxtable and A. Leger. (2005). 'Deregulation and Participation: An International Survey of Participation in Electricity Regulation'. *Governance* 18, no. 1: 53–88.

Hird, J. A. (2005a). 'Policy Analysis for What? The Effectiveness of Nonpartisan Policy Research Organizations'. *Policy Studies Journal* 33, no. 1: 83–105.

Hird, J. A. (2005b). *Power, Knowledge and Politics: Policy Analysis in the States.* Washington, DC: Georgetown University Press.

Hoberg, G. (1996). 'Putting Ideas in Their Place: A Response to "Learning and Change in the British Columbia Forest Policy Sector"'. *Canadian Journal of Political Science* 29, no. 1: 135–44.

Hoberg, G. and E. Morawaski. (1997). 'Policy Change through Sector Intersection: Forest and Aboriginal Policy in Clayoquot Sound'. *Canadian Public Administration* 40, no. 3: 387–414.

Hobson, J. and M. Ramesh. (2002). 'Globalisation Makes of States What States Make of It: Between Agency and Structure in the State/Globalisation Debate'. *New Political Economy* 7, no. 1: 5–22.

Hobson, K. and S. Niemeyer. (2013). '"What Sceptics Believe": The Effects of Information and Deliberation on Climate Change Scepticism'. *Public Understanding of Science* 22, no. 4: 396–412.

Hodge, G. A. and C. Greve. (2007). 'Public–Private Partnerships: An International Performance Review'. *Public Administration Review* (May/June): 545–58.

Hodgetts, J. E. (1955). *Pioneer Public Service: An Administrative History of the United Canadas, 1841–1867.* Toronto, ON: University of Toronto Press.

Hodgetts, J. E. (1964). 'Challenge and Response: A Retrospective View of the Public Service of Canada'. *Canadian Public Administration* 7, no. 4: 409–21.

Hodgetts, J. E. (1973). *The Canadian Public Service: A Physiology of Government 1867–1970.* Toronto, ON: University of Toronto Press.

Hodgetts, J. E., G. B. Doern, V. S. Wilson and R. Whitaker. (1972). *The Biography of an Institution: The Civil Service Commission of Canada, 1908–1967.* Kingston, ON: McGill-Queen's University Press.

Hoek, J. and B. King. (2008). 'Food Advertising and Self-Regulation: A View from the Trenches'. *Australian and New Zealand Journal of Public Health* 32, no. 3: 261–5.

Hoffmann, M. J. (2011). *Climate Governance at the Crossroads: Experimenting with a Global Response after Kyoto.* Oxford: Oxford University Press.

Hofstede, G. (1980). *Culture's Consequences: International Differences in Work-Related Values.* Beverly Hills, CA: Sage.

Hogan, J. and M. Howlett (eds). (2015). *Policy Paradigms in Theory and Practice.* Cheltenham, UK: Palgrave.

Hogan, J. and M. Howlett. (2015). 'Reflections on Our Understanding of Policy Paradigms and Policy Change'. In J. Hogan and M. Howlett (eds), *Policy Paradigms in Theory and Practice.* Studies in the Political Economy of Public Policy. Basingstoke, UK: Palgrave Macmillan, 3–18.

Hogwood, B. W. and B. G. Peters. (1982). 'The Dynamics of Policy Change: Policy Succession'. *Policy Sciences* 14, no. 3: 225–45.

Holland, S. P. and M. R. Moore. (2013). 'Market Design in Cap and Trade Programs: Permit Validity and Compliance Timing'. *Journal of Environmental Economics and Management* 66, no. 3 (November): 671–87.

Hollander, M. J. and M. J. Prince. (1993). 'Analytical Units in Federal and Provincial Governments: Origins, Functions and Suggestions for Effectiveness'. *Canadian Public Administration* 36, no. 2: 190–224.

Holmberg, S. and B. Rothstein. (2012). *Good Government: The Relevance of Political Science*. Cheltenham, UK; Northampton, MA: Edward Elgar.

Holmström, B. and P. Milgrom. (1991). 'Multitask Principal-Agent Analyses: Incentive Contracts, Asset Ownership, and Job Design'. *Journal of Law, Economics, and Organization*, 7: 24–52.

Holt, D. and R. Barkemeyer. (2012). 'Media Coverage of Sustainable Development Issues – Attention Cycles or Punctuated Equilibrium?' *Sustainable Development* 20, no. 1: 1–17.

Holzinger, K. (2005). 'Tax Competition and Tax Co-Operation in the EU: The Case of Savings Taxation'. *Rationality and Society* 17: 475–510.

Hondeghem, A. (2011). 'Changing Public Service Bargains for Top Officials'. *Public Policy and Administration* 26, no. 2 (5 April): 159–65.

Hood, C. (1983). 'Using Bureaucracy Sparingly'. *Public Administration* 61, no. 2: 197–208.

Hood, C. (1986a). *Administrative Analysis: An Introduction to Rules, Enforcement and Organizations*. Brighton, UK: Wheatsheaf.

Hood, C. (1986b). 'The Hidden Public Sector: The "Quangocratization" of the World?' In F.-X. Kaufman, G. Majone and V. Ostrom (eds), *Guidance, Control and Evaluation in the Public Sector*. Berlin, Germany: Walter de Gruyter, 183–207.

Hood, C. (1986c). *The Tools of Government*. London: Chatham House.

Hood, C. (1991). 'A Public Management for All Seasons?' *Public Administration* 69 (Spring): 3–19.

Hood, C. (1993). 'The Hidden Side of the American Welfare States'. *Political Science Quarterly* 108, no. 3: 403–36.

Hood, C. (1995). 'Contemporary Public Management: A New Global Paradigm?' *Public Policy and Administration* 10, no. 2: 104–17.

Hood, C. (1997). *The Hidden Welfare State: Tax Expenditures and Social Policy in the United States*. Princeton, NJ: Princeton University Press.

Hood, C. (2002a). 'Control, Bargains and Cheating: The Politics of Public Service Reform'. *Journal of Public Administration Research and Theory* 12, no. 3: 309–32.

Hood, C. (2002b). 'The Risk Game and the Blame Game'. *Government and Opposition* 37, no. 1: 15–54.

Hood, C. (2002c). 'Tax Expenditures'. In L. M. Salamon (ed.), *The Tools of Government: A Guide to the New Governance*. New York: Oxford University Press, 410–44.

Hood, C. (2004). 'Controlling Public Services and Government: Towards a Cross-National Perspective'. In C. Hood, O. James, B. G. Peter and C. Scott (eds), *Controlling Modern Government; Variety, Commonality and Change*. Cheltenham, UK: Edward Elgar, 3–21.

Hood, C. (2006). 'The Tools of Government in the Information Age'. In M. Moran, M. Rein and R. E. Goodin (eds), *The Oxford Handbook of Public Policy*. New York: Oxford University Press, 469–81.

Hood, C. (2007a). 'Intellectual Obsolescence and Intellectual Makeovers: Reflections on the Tools of Government After Two Decades'. *Governance* 20, no. 1: 127–44.

Hood, C. (2007b). 'What Happens When Transparency Meets Blame-Avoidance?' *Public Management Review* 9, no. 2: 191–210.

Hood, C. (2010). *The Blame Game: Spin, Bureaucracy, and Self-Preservation in Government*. Princeton, NJ: Princeton University Press.

Hood, C. and H. Z. Margetts. (2007). *The Tools of Government in the Digital Age.* Basingstoke, UK: Palgrave Macmillan.

Hood, C., C. Scott, O. James, G. Jones and T. Travers. (1999). *Regulation Inside Government: Waste-Watchers, Quality Police and Sleazebusters.* Oxford: Oxford University Press.

Hooghe, L. and G. Marks. (2003). 'Unraveling the Central State, But How? Types of Multi-Level Governance'. *American Political Science Review* 97, no. 2: 233–43.

Hoogvelt, A. (1997). *Globalisation and the Postcolonial World.* Basingstoke, UK: Macmillan, 134–9.

Hoppe, R. (1999). 'Policy Analysis, Science and Politics: From "Speaking Truth to Power" to "Making Sense Together"'. *Science and Public Policy* 26, no. 3: 201–10.

Hoppe, R. and M. Jeliazkova. (2006). 'How Policy Workers Define Their Job: A Netherlands Case Study'. In H. K. Colebatch, (ed.), *The Work of Policy: An International Survey*, New York: Rowan & Littlefield, 35–60.

Hornik, R. (1989). 'The Knowledge-Behavior Gap in Public Information Campaigns'. In C. Salmon (ed.), *Information Campaigns: Managing the Process of Social Change.* Newbury Park, CA: Sage.

Hosseus, D. and L. A. Pal. (1997). 'Anatomy of a Policy Area: The Case of Shipping'. *Canadian Public Policy* 23, no. 4: 399–416.

Hou, Y. and G. Brewer. (2010). 'Substitution and Supplementation Between Co-Functional Policy Instruments: Evidence from State Budget Stabilization Practices'. *Public Administration Review* 70, no. 6: 914–24.

Hovik, S. and K. B. Stokke. (2007). 'Network Governance and Policy Integration – The Case of Regional Coastal Zone Planning in Norway'. *European Planning Studies* 15, no. 7: 927–44.

Howard, C. (1995). 'Testing the Tools Approach: Tax Expenditures Versus Direct Expenditures'. *Public Administration Review* 55, no. 5: 439–47.

Howard, J. L. and W. T. Stanbury. (1984). 'Measuring Leviathan: The Size, Scope and Growth of Governments in Canada'. In G. Lermer (ed.), *Probing Leviathan: An Investigation of Government in the Economy.* Vancouver, BC: Fraser Institute.

Howe, R. B. and D. Johnson. (2000). *Restraining Equality: Human Rights Commissions in Canada.* Toronto, ON: University of Toronto Press.

Howell, W. G. and S. P. Jackman. (2013). 'Interbranch Negotiations over Policies with Multiple Outcomes'. *American Journal of Political Science* 57, no. 4 (1 October): 956–70.

Howells, G. (2005). 'The Potential and Limits of Consumer Empowerment by Information'. *Journal of Law and Society* 32, no. 3: 349–70.

Howlett, M. (1990). 'The Round Table Experience: Representation and Legitimacy in Canadian Environmental Policy Making'. *Queen's Quarterly* 97, no. 4: 580–601.

Howlett, M. (1991). 'Policy Instruments, Policy Styles and Policy Implementation: National Approaches to Theories of Instrument Choice'. *Policy Studies Journal* 19, no. 2: 1–21.

Howlett, M. (1996). 'Legitimacy and Governance: Re-Discovering Procedural Policy Instruments'. Vancouver, BC. Paper presented to the Annual Meeting of the British Columbia Political Studies Association.

Howlett, M. (1997). 'Issue-Attention Cycles and Punctuated Equilibrium Models Re-Considered: An Empirical Examination of Agenda-Setting in Canada'. *Canadian Journal of Political Science* 30: 5–29.

Howlett, M. (1998). 'Predictable and Unpredictable Policy Windows: Issue, Institutional and Exogenous Correlates of Canadian Federal Agenda-Setting'. *Canadian Journal of Political Science* 31, no. 3: 495–524.

Howlett, M. (1999). 'Federalism and Public Policy'. In J. Bickerton and A. Gagnon (eds), *Canadian Politics* (3rd edn). Peterborough, ON: Broadview Press.

Howlett, M. (2000a). 'Beyond Legalism? Policy Ideas, Implementation Styles and Emulation-Based Convergence in Canadian and US Environmental Policy'. *Journal of Public Policy* 20, no. 3: 305–29.

Howlett, M. (2000b). 'Complex Network Management and the Governance of the Environment: Prospects for Policy Change and Policy Stability'. In E. Parsons (ed.). *Governing the Environment: Persistent Challenges, Uncertain Innovations*. Montreal, Canada: McGill-Queens University Press, 303–44.

Howlett, M. (2000c). 'Managing the "Hollow State": Procedural Policy Instruments and Modern Governance'. *Canadian Public Administration* 43, no. 4: 412–31.

Howlett, M. (2001). 'Policy Venues, Policy Spillovers and Policy Change: The Courts, Aboriginal Rights and British Columbia Forest Policy'. In B. Cashore, G. Hoberg, M. Howlett, J. Rayner and J. Wilson (eds), *In Search of Sustainability: British Columbia Forest Policy in the 1990s*. Vancouver, BC: University of British Columbia Press, 120–40.

Howlett, M. (2002a). 'Policy Development'. In C. Dunn (ed.), *The Oxford Handbook of Canadian Public Administration*. Toronto, ON: Oxford University Press.

Howlett, M. (2002b). 'Policy Instruments and Implementation Styles: The Evolution of Instrument Choice in Canadian Environmental Policy'. In L. Debora Van Nijnatten and Robert Boardman (eds), *Canadian Environmental Policy: Context and Cases*. Toronto, ON: Oxford University Press, 25–45.

Howlett, M. (2002c). 'Understanding National Administrative Cultures and Their Impact Upon Administrative Reform: A Neo-Institutional Model and Analysis'. *Policy, Organization & Society*. 21, no. 1: 1–24.

Howlett, M. (2004a). 'Administrative Styles and the Limits of Administrative Reform: A Neo-Institutional Analysis of Administrative Culture'. *Canadian Public Administration* 46, no. 4: 471–94.

Howlett, M. (2004b). 'Beyond Good and Evil in Policy Implementation: Instrument Mixes, Implementation Styles and Second Generation Theories of Policy Instrument Choice'. *Policy and Society* 23, no. 2: 1–17.

Howlett, M. (2005). 'What Is a Policy Instrument? Policy Tools, Policy Mixes and Policy Implementation Styles'. In P. Eliadis, M. Hill and M. Howlett (eds), *Designing Government: From Instruments to Governance*. Montreal, QC: McGill-Queen's University Press, 31–50.

Howlett, M. (2007). 'Analyzing Multi-Actor, Multi-Round Public Policy Decision-Making Processes in Government: Findings from Five Canadian Cases'. *Canadian Journal of Political Science* 40, no. 3: 659–84.

Howlett, M. (2009a). 'Governance Modes, Policy Regimes and Operational Plans: A Multi-Level Nested Model of Policy Instrument Choice and Policy Design'. *Policy Sciences* 42: 73–89.

Howlett, M. (2009b). 'Government Communication as a Policy Tool: A Framework for Analysis'. *The Canadian Political Science Review* 3 (June): 2.

Howlett, M. (2009c). 'Policy Advice in Multi-Level Governance Systems: Sub-National Policy Analysts and Analysis'. *International Review of Public Administration* 13, no. 3: 1–16.

Howlett, M. (2009d). 'Policy Analytical Capacity and Evidence-Based Policy-Making: Lessons from Canada'. *Canadian Public Administration* 52, no. 2: 153–75.

Howlett, M. (2011). *Designing Public Policies: Principles and Instruments*. New York: Routledge.

Howlett, M. (2012). 'The Lessons of Failure: Learning and Blame Avoidance in Public Policy-Making'. *International Political Science Review* 33, no. 5 (24 October): 539–55.

Howlett, M. (2014a). 'From the "Old" to the "New" Policy Design: Design Thinking Beyond Markets and Collaborative Governance'. *Policy Sciences* 47, no. 3: 187–207.

Howlett, M. (2014b). 'Policy Design: What, Who, How and Why?' In C. Halpern, L. Pierre and P. L. Gales (eds), *L'instrumentation et ses effets*. Paris: Presses de Sciences Po.

Howlett, M. (2014c). 'Why Are Policy Innovations Rare and So Often Negative? Blame Avoidance and Problem Denial in Climate Change Policy-Making'. *Global Environmental Change* 29, no. 2 (November): 395–403.

Howlett, M. (2015). 'Policy Analytical Capacity: The supply and demand for policy analysis in government'. *Policy & Society* 34, no. 3: 173–82.

Howlett, M. (2016). 'Policy Tools & Their Targets: Beyond Nudges and Utility Maximization in Policy Compliance'. In *Workshop No. 2: Behavioural Change and Public Policy*. Pisa, Italy.

Howlett, M. (2018a). 'The Criteria for Effective Policy Design: Character and Context in Policy Instrument Choice'. *Journal of Asian Public Policy* 11, no. 3 (6 December): 245–66.

Howlett, M. (2018b). 'Matching Policy Tools & Their Targets: Beyond Nudges and Utility Maximization in Policy Design'. *Policy & Politics*.

Howlett, M. and B. Cashore. (2007). 'Re-Visiting the New Orthodoxy of Policy Dynamics: The Dependent Variable and Re-Aggregation Problems in the Study of Policy Change'. *Canadian Political Science Review* 1, no. 2: 50–62.

Howlett, M. and B. Cashore. (2009). 'The Dependent Variable Problem in the Study of Policy Change: Understanding Policy Change as a Methodological Problem'. *Journal of Comparative Policy Analysis: Research and Practice* 11, no. 1: 33–46.

Howlett, M. and A. Kemmerling. (2017). 'Calibrating Climate Change Policies: The Causes and Consequences of Sustained under-Reaction'. *Journal of Environmental Policy & Planning* 19, no. 6 (2 November): 625–37.

Howlett, M. and R. P. Lejano. (2013). 'Tales from the Crypt: The Rise and Fall (and Rebirth?) of Policy Design'. *Administration & Society* 45, no. 3 (1 April): 357–81.

Howlett, M. and E. Lindquist. (2004). 'Policy Analysis and Governance: Analytical and Policy Styles in Canada'. *Journal of Comparative Policy Analysis* 6, no. 3: 225–49.

Howlett, M. and A. Migone. (2011). 'Charles Lindblom is Alive and Well and Living in Punctuated Equilibrium Land'. *Policy and Society* 30, no. 1, 53–62.

Howlett, M. and A. Migone. (2013). 'Policy Advice Through the Market: The Role of External Consultants in Contemporary Policy Advisory Systems'. *Policy & Society* 32, no. 3: 241–54.

Howlett, M. and I. Mukherjee. (2014). 'Policy Design and Non-Design: Towards a Spectrum of Policy Formulation Types'. *Politics and Governance* 2, no. 2 (13 November): 57–71.

Howlett, M. and I. Mukherjee. (2018). 'The Contribution of Comparative Policy Analysis to Policy Design: Articulating Principles of Effectiveness and Clarifying

Design Spaces'. *Journal of Comparative Policy Analysis: Research and Practice* 20, no. 1 (1 January): 72–87.

Howlett, M. and S. Nair. (2017). 'From Robustness to Resilience: Avoiding Policy Traps in the Long-Term'. *Sustainability Science*.

Howlett, M. and J. Newman. (2010). 'Policy Analysts and Policy Work in Federal Systems: Policy Advice and Its Contribution to Evidence-Based Policy-Making in Multi-Level Governance Systems'. *Policy and Society* 29, no. 2: 1–14.

Howlett, M. and J. Newman. (2013). 'After "the Regulatory Moment" in Comparative Regulatory Studies: Modeling the Early Stages of Regulatory Life Cycles'. *Journal of Comparative Policy Analysis: Research and Practice* 15, no. 2: 107–121.

Howlett, M. and M. Ramesh. (1993). 'Patterns of Policy Instrument Choice: Policy Styles, Policy Learning and the Privatization Experience'. *Policy Studies Review* 12, no. 1: 3–24.

Howlett, M. and M. Ramesh. (1998). 'Policy Subsystem Configurations and Policy Change: Operationalizing the Postpositivist Analysis of the Politics of the Policy Process'. *Policy Studies Journal* 26, no. 3: 466–82.

Howlett, M. and M. Ramesh. (2002). 'The Policy Effects of Internationalization: A Subsystem Adjustment Analysis of Policy Change'. *Journal of Comparative Policy Analysis* 4, no. 1: 31–50.

Howlett, M. and M. Ramesh. (2003). *Studying Public Policy: Policy Cycles and Policy Subsystems*. Toronto, ON: Oxford University Press.

Howlett, M. and M. Ramesh. (2006). 'Globalization and the Choice of Governing Instruments: The Direct, Indirect and Opportunity Effects of Internationalization'. *International Public Management Journal* 9, no. 2: 175–94.

Howlett, M. and M. Ramesh. (2014). 'The Two Orders of Governance Failure: Design Mismatches and Policy Capacity Issues in Modern Governance'. *Policy and Society* 33, no. 4.

Howlett, M. and M. Ramesh. (2016a). 'Achilles' Heels of Governance: Critical Capacity Deficits and Their Role in Governance Failures'. *Regulation & Governance* 10, no. 4 (1 December): 301–13.

Howlett, M. and M. Ramesh. (2016b). 'Understanding the Role of Policy Capacity in Policy Success and Failure: Government Competencies and Capabilities in Public Policy and Administration'. In T. R. Klassen, D. Cepiku and T. J. Lah (eds), *Global Public Policy and Administration*. London: Routledge.

Howlett, M. and J. Rayner. (1995). 'Do Ideas Matter? Policy Subsystem Configurations and the Continuing Conflict Over Canadian Forest Policy'. *Canadian Public Administration* 38, no. 3: 382–410.

Howlett, M. and J. Rayner. (2004). '(Not So) "Smart Regulation"? Canadian Shellfish Aquaculture Policy and the Evolution of Instrument Choice for Industrial Development'. *Marine Policy* 28, no. 2: 171–84.

Howlett, M. and J. Rayner. (2006a). 'Convergence and Divergence in "New Governance", Arrangements: Evidence from European Integrated Natural Resource Strategies'. *Journal of Public Policy* 26, no. 2: 167–89.

Howlett, M. and J. Rayner. (2006b). 'Globalization and Governance Capacity: Explaining Divergence in National Forest Programmes as Instances of "Next-Generation" Regulation in Canada and Europe'. *Governance* 19, no. 2: 251–75.

Howlett, M. and J. Rayner. (2006c). 'Policy Divergence as a Response to Weak International Regimes: The Formulation and Implementation of Natural Resource New Governance Arrangements in Europe and Canada'. *Policy and Society* 24, no. 2: 16–45.

Howlett, M. and J. Rayner. (2007). 'Design Principles for Policy Mixes: Cohesion and Coherence in "New Governance Arrangements"'. *Policy and Society* 26, no. 4: 1–18.

Howlett, M. and J. Rayner. (2013). 'Patching Vs Packaging in Policy Formulation: Assessing Policy Portfolio Design'. *Politics and Governance* 1, no. 2: 170–82.

Howlett, M. and P. del Río. (2015). 'The Parameters of Policy Portfolios: Verticality and Horizontality in Design Spaces and Their Consequences for Policy Mix Formulation'. *Environment and Planning* C 33, no. 5: 1233–45.

Howlett, M. and J. Tosun (eds). (2019). *Policy Styles and Policy-Making: Exploring the National Dimension* New York: Routledge.

Howlett, M. and R. M. Walker. (2012). 'Public Managers in the Policy Process: More Evidence on the Missing Variable?' *Policy Studies Journal* 40, no. 2 (1 May): 211–33.

Howlett, M., J. Craft and L. Zibrik. (2010). 'Government Communication and Democratic Governance: Electoral and Policy-Related Information Campaigns in Canada'. *Policy and Society* 29, no. 1 (January): 13–22.

Howlett, M., A. Kekez and O. Poocharoen. (2017). 'Understanding Co-Production as a Policy Tool Integrating New Public Governance and Comparative Policy Theory'. *Journal of Comparative Policy Analysis* 19, no. 5: 487–501.

Howlett, M., J. Kim and P. Weaver. (2006). 'Assessing Instrument Mixes Through Program- and Agency-Level Data: Methodological Issues in Contemporary Implementation Research'. *Review of Policy Research* 23, no. 1: 129–51.

Howlett, M., A. McConnell and A. Perl. (2014). 'Streams and Stages: Reconciling Kingdon and Policy Process Theory'. *European Journal of Political Research* 54, no. 3: 419–34.

Howlett, M., I. Mukherjee, and J. Rayner. (2014). 'The Elements of Effective Program Design: A Two-Level Analysis'. *Politics and Governance* 2, no. 2 (June 9): 1–12.

Howlett, M., I. Mukherjee and J. J. Woo. (2015). 'From Tools to Toolkits in Policy Design Studies: The New Design Orientation Towards Policy Formulation Research'. *Policy & Politics* 43, no. 2: 291–311.

Howlett, M., I. Mukherjee, and J. J. Wu. (2014). 'The New Policy Design Orientation: From Tools to Toolkits in Policy Instrument Studies'. *Policy & Politics*.

Howlett, M., M. Ramesh and A. Perl. (2009). *Studying Public Policy*. Toronto, ON: Oxford University Press.

Howlett, M., M. Ramesh and X. Wu. (2015). 'Understanding the Persistence of Policy Failures: The Role of Politics, Governance and Uncertainty'. *Public Policy and Administration* 30, nos 3–4 (1 July): 209–20.

Howlett, M., J. Rayner and C. Tollefson. (2009). 'From Government to Governance in Forest Planning? Lesson from the Case of the British Columbia Great Bear Rainforest Initiative'. *Forest Policy and Economics* 11: 383–91.

Howlett, M., J. Vince and P. del Río. (2017). 'Policy Integration and Multi-Level Governance: Dealing with the Vertical Dimension of Policy Mix Designs'. *Politics and Governance* 5, no. 2 (5 May): 69–78.

Howlett, M., S. L. Tan, A. Migone, A. Wellstead and B. Evans. (2014). 'The Distribution of Analytical Techniques in Policy Advisory Systems: Policy Formulation and the Tools of Policy Appraisal'. *Public Policy and Administration* 29, no. 4 (24 March): 271–91.

Howse, R., J. R. S. Prichard and M. J. Trebilcock. (1990). 'Smaller or Smarter Government?' *University of Toronto Law Journal* 40: 498–541.

Huber, G. P. (1991). 'Organization Learning: The Contributing Processes and the Literatures'. *Organization Science* 2, no: 88–115.

Hudson, J., S. Lowe, N. Oscroft and C. Snell. (2007). 'Activating Policy Networks: A Case Study of Local Environmental Policy-Making in the United Kingdom'. *Policy Studies* 28, no. 1: 55–70.

Huestis, L. (1993). 'Enforcement of Environmental Law in Canada'. In M. L. McConnell and L. Huestis (eds), *Environmental Law and Business in Canada*. Aurora, ON: Thompson/Canada Law Book, 240–55.

Huitt, R. K. (1968). 'Political Feasibility'. In A. Rannay (ed.), *Political Science and Public Policy*. Chicago, IL: Markham, 263–76.

Hula, R. C. (1988). 'Using Markets to Implement Public Policy'. In R. C. Hula (ed.), *Market-Based Public Policy*. London: Macmillan, 3–20.

Hula, R., C. Jackson-Elmoore and L. Reese. (2007). 'Mixing God's Work and the Public Business: A Framework for the Analysis of Faith-Based Service Delivery'. *Review of Policy Research* 24, no. 1: 67–89.

Hull, A. (2008). 'Policy Integration: What Will It Take to Achieve More Sustainable Transport Solutions in Cities?' *Transport Policy* 15, no. 2 (March): 94–103.

Huntington, S. P. (1952). 'The Marasmus of the ICC: The Commissions, the Railroads and the Public Interest'. *Yale Law Review* 61, no. 4: 467–509.

Hupe, P. L. and M. J. Hill. (2016). 'And the Rest Is Implementation. Comparing Approaches to What Happens in Policy Processes beyond Great Expectations'. *Public Policy and Administration* 31, no. 2 (1 April): 103–21.

Hustedt, T. and S. Veit. (2017). 'Policy Advisory Systems: Change Dynamics and Sources of Variation'. *Policy Sciences* 50, no. 1 (1 March): 41–6.

Hutter, B. M. (1989). 'Variations in Regulatory Enforcement Styles'. *Law and Policy* 11, no. 2: 153–74.

Hutter, B. M. and P. K. Manning. (1990). 'The Contexts of Regulation: The Impact upon Health and Safety Inspectorates in Britain'. *Law and Policy* 12, no. 2: 103–36.

Hysing, E. (2009). 'From Government to Governance? A Comparison of Environmental Governing in Swedish Forestry and Transport'. *Governance* 22: 547–672.

Iacobucci, E., M. Trebilcock and R. A. Winter. (2006). 'The Canadian Experience with Deregulation'. *University of Toronto Law Journal* 56, no. 1: 1–63.

Iannuzzi, Alphonse. (2001). *Industry Self-Regulation and Voluntary Environmental Compliance*. Boca Raton, FL: Lewis Publishers.

ICT Export Cluster. (2017). Utilities-e-Estonia. https://e-estonia.com/the-story/digital-society/utilities. Retrieved 8 April 2017.

Igielska, B. (2008). 'Climate Change Mitigation: Overview of the Environmental Policy Instruments'. *International Journal of Green Economics* 2, no. 2: 210–25.

Ikenberry, G. J. (1990). 'The International Spread of Privatization Policies: Inducements, Learning and "Policy Bandwagoning"'. In E. N. Suleiman and J. Waterbury (eds), *The Political Economy of Public Sector Reform and Privatization*. Boulder, CO: Westview, 88–110.

Ingraham, P. (1987). 'Toward More Systematic Considerations of Policy Design'. *Policy Studies Journal* 15, no. 4: 611–28.

Ingram, H. M. and A. Schneider. (1990). 'Improving Implementation Through Framing Smarter Statutes'. *Journal of Public Policy*, 10, no. 1, 67–88.

Ingram, H. M. and D. E. Mann. (1980). 'Policy Failure: An Issue Deserving Analysis'. In H. M. Ingram and D. E. Mann (eds), *Why Policies Succeed or Fail*. Beverly Hills, CA: Sage, 11–32.

Innvaer, S., G. Vist, M. Trommald and A. Oxman. (2002). 'Health Policy-Makers' Perceptions of Their Use of Evidence: A Systematic Review'. *Journal of Health Services Research and Policy* 7, no. 4: 239–45.

IPCC (Intergovernmental Panel on Climate Change). (2001). Working Group III: 'Mitigation'. In R. T. Watson and Core Writing Team (eds), *Climate Change 2001 – IPCC Third Assessment Report*. Cambridge; New York: Cambridge University Press.

IPCC. (2014a). Annex II: Glossary (edited by K. J. Mach, S. Planton and C. von Stechow). In R. K. Pachauri, L. Mayer and IPCC (eds), *Climate Change 2014: Synthesis Report. Contribution of Working Groups I, II and III to the Fifth Assessment Report of the Intergovernmental Panel on Climate Change*. Geneva, Switzerland: IPCC, 117–30.

IPCC. (2014b). *Climate change 2014: Mitigation of Climate Change. Contribution of Working Group III to the Fifth Assessment Report of the Intergovernmental Panel on Climate Change*. In O. Edenhofer, R. Pichs-Madruga, Y. Sokona, E. Farahani, S. Kadner, K. Seyboth, . . . J. C. Minx (eds), New York: Cambridge University Press.

Ito, T. and A. O. Kreuger (eds). (2004). *Governance, Regulation and Privatization in the Asia-Pacific Region*. Chicago, IL: University of Chicago Press.

Jackson, A. and B. Baldwin. (2007). 'Policy Analysis by the Labour Movement in a Hostile Environment'. In L. Dobuzinskis, M. Howlett and D. Laycock (eds), *Policy Analysis in Canada: The State of the Art*. Toronto, ON: University of Toronto Press, 260–72.

Jackson, P. M. (2007). 'Making Sense of Policy Advice'. *Public Money & Management* 27, no. 4: 257–64.

Jacobs, A. M. and K. Weaver. (2010). *Policy Feedback and Policy Change* (19 July). SSRN Scholarly Paper. Rochester, NY: Social Science Research Network. http://papers.ssrn.com/abstract=1642636.

Jacobs, A. M. and K. Weaver. (2014). 'When Policies Undo Themselves: Self-Undermining Feedback as a Source of Policy Change'. *Governance: An International Journal of Policy, Administration, and Institutions* 28, no. 4: 441–57.

Jacobsen, J. K. (1995). 'Much Ado about Ideas: The Cognitive Factor in Economic Policy'. *World Politics* no. 47: 283–310.

Jacobzone, S. (2005). 'Independent Regulatory Authorities in OECD Countries: An Overview'. In *Designing Independent and Accountable Regulatory Authorities for High Quality Regulation – Proceedings of an Expert Meeting in London, United Kingdom 10–11 January 2005*. Paris: OECD Working Party on Regulatory Management and Reform, 72–100.

Jaffe, L. L. (1965). *Judicial Control of Administrative Action*. Boston, MA: Little, Brown.

Jahn, G., M. Schramm and A. Spiller. (2005). 'The Reliability of Certification: Quality Labels as a Consumer Policy Tool'. *Journal of Consumer Policy* 28: 53–73.

James, T. E. and P. D. Jorgensen. (2009). 'Policy Knowledge, Policy Formulation, and Change: Revisiting a Foundational Question'. *Policy Studies Journal* 37, no. 1: 141–62.

Jann, W. and K. Wegrich. (2007). 'Theories of the Policy Cycle'. In F. Fischer, G. J. Miller and M. S. Sidney (eds), *Handbook of Public Policy Analysis: Theory, Politics and Methods*. Boca Raton, FL: CRC Press, 43–62.

Jarvis, D. S. L. (2011a). *Infrastructure Regulation What Works, Why and How Do We Know? Lessons from Asia and Beyond*. Singapore: World Scientific.

Jarvis, D. S. L. (2011b). 'Theorising Risk and Uncertainty in International Relations: The Contributions of Frank Knight'. *International Relations* 25, no. 3 (1 September): 296–312.

Jarvis, D. S. L. (2014). 'Policy Transfer, Neo-Liberalism or Coercive Institutional Isomorphism? Explaining the Emergence of a Regulatory Regime for Quality Assurance in the Hong Kong Higher Education Sector'. *Policy and Society* 33, no. 3: 237–52.

Jasanoff, S. (1998). *The Fifth Branch: Science Advisers as Policymakers.* Cambridge, MA: Harvard University Press.

Jayasuriya, K. (2001). 'Globalization and the Changing Architecture of the State: The Regulatory State and the Politics of Negative Co-ordination'. *Journal of European Public Policy* 8, no. 1: 101–23.

Jayasuriya, K. (2004). 'The New Regulatory State and Relational Capacity'. *Policy and Politics* 32, no. 4: 487–501.

Jenson, J. (1994). 'Commissioning Ideas: Representation and Royal Commissions'. In S. D. Phillips (ed.), *How Ottawa Spends, 1994–95: Making Change.* Ottawa, ON: Carleton University Press, 39–69.

Jensen, O. (2017). 'Public–Private Partnerships for Water in Asia: A Review of Two Decades of Experience'. *International Journal of Water Resources Development* 33, no. 1 (2 January): 4–30.

Jentoft, S. (2000). 'Legitimacy and Disappointment in Fisheries Management'. *Marine Policy* 24: 141–8.

Jochim, A. E. and P. J. May. (2010). 'Beyond Subsystems: Policy Regimes and Governance'. *Policy Studies Journal* 38, no. 2: 303–27.

Johannesen, A. B. (2006). 'Designing Integrated Conservation and Development Projects (ICDPs): Illegal Hunting, Wildlife Conservation and the Welfare of the Local People'. *Environment and Development Economics* 11, no. 1: 247–67.

Johansson, R. and K. Borell. (1999). 'Central Steering and Local Networks: Old-Age Care in Sweden'. *Public Administration* 77, no. 3: 585–98.

Johnsen, A. (2005). 'What Does 25 Years of Experience Tell Us about the State of Performance Measurement in Public Policy and Management?' *Public Money and Management* 25, no. 1: 9–17.

Johnson, E. J. and D. Goldstein. (2003). 'Do Defaults Save Lives?' *Science* 302, 5649: 1338–9.

Johnson, E. J. and D. G. Goldstein. (2013). 'Decisions by Default'. In E. Shafir (ed.), *The Behavioral Foundations of Public Policy.* Princeton, NJ: Princeton University Press, 417–27.

Johnson, E. J., S. B. Shu, B. G. C. Dellaert, C. Fox, D. G. Goldstein, G. Häubl, R. P. Larrick, *et al.* (2012). 'Beyond Nudges: Tools of a Choice Architecture'. *Marketing Letters* 23, no. 2 (June): 487–504.

Johnson, J. and M. Cook. (2014). 'Policy Design: A New Area of Design Research and Practice'. In M. Arguierc, F. Bonlanger, D. Krub and C. Marchal (eds). *Complex Systems Design & Management.* Cham, Germany: Springer, 51–62.

Jones, B. D., G. Boushey and S.Workman. (2006). 'Behavioral Rationality and the Policy Processes: Toward a New Model of Organizational Information Processing'. In B. G. Peters and J. Pierre (eds) *Handbook of Public Policy.* London: Sage, 49–74.

Jones, B. D., H. F. Thomas III and M. Wolfe. (2014) 'Policy Bubbles'. *Policy Studies Journal* 42 no. 1, 146–71.

Jones, C. O. (1984). *An Introduction to the Study of Public Policy*. Monterey, CA: Brooks/Cole.

Jonsson, G. and I. Zakrisson. (2005). 'Organizational Dilemmas in Voluntary Associations'. *International Journal of Public Administration* 28: 849–56.

Jordan, A. (2003). 'The Europeanization of National Government and Policy: A Departmental Perspective'. *British Journal of Political Science* 33, no. 1: 261–82.

Jordan, A. and E. Matt. (2014). 'Designing Policies that Intentionally Stick: Policy Feedback in a Changing Climate'. *Policy Sciences* (11 June), 1–21.

Jordan, A., R. Wurzel and A. Zito. (2003). 'New Instruments of Environmental Governance'. *Environmental Politics* 12, no. 3: 1–24.

Jordan, A., R. Wurzel and A. Zito. (2005)'.The Rise of "New" Policy Instruments in Comparative Perspective: Has Governance Eclipsed Government?' *Political Studies* 53, 477–96.

Jordan, A., R. Wurzel and A. Zito. (2013). 'Still the Century of "New" Environmental Policy Instruments? Exploring Patterns of Innovation and Continuity'. *Environmental Politics* 22, no. 1: 155–73.

Jordan, A., D. Benson, R. Wurzel and A. Zito. (2011). 'Policy Instruments in Practice'. In J. S. Dryzek, R. B. Norgaard and D. Schlosberg (eds), *Oxford Handbook of Climate Change and Society*. Oxford: Oxford University Press, 536–49.

Jordan, A., D. Benson, A. Zito and Wurzel, R. (2012). 'Environmental Policy: Governing by Multiple Policy Instruments?' In J. J. Richardson (ed.), *Constructing a Policy State? Policy Dynamics in the EU*. Oxford: Oxford University Press.

Jordan, A. G. (1981). 'Iron Triangles, Woolly Corporatism and Elastic Nets: Images of the Policy Process'. *Journal of Public Policy* 1, no. 1: 95–123.

Jordan, A. G. (2008). 'The Governance of Sustainable Development: Taking Stock and Looking Forwards'. *Environment and Planning C: Government and Policy* 26: 17–33.

Jordan, A. J. and D. Huitema. (2014). 'Innovations in Climate Policy: The Politics of Invention, Diffusion and Evaluation Environmental Politics'. *Environmental Politics* 23 (Special Issue), no. 5: 715–34.

Jordan, A. J., D. Huistema, M. Hilden, H. van Assett, T. Rayner, J. Schoenfeld, J. Tosun, J. Forster and E. Bousson. (2015). 'Emergence of Polycentric Climate Governance and Its Future Prospects'. *Nature Climate Change* 5: 977–82.

Jordan, G. and J. Richardson. (1982). 'The British Policy Style or the Logic of Negotiation?' In J. Richardson (ed.), *Policy Styles in Western Europe*. London: Allen & Unwin, 80–110.

Jordan-Zachery, J. S. (2007). 'Policy Interaction: The Mixing of Fatherhood, Crime and Urban Policies'. *Journal of Social Policy* 27, no. 1: 81–102.

Jordana, J. and D. Levi-Faur. (2004a). 'The Politics of Regulation in the Age of Governance'. In J. Jacint and D. Levi-Faur (eds), *Politics of Regulation*. Cheltenham, UK: Edward Elgar, 1–28.

Jordana, J. and D. Levi-Faur (eds). (2004b). *The Politics of Regulation: Institutions and Regulatory Reforms for the Age of Governance*. Cheltenham, UK: Edward Elgar.

Jorgensen, H. and F. Larsen. (1997). 'The Blessings of Network Steering? Theoretical and Empirical Arguments for Coordination Concepts as Alternatives to Policy Design' (Working Paper.) Aalborg, Denmark: Aalborg University.

Jorgensen, P. (2017). 'The Politics of Policy Formulation: Overcoming Subsystem Dynamics'. In M. Howlett and I. Mukherjee (eds), *Handbook of Policy Formulation*. Cheltenham, UK: Edward Elgar, 449–62.

Junginger, S. (2013). 'Design and Innovation in the Public Sector: Matters of Design in Policy-Making and Policy Implementation'. *Annual Review of Policy Design* 1, no. 1 (13 September): 1–11.

Justen, A., J. Schippl, B. Lenz and T. Fleischer. (2013). 'Assessment of Policies and Detection of Unintended Effects: Guiding Principles for the Consideration of Methods and Tools in Policy-Packaging'. *Transportation Research Part A: Policy and Practice.*

Justen, A., N. Fearnley, M. Givoni, and J. Macmillen. (2014). 'A Process for Designing Policy Packaging: Ideals and Realities'. *Transportation Research Part A: Policy and Practice* 60 (February): 9–18.

Kagan, R. A. (1991). 'Adversarial Legalism and American Government'. *Journal of Policy Analysis and Management* 10, no. 3: 369–406.

Kagan, R. A. (1994). 'Regulatory Enforcement'. In D. H. Rosenbloom and R. D. Schwartz (eds), *Handbook of Regulation and Administrative Law*. New York: Marcel Dekker, 383–422.

Kagan, R. A. (1996). 'The Political Construction of American Adversarial Legalism'. In A. Ranney (ed.), *Courts and the Political Process*. Berkeley, CA: Institute of Governmental Studies Press, 19–39.

Kagan, R. A. (1997). 'Should Europe Worry about Adversarial Legalism?' *Oxford Journal of Legal Studies* 17, no. 2: 165–83.

Kagan, R. A. (2001). *Adversarial Legalism: The American Way of Law*. Cambridge, MA: Harvard University Press.

Kagan, R. A. and L. Axelrad. (1997). 'Adversarial Legalism: An International Perspective'. In P. S. Nivola (ed.), *Comparative Disadvantages? Social Regulations and the Global Economy*. Washington, DC: Brookings Institution, 146–202.

Kagan, R. A. and Skolnick, J. H. (1993). 'Banning Smoking: Compliance Without Enforcement'. *Smoking Policy: Law, Politics, and Culture* 69, 78–80.

Kahler, M. (2004). 'Modeling Races to the Bottom'. Unpublished paper. http://irpshome.ucsd.edu/faculty/mkahler/RaceBott.pdf.

Kahler, M. and D. Lake (eds). (2004). *Governance in a Global Economy*. Princeton, NJ: Princeton University Press.

Kahn, A. E. (1970). *The Economic of Regulation: Principles and Institutions*, Vol. 1: *Economic Principles*. New York: John Wiley.

Kahneman, D. (2003). 'Maps of Bounded Rationality: Psychology for Behavioral Economics'. *American Economic Review* 93, no. 5: 1449–75.

Kahneman, D. (2013a). Foreword. In E. Shafir (ed.), *The Behavioral Foundations of Public Policy*. Princeton, NJ: Princeton University Press.

Kahneman, D. (2013b). *Thinking, Fast and Slow* (1st edn). New York: Farrar, Straus & Giroux.

Kahneman, D. and A. Tversky. (1979). 'Prospect Theory: An Analysis of Decision Under Risk'. *Econometrica*, 47, no. 2: 263–91.

Kahneman, D. and A. Tversky (eds). (2000). *Choices, Values, and Frames* (1st edn). New York; Cambridge: Cambridge University Press.

Kaine, G., H. Murdoch, R. Lourey and D. Bewsell. (2010). 'A Framework for Understanding Individual Response to Regulation'. *Food Policy* 35, no. 6 (December): 531–37.

Kaiser, A., A. Kaiser and J. Biela. (2012). *Policy Making in Multilevel Systems: Federalism, Decentralisation, and Performance in the OECD Countries*. Exeter, UK: European Consortium for Political Research Press.

Kallbekken, S., H. Sælen and E. A. T. Hermansen. (2013). 'Bridging the Energy Efficiency Gap: A Field Experiment on Lifetime Energy Costs and Household Appliances'. *Journal of Consumer Policy*, 36, no. 1: 1–16.

Kamerman, S. B. and A. J. Kahn (eds). (1989). *Privatization and the Welfare State*. Princeton, NJ: Princeton University Press.

Kapstein, E. B. (1994). *Governing the Global Economy*. Cambridge, MA: Harvard University Press.

Karamanos, P. (2001). 'Voluntary Environmental Agreements: Evolution and Definition of a New Environmental Policy Approach'. *Journal of Environmental Planning and Management* 44, no. 1: 67–84.

Karlan, D. S. and J. Appel. (2011). *More Than Good Intentions: How a New Economics Is Helping to Solve Global Poverty*. New York: Dutton.

Kash, J. P. (2008). 'Enemies to Allies: The Role of Policy-Design Adaptation in Facilitating a Farmer-Environmentalist Alliance'. *Policy Studies Journal* 36, no. 1: 39–60.

Kassim, H. and P. Le Galès. (2010). 'Exploring Governance in a Multi-Level Polity: A Policy Instruments Approach'. *West European Politics* 33, no. 1: 1–21.

Kato, J. (1996). 'Review Article: Institutions and Rationality in Politics – Three Varieties of Neo-Institutionalists'. *British Journal of Political Science* 26: 553–82.

Katzenstein, P. J. (1977). 'Conclusion: Domestic Structures and Strategies of Foreign Economic Policy'. *International Organization* 31, no. 4: 879–920.

Katzenstein, P. J. (1985). *Small States in World Markets: Industrial Policy in Europe*. Ithaca, NY: Cornell University Press.

Katzman, M. T. (1988). 'Societal Risk Management through the Insurance Market'. In R. C. Hula (ed.), *Market-Based Public Policy*. London: Macmillan, 21–42.

Kautto, P. and J. Simila. (2005). 'Recently Introduced Policy Instruments and Intervention Theories'. *Evaluation* 11, no. 1: 55–68.

Kay, A. (2007). 'Tense Layering and Synthetic Policy Paradigms: The Politics of Health Insurance in Australia'. *Australian Journal of Political Science* 42, no. 4: 579–91.

Kay, A. (2011). 'Evidence-Based Policy-Making: The Elusive Search for Rational Public Administration'. *Australian Journal of Public Administration* 70, no. 3 (1 September): 236–45.

Kay, A. and P. Baker. (2015). 'What Can Causal Process Tracing Offer to Policy Studies? A Review of the Literature'. *Policy Studies Journal* 43, no. 1: 1–21.

Keast, R., K. Brown and M. Mandell. (2007). 'Getting the Right Mix: Unpacking Integration Meanings and Strategies'. *International Public Management Journal* 10, no. 1 (1 January): 9–33.

Keast, R., M. Mandell and K. Brown. (2006). 'Mixing State, Market and Network Governance Modes: The Role of Government in "Crowded" Policy Domains'. *International Journal of Organization Theory and Behavior* 9, no. 1: 27–50.

Kemp, R. L. (1991). *Privatization: The Provision of Public Services by the Private Sector*. Jefferson, NC: McFarland & Co.

Kempf, R. J. (2015). 'Crafting Accountability Policy: Designing Offices of Inspector General'. *Policy and Society* 34: 147–9.

Keohane, N. O., R. L. Revesz and R. N. Stavins. (1998). 'The Choice of Regulatory Instruments in Environmental Policy'. *Harvard Environmental Law Review* 22: 313–67.

Keohane, R. O. (1989). *International Institutions and State Power: Essays in International Relations Theory*. Boulder, CO: Westview, 163.

Keohane, R. O. and S. Hoffman. (1991). 'Institutional Change in Europe in the 1980s'. In R. O. Keohane and S. Hoffman (eds), *The New European Community: Decision-Making and Institutional Change*. Boulder, CO: Westview, 1–40.

Kern, F. and M. Howlett. 'Implementing Transition Management as Policy Reforms: A Case Study of the Dutch Energy Sector'. *Policy Sciences* 42, no. 4 (2009): 391–408.

Kernaghan, K. (1985). 'Judicial Review of Administration Action'. In K. Kernaghan (ed.), *Public Administration in Canada: Selected Readings*. Toronto, ON: Methuen, 358–73.

Kernaghan, K. (1993). 'Partnership and Public Administration: Conceptual and Practical Considerations'. *Canadian Public Administration* 36, no. 1: 57–76.

Kernaghan, K., B. Marson and S. Borins. (2000). *The New Public Organization*. Toronto, ON: Institute of Public Administration of Canada.

Kerr, D. H. (1976). 'The Logic of "Policy" and Successful Policies'. *Policy Sciences* 7, no. 3: 351–63.

Kersh, R. (2015). 'Of Nannies and Nudges: The Current State of US Obesity Policymaking'. *Public Health* 129, no. 8 (August): 1083–91.

Kerwin, C. M. (1994). 'The Elements of Rule-Making'. In D. H. Rosenbloom and R. D. Schwartz (eds), *Handbook of Regulation and Administrative Law*. New York: Marcel Dekker, 345–81.

Kerwin, C. M. (1999). *Rulemaking: How Government Agencies Write Law and Make Policy*. Washington, DC: CQ Press.

Kettl, D. F. (2000). *The Global Public Management Revolution: A Report on the Transformation of Governance*. Washington, DC: Brookings Institution.

Keyes, J. M. (1996). 'Power Tools: The Form and Function of Legal Instruments for Government Action'. *Canadian Journal of Administrative Law and Practice* 10: 133–74.

Keysar, E. (2005). 'Procedural Integration in Support of Environmental Policy Objectives: Implementing Sustainability'. *Journal of Environmental Planning and Management* 48, no. 4: 549–69.

Kickert, W. J. M. and J. F. M. Koppenjan. (1997). 'Public Management and Network Management: An Overview'. In W. J. M. Kickert, E.-H. Klijn and J. F. M. Koppenjan (eds), *Managing Complex Networks: Strategies for the Public Sector*. London: Sage, 35–61.

Kickert, W. J. M., E.-H. Klijn and J. F. M. Koppenjan. (1997). 'Managing Networks in the Public Sector: Findings and Reflections'. In W. J. M. Kickert, E.-H. Klijn and J. F. M. Koppenjan (eds), *Managing Complex Networks: Strategies for the Public Sector*. London: Sage, 166–91.

Kiesling, Lynne. (2001). 'Flimsy Excuse for More Regulation'. *Houston Chronicle*, 2 December.

King, D. C. and J. L. Walker. (1991). 'The Origins and Maintenance of Groups'. In J. L. Walker (ed.), *Mobilizing Interest Groups in America: Patrons, Professions and Social Movements*. Ann Arbor, MI: University of Michigan Press, 75–102.

King, G. (2003). 'The Role of Participation in the European Demonstration Projects in ICZM'. *Coastal Management* 31, no. 2: 137–43.

Kingdon, J. W. (1984). *Agendas, Alternatives and Public Policies*. Boston, MA: Little, Brown.

Kirschen, E. S., J. Benard, H. Besters, F. Blackaby, O. Eckstein, J. Faaland, F. Hartog, L. Morissens and E. Tosco (eds). (1964). *Economic Policy in Our Time. I – General Theory*. Chicago, IL: Rand McNally.

Kiss, B., C. González Manchón and L. Neij. (2012). 'The Role of Policy Instruments in Supporting the Development of Mineral Wool Insulation in Germany, Sweden and the United Kingdom'. *Journal of Cleaner Production* 48, no. 2: 187–199.

Kissane, R. J. (2007). 'How Do Faith-Based Organizations Compare to Secular Providers? Nonprofit Directors' and Poor Women's Assessments of FBOs'. *Journal of Poverty* 11, no. 4: 91–115.

Kiviniemi, M. (1986). 'Public Policies and Their Targets: A Typology of the Concept of Implementation'. *International Social Science Journal* 38, no. 108: 251–66.

Kjær, A. M. (2004). *Governance*, Cambridge: Polity Press.

Kleiman, M. A. R. and S. M. Teles. (2006). 'Market and Non-Market Failures'. In M. Moran, M. Rein and R. E. Goodin (eds), *The Oxford Handbook of Public Policy*. Oxford: Oxford University Press, 624–50.

Klein, L., C. Biesenthal and E. Dehlin. (2015). 'Improvisation in Project Management: A Praxeology'. *International Journal of Project Management* 33, no. 2 (February): 267–77.

Klijn, E.-H. (1996). 'Analyzing and Managing Policy Processes in Complex Networks: A Theoretical Examination of the Concept Policy Network and Its Problems'. *Administration and Society* 28, no. 1: 90–119.

Klijn, E.-H. (2002). 'Governing Networks in the Hollow State: Contracting Out, Process Management, or a Combination of the Two?' *Public Management Review* 4, no. 2: 149–65.

Klijn, E. H. (2010). 'Trust in Governance Networks: Looking for Conditions for Innovative Solutions and Outcome' In S. P. Osborne (ed.), *The New Public Governance: Emerging Perspectives on the Theory and Practice of Public Governance*. London: Routledge, 303–22.

Klijn, E.-H. and K. Joop. (2012). 'Governance Network Theory: Past, Present and Future'. *Policy & Politics*, 40, no. 4: 587–606.

Klijn, E. H. and J. F. Koppenjan. (2000a). 'Interactive Decision Making and Representative Democracy: Institutional Collisions and Solutions'. In O. van Heffen, W. Kickert, and J. Thomassen (eds), *Governance in Modern Society: Effects, Change and Formation of Government Institutions*. Dordrecht, Netherlands: Kluwer, 109–34.

Klijn, E. H. and J. F. Koppenjan. (2000b). 'Politicians and Interactive Decision Making: Institutional Spoilsports or Playmakers'. *Public Administration* 78, no. 2: 365–87.

Klijn, E. H. and J. F. Koppenjan. (2000c). 'Public Management and Policy Networks: Foundations of a Network Approach to Governance'. *Public Management: An International Journal of Research and Theory*, 2, no. 2, 135–58.

Klijn, E. H. and J. F. Koppenjan. (2006). 'Institutional Design: Changing Institutional Features of Networks'. *Public Management Review* 8, no. 1: 141–60.

Klijn, E. H. and J. F. Koppenjan. (2007). 'Governing Policy Networks'. In G. Morcol (ed.), *Handbook of Decision Making*. New York: CRC/Taylor & Francis, 169–87.

Klijn, E.-H. and C. Skelcher. (2007). 'Democracy and Governance Networks: Compatible or Not?' *Public Administration* 85, no. 3: 587–608.

Klijn, E. H. and G. R. Teisman. (1991). 'Effective Policymaking in a Multi-Actor Setting: Networks and Steering'. In R. T. Veld, L. Schaap, C. J. A. M. Termeer and M. J. W. Van Twist (eds), *Autopoiesis and Configuration Theory: New Approaches to Societal Steering*. Dordrecht, Netherlands: Kluwer, 99–111.

Klijn, E.-H., S. Bram and J. Edelenbos. (2010). 'The Impact of Network Management on Outcomes in Governance Network'. *Public Administration* 88, no. 4: 1063–82.

Klijn, E. H., J. F. Koppenjan and K. Termeer. (1995). 'Managing Networks in the Public Sector: A Theoretical Study of Management Strategies in Policy Networks'. *Public Administration* 73, no. 3: 437–54.

Klitgaard, M. B. (2008). 'School Vouchers and the New Politics of the Welfare State'. *Governance* 21, no. 4: 479–98.

Knaggård, Å. (2015). 'The Multiple Streams Framework and the Problem Broker'. *European Journal of Political Research* 54, no 3: 450–65.

Knill, C. (1998). 'European Policies: The Impact of National Administrative Traditions'. *Journal of Public Policy* 18, no. 1: 1–28.

Knill, C. (1999). 'Explaining Cross-National Variance in Administrative Reform: Autonomous Versus Instrumental Bureaucracies'. *Journal of Public Policy* 19, no. 2: 113–39.

Knill, C. (2001a). *The Europeanization of National Administrations: Patterns of Institutional Change and Persistence.* Cambridge: Cambridge University Press.

Knill, C. (2001b). 'Private Governance across Multiple Arenas: European Interest Associations as Interface Actors'. *Journal of European Public Policy* 8, no. 2: 227–46.

Knill, C. and D. Lehmkuhl. (2002). 'Private Actors and the State: Internationalization and Changing Patterns of Governance'. *Governance* 15, no. 1: 41–63.

Knill, C. and A. Lenschow. (2005). 'Compliance, Communication and Competition: Patterns of EU Environmental Policy Making and Their Impact on Policy Convergence'. *European Environment* 15: 114–28.

Knoepfel, P. and I. Kissling-Naf. (1998). 'Social Learning in Policy Networks'. *Policy and Politics* 26, no. 3: 343–67.

Knoke, D. (1987). *Political Networks: The Structural Perspective.* Cambridge: Cambridge University Press.

Knoke, D. (1993). 'Networks as Political Glue: Explaining Public Policy-Making'. In W. J. Wilson (ed.), *Sociology and the Public Agenda.* London: Sage, 164–84.

Knoke, D. (2004). 'The Sociopolitical Construction of National Policy Domains'. In C. H. C. A. Henning and C. Melbeck (eds), *Interdisziplinäre Sozialforschung: Theorie und empirische Anwendungen.* Frankfurt, Germany: Campus Verlag, 81–96.

Knoke, D. and J. H. Kuklinski. (1991). 'Network Analysis: Basic Concepts'. In G. Thompson, J. Frances, R. Levacic and J. Mitchell (eds), *Markets, Hierarchies and Networks: The Coordination of Social Life.* London: Sage, 173–82.

Knott, J. H. and D. McCarthy. (2007). 'Policy Venture Capital: Foundations, Government Partnerships and Child Care Programs'. *Administration and Society* 39, no. 3: 319–53.

Knudson, W. (2009). 'The Environment, Energy, and the Tinbergen Rule'. *Bulletin of Science, Technology & Society* 29, no. 4 (1 August): 308–12.

Koch, P. (2013). 'Overestimating the Shift from Government to Governance: Evidence from Swiss Metropolitan Areas'. *Governance* 26, no. 3: 397–423.

Koen, V., P. G. Roness, B. Verschuere, K. Rubecksen and M. MacCarthaigh. (2010). *Autonomy and Control of State Agencies: Comparing States and Agencies.* London: Palgrave Macmillan.

Koffijberg, J., H. De Bruijn and H. Priemus. (2012). 'Combining Hierarchical and Network Strategies. Successful Changes in Dutch Social Housing'. *Public Administration* 90, no. 1: 262–75.

Kogan, V. (2010). 'Lessons from Recent State Constitutional Conventions'. *California Journal of Politics and Policy* 2, no. 2, Article 3.

343

Kohler-Koch, B. (1996). 'Catching up with Change: The Transformation of Governance in the European Union'. *Journal of European Public Policy* 3, no. 3: 359–80.

Koliba, C., J. W. Meek and A. Zia. (2010). *Governance Networks in Public Administration and Public Policy* (1st edn). Boca Raton, FL: CRC Press.

Könnöla, T., J. E. Smith and A. Eerola. (2009). Future-Oriented Technology Analysis (FTA): Impacts and Implications for Policy and Decision Making (The 2008 FTA International Seville Conference), 76, no. 9 (November): 1135–7.

Kooiman, J. (ed.). (1993). 'Governance and Governability: Using Complexity, Dynamics and Diversity'. In *Modern Governance*. London: Sage, 35–50.

Kooiman, J. (2000). 'Societal Governance: Levels, Models and Orders of Social–Political Interaction'. In J. Pierre (ed.), *Debating Governance*. Oxford: Oxford University Press, 138–66.

Kooiman, J. (2008). 'Exploring the Concept of Governability'. *Journal of Comparative Policy Analysis* 10, no. 2: 171–90.

Koppell, J. G. S. (2003). *The Politics of Quasi-Government: Hybrid Organizations and the Dynamics of Bureaucratic Control*. Cambridge: Cambridge University Press.

Koppenjan, J. and E.-H. Klijn. (2004). *Managing Uncertainties in Networks: A Network Approach to Problem Solving and Decision Making*. London: Routledge.

Koppenjan, J., M. Kars and H. van der Voort. (2009). 'Vertical Politics in Horizontal Policy Networks: Framework Settings as Coupling Arrangement'. *Policy Studies Journal* 37, no. 4: 769–92.

Korpi, W. (1980). 'Social Policy and Distributional Conflict in Capitalist Democracies'. *West European Politics* 3: 296–316.

Krause, R. M. (2011). 'Policy Innovation, Intergovernmental Relations, and the Adoption of Climate Protection Initiatives by US Cities'. *Journal of Urban Affairs* 33 no. 1: 45–60.

Kritzinger, S. and H. Pulzl. (2008). 'Governance Modes and Interests: Higher Education and Innovation Policy in Austria'. *Journal of Public Policy* 28, no. 3: 289–307.

Krosnick, J. A., A. L. Holbrook, L. Lowe and P. S. Visser. (2006). 'The Origins and Consequences of Democratic Citizens' Policy Agendas: A Study of Popular Concern about Global Warming'. *Climatic Change*, 77, nos 1–2: 7–43.

Krysiak, F. C. and P. Schweitzer. (2010). 'The Optimal Size of a Permit Market'. *Journal of Environmental Economics and Management* 60, no. 2: 133–43.

Kuhfuss, L., R. Préget, S. Thoyer and N. Hanley. (2016). 'Nudging Farmers to Enrol Land into Agri-Environmental Schemes: The Role of a Collective Bonus'. *European Review of Agricultural Economics*, 43 no. 4: 609–36.

Kuhlmann, E. and J. Allsop. (2008). 'Professional Self-Regulation in a Changing Architecture of Governance: Comparing Health Policy in the UK and Germany'. *Policy and Politics* 36, no. 2: 173–89.

Kuhn, T. S. (1962). *The Structure of Scientific Revolutions*. Chicago, IL: University of Chicago Press.

Kuhn, T. S. (1974). 'Second Thoughts on Paradigms'. In F. Suppe (ed.) *The Structure of Scientific Theories*. Urbana, IL: University of Illinois Press, 459–82.

Kuipers, B., H., Malcolm, K., Walter, T. G. Lars, G. Jolien and V. V. Joris. (2013). 'The Management of Change in Public Organisations: A Literature Review', *Public Administration*. SSRN. http://ssrn.com/abstract=2226612.

Kwakkel, J. H., W. E. Walker and V. A. W. J. Marchau. (2010). 'Classifying and Communicating Uncertainties in Model-Based Policy Analysis'. *International Journal of Technology, Policy and Management* 10, no. 4 (1 January): 299–315.

Kwaterski, J. (2010). 'Opportunities for Rationalizing the Capacity Development Knowledge Architecture'. The World Bank Institute and Learning Network for Capacity Development.

Lackey, R. T. (2007). 'Science, Scientists, and Policy Advocacy'. *Conservation Biology* 21: 12–17.

Ladi, S. (2000). 'Globalization, Think-Tanks and Policy Transfer'. In D. Stone (ed.), *Banking on Knowledge: The Genesis of the GDN*. London: Routledge, 203–20.

Laegreid, P., P. G. Roness and K. Rubecksen. (2008). 'Controlling Regulatory Agencies'. *Scandinavian Political Studies* 31, no. 1: 1–26.

Lafferty, W. M. and E. Hovden. (2003). 'Environmental Policy Integration: Towards an Analytical Framework'. *Environmental Politics* 12, no. 3: 1–22.

Laffont, J. J. and J. Tirole. (1991). 'The Politics of Government Decision-Making: A Theory of Regulatory Capture'. *The Quarterly Journal of Economics* 106, no. 4: 1089–127.

Laforest, R. and M. Orsini. (2005). 'Evidence-Based Engagement in the Voluntary Sector: Lessons from Canada'. *Social Policy and Administration* 39, no. 5: 481–97.

Lai, A. Y. (2012). 'Organizational Collaborative Capacity in Fighting Pandemic Crises: A Literature Review From the Public Management Perspective'. *Asia-Pacific Journal of Public Health* 24, no. 1 (1 January): 7–20.

de Lancer Julnes, P. and M. Holzer. (2001). 'Promoting the Utilization of Performance Measures in Public Organizations: An Empirical Study of Factors Affecting Adoption and Implementation'. *Public Administration Review* 61, no. 6: 693–708.

Landes, W. M. and R. A. Posner. (1975). 'The Independent Judiciary in an Interest Group Perspective'. *Journal of Law and Economics* 18 (December): 875–901.

Landry, R. (1991). 'Party Competition in Quebec: Direct Confrontation or Selective Emphasis?' In H. G. Thorburn (ed.), *Party Politics in Canada*. Scarborough, ON: Prentice-Hall, 401–13.

Landry, R., M. Lamari and N. Amara. (2003). 'The Extent and Determinants of the Utilization of University Research in Government Agencies'. *Public Administration Review* 63, no. 2: 192–205.

Landry, R., F. Varone and M. L. Goggin. (1998). 'The Determinants of Policy Design: The State of the Theoretical Literature'. Paper presented to the Midwest Political Science Association, Chicago, IL.

Lane, J. E. (2000). *New Public Management*. London: Routledge.

Lang, A. (2016). 'Collaborative Governance in Health and Technology Policy: The Use and Effects of Procedural Policy Instruments'. *Administration & Society*, forthcoming.

Lange, P., P. Driessen, A. Scuerc, B. Bornemann and P. Burgen. (2013). 'Governing towards Sustainability – Conceptualizing Modes of Governance'. *Journal of Environmental Policy & Planning* 15, no. 3: 403–25.

Lanzalaco, L. (2011). 'Bringing the Olympic Rationality Back In? Coherence, Integration and Effectiveness of Public Policies'. *World Political Science Review* 7, no. 1 (25 May): 1098.

La Porte, T. (ed.). (1975). *Organized Social Complexity Challenge to Politics and Policy*. Princeton, NJ: Princeton University Press.

Larsen, T. P., P. Taylor-Gooby and J. Kananen. (2006). 'New Labour's Policy Style: A Mix of Policy Approaches'. *International Social Policy* 35, no. 4: 629–49.

Larson, J. S. (1980). *Why Government Programs Fail: Improving Policy Implementations*. New York: Praeger.

Lascoumes, P. and P. Le Galès. (2007). 'Introduction: Understanding Public Policy through Its Instruments – From the Nature of Instruments to the Sociology of Public Policy Instrumentation'. *Governance* 20, no. 1: 1–21.

Lasswell, H. D. (1951). 'The Policy Orientation'. In D. Lerner and H. D. Lasswell (eds), *The Policy Sciences: Recent Developments in Scope and Method*. Palo Alto, CA: Stanford University Press, 3–15.

Lasswell, H. D. (1954). 'Key Symbols, Signs and Icons'. In L. Bryson, L. Finkelstein, R. M. MacIver and R. McKean (eds), *Symbols and Values: An Initial Study*. New York: Harper, 77–94.

Lasswell, H. (1956). *The Decision Process: Seven Categories of Functional Analysis*. College Park, MD: University of Maryland Press.

Lasswell, H. (1958). *Politics: Who Gets What, When, How*. New York: Meridian.

Lasswell, H. (1971). *A Pre-View of Policy Sciences*. New York: Elsevier.

Lasswell, H. D. and D. Lerner. (1951). 'The Policy Orientation'. In *The Policy Sciences: Recent Developments in Scope and Method*. Stanford, CA: Stanford University Press, 3–15.

Latin, H. A. (2012). *Climate Change Policy Failures*. Hackensack, NJ: World Scientific Publishing.

Laux, J. (1993). 'How Private is Privatization'. *Canadian Public Policy* 19, no. 4: 398–411.

Laux, J. K. and M. A. Molot. (1988). *State Capitalism: Public Enterprise in Canada*. Ithaca, NY: Cornell University Press.

Lawrence, D. P. (2001). 'Choices for EIA Process Design and Management'. *Journal of Environmental Assessment Policy and Management* 3, no. 4: 437–64.

Lazarus, R. J. (2009). 'Super Wicked Problems and Climate Change: Restraining the Present to Liberate the Future'. *Cornell Law Review* 94 :1153–1234.

Lazer, D. and V. Mayer-Schonberger. (2002). 'Governing Networks: Telecommunication Deregulation in Europe and the United States'. *Brooklyn Journal of International Law* no. 3: 820–51.

Le Grand, J. (ed.). (1984). *Privatization and the Welfare State*. London: Allen & Unwin.

Le Grand, J. (1991). 'The Theory of Government Failure'. *British Journal of Political Science* 21, no. 4: 423–42.

Le Grand, J. (2007). *The Other Invisible Hand: Delivering Public Services through Choice and Competition*. Princeton, NJ: Princeton University Press.

Le Grand, J. (2009). 'Choice and Competition in Publicly Funded Health Care'. *Health Economics, Policy and Law* 4, no. 3: 479–88.

Lecuyer, O. and R. Bibas. (2012). *Combining Climate and Energy Policies: Synergies or Antagonism? Modeling Interactions with Energy Efficiency Instruments*. SSRN Scholarly Paper. Rochester, NY: Social Science Research Network. http://papers.ssrn.com/abstract=1992324. Accessed 26 January.

Lecuyer, O. and P. Quirion. (2013). 'Can Uncertainty Justify Overlapping Policy Instruments to Mitigate Emissions?' *Ecological Economics* 93 (September): 177–91.

Ledingham, J. A. (2003). 'Explicating Relationship Management as a General Theory of Public Relations'. *Journal of Public Relations Research* 15, no. 2: 181–98.

Lee, N. (2006). 'Bridging the Gap Between Theory and Practice in Integrated Assessment'. *Environmental Impact Assessment Review* 26: 57–78.

Leech, B. L., F. R. Baumgartner, T. La Pira and N. A. Semanko. (2005). 'Drawing Lobbyists to Washington: Government Activity and the Demand for Advocacy'. *Political Research Quarterly* 58, no. 1: 19–30.

Leenheer, J., M. Elsen, N. Mikola, M. Wagt., L. L. van der, European Commission, and GFK. (2014). *Study on the Effects on Consumer Behaviour of Online Sustainability Information Displays: Final Report.* Luxembourg: Publications Office of the European Union. http://bookshop.europa.eu/uri?target=EUB: NOTICE:KK0214676:EN:HTML.

Leeuw, F. L. (1991). 'Policy Theories, Knowledge Utilization, and Evaluation'. *Knowledge and Policy* 4, no. 3: 73–91.

Leeuw, F. L. (1998). 'The Carrot: Subsidies as a Tool of Government'. In M.-L. Bemelmans-Videc, R. C. Rist and E. Vedung (eds), *Carrots, Sticks and Sermons: Policy Instruments and Their Evaluation.* New Brunswick, NJ: Transaction, 77–102.

Leggett, J. A. (2011). *Climate Change: Conceptual Approaches and Policy Tools* (CRS Report for Congress No. 7-5700). Congressional Research Service. http://biotech.law.lsu.edu/blog/R41973.pdf. Washington, DC.

Lehmbruch, G. (1979). 'Consociational Democracy, Class Conflict and the New Corporatism'. In P. C. Schmitter and G. Lehmbruch (eds), *Trends Towards Corporatist Intermediation.* Beverley Hills, CA: Sage, 53–61.

Lehmbruch, G. (1991). 'The Organization of Society, Administrative Strategies and Policy Networks'. In R. M. Czada and A. Windhoff-Heritier (eds), *Political Choice: Institutions, Rules and the Limits of Rationality.* Boulder, CO: Westview, 121–55.

Lehmbruch, G. and P. Schmitter. (1982). *Patterns of Corporatist Policy-Making.* London: Sage.

Lehmkuhl, D. (2008). 'On Government, Governance and Judicial Review: The Case of European Competition Policy'. *Journal of Public Policy* 28, no. 1: 139–59.

Lehoux, P., J.-L. Denis, S. Tailliez and M. Hivon. (2005). 'Dissemination of Health Technology Assessments: Identifying the Visions Guiding and Evolving Policy Innovation in Canada'. *Journal of Health Politics, Policy and Law* 30, no. 4: 603–41.

Leik, R. K. (1992). 'New Directions for Network Exchange Theory: Strategic Manipulation of Network Linkages'. *Social Networks* 14: 309–23.

Leiss, W. and D. A. Powell. (2004). *Mad Cows and Mother's Milk: The Perils of Poor Risk Communication* (2nd edn). Montreal, QC: McGill-Queen's University Press.

Lejano, R. P. and H. Ingram. (2009). 'Collaborative Networks and New Ways of Knowing'. *Environmental Science and Policy* 12, no. 6: 653–62.

Lejano, R. P. and C. Leong. (2012). 'A Hermeneutic Approach to Explaining and Understanding Public Controversies'. *Journal of Public Administration Research and Theory* 22: 793–814.

Lejano, R. P. and S. Shankar. (2013). 'The Contextualist Turn and Schematics of Institutional Fit: Theory and a Case Study from Southern India'. *Policy Sciences* 46, no. 1 (1 March): 83–102.

Leland, S. and O. Smirnova. (2009). 'Reassessing Privatization Strategies 25 Years Later: Revisting Perry and Babitsky's Comparative Performance Study of Urban Bus Transit Services'. *Public Administration Review* 69, no. 5: 855–67.

Leman, C. K. (1989). 'The Forgotten Fundamental: Successes and Excesses of Direct Government'. In L. M. Salamon (ed.), *Beyond Privatization: The Tools of Government Action.* Washington, DC: Urban Institute, 51–92.

Leman, C. K. (2002). 'Direct Government'. In L. M. Salamon (ed.), *The Tools of Government: A Guide to the New Governance,* New York: Oxford University Press, 48–79.

Lempert, R., S. Popper and S. Bankes. (2002). 'Confronting Surprise'. *Social Science Computer Review* 20, no. 4: 420–40.

Lenihan, D. G. and R. Alcock. (2000). *Collaborative Government in the Post-Industrial Age: Five Discussion Pieces – Changing Government*, Vol. I. Ottawa, ON: Centre for Collaborative Government.

Leone, L. (2010). 'Opening Up Innovation: Strategy, Organization and Technology'. London: Imperial College Business School.

Leplay, S. and S. Thoyer. (2011). *Synergy Effects of International Policy Instruments to Reduce Deforestation: A Cross-country Panel Data Analysis* (Working Paper). Montpellier, France: LAMETA, University of Montpellier. http://ideas.repec.org/p/lam/wpaper/11-01.html.

Leroux, T., M. Hirtle and L.-N. Fortin. (1998). 'An Overview of Public Consultation Mechanisms Developed to Address the Ethical and Social Issues Raised by Biotechnology'. *Journal of Consumer Policy* 21, no. 4: 445–81.

Lester, J. P. and M. L. Goggin. (1998). 'Back to the Future: The Rediscovery of Implementation Studies'. *Policy Currents* 8, no. 3: 1–9.

Leung, W., B. Noble, J. Gunn and J. A. G. Jaeger. (2015). 'A Review of Uncertainty Research in Impact Assessment'. *Environmental Impact Assessment Review* 50 (January): 116–23.

Leutz, W. N. (1999). 'Five Laws for Integrating Medical and Social Services: Lessons from the United States and the United Kingdom'. *The Milbank Quarterly* 77, no. 1 (1 January): 77–110.

Levi-Faur, D. (2003). 'The Politics of Liberalisation: Privatisation and Regulation-For-Competition in Europe's and Latin America's Telecoms and Electricity Industries'. *European Journal of Political Research* 42, no. 5: 705–23.

Levi-Faur, D. (2009). 'Regulatory Capitalism and the Reassertion of the Public Interest'. *Policy and Society* 27, no. 3: 181–91.

Levi-Faur, D. (2012). 'From "Big Government" to "Big Governance"?' In D. Levi-Faur (ed.), *The Oxford Handbook of Governance*. Oxford: Oxford University Press, 3–18.

Levi-Faur, D. and S. Gilad. (2005). 'The Rise of the British Regulatory State – Transcending the Privatization Debate'. *Comparative Politics* 37, no. 1: 105–24.

Levin, K., B. Cashore, S. Bernstein and G. Auld. (2012). 'Overcoming the Tragedy of Super Wicked Problems: Constraining our Future Selves to Ameliorate Global Climate Change'. *Policy Sciences*. 45, no. 2: 123–52.

Levitsky, S. and L. A. Way. (2010). 'Competitive Authoritarianism: Hybrid Regimes after the Cold War'. Cambridge: Cambridge University Press.

Levitt, B. and J. G. March. (1988). 'Organizational Learning'. *Annual Review of Sociology* 14: 319–40.

Levy, B. and P. T. Spiller. (1994). 'The Institutional Foundations of Regulatory Commitment: A Comparative Analysis of Telecommunications Regulation'. *Journal of Law, Economics and Organization* 10, no. 2: 201–46.

Levy, D. and M. Scully. (2007). 'The Institutional Entrepreneur as Modern Prince: The Strategic Face of Power in Contested Fields'. *Organization Studies* 28, no. 7 (1 July): 971–91.

Lewis, M. (2007). *States of Reason: Freedom, Responsibility and the Governing of Behaviour Change*. London: Institute for Public Policy Research.

Li, C., X. Yu, J. R. G. Butler, V. Yiengprugsawan and M. Yu. (2011). 'Moving Towards Universal Health Insurance in China: Performance, Issues and Lessons from Thailand'. *Social Science & Medicine* 73, no. 3 (August): 359–66.

Li, Y., E. J. Johnson and L. Zaval. (2011). 'Local Warming: Daily Temperature Change Influences Belief in Global Warming'. *Psychological Science* 22, no. 4, 454–59.

Libecap, G. D. (1986). 'Deregulation as an Instrument in Industrial Policy: Comment'. *Journal of Institutional and Theoretical Economics* 142: 70–4.

Libecap, G. D. (2005). 'State Regulations of Open-Access, Common-Pool Resources' In C. Menard and M. M. Shirley (eds), *Handbook of New Institutional Economics*, Dordrecht, Netherlands: Springer, 545–72.

Lichtenstein, S. and P. Slovic. (2006). *The Construction of Preference*. Cambridge; New York: Cambridge University Press.

Lidskog, R. and I. Flander. (2010). 'Addressing Climate Change Democratically. Multi-level Governance, Transnational Networks and Governmental Structures'. *Sustainable Development* 18: 32–41.

Liefferink, D. (2006). 'The Dynamics of Policy Arrangements: Turning Round the Tetrahedron'. In B. Arts and P. Leroy (eds), *Institutional Dynamics in Environmental Governance*. Dordrecht, Netherlands: Springer, 45–68.

Lierse, H. (2010). 'European Economic Governance: The OMC as a Road to Integration?' *International Journal of Public Policy* 6, nos 1/2: 35–49.

Lijphart, A. (1969). 'Consociational Democracy'. *World Politics* 21, no. 2: 207–25.

Lindblom, C. E. (1955). *Bargaining: The Hidden Hand in Government*. Los Angeles, CA: Rand Corporation.

Lindblom, C. E. (1958a). 'Policy Analysis'. *American Economic Review* 48, no. 3: 298–312.

Lindblom, C. E. (1958b). 'Tinbergen on Policy-Making'. *The Journal of Political Economy* 66, no. 6 (December): 531–38.

Lindblom, C. E. (1959). 'The Science of Muddling Through'. *Public Administration Review* 19, no. 2: 79–88.

van der Linden, S. (2015). 'Exploring Beliefs about Bottled Water and Intentions to Reduce Consumption: The Dual-Effect of Social Norm Activation and Persuasive Information'. *Environment and Behavior* 47, no. 5 : 526–50.

Linder, S. H. (1999). 'Coming to Terms with Public–Private Partnership'. *American Behavioural Scientist* 43, no. 1: 35–51.

Linder, S. H. and B. G. Peters. (1984). 'From Social Theory to Policy Design'. *Journal of Public Policy* 4, no. 3: 237–59.

Linder, S. H. and B. G. Peters. (1987). 'A Design Perspective on Policy Implementation: The Fallacy of Misplaced Precision'. *Review of Policy Research* 6: 459–75.

Linder, S. H. and B. G. Peters. (1988). 'The Analysis of Design or the Design of Analysis?' *Policy Studies Review* 7, no. 4: 738–50.

Linder, S. H. and B. G. Peters. (1989). 'Instruments of Government: Perception and Contexts'. *Journal of Public Policy* 9, no. 1: 35–58.

Linder, S. H. and B. G. Peters. (1990a). 'The Design of Instruments for Public Policy'. In S. S. Nagel (ed.), *Policy Theory and Policy Evaluation: Concepts, Knowledge, Causes and Norms*. New York: Greenwood Press, 103–19.

Linder, S. H. and B. G. Peters. (1990b). 'An Institutional Approach to the Theory of Policy-Making: The Role of Guidance Mechanisms in Policy Formulation'. *Journal of Theoretical Politics* 2, no. 1 (1 January): 59–83.

Linder, S. H. and B. G. Peters. (1990c). 'Policy Formulation and the Challenge of Conscious Design'. *Evaluation and Program Planning* 13: 303–11.

Linder, S. H. and B. G. Peters. (1990d). 'Research Perspectives on the Design of Public Policy: Implementation, Formulation and Design'. In D. J. Palumbo and D. J.

Calista (eds), *Implementation and the Policy Process: Opening up the Black Box*. New York: Greenwood Press.

Linder, S. H. and B. G. Peters. (1991). 'The Logic of Public Policy Design: Linking Policy Actors and Plausible Instruments'. *Knowledge, Technology & Policy* 4, no. 1: 125–51.

Linder, S. H. and B. G. Peters. (1992). 'A Metatheoretic Analysis of Policy Design'. In W. N. Dunn and R. M. Kelly (eds), *Advances in Policy Studies Since 1950*. New Brunswick, NJ: Transaction, 201–38.

Linders, D. (2012). 'From E-Government to We-Government: Defining a Typology for Citizen Coproduction in the Age of Social Media'. *Government Information Quarterly* (Social Media in Government – Selections from the 12th Annual International Conference on Digital Government Research) dg.o2011, 29, no. 4 (October): 446–54.

Lindquist, E. A. (1992). 'Public Managers and Policy Communities: Learning to Meet New Challenges'. *Canadian Public Administration* 35, no. 2 (2000): 127–59.

Lindquist, E. A. (1998). 'A Quarter Century of Canadian Think Tanks: Evolving Institutions, Conditions and Strategies'. In D. Stone, A. Denham and M. Garnett (eds), *Think Tanks Across Nations: A Comparative Approach*. Manchester, UK: Manchester University Press, 127–44.

Lindquist, E. A. (ed.). (2000). *Government Restructuring and Career Public Service in Canada*. Toronto, ON: Institute of Public Administration of Canada.

Lindquist, E. A. (2006). 'Organizing for Policy Implementation: The Emergence and Role of Implementation Units in Policy Design and Oversight'. *Journal of Comparative Policy Analysis: Research and Practice* 8, no. 4: 311–24.

Lindquist, E. and J. Desveaux. (1998). *Recruitment and Policy Capacity in Government*. Ottawa, ON: Public Policy Forum.

Lindqvist, K. (2016). 'Dilemmas and Paradoxes of Regional Cultural Policy Implementation: Governance Modes, Discretion, and Policy Outcome'. *Administration & Society* (20 January), forthcoming.

Lindvall, J. (2009). 'The Real but Limited Influence of Expert Ideas'. *World Politics* 61, no. 4: 703–30.

Ling, T. (2002). 'Delivering Joined Up Government in the UK: Dimensions, Issues and Problems'. *Public Administration*, 80, no. 4: 615–42.

Locke, W. (2009). 'Reconnecting the Research–Policy–Practice Nexus in Higher Education: "Evidence-Based Policy" in Practice in National and International Contexts'. *Higher Education Policy* 22: 119–40.

Lockton, D., D. Harrison and N. A. Stanton. (2016). 'Design for Sustainable Behaviour: Investigating Design Methods for Influencing User Behaviour'. *Annual Review of Policy Design* 4, no. 1 (28 October): 1–10.

Lockwood, M. (2013). 'The Political Sustainability of Climate Policy: The Case of the UK Climate Change Act'. *Global Environmental Change* 23: 1339–48.

Lodge, M. (2003). 'Institutional Choice and Policy Transfer: Reforming British and German Railway Regulation'. *Governance* 16, no. 2: 159–78.

Lodge, M. (2008). 'Regulation, the Regulatory State and European Politics'. *West European Politics* 31, nos 1–2: 280–301.

Loewenstein, G. (2008). *Exotic Preferences: Behavioral Economics and Human Motivation*. Oxford; New York: Oxford University Press.

Lombardo, E. (2005). 'Integrating or Setting the Agenda? Gender Mainstreaming in the European Constitution-Making Process'. *Social Politics* 12, no. 3: 412–32.

Lombe, M. and M. Sherraden. (2008). 'Inclusion in the Policy Process: An Agenda for Participation of the Marginalized'. *Journal of Policy Practice* 7, nos 2–3: 199–213.

Lorenzoni, I. and N. F. Pidgeon. (2006). 'Public Views on Climate Change. European and USA Perspectives'. *Climate Change* 77: 73–95.

Lorenzoni, I., S. Nicholson-Cole and L. Whitmarsh. (2007). 'Barriers Perceived to Engaging with Climate Change Among the UK Public and Their Policy Implications'. *Global Environmental Change* 18, nos 3–4: 445–59.

Lourenço, J. S., E. Ciriolo, S. R. Almeida and X. Troussard. (2016). *Behavioural Insights Applied to Policy: European Report 2016*. Brussels, Belgium: European Commission.

Lovan, W. R., M. Murray and R. Shaffer. (2004). 'Participatory Governance in a Changing World'. In W. R. Lovan, M. Murray and R. Shaffer (eds), *Participatory Governance: Planning, Conflict Mediation and Public Decision-Making in Civil Society*. Aldershot, UK: Ashgate, 1–20.

Lovink, J. A. A. (1999). 'Choosing the Right Autonomy for Operators of Privatized Government Services: The Case of Nav Canada'. *Canadian Public Administration* 42, no. 3: 371–86.

Low, D. (2012). *Behavioural Economics and Policy Design: Examples from Singapore*. Singapore; Hackensack, NJ: World Scientific.

Lowi, T. J. (1966). 'Distribution, Regulation, Redistribution: The Functions of Government'. In R. B. Ripley (ed.), *Public Policies and Their Politics: Techniques of Government Control*. New York: W. W. Norton, 27–40.

Lowi, T. J. (1969). *The End of Liberalism: Ideology, Policy and the Crisis of Public Authority*. New York: Norton.

Lowi, T. J. (1972). 'Four Systems of Policy, Politics and Choice'. *Public Administration Review* 32, no. 4: 298–310.

Lowi, T. J. (1985). 'The State in Politics: The Relation between Policy and Administration'. In R. G. Noll (ed.), *Regulatory Policy and the Social Sciences*. Berkeley, CA: University of California Press, 67–105.

Lowndes, V. and C. Skelcher. (1998). 'The Dynamics of Multi-Organizational Partnerships: An Analysis of Changing Modes of Governance'. *Public Administration* 76: 313–33.

Lowry, R. C. (1999). 'Foundation Patronage toward Citizen Groups and Think Tanks: Who Gets Grants?' *The Journal of Politics* 81, no. 3: 758–76.

Lunn, P. D. (2013). 'Behavioural Economics and Policymaking: Learning from the Early Adopters'. *The Economic and Social Review* 43, no. 3 (Autumn): 423–49.

Lunn, P. (2014). *Regulatory Policy and Behavioural Economics*. Paris, France: Organisation for Economic Co-operation and Development. www.oecd-ilibrary.org/content/book/9789264207851-en.

Lutz, S. (2003). *Convergence within National Diversity: A Comparative Perspective on the Regulatory State in Finance* (Discussion Paper 03/7). Cologne, Germany: Max Planck Institute for the Study of Societies.

Lybecker, K. M. and R. A. Freeman. (2013). 'Funding Pharmaceutical Innovation Through Direct Tax Credits'. *Health Economics, Politics and Law* 2, no. 3: 267–84.

Lyden, F. J., G. A. Shipman and R. W. Wilkinson. (1968). 'Decision-Flow Analysis: A Methodology for Studying the Public Policy-Making Process'. In P. P. Le Breton (ed.), *Comparative Administrative Theory*. Seattle, WA: University of Washington Press, 155–68.

Lynn Jr, L. E. (1978). *Knowledge and Policy: The Uncertain Connection*. Washington, DC: National Academy of Sciences.

Lynn Jr, L. E. (1980). *Designing Public Policy: A Casebook on the Role of Policy Analysis*. Tucson, AZ: Goodyear Publishing.

Lynn Jr, L. E. (1986). 'The Behavioral Foundations of Public Policy-Making'. *The Journal of Business* 59, no. 4: S379–84.

Lynn Jr, L. E. (2001). 'Globalization and Administrative Reform: What is Happening in Theory?' *Public Management Review* 3, no. 2: 191–208.

Lynn Jr, L. E. (2012). 'The Many Faces of Governance: Adaptation? Transformation? Both? Neither?' In D. Levi-Faur (ed.), *The Oxford Handbook of Governance*, Oxford: Oxford University Press, 49–64.

McAllister, L. K. (2009). 'Dimensions of Enforcement Style: Factoring in Autonomy and Capacity'. *Law and Policy* 32, no. 1: 61–78.

McAllister, L. K., B. V. Rooij and R. A. Kagan. (2010). 'Reorienting Regulation: Pollution Enforcement in Industrializing Countries'. *Law and Policy* 32, no. 1: 1–13.

McArthur, D. (2007). 'Policy Analysis in Provincial Governments in Canada: From PPBS to Network Management'. In L. Dobuzinskis, M. Howlett and D. Laycock (eds), *Policy Analysis in Canada: The State of the Art*. Toronto, ON: University of Toronto Press, 132–45.

MacAvoy, P., W. T. Stanbury, G. Yarrow and R. Zeckhauser. (1989). *Privatization and State-Owned Enterprises: Lessons from the United States, Great Britain and Canada*. Boston, MA: Kluwer Academic Publishers.

McCalley, T., F. Kaiser, C. Midden, M. Keser and M. Teunissen. (2006). 'Persuasive Appliances: Goal Priming and Behavioral Response to Product-Integrated Energy Feedback'. In W. A. IJsselsteijn, Y. A. W. de Kort, C. Midden, B. Eggen and E. van den Hoven (eds), *Persuasive Technology*, Lecture Notes in Computer Science 3962. Berlin/Heidelberg, Germany: Springer, 45–9.

McConnell, A. (2010). *Understanding Policy Success: Rethinking Public Policy*. Basingstoke, UK: Palgrave Macmillan.

McCool, D. (1998). 'The Subsystem Family of Concepts: A Critique and a Proposal'. *Political Research Quarterly* 51, no. 2: 551–70.

McCourt, W. and M. Minogue (eds). (2001). *The Internationalization of Public Management: Reinventing the Third World State*. Cheltenham, UK: Edward Elgar.

McCrudden, C. (2004). 'Using Public Procurement to Achieve Social Outcomes'. *Natural Resources Journal* 28: 257–67.

McCubbins, M. D. and A. Lupia. (1994). 'Learning from Oversight: Fire Alarms and Policy Patrols Reconstructed'. *Journal of Law, Economics and Organization* 10, no.1: 96–125.

McCubbins, M. D., R. G. Noll and B. R. Weingast. (1987). 'Administrative Procedures as Instruments of Political Control'. *Journal of Law, Economics and Organization* 3, no. 2: 243–77.

McCubbins, M. D. and T. Schwartz. (1984). 'Congressional Oversight Overlooked: Policy Patrols versus Fire Alarms'. *American Journal of Political Science* 28, no. 1: 165–79.

McDavid, J. C. and E. G. Clemens. (1995). 'Contracting Out Local Government Services: The BC Experience'. *Canadian Public Administration* 38, no. 2: 177–93.

McDermott, R. (1992). 'Prospect Theory in International Relations: The Iranian Hostage Rescue Mission'. *Political Psychology* 13, no. 2: 237–63.

McDonnell, L. M. and R. F. Elmore. (1987). *Alternative Policy Instruments*. Santa Monica, CA: Center for Policy Research in Education.

McFarland, A. S. (1991). 'Interest Groups and Political Time: Cycles in America'. *British Journal of Political Science* 21, no. 3: 257–84.

McGann, J. G. and E. C. Johnson. (2005). *Comparative Think Tanks, Politics and Public Policy*. Cheltenham, UK: Edward Elgar.

McGann, J. G., A. Viden and J. Rafferty. (2014). *How Think Tanks Shape Social Development Policies*. Philadelphia, PA: University of Pennsylvania Press.

McGarity, T. O. (1991). *Reinventing Rationality: The Role of Regulatory Analysis in the Federal Bureaucracy*. New York: Cambridge University Press.

McGoldrick, D. E. and A. V. Boonn. (2010). 'Public Policy to Maximize Tobacco Cessation'. *American Journal of Preventive Medicine* 38, no. 3, Supplement 1 (March): S327–S332.

McGuire, M. (2002). 'Managing Networks: Propositions on What Managers Do and Why They Do It'. *Public Administration Review* 62, no. 5: 599–609.

McInerney, D., R. Lempert and K. Keller. (2012). 'What Are Robust Strategies in the Face of Uncertain Climate Threshold Responses?' *Climatic Change* 112, nos 3–4 (3 January): 547–68.

McKelvey, B. (1978). 'Organizational Systematics: Taxonomic Lessons from Biology'. *Management Science* 24, no. 13: 1428–40.

McKelvey, B. (1982). *Organizational Systematics: Taxonomy, Evolution, Classification*. Berkeley, CA: University of California Press.

McKenna, J. and A. Cooper. (2006). 'Sacred Cows in Coastal Management: The Need for a "Cheap and Transitory" Model'. *Area* 38, no. 4: 421–31.

McKenzie, C. R. M., M. J. Liersch and S. R. Finkelstein. (2006). 'Recommendations Implicit in Policy Defaults'. *Psychological Science* 17, 5: 414–20.

McKirnan, D. J. (1980). 'The Identification of Deviance: A Conceptualization and Initial Test of a Model of Social Norms'. *European Journal of Social Psychology* 10, no. 1: 75–93.

Macmillan, R. (2010). *The Third Sector Delivering Public Services: An Evidence Review*, Working Paper 20. Birmingham: Third Sector Research Centre.

McMillin, W. D. and J. S. Fackler. (1984). 'Monetary vs Credit Aggregates: An Evaluation of Monetary Policy Targets'. *Southern Economic Journal* 50, no. 3: 711–23.

McNees, S. K. (1990). 'The Role of Judgment in Macroeconomic Forecasting Accuracy'. *International Journal of Forecasting* 6, no. 3: 287–99.

MacRae, D. (1991). 'Policy Analysis and Knowledge Use'. *Knowledge and Policy* 4, no. 3: 27–40.

MacRae, D. and D. Whittington. (1997). *Expert Advice for Policy Choice: Analysis and Discourse*. Washington, DC: Georgetown University Press.

MacRae Jr, D. and A. James. (1985). *Wilde. Policy Analysis for Public Decisions*. Lanham, MD: University Press of America.

McWilliams, W. C. (1971). 'On Political Illegitimacy'. *Public Policy* 19, no. 3: 444–54.

Maddison, S. (2005). 'Democratic Constraint and Embrace: Implications for Progressive Non-Government Advocacy Organisations in Australia'. *Australian Journal of Political Science* 40, no. 3: 373–89.

Madrian, B. C. (2014). 'Applying Insights from Behavioral Economics to Policy Design'. *Annual Review of Economics* 6, no. 1: 663–88.

Mahoney, C. and M. J. Beckstrand. (2009). 'Following the Money: EU Funding of Civil Society Organizations'. Paper presented to the ECPR Joint Sessions of Workshops, Potsdam, Germany.

353

BIBLIOGRAPHY

Mahoney, J. and Thelen, K. (2010). *A Theory of Gradual Institutional Change. Explaining Institutional Change: Ambiguity, Agency, and Power, 1.* Cambridge: Cambridge University Press.

Majone, G. (1975). 'On the Notion of Political Feasibility'. *European Journal of Political Research* 3: 259–74.

Majone, G. (1976). 'Choice among Policy Instruments for Pollution Control'. *Policy Analysis* 2, no. 4: 589–613.

Majone, G. (1989). *Evidence, Argument, and Persuasion in the Policy Process*: New Haven, CT: Yale University Press.

Majone, G. (1997). 'From the Positive to the Regulatory State: Causes and Consequences of Changes in the Mode of Governance'. *Journal of Public Policy*, 17 no. 2: 139–67.

Majone, G. (2005). 'Strategy and Structure: The Political Economy of Agency Independence and Accountability'. In *Designing Independent and Accountable Regulatory Authorities for High Quality Regulation – Proceedings of an Expert Meeting in London, United Kingdom, 10–11 January 2005.* Paris: OECD Working Party on Regulatory Management and Reform, 126–55.

Maley, M. (2000). 'Conceptualising Advisers' Policy Work: The Distinctive Policy Roles of Ministerial Advisers in the Keating Government, 1991–96'. *Australian Journal of Political Science* 35, no. 3: 449.

Malloy, J. (1989). 'What Makes a State Advocacy Structure Effective? Conflicts Between Bureaucratic and Social Movements Criteria'. *Governance* 12, no. 3: 267–88.

Malloy, J. (2003). *Colliding Worlds: The Inherent Ambiguity of Government Agencies for Aboriginal and Women's Policy.* Toronto, ON: University of Toronto Press: IPAC Series in Public Management and Governance.

Mandell, M. P. (1994). 'Managing Interdependencies through Program Structures: A Revised Paradigm'. *American Review of Public Administration* 25, no. 1: 99–121.

Mandell, M. P. (2000). 'A Revised Look at Management in Network Structures'. *International Journal of Organizational Theory and Behavior* 3, nos 1/2: 185–210.

Mandell, S. (2008). 'Optimal Mix of Emissions Taxes and Cap-and-Trade'. *Journal of Environmental Economics and Management* 56: 131–40.

Manitoba Office of the Provincial Auditor. (2001). *A Review of the Policy Development Capacity within Government Departments.* Winnipeg, Canada: Queen's Printer.

Mann, C. and A. Simons. (2014). 'Local Emergence and International Developments of Conservation Trading Systems: Innovation Dynamics and Related Problems'. *Environmental Conservation* 42, no. 4: 1–10.

Mann, S. and H. Wustemann. (2010). 'Public Goverance of Information Asymmetries: The Gap between Reality and Economic Theory'. *The Journal of Socio-Economics* 39, no. 2: 278–85.

Manor, J. (2013). 'Post-Clientelist Initiatives'. In *Democratization in the Global South. International Political Economy.* London: Palgrave Macmillan, 243–53.

Manwaring, R. (2018). 'Understanding Impact in Policy Advisory Systems: The Australian Case of the "Thinker in Residence"'. *International Journal of Public Administration* 41, no. 11: 868–79.

Maor, M. (2012a). 'Policy Overreaction'. *Journal of Public Policy* 32, no. 3: 231–59.

Maor, M. (2012b). *Risk and Policy Underreaction.* Unpublished paper.

Maor, M. (2014a). 'Policy Bubbles: Policy Overreaction and Positive Feedback'. *Governance* 27, no. 3: 469–87.

Maor, M. (2014b). 'Policy Persistence, Risk Estimation and Policy Underreaction'. *Policy Sciences* 47, no. 4: 425–43.

Maor, M. (2015). 'Emotion-Driven Negative Policy Bubbles'. *Policy Sciences* 49, no. 2 (1 September): 191–210.

Maor, M. (2016). 'The Implications of the Emerging Disproportionate Policy Perspective for the New Policy Design Studies'. *Policy Sciences* (19 July): 1–16.

March, J. G. (1981). 'Decision Making Perspective: Decisions in Organizations and Theories of Choice'. In A. H. van de Ven and W. F. Joyce (eds), *Perspectives on Organization Design and Behaviour*. New York: Wiley.

March, J. G. (1994). *A Primer on Decision-Making: How Decisions Happen*. New York: Free Press.

March, J. G. and J. P. Olsen. (1979). *Ambiguity and Choice in Organizations*. Bergen, Norway: Universitetsforlaget.

March, J. G. and J. P. Olsen. (1983). 'Organizing Political Life: What Administrative Reorganization Tells Us about Government'. *American Political Science Review* 77, no. 2: 281–96.

March, J. G. and J. P. Olsen. (1984). 'The New Institutionalism: Organizational Factors in Political Life'. *American Political Science Review* 78: 734–49.

March, J. G. and J. P. Olsen. (1989). *Rediscovering Institutions*. New York: Free Press.

March, J. G. and J. P. Olsen. (1994). 'Institutional Perspectives on Political Institutions'. Berlin, Germany: International Political Science Association, 5.

March, J. G. and J. P. Olsen. (1996). 'Institutional Perspectives on Political Institutions'. *Governance* 9, no. 3: 247–64.

March, J. G. and J. P. Olsen. (2004). *The Logic of Appropriateness*. In M. Rein, M. Moran and R. E. Goodin (eds), *Handbook of Public Policy*. Oxford: Oxford University Press.

Marchildon, G. F. (2007). 'Royal Commissions and the Policy Cycle in Canada: The Case of Health Care'. In J. Hans, M. Donald, C. Story and J. S. Steeves (eds), *Political Leadership and Representation in Canada*. Toronto, ON: University of Toronto Press.

Margerum, R. D. (2008). 'A Typology of Collaboration Efforts in Environmental Management'. *Environmental Management* 41: 487–500.

Marier, P. (2008). 'Empowering Epistemic Communities: Specialized Politicians, Policy Experts and Policy Reform'. *West European Politics* 31, no. 3: 513–33.

Marier, P. (2009). 'The Power of Institutionalized Learning: The Uses and Practices of Commissions to Generate Policy Change'. *Journal of European Public Policy* 16, no. 8: 1204–23.

Marin, B. and R. Mayntz (eds) (1991). *Policy Networks: Empirical Evidence and Theoretical Considerations*. Boulder, CO: Westview Press.

Marion, R. (1999). *The Edge of Organization: Chaos and Complexity Theories of Formal Social Systems*. London: Sage.

Markoff, J. and V. Montecinos. (1993). 'The Ubiquitous Rise of Economists'. *Journal of Public Policy* 13, no. 1: 37–68.

Marriott, L. (2010). 'Power and Ideas: The Development of Retirement Savings Taxation in Australasia'. *Critical Perspectives on Accounting* 21, no. 7: 597–610.

Marsh, D. (1991). 'Privatization under Mrs Thatcher: A Review of the Literature'. *Public Administration* 69, no. 4: 459–80.

Marsh, D. and A. McConnell. (2010). 'Towards a Framework for Establishing Policy Success'. *Public Administration* 88, no. 2: 564–83.

Martikke, S. and C. Moxham. (2010). 'Public Sector Commissioning: Experiences of Voluntary Organizations Delivering Health and Social Services'. *International Journal of Public Administration* 33: 790–99.

Marx, S. M. and E. U. Weber. (2011). 'Decision Making Under Climate Uncertainty: The Power of Understanding Judgment and Decision Processes'. In T. Dietz, and D. Bidwell (eds), *Climate Change in the Great Lakes Region: Navigating an Uncertain Future*. East Lansing, MI: MSU Press.

Maslove, A. M. (1978). 'The Other Side of Public Spending: Tax Expenditures in Canada'. In G. B. Doern, and A. M. Maslove (eds), *The Public Evaluation of Government Spending*. Montreal, QC: Institute for Research on Public Policy, 149–68.

Maslove, A. M. (1983). 'Loans and Loan Guarantees: Business as Usual Versus the Politics of Risk'. In G. B. Doern (ed.), *How Ottawa Spends: The Liberals, the Opposition and Federal Priorities*. Toronto, ON: James Lorimer, 121–32.

Massey, E. and D. Huitema. (2013). 'The Emergence of Climate Change Adaptation as a Policy Field: The Case of England'. *Regional Environmental Change* 13, no. 2: 341–52.

Matheson, C. (2000). 'Policy Formulation in Australian Government: Vertical and Horizontal Axes'. *Australian Journal of Public Administration* 59, no. 2 (1 June): 44–55.

Mathijssen, J., A. Petersen, P. Besseling, A. Rahman and H. Don (eds). (2007). *Dealing with Uncertainty in Policy Making*. CPB/PBL/Rand Europe, Final Report of the Conference Dealing with Uncertainty in Policy Making, The Hague, Netherlands, 16–17 May 2006.

Mathur, N. and C. Skelcher. (2007). 'Evaluating Democratic Performance Methodologies for Assessing the Relationship between Network Governance and Citizens'. *Public Administration Review* 67, no. 2: 228–37.

Matland, R. E. (1995). 'Synthesizing the Implementation Literature: The Ambiguity-Conflict Model of Policy Implementation'. *Journal of Public Administration Research and Theory* 5, no. 2: 145–74.

Maxim, L. and J. P. van der Sluijs. (2011). 'Quality in Environmental Science for Policy: Assessing Uncertainty as a Component of Policy Analysis'. *Environmental Science & Policy* 14, no. 4 (June): 482–92.

May, P. J. (1981). 'Hints for Crafting Alternative Policies'. *Policy Analysis* 7, no. 2: 227–44.

May, P. J. (1991). 'Reconsidering Policy Design: Policies and Publics'. *Journal of Public Policy* 11, no. 2: 187–206.

May, P. J. (1992). 'Policy Learning and Failure'. *Journal of Public Policy* 12: 331–54.

May, P. J. (1993). 'Mandate Design and Implementation: Enhancing Implementation Efforts and Shaping Regulatory Styles'. *Journal of Policy Analysis and Management* 12, no. 4: 634–63.

May, P. J. (1996). 'Coercive Versus Cooperative Policies: Comparing Intergovernmental Mandate Performance'. *Journal of Policy Analysis and Management* 15, no. 2: 171–206.

May, P. J. (1999). 'Fostering Policy Learning: A Challenge for Public Administration'. *International Review of Public Administration* 4, no. 1: 21–31.

May, P. J. (2002). 'Social Regulation'. In L. M. Salamon (eds), *The Tools of Government: A Guide to the New Governance*. New York: Oxford University Press, 156–85.

May, P. J. (2003). 'Policy Design and Implementation'. In B. G. Peters, and J. Pierre (eds), *Handbook of Public Administration*. Beverly Hills, CA: Sage, 223–33.

May, P. J. (2005a). 'Policy Maps and Political Feasibility'. In I. Geva-May (ed.), *Thinking Like a Policy Analyst: Policy Analysis as a Clinical Profession*. London: Palgrave Macmillan, 127–51.

May, P. J. (2005b). 'Regulation and Compliance Motivations: Examining Different Approaches'. *Public Administration Review* 65, no. 1: 31–44.

May, P. J. (2007). 'Regulatory Regimes and Accountability'. *Regulation and Governance* 1, no. 1: 8–26.

May, P. J. and J. W. Handmer. (1992). 'Regulatory Policy Design: Co-operative versus Deterrent Mandates'. *Australian Journal of Public Administration* 51, no. 1: 45–53.

May, P. J. and A. E. Jochim. (2013). 'Policy Regime Perspective: Policies, Politics and Governing'. *Policy Studies Journal* 39: 285–305.

May, P. J. and S. Winter. (1999). 'Regulatory Enforcement and Compliance: Examining Danish Agro-Environmental Policy'. *Journal of Policy Analysis and Management* 18, no. 4: 625–51.

May, P. J., J. Saptichne and S. Workman. (2005). 'Policy Coherence and Policy Design'. In *Annual Research Meeting of the Association for Public Analysis and Management*. Washington, DC.

May, P. J., B. D. Jones, B. E. Beem, E. A. Neff-Sharum and M. K. Poague. (2005). 'Policy Coherence and Component-Driven Policymaking: Arctic Policy in Canada and the United States'. *Policy Studies Journal* 33, no. 1: 37–63.

May, P. J. J. Sapotichne and S. Workman. (2009). 'Widespread Policy Disruption: Terrorism, Public Risks, and Homeland Security'. *The Policy Studies Journal* 37, no. 2: 171–94.

Mayer, I., P. Bots and E. van Daalen. (2004). 'Perspectives on Policy Analysis: A Framework for Understanding and Design'. *International Journal of Technology, Policy and Management* 4, no. 1: 169–91.

Mayntz, R. (1975). 'Legitimacy and the Directive Capacity of the Political System'. In Leon N. Lindberg, Robert Alford, Colin Crouch and Claus Offe (eds), *Stress and Contradiction in Modern Capitalism*. Lexington, MA: Lexington Books, 261–74.

Mayntz, R. (1979). 'Public Bureaucracies and Policy Implementation'. *International Social Science Journal* 31, no 4: 633–45.

Mayntz, R. (1983). 'The Conditions of Effective Public Policy: A New Challenge for Policy Analysis'. *Policy & Politics* 11 (April): 123–43.

Mayntz, R. (1993). 'Modernization and the Logic of Interorganizational Networks'. In J. C. M. Crozier and R. Mayntz (eds), *Societal Change between Market and Organization*. Aldershot, UK: Avebury, 3–18.

Mazmanian, D. M. and P. A. Sabatier. (1983). *Implementation and Public Policy*. Glenview, IL: Scott, Foresman, 21–5.

Mees, H L. P., J. Dijk, D. van Soest, P. P. J. Driessen, M. H. F. M. W. van Rijswick and H. Runhaar. (2014). 'A Method for the Deliberate and Deliberative Selection of Policy Instrument Mixes for Climate Change Adaptation'. *Ecology and Society* 19, no. 2.

Mees, P. (2005). 'Privatization of Rail and Tram Services in Melbourne: What Went Wrong?' *Transport Reviews* 25, no. 4: 433–49.

Meijers, E. (2004). 'Policy Integration: A Literature Review'. In D. Stead, H. Geerlings and E. Meijers (eds), *Policy Integration in Practice: The Integration of Land Use*

Planning, Transport and Environmental Policy-Making in Denmark, England and Germany. Delft, Netherlands: Delft University Press: 9–24.

Meijers, E. and D. Stead. (2004). 'Policy Integration: What Does It Mean and How Can It Be Achieved? A Multi-Disciplinary Review'. In *2004 Berlin Conference on the Human Dimensions of Global Environmental Change: Greening of Policies – Interlinkages and Policy Integration.* Berlin, Germany: 1–15.

Meltsner, A. J. (1972). 'Political Feasibility and Policy Analysis'. *Public Administration Review* 32: 859–67.

Meltsner, A. J. (1975). 'Bureaucratic Policy Analysts'. *Policy Analysis* 1, no. 1: 115–31.

Meltsner, A. J. (1976). *Policy Analysts in the Bureaucracy.* Berkeley, CA: University of California Press.

Menahem, G. and R. Stein. (2013). 'High-Capacity and Low-Capacity Governance Networks in Welfare Services Delivery: A Typology and Empirical Examination of the Case of Israeli Municipalities'. *Public Administration* 91, no. 1: 211–31.

Menard, C. and M. Ghertman. (2009). *Regulation, Deregulation, Reregulation: Institutional Perspectives.* Cheltenham, UK: Edward Elgar.

Mendes, L. M. Z. and G. Santos. (2008). 'Using Economic Instruments to Address Emissions from Air Transport in the European Union'. *Environment and Planning A* 40: 189–209.

Merelman, R. M. (1966). 'Learning and Legitimacy'. *American Political Science Review* 60, no. 3: 548–61.

Merton, R. K. (1936). 'The Unanticipated Consequences of Purposive Social Action'. *American Sociology Review* 6: 1894–1904.

Merton, R. K. (1948a). 'The Role of Applied Social Science in the Formation of Policy: A Research Memorandum'. *Philosophy of Science* 16, no. 3: 161–81.

Merton, R. K. (1948b). 'The Self-Fulfilling Prophecy'. *The Antioch Review* 8, no. 2: 193–210.

Meseguer, C. (2003). 'The Diffusion of Privatization in OECD and Latin America Countries: What Role for Learning?' Paper presented at the Conference on The Internationalization of Regulatory Reforms, Berkeley, CA, 25–6 April.

Meseguer, C. (2005). 'Policy Learning, Policy Diffusion and the Making of a New Order'. *Annals of the American Academy of Political and Social Science* 598, no. 1: 67–82.

Meseguer, C. (2006). 'Rational Learning and Bounded Learning in the Diffusion of Policy Innovations'. *Rationality and Society* 18, no. 1: 35–66.

Metcalfe, L. (2000). 'Reforming the Commission: Will Organizational Efficiency Produce Effective Governance?' *Journal of Common Market Studies* 38, no. 5: 817–41.

van Meter, D. and C. van Horn. (1975). 'The Policy Implementation Process: A Conceptual Framework'. *Administration and Society* 6: 445–88.

Meuleman, L. (2009). 'Metagoverning Governance Styles: Increasing the Public Manager's Toolbox'. Paper presented at The ECPR General Conference, Potsdam.

Meuleman, L. (2010a). 'The Cultural Dimension of Metagovernance: Why Governance Doctrines May Fail'. *Public Organization Review* 10, no. 1: 49–70.

Meuleman, L. (2010b). *Public Management and the Metagovernance of Hierarchies, Networks and Markets: The Feasibility of Designing and Managing Governance Style Combinations.* Heidelberg, Germany: Physica-Verlag.

Meyer, A. D. (1982). 'Adapting to Environmental Jolts'. *Administrative Science Quarterly* 27: 515–37.

Meyer, J. L., P. C. Frumhoff, S. P. Hamburg and C. de la Rosa. (2010). 'Above the Din but in the Fray: Environmental Scientists as Effective Advocates'. *Frontiers in Ecology and the Environment* 8: 299–305.

Mickwitz, P. (2003). 'A Framework for Evaluating Environmental Policy Instruments: Context and Key Concepts'. *Evaluation* 9, no. 4: 415–36.

Mickwitz, P. H. H. and P. Kivimaa. (2008). 'The Role of Policy Instruments in the Innovation and Diffusion of Environmentally Friendlier Technologies: Popular Claims versus Case Study Experiences'. *Journal of Cleaner Production* 16, no. 1 (January): S162–S170.

Middleton, P. (2007). *A Brief Guide to the End of Oil*. London: Robinson.

Mikenberg, M. (2001). 'The Radical Right in Public Office: Agenda-Setting and Policy Effects'. *West European Politics* 24, no. 4: 1–21.

Milkman, K. L., M. C. Mazza, L. L. Shu, C. Tsay and M. H. Bazerman. (2011). 'Policy Bundling to Overcome Loss Aversion: A Method for Improving Legislative Outcomes'. *Organizational Behavior and Human Decision Processes* 117, no. 1: 158–67.

Miller, D. B. and L. Rudnick. (2011). 'Trying It on for Size: Design and International Public Policy'. *Design Issues* 27, no. 2 (1 April): 6–16.

Miller, R. W. (1978). 'Methodological Individualism and Social Explanation'. *Philosophy of Science* 45, no. 3: 387–414.

Miller, S. E. and B. F. Mannix. (2016). 'One Standard to Rule Them All: The Disparate Impact of Energy Efficiency Regulations'. In S. Abdukadirov (eds), *Nudge Theory in Action*. Cham, Germany: Springer, 251–87.

Miller, S. M., A. Evers and H. Winterberger. (1990). 'The Evolving Welfare State Mixes'. In *Shifts in the Welfare Mix: Their Impact on Work, Social Services and Welfare Policies*. Frankfurt, Germany: Campus Verlag, 371–88.

Mills, A., R. Meek and D. Gojkovic. (2011). 'Exploring the Relationship Between the Voluntary Sector and the State in Criminal Justice'. *Voluntary Sector Review* 2, no. 2: 195–213.

Mills, C. (2013). 'Why Nudges Matter: A Reply to Goodwin'. *Politics* 33, no. 1: 28–36.

Milner, H. V. and R. O. Keohane. (1996). 'Internationalization and Domestic Politics: A Conclusion'. In R. O. Keohane and H. V. Milner (eds), *Internationalization and Domestic Politics*. Cambridge: Cambridge University Press, 243–58.

Milward, H. B. and K. G. Provan. (2000). 'Governing the Hollow State'. *Journal of Public Administration Research and Theory* 10, no. 2: 359–80.

Milward, H. B., K. G. Provan and B. A. Else. (1993). 'What Does the "Hollow State" Look Like?' In B. Bozeman (eds), *Public Management: The State of the Art*. San Francisco, CA: Jossey-Bass, 309–23.

Minogue, M. (2002). 'Governance-Based Analysis of Regulation'. *Annals of Public and Cooperative Economics* 73, no. 4: 649–66.

Mintrom, M. (1997). 'Policy Entrepreneurs and the Diffusion of Innovation'. *American Journal of Political Science* 41, no. 3: 738–70.

Mintrom, M. (2007). 'The Policy Analysis Movement'. In, D., M. Howlett and D. Laycock (eds), *Policy Analysis in Canada: The State of the Art*. Toronto, ON: University of Toronto Press, 71–84.

Mintrom, M. and J. Luetjens. (2016). 'Design Thinking in Policymaking Processes: Opportunities and Challenges'. *Australian Journal of Public Administration* 75, no. 3 (1 July): 391–402.

Mintrom, M. and P. Norman. (2009). 'Policy Entrepreneurship and Policy Change'. *Policy Studies Journal* 37, no. 4: 649–67.

Mintz, A. (1993). 'The Decision to Attack Iraq: A Noncompensatory Theory of Decision Making'. *The Journal of Conflict Resolution* 37, no. 4: 595–618.

Mintz, A. (2004). 'How Do Leaders Make Decisions? A Poliheuristic Perspective'. *The Journal of Conflict Resolution* 48, no. 1, 3–13.

Mintz, A., N. Geva, S. B. Redd and A. Carnes. (1997). 'The Effect of Dynamic and Static Choice Sets on Political Decision Making: An Analysis Using the Decision Board Platform'. *The American Political Science Review* 91, no. 3: 553–66.

Mitnick, B. M. (1978). 'The Concept of Regulation'. *Bulletin of Business Research* 53, no. 5: 1–20.

Mitnick, B. M. (1980). *The Political Economy of Regulation: Creating, Designing and Removing Regulatory Forms*. New York: Columbia University Press, 401–4.

Mittenzwei, K., T. Persson, M. Höglind and S. Kværnø. (2017). 'Combined Effects of Climate Change and Policy Uncertainty on the Agricultural Sector in Norway'. *Agricultural Systems* 153 (May): 118–26.

Mizrahi, S. (2012). 'Self-Provision of Public Services: Its Evolution and Impact'. *Public Administration Review* 72, no. 2: 285–91.

Moffet, J. and F. Bregha. (1999). 'Non-Regulatory Environmental Measures'. In R. B. Gibson (eds), *Voluntary Initiatives: The New Politics of Corporate Greening*. Peterborough, ON: Broadview Press, 15–31.

Mols, F., S. A. Haslam, J. Jetten and N. K. Steffens. (2015). 'Why a Nudge Is Not Enough: A Social Identity Critique of Governance by Stealth'. *European Journal of Political Research* 54, no. 1: 81–98.

Mondou, M. and É. Montpetit. (2010). 'Policy Styles and Degenerative Politics: Poverty Policy Designs in Newfoundland and Quebec'. *Policy Studies Journal* 38, no. 4 (November): 703–22.

Montgomery, J. D. (2000). 'Social Capital as a Policy Resource'. *Policy Sciences* 33: 227–43.

Montpetit, É. (2002). 'Policy Networks, Federal Arrangements, and the Development of Environmental Regulations: A Comparison of the Canadian and American Agricultural Sectors. *Governance* 15, no. 1: 1–20.

Montpetit, É. (2003a). 'Biotechnology, Life Sciences and Policy Networks in the European Union'. *Swiss Political Science Review* 9, no. 2: 127–34.

Montpetit, É. (2003b). *Misplaced Distrust: Policy Networks and the Environment in France, the United States, and Canada*. Vancouver, BC: University of British Columbia Press.

Montpetit, É. (2003c). 'Public Consultations in Policy Network Environments'. *Canadian Public Policy* 29, no. 1: 95–110.

Montpetit, É. (2008). 'Policy Design for Legitimacy: Expert Knowledge, Citizens, Time and Inclusion in the United Kingdom's Biotechnology Sector'. *Public Administration* 86, no. 1: 259–77.

Moon, M. J., J. Lee and C. Roh. (2014). 'The Evolution of Internal IT Applications and E-Government Studies in Public Administration Research Themes and Methods'. *Administration & Society* 46, no. 1 (1 January): 3–36.

de Moor, A. P. G. (1997). *Perverse Incentives: Hundreds of Billions of Dollars in Subsidies now Harm the Economy, the Environment, Equity and Trade*. San Jose, CA: Earth Council.

Moore, D. A. and P. J. Healy. (2008). 'The Trouble with Overconfidence'. *Psychological Review* 115, no. 2: 502–17.

Moore, M. H. (1988). 'What Sort of Ideas Become Public Ideas?' In R. B. Reich (eds), *The Power of Public Ideas*. Cambridge, MA: Ballinger, 55–83.

Moran, M. (2002). 'Review Article: Understanding the Regulatory State'. *British Journal of Political Science* 32, no. 2: 391–413.

Morgan, M. G. and M. Henrion. (1990). *Uncertainty: A Guide to Dealing with Uncertainty in Quantitative Risk and Policy Analysis*. Cambridge: Cambridge University Press.

Moseley, A. and G. Stoker. (2015). 'Putting Public Policy Defaults to the Test: The Case of Organ Donor Registration'. *International Public Management Journal* 18, no. 2 (3 April): 246–64.

Moseley, A. and S. Tierney. (2004). 'Evidence-Based Practice in the Real World'. *Evidence & Policy* 1, no. 1: 113–19.

Mosley, L. (2003). *Global Capital and National Governments*. New York: Cambridge University Press.

Moss, D. A. (2002). *When All Else Fails: Government as the Ultimate Risk Manager*. Cambridge, MA: Harvard University Press.

de la Mothe, J. (1996). 'One Small Step in an Uncertain Direction: The Science and Technology Review and Public Administration in Canada'. *Canadian Public Administration* 39, no. 3: 403–17.

Moxey, A., B. White and A. Ozanne. (1999). 'Efficient Contract Design for Agri-Environment Policy'. *Journal of Agricultural Economics* 50, no. 2: 187–202.

Moynihan, D. P. (2008). 'Combining Structural Forms in the Search for Policy Tools: Incident Command Systems in US Crisis Management'. *Governance* 21, no. 2: 205–29.

Moynihan, D. P. (2009a). 'From Intercrisis to Intracrisis Learning'. *Journal of Contingencies and Crisis Management* 17, no. 3: 189–98.

Moynihan, D. P. (2009b). 'The Network Governance of Crisis Response: Case Studies of Incident Command Systems'. *Journal of Public Adminstration Research and Theory* 19, no. 4 (1 October): 895–915.

Mucciaroni, G. (1992). 'The Garbage Can Model And the Study of Policymaking: A Critique'. *Polity* 24, no. 3: 460–82.

Mueller, C. (1973). *The Politics of Communication: A Study in the Political Sociology of Language, Socialization and Legitimation*. New York: Oxford University Press.

Mueller, D. (2011). 'Antecedences and Determinants of Improvisation in Firms'. *Problems and Perspectives in Management* 9, no. 4: 117–30.

Mueller, J. (2005). 'Simplicity and Spook: Terrorism and the Dynamics of Threat Exaggeration'. *International Studies Perspectives* 6, no. 2: 208–34.

Mukherjee, I. and S. Giest. (2017). 'Designing Policies in Uncertain Contexts: Entrepreneurial Capacity and the Case of the European Emission Trading Scheme'. *Public Policy and Administration*, 20 September. Forthcoming.

Mukherjee, I. and M. Howlett. (2015). 'Who Is a Stream? Epistemic Communities, Instrument Constituencies and Advocacy Coalitions in Public Policy-Making'. *Politics and Governance* 3, no. 2: 65–75.

Mukherjee, I., B. G. Peters, M. Chou, P. Ravinet, M. Howlett and G. Capano. (2018). *Designing for Policy Effectiveness: Defining and Understanding a Concept*. Elements Series. Cambridge: Cambridge University Press.

Mulder, K. F. (2007). 'Innovation for Sustainable Development: From Environmental Design to Transition Management'. *Sustainability Science* 2, no. 2: 253–63.

Mulgan, G. (2008). *The Art of Public Strategy: Mobilizing Power and Knowledge for the Common Good*. Oxford; New York: Oxford University Press.

Mullainathan, S. and E. Shafir. (2013). 'Decision Making and Policy in Contexts of Poverty'. In E. Shafir (eds), *The Behavioral Foundations of Public Policy*. Princeton, NJ: Princeton University Press.

Mullainathan, S. and E. Shafir. (2014). *Scarcity: The New Science of Having Less and How It Defines Our Lives* (reprint edn). New York: Picador.

Murphy, J. J., A. Dinar, R. E. Howitt, S. J. Rassenti, V. L. Smith and M. Weinberg. (2009). 'The Design of Water Markets When Instream Flows Have Value'. *Journal of Environmental Management* 90: 1089–96.

Murray, C. (2007). 'The Media'. In L. Dobuzinskis, M. Howlett and D. Laycock (eds), *Policy Analysis in Canada: The State of the Art*. Toronto, ON: University of Toronto Press, 286–97.

Murray, F. (2013). 'The Changing Winds of Atmospheric Environment Policy'. *Environmental Science & Policy* 29 (May): 115–23.

Myers, N. and J. Kent. (2001). *Perverse Subsidies: How Tax Dollars Can Undercut the Environment and the Economy*. Washington, DC: Island Press.

Myles, J. (1989). 'Old Age in the Welfare State: The Political Economy of Public Pensions'. Lawrence, KS: University Press of Kansas.

Nair, S. and M. Howlett. (2015). 'Scaling up of Policy Experiments and Pilots: A Qualitative Comparative Analysis and Lessons for the Water Sector'. *Water Resources Management* 29, no. 14: 4945–61.

Nair, S. and M. Howlett. (2017). 'Policy Myopia as a Source of Policy Failure: Adaptation and Policy Learning under Deep Uncertainty'. *Policy & Politics* 45, no. 1: 103–18.

Natural Resources Canada. (2003). *Corporate Social Responsibility: Lessons Learned*. Ottawa, ON: Natural Resources Canada.

Nelson, M. and J. A. Vucetich. (2009). 'On Advocacy by Environmental Scientists: What, Whether, Why, and How'. *Conservation Biology* 23: 1090–1101.

Nelson, R. (1977). *The Moon and the Ghetto: An Assay on Public Policy Analysis*. Chicago, IL: W. W. Norton.

Nemetz, P. (1986). 'The Fisheries Act and Federal–Provincial Environmental Regulation: Duplication or Complementarity?' *Canadian Public Administration* 29: 401–24.

Newbery, D. M. (2003). 'Network Capacity Auctions: Promise and Problems'. *Utilities Policy* 11: 27–32.

Newman, J. (2001). *Modernising Governance: New Labour Policy and Society*. London; Newbury Park, CA: Sage.

Newman, J. (2014). 'Measuring Policy Success: Case Studies from Canada and Australia'. *Australian Journal of Public Administration* 73, no. 2 (1 June): 192–205.

Newman, J. and B. W. Head. (2015). 'Categories of Failure in Climate Change Mitigation Policy in Australia'. *Public Policy and Administration* 30, nos 3–4: 342–58.

Newman, J. and M. Howlett. (2014). 'Regulation and Time: Temporal Patterns in Regulatory Development'. *International Review of Administrative Sciences* 80, no. 3: 493–511.

Nickerson, R. S. (1998). 'Confirmation Bias: A Ubiquitous Phenomenon in Many Guises'. *Review of General Psychology* 2, no. 2: 175.

Nielsen, A. S. E., A. Sand, P. Sørensen, M.Knutsson, P. Martinsson., E. Persson and C. Wollbrant. (2017). *Nudging and Pro-environmental Behaviour*. Copenhagen, Denmark: Nordic Council of Ministers.

Nilsson, M., A. Jordan, J. Turnpenny, J. Hertin, B. Nykvist and D. Russel. (2008). 'The Use and Non-Use of Policy Appraisal Tools in Public Policy Making: An Analysis of Three European Countries and the European Union'. *Policy Sciences* 41: 335–55.

van Nispen, F. K. M. and A. B. Ringeling. (1998). 'On Instruments and Instrumentality: A Critical Assessment'. In B. G. Peters and F. K. M. V. Nispen (eds), *Public Policy Instruments: Evaluating the Tools of Public Administration*. New York: Edward Elgar, 204–17.

Nohrstedt, D. (2016). 'Collaborative Governance Regimes'. *Public Administration* 94, no. 4: 1157–9.

Nordhaus, W. D. (2015). *The Climate Casino: Risk, Uncertainty, and Economics for a Warming World*. New Haven, CT; London: Yale University Press.

Nowlan, D. M. (1994). 'Local Taxation as an Instrument of Policy'. In F. Frisken (eds), *The Changing Canadian Metropolis: A Public Policy Perspective*. Berkeley, CA: Institute of Governmental Studies, 799–841.

Nownes, A. J. (2000). 'Policy Conflict and the Structure of Interest Communities'. *American Politics Quarterly* 28, no. 3: 309–27.

Nownes, A. J. (2004). 'The Population Ecology of Interest Group Formation: Mobilizing for Gay and Lesbian Rights in the United States, 1950–98'. *British Journal of Political Science* 34, no. 1: 49–67.

Nownes, A. and G. Neeley. (1996). 'Toward an Explanation for Public Interest Group Formation and Proliferation: "Seed Money". Disturbances, Entrepreneurship and Patronage'. *Policy Studies Journal* 24, no. 1: 74–92.

Nutley, S. M., I. Walter and H. T. O. Davies. (2007). *Using Evidence: How Research Can Inform Public Services*. Bristol, UK: Policy Press.

O'Connor, A., G. Roos and T. Vickers-Willis. (2007). 'Evaluating an Australian Public Policy Organization's Innovation Capacity'. *European Journal of Innovation Management* 10, no. 4: 532–58.

O'Donoghue, T. and M. Rabin. (1999). 'Doing It Now or Later'. *The American Economic Review* 89, no. 1: 103–24.

O'Faircheallaigh, C. (2010). 'Public Participation and Environmental Impact Assessment: Purposes, Implications and Lessons for Public Policy Making'. *Environmental Impact Assessment Review* 30: 19–27.

O'Flynn, J. (2007). 'From New Public Management to Public Value: Paradigmatic Change and Managerial Implications'. *Australian Journal of Public Administration* 66, no. 3: 353–66.

O'Toole, L. J. (2000). 'Research on Policy Implementation: Assessment and Prospects'. *Journal of Public Administration Research and Theory* 10, no. 2: 263–88.

O'Toole, L. J. and K. J. Meier. (2010). 'In Defense of Bureaucracy – Public Managerial Capacity, Slack and the Dampening of Environmental Shocks'. *Public Management Review* 12, no. 3: 341.

Öberg, P., M. Lundin and J. Thelander. (2015). 'Political Power and Policy Design: Why Are Policy Alternatives Constrained?' *Policy Studies Journal* 43, no. 1 (1 February): 93–114.

Obinger, H. and U. Wagschal. (2001). 'Families of Nations and Public Policy'. *West European Politics* 24, no. 1: 99–114.

OECD (Organisation for Economic Co-operation and Development). (1995). *Recommendation of the Council of the OECD on Improving the Quality of Government Regulation*. Paris: OECD.

OECD. (1996). *Building Policy Coherence: Tools and Tensions*. Public Management Occasional Papers No. 12. Paris: OECD.

OECD. (1996–7). *Issues and Developments in Public Management: Survey*. Paris: OECD.

OECD. (2011). 'Strategic Agility for Strong Societies and Economies. Summary and Issues for Further Debate'. International Workshop, 10 November, OECD Conference Centre, Paris.

OECD. (2017). *Behavioural Insights and Public Policy*. Paris: OECD.

Offe, C. (2006). 'Political Institutions and Social Power: Conceptual Explorations'. In I. Shapiro, S. Skowronek and D. Galvin (eds), *Rethinking Political Institutions: The Art of the State*. New York: New York University Press, 9–31.

OFGEM (Office of Gas and Electricity Markets). (2011). *Energy Demand Research Project Final Analysis*. Reports and plans. https://www.ofgem.gov.uk/publications-and-updates/energy-demand-research-project-final-analysis.

Oh, C. H. (1997). 'Explaining the Impact of Policy Information on Policy-Making'. *Knowledge and Policy* 10, no. 3: 22–55.

Ohmae, K. (1990). *The Borderless World*. London: Collins.

Oikonomou, V. and C. J. Jepma. (2007). 'A Framework on Interactions of Climate and Energy Policy Instruments'. *Mitigation and Adaptation Strategies for Global Change* 13, no. 2 (15 February): 131–56.

Oikonomou, V., A. Flamos and S. Grafakos. (2010). 'Is Blending of Energy and Climate Policy Instruments Always Desirable?' *Energy Policy* 38, no. 8: 4186–95.

Oikonomou, V., A. Flamos, D. Zeugolis and S. Grafakos. (2011a). 'A Qualitative Assessment of EU Energy Policy Interactions'. *Energy Sources, Part B: Economics, Planning, and Policy* 7, no. 2: 177–87.

Oikonomou, V., A. Flamos, M. Gargiulo, G. Giannakidis, A. Kanudia, E. Spijker and S. Grafakos. (2011b). 'Linking Least-Cost Energy System Costs Models with MCA: An Assessment of the EU Renewable Energy Targets and Supporting Policies'. *Energy Policy* 39, no 5: 2786–99.

Oliphant, S. and M. Howlett. (2010). 'Assessing Policy Analytical Capacity: Comparative Insights from a Study of the Canadian Environmental Policy Advice System'. *Journal of Comparative Policy Analysis: Research and Practice* 12, no. 4: 439.

Oliver, A. (2013). 'From Nudging to Budging: Using Behavioural Economics to Inform Public Sector Policy'. *Journal of Social Policy* 42, no. 4: 685–700.

Oliver, A. (2017). 'Nudges, Shoves and Budges: Behavioural Economic Policy Frameworks'. *The International Journal of Health Planning and Management* 33, no. 1: 272–5.

Oliver, P. E. (1993). 'Formal Models of Collective Action'. *Annual Review of Sociology* 19: 271–300.

Olsen, J. P. (2005). 'Maybe It Is Time to Rediscover Bureaucracy'. *Journal of Public Administration Research and Theory* 16, no. 1: 1–24.

Olsen, J. P. and B. G. Peters (eds). (1996). *Lessons from Experience: Experiential Learning in Administrative Reforms in Eight Democracies*. Oslo, Norway: Scandinavian University Press.

Olson, M. (1965). *The Logic of Collective Action*. Cambridge, MA: Harvard University Press.

d'Ombrain, N. (1997). 'Public Inquiries in Canada'. *Canadian Public Administration* 40, no. 1: 86–107.

Oosterveer, P. (2002). 'Reinventing Risk Politics: Reflexive Modernity and the European BSE Crisis'. *Journal of Environmental Policy and Planning* 4: 215–29.

Optic Optimal Policies for Transportation in Combination. (2014). 'Best Practices and Recommendations on Policy Packaging'. *Annual Review of Policy Design* 2, no. 1 (8 November): 1–10.

Orren, K. and S. Skowronek. (1998). 'Regimes and Regime Building in American Government: A Review of Literature on the 1940s'. *Political Science Quarterly* 113, no. 4: 689–702.

Osborne, D. and E. Gaebler. (1992). *Reinventing Government*. Reading, MA: Addison-Wesley.

Osborne, K., C. Bacchi and C. Mackenzie. (2008). 'Gender Analysis and Community Consultation: The Role of Women's Policy Units'. *Australian Journal of Public Administration* 67, no. 2: 149–60.

Osborne, S. P. (2006). 'The New Public Governance?' *Public Management Review* 8, no. 3: 377–87.

Osborne, S. P. (2010). *The New Public Governance: Emerging Perspectives on the Theory and Practice of Public Governance*. London: Routledge.

Ostrom, E. (1986). 'A Method of Institutional Analysis'. In F. X. Kaufman, G. Majone and V. Ostrom (eds), *Guidance, Control and Evaluation in the Public Sector*. Berlin, Germany: de Gruyter, 459–75.

Ostrom, E. (1996). 'Crossing the Great Divide: Co-Production, Synergy, and Development'. *World Development* 24, no. 6: 1037–87.

Ostrom, E. (1999). 'Institutional Rational Choice: As Assessment of the Institutional Analysis and Development Framework'. In P. A. Sabatier (eds), *Theories of the Policy Process*. Boulder, CO: Westview, 35–71.

Ostrom, E. (2003). 'How Types of Goods and Property Rights Jointly Affect Collective Action'. *Journal of Theoretical Politics* 15, no. 3: 239–70.

Ostrom, E. and R. B. Parks. (1973). 'Suburban Police Departments: Too Many and Too Small?' In B. P. Roger, L. H. Masotti and J. K. Hadden (eds), *The Urbanization of the Suburbs*. Urban Affairs Annual Reviews 7. Beverly Hills, CA: Sage, 367–402.

Ostrom, E., J. Burger, C. B. Field, R. B. Norgaard and D. Policansky. (1999). 'Revisiting the Commons: Local Lessons, Global Challenges'. *Science* 284, no. 5412 (9 April): 278–82.

Ouimet, M., P. Bédard, J. Turgeon, J. N. Lavis, F. Gélineau, F. Gagnon and C. Dallaire. (2010). 'Correlates of Consulting Research Evidence Among Policy Analysts in Government Ministries: A Cross-Sectional Survey'. *Evidence & Policy: A Journal of Research, Debate and Practice* 6, no. 4 (22 November): 433–60.

Overbye, E. (1994). 'Convergence in Policy Outcomes: Social Security Systems in Perspectives'. *Journal of Public Policy* 14, no. 2: 147–74.

Owens, S. and T. Rayner. (1999). '"When Knowledge Matters": The Role and Influence of the Royal Commission on Environmental Pollution'. *Journal of Environmental Policy and Planning* 1: 7–24.

Packwood, A. (2002). 'Evidence-Based Policy: Rhetoric and Reality'. *Social Policy & Society* 1, no. 3: 267–72.

Padberg, D. I. (1992). 'Nutritional Labeling as a Policy Instrument'. *American Journal of Agricultural Economics* 74, no. 5: 1208–13.

Paehlke, R. (1990). 'Regulatory and Non-Regulatory Approaches to Environmental Protection'. *Canadian Public Administration* 33, no. 1: 17–36.

Page, E. C. (2001). *Governing by Numbers: Delegated Legislation and Everyday Policy-Making*. Portland, OR: Hart Publishing.

Page, E. C. (2006). *The Roles of Public Opinion Research in Canadian Government.* Toronto, ON: University of Toronto Press.

Page, E. C. (2010). 'Bureaucrats and Expertise: Elucidating a Problematic Relationship in Three Tableaux and Six Jurisdictions'. *Sociologie du Travail* 52, no. 2: 255–73.

Page, E. C. and B. Jenkins. (2005). *Policy Bureaucracy: Governing with a Cast of Thousands*. Oxford: Oxford University Press.

Painter, M. and J. Pierre (eds). (2005). *Challenges to State Policy Capacity: Global Trends and Comparative Perspectives*. London: Palgrave Macmillan.

Pal, L. A. (1987). *Public Policy Analysis: An Introduction*. Toronto, ON: Methuen.

Pal, L. A. (1993). *Interests of State: The Politics of Language, Multiculturalism and Feminism in Canada*. Montreal, QC; Kingston, ON: McGill-Queen's University Press.

Pal, L. A. (1997). *Beyond Policy Analysis: Public Issue Management in Turbulent Times*. Toronto, ON: ITP Nelson.

Palan, R. and J. Abbott. (1996). *State Strategies in the Global Political Economy*. London: Pinter.

Palumbo, D. J. and D. J. Calista. (1990). 'Opening Up the Black Box: Implementation and the Policy Process'. In D. J. Palumbo and D. J. Calista (eds), *Implementation and the Policy Process*. New York: Greenwood Press.

Papaioannou, H. R. and J. Bassant. (2006). 'Performance Management: Benchmarking as a Policy-Making Tool: From the Private to the Public Sector'. *Science and Public Policy* 33, no. 2: 91–102.

Parks, R. B., P. C. Baker, L. Kiser, R. Oakerson, E. Ostrom, V. Ostrom, S. L. Percy, M. B. Vandivort, G. P. Whitaker and R. Wilson. (1981). 'Consumers as Coproducers of Public Services: Some Economic and Institutional Considerations'. *Policy Studies Journal* 9, no. 7 (1 June): 1001–11.

Parson, E. A. and K. Fisher-Vanden. (1999). 'Joint Implementation of Greenhouse Gas Abatement under the Kyoto Protocol's "Clean Development Mechanism": Its Scope and Limits'. *Policy Sciences* 3: 207–24.

Parsons, W. (1995). *Public Policy: An Introduction to the Theory and Practice of Policy Analysis*. Aldershot, UK; Cheltenham, UK: Edward Elgar.

Parsons, W. (2001). 'Modernising Policy-Making for the Twenty First Century: The Professional Model'. *Public Policy and Administration* 16, no. 3: 93–110.

Parsons, W. (2004). 'Not Just Steering But Weaving: Relevant Knowledge and the Craft of Building Policy Capacity and Coherence'. *Australian Journal of Public Administration* 63, no. 1: 43–57.

Pasquier, M. and J. Villeneuve. (2007). 'Organizational Barriers to Transparency: A Typology and Analysis of Organizational Behaviour Tending to Prevent or Restrict Access to Information'. *International Review of Administrative Sciences* 73, no. 1: 147–62.

Patashnik, E. (2003). 'After the Public Interest Prevails: The Political Sustainability of Reforms'. *Governance* 16, no. 2: 203–34.

Patchen, M. (2010). 'What Shapes Public Reactions to Climate Change? Overview of Research and Policy Implications'. *Analyses of Social Issues and Public Policy* 10, no. 1: 47–68.

Patt, A. G. and D. Schröter. (2008). 'Perceptions of Climate Risk in Mozambique: Implications for the Success of Adaptation Strategies'. *Global Environmental Change* 18, no. 3: 458–67.

Patton, C. V. and D. S. Sawicki. (1993). 'Basic Methods of Policy Analysis and Planning'. Englewood Cliffs, NJ: Prentice Hall.

Pauly, L. W. and S. Reich. (1997). 'National Structures and Multinational Corporate Behaviour: Enduring Differences in the Age of Globalisation'. *International Organization* 51, no. 1: 1–30.

Pautz, M. C. (2009). 'Perceptions of the Regulated Community in Environmental Policy: The View from Below'. *Review of Policy Research* 26, no. 5: 533–50.

Pawson, R. (2002). 'Evidence-Based Policy: In Search of a Method?' *Evaluation* 8, no. 2: 157–81.

Pawson, R. (2006). *Evidence-Based Policy: A Realist Perspective*. London: Sage.

Pawson, R., T. Greenhalgh, G. Harvey and K. Walshe. (2005). 'Realist Review – A New Method of Systematic Review Designed for Complex Policy Interventions'. *Journal of Health Services Research Policy* 10, Supplement 1: S1:21–S1:34.

Pearse, P. H. (1980). 'Property Rights and the Regulation of Commercial Fisheries'. In P. N. Nemetz (eds), *Resource Policy: International Perspectives*. Montreal, QC: Institute for Research on Public Policy, 185–210.

Pedersen, L. H. (2007). 'Ideas Are Transformed as They Transfer: A Comparative Study of Eco-Taxation in Scandinavia'. *Journal of European Public Policy* 14, no. 1: 59–77.

Peled, A. (2002). 'Why Style Matters: A Comparison of Two Administrative Reform Initiatives in the Israeli Public Sector, 1989–98'. *Journal of Public Administration Research and Theory* 12, no. 2: 217–40.

Pellikaan, H. and R. J. van der Veen. (2002). *Environmental Dilemmas and Policy Design*. Cambridge: Cambridge University Press.

Peltzman, S. (1976). 'Toward a More General Theory of Regulation'. *Journal of Law and Economics* 19 (August): 211–40.

Pentland, B. and M. Feldman. (2008). 'Designing Routines: On the Folly of Designing Artifacts, While Hoping for Patterns of Action'. *Information and Organization* 18, no. 4 (October): 235–50.

Perez-Batres, L. A., V. V. Miller and M. J. Pisani. (2011). 'Institutionalizing Sustainability: An Empirical Study of Corporate Registration and Commitment to the United Nations Global Compact Guidelines'. *Journal of Cleaner Production* 19, no. 8: 843–51.

Pérez-Ramírez, M., G. Ponce-Díaz and S. Lluch-Cota. (2012). 'The Role of MSC Certification in the Empowerment of Fishing Cooperatives in Mexico: The Case of Red Rock Lobster Co-Managed Fishery'. *Ocean & Coastal Management* 63 (July): 24–9.

Perl, A. and D. J. White. (2002). 'The Changing Role of Consultants in Canadian Policy Analysis'. *Policy and Society* 21, no. 1: 49–73.

Perrow, C. (1984). *Normal Accidents: Living with High Risk Technologies*. New York: Basic Books.

Perry, J. L. and H. G. Rainey. (1988). 'The Public–Private Distinction in Organization Theory: A Critique and Research Strategy'. *Academy of Management Review* 13, no. 2: 182–201.

Pestoff, V. (2006). 'Citizens and Co-Production of Welfare Services'. *Public Management Review* 8, (December): 503–19.

Pestoff, V. and T. Brandsen. (2010). 'Public Governance and the Third Sector: Opportunities for Co-Production and Innovation?' In S. P. Osborne (eds), *The New Public Governance: Emerging Perspectives on the Theory and Practice of Public Governance*. London: Routledge, 223–37.

Pestoff, V., T. Brandsen and B. Verschuere. (2012). *New Public Governance, the Third Sector and Co-Production*. New York: Routledge.

Pestoff, V., S. P. Osborne and T. Brandsen. (2006). 'Patterns of Co-Production in Public Services'. *Public Management Review* 8 (December): 591–95.

Petek, A. (2011). 'Transformacija politike prema osobama s invaliditetom: analiza ciljeva' (Transformation of Policy for Persons with Disability in Croatia: Analysis of Goals). *Anali Hrvatskog politološkog društva* no. 8: 101–23.

Peters, B. G. (2017). 'Is Governance for Everybody?' *Policy and Society* 33, no. 4 (December): 317–27.

Peters, B. G. (ed.). (1988). *Comparing Public Bureaucracies: Problems of Theory and Method*. Tuscaloosa, AL: University of Alabama Press, 8.

Peters, B. G. (1990). 'Administrative Culture and Analysis of Public Organizations'. *Indian Journal of Public Administration* 36: 420–8.

Peters, B. G. (1992a). 'Government Reorganization: A Theoretical Analysis'. *International Political Science Review* 13, no. 2: 199–218.

Peters, B. G. (1992b). 'The Policy Process: An Institutionalist Perspective'. *Canadian Public Administration* 35, no. 2: 160–80.

Peters, B. G. (1996a). *The Future of Governing: Four Emerging Models*. Lawrence, KS: University Press of Kansas.

Peters, B. G. (1996b). *The Policy Capacity of Government*. Ottawa, ON: Canadian Centre for Management Development.

Peters, B. G. (1996c). 'Theory and Methodology'. In H. A. G. M. Bekke, J. L. Perry and T. A. J. Toonen (eds), *Civil Service Systems in Comparative Perspective*. Bloomington, IN: Indiana University Press. 13–41.

Peters, B. G. (1998). *Managing Horizontal Government: The Politics of Coordination*. Ottawa, ON: Canadian Centre for Management Development.

Peters, B. G. (2000a). 'Policy Instruments and Public Management: Bridging the Gaps'. *Journal of Public Administration Research and Theory* 10, no. 1: 35–48.

Peters, B. G. (2000b). 'Public-Service Reform: Comparative Perspectives'. In E. Lindquist (eds), *Government Restructuring and Career Public Services*. Toronto, ON: Institute of Public Administration of Canada, 27–40.

Peters, B. G. (2001). *The Politics of Bureaucracy*. London; New York: Routledge.

Peters, B. G. (2002). 'Governing in a Market Era: Alternative Models of Governing'. *Public Administration and Public Policy* 99: 85–97.

Peters, B. G. (2004) 'The Search for Coordination and Coherence in Public Policy: Return to the Center?' Unpublished Paper. Pittsburgh, PA: University of Pittsburgh.

Peters, B. G. (2005a). 'Conclusion: The Future of Instruments Research'. In P. Eliadis, M. Hill and M. Howlett (eds), *Designing Government: From Instruments to Governance*. Montreal, QC: McGill-Queen's University Press, 353–63.

Peters, B. G. (2005b). 'The Problem of Policy Problems'. In P. Eliadis, M. Hill and M. Howlett, (eds), *Designing Government: From Instruments to Governance*. Montreal, QC: McGill-Queen's University Press, 77–105 .

Peters, B. G. (2010). 'Meta-Governance and Public Management' In S. P. Osborne (eds), *The New Public Governance: Emerging Perspectives on the Theory and Practice of Public Governance*. London: Routledge, 36–52.

Peters, B. G. and A. Barker. (1993). *Advising West European Governments: Inquiries, Expertise and Public Policy*. Edinburgh, UK: Edinburgh University Press.

Peters, B. G. and J. A. Hoornbeek. (2005). 'The Problem of Policy Problems'. In P. Eliadis, M. Hill and M. Howlett (eds), *Designing Government: From Instruments to Governance*. Montreal, QC: McGill-Queen's University Press, 77–105.

Peters, B. G. and J. Pierre. (1998). 'Governance Without Government? Rethinking Public Administration'. *Journal of Public Administration Research and Theory* 8, no. 2: 223–44.

Peters, B. G. and J. Pierre. (2000). 'Citizens versus the New Public Manager: The Problem of Mutual Empowerment'. *Administration and Society* 32, no. 1: 9–28.

Peters, B. G. and F. K. M. Van Nispen (eds) (1998). *Public Policy Instruments: Evaluating the Tools of Public Administration.* New York: Edward Elgar.

Peters, B. G., J. C. Doughtie and M. K. McCulloch. (1978). 'Do Public Policies Vary in Different Types of Democratic System?' In P. G. Lewis, D. C. Potter and F. G. Castles (eds), *The Practice of Comparative Politics: A Reader.* London: Longman, 70–100.

Peters, B. G., P. Eliadis, M. Hill and M. Howlett. (2005). 'Conclusion: The Future of Instruments Research'. In *Designing Government: From Instruments to Governance.* Montreal, QC: McGill-Queen's University Press, 353–63.

Peters, B. G., P. Ravinet, M. Howlett, G. Capano, I. Mukherjee and M. H. Chou. (2018). *Designing for Policy Effectiveness: Defining and Understanding a Concept.* Elements Series. Cambridge: Cambridge University Press.

Pew Research Center. (2009). *Modest Support for 'Cap and Trade' Policy: Fewer Americans See Solid Evidence of Global Warming.* Washington, DC: Pew Research Center.

Pfeffer, J. (1977). 'The Ambiguity of Leadership'. *Academy of Management Review* 2, no. 1 (1 January): 104–12.

Phidd, R. W. (1975). 'The Economic Council of Canada: Its Establishment, Structure and Role in the Canadian Policy-Making System 1963–74'. *Canadian Public Administration* 18, no. 3: 428–73.

Phidd, R. W. and G. B. Doern. (1983). *Canadian Public Policy: Ideas, Structures, Process.* Toronto, ON: Methuen.

Philibert, C. (2011). 'Interactions of Policies for Renewable Energy and Climate'. IEA Energy Paper. OECD. http://econpapers.repec.org/paper/oecieaaaa/2011_2f6-en.htm.

Phillips, S. D. (1991). 'How Ottawa Blends: Shifting Government Relationships with Interest Groups'. In F. Abele (ed.), *How Ottawa Spends 1991–92: The Politics of Fragmentation.* Ottawa, ON: Carleton University Press, 183–228.

Phillips, S. D. (2001). 'From Charity to Clarity: Reinventing Federal Government–Voluntary Sector Relationships'. In L. A. Pal (eds), *How Ottawa Spends 2001–2: Power in Transition.* Toronto, ON: Oxford University Press, 145–76.

Phillips, S. D. (2007). 'Policy Analysis and the Voluntary Sector: Evolving Policy Styles'. In L. Dobuzinskis, M. Howlett and D. Laycock (eds), *Policy Analysis in Canada: The State of the Art.* Toronto, ON: University of Toronto Press, 272–84.

Phillips, S. D. and M. Orsini. (2002). *Mapping the Links: Citizen Involvement in Policy Processes.* Ottawa, ON: Canadian Policy Research Networks.

Pichert, D. and K. V. Katsikopoulos. (2008). 'Green Defaults: Information Presentation and Pro-Environmental Behaviour'. *Journal of Environmental Psychology* 28, no. 1: 63–73.

Phillips, S. D., R. Laforest and A. Graham. (2010). 'From Shopping to Social Innovation: Getting Public Financing Right in Canada'. *Policy and Society* 29, no. 3: 189–99.

Pielke Jr, R. (2010). *The Climate Fix. What Scientists and Politicians Won't Tell You About Global Warming.* New York: Basic Books.

Pierre, J. (1995). 'Conclusions: A Framework of Comparative Public Administration'. In J. Pierre (eds), *Bureaucracy in the Modern State: An Introduction to Comparative Public Administration*. Aldershot, UK: Edward Elgar, 205–18.

Pierre, J. (1998). 'Public Consultation and Citizen Participation: Dilemmas of Policy Advice'. In B. G. Peters and D. J. Savoie (eds), *Taking Stock: Assessing Public Sector Reforms*. Montreal, QC: McGill-Queen's Press, 137–63.

Pierre, J. (2012). 'Governance and Institutional Flexibility'. In D. Levi-Faur (eds), *The Oxford Handbook of Governance*. Oxford: Oxford University Press, 187–201.

Pierre, J. and B. G. Peters. (2005). *Governing Complex Societies: Trajectories and Scenarios*. London: Palgrave Macmillan.

Pierson, P. (1992). ' "Policy Feedbacks" and Political Change: Contrasting Reagan and Thatcher's Pension Reform Initiatives'. *Studies in American Political Development* 6: 359–90.

Pierson, P. (1993). 'When Effect Becomes Cause: Policy Feedback and Political Change'. *World Politics* 45: 595–628.

Pierson, P. (2000). 'Increasing Returns, Path Dependence, and the Study of Politics'. *American Political Science Review* 94, no. 2: 251–67.

Pierson, P. (2004). *Politics in Time: History, Institutions and Social Analysis*. Princeton, NJ: Princeton University Press.

Pigou, A. C. (1932). *The Economics of Welfare*. London: Macmillan.

Pina e Cunha, M., J. V. da Cunha and K. Kamoche. (1999). 'Organizational Improvisation: What, When, How and Why'. *International Journal of Management Reviews* 1, no. 3: 299–341.

Pittel, K. and D. T. G. Rubbelke. (2006). 'Private Provision of Public Goods: Incentives for Donations'. *Journal of Economic Studies* 33, no. 6: 497–519.

Pollack, M. A. (2003). 'Control Mechanism or Deliberative Democracy? Two Images of Comitology'. *Comparative Political Studies* 36, nos 1/2: 125–55.

Pollitt, C. (2001a). 'Clarifying Convergence: Striking Similarities and Durable Differences in Public Management Reform'. *Public Management Review* 4, no. 1: 471–92.

Pollitt, C. (2001b). 'Convergence: The Useful Myth?' *Public Administration* 79, no. 4: 933–47.

Pollitt, C. and G. Bouckaert. (2011). *Public Management Reform: A Comparative Analysis –New Public Management, Governance, and the Neo-Weberian State* (3rd edn). Oxford: Oxford University Press.

Pollitt, M. G. and I. Shaorshadze. (2011). 'The Role of Behavioural Economics in Energy and Climate Policy'. Cambridge Working Paper in Economics (CWPE). Cambridge: University of Cambridge.

Pontusson, J. (1995). 'From Comparative Public Policy to Political Economy: Putting Institutions in their Place and Taking Interests Seriously'. *Comparative Political Studies* 28, no. 1: 117–47.

Poocharoen, O. and B. Ting. (2015). 'Collaboration, Co-Production, Networks: Convergence of Theories'. *Public Management Review* 17, no. 4: 587–614.

Poortinga, W., A. Spence, L. Whitmarsh, S. Capstick and N. F. Pidgeon. (2011). 'Uncertain Climate: An Investigation into Public Scepticism about Anthropogenic Climate Change'. *Global Environmental Change* 21, no. 3, 1015–24.

Pope, J. and A. D. Owen. (2009). 'Emission Trading Schemes: Potential Revenue Effects, Compliance Costs and Overall Tax Policy Issues'. *Energy Policy* 37: 4595–603.

Pope, J. and J. M. Lewis. (2008). 'Improving Partnership Governance: Using a Network Approach to Evaluate Partnerships in Victoria'. *Australian Journal of Public Administration* 67, no. 4: 443–56.

Porter, T. and R. Karsten. (2006)'.Self-Regulation as Policy Process: The Multiple and Crisscrossing Stages of Private Rule-Making'. *Policy Sciences* 39: 41–72.

Porumbescu, G. A., M. I. H. Lindeman, E. Ceka and M. Cucciniello. (2017). 'Can Transparency Foster More Understanding and Compliant Citizens?' *Public Administration Review*.

Posner, R. A. (1974). 'Theories of Economic Regulation'. *Bell Journal of Economics and Management Science* 5: 335–58.

Post, L. A., T. Salmon and A. Raile. (2008). 'Using Public Will to Secure Political Will'. In S. Odugbemi and T. Jacobson (eds), *Governance Reform Under Real World Conditions. Communication for Governance and Accountability Program.* Washington, DC: World Bank, Chapter 7. www.gsdrc.org/go/display&type=Document&id=3710.

Potoski, M. (2002). 'Designing Bureaucratic Responsiveness: Administrative Procedures and Agency Choice in State Environmental Policy'. *State Politics and Policy Quarterly* 2, no. 1: 1–23.

Potoski, M. and A. Prakash (eds) (2009). *Voluntary Programs: A Club Theory Perspective.* Cambridge, MA: MIT Press.

Power, M. and L. S. McCarty. (2002). 'Trends in the Development of Ecological Risk Assessment and Management Frameworks'. *Human and Ecological Risk Assessment* 8, no. 1: 7–18.

Prasser, S. (2006). 'Royal Commissions in Australia: When Should Governments Appoint Them?' *Australian Journal of Public Administration* 65, no. 3: 28–47.

Pratt, J. W. and R. J. Zeckhauser. (1991). *Principals and Agents: The Structure of Business.* Cambridge, MA: Harvard Business School Press.

Prentice, S. (2006). 'Childcare, Co-Production and the Third Sector in Canada'. *Public Management Review* 8, no. 4: 521–36.

Preskill, H. and S. Boyle. (2008). 'A Multidisciplinary Model of Evaluation Capacity Building'. *American Journal of Evaluation* 29, no. 4: 443–59.

Pressman, J. L. and A. B. Wildavsky. (1973). *Implementation: How Great Expectations in Washington Are Dashed in Oakland.* Berkeley, CA: University of California Press.

Prichard, J. R. S. (1983). *Crown Corporations in Canada: The Calculus of Instrument Choice.* Toronto, ON: Butterworths.

Prince, M. J. (1979). 'Policy Advisory Groups in Government Departments'. In G. B. Doern and P. Aucoin (eds), *Public Policy in Canada: Organization, Process, Management.* Toronto, ON: Gage, 275–300.

Prince, M. J. (1983). *Policy Advice and Organizational Survival.* Aldershot, UK: Gower.

Prince, M. J. (2007). 'Soft Craft, Hard Choices, Altered Context: Reflections on 25 Years of Policy Advice in Canada'. In L. Dobuzinskis, M. Howlett and D. Laycock (eds), *Policy Analysis in Canada: The State of the Art.* Toronto, ON: University of Toronto Press, 95–106.

Prince, M. J. (2008). *Reviewing the Literature on Policy Instruments.* Ottawa, ON: Human Resources and Social Development Canada.

Prince, M. J. and J. Chenier. (1980). 'The Rise and Fall of Policy Planning and Research Units'. *Canadian Public Administration* 22, no. 4: 536–50.

Proag, S. and V. Proag. (2014). 'The Cost Benefit Analysis of Providing Resilience'. *Procedia Economics and Finance*, 4th International Conference on Building Resilience, Incorporating the 3rd Annual Conference of the ANDROID Disaster Resilience Network, 8–11 September 2014, Salford Quays, United Kingdom 18: 361–8.

Pross, A. P. (1992). *Group Politics and Public Policy*. Toronto, ON: Oxford University Press.

Pross, A. P. and I. S. Stewart. (1993). 'Lobbying, the Voluntary Sector and the Public Purse'. In S. D. Phillips (eds), *How Ottawa Spends 1993–94: A More Democratic Canada?* Ottawa, ON: Carleton University Press, 109–42.

Provan, K. G. and P. Kenis. (2008). 'Modes of Network Governance: Structure, Management and Effectiveness'. *Journal of Public Administration Research and Theory* 18, no. 2: 229–52.

Prpic, J., A. Taeihagh and J. Melton. (2015). 'The Fundamentals of Policy Crowdsourcing'. *Policy & Internet* 1 August.

Przeworski, A. (1990). *The State and the Economy under Capitalism*. Chur, Switzerland: Harwood.

PwC (PricewaterhouseCoopers). (2014). 'Agility: The Future of Government'. Retrieved from www.pwc.com/ca/en/public-sector-government/agility.jhtml (accessed September 13).

Qualter, T. H. (1985). *Opinion Control in the Democracies*. London: Macmillan.

Quirk, Paul J. 'In Defense of the Politics of Ideas'. *The Journal of Politics* 50: 31–45.

Qureshi, H. (2004). 'Evidence in Policy and Practice: What Kinds of Research Designs?' *Journal of Social Work* 4, no. 1: 7–23.

Raadschelders, J. C. N. (1998). *Handbook of Administrative History*. New Brunswick, NJ: Transaction.

Raadschelders, J. C. N. (2000). 'Administrative History of the United States: Development and State of the Art'. *Administration and Society* 32, no. 5: 499–528.

Raadschelders, J. C.N. and M. R. Rutgers. (1996). 'The Evolution of Civil Service Systems'. In H. A. G. M. Bekke, J. L. Perry and T. A. J. Toonen, (eds), *Civil Service Systems in Comparative Perspective*. Bloomington, IN: Indiana University Press, 67–99.

Rabe, B., C. Borick and E. Lachapelle. (2011). 'Climate Compared: Public Opinion on Climate Change in the United States and Canada'. Brookings Institution. www.brookings.edu/research/papers/2011/04/climate-change-opinion.

Radaelli, C. M. (1995). 'The Role of Knowledge in the Policy Process'. *Journal of European Public Policy* 2, no. 2: 159–83.

Radaelli, C. M. (2005). 'Diffusion without Convergence: How Political Context Shapes the Adoption of Regulatory Impact Assessment'. *Journal of European Public Policy* 12, no. 5: 924–43.

Radaelli, C. M. and C. A. Dunlop. (2013). 'Learning in the European Union: Theoretical Lenses and Meta-theory'. *Journal of European Public Policy* 20, no. 6: 923–40.

Radaelli, C. M. and A. C. M. Meuwese. (2009). 'Better Regulation in Europe: Between Public Management and Regulatory Reform'. *Public Administration* 87, no. 3: 639–54.

Radin, B. A. (2000). *Beyond Machiavelli: Policy Analysis Comes of Age*. Washington, DC: Georgetown University Press.

Radin, B. A. and J. P. Boase. (2000). 'Federalism, Political Structure, and Public Policy in the United States and Canada'. *Journal of Comparative Policy Analysis* 2, no. 1: 65–90.

Radnor, Z. J. and R. Boaden. (2004). 'Developing an Understanding of Corporate Anorexia'. *International Journal of Operations & Production Management* 24, no. 4 (1 April): 424–40.

Rajan, S. C. (1992). 'Legitimacy in Environmental Policy: The Regulation of Automobile Pollution in California'. *International Journal of Environmental Studies* 42: 243–58.

Ramesh, M. (1995). 'Economic Globalization and Policy Choices: Singapore'. *Governance* 8, no. 2: 243–60.

Ramesh, M. (2009). 'Healthcare Reforms in Thailand: Rethinking Conventional Wisdom'. In M. Ramesh and S. Fritzen (eds), *Transforming Asian Governance: Rethinking Assumptions, Challenging Practices*. London: Routledge.

Ramesh, M. and S. Fritzen (eds). (2009). *Transforming Asian Governance: Rethinking Assumptions, Challenging Practices*. New York: Routledge.

Ramesh, M. and M. Howlett (eds). (2006). *Deregulation and Its Discontents: Rewriting the Rules in Asia*. Aldershot, UK: Edward Elgar.

Ramesh, M., X. Wu and M. Howlett. (2015). 'Second Best Governance? Governments and Governance in the Imperfect World of Health Care Delivery in China, India and Thailand in Comparative Perspective'. *Journal of Comparative Policy Analysis: Research and Practice* 21 January: 1–17.

Rasmussen, K. (1999). 'Policy Capacity in Saskatchewan: Strengthening the Equilibrium'. *Canadian Public Administration* 42, no. 3: 331–48.

Rayner, J. (2013). 'On Smart Layering as Policy Design: Tackling the Biofuels Policy Mess in Canada and the United Kingdom'. *Policy Sciences* (Special Issue on Policy Design).

Rayner, J. and M. Howlett. (2009). 'Conclusion: Governance Arrangements and Policy Capacity for Policy Integration'. *Policy and Society* 28, no. 2 (July): 165–72.

Rayner, J., K. McNutt and A. Wellstead. (2013). 'Dispersed Capacity and Weak Coordination: The Challenge of Climate Change Adaptation in Canada's Forest Policy Sector'. *Review of Policy Research* 30, no. 1: 66–90.

Rayner, J., B. Cashore, M. Howlett and J. Wilson. (2001). 'Privileging the Sub-Sector: Critical Sub-Sectors and Sectoral Relationships in Forest Policy-Making'. *Forest Policy and Economics* 2, nos 3–4: 319–32.

Reagan, M. D. (1987). *Regulation: The Politics of Policy*. Boston, MA: Little, Brown.

Redström, J. (2006). 'Persuasive Design: Fringes and Foundations'. In A. I. Wijnand, Y. A. W. de Kort, C. Midden, B. Eggen and E. van den Hoven (eds), *Persuasive Technology*. Lecture Notes in Computer Science 3962. Berlin/Heidelberg: Springer, 112–22.

Regens, J. L. and R. W. Rycroft. (1988). *The Acid Rain Controversy*. Pittsburgh, PA; London: University of Pittsburgh Press.

Reich, R. B. (1991). *The Work of Nations*. New York: Alfred Knopf.

Rein, M. and D. Scholl (1991). 'Frame-reflective policy discourse'. In P. Wagner, C. H. Weiss, B. Wittrock and H. Wollman (eds), *Social Sciences and Modern States: National Experiences and Theoretical Crossroads*. Cambridge: Cambridge University Press, 262–89.

Reinicke, W. H. (1998). *Global Public Policy: Governing Without Government?* Washington, DC: Brookings Institution.

Reisch, L. A. and C. R. Sunstein. (2016). 'Do Europeans Like Nudges?' *Judgement and Decision Making* 11, no. 4: 310–25.

Relyea, H. C. (1977). 'The Provision of Government Information: The Freedom of Information Act Experience'. *Canadian Public Administration* 20, no. 2: 317–41.

Renn, O. (1995). 'Style of Using Scientific Expertise: A Comparative Framework'. *Science and Public Policy* 22, no. 3: 147–56.

Resodihardjo, S. L. (2006). 'Wielding a Double-Edged Sword: The Use of Inquiries at Times of Crisis'. *Journal of Contingencies and Crisis Management* 14, no. 4: 199–206.

Rhodes, R. A. W. (1994). 'The Hollowing Out of the State: The Changing Nature of the Public Service in Britain'. *The Political Quarterly* 65, no. 2: 138–51.

Rhodes, R. A. W. (1996). 'The New Governance: Governing Without Government'. *Political Studies* 44: 652–67.

Rhodes, R. A. W. (1997). 'From Marketisation to Diplomacy: It's the Mix that Matters'. *Australian Journal of Public Administration* 56, no. 2: 40–54.

Rhodes, R. A. W. (2007). 'Understanding Governance: Ten Years On'. *Organization Studies* 28: 1243–64.

Rhodes, R. A. W. (2012). 'Waves of Governance'. In D. Levi-Faur (eds), *The Oxford Handbook of Governance*. Oxford: Oxford University Press, 33–48.

Rhodes, R. A. W. and P. Weller. (2001). *The Changing World of Top Officials*. Buckingham, UK: Open University Press.

Rhue, L. and A. Sundararajan. (2014). 'Digital Access, Political Networks and the Diffusion of Democracy'. *Social Networks* 36 (January): 40–53.

Riccucci, N. M. and M. K. Meyers. (2008). 'Comparing Welfare Service Delivery Among Public, Nonprofit and For-Profit Work Agencies'. *International Journal of Public Administration* 31: 1441–54.

Rich, A. (2004). *Think Tanks, Public Policy, and the Politics of Expertise*. New York: Cambridge University Press.

Richardson, J. J. (ed.). (1990). *Privatisation and Deregulation in Canada and Britain*. Aldershot, UK: Dartmouth Publishing.

Richardson, J. J. and A. G. Jordan. (1979). *Governing Under Pressure: The Policy Process in a Post-Parliamentary Democracy*. Oxford: Martin Robertson.

Richardson, J., G. Gustafsson and G. Jordan. (1982). 'The Concept of Policy Style'. In J. J. Richardson (eds), *Policy Styles in Western Europe*. London: George Allen & Unwin, 1–16.

Richardson, J. J., A. G. Jordan and R. H. Kimber. (1978). 'Lobbying, Administrative Reform and Policy Styles: The Case of Land Drainage'. *Political Studies* 26, no. 1: 47–64.

Ricoeur, P. and J. B. Thompson. (1981). *Hermeneutics and the Human Sciences: Essays on Language, Action and Interpretation*. Cambridge: Cambridge University Press.

Riddell, N. (1998). *Policy Research Capacity in the Federal Government*. Ottawa, ON: Policy Research Initiative.

Riedel, J. A. (1972). 'Citizen Participation: Myths and Realities'. *Public Administration Review* (May–June): 211–20.

Riker, W. H. (1982). *Liberalism Against Populism: A Confrontation Between the Theory of Democracy and the Theory of Social Choice*. San Francisco, CA: Freeman.

Riker, W. H. (1983). 'Political Theory and the Art of Heresthetics'. In W. Finifter (ed.), *Political Science: The State of the Discipline*. Washington, DC: American Political Science Association, 47–67.

Riker, W. H. (1986). *The Art of Political Manipulation*. New Haven, CT: Yale University Press.

Rimlinger, G. V. (1971). *Welfare Policy and Industrialization in Europe, America and Russia*. New York: Wiley.

Ring, I. and C. Schroter-Schlaack. (2011). *Instrument Mixes for Biodiversity Policies*. Leipzig, Germany: Helmholtz Centre for Environmental Research.

Ring, I., M. Drechsler, A. J. A. van Teeffelen, S. Irawan and O. Venter. (2010). 'Biodiversity Conservation and Climate Mitigation: What Role Can Economic Instruments Play?' *Current Opinion in Environmental Sustainability* 2, nos 1–2: 50–8.

Ringquist, E. J., J. Worsham and M. A. Eisner. (2003). 'Salience, Complexity and the Legislative Direction of Regulatory Bureaucracies'. *Journal of Public Administration Research and Theory* 13, no. 2: 141–65.

Rittel, H. W. J. and M. M. Webber. (1973). 'Dilemmas in a General Theory of Planning'. *Policy Sciences* 4: 155–69.

Roberts, A. (1999). 'Retrenchment and Freedom of Information: Recent Experience under Federal, Ontario and British Columbia Law'. *Canadian Public Administration* 42, no. 4: 422–51.

Roberts, A. and J. Rose. (1995). 'Selling the Goods and Services Tax: Government Advertising and Public Discourse in Canada'. *Canadian Journal of Political Science* 28, no. 2: 311–30.

Roberts, R. and L. E. R. Dean. (1994). 'An Inquiry into Lowi's Policy Typology: The Conservation Coalition and the 1985 and 1990 Farm Bill'. *Environment and Planning C, Government and Policy* 12, no. 1: 71–86.

Robins, L. (2008). 'Perspectives on Capacity Building to Guide Policy and Program Development and Delivery'. *Environmental Science and Policy* 11: 687–701.

Roch, C., D. Pitts and I. Navarro. (2010). 'Representative Bureaucracy and Policy Tools: Ethnicity, Student Discipline, and Representation in Public Schools'. *Administration & Society* 42, no. 1: 38–65.

Rochefort, D. A. and R. W. Cobb (eds). (1994). *The Politics of Problem Definition: Shaping the Policy Agenda*. Lawrence, KS: University Press of Kansas.

Rochet, C. (2004). 'Rethinking the Management of Information in the Strategic Monitoring of Public Policies by Agencies'. *Industrial Management and Data Systems* 104, no. 3: 201–8.

Rodrik, D. (1997). *Has Globalization Gone Too Far?* Washington, DC: Institute for International Economics.

Rodrik, D. (1998). 'Why Do Open Economies Have Bigger Governments?' *Journal of Political Economy* 106, no. 5: 997–1032.

Roehrich, J. K., M. A. Lewis and G. George. (2014). 'Are Public–Private Partnerships a Healthy Option? A Systematic Literature Review of "Constructive" Partnerships between Public and Private Actors'. *Social Science & Medicine* 113 (July): 110–19.

Rolfstam, M. (2009). 'Public Procurement as an Innovation Policy Tool: The Role of Institutions'. *Science and Public Policy* 36, no. 5: 349–60.

Roman, A. J. and K. Hooey. (1993). 'The Regulatory Framework'. In G. Thompson, M. L. McConnell and L. B. Huestis (eds), *Environmental Law and Business in Canada*. Aurora, ON: Canada Law Books, 55–75.

Romans, J. T. (1966). 'Moral Suasion as an Instrument of Economic Policy'. *American Economic Review* 56, no. 5: 1220–26.

Ronal, G.-C., R. Guinza-Carmenates, J. Carlos Attamirans-Cabrera, P. Thalmann and L. Dronet. (2010). 'Trade-offs and Performances of a Range of Alternative Global Climate Architectures for Post-2012'. *Environmental Science & Policy* 13, no. 1 (February): 63–71.

Ronit, K. (2001). 'Institutions of Private Authority in Global Governance: Linking Territorial Forms of Self-regulation'. *Administration and Society* 33, no. 5: 555–78.

Room, G. (2013a). *Agile Policy on Complex Terrains: Nudge or Nuzzle?* 2 October. www.horizons.gc.ca/eng/content/agile-policy-complex-terrains-%E2%80%93-nudge-or-nuzzle.

Room, G. (2013b). 'Evidence for Agile Policy Makers: The Contribution of Transformative Realism'. *Evidence & Policy: A Journal of Research, Debate and Practice* 9, no. 2 (24 May): 225–44.

Roots, R. I. (2004). 'When Laws Backfire: Unintended Consequences of Public Policy'. *American Behavioural Scientist* 47, no. 11: 1376–94.

Rose, J. (1993). 'Government Advertising in a Crisis: The Quebec Referendum Precedent'. *Canadian Journal of Communication* 18: 173–96.

Rose, R. (1988a). 'Comparative Policy Analysis: The Program Approach'. In M. Dogan (ed.), *Comparing Pluralist Democracies: Strains on Legitimacy*. Boulder, CO: Westview, 219–41.

Rose, R. (1988b). 'The Growth of Government Organization: Do We Count the Number or Weigh the Programs?' In C. Campbell, and B. G. Peters (eds), *Organizing Governance/Governing Organizations*. Pittsburgh, PA: University of Pittsburgh Press, 99–128.

Rose, R. (1991). 'What is Lesson-Drawing?' *Journal of Public Policy* 11, no. 1: 3–30.

Rose, R. (1993). *Lesson-Drawing in Public Policy: A Guide to Learning Across Time and Space*. London: Chatham House.

Rose, R. (2005). *Learning from Comparative Public Policy*. London: Routledge.

Rosenau, J. N. (1980). *The Study of Global Interdependence*. London: Pinter.

Rosenau, P. V. (1999). 'The Strengths and Weaknesses of Public–Private Policy Partnerships'. *American Behavioral Scientist* 43, no. 1: 10–34.

Rosenbloom, D. H. (2007). 'Administrative Law and Regulation'. In J. Rabin, W. B. Hildreth and G. J. Miller (eds), *Handbook of Public Administration*. London: CRC/Taylor & Francis, 635–96.

Ross, H., M. Buchy and W. Proctor. (2002). 'Laying Down the Ladder: A Typology of Public Participation in Australian Natural Resource Management'. *Australian Journal of Environmental Management* 9, no. 4: 205–17.

Rotberg, R. I. (2014). 'Good Governance Means Performance and Results'. *Governance* 27, no. 3: 511–18.

Rothmayr, C. and S. Hardmeier. (2002). 'Government and Polling: Use and Impact of Polls in the Policy-Making Process in Switzerland'. *International Journal of Public Opinion Research* 14, no. 2: 123–40.

Rotmans, J., R. Kemp and M. van Asselt. (2001). 'More Evolution Then Revolution: Transition Management in Public Policy'. *Foresight* 3, no. 1: 15–31.

Rouban, L. (1999). 'Introduction Citizens and the New Governance'. In L. Rouban (ed.), *Citizens and the New Governance: Beyond New Public Management*. Amsterdam, Netherlands: IOS Press, 1–5.

Rourke, F. E. (1957). 'The Politics of Administrative Organization: A Case History'. *The Journal of Politics* 19, no. 1: 461–78.

Rowe, G. and L. J. Frewer. 'A Typology of Public Engagement Mechanisms'. *Science, Technology & Human Values* 30, no. 2: 251–90.

Rowe, M. and L. McAllister. (2006). 'The Roles of Commissions of Inquiry in the Policy Process'. *Public Policy and Administration* 21, no. 4: 99–115.

Royer, A. (2008). 'The Emergence of Agricultural Marketing Boards Revisited: A Case Study in Canada'. *Canadian Journal of Agricultural Economics* 56: 509–22.

Rubsamen, V. (1989). 'Deregulation and the State in Comparative Perspective: The Case of Telecommunications'. *Comparative Politics* 22, no. 1: 105–20.

Rudd, M. (2014). 'A Scientist's Perspectives on Global Ocean Research Priorities'. *Frontiers in Marine Science* 1: 36.

Rudd, M. (2015). 'Scientists' Framing of the Ocean Science–Policy Interface'. *Global Environmental Change* 33: 44–60.

de la Rue du Can, S., G. Leventis, A. Phadke and A. Gopal. (2014). 'Design of Incentive Programs for Accelerating Penetration of Energy-Efficient Appliances'. *Energy Policy* 72 (September): 56–66.

Rutgers, M. R. (2001). 'Traditional Flavors? The Different Sentiments in European and American Administrative Thought'. *Administration and Society* 33, no. 2: 220–44 (at p. 239).

Ryan, P. (1995). 'Miniature Mila and Flying Geese: Government Advertising and Canadian Democracy'. In S. D. Phillips (ed.), *How Ottawa Spends 1995–96: Mid-Life Crises*. Ottawa, ON: Carleton University Press, 263–86.

Sabatier, P. A. (1987). 'Knowledge, Policy-Oriented Learning, and Policy Change'. *Knowledge: Creation, Diffusion, Utilization* 8, no. 4: 649–92.

Sabatier, P. A. (1988). 'An Advocacy Coalition Framework of Policy Change and the Role of Policy-Oriented Learning Therein'. *Policy Sciences* 21, nos 2/3: 129–68.

Sabatier, P. A. (1991). 'Toward Better Theories of the Policy Process'. *PS: Political Science and Politics* 24, no. 2: 144–56.

Sabatier, P. A. (1998). 'The Advocacy Coalition Framework: Revisions and Relevance for Europe'. *Journal of European Public Policy* 5, no. 1: 98–130.

Sabatier, P. A. (1999). *Theories of the Policy Process*, Boulder, CO: Westview Press.

Sabatier, P. A. and H. Jenkins-Smith. (1993a). 'The Advocacy Coalition Framework: Assessment, Revisions, and Implications for Scholars and Practitioners'. In P. Sabatier and H. Jenkins-Smith (eds), *Policy Change and Learning: An Advocacy Coalition Approach*. Boulder, CO: Westview, 211–36.

Sabatier, P. A. and H. Jenkins-Smith (eds). (1993b). *Policy Change and Learning. An Advocacy Coalition Approach*. Boulder, CO: Westview Press.

Sabatier, P. A. and D. A. Mazmanian. (1981). *Effective Policy Implementation*. Lexington, MA: Lexington Books.

Sabatier, P. A. and N. Pelkey. (1987). 'Incorporating Multiple Actors and Guidance Instruments into Models of Regulatory Policymaking: An Advocacy Coalition Framework'. *Administration and Society* 19, no. 2: 236–63.

Sabatier, P. A. and C. M. Weible. (2007). *Theories of the Policy Process*. Boulder, CO: Westview Press.

Sadler, Barry. (2005). *Strategic Environmental Assessment at the Policy Level: Recent Progress, Current Status and Future Prospects*. Prague: Ministry of the Environment.

Sager, F. and Y. Rielle. (2013). 'Sorting through the Garbage Can: Under What Conditions Do Governments Adopt Policy Programs?' *Policy Sciences* 46, no. 1 (1 March): 1–21.

Saint-Martin, D. (1998). 'Management Consultants, the State, and the Politics of Administrative Reform in Britain and Canada'. *Administration Society* 30, no. 5 (1 November): 533–68.

Saint-Martin, D. (2013). 'Making Government More "Business-Like": Management Consultants as Agents of Isomorphism in Modern Political Economies'. In J. Mikler (eds), *The Handbook of Global Companies*. John Wiley, 173–92.

Salamon, L. M. (1981). 'Rethinking Public Management: Third-Party Government and the Changing Forms of Government Action'. *Public Policy* 29, no. 3: 255–75.

Salamon, L. M. (1987). 'Of Market Failure, Voluntary Failure, and Third-Party Government: Toward a Theory of Government–Nonprofit Relations in the Modern Welfare State'. *Journal of Voluntary Action Research* 16, nos 1/2: 29–49.

Salamon, L. M. (1989). 'The Tools Approach: Basic Analytics'. In L. S. Salamon, and M. S. Lund (eds), *Beyond Privatization: The Tools of Government Action*. Washington, DC: Urban Institute, 23–50.

Salamon, L. M. (2001). 'New Governance and the Tools of Public Action: An Introduction'. *Fordham Urban Law Journal* 28: 1611.

Salamon, L. M. (2002a). 'Economic Regulation'. In L. M. Salamon (ed.), *The Tools of Government: A Guide to the New Governance*, New York: Oxford University Press, 117–55.

Salamon, L. M. (2002b). 'The New Governance and the Tools of Public Action'. In L. M. Salamon (ed.), *The Tools of Government: A Guide to the New Governance*. New York: Oxford University Press, 1–47.

Salamon, L. M. (2002c). *The Tools of Government: A Guide to the New Governance*. New York: Oxford University Press.

Salamon, L. M. and M. S. Lund. (1989). 'The Tools Approach: Basic Analytics'. In L. M. Salamon (ed.), *Beyond Privatization: The Tools of Government Action*. Washington, DC: Urban Institute, 23–50.

Salisbury, R. H. (1969). 'An Exchange Theory of Interest Groups'. *Midwest Journal of Political Science* 13, no. 1: 1–32.

Salmon, C. (1989a). 'Campaigns for Social Improvement: An Overview of Values, Rationales and Impacts'. In C. Salmon (ed.), *Information Campaigns: Managing the Process of Social Change*. Newbury Park, CA: Sage, 1–32.

Salmon, C. (ed.). (1989b). *Information Campaigns: Managing the Process of Social Change*. Newbury Park, CA: Sage.

Salomonsen, H. H. and T. Knudsen. (2011). 'Changes in Public Service Bargains: Ministers and Civil Servants in Denmark'. *Public Administration* 89, no. 3 (1 September): 1015–35.

Salter, L. (1990). 'The Two Contradictions in Public Inquiries'. In A. P. Pross, I. Christie and J. A. Yogis (eds), *Commissions of Inquiry*. Toronto, ON: Carswell, 175–95.

Salter, L. (2003). 'The Complex Relationship between Inquiries and Public Controversy'. In A. Manson and D. Mullan (eds), *Commissions of Inquiry: Praise or Reappraise?* Toronto, ON: Irwin Law, 185–209.

Salter, L. and D. Slaco. (1981). *Public Inquiries in Canada*. Ottawa, ON: Science Council of Canada.

Sanderson, I. (2002a). 'Evaluation, Policy Learning and Evidence-Based Policy Making'. *Public Administration* 80, no. 1: 1–22.

Sanderson, I. (2002b). 'Making Sense of What Works: Evidence Based Policymaking as Instrumental Rationality?' *Public Policy and Administration* 17, no. 3: 61–75.

Sanderson, I. (2006). 'Complexity, "Practical Rationality" and Evidence-Based Policy Making'. *Policy & Politics* 34, no. 1: 115–32.

Santos, G., H. Behrendt and A. Teytelboym. (2010). 'Part II: Policy Instruments for Sustainable Road Transport'. *Research in Transportation Economics* 28, no. 1: 46–91.

Sappington, D. E. M. (1994). 'Designing Incentive Regulation'. *Review of Industrial Organization* 9, no. 3: 245–72.

Sassen, S. (1998). *Globalization and Its Discontents*. New York: New Press.

de Saulles, M. (2007). 'When Public Meets Private: Conflicts in Information Policy'. *Info* 9, no. 6: 10–16.

Savas, E. S. (1977). *Alternatives for Delivering Public Services: Toward Improved Performance*. Boulder, CO: Westview.

Savas, E. S. (1987). *Privatization: The Key to Better Government*. London: Chatham House.

Savas, E. S. (1989). 'A Taxonomy of Privatization Strategies'. *Policy Studies Journal* 18: 343–55.

Savoie, D. J. (1999). *Governing from the Centre: The Concentration of Power in Canadian Politics*. Toronto, ON: University of Toronto Press.

Saward, M. (1990). 'Cooption and Power: Who Gets What from Formal Incorporation'. *Political Studies* 38: 588–602.

Saward, M. (1992). *Co-Optive Politics and State Legitimacy*. Aldershot, UK: Dartmouth.

Schaar, John H. (1981). *Legitimacy in the Modern State*. New Brunswick, NJ: Transaction.

Scharpf, F. W. (1986). 'Policy Failure and Institutional Reform: Why Should Form Follow Function?' *International Social Science Journal* 108: 179–90.

Scharpf, F. W. (1990). 'Games Real Actors Could Play: The Problem of Mutual Predictability'. *Rationality and Society* 2: 471–94 .

Scharpf, F. W. (1991). 'Political Institutions, Decision Styles and Policy Choices'. In R. M. Czada and A. Windhoff-Heritier (eds), *Political Choice: Institutions, Rules and the Limits of Rationality*. Frankfurt, Germany: Campus Verlag, 53–86.

Scharpf, F. W. (1998). 'Globalization: The Limitations on State Capacity'. *Swiss Political Science Review* 4, no. 1: 2–8.

Scharpf, F. W. (2000). 'Institutions in Comparative Policy Research'. *Comparative Political Studies* 33, nos 6/7: 762–90.

Schattschneider, E. E. (1960). *The Semisovereign People: A Realist's View of Democracy in America*. New York: Holt, Rinehart & Winston.

Scheb, J. M. and J. M. Scheb II. (2005). *Law and the Administrative Process*. Toronto, ON: Thomson Wadsworth.

Scheraga, J. D. and J. Furlow. (2001). 'From Assessment to Policy: Lessons Learned from the US National Assessment'. *Human and Ecological Risk Assessment* 7, no. 5: 1227–46.

Scherer, F. M. (2008). 'The Historical Foundations of Communications Regulation'. In *Kennedy School Faculty Working Papers Series RWP08-050*. Boston, MA: Harvard University.

Schlager, E. (1999). 'A Comparison of Frameworks, Theories and Models of Policy Processes'. In P. A. Sabatier (ed.), *Theories of the Policy Process*. Boulder, CO: Westview, 233–60.

Schlager, E. and Blomquist W. (1996). 'Emerging Political Theories of the Policy Process: Institutional Rational Choice, the Politics of Structural Choice, and Advocacy Coalitions'. *Political Research Quarterly* 49: 651–72.

Schmalensee, R., P. L. Joskow, A. D. Ellerman, J. P. Montero and E. M. Bailey. (1998). 'An Interim Evaluation of Sulfur Dioxide Emissions Trading'. *The Journal of Economic Perspectives,* 12, no. 3 (Summer): 53–68.

Schmidt, A., A. Ivanova and M. S. Schäfer. (2013). 'Media Attention for Climate Change around the World: A Comparative Analysis of Newspaper Coverage in 27 Countries'. *Global Environmental Change* 23, no. 5: 1233–48.

Schmidt, M. G. (1996). 'When Parties Matter: A Review of the Possibilities and Limits of Partisan Influence on Public Policy'. *European Journal of Political Research* 30: 155–83.

Schmidt, V. A. (2008). 'Discursive Institutionalism: The Explanatory Power of Ideas and Discourse'. *Annual Review of Political Science* 11: 303–26.

Schmitter, P. C. (1977). 'Modes of Interest Intermediation and Models of Societal Change in Western Europe'. *Comparative Political Studies* 10, no. 1: 7–38.

Schmitter, P. C. (1985). *Neo-Corporatism and the State*. In W. Grant (ed.), *The Political Economy of Corporatism*. London: Macmillan, 32–62.

Schneider, A. and H. Ingram. (1988). 'Systematically Pinching Ideas: A Comparative Approach to Policy Design'. *Journal of Public Policy* 8, no. 1: 61–80.

Schneider, A. and H. Ingram. (1990a). 'Behavioral Assumptions of Policy Tools'. *The Journal of Politics* 52, no. 2: 510–29.

Schneider, A. and H. Ingram. (1990b). 'Policy Design: Elements, Premises and Strategies'. In S. S. Nagel (ed.), *Policy Theory and Policy Evaluation: Concepts, Knowledge, Causes and Norms*. New York: Greenwood Press, 77–102.

Schneider, A. and H. Ingram. (1993). 'Social Construction of Target Populations: Implications for Politics and Policy'. *The American Political Science Review* 87, no. 2: 334–47.

Schneider, A. and H. Ingram. (1994). 'Social Constructions and Policy Design: Implications for Public Administration'. *Research in Public Administration* 3: 137–73.

Schneider, A. and H. Ingram. (1997). *Policy Design for Democracy*. Lawrence, KS: University Press of Kansas.

Schneider, A. and H. Ingram. (2005). *Deserving and Entitled: Social Constructions and Public Policy*. SUNY Series in Public Policy. Albany, NY: State University of New York.

Schneider, A. and M. Sidney. (2009). 'What Is Next for Policy Design and Social Construction Theory?' *Policy Studies Journal* 37, no. 1: 103–19.

Schneider, J. W. (1985). 'Social Problems Theory: The Constructionist View'. *Annual Review of Sociology* 11: 209–29.

Schneider, M. and P. Teske. (1995). *Public Entrepreneurs: Agents for Change in American Government*. Princeton, NJ: Princeton University Press.

Scholte, J. A. (1997). 'Global Capitalism and the State'. *International Affairs* 73: 440–51.

Scholz, J. T. (1984). 'Cooperation, Deterrence, and the Ecology of Regulatory Enforcement'. *Law Society Review* 18, no. 2: 179–224.

Scholz, J. T. (1991). 'Cooperative Regulatory Enforcement and the Politics of Administrative Effectiveness'. *American Political Science Review* 85, no. 1: 115–36.

Schön, D. A. (1988). 'Designing: Rules, Types and Words'. *Design Studies* 9, no. 3: 181–90.

Schön, D. A. (1992). 'Designing as Reflective Conversation with the Materials of a Design Situation'. *Knowledge-Based Systems* 5, no. 1 (March): 3–14.

Schön, D. A. and M. Rein. (1994). *Frame Reflection: Solving Intractable Policy Disputes*. New York: Basic Books.

Schout, A., A. Jordan and M. Twena. (2010). 'From "Old" to "New" Governance in the EU: Explaining a Diagnostic Deficit'. *West European Politics* 33, no. 1: 154–70.

Schrader, S., W. M. Riggs and R. P. Smith. (1993). 'Choice over Uncertainty and Ambiguity in Technical Problem Solving'. *Journal of Engineering and Technology Management* 10, nos 1–2 (June): 73–99.

Schubert, C. (2007). 'Green Nudges: Do They Work? Are They Ethical?' *Ecological Economics* 132, Supplement C (February): 329–342.

Schudson, M. (2006). 'The Trouble with Experts – and Why Democracies Need Them'. *Theory & Society* 35: 491–506.

Schultz, D. (2007). 'Stupid Public Policy Ideas and Other Political Myths'. Paper presented to the American Political Science Association, Chicago, IL.

Schwartz, B. (1997). 'Public Inquiries'. *Canadian Public Administration* 40, no. 1: 72–85.

Scott, C. (2001). 'Analysing Regulatory Space: Fragmented Resources and Institutional Design'. *Public Law* (Summer): 329–53.

Scott, C., J. Jordana and D. Levi-Faur. (2004). 'Regulation in the Age of Governance: The Rise of the Post-Regulatory State'. In J. Jordane and D. Levi-Faur (eds), *The Politics of Regulation: Institutions and Regulatory Reforms for the Age of Governance*. Cheltenham, UK: Edward Elgar, 145–74.

Scrase, J. I. and W. R. Sheate. (2002). 'Integration and Integrated Approaches to Assessment: What Do They Mean for the Environment'. *Journal of Environmental Policy and Planning* 4, no. 1: 275–94.

Scruggs, L. and S. Benegal. (2012). 'Declining Concern about Climate Change: Can We Blame the Great Recession?' *Global Environmental Change* 22, no. 2: 505–15.

Seeliger, R. (1996). 'Conceptualizing and Researching Policy Convergence'. *Policy Studies Journal* 24, no. 2: 287–310.

Selznick, P. (1984). *Leadership in Administration: A Sociological Interpretation*. Berkeley, CA: University of California Press.

Sethi-Iyengar, S., G. Huberman and G. Jiang. (2004). 'How Much Choice Is Too Much? Contributions to 401(k) Retirement Plans'. In O. S. Mitchell and S. P. Utkus (eds), *Pension Design and Structure: New Lessons from Behavioural Finance*. Oxford: Oxford University Press.

Shafir, E., (ed.). (2013). *The Behavioral Foundations of Public Policy*. Princeton, NJ: Princeton University Press.

Shafir, E., I. Simonson and A. Tversky. (1993). 'Reason-Based Choice'. *Cognition* 49, nos 1–2 (November): 11–36.

Shah, A. K. and D. M. Oppenheimer. (2008). 'Heuristics Made Easy: An Effort-Reduction Framework'. *Psychological Bulletin* 134, no. 2: 207–22.

Shalev, M. (1983). 'The Social Democratic Model and Beyond: Two Generations of Comparative Research on the Welfare State'. *Comparative Social Research* 6: 315–51.

Shapiro, S. A. and C. H. Schroeder. (2008). 'Beyond Cost–Benefit Analysis: A Pragmatic Reorientation'. *Harvard Environmental Law Review* 32: 433–501.

Sharkansky, I. (1971). 'Constraints on Innovation in Policy Making: Economic Development and Political Routines'. In F. Marini (ed.), *Toward a New Public Administration: The Minnowbrook Perspective*. Scranton, PA: Chandler, 261–79.

Sharkansky, I. and Y. Zalmanovitch. (2000). 'Improvisation in Public Administration and Policy Making in Israel'. *Public Administration Review* 60, no. 4 (1 July): 321–9.

Sharma, B. and J. Wanna. (2005). 'Performance Measures, Measurement and Reporting in Government Organisations'. *International Journal of Business Performance Management* 7, no. 3: 320–33.

Sharpe, D. (2001). 'The Canadian Charitable Sector: An Overview'. In J. Phillips, B. Chapman and D. Stevens (eds), *Between State and Market: Essays on Charities Law and Policy in Canada*. Toronto, ON: University of Toronto Press, 1–30.

Shaxson, L. (2004). 'Is Your Evidence Robust Enough? Questions for Policy Makers and Practitioners'. *Evidence & Policy* 1, no. 1: 101–11.

Sheriff, P. E. (1983). 'State Theory, Social Science and Governmental Commissions'. *American Behavioural Scientist* 26, no. 5: 669–80.

Shulock, N. (1999). 'The Paradox of Policy Analysis: If It Is Not Used, Why Do We Produce So Much of It?' *Journal of Policy Analysis and Management* 18, no. 2: 226–44.

Sidney, M. S. (2007). 'Policy Formulation: Design and Tools'. In F. Fischer, G. J. Miller and M. S. Sidney (eds), *Handbook of Public Policy Analysis: Theory, Politics and Methods*. New Brunswick, NJ: CRC/Taylor & Francis, 79–87.

Simmons, A. B. and K. Keohane. (1992). 'Canadian Immigration Policy: State Strategies and the Quest for Legitimacy'. *Canadian Review of Sociology and Anthropology* 29, no. 4: 421–52.

Simmons, B. A. and Z. Elkins. (2004). 'Globalization and Policy Diffusion: Explaining Three Decades of Liberalization'. In M. Kahler and D. Lake (eds), *Governance in a Global Economy*. Princeton, NJ: Princeton University Press, 275–304.

Simmons, R. and J. Birchall. (2005). 'A Joined-Up Approach to User Participation in Public Services: Strengthening the "Participation Chain"'. *Social Policy and Administration* 39, no. 3: 260–83.

Simmons, R. H., B. W. Davis, R. J. K. Chapman and D. D. Sager. (1974). 'Policy Flow Analysis: A Conceptual Model for Comparative Public Policy Research'. *Western Political Quarterly* 27, no. 3: 457–68.

Simon, H. A. (1955). 'A Behavioral Model of Rational Choice'. *The Quarterly Journal of Economics* 69, no. 1: 99–118.

Simon, H. A. (1957). *Models of Man: Social and Rational: Mathematical Essays on Rational Human Behavior in a Social Setting*. New York: Wiley.

Simon, H. A. (1973). 'The Structure of Ill Structured Problems'. *Artificial Intelligence* 4, nos 3–4 (Winter): 181–201.

Simon, H. A. (1976). *Administrative Behavior: A Study of Decision Making Processes in Administrative Organization* (3rd edn). New York: Free Press.

Simons, A. and J.-P. Voss. (2017). 'Policy Instrument Constituencies'. In M. Howlett and I. Mukherjee (eds), *Handbook of Policy Formulation*. Cheltenham, UK: Edward Elgar, 355–72.

Simons, A. and J.-P. Voss. (2018). 'The Concept of Instrument Constituencies: Accounting for Dynamics and Practices of Knowing Governance'. *Policy and Society* 37, no. 1: 14–35.

Sinclair, D. (1997). 'Self-Regulation versus Command and Control? Beyond False Dichotomies'. *Law and Policy* 19, no. 4: 529–59.

Singleton, J. (2001). *A Review of the Policy Capacity Between Departments*. Winnipeg, MB: Office of the Auditor-General.

Skeete, J.-P. (2017). 'Examining the Role of Policy Design and Policy Interaction in EU Automotive Emissions Performance Gaps'. *Energy Policy* 104 (May): 373–81.

Skelly, J. M. and J. L. Innes. (1994). 'Waldsterben in the Forests of Central Europe and Eastern North America: Fantasy or Reality?' *Plant Disease* 78, no. 11: 1021–32.

Skodvin, T., A. T. Gullberg and S. Aakre. (2010). 'Target-Group Influence and Political Feasibility: The Case of Climate Policy Design in Europe'. *Journal of European Public Policy* 17, no. 6: 854.

Skowronek, S. (1982). *Building a New American State: The Expansion of National Administrative Capacities 1877–1920*. Cambridge: Cambridge University Press.

Slovic, P. (1992). Perception of Risk: Reflections on the Psychometric Paradigm. In S. Krimsky and D. Golding (eds), *Social Theories of Risk*. Westport, CT; London: Praeger.

Smismans, S. (2008). 'New Modes of Governance and the Participatory Myth'. *West European Politics* 31, no. 5: 874–95.

Smith, A. (2000). 'Policy Networks and Advocacy Coalitions: Explaining Policy Change and Stability in UK Industrial Pollution Policy'. *Environment and Planning C: Government and Policy* 18: 95–114.

Smith, B. L. R. (1977). 'The Non-Governmental Policy Analysis Organization'. *Public Administration Review* 37, no. 3: 253–58.

Smith, M. (2005a). *A Civil Society? Collective Actors in Canadian Political Life*. Peterborough, ON: Broadview Press.

Smith, M. (2005b). 'Diversity and Identity in the Non-Profit Sector: Lessons from LGBT Organizing in Toronto'. *Social Policy and Administration* 39, no. 5: 463–80.

Smith, M. J. (1994). 'Policy Networks and State Autonomy'. In S. Brooks and A.-G. Gagnon (eds), *The Political Influence of Ideas: Policy Communities and the Social Sciences*. New York: Praeger.

Smith, M. J. (2004). 'Mad Cows and Mad Money: Problems of Risk in the Making and Understanding of Policy'. *The British Journal of Politics and International Relations* 6, no. 3 : 312–32.

Smith, M. J., D. Marsh and D. Richards. (1993). 'Central Government Departments and the Policy Process'. *Public Administration* 71: 567–94 (at p. 580).

Smith, M. P. (2008). 'All Access Points Are Not Created Equal: Explaining the Fate of Diffuse Interests in the EU'. *British Journal of Politics and International Relations* 10: 64–83.

de Smith, S. A. (1973). *Judicial Review of Administrative Action*. London: Stevens & Son.

Smith, T. B. (1977). 'Advisory Committees in the Public Policy Process'. *International Review of Administrative Sciences* 43, no. 2: 153–66.

Sorensen, E. (2012). 'From Governance and Innovation in the Public Sector'. In D. Levi-Faur (eds), *The Oxford Handbook of Governance*. Oxford: Oxford University Press, 215–28.

Sorensen, E. and J. Torfing. (2005). 'Democratic Anchorage of Governance Networks'. *Scandinavian Political Studies* 28: 195–218.

Sorrell, S. and J. Sijm. (2003). 'Carbon Trading in the Policy Mix'. *Oxford Review of Economic Policy* 19, no. 3 (1 September): 420–37.

Sorrentino, M., C. Guglielmetti, S. Gilardi and M. Marsilio (2015). 'Health Care Services and the Coproduction Puzzle: Filling in the Blanks'. *Administration & Society* (July 9).

Sousa, D. and C. Klyza. (2007). 'New Directions in Environmental Policy Making: An Emerging Collaborative Regime or Reinventing Interest Group Liberalism'. *Natural Resources Journal* 47, no. 2: 377–444.

Sousa L. J., E. Ciriolo, A. S. Rafael, X. Troussard, European Commission, and Joint Research Centre (2016). *Behavioural Insights Applied to Policy: European Report 2016*. Luxembourg: European Commission and Joint Research Centre. http://bookshop.europa.eu/uri?target=EUB:NOTICE:KJNA27726:EN:HTML.

Sovacool, B. K. (2011). 'The Policy Challenges of Tradable Credits: A Critical Review of Eight Markets'. *Energy Policy* 39, no. 2: 575–85.

Speers, K. (2007). 'The Invisible Public Service: Consultants and Public Policy in Canada'. In L. Dobuzinskis, M. Howlett and D. Laycock (eds), *Policy Analysis in Canada: The State of the Art*. Toronto, ON: University of Toronto Press, 220–31.

Spence, A., W. Poortinga, C. Butler and N. F. Pidgeon. (2011). 'Perceptions of Climate Change and Willingness to Save Energy Related to Flood Experience'. *Nature Climate Change* 1, no. 1 : 46–9.

Spicker, P. (2005). 'Targeting, Residual Welfare and Related Concepts: Modes of Operation in Public Policy'. *Public Administration* 83, no. 2: 345–65.

Sproule-Jones, M. (1983). 'Institutions, Constitutions and Public Policies: A Public-Choice Overview'. In M. Atkinson and M. Chandler (eds), *The Politics of Canadian Public Policy*. Toronto, ON: University of Toronto Press, 127–50.

Stanbury, W. T. (1986). *Business–Government Relations in Canada: Grappling with Leviathan*. Toronto, ON: Methuen.

Stanbury, W. T. (1993). 'A Sceptic's Guide to the Claims of So-Called Public Interest Groups'. *Canadian Public Administration* 36, no. 4: 580–605.

Stanbury, W. T. and J. Fulton. (1984). 'Suasion as a Governing Instrument'. In A. Maslove (ed.), *How Ottawa Spends 1984: The New Agenda*. Toronto, ON: Lorimer, 282–324.

Stanbury, W. T., G. J. Gorn and C. B. Weinberg. (1983). 'Federal Advertising Expenditures'. In G. B. Doern (ed.), *How Ottawa Spends: The Liberals, the Opposition and Federal Priorities*. Toronto, ON: James Lorimer and Company, 133–72.

Starr, P. (1989). 'The Meaning of Privatization'. In S. B. Kamerman and A. J. Kahn (eds), *Privatization and the Welfare State*. Princeton, NJ: Princeton University Press, 15–48.

Starr, P. (1990a). 'The Limits of Privatization'. In D. J. Gayle and J. N. Goodrich (eds), *Privatization and Deregulation in Global Perspective*. New York: Quorum Books, 109–25.

Starr, P. (1990b). 'The New Life of the Liberal State: Privatization and the Restructuring of State–Society Relations'. In E. N. Suleiman and J. Waterbury (eds), *The Political Economy of Public Sector Reform and Privatization*. Boulder, CO: Westview, 22–54.

Stasiulis, D. K. (1988). 'The Symbolic Mosaic Reaffirmed: Multiculturalism Policy'. In K. A. Graham (ed.), *How Ottawa Spends 1988/89: The Conservatives Heading into the Stretch*. Ottawa, ON: Carleton University Press, 81–111.

State Services Commission. (1999a). *Essential Ingredients: Improving the Quality of Policy Advice*. Wellington, New Zealand: State Services Commission.

State Services Commission. (1999b). *High Fliers: Developing High Performing Policy Units*. Occasional Paper No. 22. Wellington, New Zealand: State Services Commission.

Statistics Canada. (2004). *Cornerstones of Community: Highlights of the National Survey of Nonprofit and Voluntary Organizations*. Ottawa, ON: Ministry of Industry.

Staub, E. (1972). 'Instigation to Goodness: The Role of Social Norms and Interpersonal Influence'. *Journal of Social Issues* 28, no. 3: 131–50.

Stavins, R. N. (1996). 'Correlated Uncertainty and Policy Instrument Choice'. *Journal of Environmental Economics and Management* 30, no. 2 (March): 218–32.

Stavins, R. N. (2001). *Lessons from the American Experiment with Market-Based Environmental Policies*. Washington, DC: Resources for the Future.

Stavins, R. N. (2008). 'A Meaningful US Cap-and-Trade System to Address Climate Change'. *Harvard Environmental Law Review* 32: 293–364.

Stead, D. and E. Meijers. (2004). 'Policy Integration in Practice: Some Experiences of Integrating Transport, Land-Use Planning and Environmental Politics in Local Government'. In *2004 Berlin Conference on the Human Dimensions of Global Environmental Change: Greening of Policies – Interlinkages and Policy Integration*, Berlin, Germany: 1–13.

Stead, D. and E. Meijers. (2009). 'Spatial Planning and Policy Integration: Concepts, Facilitators and Inhibitors'. *Planning Theory & Practice* 10, no. 3 (September): 317–32.

Stead, D., H. Geerlings and E. Meijers (eds). (2004). *Policy Integration in Practice: The Integration of Land Use Planning, Transport and Environmental Policy-Making in Denmark, England and Germany*. Delft, Netherlands: Delft University Press.

Stein, J. G., D. Cameron and R. Simeon. (1999). 'Citizen Engagement in Conflict Resolution: Lessons for Canada in International Experience'. In D. Cameron (ed.), *The Referendum Papers: Essays on Secession and National Unity*. Toronto, ON: University of Toronto Press, 144–98.

Stern, J. (1997). 'What Makes and Independent Regulator Independent?' *Business Strategy Review* 8, no. 2: 67–74.

Stern, J. and S. Holder. (1999). 'Regulatory Governance: Criteria for Assessing the Performance of Regulatory Systems – An Application to Infrastrucrure Industries in the Developing Countries of Asia'. *Utilities Policy* 8: 33–50.

Stern, N. H. (2007). *The Economics of Climate Change: The Stern Review*. Cambridge: Cambridge University Press.

Sterner, T. (2003). *Policy Instruments for Environmental and Natural Resource Management*. Washington, DC: Resources for the Future.

Steurer, R. (2009). 'The Role of Governments in Corporate Social Responsibility: Characterising Public Policies on CSR in Europe'. *Policy Sciences* 43, no. 1: 49–72.

Steurer, R. (2013). 'Disentangling Governance: A Synoptic View of Regulation by Government, Business and Civil Society'. *Policy Sciences* 46, no. 4 (1 December): 387–410.

Steurle, C. E. and E. C. Twombly. (2002). 'Vouchers'. In L. M. Salamon (ed.), *The Tools of Government: A Guide to the New Governance*. New York: Oxford University Press, 445–65.

Stevens, P. F. (1994). *The Development of Biological Systematics*. New York: Columbia University Press.

Stewart, J. (1993). 'Rational Choice Theory, Public Policy and the Liberal State. *Policy Sciences* 26, no. 4: 317–30.

Stewart, J. and R. Ayres. (2001). 'Systems Theory and Policy Practice: An Exploration'. *Policy Sciences* 34: 79–94.

Stewart, J. and A. J. Sinclair. (2007). 'Meaningful Public Participation in Environmental Assessment: Perspectives from Canadian Participants, Proponents and Government'. *Journal of Environmental Assessment Policy and Management 9*, no. 2: 161–83.

Stewart, K. and P. J. Smith. (2007). 'Immature Policy Analysis: Building Capacity in Eight Major Canadian Cities. In L. Dobuzinskis, M. Howlett and D. Laycock (eds), *Policy Analysis in Canada: The State of the Art*. Toronto, ON: University of Toronto Press, 146–58.

Stigler, G. J. (1975a). *The Citizen and the State: Essays on Regulation*. Chicago, IL: University of Chicago Press.

Stigler, G. J. (1975b). 'The Theory of Economic Regulation'. In G. Stigler (ed.), *The Citizen and the State*. Chicago, IL: University of Chicago Press, 114–41.

Stiglitz, J. (1998). 'The Private Uses of Public Interests: Incentives and Institutions'. *Journal of Economic Perspectives* 12, no. 2: 3–22.

Stillman, P. G. (1974). 'The Concept of Legitimacy'. *Polity* 7, no. 1: 32–56.

Stimson, J. A. (1991). *Public Opinion in America: Moods Cycles and Swings*. Boulder, CO: Westview Press.

Stimson, J. A., M. B. Mackuen and R. S. Erikson. (1995). 'Dynamic Representation'. *American Political Science Review* 89: 543–65.

Stirling, A. (2010). 'Keep It Complex'. *Nature* 468, no. 7327 (23 December): 1029–31.

Stokey, E. and R. Zeckhauser. (1978). *A Primer for Policy Analysis*. New York: W. W. Norton.

Stone, D. (1999). 'Learning Lessons and Transferring Policy across Time, Space and Disciplines'. *Politics* 19, no. 1: 51–9.

Stone, D. (2008). 'Global Public Policy, Transnational Policy Communities, and Their Networks'. *Policy Studies Journal* 36, no. 1: 19–38.

Stone, D. and A. Denham (eds). (2004). *Think Tank Traditions: Policy Research and the Politics of Ideas*. Manchester, UK: Manchester University Press.

Stone, D. A. (1988). *Policy Paradox and Political Reason*. Glenview, IL: Scott, Foresman.

Stone, D. A. (1989). 'Causal Stories and the Formation of Policy Agendas'. *Political Science Quarterly* 104, no. 2: 281–300.

Stone, D. A. (2001). 'Learning Lessons, Policy Transfer and the International Diffusion of Policy Ideas' (Working Paper 69/01). Coventry, UK: Centre for the Study of Globalization and Regionalization, University of Warwick.

Stouten, H., A. Heene, X. Gellynck and H. Polet. (2011). 'Policy Instruments to Meet Fisheries Management Objectives in Belgian Fisheries'. *Fisheries Research* (in press, accepted manuscript) 111, no. 1–2: 8–23.

Strange, S. (1996). *The Retreat of the State*. Cambridge: Cambridge University Press.

Strassheim, H. and R.-L. Korinek. (2015). 'Behavioural Governance in Europe'. In *Future Directions for Scientific Advice in Europe*. London: University of Cambridge/University of Sussex, 155–62.

Strassheim, H. and R.-L. Korinek. (2016). 'Cultivating "Nudge": Behavioural Governance in the UK'. In J.-P. Voß and R. Freeman (eds), *Knowing Governance*. Basingstoke: Palgrave Macmillan, 107–26.

Streeck, W. and Thelen, K. A. (2005). 'Introduction: Institutional Change in Advanced Political Economies'. In *Beyond Continuity*. Oxford: Oxford University Press, 1–39.

Stritch, A. (2007). 'Business Associations and Policy Analysis in Canada'. In L. Dobuzinskis, M. Howlett and D. Laycock (eds), *Policy Analysis in Canada: The State of the Art*. Toronto, ON: University of Toronto Press, 242–59.

Strolovitch, D. Z. (2006). 'Do Interest Groups Represent the Disadvantaged? Advocacy at the Intersections of Race, Class and Gender'. *The Journal of Politics* 68, no. 4: 894–910.

Stubbs, P. and S. Zrinščak. (2007). 'Croatia'. In B. Deacon and P. Stubbs (eds), *Social Policy and International Interventions in South East Europe*. Cheltenham, UK: Edward Elgar, 103–29.

Stutz, J. R. (2008). 'What Gets Done and Why: Implementing the Recommendations of Public Inquiries'. *Canadian Public Administration* 51, no. 3: 502–21.

Subramaniam, V. (1977). *Transplanted Indo-British Administration*. New Delhi, India: Ashish Publishing House.

Suchman, M. C. (1995). 'Managing Legitimacy: Strategic and Institutional Approaches'. *Academy of Management Review* 20, no. 3: 571–610.

Suleiman, E. N. and J. Waterbury (eds). (1990). *The Political Economy of Public Sector Reform and Privatization*. Boulder, CO: Westview Press.

Sulitzeanu-Kenan, R. (2007). 'Scything the Grass: Agenda-Setting Consequences of Appointing Public Inquiries in the UK, a Longitudinal Analysis'. *Policy and Politics* 35, no. 4: 629–50.

Sulitzeanu-Kenan, R. (2010). 'Reflection in the Shadow of Blame: When Do Politicians Appoint Commissions of Inquiry?' *British Journal of Political Science* 40, no. 3: 613–34.

Sulitzeanu-Kenan, R. and C. Hood. (2005). 'Blame Avoidance with Adjectives? Motivation, Opportunity, Activity and Outcome'. Paper for ECPR Joint Sessions, Blame Avoidance and Blame Management Workshop, Granada, Spain, 14–20 April.

Sunnevag, K. J. (2000). 'Designing Auctions for Offshore Petroleum Lease Allocation'. *Resources Policy* 26, no. 1: 3–16.

Sunstein, C. R. (1996). 'Social Norms and Social Roles'. *Columbia Law Review* 96, no. 4: 903–68.

Sunstein, C. R. (2006). 'The Availability Heuristic, Intuitive Cost-Benefit Analysis, and Climate Change'. *Climatic Change* 77, nos 1–2: 195–210.

Sunstein, C. R. (2013). *Simpler: The Future of Government* (reprint edn). New York: Simon & Schuster.

Sunstein, C. R. (2014). 'Nudging: A Very Short Guide'. *Journal of Consumer Policy* 37, no. 4: 583–88.

Sunstein, C. R. (2015). *Why Nudge? The Politics of Libertarian Paternalism* (reprint edn). New Haven, CT: Yale University Press.

Sunstein, C. R. (2016a). *The Ethics of Influence: Government in the Age of Behavioral Science*. Cambridge: Cambridge University Press.

Sunstein, C. R. (2016b). 'People Prefer System 2 Nudges (Kind Of)'. *Duke Law Journal* 66, no. 1 (1 October): 121–68.

Sunstein, C. R. and L. A. Reisch. (2013). 'Green by Default'. *Kyklos* 66, no. 3: 398–402.

Sunstein, C. R. and L. A. Reisch. (2016). *Climate-Friendly Default Rules* (Discussion Paper No. 878). Cambridge, MA: Harvard Law School. www.law.harvard.edu/programs/olin_center/papers/pdf/Sunstein_878.pdf.

Sunstein, C. R. and R. H. Thaler. (2003), 'Libertarian Paternalism Is not an Oxymoron'. *The University of Chicago Law Review*: 1159–1202.

Sunstein, C. R., D. Kahneman, D. Schkade and I. Ritov. (2001). *Predictably Incoherent Judgments* (1 July). SSRN Scholarly Paper. Rochester, NY: Social Science Research Network. Retrieved from http://papers.ssrn.com/abstract=279181.

Surel, Y. (2000). 'The Role of Cognitive and Normative Frames in Policy-Making'. *Journal of European Public Policy* 7, no. 4: 495–512.

Surrey, S. S. (1979). 'Tax Expenditure Analysis: The Concept and Its Uses'. *Canadian Taxation* 1, no. 2: 3–14.

Suzuki, M. (1992). 'Political Business Cycles in the Public Mind'. *American Political Science Review* 86: 989–96.

Svara, J. H. (1994). *Facilitative Leadership in Local Government: Lessons from Successful Mayors and Chairpersons*. San Francisco, CA: Jossey-Bass.

Swank, D. (2000). *Diminished Democracy? Global Capital, Political Institutions and Policy Change in Developed Welfare States*. New York: Cambridge University Press.

Swank, D. (2002). *Global Capital, Political Institutions and Policy Change in Developed Welfare States*. New York: Cambridge University Press.

Swann, D. (1988). *The Retreat of the State: Deregulation and Privatisation in the UK and US*. Hemel Hempstead, UK: Harvester Wheatsheaf.

Swanson, D. and S. Bhadwal (eds). (2009). *Creating Adaptive Policies: A Guide for Policy-Making in an Uncertain World*. Winnipeg, MB: IISD. www.iisd.org/publications/creating-adaptive-policies-guide-policy-making-uncertain-world.

Swanson, D., S. Barg, S. Tyler, H. Venema, S. Tomar, S. Bhadwal, S. Nair, D. Roy and J. Drexhage. (2010). 'Seven Tools for Creating Adaptive Policies'. *Technological Forecasting and Social Change* 77, no. 6 (July): 924–39.

Swedlow, B. (2011). 'Cultural Surprises as Sources of Sudden, Big Policy Change'. *PS: Political Science & Politics* 44, no. 4: 736–39.

Székely, M. (2011). 'Toward Results-Based Social Policy Design and Implementation'. CGD Working Paper 249. Washington, DC: Center for Global Development. www.cgdev.org/content/publications/detail/1425010.

Taeihagh, A., R. Bañares-Alcántara and M. Givoni. (2014). 'A Virtual Environment for the Formulation of Policy Packages'. *Transportation Research Part A: Policy and Practice* 60, no. 1: 53–68.

Taeihagh, A., R. Bañares-Alcántara and Z. Wang. (2009). 'A Novel Approach to Policy Design Using Process Design Principles'. In C. A. O. do Nascimento and E. C. B. R. M. de Brito Alves (eds), *Computer Aided Chemical Engineering* Vol. 27. London: Elsevier, 2049–54.

Taeihagh, A., M. Givoni and R. Bañares-Alcántara. (2013). 'Which Policy First? A Network-Centric Approach for the Analysis and Ranking of Policy Measures'. *Environment and Planning B: Planning and Design* 40, no. 4: 595–616.

Taeihagh, A. (2017). 'Crowdsourcing: A New Tool for Policy-Making?' *Policy Sciences* 50, no. 4 (1 December): 629–47.

Tallontire, A. (2007). 'CSR and Regulation: Towards a Framework for Understanding Private Standards Initiatives in the Agri-Food Chain'. *Third World Quarterly* 28, no. 4: 775–91.

Tanner, S. (2007). *Common Themes on Commissioning the VCS in Selected Local Authorities in Greater London*. London: London Councils.

Taylor, C., S. Pollard, S. Rocks and A. Angus. (2012). 'Selecting Policy Instruments for Better Environmental Regulation: A Critique and Future Research Agenda'. *Environmental Policy and Governance* (8 May).

Taylor, M. (2008). 'Beyond Technology-Push and Demand-Pull: Lessons from California's Solar Policy'. *Energy Economics* 30: 2829–54.

Taylor, R. and A. Migone. (2017). 'From Procurement to the Commissioning of Public Services'. Paper presented at the IPAC, Charlottetown, PE.

Teghtsoonian, K. and L. Chappell. (2008). 'The Rise and Decline of Women's Policy Machinery in British Columbia and New South Wales: A Cautionary Tale'. *International Political Science Review* 29, no. 1: 29–51.

Teghtsoonian, K. and J. Grace. (2001). ' "Something More Is Necessary": The Mixed Achievements of Women's Policy Agencies in Canada'. In A. G. Mazur (ed.), *State Feminism, Women's Movements and Job Training: Making Democracies Work in a Global Economy*. New York: Routledge, 235–69.

Teisman, G. R. (2000). 'Models for Research into Decision-Making Processes: On Phases, Streams and Decision-Making Rounds'. *Public Administration* 78, no. 4: 937–56.

Tenbensel, T. (2004). 'Does More Evidence Lead to Better Policy? The Implications of Explicit Priority-Setting in New Zealand's Health Policy for Evidence-Based Policy'. *Policy Studies* 25, no. 3: 190–207.

Tenbensel, T. (2005). 'Multiple Modes of Governance: Disentangling the Alternatives to Hierarchies and Markets'. *Public Management Review* 7, no. 2: 267–88.

Tenbensel, T. (2008). 'The Role of Evidence in Policy: How the Mix Matters'. Paper presented at the International Research Society for Public Management, Queensland University of Technology, Brisbane, QLD, Australia, 26–8 March.

Termeer, C. J. A. M. and J. F. M. Koppenjan. (1997). 'Managing Perceptions in Networks'. In W. J. M. Kickert, E.-H. Klijn and J. F. M. Koppenjan (eds), *Managing Complex Networks: Strategies for the Public Sector*. London: Sage, 79–97.

Thadani, K. B. (2014). 'Public Private Partnership in the Health Sector: Boon or Bane'. *Procedia: Social and Behavioral Sciences*. International Relations Conference on India and Development Partnerships in Asia and Africa: Towards a New Paradigm, 157 (27 November): 307–16.

Thaler, R. H. (2015). *Misbehaving: The Making of Behavioral Economics*. New York: W. W. Norton.

Thaler, R. H. and S. Mullainathan. (2008). 'Behavioral Economics'. In *The Concise Encyclopedia of Economics* (2nd edn). www.econlib.org/library/Enc/Behavioral Economics.html.

Thaler, R. H. and C. R. Sunstein. (2009). *Nudge: Improving Decisions about Health, Wealth, and Happiness* (expanded and revised edition). New York: Penguin Books.

Thaler, R. H., C. R. Sunstein and J. P. Balz. (2010). *Choice Architecture* (2 April). SSRN Scholarly Paper. Rochester, NY: Social Science Research Network. Retrieved from http://papers.ssrn.com/abstract=1583509.

Thatcher, M. (2002). 'Analyzing Regulatory Reform in Europe'. *Journal of European Public Policy* 9, no. 6: 859–72 .

Thatcher, M. and A. Stone-Sweet (eds). (2003). *The Politics of Delegation*. London: Frank Cass.

Thelen, K. (2003). 'How Institutions Evolve: Insights from Comparative Historical Analysis'. In J. Mahoney and D. Rueschemeyer (eds), *Comparative Historical Analysis in the Social Sciences*. Cambridge: Cambridge University Press, 208–40.

Thelen, K. (2004). *How Institutions Evolve: The Political Economy of Skills in Germany, Britain, the United States and Japan*. Cambridge: Cambridge University Press.

van Thiel, S. (2008). 'The "Empty Nest" Syndrome: Dutch Ministries after the Separation of Policy and Administration'. Paper presented to the IRSPM Conference, Brisbane, QLD, Australia.

Tholoniat, L. (2010). 'The Career of the Open Method of Coordination: Lessons from a "Soft" EU-Instrument'. *West European Politics* 33, no. 1: 93.

Thomas, E. V. (2003). 'Sustainable Development, Market Paradigms and Policy Integration'. *Journal of Environmental Policy and Planning* 5, no. 2: 201–16.

Thomas, H. G. (2001). 'Towards a New Higher Education Law in Lithuania: Reflections on the Process of Policy Formulation'. *Higher Education Policy* 14, no. 3: 213–23.

Thompson, G. F. (2003). *Between Hierarchies and Markets: The Logic and Limits of Network Forms of Organization*. Oxford: Oxford University Press.

Thomson, J. E. and S. D. Krasner. (1989). 'Global Transactions and the Consolidation of Sovereignty'. In E. O. Czempiel and J. N. Rosenau (eds), *Global Changes and Theoretical Challenges*. Lexington, CT: Lexington Books, 195–219.

Thorelli, H. B. (1986). 'Networks: Between Markets and Hierarchies'. *Strategic Management Journal* 7: 37–51.

Tiernan, A. (2011). 'Advising Australian Federal Governments: Assessing the Evolving Capacity and Role of the Australian Public Service'. *Australian Journal of Public Administration* 70, no. 4 (1 December): 335–46.

Tiernan, A. and J. Wanna. (2006). 'Competence, Capacity, Capability: Towards Conceptual Clarity in the Discourse of Declining Policy Skills'. Paper presented at the Govnet International Conference, Australian National University, Canberra, ACT, Australia.

Timmermans, A., C. Rothmayr, U. Serduelt and F. Varone. (1998). 'The Design of Policy Instruments: Perspectives and Concepts'. Paper presented to the Midwest Political Science Association, Chicago, IL.

Tinbergen, J. (1952). *On the Theory of Economic Policy*. Dordrecht, Netherlands: North-Holland.

Tinbergen, J. (1958). *The Design of Development*. Baltimore, MD: Johns Hopkins University Press.

Tinbergen, J. (1967). *Economic Policy: Principles and Design*. Chicago, IL: Rand McNally.

Toke, D. (2008). 'Trading Schemes, Risks, and Costs: The Cases of the European Union Emissions Trading Scheme and the Renewables Obligation'. *Environment and Planning C: Government and Policy* 26: 938–53.

Tollefson, C. (2004). 'Indigenous Rights and Forest Certification in British Columbia'. In J. Kirton and M. Trebilcock (eds), *Hard Choices, Soft Law: Voluntary Standards in Global Trade, Environment and Social Governance*. Aldershot, UK: Ashgate.

Tollefson, C. G. F. and D. Haley. (2008). *Setting the Standard: Certification, Governance and the Forest Stewardship Council*. Vancouver, BC: University of British Columbia Press.

Tollefson, C., A. R. Zito and F. Gale. (2012). 'Symposium Overview: Conceptualizing New Governance Arrangements'. *Public Administration* 90, no. 1: 3–18.

Tollison, R. D. (1991). 'Regulation and Interest Groups'. In J. High (ed.), *Regulation: Economic Theory and History*. Ann Arbor, MI: University of Michigan Press, 59–76.

Torenvlied, R. and A. Akkerman. (2004). 'Theory of "Soft" Policy Implementation in Multilevel Systems with an Application to Social Partnership in the Netherlands'. *Acta Politica* 39: 31–58.

Torgerson, D. (1985). 'Contextual Orientation in Policy Analysis: The Contribution of Harold D. Lasswell'. *Policy Sciences* 18: 240–52.

Torgerson, D. (1986). 'Between Knowledge and Politics: Three Faces of Policy Analysis'. *Policy Sciences* 19, no. 1: 33–59.

Torgerson, D. (1990). 'Origins of the Policy Orientation: The Aesthetic Dimension in Lasswell's Political Vision'. *History of Political Thought* 11 (Summer): 340–44.

Torres, L. (2004). 'Trajectories in Public Administration Reforms in European Continental Countries'. *Australian Journal of Public Administration* 63, no. 3: 99–112.

Tosun, J. (2013). 'How the EU Handles Uncertain Risks: Understanding the Role of the Precautionary Principle'. *Journal of European Public Policy* 20, no. 10: 1517–28.

Tosun, J. and K. Marcinkiewicz. (2015; online first). 'Contesting Climate Change: Mapping the Political Debate in Poland'. *East European Politics* 31, no. 2: 187–207.

Townsend, R. E., J. McColl and M. D. Young. (2006). 'Design Principles for Individual Transferable Quotas'. *Marine Policy* 30: 131–41.

Treasury Board of Canada Secretariat. (2007). *Assessing, Selecting and Implementing Instruments for Government Action*. Ottawa, ON: Treasury Board.

Trebilcock, M. J. (1983). 'Regulating Service Quality in Professional Markets'. In D. N. Dewees (ed.), *The Regulation of Quality: Products, Services, Workplaces and the Environment*. Toronto, ON: Butterworths, 83–108.

Trebilcock, M. J. (2008). 'Regulating the Market for Legal Services'. *Alberta Law Review* 45,: 215–32.

Trebilcock, M. J. and D. G. Hartle. (1982). 'The Choice of Governing Instrument'. *International Review of Law and Economics* 2: 29–46.

Trebilcock, M. J. and J. R. S. Prichard. (1983). 'Crown Corporations: The Calculus of Instrument Choice'. In J. R. S. Prichard (eds), *Crown Corporations in Canada: The Calculus of Instrument Choice*. Toronto, ON: Butterworths, 1–50.

Trebilcock, M. J., D. Dewees and D. G. Hartle. (1982). *The Choice of Governing Instrument*. Ottawa, ON: Economic Council of Canada.

Trebilcock, M. J., C. J. Tuohy and A. D. Wolfson. (1979). *Professional Regulation: A Staff Study of Accountancy, Architecture, Engineering, and Law in Ontario Prepared for the Professional Organizations Committee*. Toronto, ON: Ontario Ministry of the Attorney General.

Treib, O., H. Bahr and G. Falkner. (2007). 'Modes of Governance: Towards a Conceptual Clarification'. *Journal of European Public Policy* 14: 1–20.

Treisman, D. (2007). 'What Have We Learned about the Causes of Corruption from Ten Years of Cross-National Empirical Research?' *Annual Review of Political Science* 10: 211–44.

Tribe, L. H. (1972). 'Policy Science: Analysis or Ideology?' *Philosophy and Public Affairs* 2, no. 1: 66–110.

Trondal, J. and L. Jeppesen. (2008). 'Images of Agency Governance in the European Union'. *West European Politics* 31, no. 3: 417–41.

True, J. and M. Mintrom. (2001). 'Transnational Networks and Policy Diffusion: The Case of Gender Mainstreaming'. *International Studies Quarterly* 45: 27–57.

Truman, D. R. (1964). *The Governmental Process: Political Interests and Public Opinion*. New York: Knopf.

Tsao, K. K. (2009). 'Building Administrative Capacity: Lessons Learned from China'. *Public Administration Review* 69, no. 6: 1021–4.

Tsasis, P. (2008). 'The Politics of Governance: Government–Voluntary Sector Relationships'. *Canadian Public Administration* 51, no. 2: 265–90.

Tschakert, P. and K. A. Dietrich. (2010). 'Anticipatory Learning for Climate Change Adaptation and Resilience'. *Ecology and Society* 15, no. 2: 11.

Tsebelis, G. (2002). *Veto Players. How Political Institutions Work*. Princeton, NJ: Princeton University Press.

Tunzelmann, N. von. (2010). 'Technology and Technology Policy in the Postwar UK: Market Failure or Network Failure?' *Revue d'économie industrielle*, nos 129–30, 237–58.

Tuohy, C. (1992). *Policy and Politics in Canada: Institutionalized Ambivalence.* Philadelphia, PA: Temple University Press.

Tuohy, C. (1999). *Accidental Logics: The Dynamics of Change in the Health Care Arena in the United States, Britain and Canada.* New York: Oxford University Press.

Tuohy, C. J. and A. D. Wolfson. (1978). 'Self-Regulation: Who Qualifies?' In P. Slayton and M. J. Trebilcock (eds), *The Professions and Public Policy.* Toronto, ON: University of Toronto Press, 111–22.

Tupper, A. (1979). 'The State in Business'. *Canadian Public Administration* 22, no. 1: 124–50.

Tupper, A. and G. B. Doern. (1981). 'Public Corporations and Public Policy in Canada'. In A. Tupper, and G. B. Doern (eds), *Public Corporations and Public Policy in Canada.* Montreal, QC: Institute for Research on Public Policy, 1–50.

Turnbull, N. (2017). 'Policy Design: Its Enduring Appeal in a Complex World and How to Think It Differently'. *Public Policy and Administration* (31 May).

Turnpenny, J., M. Nilsson, D. Russel, A. Jordan, J. Hertin and B. Nykvist. (2008). 'Why is Integrating Policy Assessment so Hard? A Comparative Analysis of the Institutional Capacity and Constraints'. *Journal of Environmental Planning and Management* 51, no. 6: 759–75.

Turnpenny, J., C. M. Radaelli, A. Jordan and K. Jacob. (2009). 'The Policy and Politics of Policy Appraisal: Emerging Trends and New Directions'. *Journal of European Public Policy* 16, no. 4: 640–53.

Tversky, A. and D. Kahneman. (1973). Availability: A Heuristic for Judging Frequency and Probability. *Cognitive Psychology* 5, no. 2: 207–32.

Tversky, A. and D. Kahneman. (1974). 'Judgment under Uncertainty: Heuristics and Biases'. *Science* 185, no. 4157: 1124–31.

Tversky, A. and D. Kahneman. (1981). 'The Framing of Decisions and the Psychology of Choice'. *Science* 211, no. 4481: 453–8.

Uhr, J. (1996). Testing the Policy Capacities of Budgetary Agencies: Lessons from Finance. *Australian Journal of Public Administration* 55, no. 4: 124–34.

Uhr, J. and K. Mackay (eds). (1996). *Evaluating Policy Advice: Learning from Commonwealth Experience.* Canberra, ACT: Australian National University, Federalism Research Centre.

UK Cabinet Office. (1999). *Professional Policy Making for the Twenty-First Century.* London: Cabinet Office, Strategic Policy Making Team.

Ulrich, B. (1995). 'The History and Possible Causes of Forest Decline in Central Europe, with Particular Attention to the German Situation'. *Environmental Reviews* 3: 262–76.

Underdal, A. (1980). 'Integrated Marine Policy: What/Why/How?' *Marine Policy* 4, no. 3: 159–69.

UNFCC. (1992). 'United Nations Framework Convention on Climate Change' (Treaty). http://unfccc.int/files/essential_background/background_publications_htmlpdf/appl ication/pdf/conveng.pdf.

Ungar, S. (1992). 'The Rise and (Relative) Decline of Global Warming as a Social Problem'. *The Sociological Quarterly* 33, no. 4: 483–501.

Unger, B. and F. van Waarden. (1995). 'Introduction: An Interdisciplinary Approach to Convergence'. In B. Unger and F. van Waarden (eds), *Convergence or Diversity? Internationalization and Economic Policy Response.* Aldershot, UK: Avebury, 1–35.

Uribe, C. A. (2014). 'The *Dark Side* of Social Capital Re-Examined from a Policy Analysis Perspective: Networks of Trust and Corruption'. *Journal of Comparative Policy Analysis: Research and Practice* 16, no. 2: 175–89.

Utton, M. A. (1986). *The Economics of Regulating Industry*. London: Basil Blackwell.

Valkama, P. and S. J. Bailey. (2001). 'Vouchers as an Alternative Public Sector Funding System'. *Public Policy and Administration* 16, no. 1: 32–58.

Van Beers, C. and A. De Moor. (2001). *Public Subsidies and Policy Failures. How Subsidies Distort the Natural Environment, Equity and Trade and How to Reform Them*. Cheltenham, UK; Northampton, MA: Edward Elgar.

Vancoppenolle, D., H. Sætren and P. Hupe. (2015). 'The Politics of Policy Design and Implementation: A Comparative Study of Two Belgian Service Voucher Programs'. *Journal of Comparative Policy Analysis: Research and Practice* 17, no. 2 (21 April): 157–73.

Van Detten, R. (ed.) (2013). *Das Waldsterben. Rückblick auf einen Ausnahmezustand*. Munich, Germany: Oekom Verlag.

Van de Walle, S. (2014). 'Building Resilience in Public Organizations: The Role of Waste and Bricolage'. *The Innovation Journal: The Public Sector Innovation Journal* 19, no. 2: 1–18.

Van den Berg, C. F. (2017). 'Dynamics in the Dutch Policy Advisory System: Externalization, Politicization and the Legacy of Pillarization'. *Policy Sciences* 50, no. 1 (1 March): 63–84.

Van der Heijden, J. (2011). 'Institutional Layering: A Review of the Use of the Concept'. *Politics* 31, no. 1 (January 10): 9–18.

Van Gossum, P., B. Arts and K. Verheyen. (2009). '"Smart Regulation": Can Policy Instrument Design Solve Forest Policy Aims of Expansion and Sustainability in Flanders and the Netherlands?' *Forest Policy and Economics* 11: 616–27.

Van Heffen, O., W. J. M. Kickert and J. A. A. Thomassen. (2000a). *Governance in Modern Society: Effects, Change and Formation of Government Institutions*. Dordrecht, Netherlands: Kluwer.

Van Heffen, O., W. J. M. Kickert and J. J. A. Thomassen. (2000b). 'Introduction: Multi-Level and Multi-Actor Governance'. In O. Van Heffen, W. J. M. Kickert and J. J. A. Thomassen (eds), *Governance in Modern Society: Effects, Change and Formation of Government Institutions*. Dordrecht, Netherlands: Kluwer, 3–12.

Van Kersbergen, K. and F. Van Waarden. (2004). '"Governance" as a Bridge between Disciplines: Cross-Disciplinary Inspiration Regarding Shifts in Governance and Problems of Governability, Accountability an Legitimacy'. *European Journal of Political Research* 43, no. 2: 143–72.

Varone, F. (1998). 'Policy Design: Le choix des instruments des politiques publiques'. *Evaluation* 2: 5–14.

Varone F. (2000). 'Le choix des instruments de l'action publique analyse comparée des politiques energetiques en Europe at en Amerique du Nord'. *Revue Internationale de Politique Comparee* 7, no 1: 167–201.

Varone, F. (2001). 'Les instruments de la politique energetique: Analyse comparée du Canada et des Etats Unis'. *Canadian Journal of Political Science* 34, no. 1: 3–28.

Varone, F. and B. Aebischer. (2001). 'Energy Efficiency: The Challenges of Policy Design'. *Energy Policy* 29, no. 8: 615–29.

Vedung, E. (1997a). 'Policy Instruments: Typologies and Theories'. In M. L. Bemelmans-Videc, R. C. Rist and E. Vedung (eds), *Carrots, Sticks and Sermons: Policy Instruments and Their Evaluation*. New Brunswick, NJ: Transaction, 21–58.

Vedung, E. (1997b). 'Public Policy and Program Evaluation. Transaction Publishers of Political Feasibility'. *Futures* 1, no. 4: 282–8.

Vedung, E. and F. C. J. van der Doelen. (1998). 'The Sermon: Information Programs in the Public Policy Process – Choice, Effects and Evaluation'. In M.-L. Bemelmans-Videc, R. C. Rist and E. Vedung (eds), *Carrots, Sticks and Sermons: Policy Instruments and Their Evaluation*. New Brunswick, NJ: Transaction Publishers, 103–28.

Veggeland, N. (2008). 'Path Dependence and Public Sector Innovation in Regulatory Regimes'. *Scandinavian Political Studies* 31, no. 3: 268–90.

Veld, R. J. in't (1998). 'The Dynamics of Instruments'. In B. G. Peters and F. K. M. Van Nispen (eds), *Public Policy Instruments: Evaluating the Tools of Public Administration*. New York: Edward Elgar, 153–62.

Veljanovski, C. (1988). *Selling the State: Privatisation in Britain*. London: Weidenfeld & Nicolson.

Verheijen, T. (1999). *Civil Service Systems in Central and Eastern Europe*. Cheltenham, UK: Edward Elgar.

Verhoest, K., B. Verschuere and G. Bouckaert. (2007). 'Pressure, Legitimacy and Innovative Behavior by Public Organizations'. *Governance* 20, no. 3: 469–97.

Verhoest, K., P. G. Roness, B. Verschuere, K. Rubecksen and M. MacCarthaigh. (2010). *Autonomy and Control of State Agencies: Comparing States and Agencies*. London: Palgrave Macmillan.

Verschuere, B. (2009). 'The Role of Public Agencies in the Policy Making Process'. *Public Policy and Administration* 24, no. 1: 23–46.

Verweij, M., R. Ellis, F. Hendriks, S. Ney, M. Thompson et al. (2006). 'Clumsy Solutions for a Complex World. The Case of Climate Change'. *Public Administration* 84, no. 4: 817–43.

Vigoda, E. (2002). 'From Responsiveness to Collaboration: Governance, Citizens and the Next Generation of Public Administration'. *Public Administration Review* 62, no. 5: 527–40.

Vigoda, E. and E. Gilboa. (2002). 'The Quest for Collaboration: Toward a Comprehensive Strategy for Public Administration'. *Public Administration and Public Policy* 99: 99–117.

Vimpani, G. (2005). 'Getting the Mix Right: Family, Community and Social Policy Interventions to Improve Outcomes for Young People at Risk of Substance Misuse'. *Drug and Alcohol Review* 24: 111–25.

Vincent-Jones, P. (2006). *The New Public Contracting: Regulation, Responsiveness, Relationality*. Oxford: Oxford University Press.

Vining, A. R. and R. Botterell. (1983). 'An Overview of the Origins, Growth, Size and Functions of Provincial Crown Corporations'. In J. R. S. Pritchard (ed.), *Crown Corporations: The Calculus of Instrument Choice*. Toronto, ON: Butterworths, 303–68.

Vining, A. R. and A. E. Boardman. (2008). 'Public–Private Partnerships: Eight Rules for Governments'. *Public Works Management & Policy* 13, no. 2 (1 October): 149–61.

Vining, A. R., A. E. Boardman and F. Poschmann. (2005). 'Public–Private Partnerships in the US and Canada: "There Are No Free Lunches"'. *Journal of Comparative Policy Analysis* 7, no. 3: 199–220.

Viscusi, W. K. and T. Gayer. (2015). 'Behavioral Public Choice: The Behavioral Paradox of Government Policy'. *Harvard Journal of Law & Public Policy* 38: 973.

de Vita, C. J. and E. C. Twombly. (2005). 'Who Gains from Charitable Tax Credit Programs? The Arizona Model'. *Public Administration Review* 65, no. 1: 57–63.

Vogel, D. (1986). *National Styles of Regulation: Environmental Policy in Great Britain and the United States*. Ithaca, NY: Cornell University Press.

Vogel, D. (2001). 'Is There a Race to the Bottom? The Impact of Globalization on National Regulatory Policies'. *The Tocqueville Review/La Revue Tocqueville* 22: 1.

Vogel, D. (2005). *The Market for Virtue: The Potential and Limits of Corporate Social Responsibility*. Washington, DC: Brookings Institution.

Vogel, D. and R. A. Kagan (eds). (2002). *Dynamics of Regulatory Change: How Globalization Affects National Regulatory Policies*. Berkeley, CA: University of California Press.

Vogel, S. K. (1996). *Freer Markets, More Rules: Regulatory Reform in Advanced Industrial Countries*. Ithaca, NY: Cornell University Press.

Volkery, A. and T. Ribeiro. (2009). 'Scenario Planning in Public Policy: Understanding Use, Impacts and the Role of Institutional Context Factors'. *Technological Forecasting and Social Change* 76, no. 9: 1198–1207.

Voorberg, W. H., V. J. J. M. Bekkers and L. G. Tummers. (2015). 'A Systematic Review of Co-Creation and Co-Production: Embarking on the Social Innovation Journey'. *Public Management Review* 17, no. 9 (21 October): 1333–57.

Voss, J.-P. and B. Bornemann. (2011). 'The Politics of Reflexive Governance: Challenges for Designing Adaptive Management and Transition Management'. *Ecology and Society* 16, no. 2: 9.

Voss, J.-P. (2007). 'Innovation Process in Governance: The Development of "Emissions Trading" as a New Policy Instrument'. *Science and Public Policy* 34, no. 5: 329–43.

Voss, J.-P. and A. Simons. (2014). 'Instrument Constituencies and the Supply Side of Policy Innovation: The Social Life of Emissions Trading'. *Environmental Politics* 23, no. 5: 735–54.

Voss, J.-P., D. Bauknecht and R. Kemp (eds). (2006). *Reflexive Governance for Sustainable Development*. Cheltenham, UK: Edward Elgar.

Voss, J.-P., A. Smith and J. Grin. (2009). 'Designing Long-term Policy: Rethinking Transition Management'. *Policy Sciences* 42, no. 4: 275–302.

Voyer, J.-P. (2007). 'Policy Analysis in the Federal Government: Building the Forward-Looking Policy Research Capacity'. In. L. Dobuzinskis, M. Howlett and D. Laycock (eds), *Policy Analysis in Canada: The State of the Art*. Toronto, ON: University of Toronto Press, 123–31.

Vreugdenhil, H., S. Taljaard and J. H. Slinger. (2012). 'Pilot Projects and Their Diffusion: A Case Study of Integrated Coastal Management in South Africa'. *International Journal of Sustainable Development* 15, nos 1/2: 148.

de Vries, M. S. (1999). 'Developments in Europe: The Idea of Policy Generations'. *International Review of Administrative Sciences* 65, no. 4: 491–510.

de Vries, M. S. (2002). 'The Changing Functions of Laws and its Implication for Government and Governance'. *International Review of Administrative Sciences* 68, no. 4: 599–618.

de Vries, M. S. (2005). 'Generations of interactive Policy-Making in the Netherlands'. *International Review of Administrative Sciences* 71, no. 4: 577–91.

de Vries, M. S. (2010). *The Importance of Neglect in Policy-Making*. Basingstoke: Palgrave Macmillan.

van Waarden, F. (1995). 'Persistence of National Policy Styles: A Study of Their Institutional Foundations'. In B. Unger and F. van Waarden (eds), *Convergence or Diversity? Internationalization and Economic Policy Response*. Aldershot, UK: Avebury, 333–72.

Wagenaar, H. and S. D. N. Cook. (2003). 'Understanding Policy Practices: Action, Dialectic and Deliberation in Policy Analysis'. In M. A. Hajer and H. Wagenaar *Deliberative Policy Analysis: Understanding Governance in the Network Society*. London: Cambridge University Press, 139–71.

Waldo, D. (1984). *The Administrative State: A Study of the Political Theory of American Public Administration*. New York: Ronald Press.

Walker, A. (1984). 'The Political Economy of Privatisation'. In J. Le Grand and R. Robinson (eds), *Privatisation and the Welfare State*. London: George Allen & Unwin, 19–44.

Walker, J. L. (1969). 'The Diffusion of Innovations Among the States'. *American Political Science Review* 63, no. 3: 880–99.

Walker, J. L. (1977). 'Setting the Agenda in the US Senate: A Theory of Problem Selection'. *British Journal of Political Science* 7: 423–45.

Walker, J. L. (1983). 'The Origins and Maintenance of Interest Groups in America'. *American Political Science Review* 77, no. 2: 390–406.

Walker, J. L (1991). *Mobilizing Interest Groups in America: Patrons, Professions and Social Movements*. Ann Arbor, MI: University of Michigan Press.

Walker, W. E. (2000). 'Policy Analysis: A Systematic Approach to Supporting Policymaking in the Public Sector'. *Journal of Multi-Criteria Decision Analysis* 9, no. 1: 11–27.

Walker, W. E., R. J. Lempert and J. H. Kwakkel. (2013). 'Deep Uncertainty'. In S. I. Goss and M. C. Fu. *Encyclopaedia of Operations Research and Management Science*. New York: Springer, 395–402.

Walker, W. E., S. A. Rahman and J. Cave. (2001). 'Adaptive Policies, Policy Analysis, and Policy-Making'. *European Journal of Operational Research* 128, no. 2 (16 January): 282–9.

Walker, W. E., V. A. W. J. Marchau, and D. Swanson. (2010). 'Addressing Deep Uncertainty Using Adaptive Policies: Introduction to Section 2'. *Technological Forecasting and Social Change* 77, no. 6: 917–23.

Waller, M. (1992). 'Evaluating Policy Advice'. *Australian Journal of Public Administration* 51, no. 4: 440–9.

Walls, C. E. S. (1969). 'Royal Commissions: Their Influence on Public Policy'. *Canadian Public Administration* 12, no. 3: 365–71.

Walsh, C. (1988). 'Individual Irrationality and Public Policy: In Search of Merit/Demerit Policies'. *Journal of Public Policy* 7, no. 2: 103–34.

Walsh, C. (1990). 'Individual Irrationality and Public Policy: In Search of Merit/Demerit Policies'. In G. Brennan and C. Walsh (eds), *Rationality, Individualism and Public Policy*. Canberra, ACT: Australian National University, Centre for Research on Federal Financial Relations, 145–77.

Walsh, J. I. (1994). 'Institutional Constraints and Domestic Choices: Economic Convergence and Exchange Rate Policy in France and Italy'. *Political Studies* 42, no. 2: 243–58.

Walsh, P., M. McGregor-Lowndes and C. J. Newton. (2008). 'Shared Services: Lessons from the Public and Private Sectors for the Nonprofit Sector'. *Australian Journal of Public Administration* 67, no. 2: 200–12.

Walters, L. C., J. Aydelotte and J. Miller. (2000). 'Putting More Public in Policy Analysis'. *Public Administration Review* 60, no. 4: 349–59.

Walters, W. (2004). 'Some Critical Notes on "Governance"'. *Studies in Political Economy* 73: 27–46.

Warburton, R. N. and W. P. Warburton. (2004). 'Canada Needs Better Data for Evidence-Based Policy: Inconsistencies between Administrative and Survey Data on Welfare Dependence and Education'. *Canadian Public Policy* 30, no. 3: 241–55.

Wardekker, J. A., A. de Jong, J. M. Knoop and J. P. van der Sluijs. (2010). 'Operationalising a Resilience Approach to Adapting an Urban Delta to Uncertain Climate Changes'. *Technological Forecasting and Social Change* 77, no. 6 (July): 987–98.

Warren, R. (1987). 'Coproduction, Volunteerism, Privatization, and the Public Interest'. *Nonprofit and Voluntary Sector Quarterly* 16, no. 3 (1 January): 5–10.

Warren, R., K. S. Harlow and M. S. Rosentraub. (1982). 'Citizen Participation of Services: Methodological and Policy Issues in Coproduction Research'. *Southwest Review of Management and Economics* 2: 41–55.

Warwick, P. V. (2000). 'Policy Horizons in West European Parliamentary Systems'. *European Journal of Political Research* 38, no. 1: 37–61.

Weatherford, M. S. (1989). 'Political Economy and Political Legitimacy: The Link Between Economic Policy and Political Trust'. In H. D. Clarke, M. C. Stewart and G. Zuk (eds), *Economic Decline and Political Change: Canada, Great Britain, the United States*. Pittsburgh, PA: University of Pittsburgh Press, 225–51.

Weaver, R. K. (1986). 'The Politics of Blame Avoidance'. *Journal of Public Policy* 6, no. 4: 371–98.

Weaver, R. K. (2009a). 'If You Build It, Will They Come? Overcoming Unforeseen Obstacles to Program Effectiveness'. *The Tansley Lecture*. Saskatoon, SK: University of Saskatchewan.

Weaver, R. K. (2009b). *Target Compliance: The Final Frontier of Policy Implementation*. Washington, DC: Brookings Institution. www.brookings.edu/research/papers/2009/09/30-compliance-weaver.

Weaver, R. K. (2010a). *But Will It Work? Implementation Analysis to Improve Government Performance*. Washington, DC: Brookings Institution. www.brookings.edu/research/papers/2010/02/implementation-analysis-weaver.

Weaver, R. K. (2010b). 'Paths and Forks or Chutes and Ladders? Negative Feedbacks and Policy Regime Change'. *Journal of Public Policy* 30, no. 2: 137–62.

Weaver, R. K. (2014). 'Compliance Regimes and Barriers to Behavioral Change'. *Governance* 27, no. 2: 243–65.

Weaver, R. K. (2015). 'Getting People to Behave: Research Lessons for Policy Makers'. *Public Administration Review* 75, no. 6: 806–16.

Weaver, R. K. and B. A. Rockman. (1993a). 'Assessing the Effects of Institutions'. In R. K. Weaver and B. A. Rockman (eds), *Do Institutions Matter? Government Capabilities in the United States and Abroad*. Washington, DC: Brookings Institution, 1–41.

Weaver, R. K. and B. A. Rockman. (1993b). 'When and How Do Institutions Matter?' In R. K. Weaver and B. A. Rockman (eds), *Do Institutions Matter? Government Capabilities in the United States and Abroad*. Washington, DC: Brookings Institution, 445–63.

Webb, K. (1987). 'Between the Rocks and Hard Places: Bureaucrats, the Law and Pollution Control'. *Alternatives* 14, no. 2: 4–13.

Webb, K. (1990). 'On the Periphery: The Limited Role for Criminal Offences in Environmental Protection'. In D. Tingley (ed.), *Into the Future: Environmental Law and Policy for the 1990s*. Edmonton, AB: Environmental Law Centre, 58–69.

Webb, K. (2000). *Cinderella's Slippers? The Role of Charitable Tax Status in Financing Canadian Interest Groups*. Vancouver, BC: SFU-UBC Centre for the Study of Government and Business.

Webb, K. (2005). 'Sustainable Governance in the Twenty-First Century: Moving Beyond Instrument Choice'. In P. Eliadis, M. Hill and M. Howlett (eds), *Designing Government: From Instruments to Governance*. Montreal, QC: McGill-Queen's University Press, 242–80.

Webb, K. and J. C. Clifford. (1988). *Pollution Control in Canada: The Regulatory Approach in the 1980s*. Ottawa, ON: Law Reform Commission of Canada.

Webber, D. J. (1986). 'Analyzing Political Feasibility: Political Scientists' Unique Contribution to Policy Analysis'. *Policy Studies Journal* 14, no. 4: 545–54.

Weber, E. P. and A. M. Khademian. (2008). 'Wicked Problems, Knowledge Challenges and Collaborative Capacity Builders in Network Settings'. *Public Administration Review* 68, no. 2: 334–49.

Weber, E. U. (2016). 'What Shapes Perceptions of Climate Change? New Research Since 2010: What Shapes Perceptions of Climate Change'. *Wiley Interdisciplinary Reviews: Climate Change* 7, no. 1: 125–34.

Weber, E. U. and P. C. Stern. (2011). 'Public Understanding of Climate Change in the United States'. *American Psychologist* 66, no. 4: 315.

Weber, M. (1978). *Economy and Society: An Outline of Interpretive Sociology*. Berkeley, CA: University of California Press.

Weber, M., P. P. J. Driessen and H. A. C. Runhaar. (2011). 'Environmental Noise Policy in the Netherlands: Drivers of and Barriers to Shifts from Government to Governance'. *Journal of Environmental Policy and Planning* 13: 119–37.

Webler, T. and S. Tuler. (2000). 'Fairness and Competence in Citizen Participation'. *Administration and Society* 32, no. 5: 566–95.

WEF (World Economic Forum). (Various years). *Global Competitiveness Report*. Geneva, Switzerland: WEF.

Weible, C. M. (2008). 'Expert-Based Information and Policy Subsystems: A Review and Synthesis'. *Policy Studies Journal* 36, no. 4: 615–35.

Weible, C. M., P. A. Sabatier and K. McQueen. (2009). 'Themes and Variations: Taking Stock of the Advocacy Coalition Framework'. *Policy Studies Journal* 37, no. 1: 121–40.

Weible, C. M., P. A. Sabatier, H. C. Jenkins-Smith, D. Nohrstedt, A. D. Henry and P. deLeon. (2011). 'A Quarter Century of the Advocacy Coalition Framework: An Introduction to the Special Issue. *Policy Studies Journal* 39, no. 3: 349–60.

Weimer, D. L. (1992a). 'Claiming Races, Broiler Contracts, Heresthetics and Habits: Ten Concepts for Policy Design'. *Policy Sciences* 25: 135–59.

Weimer, D. L. (1992b). 'The Craft of Policy Design: Can It Be More Than Art?' *Policy Studies Review* 11, nos 3/4: 370–88.

Weimer, D. L. (1993). 'The Current State of Design Craft: Borrowing, Tinkering and Problem Solving'. *Public Administration Review* 53, no. 2 (April): 110–20.

Weimer, D. L. (2007). 'Public and Private Regulation of Organ Transplantation: Liver Allocation and the Final Rule'. *Journal of Health Politics, Policy and Law* 32, no. 1: 9–49.

Weimer, D. L. and A. R. Vining. (1989). *Policy Analysis: Concepts and Practice* (1st edn). Englewood Cliffs, NJ: Prentice Hall.

Weimer, D. L. and A. R. Vining. (1999). *Policy Analysis: Concepts and Practice* (3rd edn). Englewood Cliffs, NJ: Prentice Hall.

Weimer, D. L. and A. R. Vining. (2004). *Policy Analysis: Concepts and Practice* (4th edn). Englewood Cliffs, NJ: Prentice Hall.

Weimer, D. L. and A. R. Vining. (2011). *Policy Analysis: Concepts and Practice* (5th edn). Upper Saddle River, NJ: Pearson/Prentice Hall.

Weir, M. (2010). 'Collaborative Governance and Civic Empowerment: A Discussion of Investing in Democracy: Engaging Citizens in Collaborative Governance'. *Perspectives on Politics* 8, no. 2: 595–8.

Weishaar, H., A. Amos and J. Collin. (2015). 'Best of Enemies: Using Social Network Analysis to Explore a Policy Network in European Smoke-Free Policy'. *Social Science & Medicine* 133: 85–92.

Weiss, C. (1977). 'Research for Policy's Sake: The Enlightenment Function of Social Research'. *Policy Analysis* 3: 531–45.

Weiss, J. A. and J. E. Gruber. (1984). 'Using Knowledge for Control in Fragmented Policy Arenas'. *Journal of Policy Analysis and Management* 3, no. 2: 225–47.

Weiss, J. A. and M. Tschirhart. (1994). 'Public Information Campaigns as Policy Instruments'. *Journal of Policy Analysis and Management* 13, no. 1: 82–119.

Weiss, L. (1998). *The Myth of the Powerless State: Governing the Economy in a Global Era*. Cambridge: Polity Press.

Weiss, L. (1999). 'Globalization and National Governance: Antinomy or Interdependence?' *Review of International Studies* 25, no. 5: 1–30.

Weiss, L. (ed.). (2003). *States in the Global Economy: Bringing Domestic Institutions Back In*. Cambridge: Cambridge University Press.

Weiss, L. (2005). 'The State-Augmenting Effects of Globalisation'. *New Political Economy* 10, no. 3: 345–53.

Welch, E. W. and W. Wong. (2001). 'Effects of Global Pressures on Public Bureaucracy: Modeling a New Theoretical Framework'. *Administration and Society* 33, no. 4: 371–402.

Weller, P. and B. Stevens. (1998). 'Evaluating Policy Advice: The Australian Experience'. *Public Administration* 76 (Autumn): 579–89.

Wellstead, A., R. Stedman and E. Lindquist. (2007). 'Beyond the National Capital Region: Federal Regional Policy Capacity'. In *Report Prepared for the Treasury Board Secretariat of Canada*. Ottawa, ON: Treasury Board.

Wenig, M. M. and P. Sutherland. (2004). 'Considering the Upstream/Downstream Effects of the Mackenzie Pipeline: Rough Paddling for the National Energy Board'. *Resources* 86: 1–8.

Wescott, G. (2002). 'Integrated Natural Resource Management in Australia'. *Australian Journal of Environmental Management* 9, no. 3: 138–40.

West, W. (2005). 'Administrative Rulemaking: An Old and Emerging Literature'. *Public Administration Review* 65, no. 6: 655–68.

Weyland, K. (2005). 'Theories of Policy Diffusion: Lessons from Latin American Pension Reform'. *World Politics* 57, no. 2: 262–95.

Wheeler, D. (2001). 'Racing to the Bottom? Foreign Investment and Air Pollution in Developing Countries'. *Journal of Environment and Development* 10, no. 3: 225–45.

White, M. D. (2016). 'Overview of Behavioral Economics and Policy'. In S. Abdukadirov (ed.), *Nudge Theory in Action*. Cham, Germany: Springer International Publishing, 15–36.

Whiteman, D. (1985). 'The Fate of Policy Analysis in Congressional Decision Making: Three Types of Use in Committees'. *Western Political Quarterly* 38, no. 2: 294–311.

Whiteman, D. (1995). *Communication in Congress: Members, Staff and the Search for Information*. Lawrence, KS: University Press of Kansas.

Whitmarsh, L. (2009). 'What's in a Name? Commonalities and Differences in Public Understanding of "Climate Change" and "Global Warming"'. *Public Understanding of Science* 18, no. 4: 401–20.

Whitten, S. M. (2017). 'Designing and Implementing Conservation Tender Metrics: Twelve Core Considerations'. *Land Use Policy* 63 (April): 561–71.

Whyte, G. and Levi, A. S. (1994). 'The Origins and Function of the Reference Point in Risky Group Decision Making the Case of the Cuban Missile Crisis'. *Journal of Behavioral Decision Making* 7, no. 4: 243–60.

Wijen, F. and S. Ansari. (2007). 'Overcoming Inaction Through Collective Institutional Entrepreneurship: Insights from Regime Theory'. *Organization Studies* 28, no. 7 (1 July): 1079–1100.

Wildavsky, A. B. (1969). 'Rescuing Policy Analysis from PPBS'. *Public Administration Review* (March–April): 189–202.

Wildavsky, A. B. (1979). *Speaking Truth to Power: The Art and Craft of Policy Analysis*. Boston, MA: Little, Brown.

Wildavsky, A. B. (1988). *Searching for Safety*. New Brunswick, NJ: London: Transaction.

Wilder, M. and M. Howlett. (2014). 'The Politics of Policy Anomalies: Bricolage and the Hermeneutics of Paradigms. *Critical Policy Studies* 8, no. 2: 183–202.

Wilensky, H. L. (1975). *The Welfare State and Equality: Structural and Ideological Roots of Public Expenditures*. Berkeley, CA: University of California Press.

Wilensky, H. L. and L. Turner. (1987). *Democratic Corporatism and Policy Linkages: The Interdependence of Industrial, Labor-Market, Incomes, and Social Policies in Eight Countries*. Berkeley, CA: Institute of International Studies.

Wilkinson, T. M. (2013). 'Nudging and Manipulation'. *Political Studies* 61, no. 2: 341–55.

Wilks, S. and I. Battle. (2003). 'The Unanticipated Consequences of Creating Independent Competition Agencies'. In M. Thatcher and A. S. Sweet (eds), *The Politics of Delegation*. London: Frank Cass, 148–72.

Williams, A. M. and V. Balaz. (1999). 'Privatisation in Central Europe: Different Legacies, Methods and Outcomes'. *Environment and Planning C: Government and Policy* 17: 731–51.

Williams, J. A. (2000). 'The Delegation Dilemma: Negotiated Rulemaking in Perspective'. *Policy Studies Review* 17, no. 1: 125–46.

Williams, R. A. (2012). 'The Limits of Policy Analytical Capacity: Canadian Financial Regulatory Reform'. *International Journal of Public Sector Management* 25, nos 6/7: 455–63.

Williamson, O. E. (1996a). *The Mechanisms of Governance*. Oxford: Oxford University Press.

Williamson, O. E. (1996b). 'Transaction Cost Economics and Organization Theory'. In O. E. Williamson (ed.), *The Mechanisms of Governance*. New York: Oxford University Press, 219–49.

Williamson, O. E. (1975). *Markets and Hierarchies*. New York: Free Press.

Wilsford, D. (1994). 'Path Dependency, or Why History Makes It Difficult but Not Impossible to Reform Health Care Systems in a Big Way'. *Journal of Public Policy* 14, no. 3: 251–84.

Wilson, G. K. (2003). 'Changing Regulatory Systems'. Paper for the Annual Convention of the American Political Science Association, Philadelphia, August. www. lafollette.wisc.edu/facultystaff/wilson/ChangingRegulatorySystems.pdf.

Wilson, J. Q. (1974). 'The Politics of Regulation'. In J. W. McKie (ed.), *Social Responsibility and the Business Predicament*. Washington, DC: Brookings Institution, 135–68.

Wilson, V. S. (1971). 'The Role of Royal Commissions and Task Forces'. In G. B. Doern and P. Aucoin (eds), *The Structures of Policy-Making in Canada*. Toronto, ON: Macmillan, 113–29.

Wilson, W. (1887). 'The Study of Administration'. *Political Science Quarterly* 2, no. 2: 197–222.

Winter, S. C. and P. J. May. (2001). 'Motivation for Compliance with Environmental Regulations'. *Journal of Policy Analysis and Management* 20, no. 4: 675–98.

Wintges, R. (2007). *Monitoring and Analysis of Policies and Public Financing Instruments Conducive to Higher Levels of R&D Investments: The 'Policy Mix' Project: Case Study: The Netherlands*. Maastricht, Netherlands: UNU-MERIT.

Wissel, S. and F. Watzold. (2010). 'A Conceptual Analysis of the Application of Tradable Permits to Biodiversity Conservation'. *Conservation Biology* 24, no. 2: 404–11.

Wolf Jr, C. (1979). 'A Theory of Nonmarket Failure: Framework for Implementation Analysis'. *Journal of Law and Economics* 22, no. 1: 107–39.

Wolf Jr, C. (1987). 'Markets and Non-Market Failures: Comparison and Assessment'. *Journal of Public Policy* 7: 43–70.

Wolf Jr, C. (1988). *Markets or Governments: Choosing Between Imperfect Alternatives*. Cambridge, MA: MIT Press.

Wollmann, H. (1989). 'Policy Analysis in West Germany's Federal Government: A Case of Unfinished Governmental and Administrative Modernization?' *Governance* 2, no. 3: 233–66.

Wolman, H. (1981). 'The Determinants of Program Success and Failure'. *Journal of Public Policy* 1, no. 4: 433–64.

Wolman, H. (1992). 'Understanding Cross National Policy Transfers'. *Governance* 5, no. 1: 27–45.

Wonka, A. and B. Rittberger. (2010). 'Credibility, Complexity and Uncertainty: Explaining the Institutional Independence of 29 EU – Agencies'. *West European Politics* 33, no. 4: 730.

Woo, J. J., M. Ramesh and M. Howlett. (2015). 'Legitimation Capacity: System-Level Resources and Political Skills in Public Policy'. *Policy and Society* 34, no. 3–4: 271–83.

Wood, B. D. and J. Bohte. (2004). 'Political Transaction Costs and the Politics of Administrative Design'. *Journal of Politics* 66, no. 1: 176–202.

Wood, D. and L. Hagerman. (2010). 'Mission Investing and the Philanthropic Toolbox'. *Policy and Society* 29, no. 3: 257–68.

Woodley, A. (2008). 'Legitimating Public Policy'. *University of Toronto Law Journal* 58: 153–84.

Woodside, K. (1979). 'Tax Incentives vs. Subsidies: Political Considerations in Governmental Choice'. *Canadian Public Policy* 5, no. 2: 248–56.

Woodside, K. (1983). 'The Political Economy of Policy Instruments: Tax Expenditures and Subsidies in Canada'. In M. Atkinson and M. Chandler (eds), *The Politics of Canadian Public Policy*. Toronto, ON: University of Toronto Press, 173–97.

Woodside, K. (1986). 'Policy Instruments and the Study of Public Policy'. *Canadian Journal of Political Science* 19, no. 4: 775–93.

Woolley, A. (2008). 'Legitimating Public Policy'. *University of Toronto Law Journal* 58: 153–84.

World Bank. (1994). *Averting the Old Age Crisis*. Washington, DC: World Bank Group.

World Bank. (2010). *World Development Report 2010: Development and Climate Change*. Washington, DC. https://openknowledge.worldbank.org/handle/10986/4387.

World Bank. (2011). 'The Contribution of Government Communication Capacity to Achieving Good Governance Outcomes'. *Brief for Policymakers: Communication for Governance & Accountability Program*. Washington, DC: World Bank.

World Bank. (2015). *World Development Report 2015: Mind Society and Behaviour*. Washington, DC: World Bank. https://openknowledge.worldbank.org/handle/10986/20597.

Wraith, R. E. and G. B. Lamb. (1971). *Public Inquiries as an Instrument of Government*. London: George Allen & Unwin.

Wu, I. (2008). 'Who Regulates Phones, Television and the Internet? What Makes a Communications Regulator Independent and Why It Matters'. *Perspectives on Politics* 6, no. 4: 769–83.

Wu, X. and M. Ramesh. (2014). 'Market Imperfections, Government Imperfections, and Policy Mixes: Policy Innovations in Singapore'. *Policy Sciences*: 1–16.

Wu, X., M. Ramesh and M. Howlett. (2015a). 'Blending Skill and Resources Across Multiple Levels of Activity: Competences, Capabilities and the Policy Capacities of Government'. *Policy and Society* 34, nos 3–4: 271–83.

Wu, X., M. Ramesh and M. Howlett. (2015b). 'Policy Capacity: A Conceptual Framework for Understanding Policy Competences and Capabilities'. *Policy and Society* (Special Issue on The Dynamics of Policy Capacity) 34, nos 3–4 (September): 165–71.

Wu, X., M. Ramesh, M. Howlett and S. Fritzen. (2010). *The Public Policy Primer: Managing Public Policy*. London: Routledge.

Wunder, B. (1995). 'Le Modele Napoleonien d'Administration: Apercu Comparatif'. In B. Wunder (ed.), *The Influences of the Napoleonic 'Model' of Administration on the Administrative Organization of Other Countries*. Brussels, Belgium: International Institute of Administrative Sciences.

Wyborn, C. (2015). 'Co-Productive Governance: A Relational Framework for Adaptive Governance'. *Global Environmental Change* 30 (January): 56–67.

Yackee, J. W. and S. W. Yackee. (2010). 'Administrative Procedures and Bureaucratic Performance: Is Federal Rule-Making "Ossified"?' *Journal of Public Administration Research and Theory* 20, no. 2 (1 April): 261–82.

Yee, A. S. (1996). 'The Causal Effects of Ideas on Policies'. *International Organization* 50, no. 1: 69–108.

Yeung, K. and M. Dixon-Woods. (2010). 'Design-Based Regulation and Patient Safety: A Regulatory Studies Perspective'. *Social Science & Medicine* 71, no. 3: 502–9.

Yi, H. and R. C. Feiock. (2012). 'Policy Tool Interactions and the Adoption of State Renewable Portfolio Standards'. *Review of Policy Research* 29, no. 2 (1 March): 193–206.

Yi, I. (2015). *New Challenges for and New Directions in Social Policy*. New York: United Nations Research Institute for Social Development (UNRISD).

Young, K., D. Ashby, A. Boaz and L. Grayson. (2002). 'Social Science and the Evidence-Based Policy Movement'. *Social Policy and Society* 1, no. 3: 215–24.

Young, L. and J. Everitt. (2004). *Advocacy Groups*. Vancouver, BC: University of British Columbia Press.

Young, S. (2007). 'The Regulation of Government Advertising in Australia: The Politicisation of a Public Policy Issue'. *Australian Journal of Public Administration* 66, no. 4: 438–52.

Zahariadis, N. (2007). 'The Multiple Streams Framework: Structure, Limitations, Prospects'. In P. Sabatier (ed.), *Theories of the Policy Process* (2nd edn). Boulder, CO: Westview, 65–92.

Zarco-Jasso, H. (2005). 'Public–Private Partnerships: A Multidimensional Model for Contracting'. *International Journal of Public Policy* 1, nos 1/2: 22–40.

Zaval, L. and J. F. M. Cornwell. (2016). 'Cognitive Biases, Non-Rational Judgments, and Public Perceptions of Climate Change'. In M. C. Weibet, M. Schafe, E. Markowitz, S. Ho, S. O'Neill and J. Thaker (eds), *Oxford Research Encyclopaedia of Climate Science*. Oxford: Oxford University Press.

Zaval, L., E. A. Keenan, E. J. Johnson and E. U. Weber. (2014). 'How Warm Days Increase Belief in Global Warming'. *Nature Climate Change* 4, no. 2: 143–7.

Zeckhauser, R. (1981). 'Preferred Policies When There Is a Concern for Probability of Adoption'. *Journal of Environmental Economics and Management* 8: 215–37.

Zeckhauser, R. and E. Schaefer. (1968). 'Public Policy and Normative Economic Theory'. In R. A. Bauer and K. J. Gergen (eds), *The Study of Policy Formation*. New York: Free Press, 27–102.

Zehavi, A. (2008). 'The Faith-Based Initiative in Comparative Perspective: Making Use of Religious Providers in Britain and the United States'. *Comparative Politics* 40, no. 3: 331–51.

Zelli, F., I. Möller and H. van Asselt. (2017). 'Institutional Complexity and Private Authority in Global Climate Governance: The Cases of Climate Engineering, REDD+ and Short-Lived Climate Pollutants'. *Environmental Politics* 26, no. 4 (5 May): 669–93.

Zerbe, R. O. and H. E. McCurdy. (1999). 'The Failure of Market Failure'. *Journal of Policy Analysis and Management* 18, no. 4: 558–78.

Zhang, Y., R. Lee and K. Yang. (2012). 'Knowledge and Skills for Policy-Making: Stories from Local Public Managers in Florida'. *Journal of Public Affairs Education* 18, no. 1: 183–208.

Zielonka, J. (2007). 'Plurilateral Governance in the Enlarged European Union'. *Journal of Common Market Studies* 45, no. 1: 187–209.

Ziller, J. (2005). 'Public Law: A Tool for Modern Management, Not an Impediment to Reform'. *International Review of Administrative Sciences* 71, no. 2: 267–77.

Zito, A. R. (2001). 'Epistemic Communities, Collective Entrepreneurship and European Integration'. *Journal of European Public Policy* 8, no. 4: 585–603.

Zito, A. R., A. Jordan, R. Wurzel and L. Brueckner. (2003). 'Instrument Innovation in an Environmental Lead State: "New" Environmental Policy Instruments in the Netherlands'. *Environmental Politics* 12, no. 1: 157–78.

Zysman, J. (1994). 'How Institutions Create Historically Rooted Trajectories of Growth'. *Industrial and Corporate Change* 3, no. 1: 243–83.

BIBLIOGRAPHY

Index

Page numbers in *italics* refer to figures. Page numbers in **bold** refer to tables.

Abelson, D. E. 205
ad hoc task forces 183–4
adaptive policy-making 34
Adler, R. S. 226, 227, 235
administrative edicts 192
adversarial legalism 152
Advisory Committee Act (US; 1972) **204**, 205
advisory councils/boards 203–5, **203**, **204**
advocacy coalitions 122, 124–5, 129
agenda-setting 115
Agranoff, R. 29, 179
alternative service delivery 172–3
analytical units 182, **183**
Anderson, C. 104
applied problem-solving 46, *47*
appraisal 101
attitude and objectives problems 90
authoritative implementation tools 191–207, 241–4
authority 82, **83**, 142, **143**, **149**, **150**, 154
authority instruments 147–8
auto-adaptation to initial conditions 271–2
automaticity 150–1
autonomy problems 90

Balch, G. I. 142
Bardach, E. 6, 137, 142
Baxter-Moore, N. 146–7

Becker, S. W. 12
Beckstrand, M. J. 222
behavioural change 77–81, *79*, 264–5
behavioural tools 34–5, 36
Bekke, H. A. G. M. 250
Béland, D. 61
Berg, S. V. 196
Bernstein, M. H. 242–3
best practices 13
Bhadwal, S. 271
biases 127
Bobrow, D. 3, 257
bounded rationality 72
Brandsen, T. 178
Bregha, F. 199
Bressers, H. T. A. 147–8
Brewer, G. 261
Brockman, J. 198
Brown, D. S. 204, 243
Brown-John, C. L. 204
Brownson, F. O. 12

capacity issues 125–6, **126**, 267–8, 279
capacity-building instruments 147–8
'cap and trade' systems 201
Capano, G. 35
Carstensen, M. 106
cash-based financial tools 212–13, 214–17
causal stories 115–16

censorship 234
central support agencies 169
certification 176–8
Chapman, R. 153, 184
Christensen, T. 268, 278
Churchman, C. W. 16
citizen involvement 243–4
civil society governance 29
clientele units 182
Cnossen, S. 214
Cochran, C. L. 99
co-design 34–7
coercion spectrum 144–6, *145*, 191
coherence 67–8, 260–1, 279
collaborative governance 35–6, 185, 186
'command and control' regulation 192–3
commissioning 173–5
commissions 183–4, 231
competences 267, 279
complementary effects, maximizing
    261–3
compliance issues 75–7, **76**
compliance regimes/compliance regime
    design 89–91, 264–5
compliance-deterrence model 73–5
confirmation bias 127
congruence 67–8, 260–1, 279
consensus democracies 252
Considine, M. 29, 249
consistency 67–8, 260–1, 279
consolidation phase 101
consultations/co-optation tools 233
contemporary design orientation 8–10
contextual barriers and constraints 80–1,
    80, 86
contracting out 173–4, 175–6
controlled experimentation 90–1
co-production 34–7, 89, 176–7, 178–9
core actors 119, **119**, **120**, 129
corporate forms 170–2
corporate social responsibility (CSR) 201
corporatism 217, 240–1
corruption 167
cost 150–1
counter-productive effects, minimizing
    261–3
credibility 83, 86, 88, 154
cupidity 84, 86, 88, 154
Cushman, R. E. 141–2, *141*, 146
customization of policy 106

Dahl, R. A. 144
de Groot 75
decision-maker heuristics 126–7
'degree of government coercion' 144–6,
    145
del Río, P. 262
delegated professional regulation 198
Delmas, M. A. 200–1
deregulation 26–8, 196–7, 207, 242–3,
    247
design choices, temporality of 278–9
design context 265–8
design space 12, 157–9, **160**, 275–8
design with intent 73
'design-as-noun' 23
'design-as-verb' 23
dialog phase 101
digital government legislation 226,
    233–4
Dion, L. 206, 243
direct government regulation 192–7
direct government tools 165, 166–9
disproportionality in policy designing
    127–9
Doern, B. 144–5, *145*, 146–7, 153, 259,
    282
drift *63*, 106, 261, 264
Dunsire, A. 142
Dye, T. 43

Economy and Society (Weber) 166
effectiveness 12–14, *13*, 83, **83**
efficiency 12
Eichbaum, C. 113–14
Eisner, M. A. 243, 250
Elkins, Z. 26
Elmore, R. F. 142, 147
empirical inventories 140
emulation 26–7
entrepreneurship 279–80
Eping-Andersen, G. 249
epistemic communities 121–3, 129, 158,
    203
equity 12
European Environment Agency 271
evidence-based policy-making 64–6
excise tax 214
exhortation and moral suasion 227
experimentation 90–1, 268–9
expertise, role of 112–14

feasibility 98, 100
Feindt, P. H. 63
financial implementation tools: overview
    of 211; patterns of use of 244–6;
    procedural 217–22; substantive 211–17;
    summary of 222–3
financial network mobilization tools
    220–2
financial policy network creation tools
    219–20
Fischer, F. 115
fit, goodness of 267–8
Flynn, A. 63
Forester, J. 115
formulation phase 101
freedom, degrees of 267, 268
freedom of information (FOI) 226, 233–4,
    246
Fulton, J. 227, 233

Gibson, R. B. 200
Givoni, M. 153
Glicken, J. 205
globalization: effects of 25–8; and
    governance turn 8, 23–5
Goldstein, J. 116
governance: description of 28–9, 32;
    models of *30*, **31**
governance, modes of 238–40, **239**
governance modes 249, 276–7
government agencies **168**, 181–4, 187–8
government information campaign 226
government reviews 183–4
'government to governance' hypothesis
    28–32
governmental/public sector insiders 119,
    119, **120**
Grabosky, P. N. 152, 261
grants 212–13
green taxes 214
Grossback, L. J. 250
group level mechanisms *82*, 84
Gunningham, N. 67, 147, 152

Haas, E. B. 122
Hacker, J. 61, 261
Hagman, W. 230
Haider, D. 212
Halligan, J. 129
'hard' law 32

Harris, R. 249–50
Held, D. A. 24
Hennicke, P. 153
herd behaviour 128
Héritier, A. 250
Holder, S. 196
Hood, C. 55, 142, **143**, 149, 154, 161, 222,
    225, 226, 231, 232, 248, 257, 282
horizontal mixes 157–9, 266
Hou, Y. 261
Howard, C. 222, 244
Howlett, M. 97, 279

ideology, role of 250
implementation tools *see* tools; *individual*
    types of tools
improvisation 269–72
incentive and sanction problems 90
incentive regulation 199–201
incentives instruments 147–8
independent regulatory commissions
    (IRCs) 194–7, **195**
indirect effects 26
indirect government regulation 197–201
individual level mechanisms 81–4, *82*
individual transferable quotas (ITQs)
    201
information **150**
information and knowledge collection
    tools 231
information disclosure 233
information dissemination tools 226–9
information problems 90
information release prevention tools
    234–5
information release tools 233–4
informational tools 246–7
information-based choice architectures
    229–31
information-based implementation tools
    225–36, 248
information campaigns 227–9
Ingraham, P. 257
Ingram, H. M. 7–8, 76–7, **77**, 147–8,
    153–4, 282
inquiries 183–4, 231
instrument choice: analyzing policy mixes
    and 152–5; conceptions of 143–7
instrumental orientation/knowledge
    10–11

instrument constituencies 122, 123–4, 129
instruments, attributes of 67, 150–1
insurance, favorable 215–16
interest articulation systems 217–18, *218*, 245–6
interest group alteration/manipulation/ co-optation 220–2, **222**
interest group creation 219–20
international agreements 27–8
internationalization 25–8
intrusiveness 150–1

Jenkins-Smith, H. 124–5
Jones, B. D. 128
Jones, C. O. 96, 100

Kagan, R. 152
Kallgren 75
Keohane, R. O. 116
Kern, F. 279
Keyes, J. M. 193
Kingdon, J. W. 123, 125
Kirschen, E. S. 140–1, 143, 146, 266
Klijn, E. H. 56
Klok, P.-J. 147–8
Knill, C. 32, 250, 251–2
knowledge and comprehension matrix **17**
knowledge brokers 118–19
knowledge producers 118

Laforest, R. 245
Lai, A. Y. 271–2
Lasswell, H. D. 6, 43–4, 45–6, 97, 136, 138, 266
laws 192, 193–4, **194**
layering 61–4, 106, 261, 264, 265, 276, 278
leadership 279–80
learning 26–7
learning instruments 147–8
legalism, adversarial 152
legitimacy 83, 86, 88, 116, 154
Lehmkuhl, D. 32
Lijphart, A. 252
Lindblom, C. E. 144
Linder, S. H. 5, 11, 48–9, 50, 52, 54–5, 67, 112, 143, 150, 257, 282
Lindquist, E. 253
line departments 166–9

loan guarantees 215–16
Lowi, T. 141–2, **142**, 144, 161, 248
Lowry, R. C. 221
Lund, M. S. 144

Mahoney, J. 222
Majone, G. 248
majoritarian democracies 252
Maley, M. 114
Malone, E. F. 99
Maor, M. 128
market creation and maintenance 201
market governance 29
Maslove, A. M. 213
May, P. J. 9, 257
Mayntz, R. 142, 161, 257
McGuire, M. 179
Meijers, E. 61
mental models 127
Meseguer, C. 26
Migone, A. 174–5
Milkis, S. 249–50
Milkman, K. L. 153
Mitnick, B. 192
model-building strategy *139*, 140–55
Moffet, J. 199
monitoring problems 90
'MUSH' sector (municipalities, universities, schools and hospitals) 187

Neeley, G. 219
neo-pluralism 218
network governance 29
network management tools 180–1, **183**
'networkization' of society 24–5, 29, 32
New Public Governance (NPG) approach 35
New Public Management (NPM) 186
nodality 82, **83**, 88, 142, **143**, **149**, 154, 225, 232
non-design processes and situations 9–10, 58, **59**, *63*, 64
non-state market-based (NSMD) tools 177
non-state tools 176–9
notification instruments 227
Nownes, A. J. 219
nudges 34–7, 72, 73–4, 78, 88, 229–31, 246–7

official secrets acts 234
Olson, M. 218
organization 82, **83**, 142, **149**, **150**, 154
organizational capacity 154–5, *154*
organizational hybrids 172–3
organizational implementation tools: cost of 185–6; overview of 165; patterns of use of 240–1, 247; procedural 179–85; substantive 165–79; summary of 185–8
Orsini, M. 203, 245
Osters 243
Ostrom, E. 151, **152**, 178
outsiders 119, **119**, **120**
outsourcing 173, 174
over-design 14–17, **15**, 95–6, 263
over-reactions 127–9
oversight agencies 184–5

packaging 61–4, *63*, 106–7, 263–4, 276
Pal, L. A. 219, 221
parsimonious tool use 259
partnerships 173–4
patching 61–4, *63*, 106–7, 263–4, 276
path dependency 27, 250
pension plans 169–70
peripheral actors **119**
Perry, J. L. 170
persuasion instruments 226
persuasive design 72–3
Pestoff, V. 178
Peters, B. G. 5, 11, 48–9, 50, 52, 54–5, 67, 112, 143, 150, 187–8, 257, 282
Phidd, R. 144–5, 259
Phillips, S. D. 203, 221
Pierson, P. 250
pilot projects 268–9
Pittle, R. D. 226, 227, 235
pluralism 217–18
policy advice: actors in **119**, **120**, 122–5; capacity and 125–6; content of 114–17; expertise and 112–14; organization of 117–20; over-design 111–12; problems in 126–9; sources of 120–2; summary of 129
policy advisory systems 117–20
policy analysis/policy analytical capacity 66, 97, 125–6
policy compliance 71–91
policy contents, ideational components of 116–17, **117**

policy design: assembling and evaluating 257–72; capacity challenges of 275–82; in contemporary era 23–37; contemporary trends in 237–53; definitions and concepts of 43–68; description of 3–4, 47–52, 57–9; evidence-based 64–6; as field of study 10–12; as implementation tool mixes 135–61; as instrumental knowledge mobilization 17, 19; logic of 77–81; role of 3–20; studies of 4; timing of 95–109
policy designers 111–29
policy dynamics 33–4
policy formulation: altering status quo and **106**; meaning of 99–100; over-design 95–6; pre-conditions of 107–8; process of 100–7; as stage in policy cycle 96–8; studying 98–9; summary of 108–9
policy formulation spaces **59**
policy goals 44
policy instrument studies 98–9
policy instruments: description of 52–4; development of models of 139–55; as field of study 136–8; policy formulation and 104–5; portfolio analyses and 155–7; range of *53*; vertical and horizontal complexity and 157–8; *see also individual types of instruments*
policy means 44
policy mechanisms 81–6
policy mixes 33–4, 67–8, 156–7, 158–9, **160**, 260–5
policy network activation and mobilization tools 202–5
policy paradigms 116–17
policy prototypes 268–9
policy sectors 71
policy style 10, 249–53
Policy Styles in Western Europe (Richardson) 251
policy targets 7–8, 75–7, **76**, **77**
policy formulation, context and influence and 105–7
policy-takers, behaviour of 75–7
political advice 112–14, 129
politics-centered design 10
preferential procurement 215
principles of policy design: articulating 258; character of tools and 258–60; design context and 265–8

privacy and data protection acts 234–5
private governance 29
private sector insiders 119, **119**, **120**
privatization 26–8, 196–7, 241
problem conceptualization 96
procedural component 6
procedural constraints 104
procedural instruments 55, 56–7, **83**, 85–6, **87**, 147–50, **149**, **150**, 179–85, 187–8, 202–6, **202**, 232–5
procedural politicization 114
programme design 96
programme ideas 117
programme structure 96
proportionality 127–9
proximate actors **119**
proximate decision-makers 118
public consultation 205–6, **205**
public enterprises 170–2, **171**, 241
public hearings 183–4
public participation 243–4
public policy: components of **45**; description of 43–7
public sentiments 116
public services, vouchers for 216
public-private partnerships (P3) 174, 175–6, 186

quasi-autonomous non-governmental organization (quango) 173
quasi-governmental tools 165, 170–6
quasi-judicial bodies 181

Rainey, H.G. 170
Ramesh, M. 97
Rayner, J. 279
Reagan, M. 192
Reagan, R. 207
regulation: authoritative tool use and 241–3, 247; direct government 192–7; indirect government 197–201; introduction to 191–2; moral suasion and 227; summary of 206–7
replacement 60, 106–7
resource availability 154–5, *154*, 267
resource effectiveness, behavioural needs and **83**
resource problems 90
Richardson, J. 251
Riddell, N. 66

Rittel, H. W. J. 15, 16
Roberts, A. 228
robustness, designing for 269–72
Rose, J. 228
royalty-based financial instruments 213
Rudd, M. 123
Ryan, P. 228

Sabatier, P. 84, 115, 124–5
Salamon, L. M. 6, 8, 137, 138–9, 144, 147, 282
Sappington, D. E. M. 200
Saward, M. 148
Schmitter, P. 217
Schneider, A. 7–8, 76–7, **77**, 147–8, 153–4, 282
Schuitema 75
seed money 219–20, **220**
self-regulation 192, 199, 200, 259
sequencing 259–60, 265
Shaw, R. 113–14
Simmons, B. A. 26
Simmonset 250
Simon, H. 15, 72
Simons, A. 124
smart regulation 152–3, 261
Smith, B. L. R. 204
Smoth 243
social and health insurance 169–70
social construction of policy targets 127
social marketing 78, 88
social media 34–7
society-based tools 176–9
'soft' law 32
special operating agencies (SOAs) 173
specification of objectives 96
'spill-over' effects 26
staff or central agencies 180–1
stakeholder and consensus conferences 205–6
Stanbury, W. T. 146, 221, 227, 233
state assets, sale of 216–17
state-owned enterprises (SOEs) 170–2
statistical agencies and units 231–2
Stead, D. 61
Stern, J. 196
Steurer, R. 29
Stone, D. 115, 116
stretching 61–4, *63*
structural level mechanisms 84–6

student loads 216
subsidies 212–13
substantive constraints analysis 104
substantive element 6
substantive instruments 55–6, 82, **83**, 86, 138, **150**, 165–79, 191–2, 226–32
substantive politicization 114
sub-system level mechanisms 84–6
subsystems 120–2
sunk cost bias 127
Sunstein, C. R. 36, 72, 229
surveys and polling 226, 232
Swanson, D. 271
symbolic and hortatory instruments 147–8
symbolic frames 117
'system 2' mechanisms 81

'tame' policy problems 16, **16**
target behaviour 72–3
target beliefs 154–5, *154*
targeting, precision of 150–1
tax credits 213
tax incentives 213
tax-based financial instruments 213–14, 222–3, 244–5
tax-equivalent financial tools 214–17
taxonomies, development of 140–3
Taylor, R. 174–5
technical advice 112–14, 129
temporality of design choices 278–9
tense layering 63, *63*
Terlaak, A. K. 200–1
Thaler, R. H 72
Thatcher, M. 207
Thelen, K. 33, 61, 105, 260, 261
theory evaluation and selection 96
Thomas, H. G. 101, 111
Thompson 146
Tinbergen, J. 140, 155–6, 259
Tinbergen Rule 157, 259, 263
Tinbergen-Mundell theorem 162n2
tool complementarity 155
tools: description of 54–7; effective policy design and 258–60; selection process for *151*; *see also individual types of tools*
tools approach 138–40

tools orientation 6–8
traditional policy styles 237–53
treasure 82, **83**, 142, **143**, **149**, **150**, 154
treaties 27
Trebilcock, M. J. 146
tribunals 181
trilateral arrangements 29
trust 84, 86, 88, 154

uncertain compliance 72–3
uncertainty 12–17, *18*, 102–4, **103**, 269–72, 280–2
under-design 14–17, **15**, 263
under-reactions 127–9
US Clean Air Act 60, 61–2
user fees 212–13
utilitarian paradigm 72, 73–4, 75, 77–8

Vedung, E. 55, 225
vertical mixes 157–9, 266
vice taxes 214
virtuous taxes 214
visibility 150–1
Vogel, D. 201
voluntary regulation 192, 199–201, **199**, 207
Voss, J.-P. 124
vouchers for public services 216

Weaver, R. K. 76, 89, 265
Webber, M. M. 15, 16
Weber, M. 166–7, 250
Weberian 'monocratic bureaucracy' 166–7
Weimer, D. 105
Westminster model 113, 114, 180, 252
whistleblower acts 233
'wicked' policy problems 16, **16**
Wildavsky, A. 97
Wilkinson, T. M. 36–7
Wilson, S. 144–5, 259
Wilson, W. 136
Woodside, K. 146
Wu, I. 195

Young, M. D. 152

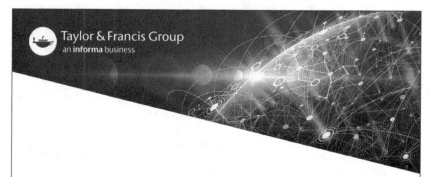